The
Supercook's
Cookbook

LA

Edited by Isabel Moore

Published by Marshall Cavendish Limited
58 Old Compton Street
London W1V 5PA

© Marshall Cavendish Limited 1973, 1974,
1975, 1976

This material was first published by
Marshall Cavendish Limited
in the partwork *Supercook*.

First published 1976

Printed in Belgium by Henri Proost, Turnhout.

ISBN 0 8148 0657 0

Introduction

To have one compact cookery book that encompasses the entire range of eating experience —it's the dream of every cook.

The Supercook's Cookbook makes that dream come true: with 384 pages absolutely crammed full of fabulous, easy to follow recipes, many of them illustrated in color (it always helps to know what your experiments should look like!) and ranging from simple, economical family meals to the more elaborate offerings usually reserved for entertaining or other special occasions.

The book begins with lots of satisfying soups, which are followed by a mouth-watering selection of hearty stews; the economical and exotic delights of rice and pasta; the delicate freshness of fish and seafood and the nutritional goodness of vegetables and salads. Cheese and eggs come next, with an amazing range of recipes, from rarebits, to meringues and, finally, the 'icing on the cake'; a wide selection of luscious sweets and puddings that just demand to be eaten.

The Supercook's Cookbook is an invaluable investment for every cook.

Key to symbols

☆ This is a guide to each recipe's preparation and cooking

      ☆ **Easy**

    ☆ ☆ **Requires special care**

☆ ☆ ☆ **Complicated**

① This is a guide to the cost of each dish and will, of course, vary according to region and season.

      ① **Inexpensive**

    ① ① **Reasonable**

① ① ① **Expensive**

⧖ This is a guide to the preparation and cooking time required for each dish and will vary according to the skill of the individual cook.

      ⧖ **Less than 1 hour**

    ⧖ ⧖ **1 hour to 2½ hours**

⧖ ⧖ ⧖ **Over 2½ hours**

Basic metric conversions

Solid measures

15 grams	=	½ ounce
25 grams	=	1 ounce
50 grams	=	2 ounces
125 grams	=	4 ounces
225 grams	=	8 ounces
450 grams	=	1 pound
1 kilogram	=	2 pounds 2 ounces

Liquid measures

25 millilitres	=	1 fluid ounce
50 millilitres	=	2 fluid ounces
125 millilitres	=	4 fluid ounces
150 millilitres	=	5 fluid ounces
300 millilitres	=	10 fluid ounces
600 millilitres	=	1 pint
1 litre	=	1¾ pints

Linear measures

0·6 centimetre	=	¼ inch
1·3 centimetres	=	½ inch
2·5 centimetres	=	1 inch
10 centimetres	=	4 inches
15 centimetres	=	6 inches
23 centimetres	=	9 inches
30 centimetres	=	1 foot
1 metre	=	40 inches

American equivalents of food and measurements are shown in brackets.

Contents

Soups and stews for the family

Soups and Stews are basic to all cuisines and have been concocted, cooked — and enjoyed — almost since Man first discovered fire. They are flexible dishes, too, that actually taste even better a day or two after they're cooked (although we won't actually guarantee that these delicious recipes will last that long!).

With practically the whole world to choose from, it has been difficult to decide what to include in this book but, in the end, the compromise was made between the tried and true (such old favourites as Onion Soup, pictured below, recipe on page 6, Tomato Soup on page 9 and Lancashire Hot Pot on page 19) and the new-and-unfamiliar-but-delicious (see page 8 for our unusual recipe for Revythia, a Greek chick-pea soup and page 22 for the exotic Near Eastern Pork with Peanuts and Grapes).

All of these attractive dishes are sustaining enough to satisfy the most demanding family and economical enough not to shatter the family budget. But, of course, there are those special occasions (birthdays, anniversaries and so on) when you'll want to spend a bit more money on the food, a bit more time in the kitchen and, recognizing this, we have provided some specially selected recipes **For Special Occasions.** And this collection of slightly extravagant but superb dishes, all fit to grace the most elegant table, are absolutely guaranteed to make your party 'go' right from the start.

But perhaps the ultimate virtues of these recipes are that they're FUN to cook, and easy too. They take the monotony out of daily cooking and enable a busy mum to sit down with the family and actually enjoy the meal she has just prepared. And any recipes that do that make good cooking — and good eating — automatic!

Bean and Bacon Soup

This filling and tasty soup may be served at an informal lunch or dinner. It also makes a good main course, served with crusty French bread, for a family lunch or supper.

6 SERVINGS

12 oz. [1½ cups] dried butter [lima] beans
2 lb. bacon hock with bone
1 large onion, cut in quarters
1 large garlic clove, crushed
3½ pints [8¾ cups] water
    bouquet garni, consisting of 4 parsley sprigs, 1 thyme spray, and 1 bay leaf tied together
½ teaspoon white pepper
20 large black olives, cut in half and stoned
3 tablespoons chopped parsley

Delicious and nutritious, Bean and Bacon Soup is a perfect family meal.

Put the beans in a bowl and cover with water. Leave them to soak overnight.

Drain the beans and put them in a large saucepan with the bacon, onion and garlic. Cover with the water, place the pan on high heat and bring to the boil.

Add the bouquet garni and pepper to the pan and stir well. Lower the heat and simmer the soup for 1½ to 2 hours, or until the beans and bacon are cooked and tender.

Remove the bacon hock and cut the meat into pieces. Remove the bouquet garni and discard. Purée some of the beans, using a fork or an electric blender and add to the soup to thicken it. Stir in the bacon pieces and olives. Taste and add salt and more pepper, if necessary.

Pour the soup into individual bowls, sprinkle with the parsley and serve hot.

Carrot Soup

Good quality, young carrots are necessary to provide a clear fresh colour and flavour for this soup. Carrot Soup may be served plain, or with croûtons of bread, fried diced potatoes, or a spoonful of boiled rice.

4 SERVINGS

1½ oz. [3 tablespoons] butter
1 lb. carrots, scraped and coarsely grated
8 oz. potatoes, peeled and roughly diced
1 medium-sized onion, finely chopped
1½ pints [3¾ cups] chicken stock or water

½ teaspoon salt
½ teaspoon freshly ground white
pepper
2 tablespoons double [heavy] cream

In a medium-sized saucepan, melt the butter over moderate heat. Reduce the heat to low and add the carrots, potatoes and onion. Cook for 15 minutes, stirring occasionally with a wooden spoon to prevent the vegetables from sticking to the pan. Add the stock or water, salt and pepper and simmer for another 20 minutes, or until the vegetables are quite soft.

Remove the pan from the heat. Pour the contents of the pan through a strainer placed over a medium-sized mixing bowl. With a wooden spoon press the vegetables through the strainer, or put them through a blender.

Return the soup to the saucepan and reheat it. If the soup is too thin, simmer, uncovered, until the soup thickens. Stir in the cream, taste and add more salt and pepper if necessary. Serve immediately, in hot bowls.

Colourful Cock-a-Leekie is a soup invented by the Scots that's absolutely guaranteed to sustain the family on cold winter days!

Cock-a-Leekie

A warming, traditional Scots soup of chicken and leeks, Cock-a-Leekie is served with hot crusty bread. It may be served as a filling first course to a dinner, or as a light but sustaining lunch or supper for the whole family.

6 SERVINGS

1 x 4 lb. chicken
4 pints [5 pints] water
7 leeks, including 2 inches of the
    green stems, thoroughly washed,
    trimmed and cut into ½-inch
    long slices
2 celery stalks, trimmed and
    coarsely chopped into ½-inch
    lengths
2 oz. [⅓ cup] pearl barley
bouquet garni, consisting of 4
    parsley sprigs, 1 thyme spray,
    1 bay leaf and 6 peppercorns
    tied together in a piece of
    cheesecloth
1 teaspoon salt
½ teaspoon freshly ground black
    pepper
1 tablespoon finely chopped fresh
    parsley

Place the chicken in a large saucepan and pour over the water. The chicken should be covered with water so add more if necessary. Place the pan over moderately high heat and bring the water to the boil. With a metal spoon, carefully skim off any scum that rises to the surface of the liquid.

Add the leeks, celery, barley, bouquet garni, salt and pepper and reduce the heat to very low.

Partly cover the pan with the lid on a slant and simmer the chicken for 1½ to 2 hours, or until the meat is almost falling off the bones.

Remove the pan from the heat and transfer the chicken to a wooden board or platter. Leave it to cool slightly. With a metal spoon, skim the fat off the surface of the cooking liquid. Remove and discard the bouquet garni.

With a small, sharp knife, carefully detach the chicken meat from the skin and bones. Discard the skin and bones. With your hands, shred the chicken coarsely and return it to the cooking liquid in the saucepan.

Place the pan over moderate heat and simmer the soup for 5 minutes to reheat it thoroughly.

Remove the pan from the heat and pour the soup into a warmed soup tureen or individual warmed soup bowls. Sprinkle the parsley over the soup and serve at once.

Cream of Chicken Soup

This is a simple, but nevertheless delicious, Cream of Chicken Soup. To add colour, it may be sprinkled with chopped parsley.

6 SERVINGS

2 lb. chicken backs and wings
2½ pints [6¼ cups] water
2 celery stalks, trimmed
1 bay leaf
1 small onion studded with 2 cloves
1 teaspoon salt
10 peppercorns
8 fl. oz. single cream [1 cup light cream]
8 fl. oz. [1 cup] milk
1½ oz. [3 tablespoons] butter blended with 1½ oz. [⅓ cup] flour

Place the chicken pieces in a large saucepan and cover them with the water. Add the celery, bay leaf, onion, salt and peppercorns. Place the pan over high heat and bring to the boil.

Reduce the heat to low, cover the pan and simmer for 2 hours.

Remove the pan from the heat and strain the liquid into a bowl. Pick out the chicken pieces, detach the meat from the bones and set the meat aside. Discard the skin, bones, vegetables and flavourings.

Return the strained liquid to the saucepan and stir in the cream and milk. Place the pan over moderate heat and bring the soup to the boil.

Roll the butter mixture into small pieces and add them, one by one, to the soup, stirring continuously.

Add the meat to the soup and bring to the boil again. Serve at once.

Cucumber and Pork Soup

A simple yet exotic Chinese soup with a fresh flavour, Cucumber and Pork Soup makes an interesting and different first course for a family meal.

6 SERVINGS

2¼ pints [5⅝ cups] chicken stock
1 teaspoon salt
1 tablespoon soy sauce
8 oz. pork fillets, cut into very thin strips
2 medium-sized cucumbers, peeled, halved lengthways, seeded, and cut into ¼-inch slices

In a large, heavy saucepan, combine the chicken stock, salt and soy sauce together. Add the strips of pork to the pan and bring the mixture to the boil over moderate heat. Cook for 10 minutes.

Add the cucumbers to the pan and

Exotic Cucumber and Pork Soup.

bring the soup back to the boil. Boil for 3 minutes, or until the cucumbers are translucent. Pour the soup into a warmed tureen and serve at once.

Georgian Vegetable Soup

An inexpensive and easy-to-make soup, Georgian Vegetable Soup may be served with crusty bread and butter for a light and warming winter lunch or dinner.

4-6 SERVINGS

1 oz. [2 tablespoons] butter
1 large onion, thinly sliced and pushed out into rings
2 tablespoons flour
2 pints [5 cups] chicken stock
1 lb. tomatoes, blanched, peeled, seeded and coarsely chopped
1 lb. leeks, washed, trimmed and cut into ½-inch lengths
1 teaspoon salt
½ teaspoon black pepper
½ teaspoon dried oregano
1 bay leaf
1 tablespoon chopped fresh chives

In a large saucepan, melt the butter over moderate heat. When the foam subsides, add the onion and cook, stirring occasionally, for 5 to 7 minutes, or until it is soft and translucent but not brown. Remove the pan from the heat and, with a wooden spoon, stir in the flour to make a smooth paste.

Gradually stir in the chicken stock. Add the tomatoes, leeks, salt, pepper, oregano and the bay leaf to the pan.

Return the pan to high heat and bring the soup to the boil, stirring constantly. Reduce the heat to low, cover the pan and simmer for 20 minutes or until the leeks are soft.

Remove the pan from the heat. Remove and discard the bay leaf. Pour the soup into a warmed soup tureen, sprinkle on the chives and serve immediately.

Knuckle of Lamb and Tomato Soup

Serve this substantial main dish soup with plenty of crusty bread.

4 SERVINGS

3 lamb's knuckles, each sawn into 2 pieces
4 peppercorns
1½ teaspoons salt
    large bouquet garni, consisting of 8 parsley sprigs, 2 thyme sprays and 2 bay leaves tied together
1 onion, halved
1 oz. [2 tablespoons] butter
1 onion, finely chopped
1 garlic clove, chopped
1 tablespoon flour
2 lb. canned peeled tomatoes, drained and coarsely chopped
1 teaspoon dried basil
¼ teaspoon pepper

Put the knuckles, peppercorns, 1 teaspoon salt, the bouquet garni and the halved onion in a large saucepan. Pour in enough water just to cover the knuckles.

Place the pan over high heat and bring the water to the boil. Reduce the heat to low, cover the pan and simmer for 1 hour.

Remove the pan from the heat and lift out the knuckles. Strain the liquid into a mixing bowl and set aside.

With a sharp knife, remove the meat from the knuckle bones and cut it into 1-inch pieces. Set the meat aside.

When the cooking liquid is cold, skim the fat off the surface with a metal spoon. Reserve 5 fluid ounces [⅝ cup].

In a medium-sized saucepan, melt the butter over moderate heat. When the foam subsides, add the chopped onion and garlic and fry, stirring occasionally, for 5 to 7 minutes, or until the onion is soft and translucent but not brown.

With a wooden spoon, stir in the flour. Cook, stirring constantly, for 2 minutes.

Remove the pan from the heat and stir in the reserved cooking liquid. Return the pan to the heat and add the tomatoes, basil, the remaining salt and the pepper. Bring the mixture to the boil, stirring.

Reduce the heat to low and add the knuckle meat. Simmer gently for 10 minutes, or until the meat is reheated.

Remove the pan from the heat and serve at once.

Mushroom Soup

This easy-to-make Mushroom Soup, flavoured with oregano and cayenne pepper, tastes delicious served with croûtons.

4-6 SERVINGS

1 oz. [2 tablespoons] butter
1 small onion, finely chopped
3 tablespoons flour
1 teaspoon salt
½ teaspoon black pepper
¼ teaspoon dried oregano
⅛ teaspoon cayenne pepper
1½ pints [3¾ cups] chicken stock
1 lb. mushrooms, stalks removed, wiped clean and sliced
1 bay leaf
5 fl. oz. double cream [⅝ cup heavy cream]

In a large saucepan, melt the butter over moderate heat. When the foam subsides, add the onion and fry, stirring occasionally, for 5 to 7 minutes, or until the onion is soft and translucent but not brown.

Remove the pan from the heat. With a wooden spoon, stir in the flour, salt, pepper, oregano and cayenne to make a smooth paste. Gradually stir in the stock, being careful to avoid lumps. Stir in the mushrooms and bay leaf.

Return the pan to the heat and bring the soup to the boil, stirring constantly. Reduce the heat to low, cover the pan and simmer for 30 minutes.

Uncover the pan and stir in the cream. Cook the soup, stirring constantly, for 2 to 3 minutes or until it is hot.

Remove the pan from the heat. Remove and discard the bay leaf and serve.

Mushroom Soup is easy to make.

Onion Soup

Onion Soup (pictured on page 1) *may be served for lunch with croûtons and chopped spring onions* [scallions], *chives or watercress.*

4 SERVINGS

1 tablespoon butter
2 tablespoons vegetable oil
1 garlic clove, crushed
1 small potato, peeled and chopped
8 medium-sized onions, peeled
1 pint [2½ cups] milk
1 pint [2½ cups] water
½ teaspoon salt
½ teaspoon freshly ground black pepper
¼ teaspoon dried sage
¼ teaspoon dried thyme
1 tablespoon cornflour [cornstarch] dissolved in 3 tablespoons water
4 fl. oz. single cream [½ cup light cream]

In a medium-sized frying-pan, melt the butter with the oil over low heat. When the foam subsides, add the garlic and cook, stirring occasionally, for 4 minutes. Increase the heat to moderately high. Add the potato and cook, stirring frequently, for 4 minutes or until it is brown.

Meanwhile, thinly slice two of the onions and push the slices out into rings.

Using a slotted spoon, remove the potato from the pan and drain it on kitchen paper towels.

Add the onion rings to the frying-pan and cook them, stirring occasionally, for 5 to 7 minutes or until they are soft and translucent but not brown. Remove the pan from the heat. Using the slotted spoon, remove the onion rings from the pan and place them to drain on kitchen paper towels. Set aside.

Place the remaining onions on a chopping board and, using a sharp knife, chop them finely.

Pour the milk and water into a large saucepan. Add the salt, pepper, sage, thyme, potato and chopped onions. Place the pan over low heat and bring the liquid to the boil. Cover the pan and simmer for 30 minutes or until the onions are tender.

Remove the pan from the heat. Strain the onion mixture into a large mixing bowl. Using the back of a wooden spoon, press down on the vegetables in the strainer to extract all the juices. Discard the contents of the strainer.

Rinse out the saucepan and wipe it dry. Return the strained soup to the saucepan. Add the reserved onion rings and stir in the cornflour [cornstarch] mixture. Place the pan over moderate heat and, stirring constantly, bring the soup to the boil.

Simmer for 1 minute, stirring constantly.

Remove the pan from the heat. Stir in the cream and pour the soup into warmed individual soup bowls.

Serve immediately.

Pea Soup with Ham

A warming winter soup, Pea Soup with Ham may be served on its own or with French bread for a sustaining lunch or supper. For the best results, make the soup the day before you intend to serve it and reheat.

4-6 SERVINGS

1 ham hock, soaked overnight and drained
5 pints [6¼ pints] water
bouquet garni, consisting of 4 parsley sprigs, 1 thyme spray and 1 bay leaf tied together
1 teaspoon freshly ground black pepper
1 oz. [2 tablespoons] butter
1 medium-sized onion, thinly sliced
1 medium-sized garlic clove, crushed
2 small carrots, scraped and thinly sliced
8 oz. [1 cup] split peas, soaked overnight and drained

Place the ham hock in a large saucepan and pour over 4 pints [5 pints] of the water. Add the bouquet garni and black pepper. Place the pan over moderate heat and bring the water to the boil, skimming off any scum that rises to the surface. Reduce the heat to low, cover the pan and simmer for 1½ to 2 hours or until the meat is very tender and nearly falling off the bone.

Remove the pan from the heat. Using tongs or two large spoons, transfer the ham hock to a plate. Cover it with aluminium foil. Set aside.

Strain the cooking liquid into a large mixing bowl and set aside to cool to room temperature. Then place the bowl in the refrigerator and chill for 2 hours or until a layer of fat has formed on the top of the liquid. Remove and discard the layer of fat. Set the cooking liquid aside.

In a large saucepan, melt the butter over moderate heat. When the foam subsides, add the onion, garlic and carrots and fry, stirring occasionally, for 5 to 7 minutes or until the onion is soft and translucent but not brown.

Add the split peas to the pan and cook, stirring constantly, for 5 minutes.

Add the cooking liquid and the remaining water and bring it to the boil over high

Thick and warming, Pea Soup with Ham is full of goodness for family meals, yet elegant enough to serve as a first course to a special dinner party.

heat, stirring occasionally. Cover the pan, reduce the heat to low and simmer for 2 hours or until the peas are tender. Remove the pan from the heat and set aside to cool for 15 minutes. Then purée the mixture in a food mill or electric blender. Return the puréed soup to the pan. Add more water if the soup is too thick for your taste. Set aside.

Cut the meat from the ham hock bone, discarding any fat. Using a sharp knife, chop the meat into very small pieces.

Add the meat to the pan and return the pan to low heat. Simmer the soup for a

further 10 minutes or until the meat is heated through and the soup is hot but not boiling.

Remove the pan from the heat and transfer the soup to a warmed tureen or individual warmed soup bowls. Serve immediately.

Potato Soup

A warm soup, easy-to-make and inexpensive, Potato Soup makes a tasty lunch for the whole family. Serve with lots of brown bread and butter.

4-6 SERVINGS

2 oz. [¼ cup] butter
2 tablespoons vegetable oil
1 medium-sized onion, finely chopped
3 medium-sized leeks, white parts only, trimmed and very thinly sliced
6 potatoes, peeled and finely chopped
1 teaspoon salt
½ teaspoon freshly ground black pepper
1 pint [2½ cups] home-made chicken stock
10 fl. oz. [1¼ cups] milk

In a medium-sized saucepan, melt the butter with the oil over moderate heat. When the foam subsides, add the onion and cook, stirring occasionally, for 5 to 7 minutes or until the onion is soft and translucent but not brown. Add the leeks and potatoes and cook, stirring and turning occasionally, for 10 to 12 minutes or until the potatoes are lightly and evenly browned. Season with the salt and pepper and pour over the chicken stock and milk. Increase the heat to high and bring the liquid to the boil, stirring constantly. Reduce the heat to moderately low, cover the saucepan and simmer the liquid for 25 minutes.

Remove the pan from the heat and pour the soup through a fine wire strainer held over a large mixing bowl. Using the back of a wooden spoon, rub the vegetables through the strainer. Discard the pulp left in the strainer.

Return the soup to the saucepan and place the pan over moderately low heat. Cook the soup, stirring occasionally, for 5 minutes.

Remove the pan from the heat. Pour the soup into a large warmed soup tureen or individual soup bowls and serve immediately.

Quebec Vegetable Soup

This soup originates from Canada, although soups bearing similar names and having similar ingredients are found throughout the world. It is a rich and simple-to-make soup.

4 SERVINGS

1 oz. [2 tablespoons] butter
2 tablespoons flour
2 pints [5 cups] chicken stock
1 carrot, scraped and chopped
1 celery stalk, trimmed and
   chopped
1 teaspoon salt
½ teaspoon black pepper
¼ teaspoon grated nutmeg
4 egg yolks
8 fl. oz. double cream [1 cup heavy
   cream]

In a large, heavy saucepan, melt the butter over moderate heat. When the foam subsides, remove the pan from the heat and stir in the flour to make a smooth paste. Gradually stir in the stock, being careful to avoid lumps. Stir in the carrot, celery, salt, pepper and nutmeg.

Return the pan to the heat and bring the soup to the boil, stirring constantly.

Reduce the heat to low, cover the pan and simmer the soup for 30 to 35 minutes or until the vegetables are very tender.

In a small mixing bowl, beat the egg yolks and the cream together with a fork until they are thoroughly combined.

Stir the cream and egg yolk mixture into the soup and cook, stirring constantly, for 4 to 5 minutes or until the soup is thick and smooth. Do not let the soup boil or it will curdle.

Remove the pan from the heat. Pour the soup into a warmed soup tureen or individual soup bowls and serve.

Revythia

GREEK CHICK-PEA SOUP

A filling soup from Greece made with chick-peas, Revythia will be a warming, nourishing dish for the family during even the coldest weather.

3-4 SERVINGS

2 pints [5 cups] chicken stock
12 oz. [2 cups] dried chick-peas,
   soaked overnight and drained
2 fl. oz. [¼ cup] olive oil
   bouquet garni, consisting of 4
   parsley sprigs, 1 thyme spray

and 1 bay leaf tied together
1 teaspoon salt
1 teaspoon freshly ground black
   pepper
1 teaspoon lemon juice
2 medium-sized onions, chopped
1 tablespoon chopped fresh parsley

In a large, heavy-based saucepan, bring the stock and the chick-peas to the boil over high heat, skimming off any scum which rises to the surface with a metal spoon.

Reduce the heat to low and add the olive oil, bouquet garni, salt, pepper and lemon juice. Cover the pan and simmer for 1 hour. Add the onions and continue simmering the soup for a further ½ hour, or until the chick-peas are very tender.

Remove the pan from the heat. Using a slotted spoon, remove about half the chick-pea mixture and either rub it through a strainer, using the back of a wooden spoon, or purée the mixture in a blender. Return the puréed chick-pea mixture to the pan. Return the pan to the heat and bring the soup to the boil over

Delicate but sustaining Quebec Vegetable Soup.

This satisfying Tomato Soup is a traditional British favourite.

moderate heat, stirring constantly. Taste the soup and, if necessary, add more salt and pepper.

Remove the pan from the heat and pour the soup into a warmed soup tureen. Sprinkle over the parsley and serve immediately.

Thrifty Soup

A filling and, as its name suggests, economical soup, Thrifty Soup may be served as a light lunch or supper.

8 SERVINGS

2 oz. [¼ cup] pearl barley
1½ lb. pork shoulder, excess fat removed, boned and cut into 1-inch cubes
3 pints [7½ cups] cold water
large bouquet garni consisting of 8 parsley sprigs, 2 thyme sprays and 2 bay leaves, tied together
1½ teaspoons salt
1 teaspoon white pepper
3 carrots, scraped and diced
1 large leek, trimmed, cleaned and chopped
3 celery stalks, trimmed, cleaned and chopped
6 potatoes, peeled and thinly sliced
1 pint [2½ cups] milk
1 tablespoon chopped fresh parsley

Place the pearl barley, pork, water, bouquet garni, salt and pepper in a large saucepan and bring the mixture to the boil over high heat. Reduce the heat to low, cover the pan and cook for 1½ hours, stirring occasionally.

Add the carrots, leek, celery and potatoes, increase the heat to high and bring the liquid to the boil, stirring constantly. Reduce the heat to moderate, cover the pan and cook for a further 15 to 20 minutes or until the vegetables are very tender. Stir in the milk and continue cooking for 4 to 5 minutes or until the liquid is hot.

Remove and discard the bouquet garni. Pour the soup into a warmed soup tureen and sprinkle over the parsley. Serve immediately.

Tomato Soup

This Tomato Soup allows the fresh taste of the tomatoes to predominate. For the family serve the soup with fresh bread or toasted rounds of French bread.

4 SERVINGS

1 oz. [2 tablespoons] butter
1½ lb. tomatoes, quartered
1½ pints [3¾ cups] chicken stock
1 medium-sized onion, finely chopped
1 bay leaf
½ teaspoon black pepper
¼ teaspoon salt
thinly pared rind of ¼ orange
2 teaspoons lemon juice
1 teaspoon sugar

In a medium-sized saucepan, melt the butter over low heat. When the foam subsides, add the tomatoes and cook for 10 minutes, stirring frequently. Increase the heat to moderate and add the stock, onion, bay leaf, pepper, salt and orange rind. When the liquid comes to the boil, reduce the heat to low, cover the pan and simmer for 45 minutes.

Remove the pan from the heat and pour the contents through a strainer into a medium-sized saucepan. Using the back of a wooden spoon, rub the tomato mixture through the strainer until only a dry pulp is left. Discard the pulp.

Add the lemon juice and sugar to the pan and place it over low heat. Bring the soup to the boil, stirring frequently. Remove the pan from the heat and pour the soup into a warmed soup tureen. Serve immediately.

Turkish Yogurt, Chicken and Barley Soup

This a refreshing and filling soup. Serve before a rather light main course.

4-6 SERVINGS

1 oz. [2 tablespoons] butter
2 medium-sized onions, finely chopped
2 pints [5 cups] home-made chicken stock
3 oz. [⅜ cup] pearl barley, soaked overnight and drained
1 tablespoon chopped fresh parsley
2 oz. cooked chicken, shredded
½ teaspoon salt
¼ teaspoon white pepper
1 pint [2½ cups] yogurt
1 tablespoon chopped fresh mint

In a large saucepan, melt the butter over moderate heat. When the foam subsides, add the onions and fry, stirring occasionally, for 5 to 7 minutes or until the onions are soft and translucent but not brown. Pour in the chicken stock, increase the heat to high and bring the liquid to the boil.

Reduce the heat to low and add the barley. Cover the pan and simmer for 30 minutes or until the barley is tender. Add the parsley, chicken, salt and pepper and simmer for 10 minutes. Remove the pan from the heat.

Pour the yogurt into a medium-sized mixing bowl. Using a fork, beat the yogurt until it is smooth. Pour in a little of the soup, beating constantly. Gradually pour the yogurt into the soup, beating all the time. Place the saucepan over moderate heat and heat the soup until it is very hot. Do not allow it to boil or it will curdle.

Stir the mint into the soup. Pour the soup into a warmed tureen and serve.

Vegetable Soup

One of the simplest and most economical soups, Vegetable Soup is warm and welcoming for the family on a cold day.

8 SERVINGS

2 oz. [¼ cup] vegetable fat
3 large carrots, scraped and diced
1 small swede [rutabaga], peeled and diced
2 large leeks, trimmed and coarsely chopped
2 large potatoes, peeled and diced
3 celery stalks, trimmed and coarsely chopped
6 tomatoes, blanched, peeled and coarsely chopped
4 oz. dried butter [lima] beans,

soaked overnight and drained
1½ teaspoons salt
1 teaspoon freshly ground black pepper
3½ pints [8¾ cups] home-made beef stock
2 bay leaves
2 oz. frozen peas, thawed
1 tablespoon finely chopped fresh parsley

In a large, heavy-based saucepan, melt the vegetable fat over moderate heat. When the foam subsides, add the carrots, swede [rutabaga], leeks, potatoes and celery and cook, stirring occasionally, for 10 minutes.

Stir in the tomatoes, beans, salt and pepper and pour over the beef stock. Add the bay leaves, increase the heat to high and bring the mixture to the boil, stirring constantly.

Reduce the heat to moderately low, cover the pan and simmer, stirring occasionally, for 20 minutes or until the vegetables are soft.

Remove the pan from the heat and strain the soup through a large, fine wire strainer into a large mixing bowl. Remove and discard the bay leaves.

Remove about half the vegetables remaining in the strainer and add them to the strained stock in the bowl. With the back of a wooden spoon, rub the remaining vegetables through the strainer into a small mixing bowl. Alternatively, place the remaining half of the vegetables in the jar of an electric blender and blend at high speed for 30 seconds or until a purée is formed.

Transfer the purée to the saucepan and stir in the reserved stock and vegetable mixture. Place the saucepan over high heat, add the peas and bring the liquid back to the boil, stirring frequently. Reduce the heat to moderately low and simmer for a further 5 minutes or until the peas are tender.

Remove the pan from the heat and pour the soup into a warmed tureen or individual bowls. Sprinkle over the parsley and serve immediately.

Vegetable and Lentil Soup

A hearty and warming winter soup, Vegetable and Lentil Soup is almost a meal in itself served with crisp rolls and butter.

6 SERVINGS

1 lb. [2 cups] lentils, soaked overnight
4 pints [5 pints] cold water
1 ham bone or knuckle (optional)
8 oz. lean bacon, in one piece

1 leek, trimmed, cleaned and chopped
2 large carrots, scraped and chopped
1 medium-sized parsnip, peeled and chopped
2 celery stalks, trimmed and chopped
1½ teaspoons salt
2 tablespoons vegetable oil
2 medium-sized onions, finely chopped
2 tablespoons flour
1½ tablespoons cider vinegar
8 oz. garlic sausage, diced
¼ teaspoon dried thyme
½ teaspoon freshly ground black pepper

Drain the lentils in a colander and set aside.

In a large, heavy saucepan, bring the water to the boil over high heat. Remove the pan from the heat and add the lentils, ham bone or knuckle, if you are using it, bacon, leek, carrots, parsnip, celery and ½ teaspoon of the salt. Return the pan to moderate heat and bring to the boil. Reduce the heat to low and simmer the soup for 45 minutes.

Meanwhile, in a heavy frying-pan heat the oil over moderate heat. When the oil is hot, add the onions and cook, stirring occasionally, for 5 to 7 minutes, or until the onions are soft and translucent but not brown. Sprinkle the flour over the onions, reduce the heat to low and cook, stirring constantly, for 3 to 4 minutes or until the flour turns golden brown. Do not let the flour burn.

Remove the frying-pan from the heat and add about a cupful of the soup to the mixture, stirring well with a wooden spoon until the mixture is thick and creamy. Stir in the vinegar.

Pour the mixture in the frying-pan into the soup, stirring with a wooden spoon until the ingredients are well blended.

Cover the pan and simmer the soup over low heat for a further 1 hour, or until the lentils are tender. Add more water if the soup gets too thick.

Remove the ham bone or knuckle from the soup and discard it. Remove the bacon from the soup and cut it into small pieces.

Return the bacon pieces to the soup and add the sausage, thyme, the remaining salt and the pepper. Simmer for a further 4 to 5 minutes, or until the sausage is heated through.

Remove the pan from the heat and serve the soup at once.

Hearty Vegetable and Lentil Soup is adapted from a German recipe.

Yablonchni Apple Soup

Yablonchni Apple Soup is a traditional Russian soup. It is delicious served ice cold with finely diced apple and croûtons fried in bacon fat.

4-6 SERVINGS

6 large cooking apples, peeled, cored and sliced
12 fl. oz. [1½ cups] water
1-inch strip pared lemon rind
2 tablespoons sugar
4 tablespoons blackcurrant jelly
26 fl. oz. [3¼ cups] (1 bottle) red wine
4 oz. [2 cups] fresh brown breadcrumbs

juice of 1 lemon
½ teaspoon ground cinnamon

Put the apples in a large saucepan and add the water, lemon rind and sugar. Place the pan over moderate heat and bring the liquid to the boil. Reduce the heat to low and simmer for 6 to 8 minutes or until the apples are tender. Remove and discard the lemon rind. Add the blackcurrant jelly, wine, breadcrumbs and lemon juice. Increase the heat to high and bring the mixture to the boil, stirring constantly. Add the cinnamon and remove the pan from the heat.

Pour the ingredients into a large fine strainer held over a large mixing bowl.

The Russians love rich fruit soups - hence Yablonchni Apple Soup with its fabulous blend of apples, blackcurrant jelly and red wine. Serve as first course to a special meal.

Using the back of a wooden spoon, rub the ingredients through the strainer until only a dry pulp is left. Discard the contents of the strainer. Set the purée aside to cool.

Place the bowl in the refrigerator and chill the soup overnight. Remove the bowl from the refrigerator and pour the soup into a soup tureen. Serve immediately.

Lamb and Lemon Soup

This thick, lemony lamb soup, flavoured with paprika and mint, is a traditional Turkish wedding soup. Ideally, it should be served with hot, flat Turkish bread.

6 SERVINGS

1 lb. boned leg of lamb, cut into
    1-inch cubes
2 oz. [½ cup] flour
3 tablespoons olive oil
2 pints [5 cups] water
2 medium-sized onions, quartered
2 medium-sized carrots, scraped
    and quartered
1 teaspoon salt
½ teaspoon black pepper
1 teaspoon cayenne pepper
3 egg yolks
2 tablespoons fresh lemon juice
2 oz. [¼ cup] butter, melted
2 teaspoons paprika
½ teaspoon ground cinnamon
2 tablespoons finely chopped fresh
    mint

Coat the lamb cubes with the flour, shaking off any excess.

In a large saucepan, heat the oil over moderate heat. Add the lamb cubes and cook them, stirring occasionally, for 4 to 5 minutes, or until they are lightly browned on all sides.

Pour the water into the pan and bring it to the boil.

With a metal spoon, skim any scum from the surface. Add the onions, carrots, salt, pepper and cayenne.

Reduce the heat to low, cover the pan and simmer for 1½ to 1¾ hours, or until the meat is very tender.

In a small mixing bowl, beat the egg yolks with a wire whisk. Beat in the lemon juice and 2 tablespoons of the hot lamb mixture in the saucepan.

Remove the pan from the heat and gradually beat in the egg yolk mixture. Return the pan to very low heat and, stirring constantly, warm the soup until it is hot. Do not allow it to boil or it will curdle.

Remove the pan from the heat and pour the soup into a warmed soup tureen.

In a small bowl, combine the melted butter, paprika and cinnamon. Spoon the mixture over the soup. Sprinkle on the mint and serve at once.

Windsor Soup

A traditional British recipe, Windsor Soup makes a sustaining first course. Serve with brown bread and butter.

8 SERVINGS

2 oz. [¼ cup] butter
8 oz. boned shin of beef, trimmed
    of fat and cubed
8 oz. lean boned leg of lamb,
    cubed
1 large onion, sliced
1 large carrot, scraped and sliced
2 oz. [½ cup] flour
4 pints [5 pints] home-made beef
    stock
    bouquet garni, consisting of 4
    parsley sprigs, 1 thyme spray
    and 1 bay leaf tied together
1 teaspoon salt
½ teaspoon cayenne pepper
4 fl. oz. [½ cup] Madeira

In a large saucepan, melt the butter over moderate heat. When the foam subsides, add the beef, lamb, onion and carrot and fry, stirring frequently, for 8 to 10 minutes or until the ingredients are lightly browned. Add the flour and cook for a further 5 minutes, stirring constantly.

Remove the pan from the heat. Gradually pour in the stock, stirring constantly and being careful to avoid lumps.

Lamb and Lemon Soup has the distinctively Middle Eastern flavour of lemon and mint, and is traditionally served at wedding feasts in Turkey.

Return the pan to the heat, increase the heat to high and bring the soup to the boil, stirring constantly. Reduce the heat to low and add the bouquet garni, salt and cayenne. Cover the pan and simmer the soup for 1½ hours or until the meat is very tender. Remove the pan from the heat.

Pour the soup through a fine strainer held over a large bowl and, using the back of a wooden spoon, rub the meat and vegetables through the strainer to form a purée. Alternatively, purée the meat and vegetables in an electric blender.

Return the soup to the saucepan and set the pan over moderate heat. Add the Madeira and cook the soup, stirring constantly, until it is very hot but not boiling. Remove the pan from the heat. Pour the soup into a warmed soup tureen or individual warmed soup bowls and serve at once.

Beef with Dumplings

This beef stew with mushrooms, dumplings and sour cream is a substantial and satisfying main dish. Serve it with a green vegetable or a fresh green salad and French bread.

4 SERVINGS

4 tablespoons flour
1 teaspoon salt
¼ teaspoon black pepper
2 lb. stewing steak, trimmed of fat and cut into 1-inch cubes
1 oz. [2 tablespoons] butter
1 tablespoon vegetable oil
1 large onion, finely diced
2 tablespoons brandy, warmed (optional)
1 bay leaf
2 pints [5 cups] home-made beef stock
6 oz. mushrooms, wiped clean
5 fl. oz. [⅝ cup] sour cream
DUMPLINGS
8 oz. breadcrumbs made from day-old white bread
4 tablespoons water
2 eggs, lightly beaten
¼ teaspoon salt
¼ teaspoon black pepper
1½ tablespoons chopped fresh parsley
1 onion, grated
½ teaspoon ground mace

Preheat the oven to warm 325°F (Gas Mark 3, 170°C).

Mix the flour, salt and pepper together on a large plate. Roll the beef cubes in the flour mixture until they are lightly coated.

In a large frying-pan heat the butter and oil over moderate heat. Add the onion and cook, stirring occasionally, for 5 to 7 minutes, or until it is soft and translucent. With a slotted spoon, remove the onion and set aside on a plate.

Add the beef cubes to the pan, a few at a time. Brown them well, adding more butter and oil if necessary. Remove the beef cubes as they brown and place them in a large ovenproof casserole.

If you are using the brandy, put it in a metal ladle. Set it alight and pour it, still burning, over the beef cubes in the casserole. When the brandy has stopped burning, add the onion to the casserole with the bay leaf and stock.

Cover the casserole and place in the oven to cook for 2 hours.

While the meat is cooking, make the dumplings. Put the breadcrumbs into a large mixing bowl. Add the water, a little at a time, and toss lightly with a fork. The breadcrumbs should be just moistened, not soggy. Still using the fork, lightly mix in the eggs. Add the salt, pepper, parsley, onion and mace.

With floured hands, shape the mixture into walnut-sized balls. Add the dumplings to the casserole, with the mushrooms, cover and cook for 30 minutes. Spoon over the sour cream just before serving.

Filling Beef with Dumplings needs only salad and lots of crusty bread to make a complete meal.

Beef Stew

This tasty Beef Stew may be served with boiled potatoes and braised carrots.

4 SERVINGS

2 lb. brisket of beef, trimmed of
  excess fat and cut into 1-inch cubes
3 tablespoons Dijon mustard
2 garlic cloves, crushed
2 tablespoons vegetable oil
2 lb. leeks, trimmed, washed and
  cut into 1-inch lengths
1 teaspoon sugar
2 tablespoons Worcestershire sauce
8 fl. oz. [1 cup] beef stock
8 oz. [2 cups] Gruyère cheese,
  finely grated

Preheat the oven to moderate 350°F (Gas Mark 4, 180°C).

Place the meat, mustard and garlic in a large mixing bowl and stir the ingredients together until the meat is coated with the mustard and garlic. In a large flameproof casserole, heat the oil over moderate heat. When the oil is hot, add the meat cubes and fry, stirring constantly, for 6 to 8 minutes or until the meat is lightly browned all over. Add the leeks, sugar and Worcestershire sauce.

Pour over the stock, increase the heat to high and bring the contents of the casserole to the boil. Remove the casserole from the heat and transfer it to the oven. Cook the meat, uncovered, for 2 hours, stirring occasionally.

Remove the casserole from the oven. Sprinkle over the cheese and return it to the oven. Cook for a further 10 to 15 minutes or until the cheese is bubbling and golden brown. Remove the casserole from the oven. Serve immediately, straight from the casserole.

Chilli Stew

Serve Chilli Stew with mashed potatoes or rice, bean salad and chilled lager.

4 SERVINGS

3 tablespoons vegetable oil
1 large onion, finely chopped
2 celery stalks, chopped
1 green pepper, white pith
  removed, seeded and chopped
2 garlic cloves, crushed
2 lb. minced [ground] beef
14 oz. canned peeled tomatoes, with
  the can juice reserved
5 oz. tomato purée

Beef Stew is an unusual blend of brisket, mustard and cheese.

1 teaspoon hot chilli powder
14 oz. canned kidney beans, drained
2 medium-sized cooking apples,
  cored and chopped
2 oz. prunes, stoned and chopped
2 tablespoons slivered almonds
4 oz. frozen French beans, thawed
  and chopped
$\frac{1}{4}$ teaspoon salt
$\frac{1}{2}$ teaspoon grated nutmeg

In a large, deep frying-pan, heat the oil over moderate heat. When the oil is hot, add the onion, celery, green pepper and garlic and fry, stirring occasionally, for 5 to 7 minutes or until the onion is soft and translucent but not brown. Stir in the minced [ground] beef and continue to fry, stirring frequently, for 5 minutes.

Add all of the remaining ingredients and stir well to mix. Bring the liquid to the boil. Reduce the heat to low, cover and simmer the mixture for 30 minutes. Uncover the pan and continue to simmer for a further 10 minutes.

Remove the pan from the heat and serve at once.

Flank Steak Stew with Herbs

  ①

A delicious and economical dish, Flank Steak Stew with Herbs makes a substantial dinner meal. Serve with green vegetables and a light, tossed salad.

6 SERVINGS

- 6 tablespoons seasoned flour, made with 6 tablespoons flour, 1 teaspoon salt and ½ teaspoon black pepper
- 3 lb. flank steak, cut into 1-inch cubes
- 3 oz. [⅜ cup] butter
- 2 tablespoons vegetable oil
- 3 medium-sized onions, thinly sliced
- 3 garlic cloves, crushed
- 1 large green pepper, white pith removed, seeded and chopped

- 2 oz. [⅓ cup] walnuts, finely chopped
- 2 tablespoons finely chopped fresh parsley
- ½ teaspoon dried oregano
- ½ teaspoon dried thyme
- 2 bay leaves
- 1 teaspoon salt
- 16 fl. oz. [2 cups] home-made beef stock
- 2 tablespoons tomato purée
- 1 tablespoon cornflour [cornstarch] mixed to a paste with 2 tablespoons water

Place the seasoned flour on a large, shallow plate. Roll the meat cubes in the flour, shaking off any excess. Set them aside.

In a large flameproof casserole, melt 2 ounces [¼ cup] of the butter with the oil over moderate heat. When the foam sub-

sides, add the meat cubes, a few at a time. Fry them, turning occasionally, for 5 minutes, or until they are lightly browned on all sides. With a slotted spoon, remove the meat from the pan and keep it warm while you fry the remaining cubes in the same way. Set the meat aside and keep it warm.

Add the remaining butter to the casserole and melt it over moderate heat. When the foam subsides, add the onions, garlic and green pepper. Cook, stirring occasionally, for 5 to 7 minutes, or until the onions are soft and translucent but not brown.

Stir in the walnuts, parsley, oregano, thyme, bay leaves and salt and cook the mixture, stirring occasionally, for 3 minutes. Pour in the beef stock and add the tomato purée. Stirring constantly, bring the liquid to the boil.

These colourful Yiddish Meatballs taste even better than they look - AND they make an economical family lunch or supper, served with rice!

drink, some well chilled cider, lager or beer.

4-6 SERVINGS

2 oz. [¼ cup] butter
2 lb. potatoes, scrubbed and thinly sliced
2 medium-sized onions, thinly sliced
1 small swede [rutabaga], peeled and thinly sliced
1 lb. skirt or flank steak, cut into 1-inch pieces
2 teaspoons salt
½ teaspoon freshly ground black pepper
2 teaspoons chopped fresh thyme or 1 teaspoon dried thyme
1 tablespoon flour
1½ tablespoons Worcestershire sauce
10 fl. oz. [1¼ cups] water

Using ½ ounce [1 tablespoon] of the butter, grease a 5-pint [2-quart] hot pot or casserole.

Preheat the oven to warm 325°F (Gas Mark 3, 170°C).

Beginning and ending with the potatoes, layer the vegetables and the meat in the casserole. Sprinkle the layers with the salt, pepper, thyme, flour and Worcestershire sauce.

Pour in the water. Cut the remaining butter into small pieces and scatter them over the top layer of potatoes.

Cover the casserole and place it in the centre of the oven. Bake for 2½ to 3 hours, or until the vegetables and meat are tender when pierced with the point of a sharp knife.

Remove the casserole or hot pot from the oven and serve immediately, straight from the dish.

2 medium-sized onions, finely grated
2 eggs, lightly beaten
2 teaspoons salt
1 teaspoon freshly ground black pepper
1 tablespoon Worcestershire sauce
2 tablespoons tomato ketchup
1 teaspoon grated nutmeg
3 fl. oz. [⅜ cup] vegetable oil or ground-nut oil

SAUCE
14 fl. oz. [1¾ cups] canned tomato juice
8 fl. oz. [1 cup] home-made beef stock
2 tablespoons tomato purée
1 teaspoon salt
½ teaspoon freshly ground black pepper
3 fl. oz. [⅜ cup] distilled malt vinegar
2 oz. [⅓ cup] soft brown sugar
1 tablespoon cornflour [cornstarch] mixed to a paste with 2 tablespoons water

In a large mixing bowl, combine the beef, bread, onions, eggs, salt, pepper, Worcestershire sauce, tomato ketchup and nutmeg. Using your hands, mix and knead the ingredients together for 5 minutes or until the meat mixture is thoroughly combined. Shape the meat mixture into 40 balls, approximately 1-inch in diameter. Set the meatballs aside.

In a large, flameproof casserole, heat the oil over moderate heat. When the oil is hot, add the meatballs, a few at a time, and fry, turning them frequently, for 6 to 8 minutes or until they are lightly browned all over. With a slotted spoon, remove the meatballs from the casserole as they brown and set them aside while you cook the remaining meatballs in the same way.

When all the meatballs have been cooked, add the tomato juice, beef stock, tomato purée, salt, pepper, vinegar, sugar and the cornflour [cornstarch] mixture to the casserole. Bring the mixture to the boil, stirring constantly.

When the sauce has thickened slightly, return the meatballs to the casserole. Reduce the heat to low, cover the casserole and simmer for 50 minutes to 1 hour or until the meatballs are cooked and very tender.

Remove the casserole from the heat. With a slotted spoon, remove the meatballs from the casserole and transfer them to a warmed serving dish. Taste the sauce and add salt and pepper if necessary. Pour the sauce over the meatballs and serve immediately.

Return the meat cubes to the casserole. Reduce the heat to low, cover the casserole and simmer for 1½ hours, or until the meat is tender when pierced with the point of a sharp knife. Stir the stew from time to time during the cooking period.

Stir in the cornflour [cornstarch] mixture and simmer for 5 minutes, or until the sauce has thickened.

Remove the casserole from the heat and serve the stew at once, straight from the casserole.

Meat and Potato Hot Pot

An inexpensive satisfying dish, this Meat and Potato Hot Pot is simple to make. Serve with a mixed green salad and, to

Yiddish Meatballs

An adaptation of a traditional Jewish recipe, Yiddish Meatballs are delicious meatballs in a sweet and sour tomato sauce. Serve with plain boiled rice and a mixed green salad and, to drink lots of chilled lager or dry white wine.

6 SERVINGS

2½ lb. lean beef, very finely minced [ground]
6 slices white bread, crusts removed, soaked in cold water and squeezed

Lamb

Lamb Ragoût

A simple brown stew, Lamb Ragoût can be made early in the day and reheated immediately before serving.

4 SERVINGS

2 lb. shoulder of lamb, boned
3 tablespoons vegetable oil
2 tablespoons flour
1 teaspoon salt
½ teaspoon black pepper
1¼ pints [3⅛ cups] beef stock
2 small garlic cloves, crushed
   bouquet garni, consisting of 4
   parsley sprigs, 1 thyme spray
   and 1 bay leaf tied together
½ teaspoon dried thyme
8 small potatoes, peeled
12 small onions, peeled
12 small whole carrots, scraped
2 oz. [⅓ cup] raisins

Cut the lamb into 2-inch cubes and dry them well on kitchen paper towels. In a large, heavy saucepan, heat the oil over moderate heat. Add the meat, a few pieces at a time, and brown on all sides. As the cubes are done, transfer them to a dish and keep warm.

When all the pieces have been browned, return them to the pan and sprinkle with the flour, salt and pepper. Toss the pieces of meat with a spoon to coat them with the other ingredients. Cook over moderate heat, mixing occasionally, until the flour is lightly browned.

Add the stock, garlic, bouquet garni and thyme. Cover the pan and bring the stock to the boil. Reduce the heat to low and simmer for 40 minutes.

Add the potatoes, onions, carrots and raisins. Replace the lid and simmer for another 45 minutes or until the meat is tender when pierced with a sharp knife and the vegetables are cooked. Taste the stock and add more seasoning if necessary.

To serve, remove the bouquet garni and transfer the mixture to a warmed serving dish.

Lamb and Mushroom Stew

A simple and nourishing dish, Lamb and Mushroom Stew makes a delicious family supper. Serve on a bed of rice.

4 SERVINGS

2 oz. [½ cup] seasoned flour, made
   with 2 oz. [½ cup] flour, 2
   teaspoons dried rosemary,
   1 teaspoon salt and ½ teaspoon
   black pepper
2 lb. boned leg of lamb, cut into
   1½-inch cubes

2 oz. [¼ cup] butter
3 medium-sized onions, thinly
   sliced
1 lb. mushrooms, wiped clean and
   sliced
½ teaspoon salt
¼ teaspoon black pepper
4 fl. oz. [½ cup] chicken stock
12 fl. oz. [1½ cups] sour cream

Place the seasoned flour on a shallow plate. Roll the meat cubes in it, shaking off any excess flour. Set the cubes aside.

In a large, deep frying-pan, melt the butter over moderate heat. When the foam subsides, add the onions and cook, stirring occasionally, for 5 to 7 minutes, or until they are soft and translucent but not brown. Add the lamb cubes and, stirring and turning occasionally, cook the mixture for 5 minutes, or until the meat is lightly and evenly browned.

Add the mushrooms, salt, pepper and chicken stock to the pan and mix well to blend. Bring the liquid to the boil. Reduce the heat to low, cover the pan and cook the mixture for 1 to 1¼ hours, or until the meat is very tender.

Stir in the sour cream and mix well to blend. Heat the mixture gently over low

Lamb Ragoût is a nutritious mixture of meat and vegetables.

heat until the sauce is hot but not boiling. Remove the pan from the heat and transfer the mixture to a warmed serving dish. Serve at once.

Lancashire Hot Pot

Lancashire Hot Pot is a traditional British dish made with lamb chops, kidneys and oysters.

4 SERVINGS

1½ lb. potatoes, peeled and thickly sliced
1½ teaspoons salt
8 small lamb chops, trimmed of excess fat
4 oz. mushrooms, sliced
4 lambs' kidneys, cleaned, prepared and sliced
1 large onion, sliced
½ teaspoon black pepper
1 teaspoon dried thyme
12 oysters
10 fl. oz. [1¼ cups] beef stock

Preheat the oven to moderate 350°F (Gas Mark 4, 180°C).

Cover the bottom of a deep ovenproof casserole with a layer of half the potatoes. Sprinkle over ¼ teaspoon of salt. Arrange the chops on the potatoes and cover them with the mushrooms, kidneys and onion.

Sprinkle over 1 teaspoon of the salt, pepper and thyme. Cover with the oysters and the remaining potatoes. Pour in the stock and sprinkle the remaining salt over the potatoes.

Cover the casserole and place it in the oven. Cook for 2 hours. Remove the lid and increase the heat to fairly hot 400°F (Gas Mark 6, 200°C). Cook for a further 30 minutes, or until the potatoes are tender and golden brown.

Remove the casserole from the oven and serve at once.

Meatballs with Spicy Sauce

This is a tasty dish, adapted from a North African recipe. Serve with boiled rice.

4 SERVINGS

2 lb. shoulder of lamb, boned and minced [ground]
2 onions, finely chopped
1 tablespoon chopped fresh parsley
1 teaspoon chopped fresh thyme
1 teaspoon salt
1 oz. [2 tablespoons] butter
2 tablespoons vegetable oil
1 small potato, finely chopped
1-inch piece of fresh root ginger, peeled and very finely chopped
1 teaspoon ground cumin
1 teaspoon ground coriander
½ teaspoon freshly ground black pepper
½ teaspoon sugar
½ teaspoon hot chilli powder
1 tablespoon white wine vinegar
⅛ teaspoon ground saffron, soaked in 2 tablespoons hot water
6 fl. oz. [¾ cup] water

Lancashire Hot Pot is a traditional favourite all over Britain.

In a large mixing bowl, combine the lamb, half the onions, the parsley, thyme and ½ teaspoon of the salt. Mix and knead the ingredients well. Shape the mixture into balls 1-inch in diameter.

In a large frying-pan, melt the butter with the oil over moderate heat. When the foam subsides, add the meatballs, a few at a time, and fry them, turning frequently, for 6 to 8 minutes, or until they are well browned. With a slotted spoon, transfer the meatballs to a plate.

In the same frying-pan, adding more oil and butter if necessary, fry the remaining onion and the potato, stirring occasionally, for 5 to 7 minutes or until the onion is soft and translucent but not brown and the potato is almost tender.

Add the ginger and cook, stirring occasionally, for 3 minutes. Add the cumin, coriander, pepper, sugar, chilli powder and the remaining salt and cook for 5 minutes, stirring frequently to prevent the spices from sticking to the bottom of the pan. Stir in the vinegar, saffron mixture and water. Reduce the heat to low and simmer for 2 minutes.

Return the meatballs to the pan and stir carefully to coat them with the spices. Cover the pan and simmer the mixture for 15 minutes or until the meatballs are just pink in the centre when broken open.

Remove the pan from the heat. Place the mixture on a serving dish and serve.

Whitsun Lamb

A delicious combination of lamb and asparagus, Whitsun Lamb is an ideal lunch or supper dish. Serve with creamed potatoes.

4 SERVINGS

2 lb. asparagus, cooked and drained

2 lb. leg of lamb, cut into 2-inch cubes

2 oz. [½ cup] seasoned flour, made with 2 oz. [½ cup] flour, 1 teaspoon salt and ½ teaspoon black pepper

2 oz. [¼ cup] butter

2 medium-sized onions, thinly sliced

10 fl. oz. [1¼ cups] chicken stock

5 fl. oz. double cream [⅝ cup heavy cream]

1 teaspoon salt

1 teaspoon black pepper
juice of ½ lemon

With a sharp knife, cut off the asparagus tips and set them aside. Keep hot.

Place the stems in the jar of an electric blender and blend until they form a smooth purée. Set aside.

Roll the lamb cubes in the seasoned flour, shaking off any excess.

In a large flameproof casserole, melt the butter over moderate heat. When the foam subsides, add the onions and fry, stirring occasionally, for 5 to 7 minutes or until they are soft and translucent but not brown.

Add the lamb cubes and fry, stirring and turning occasionally, for 5 to 8 minutes or until they are lightly and evenly browned. Stir in the stock and bring the liquid to the boil. Reduce the

Serve Whitsun Lamb, a super blend of meat and asparagus, as a special treat for Sunday lunch!

heat to low and simmer the mixture for 50 minutes to 1 hour or until the meat is tender when pierced with the point of a sharp knife.

Remove the casserole from the heat and, with a slotted spoon, transfer the lamb cubes to a plate. Keep hot.

Stir the puréed asparagus and cream into the sauce in the casserole. Add the salt, pepper and lemon juice and cook, stirring frequently, for 3 to 5 minutes or until the sauce is thick and smooth.

Place the meat on a serving dish and pour the sauce around the meat. Garnish with the reserved asparagus tips and serve immediately.

Meatballs with Hot Mexican Sauce

  ☆ ① ⧖

This recipe is for those who enjoy spicy food. Meatballs with Hot Mexican Sauce is an ideal dish for supper, served with noodles.

4-6 SERVINGS

MEATBALLS
2 lb. minced [ground] pork
1 large onion, finely grated
2 garlic cloves, crushed
2 oz. [⅓ cup] ground almonds
2 oz. [1 cup] fresh breadcrumbs
1 egg, lightly beaten
1 tablespoon chopped fresh parsley
¾ teaspoon ground cinnamon
½ teaspoon black pepper
1 teaspoon salt
3 tablespoons medium dry sherry
1 tablespoon butter
2 tablespoons olive oil

SAUCE
1 large onion, finely chopped
1 garlic clove, crushed
½ tablespoon soft brown sugar
6 medium-sized tomatoes, blanched, peeled, seeded and chopped
1 green pepper, white pith removed, seeded and sliced
1 red pepper, white pith removed, seeded and sliced
1 green chilli, finely chopped
¼ teaspoon cayenne pepper
1 teaspoon paprika
1 tablespoon chopped fresh parsley
5 fl. oz. [⅝ cup] beef stock
1 teaspoon salt
¼ teaspoon black pepper
2 teaspoons cornflour [cornstarch] dissolved in 4 tablespoons medium dry sherry

In a large mixing bowl, combine the pork, onion, garlic, almonds, breadcrumbs, egg, parsley, cinnamon, pepper, salt and sherry. Using your hands, mix and knead the ingredients well. Shape the meat mixture into about 36 walnut-sized balls.

In a large deep frying-pan, melt the butter with the oil over moderate heat. When the foam subsides, add the meatballs, a few at a time, and fry them, turning occasionally, for 6 to 8 minutes or until they are well browned. Transfer the meatballs to a plate. Set aside.

Add the onion, garlic and brown sugar to the frying-pan and fry, stirring occasionally, for 6 to 8 minutes, or until the onion is soft and golden brown. Add the tomatoes, green and red peppers, the chilli, cayenne, paprika and parsley and cook for 3 minutes, stirring occasionally.

Pour in the stock and season with the salt and pepper. Increase the heat to high and bring the mixture to the boil. Reduce the heat to low and stir in the cornflour [cornstarch] mixture. Add the meatballs to the sauce, cover the pan and continue cooking for a further 20 to 25 minutes or until the meatballs are thoroughly cooked.

Serve at once.

Meatballs with Hot Mexican Sauce will satisfy the whole family.

Near Eastern Pork with Peanuts and Grapes

Tender pork fillet, gently cooked with juicy grapes and sprinkled with toasted peanuts, Near Eastern Pork with Peanuts and Grapes is an exotic dish to serve at a special dinner party. If peanuts are not available, use any type of nut — although the flavour will, naturally, be slightly different.

6 SERVINGS

2 tablespoons peanut oil
2 lb. pork fillet, cut into 1-inch cubes
1 teaspoon salt
½ teaspoon black pepper
2½ oz. [½ cup] unsalted peanuts, ground
2 tablespoons soy sauce
¼ teaspoon mild chilli powder
1 lb. seedless white grapes, halved
2½ oz. [½ cup] unsalted peanuts, finely chopped and toasted

In a large frying-pan, heat the oil over moderate heat. When the oil is hot, add the pork cubes. Cook the pork, stirring and turning occasionally, for 6 to 8 minutes or until the cubes are lightly and evenly browned.

Add the salt, pepper, ground peanuts, soy sauce and chilli powder and mix well.

Exotic Near Eastern Pork with Peanuts and Grapes will provide a new - and delicious - taste experience for the family.

Reduce the heat to low. Add the grapes and simmer the mixture for 40 to 50 minutes, or until the pork is very tender when pierced with the point of a sharp knife.

Remove the pan from the heat and transfer the mixture to a warmed serving dish. Sprinkle with the chopped peanuts and serve at once.

Pork Casserole with Lemon

The lemon flavouring in this recipe counteracts the richness of the pork and enhances its flavour. Serve the casserole with jacket potatoes and steamed French beans. Pare the lemon rind in one piece so that it will be easy to remove.

8 SERVINGS

4 lb. pork fillet, cut into 1-inch cubes
2 oz. [½ cup] seasoned flour, made with 2 oz. [½ cup] flour, ½ teaspoon salt and ½ teaspoon black pepper
2 fl. oz. [¼ cup] olive oil

2 garlic cloves, crushed
3 medium-sized onions, roughly chopped
6 celery stalks, trimmed and cut into ½-inch lengths
1½ pints [3¾ cups] chicken stock
1 teaspoon dried marjoram
1 teaspoon dried chervil
½ teaspoon dried thyme
finely pared rind and juice of 2 lemons
2 lemons, peeled, white pith removed, segmented and finely chopped
1 tablespoon butter blended with ½ tablespoon flour

Coat the pork cubes in the seasoned flour, shaking off any excess. Set aside.

In a very large flameproof casserole, heat the oil over moderate heat. When the oil is hot, add the garlic and onions and cook them, stirring occasionally, for 5 to 7 minutes or until the onions are soft and translucent but not brown. Using a slotted spoon, transfer the onions and garlic to a plate. Set aside.

Add the pork cubes to the pan, a few at a time, and fry them, turning them frequently, for 6 to 8 minutes or until they are lightly and evenly browned. With a slotted spoon, transfer the cubes to a plate as they brown.

Return the onions and garlic to the casserole. Add the celery and pour in the chicken stock. Increase the heat to high and bring the stock to the boil, stirring constantly. Add the pork cubes and, when the mixture comes to the boil again, reduce the heat to low. Stir in the marjoram, chervil, thyme, lemon rind and juice. Cover the casserole and simmer the meat for 50 minutes or until it is very tender when pierced with the point of a sharp knife.

Remove and discard the lemon rind. Increase the heat to moderate and stir in the lemon segments. Add the butter mixture, in small pieces, stirring constantly, making sure that each piece is absorbed before adding the next. Reduce the heat to low and simmer the sauce for 2 minutes, stirring frequently. Remove the casserole from the heat and serve immediately.

Pork Stew

A delicious and inexpensive dinner dish, Pork Stew may be served with rice, courgettes grillées and a tomato salad. Some well-chilled white wine or lager would complement this dish very well.

4-6 SERVINGS

2 fl. oz. [¼ cup] vegetable oil
2 lb. lean pork fillet, cut into
   1-inch strips
1 medium-sized onion, thinly sliced
4 oz. mushrooms, wiped clean
   and sliced
3 celery stalks, trimmed and
   thinly sliced
1 tablespoon finely chopped
   orange rind
16 fl. oz. [2 cups] chicken stock
1 teaspoon curry powder
½ teaspoon salt
¼ teaspoon black pepper
2 teaspoons cornflour [cornstarch],
   dissolved in 3 tablespoons water
5 fl. oz. double cream [⅝ cup heavy
   cream]
2 teaspoons lemon juice

In a large flameproof casserole or saucepan, heat the oil over moderate heat. When the oil is hot, add the pork strips and cook them, turning occasionally, for 6 to 8 minutes, or until they are lightly and evenly browned. With a slotted spoon, transfer the pork to a bowl and set aside.

Add the onion to the casserole and cook, stirring occasionally, for 5 to 7 minutes, or until it is soft and translucent but not brown. Add the mushrooms, celery and orange rind. Add the stock and cook, stirring occasionally, for 3 to 5 minutes or until the stock has come to the boil. Stir in the curry powder, salt and pepper, and mix well to blend.

Return the pork to the casserole. Reduce the heat to low, cover the pan and simmer the mixture for 35 to 40 minutes, or until the pork is tender when pierced with a sharp knife.

Remove the pan from the heat and stir in the cornflour [cornstarch] mixture, stirring until it has dissolved. Stir in the cream and lemon juice and return the pan to low heat. Simmer the mixture gently for 2 to 3 minutes, or until the sauce is hot but not boiling.

Remove the pan from the heat and transfer the mixture to a warmed serving dish. Serve at once.

Spanish Pork Casserole

This flavourful Spanish Pork Casserole is ideal for an informal dinner or lunch. Serve it with saffron-flavoured rice for a really authentic touch!

6 SERVINGS

2 oz. [½ cup] seasoned flour, made
   with 2 oz. [½ cup] flour, ½ teaspoon
   salt and ¼ teaspoon black pepper
3 lb. lean pork fillet, cut into
   ¼-inch thick slices
4 tablespoons vegetable oil
2 medium-sized onions, sliced
2 garlic cloves, finely chopped
6 tomatoes, blanched, peeled,
   seeded and chopped
12 fl. oz. [1½ cups] dry white wine or
   chicken stock
1 teaspoon dried sweet basil
1 tablespoon chopped fresh parsley

Sprinkle the seasoned flour on to a plate. Coat the pork slices on both sides with the seasoned flour.

In a large frying-pan, heat the oil over moderate heat. When the oil is hot, add the pork slices and brown them for 4 minutes on each side. With tongs, transfer the slices from the pan to a flameproof casserole or saucepan.

Add the onions and garlic to the frying-pan and fry them for 8 to 10 minutes, or until they are golden brown.

Add the tomatoes, wine or stock and basil to the frying-pan and continue cooking for 2 to 3 minutes.

Pour the sauce over the meat. Cover the casserole or saucepan and place it over low heat. Simmer for 1 hour.

Remove the casserole from the heat and sprinkle the meat with parsley. Serve at once, from the casserole.

Serve Spanish Pork Casserole with saffron-flavoured rice for a really authentic Iberian touch!

Breast of Veal with Vegetables

A relatively inexpensive dish, Breast of Veal with Vegetables is colourful and quick to make. Serve with mashed potatoes and crusty bread for a satisfying family meal.

6 SERVINGS

1 x 3 lb. breast of veal, trimmed of excess fat
3 tablespoons vegetable oil
½ teaspoon salt
½ teaspoon freshly ground black pepper
10 fl. oz. [1¼ cups] home-made chicken stock
12 oz. small fresh or frozen carrots, scraped and cut into ¼-inch slices
8 oz. fresh or frozen and thawed peas, weighed after shelling
1 teaspoon soft brown sugar

Place the meat on a board and, using a sharp knife, cut it into 2- by 3-inch pieces.

In a large frying-pan, heat the oil over moderate heat. When the oil is hot, add the meat and cook, turning once, for 8 to 10 minutes or until it is lightly browned all over. Remove the pan from the heat. Pour off and discard the oil in the pan. Return the pan to the heat and sprinkle over the salt and pepper and pour in the stock. Bring the liquid to the boil, add the carrots and reduce the heat to moderately low. Simmer the mixture for 15 minutes.

Add the peas and sugar to the pan and continue cooking for 15 to 20 minutes or until the meat is tender when pierced with the point of a sharp knife.

Remove the pan from the heat and pour the meat and vegetables into a warmed serving dish.

Serve immediately.

Curried Veal Stew

Curried Veal Stew is a delicious way of preparing veal, and the spicy and creamy sauce gives the dish a delicate and subtle flavour. Serve with plain boiled rice and a tossed mixed salad. For special occasions, accompany it with dry white wine.

4 SERVINGS

2 lb. lean boned veal, cut into 1-inch cubes
1 teaspoon salt
1 teaspoon freshly ground black pepper
¼ teaspoon cayenne pepper
3 oz. [⅜ cup] butter
2 medium-sized onions, finely chopped
1 garlic clove, crushed
1 large tart apple, cored and chopped
2 celery stalks, trimmed and chopped
2 teaspoons curry powder
1 pint [2½ cups] chicken or veal stock
2 oz. [⅓ cup] sultanas or seedless raisins
2 tablespoons chopped blanched almonds
2 tablespoons double [heavy] cream
2 tablespoons cornflour [cornstarch] dissolved in 3 tablespoons chicken or veal stock

Place the veal on a working surface and rub in the salt, pepper and cayenne. Set aside.

Breast of Veal with Vegetables may be served with mashed potatoes and brown bread for a wholesome family meal.

White Meat Casserole is easy to make - and even easier to eat!

In a large flameproof casserole, melt the butter over moderate heat. When the foam subsides, add the onions and garlic and cook, stirring occasionally, for 5 to 7 minutes or until the onions are soft and translucent but not brown. Add the veal cubes and cook, turning and stirring, for 8 to 10 minutes or until they are evenly browned. Stir in the apple, celery and curry powder and mix well. Cook, stirring frequently, for 3 minutes. Pour over the stock and bring the liquid to the boil. Reduce the heat to low, cover and simmer the mixture for 40 minutes. Stir in the sultanas or seedless raisins and the almonds and continue to simmer the mixture for a further 20 minutes or until the meat is tender when pierced with the point of a sharp knife. Add the cream and cook for 1 minute.

Stir in the cornflour [cornstarch] mixture, and cook, stirring constantly, for 2 to 3 minutes or until the liquid has thickened. Remove the casserole from the heat and serve at once, straight from the casserole.

White Meat Casserole

A super way to prepare veal, White Meat Casserole is easy to make and tastes simply delicious served with rice and a crisp green salad. Accompany this dish with some well chilled white wine, such as Liebfraumilch, for a special treat.

6 SERVINGS

2 oz. [¼ cup] plus 2 tablespoons butter
1 medium-sized onion, finely chopped
3 lb. lean shoulder or breast of veal, cut into 1-inch cubes
28 fl. oz. [3½ cups] canned cream of mushroom soup
1 teaspoon paprika
¼ teaspoon grated nutmeg
1 teaspoon salt
½ teaspoon freshly ground white pepper
8 oz. button mushrooms, wiped clean and halved

Preheat the oven to moderate 350°F (Gas Mark 4, 180°C).

In a large flameproof casserole, melt the 2 ounces [¼ cup] of butter over moderate heat. When the foam subsides, add the onion and fry, stirring occasionally, for 5 to 7 minutes or until it is soft and translucent but not brown. Add the veal cubes and fry, stirring occasionally, for 6 to 8 minutes or until the meat is lightly browned all over. Pour over the soup. Season the mixture with the paprika, nutmeg, salt and pepper. Stir the ingredients together to mix well. Cover the casserole and transfer it to the oven. Cook the veal for 2 hours.

Meanwhile, in a small frying-pan, melt the remaining butter over moderate heat. When the foam subsides, add the mushrooms and fry, stirring constantly, for 3 minutes. Remove the pan from the heat and add the mushrooms to the casserole. Cook the mixture, covered, for a further 30 minutes or until the veal is very tender when pierced with the point of a sharp knife.

Remove the casserole from the oven. Serve immediately, straight from the casserole.

Brunswick Stew

This famous American stew, which is ideal for a family lunch or dinner, may be served with hot crusty bread.

4 SERVINGS

2 oz. [4 tablespoons] butter
8 chicken pieces
1 large onion, sliced
1 green pepper, white pith removed, seeded and coarsely chopped
10 fl. oz. [1¼ cups] chicken stock
14 oz. canned peeled tomatoes, drained
½ teaspoon salt
½ teaspoon cayenne pepper
1 tablespoon Worcestershire sauce
8 oz. canned and drained or frozen and thawed sweetcorn

1 lb. canned and drained or frozen and thawed lima beans or 1 lb. broad beans
1 tablespoon cornflour [cornstarch] mixed with 2 tablespoons water

In a flameproof casserole, heat the butter over moderate heat. Add the chicken pieces and fry them for 3 to 5 minutes on each side or until they are golden brown. Remove the chicken pieces and set them aside on a plate.

Add the onion and green pepper to the casserole and cook for 5 to 7 minutes, or until the onion is soft and translucent.

Add the stock, tomatoes, salt, cayenne

Brunswick Stew is a colourful and tasty mixture of chicken pieces and various vegetables.

and Worcestershire sauce. Stir to mix, return the chicken to the casserole and bring to the boil. Cover and reduce the heat to low. Simmer gently for 40 minutes.

Add the sweetcorn and lima or broad beans. Re-cover the casserole and continue to simmer for another 15 minutes.

Add the cornflour [cornstarch] mixture to the stew, stirring constantly. Cook, stirring, for 10 minutes.

Serve at once from the casserole.

Duck Curry

A rich, spicy dish, Duck Curry is easy to make. Serve it with plain boiled rice, fresh home-made chutney and a tomato and onion salad.

4 SERVINGS

5 tablespoons vegetable oil
1 x 6 lb. duck, cut into serving
   pieces
1 teaspoon mustard seeds
3 medium-sized onions, finely
   chopped
2 garlic cloves, finely chopped
1½-inch piece root ginger, peeled
   and finely chopped
1 green chilli, finely chopped
1 teaspoon ground cumin
1 teaspoon hot chilli powder
1 tablespoon ground coriander
1 tablespoon garam masala
1 teaspoon turmeric
½ teaspoon salt
3 tablespoons vinegar
½-inch slice creamed coconut
10 fl. oz. [1¼ cups] boiling water

In a large saucepan, heat the oil over moderate heat. Add the duck pieces and fry them for 4 to 5 minutes on each side or until they are golden brown. Using tongs, remove the duck pieces as they brown and set them aside on a plate.

Add the mustard seeds, cover the pan and fry them for 2 minutes. Keep the pan covered or the mustard seeds will spatter. Remove the cover and add the onions. Fry them for 8 minutes or until they are golden brown. Add the garlic, ginger and green chilli and fry, stirring constantly, for 2 to 3 minutes.

Put the cumin, chilli powder, coriander, garam masala, turmeric and salt in a small bowl. Add the vinegar and mix well to make a paste. Add the paste to the saucepan and fry, stirring constantly, for 8 minutes.

This rich, hot Duck Curry is an authentic Indian dish. The spices used may be obtained from Oriental delicatessens.

Add the duck pieces and turn them over several times so that they are well coated with the spices. Continue frying for 2 to 3 minutes.

Meanwhile, in a small bowl, dissolve the creamed coconut in the water to make coconut milk. Pour the coconut milk over the duck pieces in the pan and stir to mix the coconut milk into the spices. Reduce the heat to moderately low, cover the pan and simmer for 40 minutes or until the duck is tender and the gravy thick.

Taste the curry and add more salt if necessary. Serve hot.

Liver with Olives and Mushrooms

A tasty and inexpensive meal, Liver with Olives and Mushrooms may be served with puréed potatoes and fresh peas cooked with mint.

4 SERVINGS

1 tablespoon vegetable oil
4 streaky bacon slices, chopped
4 medium-sized onions, finely chopped
4 oz. mushrooms, wiped clean and sliced
1½ oz. [3 tablespoons] butter
1 lb. pig's liver, trimmed and thinly sliced
12 fl. oz. [1½ cups] beef stock
1 teaspoon salt
½ teaspoon black pepper
½ teaspoon dried thyme
1 tablespoon cornflour [cornstarch] dissolved in 1 tablespoon water
12 green olives, halved and stoned
juice of ½ lemon

Preheat the oven to moderate 350°F (Gas Mark 4, 180°C).

In a medium-sized frying-pan, heat the vegetable oil over moderate heat. When the oil is hot, add the bacon and cook, stirring and turning occasionally, for 3 minutes. Add the onions and cook, stirring occasionally, for 5 to 7 minutes, or until they are soft and translucent but not brown. Stir in the mushrooms and cook, stirring occasionally, for 3 minutes.

With a slotted spoon, transfer the bacon and vegetables to a medium-sized oven-proof casserole.

Add the butter to the oil remaining in the frying-pan and melt it over moderate heat. When the foam subsides, add the liver to the pan and cook, turning occasionally, for 5 to 6 minutes, or until the meat is lightly and evenly browned. With a slotted spoon, remove the meat from the pan and add it to the casserole.

Pour the stock into the frying-pan and add the salt, pepper and thyme. Bring the liquid to the boil, stirring and scraping in any brown bits adhering to the bottom. Stir in the cornflour [cornstarch] mixture and cook, stirring constantly, for 1 minute, or until the liquid has thickened and is smooth. Remove the pan from the heat and pour the mixture into the casserole.

Stir in the olives and lemon juice and place the casserole in the oven. Bake for 1 to 1¼ hours, or until the meat is tender when pierced with the point of a sharp knife.

Remove the casserole from the oven and serve at once.

Oxtail Casserole

Oxtail is a comparatively inexpensive cut of meat, and when cooked in this manner makes a delightful, rich dish for the family. Serve the meat on the bones; however, if you are serving the oxtail at a dinner party, remove the meat from the bones. Serve Oxtail Casserole with a mixture of sautéed root vegetables, chipolata sausages and buttered noodles.

4 SERVINGS

1 oxtail, skinned and cut into pieces
½ teaspoon salt
½ teaspoon freshly ground black pepper
¼ teaspoon mixed spice or ground allspice
1 tablespoon brandy
1 oz. [2 tablespoons] butter
2 medium-sized onions, finely chopped
2 medium-sized carrots, scraped and chopped
bouquet garni, consisting of 4 parsley sprigs, 1 thyme spray and 1 bay leaf tied together
6 fl. oz. [¾ cup] home-made beef stock
6 fl. oz. [¾ cup] dry red wine
2 tablespoons tomato purée

Place the oxtail pieces on a plate and rub them all over with the salt, pepper and mixed spice or allspice. Pour over the brandy and set the pieces aside for 20 minutes.

In a large, flameproof casserole, melt the butter over moderate heat. When the foam subsides, add the oxtail pieces and fry them, turning frequently, for 5 minutes or until they are evenly browned.

Using tongs or a slotted spoon, transfer the oxtail pieces to a plate and keep warm.

Add the onions and carrots to the casserole and cook them, stirring occasionally, for 5 to 7 minutes or until the onions are soft and translucent but not brown. Return the oxtail pieces to the casserole and add the bouquet garni, stock, wine and tomato purée. The liquid should almost cover the meat so add a little more stock if necessary.

Bring the liquid to the boil, skimming off any scum that rises to the surface. Cover the casserole and reduce the heat to very low. Simmer the oxtail for 4 hours or until the meat is very tender and comes away from the bones. Remove and discard the bouquet garni.

Remove the casserole from the heat and set it aside to cool completely. Place the casserole in the refrigerator to chill for at least 8 hours or overnight.

Remove the casserole from the refrig-

This delicious Oxtail Casserole makes an inexpensive and satisfying supper for the family.

erator. Remove and discard the fat that has risen to the surface.

Place the casserole over moderate heat and bring the liquid slowly to the boil. Reduce the heat to low and simmer for 10 minutes. Using a slotted spoon, transfer the oxtail pieces to a heated serving dish. Keep warm.

Increase the heat to moderately high and boil the braising liquid until it has reduced by about one-third. Remove the pan from the heat. Pour a little of the

braising liquid over the oxtail pieces and pour the remainder into a warmed sauceboat.

Serve immediately.

Paprika Vegetable and Sausage Stew

  ①

A tasty adaptation of a traditional Hungarian dish, Paprika Vegetable and Sausage Stew is a meal in itself.

4 SERVINGS

2 fl. oz. [¼ cup] vegetable oil
2 onions, finely chopped
2 garlic cloves, crushed
1 green pepper, white pith removed, seeded and chopped
1 red pepper, white pith removed, seeded and chopped
1 tablespoon paprika
½ teaspoon salt
¼ teaspoon black pepper
½ teaspoon dried dill
1 lb. canned peeled tomatoes
1 lb. potatoes, cooked and sliced
8 oz. garlic sausage, chopped
5 fl. oz. [⅝ cup] sour cream

In a medium-sized flameproof casserole, heat the oil over moderate heat. When the oil is hot, add the onions and garlic and cook, stirring occasionally, for 5 to 7 minutes or until the onions are soft and translucent but not brown. Add the green and red peppers and cook, stirring occasionally, for a further 5 minutes.

Remove the casserole from the heat and stir in the paprika, salt, pepper, dill and the tomatoes with the can juice mixing well to blend.

Return the casserole to low heat and simmer the mixture for 25 to 30 minutes or until the vegetables are tender. Stir in the potatoes, sausage and sour cream and simmer over low heat for a further 5 minutes or until the potatoes and sausage are heated through.

Remove the casserole from the heat and serve at once.

Daube de Lapin

RABBIT STEW

Daube de Lapin is not one of the great French daubes but it is, nevertheless, a popular and quite economical version of the classic beef daubes. Served with mashed potatoes and green vegetables, it makes a richly sustaining winter meal.

6 SERVINGS

1 x 3 lb. rabbit, cut into serving
   pieces
8 oz. streaky bacon slices, cut into
   2-inch strips
2 onions, thinly sliced
1 garlic clove, finely chopped
3 carrots, scraped and thinly sliced

MARINADE

16 fl. oz. [2 cups] dry white wine
1 tablespoon olive oil
1 teaspoon salt
6 black peppercorns
2 parsley sprigs
1 bay leaf
2 garlic cloves, crushed
½ teaspoon dried thyme

In a large shallow bowl, combine all the marinade ingredients together and stir well to mix. Add the rabbit pieces and baste them thoroughly. Cover the dish and leave the rabbit to marinate overnight, or for at least 12 hours.

Remove the rabbit pieces from the marinade and dry them on kitchen paper towels. Strain the marinade into a jug and reserve it. Remove the bay leaf.

Preheat the oven to moderate 350°F (Gas Mark 4, 180°C).

An adaptation of a classic French dish, Daube de Lapin makes an exciting dish for a special occasion.

In a large, flameproof casserole, fry the bacon strips over moderate heat until they are quite crisp. With a slotted spoon remove the bacon pieces from the pan and drain them on kitchen paper towels.

Add the onions, garlic and carrots to the fat in the casserole and cook them for 5 to 6 minutes, or until they are lightly coloured. Add the rabbit pieces and turn frequently to brown them evenly and quickly. If there is not enough fat in the pan, add a little butter or oil.

Add the reserved marinade to the casserole and bring the liquid to the boil.

Remove the casserole from the heat, add the bacon pieces to the mixture and place the casserole in the oven. Braise for 1 hour, or until the rabbit is tender. Remove from the oven and serve.

Lamb Stew with Sherry

Lamb Stew with Sherry is a flavourful Spanish dish in which pieces of lamb are marinated in sherry.

6 SERVINGS

10 fl. oz. [1¼ cups] dry sherry
2 garlic cloves, crushed
3 lb. boned lamb, cut into 2-inch
   pieces
1 teaspoon salt
½ teaspoon black pepper
1 teaspoon ground cumin
4 tablespoons vegetable oil
2 medium-sized onions, sliced
2 tablespoons flour

Combine the sherry and garlic in a large mixing bowl. Add the pieces of lamb, and mix well. Cover the bowl and leave the meat to marinate for 3 hours.

Remove the lamb from the marinade. Drain well and dry the meat on kitchen

paper towels. Reserve the marinade.

Sprinkle the salt, pepper and cumin over the lamb.

In a large saucepan, heat the oil over moderate heat. Add the pieces of lamb and fry them for 3 to 5 minutes or until they are brown. Add the onions and fry for 3 minutes.

Add the flour and mix it well with the lamb and onions. Pour over the reserved marinade and, stirring constantly, bring to the boil.

Cover the saucepan and reduce the heat to moderately low. Simmer the stew for at least 1 hour, or until the lamb is tender. Serve very hot.

Sautéed Kidneys with Chipolatas and Wine

This is a superb informal dinner dish. Serve with creamed potatoes and buttered broccoli.

4 SERVINGS

2 oz. [¼ cup] butter
12 lambs' kidneys, cleaned, and halved
4 pork chipolata sausages, twisted
   and halved
1 tablespoon flour
4 fl. oz. [½ cup] red wine
8 fl. oz. [1 cup] beef stock
1 tablespoon tomato purée
2 tablespoons brandy
½ teaspoon salt
½ teaspoon black pepper
12 button (pearl) onions, blanched
2 teaspoons chopped fresh parsley

In a large frying-pan, melt the butter over moderate heat. When the foam subsides, add the kidneys and chipolata halves to the pan. Cook them, stirring frequently, for 8 minutes or until the kidneys are tender and the chipolatas are lightly browned. With a slotted spoon, transfer the kidneys and chipolatas to a plate.

Remove the pan from the heat and stir in the flour with a wooden spoon. Return the pan to the heat and cook the mixture for 30 seconds. Gradually add the wine and stock, stirring constantly. Bring the mixture to the boil, stirring occasionally. Add the tomato purée, brandy, salt and pepper, stirring constantly. Return the kidneys and chipolatas to the pan and add the onions. Reduce the heat to low, cover the pan and cook the mixture for 25 minutes, stirring occasionally.

Remove the pan from the heat and transfer the contents to a warmed serving dish. Sprinkle over the parsley and serve.

Sautéed Kidneys with Chipolatas and Wine makes a superb dinner dish.

Spanish Beef Stew with Rice, Tomatoes and Herbs

A delicious stew from the Spanish border country on the Mediterranean coast, Spanish Beef Stew with Rice, Tomatoes and Herbs may be served with a green salad, French bread and a young red wine, such as Beaujolais.

6 SERVINGS

2 slices streaky bacon, diced
1 pint [2½ cups] water
2 tablespoons olive oil
3 lb. stewing steak, cut into 1-inch thick 2½-inch squares
2 medium-sized onions, sliced
8 oz. [1⅓ cups] long-grain rice
10 fl. oz. [1¼ cups] dry white wine
15 fl. oz. [1⅞ cups] beef stock
½ teaspoon salt
¼ teaspoon black pepper
2 garlic cloves, crushed
¼ teaspoon dried thyme
¼ teaspoon dried basil
¼ teaspoon dried oregano
⅛ teaspoon ground saffron
1 bay leaf
1 lb. ripe tomatoes, blanched, peeled, seeded and roughly chopped
4 oz. [1 cup] Gruyère or Parmesan cheese, grated

Preheat the oven to warm 325°F (Gas Mark 3, 170°C).

Place the diced bacon in a medium-sized pan and cover with the water. Bring the water to the boil over moderate heat. Reduce the heat and simmer gently for 10 minutes. Drain off the water and dry the bacon on kitchen paper towels.

In a heavy, large frying-pan, heat the oil over moderate heat and add the bacon. Fry the bacon for 3 minutes, turning it several times so that it browns. Remove the bacon with a slotted spoon and put it in a large flameproof casserole.

Dry the meat on kitchen paper towels. Over moderate heat, reheat the oil in the frying-pan until it is very hot. Quickly brown the meat a few pieces at a time. With a slotted spoon, transfer the pieces of meat as they brown to the casserole.

Reduce the heat to moderately low, add the onions to the pan and fry them lightly for 5 minutes, stirring occasionally. Remove the onions with a slotted spoon and add them to the casserole. Add the rice to the frying-pan, still using the same fat, and stir and cook for 2 to 3 minutes, or until the rice looks milky. Turn the rice into a medium-sized bowl.

Add the wine to the frying-pan, stir for 1 minute to dissolve the coagulated juices and pour the liquid into the casserole. Add the stock to the casserole

Spanish Beef Stew with Rice, Tomatoes and Herbs is surprisingly easy to make - and looks and tastes delicious. Serve with salad.

and place it over moderate heat. Stir in the salt, pepper, garlic, thyme, basil, oregano, saffron and bay leaf. Bring the liquid to the boil. Cover the casserole and place it in the lower part of the oven. Leave to cook for 1 hour.

Remove the casserole from the oven, stir in the tomatoes, bring to the boil on top of the stove, cover and return the casserole to the oven for an additional 2 hours, or until the meat is tender when pierced with a fork.

Tilt the casserole and skim off the fat. Stir the rice into the casserole. Place the casserole on top of the stove and bring the liquid to the boil over moderate heat.

Raise the oven heat to fairly hot 375°F (Gas Mark 5, 190°C).

Return the casserole to the lower part of the oven. Cook for 20 minutes, or until the rice is tender and the liquid is absorbed.

Remove the casserole from the oven, taste and add more salt and pepper if necessary. Remove the bay leaf. Stir the cheese into the mixture and serve.

Soups and stews for entertaining

The first half of the book concentrated on the basics — those useful dishes that the family will happily eat till Kingdom come and that won't break the budget every time you even contemplate cooking them.

But entertaining is part of living, too, whether it be family, friends or just an end-of-the-week, whoopee-it's-payday binge and the recipes in this section therefore concentrate on luscious-to-look-at, easy-to-cook classics absolutely guaranteed to vastly impress any guests lucky enough to sample them — just check the recipes for Boeuf Bourguinonne (page 48), Vichyssoise (page 44) or the colourful Danish Chicken Casserole (pictured above, recipe page 62) if you need convincing!

Most are a bit more expensive than the 'family-type' recipes (everyone, after all, longs for, and needs, the occasional bit of caviar on a beer budget!) but for those occasions when the boss and his wife are definitely, unputoffably coming to dinner and payday is still a long way off, we've constructed some less expensive, but still festive, dishes in **For Budget Occasions.**

Like the first section, all of the recipes on the following pages are specially chosen for their flexibility and the fact that almost all their preparation can be done ahead of time, as well as for their delicious taste. All make nourishing meals for ANY occasion, and without wearing you to a frazzle cooking them. So — try them, enjoy them — and good eating!

Asparagus Cream Soup

☆ ☆　①①①　▨▨▨

This delicious soup is made with fresh asparagus, cream and eggs. You can hasten the making process by using commercial vegetable stock, but the home-made stock given below tastes infinitely better and is well worth preparing.

4 SERVINGS

2 lb. asparagus
1 small onion, thinly sliced
10 fl. oz. [1¼ cups] water
1 teaspoon salt
½ teaspoon white pepper
1 oz. [4 tablespoons] flour
1 oz. [2 tablespoons] butter
2 egg yolks
5 fl. oz. single cream [⅝ cup light cream]

STOCK

1 oz. [2 tablespoons] butter
1 lb. carrots, scraped and chopped
1 lb. onions, thinly sliced
4 celery stalks, trimmed and chopped
1 small turnip, peeled and chopped
6 peppercorns
  bouquet garni, consisting of 4 parsley sprigs, 1 thyme spray and 1 bay leaf tied together
1 teaspoon salt
5 pints [6¼ pints] hot water

First, make the stock. In a large saucepan, melt the butter over moderate heat. When the foam subsides, add the carrots, onions, celery and turnip to the pan and cook, stirring occasionally, for 5 to 7 minutes or until the onions are soft and translucent but not brown. Add the peppercorns, bouquet garni, salt and hot water. Bring the water to the boil, half-cover the pan, reduce the heat to low and simmer the stock for 2 hours or until it has been reduced to about 1½ pints [3¾ cups].

Remove the pan from the heat and pour the stock through a strainer into a large jug, pressing down on the vegetables with the back of a wooden spoon to extract all the liquid. Set aside.

Trim and wash the asparagus. With a sharp knife, cut off 2 inches from the tips and set them aside. Peel the stalks and cut them into 1-inch lengths.

Place the sliced onion and asparagus stalks in a medium-sized saucepan. Add the strained stock and place the pan over low heat. Simmer the soup for 30 minutes.

Meanwhile, put the water and ½ teaspoon of salt into another saucepan. Place it over moderate heat and bring the water to the boil. Drop in the asparagus tips and boil for 5 to 8 minutes

or until they are tender. Drain the tips and set aside.

Pour the asparagus stock through a fine strainer into a medium-sized bowl. With the back of a wooden spoon, rub the asparagus stalks and onion through the strainer. Rinse and wipe dry the saucepan and pour back the stock. Reheat, adding the remaining salt, and the white pepper.

Roll the flour and butter together and work them into a soft paste. Roll the mixture into small balls.

Remove the stock from the heat and add the butter and flour balls, one at a time, stirring constantly with a wooden spoon. When the stock is thoroughly blended and smooth, place the pan over moderate heat and cook, stirring constantly until it boils. Remove the stock from the heat.

In a medium-sized bowl, beat the egg yolks and stir in the cream. Stirring constantly, add 10 fluid ounces [1¼ cups] of hot stock. Stirring constantly, pour the mixture into the remaining stock and replace the pan over very low heat. Simmer the soup, whisking constantly, for 2 minutes. Do not allow it to boil.

Remove the pan from the heat and pour the soup into a large, warmed tureen. Decorate with the reserved asparagus tips and serve at once.

Borscht

BEETROOT [BEET] SOUP

☆　①　▨▨

This is a classic summer Borscht, a light soup that is usually served hot. It is traditionally served hot with boiled potatoes as well as with sour cream. This recipe can be varied by whisking two beaten eggs into the hot soup just before serving.

6 SERVINGS

5 large raw beetroots [beets], peeled and coarsely grated
3 pints [7½ cups] water
1 onion, chopped
3 oz. tomato purée
1 tablespoon lemon juice
1 teaspoon salt
½ teaspoon black pepper
1 teaspoon sugar
10 fl. oz. [1¼ cups] sour cream

Place the beetroots [beets], water and onion in a large saucepan over high heat. Bring the liquid to the boil, cover the pan, reduce the heat to low and simmer for 45 minutes.

Add the tomato purée, lemon juice, salt, pepper and sugar to the saucepan. Cover and cook the soup over moderately low heat for 45 minutes.

Remove the pan from the heat. Strain the soup into a soup tureen, discarding the vegetables. Serve topped with spoonfuls of sour cream.

Cod Bouillabaisse

☆　①①　▨

This simplified version of bouillabaisse is made only with cod, unlike the classic Mediterranean version, but it tastes just as good. The fish and potatoes are served separately from the soup, so that the dish is almost a meal in itself.

6-8 SERVINGS

3 tablespoons olive oil
3 onions, chopped
3 garlic cloves, crushed
4 large tomatoes, blanched, peeled and chopped
4 pints [5 pints] water
½ teaspoon crushed saffron threads
  bouquet garni, consisting of 4 parsley sprigs, 1 thyme spray and 1 bay leaf tied together
1 teaspoon grated orange rind
½ teaspoon cayenne pepper
¼ teaspoon black pepper
¼ teaspoon salt
10 potatoes, peeled and sliced into ½-inch rounds
2 lb. cod fillets, cut into chunks

In a large saucepan, heat the oil over moderate heat. When the oil is hot, add the onions and garlic and cook, stirring frequently, for 7 minutes. Add the tomatoes, stir to mix and cook for another 2 minutes. Stir in the water, saffron, bouquet garni, orange rind, cayenne, black pepper and salt. Reduce the heat to very low and simmer the soup for 20 minutes.

Drop the potato slices into the soup and cook for 10 minutes. Add the pieces of cod and cook, stirring occasionally, for another 15 minutes, or until the fish is cooked.

With a slotted spoon, remove the fish and potatoes from the soup and place them on a heated dish. Pour the soup through a strainer into a large, warmed tureen, pressing the vegetables and flavourings with the back of a wooden spoon to extract as much of their juices as possible. Discard the vegetables and flavourings.

Serve immediately.

A delicious, rich, creamy soup, Asparagus Cream Soup is not difficult to make and is fit to grace the finest table. Serve as a very special first course for a dinner party.

Cold Fruit Soup

Fruit soup makes a delicious, cooling first course for a summer's meal. Any fruit may be used, but a mixture of tart and sweet fruit makes a particularly good soup. Fruit soup may be served with whipped or sour cream.

4 SERVINGS

2 lb. mixed fruit, washed, peeled and chopped
2 oz. [¼ cup] sugar
⅛ teaspoon salt
1 clove
1 x 2-inch cinnamon stick
   juice and finely grated rind of 1 lemon
2 pints [5 cups] water

Place the fruit in a medium-sized saucepan. Add the sugar, salt, clove, cinnamon stick and lemon juice and lemon rind. Pour in the water and bring the mixture to the boil over moderately high heat, stirring occasionally. Reduce the heat to low, cover the pan and cook the fruit for

Cold Fruit Soup makes a refreshing first course for a summer meal. Or you could serve it as a very different, and light, dessert.

10 to 15 minutes, or until it is tender but still firm.

Remove and discard the cinnamon stick.

Strain the contents of the pan into a large serving bowl, rubbing the fruit through the strainer with the back of a wooden spoon. Discard any pulp remaining in the strainer. Set the soup aside to cool for 15 minutes.

Then place the bowl in the refrigerator and chill the soup for 1 hour before serving.

Vegetable Consommé

This light and elegant soup is a simple variation on the classic consommé. It is easy to make and is a good starter when

followed by a rather rich and heavy main course.

4 SERVINGS

1 oz. [2 tablespoons] butter
2 small carrots, scraped and finely diced
1 small turnip, peeled and finely diced
2 leeks, white part only, cleaned and finely diced
1 small celery stalk, trimmed and finely diced
½ teaspoon salt
¼ teaspoon freshly ground black pepper
1 tablespoon green peas
2 pints [5 cups] strong clarified meat bouillon
3 fl. oz. [⅜ cup] sherry
1 teaspoon fresh chervil or ½ teaspoon dried chervil

In a medium-sized saucepan, melt the butter over moderate heat. When the foam subsides, add the carrots, turnip, leeks and celery and stir well with a wooden spoon. Add the salt and pepper.

36

Reduce the heat to low, cover the pan and cook for 5 minutes.

Add the peas and 5 fluid ounces [⅝ cup] of the bouillon and cook for a further 20 minutes.

Add the remaining bouillon to the pan with the sherry. Increase the heat to moderately high, stir the soup and bring it to the boil. Boil for 2 minutes. Pour the soup into a large, warmed tureen or individual serving bowls and sprinkle the chervil on top.

Serve at once.

Gazpacho

A classic Spanish soup, cold Gazpacho makes a refreshing summer lunch served with croûtons, small bowls of chopped olives, cucumbers, hard-boiled eggs and onion. Each guest then sprinkles his soup with a little of these accompaniments. It is easiest to make this soup with an electric blender.

4 SERVINGS

3 slices of brown bread, cut into 1-inch cubes
10 fl. oz. [1¼ cups] canned tomato juice
2 garlic cloves, finely chopped
½ cucumber, peeled and finely chopped
1 medium-sized green pepper, white pith removed, seeded and finely chopped
1 medium-sized red pepper, white pith removed, seeded and finely chopped
1 medium-sized onion, finely chopped
1½ lb. tomatoes, blanched, peeled, seeded and chopped
3 fl. oz. [⅜ cup] olive oil
2 tablespoons red wine vinegar
½ teaspoon salt
¼ teaspoon freshly ground black pepper
½ teaspoon fresh marjoram or ¼ teaspoon dried marjoram
½ teaspoon fresh basil or ¼ teaspoon dried basil
4 ice cubes [optional]

This exotic recipe for Gazpacho originated in Spain but is now enjoyed throughout the world. Serve with the accompaniments pictured here.

Place the bread cubes in a medium-sized mixing bowl and pour over the tomato juice. Leave the bread cubes to soak for 5 minutes, then squeeze them carefully to extract the excess juice. Transfer them to a large mixing bowl. Reserve the tomato juice.

Add the chopped garlic, cucumber, peppers, onion and tomatoes to the soaked bread cubes and stir to mix thoroughly. Purée the ingredients by pounding them in a mortar with a pestle to a paste and then rubbing them through a strainer, or by putting them through a food mill. Stir in the reserved tomato juice. If you are using a blender, purée all of the vegetables and bread cubes with the reserved tomato juice.

Add the oil, vinegar, salt, pepper, marjoram and basil to the purée and stir well. The soup should be the consistency of single [light] cream, so add more tomato juice if necessary.

Turn the soup into a deep serving bowl and place it in the refrigerator to chill for at least 1 hour.

Just before serving, stir the soup well and drop in the ice cubes, if you are using them.

Serve the Gazpacho immediately.

Greek Egg and Lemon Soup

 ✩ ✩　　① 　　✕

This traditional soup has an unusual lemon flavour. Serve as a first course to a special dinner.

6 SERVINGS

3 pints [7½ cups] chicken stock
3 oz. [½ cup] long-grain rice, washed, soaked in cold water for 30 minutes and drained
4 eggs
juice of 2 lemons
¼ teaspoon freshly ground black pepper
1 tablespoon finely chopped fresh parsley

Put the stock in a large saucepan and bring it to the boil. Add the rice and simmer over low heat for 15 to 20 minutes, or until the rice is tender. Remove the pan from the heat.

Break the eggs into a medium-sized mixing bowl and beat with a wire whisk until they are light and fluffy.

Gradually add the lemon juice, beating constantly. Add a few spoonfuls of stock, a little at a time, beating constantly until it is well mixed. Carefully stir this mixture into the saucepan containing the rest of the stock.

Continue to cook the soup over moderate heat for 2 minutes. Do not let it boil or it will curdle. Add the pepper, sprinkle over the chopped parsley and serve immediately.

Haricot Bean Cream Soup

✩ ✩　　① ① 　　✕

A thick, rich soup, Haricot Bean Cream Soup is an ideal light supper dish. Serve with crispbreads and cheese for a delightful meal.

8 SERVINGS

5 oz. [⅝ cup] butter
2 oz. [½ cup] flour
2 pints [5 cups] chicken stock
1 pint [2½ cups] chicken consommé
12 oz. white haricot beans, soaked in cold water overnight, drained, cooked and puréed
1 teaspoon salt
1 teaspoon freshly ground black pepper
8 fl. oz. single cream [1 cup light cream]
6 egg yolks, lightly beaten

In a large saucepan, melt 2 ounces [¼ cup] of the butter over moderate heat. Remove the pan from the heat. Stir in the flour until the mixture forms a thick paste. Gradually add the stock, stirring constantly and being careful to avoid lumps. Return the pan to the heat and cook, stirring constantly, for 2 to 3 minutes or until the soup is thick and smooth. Stir in the consommé, then the bean purée. Season with the salt and pepper. Cook, stirring constantly, for a further 3 minutes.

Stir in the cream and the remaining butter. Place the egg yolks in a small mixing bowl. Using a kitchen fork, beat in 4 tablespoons of the hot soup. Stir the egg yolk mixture into the soup. Reduce the heat to low and cook, stirring constantly, for a further 10 minutes. Do not allow the soup to come to the boil or the egg yolks will scramble.

Remove the pan from the heat. Ladle the soup into a large, warmed soup tureen or individual soup bowls and serve at once.

This traditional Greek Egg and Lemon Soup makes a colourful and elegant start to a meal. The soup has a distinctively lemon flavour.

Hungarian Apricot Soup

  ① ① ① ⌧ ⌧ ⌧

An unusual soup made from apricots, chicken, wine and sour cream, Hungarian Apricot Soup may be served as a first course or as a light summer lunch.

4 SERVINGS

4 oz. [⅔ cup] dried apricots, chopped
10 fl. oz. [1¼ cups] dry white wine
1 oz. [2 tablespoons] butter
1 garlic clove, crushed
2 tablespoons flour
1 pint [2½ cups] chicken stock
4 oz. cooked chicken, diced
1 tablespoon chopped fresh chives
½ teaspoon salt
¼ teaspoon black pepper
⅛ teaspoon grated nutmeg
5 fl. oz. [⅝ cup] sour cream

Soak the apricots in the wine for 6 hours.

In a large saucepan, melt the butter over moderate heat. When the foam subsides, add the garlic and cook, stirring occasionally, for 4 minutes.

Remove the pan from the heat. With a wooden spoon, stir in the flour to make a smooth paste. Add the stock, stirring constantly. Stir in the apricots, wine, chicken, chives, salt, pepper and nutmeg.

Set the pan over high heat and bring the soup to the boil, stirring constantly. Reduce the heat to low, cover the pan and simmer the soup, stirring occasionally, for 30 minutes.

Remove the pan from the heat. Stir in the sour cream. Pour the soup into a warmed soup tureen or individual soup bowls and serve immediately.

Manhattan Clam Chowder

☆ ① ⌧

One of the most popular of American chowders, Manhattan Clam Chowder traditionally contains tomatoes, potatoes, thyme and, in some recipes, salt pork. Serve the chowder as a light lunch or dinner, with crusty bread or rolls and butter.

6 SERVINGS

4 oz. salt pork, diced
1 medium-sized onion, chopped
4 large tomatoes, blanched, peeled, seeded and coarsely chopped
3 medium-sized potatoes, diced
½ teaspoon black pepper
½ teaspoon salt
½ teaspoon dried thyme
5 fl. oz. [⅝ cup] tomato juice
1 pint [2½ cups] water
5 fl. oz. [⅝ cup] clam liquid
24 small clams, steamed, removed from their shells and finely chopped or 1 lb. canned clams, drained and with the juice reserved

Manhattan Clam Chowder is one of the most popular of the traditional American soups. Served with crusty rolls it's almost a meal in itself.

In a large, heavy saucepan, fry the salt pork over moderate heat for 5 to 8 minutes, or until it has rendered its fat and is golden brown. Scrape the bottom of the pan frequently with a wooden spoon to prevent the pork from sticking.

With a slotted spoon, remove the salt pork from the pan and set aside.

Add the onion to the pan and fry, stirring occasionally, for 5 to 7 minutes, or until it is soft and translucent but not brown.

Add the chopped tomatoes, potatoes, pepper, salt and thyme. Stir in the tomato juice, water and the clam liquid. Return the salt pork to the pan and bring the soup to the boil, stirring constantly.

Reduce the heat to low, cover the pan and simmer for 15 minutes, or until the potatoes are just tender when pierced with the point of a sharp knife.

Add the clams and cook, stirring, for a further 4 to 5 minutes, or until they are heated through. Taste the chowder and add a little more salt if necessary.

Remove the pan from the heat. Pour the soup into a warmed soup tureen or individual soup bowls and serve.

Mexican Chicken and Bean Soup

The ingredients for this soup may surprise you, but the blend of flavours is delicious. It is a meal in itself, accompanied by crusty bread or — to be really authentic — hot tortillas.

6 SERVINGS

1 x 5 lb. boiling chicken
1 medium-sized onion, quartered
1 carrot, scraped and sliced
2 teaspoons salt
4 peppercorns
  bouquet garni, consisting of 4 parsley sprigs, 1 thyme spray and 1 bay leaf tied together
5 pints [6¼ pints] water
2 green peppers, white pith removed, seeded and sliced
1 large onion, sliced and pushed out into rings
14 oz. canned chick-peas, drained
¼ teaspoon black pepper
8 oz. Wensleydale or any white cheese, cubed
1 avocado, peeled, stoned, sliced and sprinkled with lemon juice

Put the chicken in a large saucepan with the quartered onion, carrot, 1 teaspoon of salt, the peppercorns and bouquet garni. Pour over the water, adding more if necessary to cover the chicken completely.

Place the saucepan over high heat. Bring the liquid to the boil and reduce the heat to moderately low. Simmer the chicken for 2 hours or until it is tender.

Remove the chicken from the pan. Set it on a board and cover it with aluminium foil to keep it warm.

Increase the heat under the saucepan to moderately high and bring the liquid back to the boil. Boil it for 15 minutes to reduce it slightly. Then strain the liquid, discarding the vegetables and seasonings. Rinse out the saucepan and return the liquid to it.

Bring the liquid back to the boil, using a metal spoon to skim off any fat that rises to the surface. Add the sliced green peppers and onion rings. Reduce the heat to moderately low and simmer for 10 minutes. Then add the chick-peas and continue simmering for 5 minutes.

While the chick-peas, peppers and onions are cooking, cut the chicken into serving pieces. Return the chicken pieces to the saucepan. Add the remaining 1 teaspoon salt and the pepper, and cook the soup for 5 minutes longer or until the chicken pieces are heated through. Stir in the cheese. As soon as the cheese begins to melt, transfer the soup to a warmed tureen. Add the avocado slices and serve.

Minestrone

A nourishing Italian vegetable and pasta soup, Minestrone is easily made. It makes a hearty meal on its own, served with crisp rolls and butter. The vegetables and dried beans used in this recipe are the traditional ingredients but they can be varied according to taste.

8 SERVINGS

1½ pints [3¾ cups] water
4 oz. [½ cup] dried red kidney beans

Chicken, chick-peas, green peppers and cheese are the principal ingredients in this delightfully unusual soup which originated in Mexico.

2 oz. [¼ cup] dried chick-peas
6 oz. salt pork, cut into cubes
4 tablespoons olive oil
2 medium-sized onions, finely chopped
1 garlic clove, crushed or finely chopped
2 medium-sized potatoes, peeled and diced
4 carrots, scraped and cut into ½-inch lengths
4 celery stalks, trimmed and cut into ½-inch lengths
½ small cabbage, coarse outer leaves removed, washed and finely shredded
6 medium-sized tomatoes, blanched, peeled, seeded and coarsely chopped
4 pints [5 pints] chicken stock

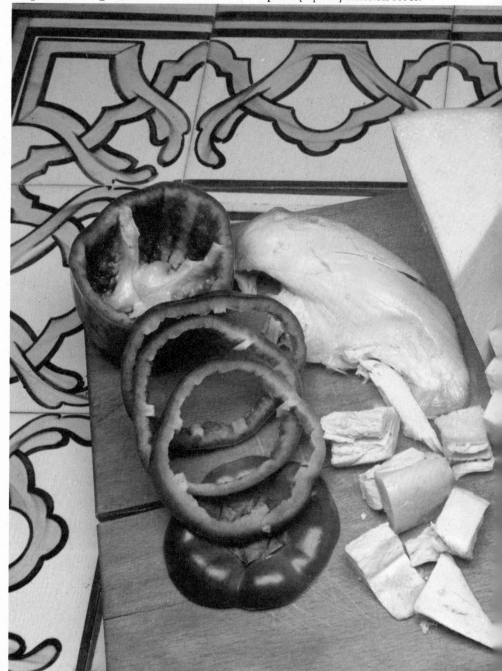

bouquet garni, consisting of 4
parsley sprigs, 1 thyme spray and
1 bay leaf tied together
½ teaspoon salt
1 teaspoon freshly ground black
pepper
8 oz. fresh peas, weighed after
shelling
4 oz. macaroni
2 oz. [½ cup] Parmesan cheese,
finely grated

In a medium-sized saucepan, bring the
water to the boil over high heat. Add the
beans and chick-peas and boil them for 2
minutes. Remove the pan from the heat
and leave the beans to soak in the pan for
1½ hours.

Replace the pan over high heat and
bring the water to the boil. Reduce the
heat to low and simmer the beans and
chick-peas for 1½ hours, or until they are
almost tender. Remove the pan from the
heat and drain the beans and peas in a
colander. Set aside.

In a large heavy saucepan, fry the salt
pork over moderate heat for 5 to 8
minutes, or until it is golden brown all
over and has rendered most of its fat.
With a slotted spoon, transfer the salt
pork to a plate and set aside while you
cook the vegetables.

Pour the olive oil into the pork fat and
add the onions and garlic to the pan. Fry
them, stirring occasionally, for 5 to 7
minutes, or until the onions are soft and
translucent but not brown. Add the
potatoes, carrots and celery to the pan
and continue to cook for a further 5
minutes, stirring constantly. Stir in the
cabbage and tomatoes and cook for 5
minutes.

Pour in the chicken stock and add the
bouquet garni, chick-peas, beans, salt
pork, salt and pepper. Increase the heat
to high and bring the soup to the boil.
Reduce the heat to low, cover the saucepan and simmer the minestrone for 35
minutes.

Uncover the saucepan and remove and
discard the bouquet garni. Add the fresh
peas and macaroni and continue to cook
the soup for another 10 to 15 minutes, or
until the macaroni is 'al dente', or just
tender.

Remove the pan from the heat and
spoon the soup into serving bowls or into
a large, warmed soup tureen. Sprinkle
over the Parmesan cheese and serve
immediately.

Peasant Soup

A country-style German dish, Peasant Soup may be served either as a first or as a main course. The quantity given in this recipe will be sufficient for 4 people as a main course. Serve this hearty soup with lots of crusty French bread or rolls and butter.

6 SERVINGS

2 oz. [¼ cup] butter
2 lb. stewing steak, cut into small cubes
2 medium-sized onions, roughly chopped
  bouquet garni, consisting of 4 parsley sprigs, 1 thyme spray and 1 bay leaf tied together
1 garlic clove, crushed or finely chopped
1 teaspoon paprika
1 teaspoon salt
½ teaspoon freshly ground black pepper
4 tablespoons flour
4½ pints [5½ pints] home-made beef stock
2 large potatoes, peeled and roughly diced
½ tablespoon finely chopped fresh dill or 1 teaspoon dried dill
2 oz. [½ cup] Parmesan cheese, grated

In a large, heavy saucepan, melt the butter over moderate heat. When the foam subsides, add the beef cubes and fry them, turning occasionally, for 5 to 8 minutes or until they are lightly and evenly browned.

Add the onions and fry for 5 to 7 minutes, or until they are soft and translucent but not brown. Add the bouquet garni, garlic, paprika, salt and pepper and stir well.

Mix in the flour, reduce the heat to moderately low and cook, stirring, for 5 minutes. Gradually stir in the stock. Bring to the boil. Cover the pan and simmer for 2 hours, stirring occasionally. Add the potatoes, cover and simmer for a further 45 minutes.

Remove and discard the bouquet garni.

Ladle the soup into a large, warmed tureen or individual soup bowls. Sprinkle the top with the dill and grated Parmesan cheese.

Serve very hot.

This meaty soup from Germany is sturdy and nourishing and makes an appetizing, filling meal on its own. Or serve it as a winter first course – but follow it with a light main course!

Pistou

ITALIAN VEGETABLE SOUP

A warming, filling soup made with vegetables and spaghetti, Pistou is given its distinctive flavour by the addition of garlic and basil, pounded together. Serve with crisp bread.

4 SERVINGS

1½ pints [3¾ cups] water
1 teaspoon salt
1 lb. French beans, trimmed, washed and chopped
4 medium-sized potatoes, peeled and cubed
14 oz. canned peeled tomatoes, drained
½ teaspoon freshly ground black pepper
4 oz. spaghetti
2 garlic cloves
3 tablespoons chopped fresh basil or 1½ tablespoons dried basil
2 tablespoons olive oil
2 oz. [½ cup] Parmesan cheese, grated

Fill a large saucepan with the water and add the salt. Place the saucepan over high heat and bring the water to the boil. Add the beans, potatoes, tomatoes and pepper. Reduce the heat to moderately low, cover the pan and cook the vegetables for 20 to 25 minutes or until they are tender.

Uncover the pan and add the spaghetti. Continue to cook for a further 12 to 15 minutes, or until the spaghetti is 'al dente' or just tender.

Meanwhile, place the garlic and basil in a mortar. Pound them together with a pestle until they are well mixed. Add the oil and 2 tablespoons of the soup and continue pounding until the mixture is thoroughly combined.

When the spaghetti is cooked, stir the garlic and basil mixture into the soup.

Remove the pan from the heat. Ladle the soup into individual warmed soup bowls and sprinkle with the Parmesan cheese. Serve at once.

Shrimp Bisque

A rich and delicious first course, Shrimp Bisque makes a marvellous start to a meal. Or, serve it with lots of crusty bread and butter for a warming, satisfying lunch.

4 SERVINGS

1 pint [2½ cups] milk
8 fl. oz. double cream [1 cup heavy cream]
8 oz. cooked shrimps, shelled and chopped

12 oz. canned condensed mushroom soup
¼ teaspoon Tabasco sauce
2 tablespoons dry sherry
1 tablespoon chopped fresh dill or 1½ teaspoons dried dill

In a large saucepan, scald the milk over moderate heat (bring just to below boiling point). Remove the pan from the heat and stir in the cream, shrimps, mushroom soup and Tabasco sauce, stirring with a wooden spoon until all the ingredients are well blended.

Return the pan to low heat and gently warm the soup until it is hot but not boiling. Remove the pan from the heat and stir in the sherry.

Transfer the soup to a warmed tureen or individual serving bowls and sprinkle on the dill.

Serve at once.

Tapioca Soup

A Thai soup with a delicate flavour, Tapioca Soup should be served very hot and accompanied by bowls of finely chopped spring onions [scallions], finely chopped fresh coriander leaves and diced cucumber.

6-8 SERVINGS

2 pints [5 cups] home-made chicken stock
8 oz. finely minced [ground] pork
½ teaspoon salt
¼ teaspoon freshly ground black pepper
4 oz. [⅔ cup] tapioca
8 oz. crabmeat, fresh or canned, with the shell and cartilage removed
1 small Chinese cabbage, coarse outer leaves removed, washed and shredded
1 tablespoon soy sauce

In a large saucepan, bring the chicken stock to the boil over moderate heat. Add the pork, salt and pepper to the pan, a little at a time, stirring constantly to prevent the meat from sticking together. When all the pork has been added, reduce the heat to moderately low and stir in the tapioca. Simmer the soup, stirring from time to time, for 20 minutes, or until the pork is cooked.

Flake the crabmeat with a fork and stir it into the soup. Add the cabbage. Cover the pan and simmer for a further 2 to 4 minutes, or until the crabmeat is heated through.

Stir in the soy sauce and serve the soup at once.

Vichyssoise

COLD CREAM OF LEEK AND POTATO SOUP

A classic cold soup, Vichyssoise, in spite of its French name, is supposed to have been invented in the United States. Whether it is from the New World or the Old, this soup is simply delicious. If you prefer more traditional garnishes, the soup may be sprinkled with chopped chives or parsley rather than the curry powder suggested here.

6 SERVINGS

4 oz. [½ cup] butter
2 lb. leeks, washed, trimmed and chopped
1 lb. potatoes, peeled and roughly chopped

Leeks and cream are the main components of this delicious and elegant version of the classic Vichyssoise.

2 celery stalks trimmed and chopped
1 pint [2½ cups] home-made chicken stock
1 pint [2½ cups] milk
1 teaspoon salt
½ teaspoon freshly ground black pepper
½ teaspoon sugar
¼ teaspoon grated nutmeg
10 fl. oz. double cream [1¼ cups heavy cream]
¼ teaspoon curry powder

In a large saucepan, melt the butter over moderate heat. When the foam subsides, add the leeks, potatoes and celery and fry, stirring constantly, for 8 minutes. Pour in the stock and milk and bring the mixture to the boil. Season the mixture with the salt, black pepper, sugar and nutmeg. Reduce the heat to moderately low, cover the pan and simmer the mixture, stirring occasionally, for 30 to 40 minutes or until the vegetables are soft and cooked through.

Remove the pan from the heat and pour the mixture through a fine strainer into a large mixing bowl. Using the back of a wooden spoon, rub the vegetables through the strainer until only a dry pulp remains. Discard the contents of the

44

strainer. Alternatively, purée the ingredients in an electric blender.

Stir half of the cream into the purée and set aside to cool. Place the bowl in the refrigerator to chill for at least 4 hours before serving.

To serve, remove the bowl from the refrigerator. Spoon the soup into a large, chilled soup tureen or individual soup bowls and pour a little of the remaining cream into each bowl.

Sprinkle a little curry powder over the soup and serve immediately.

Wonton Soup

Wonton literally means 'swallowing a cloud' in Chinese, and wontons floating in a clear soup do look rather like clouds billowing in the sky. This delicious soup makes a meal in itself, served with crispy Chinese noodles. You can obtain wonton dough or wrappers from Chinese delicatessens.

6 SERVINGS

1 lb. lean pork or beef, minced [ground]

Wonton Soup is one of the mainstays of Chinese cuisine and you can see why when you sample this delicate yet filling version.

2 tablespoons soy sauce
1-inch piece fresh root ginger, peeled and very finely chopped
1 teaspoon salt
1 teaspoon grated nutmeg
10 oz. frozen chopped spinach, thawed and drained
8 oz. wonton dough, thinly rolled and cut into 36 x 3-inch squares, or 36 bought wonton wrappers
3 pints [7½ cups] home-made chicken stock
1 bunch watercress, washed, shaken dry and very finely chopped

Place the pork or beef, soy sauce, ginger, salt, nutmeg and spinach in a large bowl. Using your fingers, knead well until they are thoroughly blended.

Place the wonton wrappers on a flat working surface. Place a teaspoon of the filling just below the centre of each

wrapper. Using a pastry brush dipped in water, wet the edges of the dough. Fold one corner of the dough over the filling to make a triangle and pinch the edges together to seal. Pull the corners at the base of the triangle together and pinch them to seal. As each wonton is ready, place it on a plate.

Repeat until all the wontons are filled and sealed.

Half-fill a large saucepan with water and place it over high heat. Bring the water to the boil and drop in the wontons. Bring the water to the boil again, reduce the heat to moderate and cook for 5 minutes or until the wontons are tender but still firm.

Remove the pan from the heat. Remove the wontons from the pan and pour off the water. Return the wontons to the pan and pour in the stock. Place the pan over high heat and bring the stock to the boil. Add the watercress. Allow the liquid to come to the boil again. Remove the pan from the heat.

Ladle the soup and wontons into a large, warmed soup tureen or warmed individual soup bowls and serve them at once.

Bread and Cheese Soup

This super soup consists of layers of fried bread and Fontina cheese in beef stock. It is very filling, takes little time to prepare and may be served as a first course or on its own as a luncheon.

4-6 SERVINGS

- **3 oz. [$\frac{3}{8}$ cup] butter**
- **12 slices French bread**
- **12 slices Fontina cheese**
- **3 pints [$7\frac{1}{2}$ cups] boiling beef stock**

In a large frying-pan, melt the butter over moderate heat. When the foam subsides, add the bread slices and fry them for 3 or 4 minutes on each side or until they are crisp and golden. Remove the pan from the heat and transfer the bread to kitchen paper towels to drain.

Preheat the oven to moderate 350°F (Gas Mark 4, 180°C).

Lay the bread slices on the bottom of an ovenproof soup tureen or individual ovenproof serving bowls and top with the cheese slices.

Pour the boiling stock over the bread and cheese and place the tureen or serving bowls in the oven for 10 minutes or until the cheese has nearly melted.

Remove the tureen or serving bowls from the oven and serve at once.

Garbure

SAUSAGE AND CABBAGE SOUP

Garbure is a classic meat and vegetable soup from the Basque country of France. Our adaptation is a somewhat simplified version of the original but loses none of its fine flavour. Served with lots of crusty bread and a tossed salad, it makes a sustaining main meal.

6-8 SERVINGS

- **1 ham bone**
- **1 teaspoon dried thyme**
- **$\frac{1}{2}$ teaspoon salt**
- **$\frac{1}{4}$ teaspoon hot chilli powder**
- **1 large bay leaf**
- **2 pints [5 cups] chicken stock**
- **1 pint [$2\frac{1}{2}$ cups] beef stock**
- **1 medium-sized green cabbage, coarse outer leaves removed, washed and coarsely shredded**
- **2 large onions, sliced**
- **3 large carrots, scraped and sliced**
- **12 oz. French beans, washed, trimmed and sliced**
- **8 oz. frozen petits pois**
- **3 large potatoes, thickly sliced**
- **1 celery stalk, cut into $\frac{1}{2}$-inch slices**
- **1 lb. French garlic sausage, skinned and thickly sliced**
- **croûtons, made from day-old white or French bread**
- **1 tablespoon chopped fresh parsley**

Place the ham bone, thyme, salt, chilli powder and bay leaf in a large saucepan. Pour in the chicken and beef stock. Stir well and place the pan over high heat. Bring the stock mixture to the boil, stirring constantly.

Add the cabbage, onions, carrots, beans, peas, potatoes and celery. Bring the soup back to the boil. Reduce the heat to low, cover the pan and simmer, stirring occasionally, for 1 hour.

Remove and discard the ham bone and bay leaf. Add the sausage slices and simmer the mixture for 20 minutes.

Remove the pan from the heat and pour the soup into a large warmed soup tureen. Float the croûtons on top, sprinkle on the parsley and serve immediately.

Mussel Chowder

An adaptation of the traditional New England Clam Chowder, Mussel Chowder makes a delicious and rich meal. Serve with warm crusty bread and butter. If fresh mussels are unobtainable, 1 pound of canned and drained mussels may be substituted, omitting the mussel cooking liquid.

4-6 SERVINGS

- **3 oz. salt pork, diced**
- **2 oz. [$\frac{1}{4}$ cup] butter**
- **2 medium-sized onions, finely chopped**
- **3 potatoes, peeled and chopped**
- **16 fl. oz. [2 cups] chicken stock**
- **2 quarts mussels, scrubbed, steamed, removed from their shells and 5 fl. oz. [$\frac{5}{8}$ cup] of the cooking liquid reserved**
- **$\frac{1}{2}$ teaspoon salt**
- **$\frac{1}{4}$ teaspoon black pepper**
- **$\frac{1}{4}$ teaspoon cayenne pepper**
- **10 fl. oz. double cream [$1\frac{1}{4}$ cups heavy cream]**
- **1 tablespoon chopped fresh parsley**

In a large saucepan, fry the salt pork over moderate heat for 5 to 8 minutes or until there is a film of fat covering the bottom of the pan and the cubes resemble small croûtons. With a slotted spoon, transfer the salt pork to kitchen paper towels to drain. Set aside and keep warm.

Add the butter to the pan. When the foam subsides, add the onions and potatoes and cook, stirring occasionally, for 5 to 7 minutes or until the onions are soft and translucent but not brown. Pour over the chicken stock and bring to the boil, stirring occasionally.

Garbure is a classic soup from the Basque country of France and is excellent for informal parties.

Reduce the heat to low, cover the pan and simmer for 5 minutes or until the potatoes are tender but still firm.

Add the mussels with their cooking liquid, the salt, pepper, cayenne and reserved salt pork, stirring to mix well. Increase the heat to high and bring the chowder to the boil. Remove the pan from the heat and gradually stir in the cream.

Pour the chowder into a heated soup tureen, sprinkle over the parsley and serve at once.

Tomato Consommé

Although this consommé is generally served cold and jellied, it is equally delicious hot.

4 SERVINGS

- **2 egg whites**
- **1 lb. tomatoes, chopped**
- **2 oz. canned pimientos**
- **2 pints [5 cups] strong cold clarified chicken bouillon**
- **3 fl. oz. [$\frac{3}{8}$ cup] dry sherry**
- **strip of lemon rind**
- **4 celery stalks, finely chopped**

In a small bowl, beat the egg whites with a wire whisk until they are frothy.

Put the tomatoes, pimientos and bouillon into a large saucepan. Whisk in the egg whites, the sherry, the lemon rind and the celery. Place the pan over moderate heat and bring to the boil, whisking constantly. When the mixture comes to the boil, stop whisking and let the boiling liquid rise in the pan. Remove the pan from the heat.

Reduce the heat to very low, return the pan to the heat and simmer gently for 45 minutes.

Let the consommé stand for 15 minutes. Lift off the egg white crust and place it in a strainer lined with cheesecloth. Pour the consommé through the lined strainer into a large bowl.

Serve hot or cold.

Tomato and Courgette [Zucchini] Soup

Delicious Tomato and Courgette [Zucchini] Soup is a meal in itself, served with crusty bread.

6 SERVINGS

- **2 lb. ripe tomatoes, blanched, peeled and chopped**

6 courgettes [zucchini], trimmed,
  blanched and chopped
3 pints [7½ cups] chicken stock
2 oz. [¼ cup] butter
1 oz. [¼ cup] flour
1 teaspoon salt
1 teaspoon freshly ground black
  pepper
1 teaspoon grated nutmeg
2 teaspoons sugar
1 tablespoon chopped fresh parsley
1 tablespoon chopped fresh dill
4 fl. oz. [½ cup] sour cream

Place the tomatoes, courgettes [zucchini] and half the chicken stock in a large saucepan. Set the pan over high heat and bring the liquid to the boil, stirring frequently. Reduce the heat to moderately low and simmer for 15 to 20 minutes or until the vegetables are soft.

In a small saucepan, melt the butter over moderate heat. Remove the pan from the heat and, with a wooden spoon, stir in the flour to make a smooth paste. Stir in 4 tablespoons of the soup liquid and stir until the mixture is well blended.

Pour the mixture back into the saucepan containing the soup. Cook, stirring constantly, for 2 to 3 minutes or until the soup is smooth and has thickened. Gradually add the remaining stock, stirring constantly, and bring the mixture to the boil. Add the salt, pepper, nutmeg, sugar, parsley and dill, stirring constantly. Remove the pan from the heat and pour the soup into a large, warmed tureen or individual soup bowls.

Stir in the sour cream and serve the soup at once.

47

Beef Stew with Corn and Tomatoes

 ① ① ① ✕ ✕

This hearty winter stew is best if served straight from the casserole, accompanied by a mixed salad.

4 SERVINGS

4 tablespoons paprika
2 lb. topside [top round] of beef, cut into 2-inch cubes
2 oz. [¼ cup] butter
2 medium-sized onions, chopped
2 garlic cloves, crushed
8 oz. canned tomatoes
1 teaspoon dried thyme
1 bay leaf
1 teaspoon salt
½ teaspoon black pepper
2 carrots, scraped and cut into ½-inch rounds
8 fl. oz. [1 cup] dry white wine
1 lb. canned drained sweetcorn
5 fl. oz. single cream [⅝ light cream]
6 tablespoons brandy
2 tablespoons flour

Sprinkle the paprika on a large plate. Roll the beef cubes in the paprika so that they are well coated. Set aside.

In a flameproof casserole, melt the butter over moderate heat. When the foam subsides, add the onions and garlic, reduce the heat to very low and cook for 4 minutes. Add the meat cubes to the casserole, a few at a time, and brown them well. Mix in the tomatoes, thyme, bay leaf, salt, pepper and carrots. Cover the casserole and simmer the stew for 25 minutes.

Pour in the wine, mixing well with a large spoon. Simmer the stew, covered, for another 45 minutes. Add the sweetcorn to the casserole, re-cover and cook the stew for a further 20 minutes.

In a medium-sized mixing bowl, beat the cream, brandy and flour together with a wire whisk. Add the mixture to the stew, stirring to blend thoroughly. Simmer for 15 minutes and serve.

Boeuf Bourguignonne

BEEF AND RED WINE STEW WITH ONIONS AND MUSHROOMS

 ① ① ① ✕ ✕

Possibly THE *classic French country stew, Boeuf Bourguignonne makes a perfect main dish for a special dinner party. Serve with potatoes, green vegetables and a mixed salad, and accompany it with a hearty Burgundy wine.*

6-8 SERVINGS

1 tablespoon cooking oil
4 oz. salt pork, cubed

3 lb. topside [top round] of beef, cut into 2-inch cubes
1 carrot, scraped and sliced
1 onion, thinly sliced
1 garlic clove, crushed
1 teaspoon salt
½ teaspoon black pepper
bouquet garni, consisting of 4 parsley sprigs, 1 thyme spray and and 1 bay leaf tied together
½ teaspoon dried thyme
2 tablespoons finely chopped fresh parsley
1¼ pints [3⅛ cups] red wine
1 tablespoon tomato purée
ONIONS
2 oz. [¼ cup] butter
15 small pickling (pearl) onions
½ teaspoon salt
½ teaspoon black pepper
MUSHROOMS
2 oz. [¼ cup] butter
1 lb. button mushrooms, wiped clean and quartered
½ teaspoon grated nutmeg

In a large flameproof casserole, heat the oil over moderate heat. Add the salt pork cubes and fry, stirring occasionally, for 5 to 8 minutes or until they resemble small croûtons and have rendered their fat. With a slotted spoon, transfer them to kitchen paper towels to drain.

Add the beef cubes, a few at a time, and fry them, stirring occasionally, for 5 to 8 minutes or until they are lightly and evenly browned. With a slotted spoon, remove the cubes from the casserole as they brown and set aside.

Add the carrot, onion and garlic to the casserole and fry, stirring occasionally, for 5 to 7 minutes or until the onion is soft and translucent but not brown. Stir in the salt, pepper, bouquet garni, thyme and parsley.

Return the beef cubes and salt pork cubes to the casserole and pour over the wine. Stir in the tomato purée. Bring the liquid to the boil, reduce the heat to very low, cover the casserole tightly and simmer the stew for 1½ hours.

Shortly before the end of the cooking time prepare the onions. In a medium-sized frying-pan, melt the butter over moderate heat. When the foam subsides, add the onions, salt and pepper and fry, stirring occasionally, for 8 to 10 minutes or until the onions are golden brown. With a slotted spoon, transfer the onions to the casserole.

Now prepare the mushrooms. Add the butter to the frying-pan and melt over moderate heat. When the foam subsides, add the mushrooms and nutmeg and fry, stirring occasionally, for 3 minutes or until they are just tender. Using the

slotted spoon, transfer the mushrooms to the casserole.

Re-cover the casserole and simmer for a further 15 minutes or until the onions are tender but still firm and the meat is very tender.

Remove the casserole from the heat and serve at once.

Carbonnades à la Flamande

FLEMISH BEEF STEW WITH BEER

 ① ① ✕ ✕ ✕

A beef stew made with beer, Carbonnades à la Flamande is one of Belgium's classic dishes. Serve with buttered noodles and plenty of ice-cold beer.

4 SERVINGS

2 oz. [½ cup] flour
1 teaspoon salt
¼ teaspoon black pepper
2 lb. chuck steak, cut into 1-inch cubes
4 tablespoons vegetable oil
6 medium-sized onions, thinly sliced
2 garlic cloves, crushed
18 fl. oz. [2¼ cups] beer
1 tablespoon soft brown sugar
bouquet garni, consisting of 4 parsley sprigs, 1 thyme spray and 1 bay leaf tied together

Sift the flour, salt and pepper into a small mixing bowl. Roll the cubes of meat in the seasoned flour until they are well coated.

In a flameproof casserole, heat the oil over moderate heat. When the oil is hot, add the meat cubes, a few at a time, and brown them on all sides. As they brown remove them with a slotted spoon and set them aside on a plate.

When all the meat cubes have been browned, add the onions and garlic to the pan and fry them for 8 to 10 minutes or until the onions are soft and translucent but not brown. Add more oil if necessary. Return the meat to the casserole and add the beer, sugar and bouquet garni.

Cover the casserole, reduce the heat to low and simmer the stew gently for about 2¼ to 2½ hours, or until the meat is very tender. After about 2 hours cooking, remove the lid and simmer the stew uncovered for the remaining cooking time. (This will reduce the liquid slightly.) Remove the casserole from the heat, remove and discard the bouquet garni and serve.

Boeuf Bourguignonne – one of the glories of French cuisine.

Daube de Boeuf

FRENCH BEEF STEW

This classic and surprisingly simple Daube de Boeuf makes an ideal main dish for an informal dinner party. Accompany it with noodles, a green salad and a hearty red vin ordinaire.

6 SERVINGS

3 lb. lean stewing steak, cut into 2-inch cubes
8 oz. streaky bacon, cut into 1-inch strips
4 oz. [1 cup] flour

6 oz. mushrooms, wiped clean and sliced
2 lb. tomatoes, blanched, peeled, seeded and roughly chopped
6 fl. oz. [¾ cup] beef stock

MARINADE

10 fl. oz. [1¼ cups] red wine
2 fl. oz. [¼ cup] brandy
2 tablespoons olive oil
2 teaspoons salt
6 black peppercorns
½ teaspoon dried thyme
1 bay leaf
2 garlic cloves, crushed
4 onions, thinly sliced

4 carrots, scraped and sliced

In a large bowl, combine all the marinade ingredients together and stir well to mix. Add the beef and baste it thoroughly. Cover the dish and place it in the refrigerator. Marinate the beef overnight or for at least 12 hours, basting occasionally.

Half fill a medium-sized saucepan with water and bring it to the boil over moderate heat. Reduce the heat to low, add the bacon and simmer it for 10 minutes. Drain the bacon and pat it dry with kitchen paper towels.

Remove the beef from the marinade and dry it on kitchen paper towels. Strain the marinade into a bowl, reserving both the liquid and the vegetables. Remove and discard the bay leaf.

Preheat the oven to moderate 350°F (Gas Mark 4, 180°C).

Put the flour into a medium-sized bowl. Dip the beef cubes into the flour so that they are well coated on all sides. Shake the cubes to remove any excess flour.

Arrange 2 or 3 strips of the bacon on the bottom of a large flameproof casserole. Spoon a few of the marinade vegetables, mushrooms and tomatoes over the top.

Arrange a layer of beef over the vegetables. Continue making layers of bacon, vegetables and beef, ending with a layer of bacon. Pour the stock and the reserved marinating liquid over the mixture.

Place the casserole over moderate heat and bring the liquid to the boil. Transfer the casserole to the oven and braise for 3½ to 4 hours, or until the meat is very tender.

Remove the casserole from the oven and skim any grease from the surface. Taste and add more salt and pepper if necessary. Serve immediately.

Hungarian Beef Goulasch

A variation of traditional goulasch, this sauce is flavoured with wine. Serve with noodles.

4 SERVINGS

2 lb. chuck steak
4 tablespoons vegetable oil
3 large onions, chopped
2 garlic cloves, crushed
1½ tablespoons paprika
1 tablespoon flour
2 tablespoons tomato puree
1 pint [2½ cups] red wine
    bouquet garni, consisting of 4
    parsley sprigs, 1 thyme spray and
    1 bay leaf tied together
1 teaspoon salt
1 teaspoon black pepper
½ teaspoon dried marjoram
1 red pepper, white pith removed
    and seeded
3 large tomatoes
5 fl. oz. [⅝ cup] sour cream

Trim any excess fat from the meat and cut it into 1-inch cubes. Dry the cubes on kitchen paper towels.

In a large, flameproof casserole, heat the oil over moderate heat. When the oil is hot add the meat cubes, a few at a time, and brown them all over. With a slotted spoon, remove the meat cubes from the casserole as they brown and set them aside.

When all the meat has been browned, reduce the heat to low, add the onions and garlic to the casserole and fry for 5 minutes, stirring occasionally. Add the paprika and stir until the onions are well coated. Stir in the flour, tomato purée and wine. Continue stirring until the liquid comes to the boil.

Return the meat to the casserole with

This colourful Hungarian Beef Goulasch makes a marvellous main course for a festive meal.

the bouquet garni, salt, pepper and marjoram. Cover and simmer over low heat for 2 hours.

While the meat is cooking, cut the red pepper into thin strips. Put the tomatoes in a bowl, cover with boiling water and leave to stand for 1 minute. Pour off the water, peel and chop the tomatoes coarsely.

Add the pepper and tomatoes to the casserole and simmer the mixture for 15 minutes or until the meat is very tender. Remove the bouquet garni and discard it.

Stir in the sour cream, cook for a further 5 minutes and serve.

Umido di Carne
ITALIAN MEAT STEW

Umido di Carne is a very simple but appetizing dish to serve for a festive supper or lunch. Serve with crusty bread.

4-6 SERVINGS

1 oz. [2 tablespoons] butter
2 tablespoons vegetable oil
2 onions, finely chopped
3 garlic cloves, crushed
1 lb. lean beef, cubed
1 lb. lean veal, cubed
3 celery stalks, trimmed and
    finely chopped
2 carrots, scraped and chopped
14 oz. canned peeled tomatoes
1 teaspoon salt
1 teaspoon black pepper
1 teaspoon dried oregano
4 parsley sprigs
1 bay leaf
8 fl. oz. [1 cup] red wine
1 lb. potatoes, peeled and halved

In a large flameproof casserole, melt the butter with the oil over moderate heat. When the foam subsides, add the onions and garlic and fry, stirring occasionally, for 5 to 7 minutes or until the onions are soft and translucent but not brown.

Add the beef and veal to the casserole and fry, stirring frequently, for 6 to 8 minutes or until the meat is browned.

Add the celery, carrots, tomatoes with the can juice, the salt, pepper, oregano, parsley and bay leaf. Pour over the wine. Increase the heat to high and bring the liquid to the boil. Reduce the heat to low, cover the casserole and simmer for 1½ hours. Add the potatoes. Re-cover the casserole and continue cooking for a further 45 minutes or until the meat is very tender when pierced with the point of a sharp knife.

Remove the casserole from the heat. Remove and discard the parsley sprigs and bay leaf. Serve at once.

Ecuadorian Lamb Stew

A tasty and colourful dish, Ecuadorian Lamb Stew should be served in a ring of saffron rice. A well-chilled bottle of light white wine, such as Sylvaner or Riesling would go well with this dish.

4 SERVINGS

- 3 fl. oz. [⅜ cup] olive oil
- 1 medium-sized onion, roughly chopped
- 2 garlic cloves, crushed
- 14 oz. canned peeled tomatoes, drained and chopped
- 1 red pepper, white pith removed, seeded and thinly sliced
- 1 green pepper, white pith removed seeded and thinly sliced
- ½ teaspoon hot chilli powder
- 1 teaspoon coriander seeds, coarsely crushed
- 1 teaspoon salt
- 2 lb. boned leg of lamb, cubed
- 8 fl. oz. [1 cup] dry white wine
- 2 tablespoons chopped fresh coriander leaves

In a medium-sized saucepan, heat half the oil over moderate heat. Add the onion and garlic and fry them for 5 to 7 minutes, or until the onion is soft and translucent but not brown. Add the tomatoes, red and green peppers, chilli powder, coriander seeds and salt and stir to mix. Reduce the heat to low, cover the pan and simmer for 15 minutes.

In a large frying-pan, heat the remaining oil over moderate heat. When the oil is hot, add the lamb cubes a few at a time and fry them for 6 to 8 minutes, or until they are browned all over. As the meat browns, remove it from the pan with a slotted spoon and transfer it to the pan with the vegetables. Stir in the wine and fresh coriander leaves. Cook, covered, for 50 minutes to 1 hour or until the meat is tender.

Remove from the heat and serve the stew immediately.

Serve exotic Ecuadorian Lamb Stew with saffron-flavoured rice for a really different dish.

Greek Lamb Stew

Delicious and easy-to-make, Greek Lamb Stew makes a warming main dish. Serve with lots of flat Greek bread, a tossed mixed salad and some light red wine, such as Demestica.

6 SERVINGS

- 4 fl. oz. [½ cup] olive oil
- 2½ lb. lean lamb, cut into 2-inch cubes
- 2 lb. small new potatoes, scrubbed and halved
- 8 oz. small pickling (pearl) onions, peeled
- 14 oz. canned peeled tomatoes, drained and chopped
- 5 oz. tomato purée
- 6 fl. oz. [¾ cup] red wine
- 2 tablespoons wine or malt vinegar
- 2 teaspoons salt
- 3 bay leaves
- 1 tablespoon lemon juice
- 3 oz. [½ cup] blanched almonds
- 6 oz. feta cheese

Greek Lamb Stew is a super mixture of lamb, potatoes, onions, wine and cheese. Serve with lots of pita (flat Greek bread) and red wine.

In a large, deep frying-pan, heat the olive oil over moderate heat. When the oil is hot, add the meat to the pan and, stirring and turning occasionally, cook for 5 minutes, or until the meat is lightly browned on all sides. With a slotted spoon remove the meat from the pan and set it aside.

Add the potatoes and onions to the pan and, stirring and turning occasionally, cook the vegetables for 8 minutes, or until the onions are lightly browned.

Meanwhile, in a small saucepan bring the tomatoes, tomato purée, red wine, vinegar and salt to the boil, stirring frequently. Remove the pan from the heat and set the tomato sauce aside.

When the onions are browned, return the meat to the frying-pan and stir in the tomato sauce. Add the bay leaves. Reduce the heat to low, cover and simmer the stew, stirring occasionally, for 1 to 1¼ hours, or until the lamb is tender when pierced with the point of a sharp knife.

Stir in the lemon juice and blanched almonds and crumble the cheese on top of the stew. Cook the mixture for a further 5 to 8 minutes, or until the cheese has melted.

Remove the pan from the heat and transfer the stew to a warmed serving dish. Serve at once.

Navarin Printanier
MUTTON STEW WITH FRESH SPRING VEGETABLES

A traditional French country dish, Navarin Printanier is the perfect dish for a dinner party. It is traditionally made with fresh young spring vegetables, but frozen vegetables may be substituted if necessary. Serve with a tomato salad and lots of light red wine, such as Brouilly.

6 SERVINGS

4 oz. salt pork, diced
1½ lb. boned breast of mutton, trimmed of excess fat and cut into 2-inch cubes
1½ lb. boned shoulder of mutton, trimmed of excess fat and cut into 2-inch cubes
2 tablespoons soft brown sugar
1 teaspoon salt
½ teaspoon freshly ground black pepper
½ tablespoon flour

6 medium-sized tomatoes, blanched peeled, seeded and chopped
2 pints [5 cups] chicken stock bouquet garni, consisting of 4 parsley sprigs, 1 thyme spray and 1 bay leaf tied together
2 oz. [¼ cup] butter
12 small potatoes, peeled
6 small turnips, peeled
6 small carrots, scraped
12 small pickling (pearl) onions, peeled
½ tablespoon white sugar

In a large, heavy-bottomed saucepan, fry the salt pork over moderate heat for 5 to 8 minutes, or until it resembles small croûtons and has rendered most of its fat. Stir occasionally to prevent it from sticking to the bottom of the pan. With a slotted spoon, transfer the salt pork to a large plate.

Add the meat cubes, a few at a time, to the pan and fry, stirring and turning occasionally, for 6 to 8 minutes, or until all of the cubes are lightly and evenly browned.

With a slotted spoon, transfer the meat to the plate with the salt pork. Keep warm while you brown the remaining meat cubes in the same way.

Remove the pan from the heat and pour off half of the fat. Return the meat cubes and salt pork to the pan and sprinkle over the brown sugar, salt and pepper. Place the pan over moderate heat and cook, stirring constantly with a

wooden spoon, for 3 minutes, or until the sugar has caramelized. Add the flour to the pan and cook for a further 3 minutes, stirring constantly with the wooden spoon.

Stir in the tomatoes, chicken stock and bouquet garni. Increase the heat to moderately high and bring the liquid to the boil. Reduce the heat to low, cover and simmer for 1 hour.

Meanwhile, prepare the vegetables. In a large frying-pan, melt the butter over moderate heat. When the foam subsides, add the potatoes, turnips, carrots and onions and cook, stirring occasionally, for 8 to 10 minutes or until the onions are golden brown. Stir in the white sugar and cook for a further 3 minutes or until the sugar has dissolved. Remove the pan from the heat. With a slotted spoon, transfer all of the vegetables to a dish and keep warm.

Remove the saucepan from the heat. With a metal spoon, skim off any scum from the surface of the cooking liquid. Add the browned vegetables and stir well. Return the pan to the heat and cook for 25 minutes, or until the meat and vegetables are tender when pierced with the point of a sharp knife.

Remove the pan from the heat. With a metal spoon, skim off any scum from the surface of the cooking liquid. Remove and discard the bouquet garni. Transfer the stew to a warmed, deep serving dish or individual serving plates.

Serve immediately.

Saute d'Agneau

LAMB SAUTE

A sophisticated meat dish, Sauté d'Agneau is simple to prepare and cook. To make the dish slightly richer, espagnole or demi-glace sauce may be used instead of the stock suggested here, although this will increase the length of preparation time. Serve with petits pois and sautéed potatoes.

4 SERVINGS

- 3 tablespoons olive oil
- 2 lb. boned shoulder of lamb, trimmed of excess fat and cut into ½-inch cubes
- 1 celery stalk, trimmed and chopped
- 1 medium-sized onion, finely chopped
- 4 fl. oz. [½ cup] red wine
- 8 fl. oz. [1 cup] beef stock

- 1 tablespoon cornflour [cornstarch], mixed to a paste with 2 tablespoons water
- 2 tablespoons tomato purée
- ½ teaspoon salt
- ½ teaspoon freshly ground black pepper
- 1 teaspoon finely grated lemon rind
- 4 oz. button mushrooms, wiped clean and thinly sliced

In a large flameproof casserole, heat 2 tablespoons of the olive oil over moderately high heat. When the oil is hot, add the lamb cubes and fry them, stirring frequently, for 10 to 12 minutes or until they are well browned all over. Using a slotted spoon, transfer the meat to a plate and keep warm.

Reduce the heat to moderate and add the remaining tablespoon of oil to the

Smooth and creamy, Sauté d'Agneau is the perfect main dish for that mid-week dinner party – it's quick and easy to make and inexpensive, too.

casserole. Add the celery and onion and fry them, stirring occasionally, for 5 to 7 minutes or until the onion is soft and translucent but not brown. Pour the wine and stock into the casserole, stir in the cornflour [cornstarch] mixture and bring the liquid to the boil, stirring constantly. Return the meat to the pan and add the tomato purée, salt, pepper, lemon rind and mushrooms. Cover the casserole and cook the mixture for 20 minutes, stirring occasionally. (If you prefer your meat well done, increase this final cooking time by 10 minutes.)

Remove the casserole from the heat and serve immediately.

Pork Balls in Wine Sauce

Serve this tasty dish with buttered rice, spinach and a lightly chilled rosé wine.

4 SERVINGS

1½ lb. minced [ground] pork
 8 oz. lean bacon or gammon, minced [ground]
 4 oz. [2 cups] fresh breadcrumbs
 1 large egg
 1 teaspoon salt
 ½ teaspoon black pepper
 ½ teaspoon ground allspice
 2 tablespoons chopped fresh parsley
 8 fl. oz. [1 cup] dry sherry
 8 fl. oz. [1 cup] chicken stock
 2 tablespoons wine vinegar
 1 tablespoon sugar
 1 teaspoon salt
 4 teaspoons cornflour [cornstarch] dissolved in 3 tablespoons water

Preheat the oven to moderate 350°F (Gas Mark 4, 180°C).

In a large mixing bowl, combine the pork, bacon or gammon, breadcrumbs, egg, salt, pepper, allspice and parsley. Using your hands, mix and knead the ingredients until they are well combined.

Shape the mixture into 12 balls. Place the balls, in one layer, in a large baking dish.

In a small saucepan, combine the sherry, stock, vinegar, sugar and salt over low heat, stirring constantly. When the sugar has dissolved, bring the mixture to the boil. Reduce the heat to low and stir in the cornflour [cornstarch] mixture. Cook, stirring constantly, until the sauce has thickened slightly.

Remove the pan from the heat and pour the sauce over the meatballs. Put the meatballs in the oven and bake them for 1½ hours, basting occasionally.

Remove the baking dish from the oven and serve immediately, from the dish.

Pork Goulasch

Serve this delicious stew with buttered noodles, tomato salad and a well-chilled Hungarian Riesling.

4 SERVINGS

2 oz. [¼ cup] butter
2 lb. pork fillets, cubed
3 onions, thinly sliced
2 garlic cloves, crushed
1½ lb. canned sauerkraut, drained
½ teaspoon dried dill
1 teaspoon caraway seeds
1 teaspoon salt
1 teaspoon black pepper
8 fl. oz. [1 cup] chicken stock
8 fl. oz. [1 cup] sour cream

In a large, flameproof casserole, melt the butter over moderate heat. When the foam subsides, add the pork cubes, a few at a time, and cook them, turning occasionally, for 6 to 8 minutes or until they are lightly and evenly browned. Transfer the cubes, as they brown, to a plate.

Add the onions and garlic to the casserole and cook, stirring occasionally, for 5 to 7 minutes or until the onions are soft and translucent but not brown. Stir in the sauerkraut, dill, caraway seeds, salt, pepper and stock and bring to the boil.

Return the pork cubes to the casserole and stir well to mix. Reduce the heat to low, cover the casserole and simmer the goulasch for 1 to 1¼ hours or until the pork is very tender.

Stir in the sour cream and serve at once.

Tasty Pork Balls in Wine Sauce.

Pork and Pineapple Casserole

This delicately-flavoured dish of pork fillets cooked with herbs, pineapple, orange, wine and green peppers makes a superb Sunday lunch. Serve with creamed potatoes and buttered green beans.

4 SERVINGS

4 pork fillets, beaten until thin
1 garlic clove, halved
1 teaspoon salt
½ teaspoon black pepper
1 tablespoon grated orange rind
½ teaspoon dried marjoram
½ teaspoon dried sage
1 oz. [2 tablespoons] butter
2 medium-sized green peppers, white pith removed, seeded and cut into julienne strips
10 fl. oz. [1¼ cups] dry white wine
16 oz. canned pineapple rings, drained and coarsely chopped
1 tablespoon cornflour [cornstarch] dissolved in 2 tablespoons orange juice

Rub the pork fillets all over with the garlic clove halves and half of the salt and pepper. Discard the garlic clove halves and lay the pork fillets flat on a working surface. Sprinkle over the orange rind, marjoram and sage. Roll up the fillets and secure the rolls with trussing thread or string. Set aside.

In a medium-sized flameproof casserole, melt the butter over moderate heat. When the foam subsides, add the green peppers and fry them, stirring frequently, for 4 minutes. With a slotted spoon, remove the peppers from the casserole and set them aside.

Add the pork fillets to the casserole and fry for 6 to 8 minutes, turning the rolls occasionally with tongs, or until they are lightly browned.

Pour the wine into the casserole and stir in the remaining salt and pepper, the pineapple pieces and fried green peppers. Bring the liquid to the boil, stirring constantly. Reduce the heat to low, cover the casserole and simmer for 50 minutes to 1 hour, or until the pork fillets are cooked and tender when pierced with the point of a sharp knife.

Remove the casserole from the heat. Using a slotted spoon, remove the pork rolls from the casserole and transfer them to a warmed serving dish. Remove and discard the trussing thread or string.

Tender pork fillet rolls cooked with pineapple chunks, green pepper and white wine, Pork and Pineapple Casserole tastes as superb as it looks.

Remove the pineapple pieces and green peppers from the casserole and arrange them around the meat. Keep the mixture warm.

With a metal spoon, skim off and discard any fat from the surface of the cooking liquid in the casserole. Pour the liquid through a fine wire strainer into a medium-sized saucepan and stir in the cornflour [cornstarch] mixture. Set the pan over moderate heat and cook the sauce, stirring constantly with a wooden spoon, for 5 minutes or until it is thick and smooth.

Remove the pan from the heat. Pour the sauce over the pork rolls and serve immediately.

Pork Ratatouille

  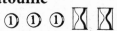

This adaptation of a Belgian recipe may be served with mashed potatoes or fried rice for a superb lunch or supper.

4 SERVINGS

2 lb. pork fillets, cut into 2-inch cubes
2 teaspoons salt
1 teaspoon black pepper
2 fl. oz. [¼ cup] olive oil
1 large onion, finely chopped
2 garlic cloves, crushed
1 large red pepper, white pith removed, seeded and chopped
1 large green pepper, white pith removed, seeded and chopped
3 large courgettes [zucchini], trimmed and sliced
1 small aubergine [eggplant], chopped and dégorged
14 oz. canned peeled tomatoes
4 fl. oz. [½ cup] dry white wine
2 teaspoons grated lemon rind
14 oz. canned white haricot beans, drained

Rub the pork cubes with the salt and pepper and set aside.

In a large flameproof casserole, heat the oil over moderate heat. When the oil is hot, add the onion, garlic, peppers, courgettes [zucchini], aubergine [eggplant] and tomatoes with the can juice. Fry, stirring and turning occasionally, for 8 to 10 minutes or until the onion is soft. Add the pork, pour over the white wine and stir in the lemon rind. Bring the liquid to the boil.

Reduce the heat to low and simmer the mixture for 1 hour. Add the haricot beans and simmer for a further 20 minutes or until the pork is very tender when pierced with the point of a sharp knife.

Remove the casserole from the heat and serve at once.

Pork Vindaloo

A pungent, strongly flavoured curry from the west coast of India, Pork Vindaloo is for those who like really hot curries. If you do not have an electric blender, use ground spices.

4-6 SERVINGS

2-inch piece fresh root ginger, peeled and chopped
4 garlic cloves, chopped
1½ teaspoons hot chilli powder
2 teaspoons turmeric
1 teaspoon salt
seeds of 6 whole cardamom
6 cloves
6 peppercorns
1 x 2-inch cinnamon stick
2 tablespoons coriander seeds
1 tablespoon cumin seeds
5 fl. oz. [⅝ cup] wine vinegar
2 lb. pork fillets, cut into large cubes
4 curry leaves (optional)
3 tablespoons vegetable oil
1 teaspoon mustard seeds
5 fl. oz. [⅝ cup] water

Put the ginger, garlic, chilli powder, turmeric, salt, cardamom seeds, cloves, peppercorns, cinnamon stick, coriander seeds, cumin seeds and the vinegar into an electric blender. Blend the mixture at high speed for 30 seconds. Scrape down the sides of the blender and blend for another 30 seconds. Add more vinegar if necessary and blend until the mixture forms a smooth liquid paste.

Place the pork in a large mixing bowl and mix in the spice paste. Cover the bowl and set it aside to marinate for 1 hour at room temperature. Lay the curry leaves, if you are using them, on top. Re-cover the bowl and place it in the refrigerator for 24 hours, turning the meat 2 or 3 times during that time.

Two hours before cooking time, remove the bowl from the refrigerator and set aside at room temperature.

In a large saucepan, heat the oil over moderate heat. When the oil is hot, add the mustard seeds. Cover the pan to stop the seeds from spattering and, when they stop popping, add the pork, all the marinade and the water. Stir to mix and bring the mixture to the boil. When the curry boils, reduce the heat to low, cover the pan and simmer for 40 minutes. Uncover the pan and continue cooking for a further 40 minutes or until the pork is very tender and the sauce is neither too thick nor too thin.

Remove the pan from the heat. Spoon the vindaloo into a large warmed serving dish. Serve immediately.

Blanquette de Veau

Served with boiled rice and garnished with sautéed mushrooms, Blanquette de Veau is an ideal main dish to serve for a dinner party.

4 SERVINGS

1½ lb. lean boned veal, cut into
    1½-inch cubes
2 medium-sized onions, studded
    with 2 cloves each
2 carrots, scraped and quartered
3 fl. oz. [⅜ cup] white wine
    bouquet garni, consisting of 4
    parsley sprigs, 1 thyme spray and
    1 bay leaf tied together
½ teaspoon salt
⅛ teaspoon white pepper
1½ oz. [3 tablespoons] butter
6 tablespoons flour
5 fl. oz. single cream [⅝ cup light cream]
2 egg yolks
8 toast triangles

Put the veal cubes in a large saucepan and pour in enough water to cover. Bring the water to the boil over moderate heat and cook the veal for 2 minutes.

Skim off any scum from the top of the liquid and reduce the heat to low. Add the onions, carrots, wine, bouquet garni, salt and pepper. Cover the saucepan and simmer over low heat for 1½ hours, or

Lean veal chunks in a rich cream sauce, Blanquette de Veau is a classic French dish which makes an excellent centrepiece for a special dinner.

until the meat is tender when pierced with the point of a sharp knife.

Strain off the liquid into a bowl and reserve 1¼ pints [3⅛ cups] for the sauce. Keep warm while you make the sauce.

In a saucepan, melt the butter over low heat. Remove the pan from the heat and stir in the flour with a wooden spoon. Stirring constantly, gradually add the reserved stock. Return the pan to the heat and cook, stirring constantly, for 2 to 3 minutes or until the sauce becomes thick and smooth. Remove the sauce from the heat.

In a small bowl, beat the cream and egg yolks together with a wooden spoon. Stir 4 tablespoons of the hot sauce, a spoonful at a time, into the cream-and-egg yolk mixture. When the sauce is well mixed with the cream and egg yolks, return it to the saucepan gradually, beating it with a wire whisk. Replace the saucepan on low heat and cook, stirring, until the sauce just boils.

Transfer the veal to a heated serving dish and pour the sauce over it.

Garnish with the toast triangles and serve immediately.

Osso Buco

STEWED VEAL KNUCKLE OR SHANK

One of the internationally recognized classics of Italian cuisine, Osso Buco is made from veal knuckle or shank with a sauce of tomatoes and wine. Osso Buco is traditionally served with risotto milanese.

6 SERVINGS

3 oz. [¾ cup] seasoned flour, made
    with 3 oz. [¾ cup] flour, 1 teaspoon
    salt and ½ teaspoon black pepper
3 lb. veal knuckle or shank, sawn
    into 3-inch pieces
4 oz. [½ cup] butter
1 large onion, thinly sliced
14 oz. canned peeled tomatoes
2 tablespoons tomato purée
6 fl. oz. [¾ cup] dry white wine
1 teaspoon salt
½ teaspoon black pepper
1 teaspoon sugar
GREMOLADA
1 tablespoon grated lemon rind
2 garlic cloves, crushed
1½ tablespoons chopped fresh
    parsley

Place the flour on a plate and dip in the veal pieces, one by one, to coat them. Shake off any excess. Set aside.

In a large, flameproof casserole, melt the butter over moderate heat. When the foam subsides, add the veal pieces and cook, turning occasionally, for 5 to 8 minutes or until they are evenly browned. Transfer the veal to a plate. Set aside.

Add the onion to the casserole and cook, stirring occasionally, for 5 to 7 minutes or until it is soft and translucent but not brown. Add the tomatoes with the can juice and the tomato purée and cook, stirring occasionally, for 3 minutes. Add the wine, salt, pepper and sugar. Bring the mixture to the boil.

Return the veal pieces to the casserole and stir well. Reduce the heat to low, cover the casserole and simmer the veal for 1½ to 2 hours or until it is very tender.

Meanwhile make the gremolada. In a small mixing bowl, combine the lemon rind, garlic and parsley.

Stir the gremolada into the veal mixture. Cook for a further 1 minute. Remove the casserole from the heat and transfer the veal pieces to a warmed serving dish. Spoon over the sauce and serve at once.

Veal Marengo

  ① ① ① ✄ ✄

This classic French stew may be served with puréed potatoes, French beans and a well-chilled strong white wine such as Meursault.

6 SERVINGS

3 lb. lean boned veal, cubed
2 teaspoons salt
2 teaspoons black pepper
3 oz. [⅜ cup] butter
2 fl. oz. [¼ cup] vegetable oil
2 onions, thinly sliced
2 garlic cloves, crushed
4 fl. oz. [½ cup] dry white wine
4 fl. oz. [½ cup] veal or chicken stock
   bouquet garni, consisting of 4
   parsley sprigs, 1 thyme spray and
   1 bay leaf tied together
8 oz. canned tomatoes, chopped
2½ oz. tomato purée
1 teaspoon paprika
12 small pickling (pearl) onions,
   peeled
12 oz. button mushrooms, wiped
   clean and sliced
1 tablespoon flour

Place the veal cubes on a working surface and sprinkle over 1 teaspoon of salt and 1 teaspoon of pepper. Set aside.

In a large flameproof casserole, melt 2 ounces [¼ cup] of the butter with the oil over moderate heat. When the foam subsides, add the onions and garlic and cook, stirring occasionally, for 5 to 7 minutes or until the onions are soft and translucent but not brown. Stir in the veal cubes and cook them, turning from

time to time, for 8 to 10 minutes or until they are evenly browned.

Pour in the wine and stock and stir in the bouquet garni, the tomatoes with the can juice, the tomato purée and paprika. Bring the liquid to the boil, stirring occasionally. Reduce the heat to low, cover the casserole and simmer the mixture for 1½ hours. Add the pickling (pearl) onions and simmer for a further 30 minutes or until the meat is very tender.

Meanwhile, in a large frying-pan, melt the remaining butter over moderate heat. When the foam subsides, add the mushrooms and cook, stirring frequently, for 3 minutes. Remove the pan from the heat and, with a slotted spoon, transfer the mushrooms to a deep, warmed serving dish. When the veal is cooked, using a slotted spoon, add the veal cubes and pickling (pearl) onions to the serving dish. Set the mixture aside.

Remove the casserole from the heat and strain the contents into a saucepan, pressing the vegetables and flavourings with the back of a wooden spoon to extract all the juices. Place the pan over moderately high heat, bring the liquid to the boil and boil for 10 minutes or until the liquid has reduced by about one-third. Stir in the flour, a little at a time, and cook, stirring constantly, for 2 to 3 minutes or until the sauce has thickened slightly.

Remove the pan from the heat and pour the sauce over the meat and vegetable mixture. Serve at once.

Veal and Rice Casserole

 ① ①

This delicious Austrian casserole is quick and easy to prepare. Serve it with a green salad.

4 SERVINGS

2 oz. [¼ cup] butter
4 tablespoons vegetable oil
2 lb. boned veal shoulder, cubed
2 onions, finely chopped
2 tablespoons paprika
1 pint [2½ cups] chicken stock
2 fl. oz. [¼ cup] white wine
1 teaspoon salt
½ teaspoon black pepper
1 teaspoon dried thyme
10 oz. [1⅔ cups] long-grain rice,
   washed, soaked in cold water for
   30 minutes and drained

In a large flameproof casserole, melt the butter with the oil over moderate heat. When the foam subsides, add the meat and onions and fry, stirring frequently, for 5 to 8 minutes or until they are brown.

Stir in the paprika. Add the stock, wine, salt, pepper and thyme. Bring to the boil. Reduce the heat to low, cover the casserole and simmer for 1¼ hours.

Stir in the rice, re-cover the casserole and simmer for a further 20 to 25 minutes, or until the rice is tender and has absorbed all the liquid. Serve at once.

Veal and Rice Casserole.

Coq au Vin

CHICKEN COOKED IN RED WINE

 ① ① ① ⋈ ⋈

One of the great classics of French cuisine, Coq au Vin makes an ideal dish for a dinner party. Serve with boiled new potatoes and steamed broccoli.

4 SERVINGS

3 oz. [⅜ cup] butter
4 slices bacon, finely chopped
1 x 4 lb. chicken, cut into serving
   pieces
1 teaspoon salt
1 teaspoon black pepper
2 fl. oz. [¼ cup] brandy, warmed
1¼ pints [3⅛ cups] red wine
10 fl. oz. [1¼ cups] chicken stock
1 tablespoon tomato purée
1 garlic clove, crushed
   bouquet garni, consisting of 4
   parsley sprigs, 1 thyme spray and
   1 bay leaf tied together
16 small onions, peeled
8 oz. mushrooms, wiped clean and
   sliced
1 oz. [2 tablespoons] butter blended
   to a paste with 1 oz. [4 tablespoons]
   flour
2 tablespoons finely chopped fresh
   parsley

Preheat the oven to moderate 350°F (Gas Mark 4, 180°C).

In a large flameproof casserole, melt 1 ounce [2 tablespoons] of butter over moderate heat. When the foam subsides, add the bacon and fry, stirring occasionally, for 5 to 8 minutes or until it is crisp. With a slotted spoon, remove the bacon to a plate.

Add the chicken pieces and fry, stirring and turning occasionally, for 8 to 10 minutes or until they are lightly but evenly browned. Stir in the salt and black pepper. Carefully pour over the brandy and ignite, shaking the casserole gently until the flames die away.

Return the bacon to the casserole and pour over the wine and stock; add the tomato purée, garlic and bouquet garni. Stir well to mix and bring the liquid to the boil.

Cover the casserole and place it in the oven. Braise the chicken for 40 minutes.

Meanwhile, prepare the onions and mushrooms. In large frying-pan, melt 1 ounce [2 tablespoons] of butter over moderate heat. When the foam subsides, add the onions and cook, stirring and turning occasionally, for 8 to 10 minutes or until they are golden brown. Reduce the heat to low and simmer the onions, stirring occasionally, for a further 15 minutes or until they are just tender.

In a second frying-pan, melt the re-

Chicken cooked slowly in red wine – that's succulent Coq au Vin, a classic French country dish.

maining butter over moderate heat. When the foam subsides, add the mushrooms and fry, stirring occasionally, for 3 minutes or until they are just tender.

Remove the casserole from the oven and add the onions and mushrooms to the mixture. Return the casserole to the oven and continue to braise the chicken for a further 15 to 20 minutes or until it is tender.

Remove the casserole from the oven and, using a slotted spoon, transfer the chicken, onions and mushrooms to a warmed plate. Cover and keep warm while you finish off the sauce.

Place the casserole over high heat and bring the liquid to the boil. Boil the liquid until it has reduced to about 1 pint [2½ cups]. Using a slotted spoon, skim any scum from the surface of the liquid and remove and discard the bouquet garni. Stir in the butter and flour mixture, a little at a time, and cook the sauce, stirring constantly, for 2 minutes or until it is smooth and has thickened.

Return the chicken, onions and mushrooms to the casserole and stir well to blend. Simmer for 2 minutes, then remove the casserole from the heat. Sprinkle over the parsley and serve at once.

Venison Stew

Serve Venison Stew with a tossed green salad, crusty bread and some red wine for a really special meal.

4 SERVINGS

2 lb. lean venison, cut into 2-inch cubes
2 oz. [¼ cup] butter
1 teaspoon salt
½ teaspoon freshly ground black pepper
1 teaspoon dried rosemary
3 medium-sized carrots, scraped and quartered
1 small turnip, peeled and roughly chopped
8 oz. small onions, peeled
3 medium-sized potatoes, peeled and halved
14 oz. canned peeled tomatoes
3 tablespoons tomato purée

MARINADE
12 fl. oz. [1½ cups] red wine
8 fl. oz. [1 cup] beef stock
3 tablespoons olive oil
1 large onion, thinly sliced
8 black peppercorns
3 garlic cloves, crushed
2 tablespoons chopped fresh parsley
1 teaspoon dried rosemary
bouquet garni, consisting of 4 parsley sprigs, 1 thyme spray and 1 bay leaf tied together

In a large, shallow dish, combine all the marinade ingredients. Add the venison cubes and mix well. Set aside and marinate the meat at room temperature for at least 12 hours, basting it from time to time.

Remove the meat from the marinade and dry it on kitchen paper towels. Reserve the marinade.

In a large flameproof casserole, melt the butter over moderate heat. When the foam subsides, add the meat cubes and cook, stirring and turning occasionally, for 8 minutes, or until the cubes are lightly and evenly browned. Add the reserved marinade, the salt, pepper and rosemary and stir well. Bring the liquid to the boil, skimming off any scum that rises to the surface. Reduce the heat to low, cover and simmer the stew for 1½ hours.

Add the carrots, turnip, onions, potatoes, tomatoes with the can juice and the tomato purée and stir thoroughly to blend.

Re-cover the casserole and continue to simmer the stew for a further 1 hour, or until the meat is tender when pierced with the point of a sharp knife.

Remove the casserole from the heat and remove and discard the bouquet garni. Serve at once.

Lean venison chunks marinated overnight then cooked with vegetables, Venison Stew makes a really hearty sustaining main course for a winter meal.

Couscous

Serve Couscous with a green salad. If you do not have a couscoussier, you can construct a temporary one by placing a cheesecloth-lined colander on top of a saucepan, sealing the space between the colander and the rim of the pan with a twisted, damp tea towel.

6 SERVINGS

5 tablespoons vegetable oil
3 garlic cloves, crushed
4 green chillis, finely chopped
3 lb. boned leg of lamb, cubed
2 teaspoons salt
¾ teaspoon black pepper
1 teaspoon cayenne pepper
2 teaspoons ground cumin
2 teaspoons paprika
1 lb. couscous
18 fl. oz. [2¼ cups] lukewarm salted
   water
4 oz. [⅔ cup] raisins
2 oz. [¼ cup] chick-peas, soaked
   overnight and drained
½ teaspoon saffron threads soaked
   in 1 teaspoon water
3 teaspoons turmeric
2 teaspoons ground coriander
4 tablespoons melted butter

In the lower part of a *couscoussier*, heat 4 tablespoons of the vegetable oil over moderate heat. Add the garlic and chillis and cook, stirring occasionally, for 3 minutes. Add the meat, salt, pepper, cayenne, cumin and paprika to the *couscoussier* and stir to mix well. Pour in 2 pints [5 cups] of water. Bring the water to the boil over high heat, reduce the heat to low and simmer the mixture, covered, for 1 hour.

Meanwhile, put the couscous grains into a large mixing bowl. Pour over 16 fluid ounces [2 cups] of the lukewarm salted water. Leave the couscous to soak for 1 hour, or until it swells slightly. Drain the grains and set them aside.

Pour a further 1 pint [2½ cups] water into the *couscoussier*, increase the heat to high and bring the liquid to the boil. Reduce the heat to low and simmer for a further 30 minutes.

Add the raisins, chick-peas, saffron, turmeric and coriander to the *couscoussier* and mix well. Pour the couscous grains into the steamer or top part of the *couscoussier* and fit it on to the lower part. Steam the couscous, covered, for 40 minutes.

Remove the top part from the *couscoussier* and set it aside. Transfer the couscous grains to a large mixing bowl and pour on the melted butter, the remaining 2 fluid ounces [¼ cup] of lukewarm salted water and 1 tablespoon vegetable oil. Leave the mixture for 15 minutes. Stir the couscous, breaking up any lumps that have formed, and return the grains to the steamer. Fit the steamer on top of the *couscoussier* again. Steam over low heat, covered, for a further 20 minutes. Remove the *couscoussier* from the heat and serve.

Danish Chicken Casserole

A tempting and easy-to-make dish, Danish Chicken Casserole is ideal to serve for lunch or supper.

6 SERVINGS

2 oz. [½ cup] flour
1 teaspoon salt
½ teaspoon black pepper
2 teaspoons dried dill
1 x 5 lb. chicken, skinned and cut
   into 8 serving pieces
2 eggs, lightly beaten
2 oz. [¼ cup] butter
2 tablespoons vegetable oil
10 fl. oz. [1¼ cups] chicken stock
1 medium-sized green pepper,
   white pith removed, seeded and
   cut into thin rings
2 tomatoes, blanched, peeled and
   sliced
4 fl. oz. double cream [½ cup heavy
   cream]
2 oz. [½ cup] Samsoe or Cheddar
   cheese, grated

In a plate or bowl, combine the flour, salt, pepper and dill together. Dip the chicken pieces in the beaten eggs and then in the flour mixture.

In a large flameproof casserole, melt the butter and oil over moderate heat. When the foam subsides, add the chicken pieces to the pan and fry them for about 8 minutes, or until they are lightly browned on all sides, turning frequently with tongs or large spoons.

Add the chicken stock to the pan and bring the liquid to the boil. Reduce the heat to low, cover the pan and simmer the chicken gently for 50 minutes, or until it is tender.

With a slotted spoon, remove the chicken pieces from the pan and arrange them in the centre of a warmed, large flameproof serving dish. Keep the chicken warm while you are finishing the sauce.

Preheat the grill [broiler] to moderate.

Add the green pepper to the liquid in the frying-pan and simmer for 4 minutes. Add the tomatoes and cook for a further 2 minutes.

With a slotted spoon, remove the vegetables from the liquid and arrange them around the chicken pieces. Remove the pan from the heat and stir the cream into the liquid. Return the pan to the heat and cook gently for 2 to 3 minutes.

Pour the sauce over the chicken. Sprinkle the cheese on top and place the dish under the grill [broiler] for 5 minutes or until the cheese is bubbling.

Serve immediately.

Pork Curry

This is a spicy, pungent curry which is best served with plain boiled rice and an onion and tomato salad.

6 SERVINGS

1 tablespoon ground coriander
1 teaspoon ground cumin
1 teaspoon hot chilli powder
1½ teaspoons turmeric
½ teaspoon ground cinnamon
½ teaspoon ground cardamom
½ teaspoon ground cloves
½ teaspoon black pepper
3 tablespoons vinegar
4 tablespoons vegetable oil
3 onions, finely chopped
3 garlic cloves, crushed
2-inch piece fresh root ginger,
   peeled and finely chopped
2 to 3 green chillis, finely chopped
3 lb. pork fillets, cubed
1½ teaspoons salt
1 teaspoon sugar
1½-inch slice creamed coconut
   dissolved in 1 pint [2½ cups]
   boiling water

In a small mixing bowl, combine the coriander, cumin, chilli powder, turmeric, cinnamon, cardamom, cloves and black pepper. Pour over the vinegar and stir until the mixture forms a smooth paste.

In a large saucepan, heat the oil over moderate heat. When the oil is hot, add the onions and fry, stirring occasionally, for 8 to 10 minutes or until they are golden brown.

Add the garlic, ginger and chillis and fry, stirring frequently, for 3 minutes. Add the spice paste and fry, stirring constantly, for 10 minutes. If the mixture gets too dry add a spoonful of vinegar or water. Add the pork cubes and fry, stirring frequently, for 6 to 8 minutes or until the pork no longer looks raw. Add the salt and sugar and pour over the coconut mixture. Stir the mixture and bring it to the boil. Cover the pan, reduce the heat to low and simmer the curry for 1 to 1¼ hours or until the pork is very tender. Serve immediately.

Couscous is ideal for entertaining.

Rabbit Stew

This delicious country stew is an excellent supper party dish. Accompany it with a full-bodied Burgundy wine, such as Nuits St. Georges, or a well-chilled white wine, such as Vouvray.

4 SERVINGS

1 x 4 lb. rabbit, cleaned and cut into serving pieces
2 oz. [¼ cup] butter
½ teaspoon salt
½ teaspoon white pepper
½ teaspoon dried thyme
½ teaspoon dried rosemary
1 tablespoon prepared French mustard
1 tablespoon cornflour [cornstarch] dissolved in 2 tablespoons single [light] cream
4 fl. oz. [½ cup] port
3 oz. [½ cup] sultanas or seedless raisins
3 oz. [½ cup] currants

MARINADE
16 fl. oz. [2 cups] dry white wine
4 fl. oz. [½ cup] olive oil
10 oz. dried prunes
2 garlic cloves, crushed
1 teaspoon salt
½ teaspoon freshly ground black pepper
1 medium-sized onion, thinly sliced
1 carrot, scraped and thinly sliced

GARNISH
1 tablespoon chopped fresh parsley
6 crescent-shaped croûtons

First prepare the marinade. Place all the marinade ingredients in a large, shallow bowl and stir well to blend. Add the rabbit pieces and marinate them at room temperature, basting occasionally, for at least 6 hours.

Remove the rabbit pieces from the marinade and pat them dry with kitchen paper towels. Reserve the marinade.

In a large, deep frying-pan, melt the butter over moderate heat. When the foam subsides, add the rabbit pieces to the pan and fry them, turning occasionally with tongs, for 8 to 10 minutes or until they are lightly and evenly browned.

Add the marinade to the pan and bring the liquid to the boil, stirring occasionally. Stir in the salt and pepper. Reduce the heat to low, cover the pan and simmer the rabbit for 1 to 1¼ hours or until it is

This warming, satisfying Rabbit Stew takes quite a long time to prepare and cook, but the end result is well worth the effort. Serve with red wine for a special dinner.

very tender when pierced with the point of a sharp knife.

Remove the pan from the heat and transfer the rabbit pieces to a heated serving dish. Keep warm while you prepare the sauce.

Strain the cooking liquids into a medium-sized saucepan and, using tongs, remove the cooked prunes and add them to the saucepan. Discard any pulp left in the strainer. Place the pan over moderate heat and bring the liquid to the boil. Stir in the thyme and rosemary. Reduce the heat to low and add the mustard and the cornflour [cornstarch] mixture, stirring gently. Add the port, sultanas or seedless raisins and currants and simmer gently for 10 minutes.

Pour the sauce over the rabbit in the heated serving dish. Sprinkle with chopped parsley and arrange the croûtons around the sides of the serving dish.

Serve immediately.

Rice and pasta

Rice and pasta dishes were, not so long ago, firmly classed in the 'different therefore suspect' category by most of the English-speaking world. Occasionally, perhaps rice was used to make a warming pudding and pasta was legitimatized by the addition of a basic cheese sauce — but otherwise their potential was politely ignored and their popularity in other lands put down to foreign perversity.

Now, however, the word is out: the addition of staples such as rice and pasta to meat, fish and vegetables can eke out a meal, can make that end-of-the-week supper into an exotically acceptable dish, fit for any and all occasions. And economical needn't mean dull uninteresting cooking, as can be seen from a glance at the selection of recipes in this book — recipes such as hearty Russian Lamb Pilaff (pictured below, page 79), or Spaghetti alla Carbonara (page 110), a delicious mixture of pasta, bacon, eggs, cream and grated cheese.

And for those occasions when you've got people coming and don't mind spending a bit more time in the kitchen — well, rice and pasta can be festive too, as you can see from the colourful selection of recipes specially designed for worry-free entertaining — Lasagne (page 114), for instance, or Risotto alla Bolognese (page 92).

Any dishes that provide good eating at prices that won't empty your purse can only be welcome these days — and all of the recipes in this book are guaranteed to do just that.

Rice

Rice is one of the most important food grains in the world and is the staple food of millions of people. Cultivated rice, *oryza sativa*, has been known in India, where it is supposed to have originated, since about 3,000 B.C.

Rice is now produced in Asia, Africa, Latin America, parts of Europe, Australia and the United States. The latter is one of the world's largest exporters of rice; although the Asian countries grow a large amount, very little is exported as they require most of it for their own use. Most varieties grow on land submerged in water although there is a variety known as upland rice which grows well on dry land.

Because it keeps well, cooks more quickly and has a better appearance, most rice is milled before it is marketed. Milling removes the bran skin which lies under the husk, therefore some of the protein, minerals and vitamins are lost. Brown rice which has only the husk removed is more nutritious than other varieties and is often used in vegetarian dishes.

There are about 7,000 varieties of rice in almost as many colours — rice may be red, brown, blue, purple, black or ivory. Long, short and round-grain rice are the three most commonly used varieties in Western cooking.

Rice can be bought in several forms, among them are parboiled, pre-cooked (which only requires reconstituting in hot water) and boil-in-bag packs. Rice is also ground and used for puddings, or very finely ground to make rice flour for use in cakes and biscuits [cookies].

Wild rice, *zinzania aquatica*, is not a true rice, but a water grass which grows only in North America in swamps and shallow coastal waters.

Rice which is to be served as an accompaniment for a curry or used to make a pilaff or biryani should be a long-grain variety such as Patna or basmati, the latter being the better. Risottos are best made with absorbent Italian rice such as avorio or crystalo. Round-grain rice is most suitable for rice puddings.

Rice absorbs liquids in varying amounts. Each variety, and sometimes different crops of the same variety, have unequal powers of absorption. The amount of liquid given in any recipe, therefore, can only be approximate. When cooking rice, check halfway through the cooking time and add more liquid if necessary.

Rice, when cooked, increases $2\frac{1}{2}$ to 3 times in bulk, so 1 cup of uncooked rice will yield between $2\frac{1}{2}$ and 3 cups of cooked rice.

Servings vary with appetite and custom but, on average, allow about $2\frac{1}{2}$ ounces [1 cup] of cooked rice per person.

BOILED RICE

To cook 10 ounces [1⅔ cups] of uncooked long-grain rice, wash thoroughly in cold running water. When the water runs clear, leave the rice to soak for 30 minutes, then drain.

Put the rice in a medium-sized sauce-pan. Pour over 1 pint [2½ cups] of water and add 1 teaspoon of salt. Place the pan over high heat and bring the water to the boil. Cover the pan, reduce the heat to low and simmer for 15 to 20 minutes or until the rice is tender and all the liquid has been absorbed.

FRIED RICE

In a large frying-pan, heat 3 tablespoons of vegetable oil over moderately high heat. When the oil is very hot, add 3 lightly beaten eggs. Before the eggs set too firmly, add 1¼ pounds [8 cups] cold, cooked long-grain rice and ½ teaspoon of salt. Fry, stirring constantly, for 3 to 4 minutes or until all the grains of rice are coated with the oil. (Other ingredients such as diced cooked ham and spring onions [scallions] may be added at this point to make a more substantial dish.)

Italian rice is cooked in a completely different way. It is a thick, short-grain, highly absorbent rice and requires slow cooking. The liquid is added a little at a time, the first amount being absorbed before more is added. (See recipe for Green Rice on page 8.)

BASIC RICE PUDDING

Preheat the oven to cool 300°F (Gas Mark 2, 150°C). Grease a 2-pint [1½-quart] baking dish with 2 teaspoons of butter. Place 1½ ounces [¼ cup] of round-grain rice, 2 tablespoons sugar, 1½ pints [3¾ cups] milk and 1 teaspoon vanilla essence or ⅛ teaspoon grated nutmeg in the dish. Place the dish in the oven and bake the pudding for 3 hours. If a richer pudding is required, beat in 2 egg yolks 30 minutes before the end of the cooking

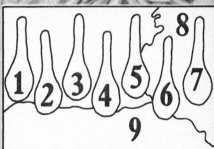

1 Brown rice 2 Avorio rice 3 Basmati rice 4 Wild rice 5 Round-grain rice 6 Ground rice 7 Rice flour 8 Natural rice 9 Rice paper, similar in name only, comes from an Asiatic tree.

time. For a more attractive appearance remove the dish from the oven, sprinkle the top of the pudding with 1 tablespoon of sugar and place the dish under a hot grill [broiler] for 1 minute to glaze.

Rice with Aubergine [Eggplant] **and Potatoes**

An adaptation of a recipe from the west coast of India, Rice with Aubergine [Eggplant] and Potatoes may be served as a filling accompaniment to curries or roast pork.

6 SERVINGS

10 oz. [1⅔ cups] long-grain rice, washed, soaked in cold water for 30 minutes and drained
1 pint [2½ cups] water
1½ teaspoons salt
1 teaspoon turmeric
1 teaspoon ground cumin
1 tablespoon ground coriander
½ teaspoon cayenne pepper
½ teaspoon sugar
1 tablespoon lemon juice
2 teaspoons chick-pea flour
2 oz. [¼ cup] butter
12 oz. potatoes, peeled and cut into ½-inch cubes
1 large aubergine [eggplant], cubed and dégorged
2 oz. [¼ cup] butter, melted

Put the rice in a large saucepan. Pour over the water and add 1 teaspoon of the salt. Bring to the boil over high heat. Cover the pan, reduce the heat to low and simmer for 15 to 20 minutes or until the rice is tender and all the water has been absorbed. Remove the pan from the heat. Set aside and keep warm.

Meanwhile, in a small mixing bowl, mix the turmeric, cumin, coriander, cayenne, sugar, lemon juice, chick-pea flour and the remaining salt to a paste, adding more lemon juice if necessary. Set aside.

Preheat the oven to moderate 350°F (Gas Mark 4, 180°C).

In a large frying-pan, melt the butter over moderate heat. When the foam subsides, add the potato and aubergine [eggplant] cubes and fry, stirring frequently, for 5 minutes. Add the spice paste and fry, stirring constantly, for 10 minutes, adding a spoonful or two of water if the mixture becomes too dry. Cover the pan, reduce the heat to low and cook the vegetables for 15 to 20 minutes or until they are tender when pierced with the point of a sharp knife. Remove the pan from the heat and set aside.

Spread half the rice over the bottom of an ovenproof dish. Sprinkle 1 ounce [2 tablespoons] of the melted butter over the rice. Spread the vegetable mixture over the rice and cover with the remaining rice. Sprinkle the remaining melted butter over the top.

Cover the dish and place it in the centre of the oven. Cook for 20 to 25 minutes or until all of the ingredients are very hot.

Remove the dish from the oven and serve the mixture immediately, straight from the dish.

Brazilian Rice

This is a tasty and simple Brazilian way of cooking rice. It may be served instead of plain boiled rice with roast chicken or grilled [broiled] steaks.

4-6 SERVINGS

4 tablespoons olive oil
1 medium-sized onion, thinly sliced
12 oz. [2 cups] long-grain rice, washed, soaked in cold water for 30 minutes and drained
2 tomatoes, blanched, peeled and chopped
1 teaspoon salt
1¼ pints [3⅛ cups] boiling water

In a large saucepan, heat the oil over moderate heat. Add the onion and fry, stirring constantly, for 5 to 7 minutes or until the onion is soft and translucent but not brown. Add the rice and fry for 5 minutes, stirring constantly.

Add the tomatoes and salt. Cook for 2 minutes and then pour in the boiling water.

Reduce the heat to low, cover the pan and simmer for 15 to 20 minutes, or until the rice is cooked and all the liquid has

Rice with Aubergine [Eggplant] and Potatoes is an exotic accompaniment to meat curries.

been absorbed.

Turn the rice into a warmed serving dish and serve immediately.

Russian Rice

This dish from the USSR is delicately flavoured with sesame seeds and a little ginger. It makes an excellent accompaniment to roast chicken, roast lamb or a hot curry.

4 SERVINGS

2 oz. [¼ cup] butter
10 oz. [1⅔ cups] long-grain rice, washed, soaked in cold water for 30 minutes and drained
½ teaspoon ground ginger
1½ teaspoons sesame seeds
1 pint [2½ cups] chicken stock
½ teaspoon salt
½ teaspoon freshly ground black pepper
2 oz. [½ cup] slivered, toasted almonds

Preheat the oven to moderate 350°F (Gas Mark 4, 180°C).

In a flameproof casserole, melt the butter over moderate heat. Add the rice and cook for 10 minutes, stirring constantly. Add the ginger and sesame seeds and cook for 3 minutes. Pour in the stock, salt and pepper and bring to the boil, stirring constantly.

Put the caserole in the oven, uncovered, for 35 minutes or until all the liquid is absorbed and the rice is cooked. Toss the rice with a fork after 10 minutes and again after 20 minutes. Taste and add more salt if necessary. Sprinkle with the almonds and serve immediately.

Saffron Rice

Aromatic Saffron Rice is an Indian dish which may be served as part of an Indian meal, or with kebabs and yogurt.

4-6 SERVINGS

2 oz. [¼ cup] butter
seeds of 4 whole cardamom pods
4 cloves
3 x 1-inch pieces cinnamon stick
1 medium-sized onion, finely chopped
12 oz. [2 cups] long-grain rice, washed, soaked in cold water for 30 minutes and drained
1¼ pints [3⅛ cups] home-made boiling chicken stock
1 teaspoon salt
¾ teaspoon crushed saffron threads, soaked in 2 tablespoons boiling

water for 20 minutes

In a medium-sized saucepan, melt the butter over moderate heat. When the foam subsides, add the cardamom seeds, cloves and cinnamon sticks to the pan and fry, stirring constantly, for 2 minutes.

Add the onion and fry, stirring occasionally, for 8 to 10 minutes or until it is golden brown. Add the rice, reduce the heat to moderately low and fry gently, stirring constantly, for 5 minutes.

Pour the boiling stock over the rice, add the salt and stir in the saffron mixture.

Cover the pan, reduce the heat to low and cook for 15 to 20 minutes or until the rice is tender and all the liquid has been absorbed. Remove and discard the cinnamon sticks.

Remove the pan from the heat. Spoon the rice on to a warmed serving platter and serve immediately.

Yellow Rice

This simple dish of rice flavoured and coloured with turmeric is a good accompaniment for roast chicken or lamb, or any strongly flavoured beef dish. Use a good quality long-grain rice such as basmati. If basmati is not available use any rice you are familiar with and alter the amount of water used accordingly.

4-6 SERVINGS

2 oz. [¼ cup] butter
12 oz. [2 cups] long-grain rice, washed, soaked in cold water for 30 minutes and drained
1 teaspoon turmeric
1 teaspoon salt
3 oz. [½ cup] sultanas or seedless raisins
1 cinnamon stick
1 bay leaf
1¼ pints [3⅛ cups] boiling water

In a medium-sized saucepan, melt the butter over moderate heat. When the foam subsides, add the rice. Reduce the heat to moderately low and, stirring constantly, fry the rice gently for 5 minutes. Add the turmeric, salt, sultanas or seedless raisins, cinnamon stick and bay leaf and stir well to mix.

Pour in the boiling water and increase the heat to moderately high. When the rice is bubbling, cover the pan, reduce the heat to low and cook the rice for 15 to 20 minutes or until it is tender and all the water has been absorbed. Remove and discard both the bay leaf and cinnamon stick.

Turn the rice into a warmed serving dish and serve.

African Vegetable Rice

This appetizing vegetable rice dish from West Africa makes an ideal light supper or lunch dish. It also makes an excellent stuffing for joints of meat or poultry.

2-3 SERVINGS

12 oz. [2 cups] long-grain rice, washed, soaked in cold water for 30 minutes and drained
1¼ pints [3⅛ cups] water
2 teaspoons salt
2 oz. [¼ cup] butter
1 medium-sized onion, finely chopped
2 large tomatoes, blanched, peeled and chopped
1 large red pepper, white pith removed, seeded and finely chopped
2 celery stalks, trimmed and finely chopped
4 oz. broccoli, trimmed and chopped
4 oz. mushrooms, wiped clean and finely chopped
¼ teaspoon cayenne pepper

Put the rice in a large saucepan. Pour over the water and add 1½ teaspoons of the salt.

Place the pan over moderately high heat and bring the water to the boil. Cover the pan, reduce the heat to low and simmer the rice for 15 to 20 minutes or until all the liquid has been absorbed and the rice is tender. Remove the pan from the heat and set aside.

In a large frying-pan, melt the butter over moderate heat. When the foam subsides, add the onion and fry, stirring occasionally, for 5 to 7 minutes or until it is soft and translucent but not brown. Add the tomatoes, red pepper, celery and broccoli. Fry, stirring frequently, for 10 minutes or until the vegetables begin to soften. Add the mushrooms to the pan and fry, stirring frequently, for a further 3 minutes. Season with the remaining salt and the cayenne.

Add the rice to the pan and stir the mixture until it is combined. Cook, stirring frequently, for a further 10 minutes or until the mixture is thoroughly heated through.

Remove the pan from the heat and serve at once.

African Vegetable Rice makes an appetizing light supper, or an unusual stuffing for poultry.

Balkan Chicken Pilaff

This pilaff depends on a strong chicken stock for its flavour. For convenience, cook the chicken and make the stock the day before. Serve the pilaff for a delicious family supper with ratatouille and a salad of yogurt with chopped cucumber and mint leaves.

6-8 SERVINGS

STOCK
1 x 3 lb. chicken
1 teaspoon salt
1 medium-sized onion, halved
2 carrots, scraped
4 peppercorns
PILAFF
3 oz. [⅜ cup] butter
1 medium-sized onion, finely chopped
3 tomatoes, blanched, peeled and chopped
1 teaspoon salt
½ teaspoon freshly ground black pepper
2 teaspoons chopped fresh basil or 1 teaspoon dried basil
2 oz. [⅓ cup] walnuts, chopped
1 lb. [2⅔ cups] long-grain rice, washed, soaked in cold water for

30 minutes and drained

First make the stock. Put the chicken in a pot large enough to hold it comfortably. Pour in enough water to come halfway up the sides. Add the salt, onion, carrots and peppercorns and bring to the boil. Reduce the heat to low and simmer the chicken for 1¼ hours or until it is tender and cooked. Remove the saucepan from the heat and let the chicken cool.

When the chicken is cool enough to handle, remove it from the stock. Put it on a board and cut off all the meat. Put the meat in a bowl, cover and place in the refrigerator.

Return the chicken bones to the pan, adding more water if necessary to cover, and simmer for 1½ hours. Strain the stock into a bowl, cool, cover and refrigerate. When the fat hardens on the top of the stock, skim it off with a spoon.

To make the pilaff, heat 1½ pints [3¾ cups] of the stock until it boils. Cut the chicken meat into bite-sized pieces.

In a large flameproof casserole, melt the butter over moderate heat. Add the chopped onion and fry for 8 minutes. Add the chicken pieces, stir and cook for 2 minutes. Add the tomatoes, salt, pepper, basil and walnuts and cook for 1 minute. Add the rice and cook for 2 minutes, stirring constantly. Pour in the hot stock, raise the heat to high and bring the rice to the boil. When it is bubbling briskly,

cover, reduce the heat to low and simmer for 15 to 20 minutes, or until all the liquid is absorbed and the rice is tender. Serve at once, straight from the casserole.

Chicken Pilaff

 ①

The tastiest way to make this dish is to use a whole chicken so that you can make the stock from the carcass and giblets. If you do not have the time to do this, chicken pieces and a stock cube will do, though the flavour of the pilaff will not be as good.

4 SERVINGS

2 oz. [¼ cup] butter
1 x 4 lb. chicken, cut into serving pieces, or 8 chicken pieces
1 teaspoon salt
½ teaspoon freshly ground black pepper
1 teaspoon chopped fresh tarragon or ½ teaspoon dried tarragon
8 oz. button mushrooms, wiped clean
12 oz. [2 cups] long-grain rice, washed, soaked in cold water for 30 minutes and drained
1 pint [2½ cups] home-made chicken stock
5 fl. oz. single cream [⅝ cup light cream]

In a large saucepan, melt the butter over

This delicately creamy Chicken Pilaff is best made with home-made stock, but you can save time and use a stock cube and water. Serve with a tossed mixed salad, crusty bread and lots of ice-cold lager.

moderate heat. When the foam subsides, add the chicken pieces and cook them, turning them frequently, for 6 to 8 minutes or until they are lightly browned. Sprinkle the chicken pieces with half of the salt, the pepper and tarragon. Reduce the heat to low, cover the pan and cook the chicken pieces, turning occasionally, for 35 minutes.

Uncover the pan, increase the heat to moderate and add the mushrooms. Continue cooking for 10 minutes, stirring occasionally.

Add the drained rice and the remaining salt and cook, stirring constantly, for 5 minutes.

Pour in the chicken stock and bring the mixture to the boil. Cover the pan, reduce the heat to low and cook the pilaff for 15 to 20 minutes or until the rice is tender and all the liquid has been absorbed, and the chicken pieces are tender when pierced with the point of a sharp knife. Remove the pan from the heat and stir in the cream.

Spoon the pilaff on to a warmed serving platter, and serve immediately.

Chicken Liver Risotto

Tasty and inexpensive, Chicken Liver Risotto is very simple to prepare and ideal to serve as a main dish for lunch or supper accompanied by a green salad.

4 SERVINGS

2 oz. [¼ cup] butter
1 onion, finely chopped
4 oz. mushrooms, wiped clean and sliced
10 oz. [1⅔ cups] long-grain rice, washed, soaked in cold water for 30 minutes and drained
1 pint [2½ cups] boiling chicken stock
8 chicken livers, cut into small pieces
2 tablespoons chopped fresh parsley
2 oz. [½ cup] Parmesan cheese, grated

In a large, heavy saucepan, melt three-quarters of the butter over moderate heat. Add the onion and cook, stirring occasionally, for 5 to 7 minutes or until the onion is soft and translucent but not brown. Add the mushrooms and cook for a further 3 minutes.

Add the rice to the saucepan and cook, stirring constantly, for 2 minutes. Pour on the stock and let the rice cook over high heat for 15 seconds. Cover the saucepan, reduce the heat to low and simmer gently for 15 to 20 minutes, or until the liquid is absorbed and the rice is tender.

While the rice is cooking, prepare the chicken livers. In a medium-sized frying-pan, melt the remaining butter over moderate heat. Add the chicken livers and cook them for 10 minutes, stirring

occasionally.

When the rice is cooked, stir in the chicken livers and parsley. Put the mixture into a warmed serving dish and sprinkle on the Parmesan cheese. Serve immediately.

Rice Croquettes

These tasty rice and shrimp croquettes may be served with a hot tomato sauce for a superb dinner.

4 SERVINGS

1 oz. [2 tablespoons] butter
1 oz. [¼ cup] flour
4 fl. oz. double cream [½ cup heavy cream]
1 teaspoon salt
1 teaspoon black pepper
¼ teaspoon hot chilli powder
1 tablespoon ground coriander
1 teaspoon garam masala
1 tablespoon tomato purée
8 oz. [3 cups] cooked long-grain rice
4 tablespoons canned sweetcorn
8 oz. peeled frozen shrimps, thawed and drained
1 egg, lightly beaten
4 oz. [1⅓ cups] dry white breadcrumbs
4 fl. oz. [½ cup] vegetable oil

In a large saucepan, melt the butter over moderate heat. Remove the pan from the heat and, using a wooden spoon, stir in the flour to make a smooth paste. Gradually add the cream, stirring constantly and being careful to avoid lumps.

Chicken Liver Risotto is super to eat, easy to prepare and it makes an inexpensive family supper dish.

Return the pan to the heat and cook the sauce, stirring constantly, for 2 to 3 minutes or until it is very thick. Stir in the salt, pepper, chilli powder, coriander, garam masala and tomato purée. Cook the sauce, stirring constantly, for a further 2 minutes.

Remove the pan from the heat and stir in the rice, sweetcorn and shrimps. Combine the mixture thoroughly and then chill it in the refrigerator for 1 hour.

Remove the pan from the refrigerator. Place the egg on one plate and the breadcrumbs on another. Break off pieces of the mixture and shape them into balls. Slightly flatten the balls between the palms of your hands and roll them, first in the egg and then in the breadcrumbs, coating them thoroughly and shaking off any excess crumbs.

In a large, heavy-based frying-pan, heat the oil over moderate heat. When the oil is hot, add half the croquettes and fry them for 3 to 4 minutes on each side or until they are heated through and crisp and golden on the outside.

Using a fish slice or spatula, transfer the croquettes from the pan to kitchen paper towels to drain. Arrange the croquettes on a warmed serving dish and keep them hot while you fry and drain the remaining croquettes in the same way.

When all the croquettes have been fried, serve immediately.

Green Rice

This delicious and very attractive Italian dish may be served for supper with a tomato salad.

4 SERVINGS

2½ oz. [5 tablespoons] butter
6 oz. [1 cup] Italian rice, such as avorio
15 fl. oz. [1⅞ cups] chicken stock
3 teaspoons salt
1 lb. fresh green peas, shelled
7 fl. oz. [⅞ cup] water
2 lb. spinach, thoroughly washed
1 teaspoon black pepper
1 teaspoon chopped fresh basil
1 teaspoon chopped fresh marjoram
2 oz. [½ cup] Parmesan cheese, grated

In a large saucepan, melt 1 ounce [2 tablespoons] of butter over moderate heat. When the foam subsides, add the rice and fry, stirring constantly, for 1 minute. Pour over about one-third of the stock and 1 teaspoon of salt. Regulate the heat so that the rice is bubbling all the time. Stir the rice occasionally with a fork. When the rice swells and the liquid is absorbed, add another one-third of the stock. Continue cooking the rice in this way until it is tender and moist but still firm.

Meanwhile, in a medium-sized saucepan, cook the peas with the water and 1 teaspoon of salt over moderate heat for 8 minutes, or until they are tender. Drain the peas and set them aside.

In another medium-sized saucepan, cook the spinach with the remaining salt over moderate heat for 7 to 12 minutes, or until it is just tender. Do not add any water because there should be enough left on the spinach leaves after they are washed.

Drain the spinach, pressing down with a wooden spoon to extract any excess liquid. Chop the spinach and sprinkle with the pepper. Arrange one-third on the bottom of a shallow heatproof dish.

When the rice is cooked add 1 ounce [2 tablespoons] of the butter, the basil and marjoram and toss until the rice is well coated. Spoon one-third over the spinach.

Purée the peas in a blender or mash them through a strainer. Spread one-third of the pea purée over the rice. Continue making layers of spinach, rice and peas, until all the ingredients have been used up.

Preheat the grill [broiler] to high.

Sprinkle the cheese over the top and dot with the remaining butter, cut into small pieces. Place the dish under the grill [broiler]. Grill [broil] for 3 to 4 minutes, or until the cheese is bubbling and beginning to brown. Serve at once.

Ham and Fried Rice

A delicious dish, cooked quickly in the Chinese way, Ham and Fried Rice may be served for supper or as part of a Chinese meal. Serve with a cucumber and tomato salad.

3-4 SERVINGS

8 oz. [1⅓ cups] long-grain rice, washed, soaked in cold water for 30 minutes and drained
16 fl. oz. [2 cups] water
½ teaspoon salt
1 tablespoon butter
2 eggs, lightly beaten
4 tablespoons vegetable oil
4 oz. French beans, cut into small pieces, blanched and drained

Ham and Fried Rice, an unusual mixture of vegetables, ham and rice cooked the Chinese way, makes a filling supper dish for family or friends.

10 oz. cooked ham, cut into very small dice
½ teaspoon black pepper
4 small spring onions [scallions]
1 tablespoon chopped fresh coriander

Put the rice, water and salt in a medium-sized saucepan. Bring the water to the boil over high heat. Cover the pan, reduce the heat to low and simmer for 15 to 20 minutes or until the rice is tender and all the water has been absorbed. Remove the pan from the heat and set aside.

In a large frying-pan, melt the butter over moderate heat. Add the eggs and cook for 2 to 3 minutes or until they are set on the underside. Stir the eggs with a fork and cook for 2 to 3 minutes more or until they are just set. Remove the pan from the heat and transfer the eggs to a small mixing bowl. Break up with the fork. Set aside.

Add the oil to the frying-pan and heat it over moderately high heat. Add the cooked rice, beans, diced ham and pepper to the pan and cook, stirring constantly, for 2 minutes or until the rice is well coated with the oil. Reduce the heat to moderate and add the spring onions [scallions] and eggs. Cook, stirring constantly, for 2 minutes or until the mixture is hot.

Remove the pan from the heat and transfer the mixture to a warmed serving dish. Sprinkle with the coriander and serve immediately.

Japanese Mixed Vegetables and Rice

Japanese Mixed Vegetables and Rice may be served as part of a Japanese meal, or with a salad for an unusual and exotic lunch, followed by a light fruit dessert. Canned ginko nuts can be bought at most oriental food stores, but if you cannot obtain them, you can omit them without spoiling the dish. Ground ginger can be substituted for the root ginger if necessary.

4 SERVINGS

1 large dried mushroom, soaked for 30 minutes in cold water and drained
2 carrots, scraped and thinly sliced
1-inch piece fresh root ginger, peeled and chopped
2 celery stalks, trimmed and chopped
12 canned ginko nuts, drained
2 tablespoons soy sauce
1 tablespoon sake or dry sherry
½ teaspoon salt
12 oz. [2 cups] long-grain rice, washed, soaked in cold water for 30 minutes and drained
1¼ pints [3⅛ cups] water

4 oz. fresh peas, shelled
4 oz. cooked shrimps, shelled

Chop the mushroom finely and place it in a large saucepan. Add the carrots, ginger, celery, ginko nuts, soy sauce, sake or sherry, salt and rice.

Pour in the water, place the pan over moderate heat and bring the water to the boil. Reduce the heat to low, cover the pan and cook for 15 to 20 minutes or until the rice is tender and has absorbed most of the liquid.

Stir in the peas and shrimps and cook the mixture for a further 8 to 10 minutes or until the peas are cooked and the shrimps are heated through. If the mixture becomes too dry add a little more water.

Remove the pan from the heat and transfer the mixture to a warmed serving dish.

Serve at once.

Khichri

Khichri is a lightly aromatic mixture of rice and lentils from India and is the dish from which the English evolved Kedgeree. Serve it with spiced vegetables for a sustaining

This exotic dish from the Orient (Japanese Mixed Vegetables and Rice) includes vegetables, shrimps, rice, ginger and a Japanese speciality called ginko nuts.

meal in itself, or as a filling accompaniment to meat curries.

4 SERVINGS

2½ oz. [5 tablespoons] butter
1 medium-sized onion, finely chopped
1-inch piece fresh root ginger, peeled and very finely chopped
1 garlic clove, finely chopped
6 peppercorns
1 bay leaf
8 oz. [1⅓ cups] long-grain rice, washed, soaked in cold water for 30 minutes and drained
4 oz. [½ cup] yellow moong dhal, washed, soaked in cold water for 1 hour and drained
1 teaspoon salt
½ teaspoon turmeric
1 pint [2½ cups] boiling water fried onion slices to garnish

In a large saucepan, melt 1½ ounces [3

tablespoons] of the butter over moderate heat. When the foam subsides, add the onion and fry, stirring occasionally, for 4 minutes. Add the ginger, garlic, peppercorns and bay leaf and continue frying, stirring occasionally, for 3 minutes or until the onion is soft and translucent but not brown.

Add the rice, moong dhal, salt and turmeric. Stir and toss the mixture gently. Reduce the heat to moderately low and continue cooking and stirring gently for 5 minutes.

Pour in the boiling water and stir once. Cover the pan, reduce the heat to low and cook for 15 to 20 minutes, or until the rice and moong dhal are cooked and tender and all the water has been absorbed. With a fork, stir in the remaining butter.

Remove the pan from the heat and turn the khichri into a heated serving dish. Scatter the fried onion slices on top and serve at once.

Leftover Pork with Fried Rice

This is a wonderful way to use up leftover roast pork. Serve on its own as a light luncheon dish, or for supper accompanied by a salad. Chicken or beef may be substituted for the pork if you prefer—and in similar quantities.

4 SERVINGS

3 tablespoons vegetable oil
1 medium-sized onion, finely chopped
2 celery stalks, trimmed and finely chopped
2 small carrots, scraped and finely chopped
8 oz. roast pork, cut into strips 1-inch long
½ small cabbage, coarse outer leaves removed, washed and with the leaves finely shredded
½ teaspoon freshly ground black pepper
2 tablespoons soy sauce
8 oz. [3 cups] cooked long-grain rice
2 eggs, lightly beaten
¼ teaspoon salt

In a large frying-pan, heat 2 tablespoons of the oil over moderate heat. When the oil is hot, add the onion, celery and carrots and cook, stirring constantly, for 5 minutes. Stir in the pork, cabbage, pep- per, soy sauce and rice and cook, stirring constantly, for a further 2 to 3 minutes or until the mixture is hot. Moisten with a little water or chicken stock if the mixture is dry. Set aside and keep hot while you make the garnish.

In a small frying-pan, heat the remaining oil over moderate heat. When the oil is hot, add the beaten eggs and salt and cook for 2 minutes. When the bottom is set and lightly browned turn the omelet over, using a fish slice. Cook for a further 2 to 3 minutes or until the omelet is completely set. Remove the pan from the heat and, using the fish slice, remove the omelet from the pan. Using a sharp knife, cut the omelet into strips 1-inch by ¼-inch.

Spoon the rice mixture on to a warmed serving dish. Garnish with the omelet strips.

Serve at once.

Leftover Pork with Fried Rice uses up cooked pork in this recipe, but you can substitute leftover poultry, lamb or beef if you prefer. Serve as a light but filling supper dish, with salad and a bottle of well-chilled white wine, such as Soave.

Meat and Fruit Pilaff

A festive dish of rice with lamb, fruit and nuts, Meat and Fruit Pilaff may be served as part of an Indian meal or on its own accompanied by yogurt and chutneys.

6-8 SERVINGS

2 oz. [¼ cup] butter
2 onions, sliced
1-inch piece of fresh root ginger, peeled and finely chopped
1 garlic clove, crushed
1 teaspoon ground cumin
1 tablespoon coriander seeds, crushed
1 teaspoon cardamom seeds, crushed
1 teaspoon peppercorns, crushed
1 cinnamon stick, broken in half
1 lb. boned leg of lamb, cut into ¾-inch cubes
4 oz. [⅔ cup] dried apricots
4 oz. [⅔ cup] sultanas or seedless raisins
2 oz. [½ cup] cashew nuts, slit in half
2 oz. [½ cup] slivered almonds
2 bay leaves
2 teaspoons salt
15 fl. oz. [1⅞ cups] chicken stock
3 pints [7½ cups] water
12 oz. [2 cups] basmati rice, washed, soaked in cold water for 30 minutes and drained
1½ oz. [3 tablespoons] butter, melted
½ teaspoon saffron threads soaked in 2 tablespoons boiling water for 10 minutes
2 oz. [½ cup] pistachio nuts

In a medium-sized saucepan, melt the butter over moderate heat. When the foam subsides, add the onions, ginger and garlic and fry, stirring occasionally, for 5 to 7 minutes or until the onions are soft and translucent but not brown. Add the cumin, coriander, cardamom, peppercorns and cinnamon and fry, stirring constantly, for 2 minutes.

Add the lamb cubes and fry, turning the cubes over frequently, for 10 to 15 minutes or until they are browned. Add the apricots, sultanas or raisins, cashew nuts, half the almonds, the bay leaves and 1 teaspoon of the salt. Pour in the chicken stock, cover the pan and simmer the mixture for 35 minutes or until the lamb is tender. Taste the mixture and add more salt if necessary. Remove the pan from the heat. Remove and discard the cinnamon stick. Set aside and keep warm.

Preheat the oven to moderate 350°F

Serve Meat and Fruit Pilaff with lots of yogurt, poppadums and chutney.

(Gas Mark 4, 180°C).

In a large saucepan, bring the water to the boil over high heat. Add the remaining salt and the rice and boil for 1½ minutes. Remove the pan from the heat and drain the rice in a strainer.

Pour 1 tablespoon of the melted butter into a large ovenproof casserole. Put one-third of the rice in the bottom of the casserole. Sprinkle the rice with one-third of the saffron water. With a slotted spoon, transfer half of the meat and fruit mixture to the casserole. Put in another one-third of the rice and saffron water. Add the remaining meat and fruit mixture, reserving the pan juices. Finish with a last layer of rice sprinkled with the remaining saffron water. Pour over all the reserved pan juices. Sprinkle the top with the pistachio nuts, the remaining almonds and the remaining melted butter.

Cover the casserole and put it in the oven. Bake for 20 to 30 minutes or until the rice has absorbed all the liquid.

Remove the casserole from the oven and serve the pilaff immediately.

Mee Feng Jou
PORK IN GROUND RICE

Serve Mee Feng Jou, a delicious and unusual pork dish, with a variety of dips, such as Tomato-Soy Dip (mix together equal quantities of tomato ketchup and soy sauce), Garlic-Soy Dip (finely chop 2 or 3 cloves and mix with 3 to 4 tablespoons of soy sauce) and Soy-Sherry-Chilli Dip (combine 3 tablespoons each of soy sauce and sherry with 1 tablespoon of chilli sauce).

4 SERVINGS

2 lb. leg or belly of pork
2 slices of fresh root ginger, peeled and finely chopped
2 tablespoons soy sauce
1½ teaspoons chilli sauce
5 oz. [1¼ cups] coarsely ground rice

With a sharp knife, cut the pork into 2½-by 1½-inch slices, about ¼-inch thick.

In a small bowl, mix together the ginger, soy sauce and chilli sauce. With your fingertips, rub the mixture over the pork slices to coat them evenly. Set the pork aside to marinate for 1 hour.

Heat a large dry frying-pan over moderate heat. Add the rice to the pan and cook, stirring constantly, until it begins to turn brown. Place the pork slices in the pan and turn them so that they become thickly coated with the rice. Remove the pan from the heat.

Transfer the rice-coated pork slices to a heatproof dish. Place the dish in a

steamer, cover and steam over moderate heat for 35 to 40 minutes, or until the pork is well cooked and tender.

Remove the dish from the steamer and serve, with the dips.

Mexican Pork and Rice

Mexican Pork and Rice is a colourful and spicy dish to serve at an informal supper.

4 SERVINGS

2 tablespoons vegetable oil
1 medium-sized onion, chopped
1 lb. minced [ground] pork
8 oz. sausage meat
2 celery stalks, chopped
1 green pepper, white pith removed, seeded and cut into rings
3 oz. [½ cup] raisins
1 garlic clove, crushed
¼ teaspoon ground cumin
½ teaspoon hot chilli powder
1 tablespoon chopped fresh parsley
1 teaspoon salt
½ teaspoon black pepper
6 oz. [1 cup] long-grain rice, washed, soaked in cold water for 30 minutes and drained
14 oz. canned peeled tomatoes
4 fl. oz. [½ cup] water
2 tablespoons tomato purée
juice of ½ lemon
3 tablespoons pine nuts

Preheat the oven to moderate 350°F (Gas Mark 4, 180°C).

In a large flameproof casserole, heat the oil over moderate heat. When the oil is hot, add the onion and fry, stirring occasionally, for 5 to 7 minutes, or until it is soft and translucent but not brown. Add the pork and sausage meat and cook, stirring frequently, for 3 to 5 minutes, or until the meat is lightly browned all over.

Add the celery, green pepper, raisins, garlic, cumin, chilli powder, parsley, salt, pepper and rice. Fry the mixture, stirring constantly, for 5 to 7 minutes or until the rice has changed colour. Add the tomatoes with the can juice, the water and tomato purée and stir to mix. Simmer for 5 minutes. Reduce the heat to low, cover the casserole and cook for a further 10 minutes.

Remove the casserole from the heat and place it in the oven. Bake, covered, for 25 minutes.

Remove the casserole from the oven and sprinkle the lemon juice and the pine nuts over the top. Return the casserole to the oven, uncovered, and bake for a further 10 minutes.

Remove the casserole from the oven and serve immediately.

Risotto with Leeks and Bacon

This delightful dish is a perfect mid-week lunch or supper for the family.

4 SERVINGS

1 lb. streaky bacon slices, chopped
2 fl. oz. [¼ cup] vegetable oil
4 leeks, cleaned and chopped
1 lb. [2⅔ cups] long-grain rice, washed, soaked in cold water for 30 minutes and drained
14 oz. canned peeled tomatoes
1 teaspoon salt
1 teaspoon black pepper
½ teaspoon cayenne pepper
½ teaspoon ground cumin
1 teaspoon grated lemon rind
1½ pints [3¾ cups] chicken stock

In a flameproof casserole, fry the bacon over moderate heat for 6 to 8 minutes or until it is crisp and brown and has rendered most of its fat. Transfer the pieces to a plate and set aside.

Add the oil and heat it over moderate heat. When the oil is hot, add the leeks and fry, stirring occasionally, for 12 minutes. Stir in the rice and fry, stirring frequently, for 5 minutes. Add the tomatoes with the can juice, salt, pepper, cayenne, cumin and lemon rind and stir to mix. Pour over the stock and bring the liquid to the boil.

Return the bacon pieces to the casserole, reduce the heat to low and simmer the mixture for 15 to 20 minutes or until the rice is cooked and tender and all the liquid has been absorbed.

Remove the casserole from the heat and serve at once.

Russian Lamb Pilaff

This simple dish (pictured on page 65) *may be served with a mixed salad.*

4-6 SERVINGS

2 oz. [¼ cup] butter
1 tablespoon vegetable oil
2 lb. boned leg of lamb, cubed
3 onions, finely chopped
1 garlic clove, crushed
1 lb. carrots, scraped and chopped
1 lb. [2⅔ cups] long-grain rice, washed, soaked in cold water for 30 minutes and drained
1½ teaspoons dried marjoram
1½ pints [3¾ cups] strong beef stock

In a large, flameproof casserole, melt the butter with the oil over moderate heat.

Spanish Chicken with Rice.

When the foam subsides, add the lamb cubes and fry, stirring frequently, for 10 to 15 minutes or until the meat is golden brown. With a slotted spoon, transfer the meat to a plate.

Add the onions, garlic, carrots, rice and marjoram and fry, stirring constantly, for 5 to 7 minutes or until the onions are soft and translucent but not brown.

Return the meat to the casserole. Pour over the stock and bring the liquid to the boil. Reduce the heat to low, cover the casserole and simmer the mixture for 35 to 40 minutes or until the meat is tender and the liquid is absorbed.

Remove the casserole from the heat. Serve the pilaff immediately.

Spanish Chicken with Rice

This delicious chicken and rice dish is flavoured with saffron and spices.

4 SERVINGS

3 tablespoons vegetable oil
6 slices streaky bacon, chopped
1 x 5 lb. chicken, cut into serving pieces
6 tablespoons seasoned flour
2 onions, chopped
1 garlic clove, crushed
14 oz. canned peeled tomatoes
3 oz. canned pimientos, drained
2 teaspoons paprika
¼ teaspoon ground saffron
1 teaspoon salt
1 pint [2½ cups] water
8 oz. [1⅓ cups] long-grain rice, washed, soaked in cold water for 30 minutes and drained
6 oz. frozen peas, thawed

In a flameproof casserole, heat the oil over moderate heat. Add the bacon and fry until crisp. Transfer the bacon to kitchen paper towels to drain.

Coat the chicken pieces in the flour, and add to the casserole. Place over moderate heat and fry on all sides until the pieces are golden. Remove the pieces from the casserole and set aside.

Preheat the oven to moderate 350°F (Gas Mark 4, 180°C).

Drain off most of the oil from the casserole. Add the onions and garlic and fry over moderate heat for 5 minutes.

Place the chicken over the onions and add the tomatoes, with the can juice, the pimientos, paprika, saffron, salt and water. Bring to the boil. Stir in the rice.

Cover the casserole and place in the oven to cook for 35 minutes.

Add the peas and bacon and cook for a further 15 minutes or until the chicken is tender. Serve at once.

Coconut Rice

Coconut Rice is particularly good if made with fresh coconut. If it is not available, use creamed coconut instead.

6 SERVINGS

1 oz. [2 tablespoons] butter
1 medium-sized onion, finely chopped
1 lb [2⅔ cups] basmati rice, washed, soaked in cold water for 30 minutes and drained
1½ pints [3¾ cups] water
coconut milk made from ½ coconut, or 4 oz. slice of creamed coconut dissolved in 10 fl. oz. [1¼ cups] boiling water
1½ teaspoons salt
½ coconut

Preheat the oven to fairly hot 400°F (Gas Mark 6, 200°C).

In a saucepan, heat the butter over moderate heat. Add the onion and fry, stirring occasionally, for 5 to 7 minutes or until it is translucent but not brown.

Reduce the heat to low and add the rice. Cook, stirring constantly, for 5 minutes or until the rice is soft.

Add the water, coconut milk and salt. Increase the heat to moderately high. When the liquid is bubbling vigorously, cover the pan, reduce the heat to low and cook for 15 to 20 minutes or until the rice is tender and all the liquid absorbed.

Remove the brown outer skin of the half coconut with a sharp knife. Cut the coconut into little flakes. Spread the flaked coconut on a baking sheet lined with aluminium foil. Place the sheet in the oven and bake for 10 minutes or until the coconut turns golden brown.

When the rice is cooked, heap it on a heated serving dish. Sprinkle the top with the toasted flaked coconut and serve at once.

Hoppin' John

A traditional West Indian recipe now firmly incorporated into the American Southern 'soul' food repertoire, Hoppin' John is a spicy mixture of black-eye beans, rice, tomatoes and onion. It is particularly tasty when served with the other staples of 'soul', such as ham hocks, smothered pork chops and collard greens. Some ice-cold beer is best with this delicious but spicy food.

4-6 SERVINGS

8 oz. [1⅓ cups] dried black-eye beans, soaked in cold water overnight and drained
2 pints [5 cups] water
1½ teaspoons salt
8 oz. [1⅓ cups] long-grain rice, washed, soaked in cold water for 30 minutes and drained
1 tablespoon vegetable oil
1 medium-sized onion, finely chopped
14 oz. canned peeled tomatoes
¼ teaspoon cayenne pepper
½ teaspoon black pepper

Place the beans in a large saucepan and pour in the water and 1 teaspoon of salt. Place the pan over moderately high heat and bring to the boil. Reduce the heat to low, partially cover the pan and simmer the beans for 1½ hours.

Stir in the rice, cover the pan and simmer for 15 minutes.

Hoppin' John, a spicy soulfood dish from America, is a mixture of rice, beans, onions and tomatoes.

Meanwhile, in a small frying-pan, heat the oil over moderate heat. When the oil is hot, add the onion and cook, stirring occasionally, for 5 to 7 minutes or until the onion is soft and translucent but not brown. Remove the pan from the heat and stir in the tomatoes with the can juice, the cayenne, pepper and the remaining salt.

Pour the onion and tomato mixture into the beans and rice mixture and stir to blend the ingredients. Re-cover the pan and continue to simmer the mixture for a further 15 to 20 minutes or until the rice and beans are tender.

Remove the pan from the heat and serve at once.

Pilaff with Almonds and Mixed Fruit

This is a moist, delicately flavoured pilaff to serve with roast or fried chicken or with a vegetable casserole. Use a good quality long-grain rice such as basmati so that when the pilaff is cooked each grain remains separate.

6-8 SERVINGS

3 oz. [⅜ cup] butter
1 medium-sized onion, roughly chopped
1 large green pepper, white pith removed, seeded and roughly chopped
½ teaspoon turmeric
1 teaspoon salt
6 oz. [1 cup] dried apricots, soaked in water for 30 minutes, drained and chopped
3 oz. [½ cup] sultanas or seedless raisins
12 oz. [2 cups] long-grain rice, washed, soaked in cold water for 30 minutes and drained
1½ pints [3¾ cups] boiling chicken stock
4 oz. [1 cup] blanched flaked almonds, toasted

In a medium-sized saucepan, melt the butter over moderate heat. When the foam subsides, add the onion and green pepper and fry, stirring occasionally, for 5 to 7 minutes or until the onion is soft and translucent but not brown and the green pepper is soft.

Stir in the turmeric and salt. Add the apricots and sultanas or seedless raisins and cook, stirring constantly, for 2 minutes.

Add the rice and cook, stirring constantly, for 5 minutes. Pour in the chicken stock.

When the mixture comes to the boil,

cover the pan, reduce the heat to low and simmer the pilaff for 15 to 20 minutes or until the rice is tender and all the liquid has been absorbed. Stir in the toasted almonds.

Spoon the pilaff on to a warmed serving platter and serve immediately. Alternatively, cover the pan tightly and put it in a warm oven until you are ready to serve it.

Wild Rice with Mushrooms

A delicious dish, Wild Rice with Mushrooms may be served as a vegetable accompaniment to duck, chicken or venison. Or serve it by itself as the main course for a vegetarian meal, substituting the chicken stock with vegetable stock.

6 SERVINGS

2 oz. [¼ cup] butter
1 medium-sized onion, finely chopped
1 celery stalk, trimmed and finely chopped
8 oz. [1⅓ cups] wild rice, washed, soaked overnight and drained
6 oz. button mushrooms, wiped clean and halved
16 fl. oz. [2 cups] home-made

Wild Rice with Mushrooms is a deliciously extravagant dish—perfect for a light vegetarian meal, or as an accompaniment to roasts.

chicken stock
1 teaspoon salt
½ teaspoon freshly ground black pepper
2 oz. [½ cup] slivered almonds, toasted

In a large, heavy-based saucepan, melt the butter over moderate heat. When the foam subsides, add the onion and celery and fry, stirring occasionally, for 5 to 7 minutes or until the onion is soft and translucent but not brown.

Stir in the rice and mushrooms and fry, stirring constantly, for 3 minutes. Pour over the stock and season the mixture with the salt and pepper. Increase the heat to high and bring the liquid to the boil. Reduce the heat to low, cover the pan and simmer the mixture for 20 minutes or until the rice is tender and all the liquid has been absorbed. Remove the pan from the heat. Spoon the mixture into a warmed serving dish. Sprinkle over the toasted almonds and serve immediately.

Biryani

SPICED RICE WITH LAMB

A North Indian dish of Moghul origin, Biryani is a fragrant mixture of meat, spices, nuts and saffron rice. The traditional meat in a Biryani is lamb, but today prawns, chicken or other meats are also used by Indian cooks. It is a main dish, the quantity of lamb being double that of the rice, and so it may be served alone with a yogurt salad or as a part of a much larger and elaborate Indian meal consisting of other meat and vegetable dishes with chutneys and pickles.

6 SERVINGS

8 tablespoons butter or cooking oil
2 garlic cloves, crushed
1-inch piece fresh ginger, peeled and finely chopped
¼ teaspoon cayenne pepper
1½ teaspoons cumin seeds
2 lb. lean boned lamb, cut into 1-inch cubes
4-inch piece of cinnamon stick

10 cloves
8 peppercorns
1 teaspoon cardamom seeds
10 fl. oz. [1¼ cups] yogurt
2 teaspoons salt
1 lb. [2⅔ cups] basmati rice, washed, soaked in cold water for 30 minutes and drained

Biryani, a combination of rice and lamb, spices and yogurt, is one of the great classics of Indian cuisine.

½ teaspoon saffron threads soaked in 2 tablespoons boiling water for 10 minutes
2 onions, thinly sliced
1½ oz. [⅓ cup] almonds, slivered
1½ oz. [⅓ cup] pistachio nuts
2 oz. [⅓ cup] sultanas or raisins

In a large saucepan, heat 4 tablespoons of the butter or cooking oil over moderate heat.

Add the garlic, ginger, cayenne pepper and cumin seeds to the pan. Fry for 3 minutes. Raise the heat to moderately high, add the lamb cubes and fry for 10 to 15 minutes or until they are evenly browned. Stir in the cinnamon, cloves, peppercorns, cardamom, yogurt and 1 teaspoon of salt. Mix well and add 5 fluid ounces [⅝ cup] of water. Bring the mixture to the boil. Reduce the heat to low, cover the pan and simmer for 40 minutes or until the lamb is tender.

In a second saucepan, bring 3 pints of water to the boil over moderate heat. Add the remaining salt and pour in the rice. Boil briskly for 1½ minutes. Remove the pan from the heat, drain the rice thoroughly and set aside.

Preheat the oven to moderate 350°F (Gas Mark 4, 180°C).

Pour 1 tablespoon of butter or oil into a large ovenproof casserole dish. Put one-third of the parboiled rice in the bottom of the casserole. Sprinkle one-third of the saffron water over it. With a slotted spoon, remove one-third of the lamb cubes from the saucepan and put them over the rice. Cover with another one-third of the rice sprinkled with saffron water. Remove all the remaining meat cubes from the pan with the slotted spoon and put them on top, then finish with a last layer of the remaining rice. Pour all the liquid left in the saucepan in which the lamb was cooked carefully over the rice and meat. Sprinkle the remaining saffron water over the top layer of rice.

Cover the casserole with aluminium foil. Place the casserole in the oven and cook for 20 to 30 minutes or until the rice is cooked and has absorbed all the liquid.

In a small frying-pan, heat the remaining butter or oil over high heat. Add the onions, reduce the heat to moderate and, stirring frequently, fry for 8 to 10 minutes or until they are golden brown. With a slotted spoon, remove the onions and set aside on kitchen paper towels to drain.

Add the almonds, pistachio nuts and sultanas or raisins to the pan, adding more butter or oil if necessary. Fry them for 3 minutes or until the nuts are lightly browned. With a slotted spoon, remove the mixture from the pan and set aside on a plate.

Pile the rice and lamb attractively on a large heated serving dish and sprinkle the top with the nuts, sultanas and onions. Serve immediately.

Gamberi con Riso

 ① ① ✕

A delicious rice dish from Italy, Gamberi con Riso may be eaten on its own with only a green salad to follow. Serve it with a well-chilled Toscano Bianco. Italian rice, unlike basmati or patna, needs no washing or soaking.

4 SERVINGS

2 oz. [¼ cup] butter
2 tablespoons olive oil
1 large onion, finely chopped
1 garlic clove, finely chopped
1 medium-sized red pepper, white pith removed, seeded and chopped
4 oz. button mushrooms, wiped clean and chopped
½ teaspoon dried basil
1 teaspoon salt
½ teaspoon black pepper
12 oz. [2 cups] Italian rice, such as avorio
12 oz. frozen shrimps, thawed and shelled
1½ pints [3¾ cups] boiling water

2 oz. [½ cup] Parmesan cheeese, grated

In a large, heavy frying-pan, melt half the butter with the oil over moderately high heat. When the foam subsides, reduce the heat to moderate. Add the onion, garlic and pepper and fry them, stirring occasionally, for 5 to 7 minutes, or until the onion is soft and translucent but not brown. Stir in the mushrooms, basil, salt and pepper. Cook, stirring occasionally, for 5 minutes.

Add the rice, reduce the heat to low, and cook, stirring frequently, for 5 minutes. Stir in the shrimps and cook for 1 minute. Add approximately one-third of the boiling water. Regulate the heat so that the rice is bubbling all the time. Stir the rice occasionally with a fork. When the rice swells and the liquid is absorbed, add another one-third of the water. Continue cooking the rice in this way until the rice is tender and moist but still firm.

Remove the pan from the heat and stir in the remaining butter and the cheese. Turn the mixture into a warmed serving dish and serve at once.

Gamberi con Riso is a succulent Italian mixture of rice, shrimps, vegetables and Parmesan cheese.

Jambalaya

One of the most popular Creole dishes from the southern United States, Jambalaya is a delicious dinner party dish. Serve with crusty bread and a tossed green salad and, to drink, some well-chilled white wine, such as Californian Chablis.

4-6 SERVINGS
1 tablespoon vegetable oil
3 lean bacon slices, rinds removed and chopped
1 medium-sized onion, finely chopped
2 celery stalks, trimmed and chopped
12 oz. [2 cups] long-grain rice, washed, soaked in cold water for 30 minutes and drained
1 pint [2½ cups] chicken stock
½ teaspoon salt
½ teaspoon freshly ground black pepper
⅛ teaspoon cayenne pepper
1 bay leaf
1 large green pepper, white pith removed, seeded and roughly chopped
14 oz. canned peeled tomatoes
4 oz. cooked ham
8 oz. cooked shrimps, shelled
8 oz. cooked chicken meat, chopped
1 tablespoon finely chopped fresh parsley

Jambalya, a fabulous mixture of rice, vegetables, meat and shrimps, comes from the southern part of the United States.

In a large saucepan, heat the oil over moderate heat. When the oil is hot, add the bacon and fry, stirring occasionally, for 6 minutes or until it is crisp and golden brown. With a slotted spoon, remove the bacon from the pan and drain on kitchen paper towels. Set the bacon aside.

Add the onion to the frying-pan and cook, stirring occasionally, for 8 to 10 minutes or until it is golden brown. Add the celery, then stir in the rice. Cook, stirring constantly, for 3 minutes or until the rice is well coated with the fat. Pour in the chicken stock, stirring constantly. Add the salt, pepper, cayenne and bay leaf. Reduce the heat to low, cover the pan and simmer the mixture for 10 minutes.

Add the green pepper and tomatoes with the can juice and simmer, covered, for a further 5 minutes.

Add the ham, shrimps, chicken and reserved bacon pieces and stir well. Re-cover the pan and cook the mixture for a further 5 minutes or until the meats and shrimps are heated through and the rice is tender.

Remove the pan from the heat and

transfer the mixture to a warmed serving dish. Sprinkle over the parsley and serve at once.

Kedgeree of Salmon

Kedgeree of Salmon is a richer version of plain kedgeree and makes an excellent family supper or a festive meal for unexpected guests. Accompany with a colourful tossed mixed salad and lots of generously buttered toast.

4 SERVINGS
1¼ lb. canned salmon, drained and flaked
10 fl. oz. double cream [1¼ cups heavy cream], beaten until thick but not stiff
½ teaspoon grated nutmeg
2 oz. [¼ cup] butter
1 medium-sized onion, finely chopped
10 oz. [4 cups] cooked long-grain rice
2 hard-boiled eggs, finely chopped
½ teaspoon salt
¼ teaspoon freshly ground black pepper
2 teaspoons curry powder

In a medium-sized saucepan, combine the salmon, cream and nutmeg together, stirring to mix. Set the pan over moderate heat and cook the mixture, stirring occasionally, for 3 to 5 minutes, or until the fish is heated through. Remove the pan from the heat.

In a large saucepan, melt the butter over moderate heat. When the foam subsides, add the onion and cook, stirring occasionally, for 5 to 7 minutes, or until it is soft and translucent but not brown. Stir in the cooked rice and half of the chopped eggs, then stir in the salmon mixture, the salt, black pepper and curry powder.

Remove the pan from the heat and pile the mixture on to a large warmed serving dish. Sprinkle over the remaining chopped egg.

Serve immediately.

Lamb and Mixed Fruit Pilaff

An exotic and satisfying dish, Lamb and Mixed Fruit Pilaff makes a delicious dinner party centrepiece. Serve with a tossed green salad, some crusty bread and a well-chilled bottle of Greek white wine, such as Hymettus or Retsina.

4 SERVINGS

4 oz. [½ cup] butter
1 medium-sized onion, thinly sliced
1½ lb. boned leg of lamb, cut into

1-inch cubes
3 oz. [½ cup] dried apricots, soaked overnight in cold water, drained and halved
3 tablespoons sultanas or seedless raisins
2 teaspoons salt
½ teaspoon ground cinnamon
¼ teaspoon freshly ground black pepper
1½ pints [3¾ cups] water
8 oz. [1⅓ cups] long-grain rice, washed, soaked in cold water for 30 minutes and drained

In a large, deep frying-pan, melt the butter over moderate heat. When the foam subsides, add the onion and cook, stirring occasionally, for 5 to 7 minutes, or until it is soft and translucent but not brown.

Add the lamb and cook, stirring and turning occasionally, for 5 to 8 minutes, or until it is lightly browned all over. Stir in the apricots, sultanas or seedless raisins, 1 teaspoon of the salt, the cinnamon and pepper.

Pour in 16 fluid ounces [2 cups] of the water and bring to the boil, stirring occasionally. Reduce the heat to moderately low, cover the pan and simmer the meat for 1 hour, or until the meat is tender when pierced with the point of a sharp knife.

Meanwhile, put the rice in a medium-sized saucepan. Pour over the remaining water and add the remaining salt. Place the saucepan over high heat and bring the water to the boil. Reduce the heat to low, cover the pan and simmer the rice for 15 to 20 minutes. If all the liquid is not absorbed, continue to cook the rice, uncovered, over low heat until the rice is dry. Remove the saucepan from the heat and set aside.

Preheat the oven to moderate 350°F (Gas Mark 4, 180°C). Place one-third of the rice in a medium-sized ovenproof casserole. Cover with a layer of one-half of the meat mixture, then top with another one-third of the rice. Continue to make layers in this manner until all the ingredients have been used up, finishing with a layer of rice. Cover the casserole with a lid and carefully place it in the centre of the oven. Bake the pilaff for 20 minutes.

Remove the casserole from the oven and serve the pilaff at once, straight from the casserole.

A rice dish from the Balkans, Lamb and Mixed Fruit Pilaff makes a superb and relatively inexpensive main course for a family supper or informal entertaining. Serve with some well-chilled white wine.

Liver and Rice

This delicious dish is traditionally Indonesian and makes a festive main course.

6-8 SERVINGS

1 lb. [2⅔ cups] long-grain rice, washed, soaked in cold water for 30 minutes and drained
2 pints [5 cups] water
1 teaspoon salt
3 tablespoons peanut oil
3 eggs, lightly beaten
4 spring onions [scallions], trimmed and chopped
3 oz. button mushrooms, wiped clean and sliced
1 red chilli, finely chopped
2 garlic cloves, crushed
2-inch piece fresh root ginger, peeled and very finely chopped
2 tablespoons soy sauce

LIVER
4 tablespoons soy sauce
4 tablespoons beef stock
1 tablespoon wine vinegar
2 tablespoons water
1 teaspoon black pepper
4-inch piece fresh root ginger, peeled and very finely chopped
2 teaspoons cornflour [cornstarch]
3 lb. lamb's liver, thinly sliced
2 fl. oz. [¼ cup] peanut oil
2 celery stalks, finely chopped
12 oz. bean sprouts

First prepare the liver. In a large, shallow dish, combine the soy sauce, beef stock,

Liver and Rice is a Dutch adaptation of a traditional Indonesian dish called Nasi Goreng.

vinegar, water, pepper, half of the ginger and the cornflour [cornstarch]. Place the liver slices in the mixture and baste well. Set aside to marinate for 45 minutes, basting frequently.

Meanwhile, prepare the rice. Put the rice in a large saucepan. Pour over the water and add the salt. Bring the water to the boil over high heat. Cover the pan, reduce the heat to low and simmer for 15 to 20 minutes or until the rice is tender and has absorbed all the liquid. Remove the pan from the heat.

In a small frying-pan, heat 1 tablespoon

of the oil over moderate heat. When the oil is hot, add the eggs and fry for 3 minutes on each side or until they are set in a thin omelet. Remove the pan from the heat. Cut the omelet into thin strips about 2-inches long and ½-inch wide.

Preheat the oven to very cool 250°F (Gas Mark ½, 130°C).

In a large frying-pan, heat the remaining oil over moderate heat. When the oil is hot, add the spring onions [scallions], mushrooms, chilli, garlic and ginger and fry, stirring occasionally, for 3 to 4 minutes or until the spring onions [scallions] are soft and translucent but not brown. Stir in the cooked rice, soy sauce and omelet strips and fry, stirring occasionally, for 3 minutes or until all the ingredients are warmed through.

Transfer the mixture to a warmed, ovenproof serving dish. Place in the oven and keep hot while you cook the liver.

In a large frying-pan, heat the oil over moderate heat. When the oil is hot, add the remaining ginger and fry, stirring constantly, for 2 minutes. Increase the heat to moderately high and add the liver slices and marinade to the pan. Fry, stirring and turning occasionally, for 6 minutes. Stir in the celery and bean sprouts and continue to fry, stirring and turning occasionally, for a further 3 minutes or until the liver is cooked.

Remove the serving dish from the oven and arrange the liver slices decoratively over the rice. Spoon over the sauce and vegetables and serve at once.

Morue à l'Americaine
SALT COD WITH RICE AND BRANDY AND WINE SAUCE

Salt cod is a relatively exotic delicacy in the English-speaking world, but around the Mediterranean it is consumed with great relish. The recipe below for Morue à l'Americaine is easy to prepare — and makes a deliciously different dinner dish.

4 SERVINGS

10 oz. [1⅔ cups] long-grain rice, washed, soaked in cold water for 30 minutes and drained
1 pint [2½ cups] water
1½ teaspoons salt
2 lb. salt cod, soaked in cold water for 24 hours
3 tablespoons olive oil
1 large onion, finely chopped
1 garlic clove, crushed
5 oz. canned tomato purée
½ teaspoon black pepper
8 fl. oz. [1 cup] dry white wine
2 fl. oz. [¼ cup] brandy
1 oz. [2 tablespoons] butter

Put the rice in a saucepan. Pour over the water and add 1 teaspoon of the salt. Place the pan over moderate heat and bring the water to the boil. Cover the pan, reduce the heat to low and simmer the rice for 15 to 20 minutes, or until all the liquid has been absorbed and the rice is tender. Remove the pan from the heat.

Drain the salt cod and dry it on kitchen paper towels. Skin the cod and chop into 1½-inch pieces. Set aside.

In a large frying-pan, heat the oil over moderate heat. When the oil is hot, add the onion and garlic and cook, stirring occasionally, for 5 to 7 minutes, or until the onion is soft and translucent but not brown. Stir in the tomato purée, the remaining salt and the pepper and cook, stirring occasionally, for 3 minutes. Stir in the wine and bring the mixture to the boil, stirring frequently.

Add the salt cod and brandy to the pan, stirring to combine. Reduce the heat to low, cover the pan and cook, stirring and turning from time to time, for 15 to 20 minutes, or until the fish flakes easily.

Meanwhile, in a saucepan, melt the butter over moderate heat. When the foam subsides, add the rice to the pan. Cook, stirring frequently, for 3 to 5 minutes, or until the rice is heated through and is coated with the butter.

Remove the pan from the heat. Arrange the rice in a ring on a warmed serving platter. Remove the frying-pan from the heat, spoon the fish and sauce into the centre and serve.

Morue à l'Americaine is a popular French dish of salt cod and rice.

Paella

SPANISH RICE WITH CHICKEN AND SEAFOOD

Traditionally, Paella is made from a combination of chicken, seafood, sausage, vegetables and rice. It can vary from a simple supper dish made with a few inexpensive chicken pieces and a handful of shrimps to an elaborate party dish with lobster and mussels.

4-6 SERVINGS

1 x 1½ lb. cooked lobster, shell split, claws cracked and grey sac removed
2 tablespoons olive oil
1 x 2 lb. chicken, cut into 8 serving pieces
1 chorizo sausage, sliced
1 onion, thinly sliced
1 garlic clove, crushed
3 tomatoes, blanched, peeled, seeded and chopped or 8 oz. canned peeled tomatoes, drained
1 large red pepper, white pith removed, seeded and chopped
1 teaspoon salt
½ teaspoon black pepper
1 teaspoon paprika
12 oz. [2 cups] long-grain rice, washed, soaked in cold water for 30 minutes and drained
1 pint [2½ cups] water
juice of 1 lemon
⅛ teaspoon ground saffron, soaked in 4 fl. oz. [½ cup] hot water for 20 minutes
8 oz. fresh peas, shelled
6 oz. large prawns or shrimps, shelled
1 quart mussels, scrubbed, steamed and removed from their shells
1 tablespoon chopped fresh parsley

Remove the lobster meat from the shell and claws and cut it into 1-inch pieces.

In a large flameproof casserole, heat the olive oil over moderate heat. When it is hot, add the chicken pieces and chorizo sausage slices and fry, turning occasionally, for 10 to 15 minutes or until the chicken is evenly browned.

Using tongs or a slotted spoon, remove the chicken pieces and sausage slices from the pan. Set aside and keep hot.

Add the onion and garlic to the casserole and fry, stirring occasionally, for 5 to 7 minutes or until the onion is soft and translucent but not brown. Add the tomatoes, red pepper, salt, pepper and paprika and cook, stirring occasionally, for 10 to 12 minutes or until the mixture

The Spanish national dish—Paella.

is thick and pulpy.

Add the rice and, shaking the casserole frequently, fry it for 3 minutes or until it is transparent. Add the water, lemon juice and saffron, and bring to the boil. Reduce the heat to low and stir in the peas. Return the chicken pieces and sausage slices to the pan and cook for 15 minutes, stirring occasionally. Add the lobster, prawns or shrimps and mussels and cook for a further 5 minutes or until the chicken is cooked and the cooking liquid has been absorbed.

Remove from the heat. Sprinkle over the parsley and serve immediately.

Picardy Rice

Picardy Rice, a tasty mixture of rice, chicken, tomatoes, bacon and vegetables, may be served as a meal in itself.

4-6 SERVINGS

4 streaky bacon slices, diced
1 oz. [2 tablespoons] butter
2 shallots, finely chopped
2 small green peppers, white pith removed, seeded and cut into julienne strips
2 medium-sized tomatoes, blanched, peeled and chopped
1 teaspoon salt
½ teaspoon black pepper
½ teaspoon dried thyme
12 oz. [2 cups] long-grain rice, washed, soaked in cold water for 30 minutes and drained
1 pint [2½ cups] hot chicken stock
1 lb. lean cooked chicken, cut into strips

In a flameproof casserole, fry the bacon over moderate heat for 5 minutes or until it is crisp and has rendered most of its fat. Scrape the bottom of the casserole frequently with a wooden spoon to prevent the bacon from sticking.

With a slotted spoon, remove the bacon from the casserole and drain it on kitchen paper towels. Set aside.

Add the butter to the casserole. When the foam subsides, add the shallots and green peppers and fry, stirring frequently, for 3 to 4 minutes or until the shallots are soft and translucent but not brown. Stir in the tomatoes, salt, pepper and thyme. Add the rice and stir well to coat the grains. Pour in the stock and bring to the boil, stirring occasionally.

Reduce the heat to low and simmer stirring occasionally, for 15 to 20 minutes. Stir in the chicken and simmer for a further 5 minutes, or until the rice is cooked and tender and has absorbed the cooking liquid.

Remove the casserole from the heat and spoon the rice mixture into a large warmed serving dish. Sprinkle over the fried bacon and serve immediately.

Pilaff à la Grecque

RICE COOKED WITH MUSHROOMS

Use a good quality long-grain rice for this dish to ensure that the grains of rice remain separate when cooked. Pilaff à la Grecque may be served by itself or with kebabs.

4-6 SERVINGS

2 oz. [¼ cup] plus 1 tablespoon butter
1 onion, finely chopped
2 garlic cloves, crushed
12 oz. [2 cups] long-grain rice, washed, soaked in cold water for 30 minutes and drained
8 oz. button mushrooms, wiped clean
1 teaspoon salt
½ teaspoon black pepper
1½ pints [3¾ cups] hot chicken stock
1 bay leaf
thinly pared rind of 1 lemon, in one piece

GARNISH

2 tablespoons slivered almonds
2 tablespoons raisins
8 large black olives, stoned

In a saucepan, melt 2 ounces [¼ cup] of the butter over moderate heat. When the foam subsides, add the onion and garlic and fry for 5 to 7 minutes or until the onion is soft and translucent but not brown. Add the rice and cook, stirring constantly, for 5 minutes. Add the mushrooms, and cook, stirring constantly, for 3 minutes.

Stir in the salt and pepper and pour in the stock.

Increase the heat to high and add the bay leaf and lemon rind. When the stock is boiling vigorously, cover the pan, reduce the heat to low and simmer for 15 to 20 minutes or until the rice is tender and all the liquid has been absorbed.

Meanwhile, in a small frying-pan, melt the remaining butter over moderate heat. When the foam subsides, add the almonds and raisins and fry them, stirring constantly, for 5 minutes or until the almonds are browned and the raisins puffed up.

Remove the pan from the heat.

Remove the pilaff from the heat. Remove and discard the bay leaf and the lemon rind. Spoon the pilaff on to a warmed serving platter and scatter the almonds, raisins and the olives over the top. Serve immediately.

Pilaff with Pineapple and Cashew Nuts

☆ ①

A subtle mixture of taste and texture makes this pilaff an exciting accompaniment to roast lamb. Or serve it on its own, accompanied by a green salad.

4 SERVINGS

3 oz. [⅜ cup] butter
1 small pineapple, peeled, cored and cut into chunks
3 tablespoons raisins
12 spring onions [scallions], chopped
2½ oz. [½ cup] cashew nuts
1 tablespoon coriander seeds, coarsely crushed
¼ teaspoon cayenne pepper
12 oz. [2 cups] long-grain rice, washed, soaked in cold water for 30 minutes and drained
1 teaspoon salt
1 pint [2½ cups] chicken stock
2 hard-boiled eggs, quartered
1 tablespoon chopped coriander leaves

In a frying-pan, melt half of the butter over moderate heat. When the foam subsides, add the pineapple chunks and raisins and fry, turning them frequently, for 2 to 3 minutes or until the pineapple is lightly coloured. Remove the pan from the heat and set aside.

In a large saucepan, melt the remaining butter over moderate heat. When the foam subsides, add the spring onions [scallions] and fry them, stirring occasionally, for 4 to 6 minutes or until they are golden brown.

Add the cashew nuts, coriander seeds and cayenne and fry, stirring occasionally, for 4 minutes.

Add the rice and the salt and fry, stirring constantly, for 5 minutes. Stir in the pineapple mixture. Pour in the chicken stock and bring the mixture to the boil.

Cover the pan, reduce the heat to low and cook the pilaff for 15 to 20 minutes or until the rice is tender and all the liquid has been absorbed.

Pilaff with Pineapple and Cashew Nuts is a delicate rice dish from India. Serve on its own or with meat.

Taste the pilaff and add more salt and pepper if necessary.

Remove the pan from the heat and spoon the pilaff on to a warmed serving platter. Garnish with the hard-boiled eggs and the chopped coriander leaves.

Serve immediately.

Rice with Shellfish

☆ ① ① ①

Serve this sustaining dish with a tossed green salad and a well-chilled dry white wine, such as Muscadet.

4 SERVINGS

2 oz. [¼ cup] butter
8 oz. [1⅓ cups] long-grain rice, washed, soaked in cold water for 30 minutes and drained
8 fl. oz. [1 cup] fish stock
10 fl. oz. [1¼ cups] water
1½ teaspoons salt
1 teaspoon black pepper
3 large tomatoes, blanched, peeled, seeded and chopped
2 garlic cloves, crushed
1 tablespoon flour

2 quarts mussels, scrubbed,
   steamed, removed from their
   shells and 4 fl. oz. [½ cup] of the
   cooking fluid reserved
8 fl. oz. [1 cup] dry white wine
1 tablespoon lemon juice
1 tablespoon sweet vermouth
1 lb. scallops, scrubbed and
   removed from their shells
8 oz. frozen Dublin Bay prawns
   [large Gulf shrimps], thawed
4 oz. [1 cup] Parmesan cheese,
   grated

In a large saucepan, melt 1 ounce [2
tablespoons] of the butter over moderate
heat. When the foam subsides, add the
rice and fry, stirring constantly, for 3
minutes. Pour over the stock and water
and add half the salt and pepper, the
tomatoes and garlic. Bring the liquid to
the boil, stirring constantly. Reduce the
heat to low, cover tightly and simmer for
20 minutes or until the rice is cooked and
tender and has absorbed all the liquid.

Meanwhile, in a medium-sized saucepan, melt the remaining butter over
moderate heat. Remove the pan from the
heat. Stir in the flour and the remaining
salt and pepper with a wooden spoon to
make a smooth paste. Gradually add the
reserved mussel liquid, the wine, lemon
juice and vermouth, stirring constantly
and being careful to avoid lumps.

*Rice with Shellfish is rice, mussels,
scallops and prawns or shrimps in
a creamy white wine sauce.*

Return the pan to the heat and cook
the sauce, stirring constantly, for 3
minutes or until it is smooth and has
thickened slightly. Remove from the
heat and spoon half the sauce into a
warmed sauceboat. Set aside and keep
warm.

Return the pan to the heat and add the
mussels, scallops and prawns [shrimps].
Cook the shellfish, stirring frequently, for
5 minutes. Remove the pan from the heat
and keep warm.

Remove the rice from the heat and stir
in half the grated cheese. Spoon the rice
mixture into a warmed serving dish and
spoon over the fish mixture. Place the
remaining cheese in a small serving bowl
and serve immediately, with the sauce.

Spanish Rice

*Spanish Rice may be served with crusty
bread and a mixed salad, as a light luncheon
dish.*

3-4 SERVINGS

3 tablespoons olive oil
2 onions, thinly sliced

1 garlic clove, crushed
1 green pepper, white pith
   removed, seeded and thinly sliced
2 red peppers, white pith removed,
   seeded and thinly sliced
12 oz. mushrooms, wiped clean and
   sliced
14 oz. canned peeled tomatoes,
   chopped
1½ oz. [⅓ cup] stoned green olives
1 teaspoon dried oregano
½ teaspoon dried basil
½ teaspoon salt
¼ teaspoon black pepper
5 oz. [2 cups] cooked rice

In a large frying-pan, heat the oil over
moderate heat. When the oil is hot, add
the onions and garlic to the pan and cook,
stirring occasionally, for 5 to 7 minutes
or until the onions are soft and translucent
but not brown.

Add the green and red peppers and
cook for 4 minutes, stirring frequently.
Add the mushrooms, tomatoes with the
can juice, olives, oregano, basil, salt and
pepper to the pan and cook, stirring
occasionally, for 3 minutes.

Add the rice to the pan and cook for 3
to 4 minutes, stirring constantly, or until
the rice is heated through.

Transfer the mixture to a warmed
serving dish. Serve immediately, if you
are serving it hot.

Risi e Bisi
RICE WITH PEAS

A classic Venetian dish, Risi e Bisi is a delicious combination of rice, peas and bacon. Serve Risi e Bisi as a deliciously different first course to an Italian meal or, with lots of crusty bread and mixed salad, for a sustaining lunch or supper. A well-chilled Frascati wine would complement this dish.

4-6 SERVINGS

1 tablespoon olive oil
6 oz. lean bacon, chopped
2 oz. [¼ cup] butter
1 onion, thinly sliced
1 lb. peas, weighed after shelling
1 lb. [2⅔ cups] Italian rice, such as avorio
3 fl. oz. [⅜ cup] dry white wine
2 pints [5 cups] boiling chicken stock
1 teaspoon salt
½ teaspoon black pepper
4 oz. [1 cup] Parmesan cheese, grated

In a large, heavy saucepan, heat the oil over moderate heat. When the oil is hot, add the bacon and fry, stirring occasionally, for 5 minutes or until it is crisp and golden brown. With a slotted spoon, transfer the bacon to kitchen paper towels to drain.

Add 1 ounce [2 tablespoons] of butter to the pan and melt it over moderate heat. When the foam subsides, add the onion and cook, stirring occasionally, for 5 to 7 minutes or until the onion is soft and translucent but not brown.

Add the peas and rice to the pan, reduce the heat to low and cook, stirring frequently, for 5 minutes. Pour over the wine and approximately one-third of the boiling stock. Regulate the heat so that the rice is bubbling all the time. Stir the rice occasionally with a fork. When the rice swells and the liquid is absorbed add another one-third of the stock. Continue cooking the rice in this way until it is tender and moist but still firm.

Stir in the bacon, the remaining butter, the salt, pepper and grated cheese and mix well to blend. Simmer for 1 minute, stirring frequently.

Remove the pan from the heat and transfer the risotto to a warmed serving bowl. Serve at once.

Risotto alla Bolognese
BRAISED RICE WITH HAM AND
BOLOGNESE SAUCE

This light dish is a mixture of Italian rice, Parma ham, meat sauce and grated cheese. *Serve as a light lunch or supper with garlic bread and a mixed salad.*

4-6 SERVINGS

4 oz. [½ cup] butter
1 medium-sized onion, thinly sliced
4 oz. Parma ham, chopped
1 lb. [2⅔ cups] Italian rice, such as avorio
3 fl. oz. [⅜ cup] dry white wine
2 pints [5 cups] boiling beef stock
1 oz. [¼ cup] Parmesan cheese, grated

BOLOGNESE SAUCE
1 oz. [2 tablespoons] butter
2 oz. lean ham, chopped
1 small onion, chopped
½ carrot, scraped and chopped
1 celery stalk, trimmed and chopped
4 oz. lean minced [ground] beef
2 oz. chicken livers, chopped
8 oz. canned peeled tomatoes, drained
2 tablespoons tomato purée
3 fl. oz. [⅜ cup] dry white wine
6 fl. oz. [¾ cup] chicken stock
½ teaspoon dried basil
½ teaspoon salt
¼ teaspoon black pepper

First make the sauce. In a large saucepan, melt the butter over moderate heat. When the foam subsides, add the ham, onion, carrot and celery. Cook, stirring occasionally, for 8 to 10 minutes or until the onion is golden brown. Add the beef to the pan and cook, stirring occasionally, for 10 minutes or until it is well browned.

Add all the remaining ingredients and stir well to mix. Reduce the heat to low, cover and simmer the mixture for about 1 hour.

Meanwhile, make the rice. In a large saucepan, melt 3 ounces [⅜ cup] of the butter over moderate heat. When the foam subsides, add the onion and cook, stirring occasionally, for 5 to 7 minutes or until it is soft and translucent but not brown.

Add the ham and rice, reduce the heat to low and cook, stirring frequently, for 5 minutes. Pour over the wine and approximately one-third of the boiling stock. Regulate the heat so that the rice is bubbling all the time. Stir the rice occasionally with a fork. When the rice

Three of the glories of Italian cuisine (from left to right) Risotto con Funghi (rice with mushrooms), Risi e Bisi (rice with peas) and Risotto alla Bolognese (rice with ham and bolognese sauce). Serve them as filling first courses.

swells and the liquid is absorbed, add another one-third of the stock. Continue cooking the rice in this way until it is tender and moist but still firm.

Stir in the remaining butter, the bolognese sauce and grated cheese and mix well to blend. Simmer for 1 minute, stirring frequently.

Remove the pan from the heat and transfer the risotto to a warmed serving bowl. Serve at once.

Risotto con Funghi
BRAISED RICE WITH MUSHROOMS

A light, attractive dish, Risotto con Funghi is a mixture of Italian rice, mushrooms, onion and grated cheese. It may be served with garlic bread and a mixed salad as a light lunch or supper.

4-6 SERVINGS

- 3 oz. [⅜ cup] butter
- 1 medium-sized onion, finely chopped
- 1 garlic clove, crushed
- 1 lb. [2⅔ cups] Italian rice, such as avorio
- 3 fl. oz. [⅜ cup] dry white wine
- 2 pints [5 cups] boiling beef stock
- 10 oz. mushrooms, wiped clean and sliced
- ½ teaspoon grated nutmeg
- ⅛ teaspoon cayenne pepper
- ½ teaspoon salt
- ¼ teaspoon black pepper
- 2 oz. [½ cup] Parmesan cheese, grated

In a large, heavy saucepan, melt 2 ounces [¼ cup] of the butter over moderate heat. When the foam subsides, add the onion and garlic and cook, stirring occasionally, for 5 to 7 minutes or until the onion is soft and translucent but not brown.

Add the rice to the pan, reduce the heat to low and cook, stirring frequently, for 5 minutes. Pour over the wine and approximately one-third of the boiling stock. Regulate the heat so that the liquid is bubbling all the time. Stir the rice occasionally with a fork. When the rice swells and the liquid is absorbed add another one-third of the stock. Continue cooking the rice in this way until it is tender and moist but still firm.

Stir in the mushrooms, nutmeg, cayenne, salt and pepper and cook, stirring occasionally, for 3 minutes. Stir in the remaining butter and the grated cheese and mix well to blend. Simmer for 1 minute, stirring frequently.

Remove the pan from the heat and transfer the risotto to a warmed serving bowl. Serve at once.

Rizotto Corine

RICE WITH CHICKEN AND VEGETABLES

A hearty, nourishing rice dish from Belgium, Rizotto Corine is a complete meal served with brown bread and butter.

4-6 SERVINGS

6 streaky bacon slices, diced
2 oz. [¼ cup] butter
2 chicken breasts, skinned, boned and cut into strips
2 medium-sized onions, thinly sliced and pushed out into rings
2 large green peppers, white pith removed, seeded and coarsely chopped
8 oz. small button mushrooms, wiped clean and halved
10 oz. [1⅔ cups] long-grain rice, washed, soaked in cold water for 30 minutes and drained
5 medium-sized tomatoes, blanched, peeled and chopped
10 oz. canned sweetcorn, drained
½ teaspoon dried thyme
1 teaspoon salt
½ teaspoon black pepper
¼ teaspoon celery salt
¼ teaspoon cayenne pepper
2 teaspoons Worcestershire sauce (optional)
15 fl. oz. [1⅞ cups] chicken stock
2 oz. [½ cup] Parmesan cheese, grated

In a medium-sized flameproof casserole, fry the bacon over moderate heat for 5 minutes or until it is crisp and golden and has rendered most of its fat. Scrape the bottom of the pan frequently with a spatula to prevent the bacon from sticking.

Using a slotted spoon, remove the bacon from the casserole and drain it on kitchen paper towels. Set aside on a large plate.

Add half of the butter to the casserole. When the foam subsides, add the chicken strips and fry them, stirring frequently, for 6 to 8 minutes or until the chicken is lightly browned.

Using the slotted spoon, remove the chicken from the casserole and set it aside with the bacon.

Add the onions and peppers to the casserole and fry, stirring frequently, for 5 minutes. Add the mushrooms and fry, stirring frequently, for a further 3 minutes.

Using the slotted spoon, remove the vegetables from the casserole and set them aside with the chicken.

Add the remaining butter to the casserole and, when the foam subsides, add the rice. Fry, stirring constantly, for 3 minutes. Stir in the chicken, bacon and vegetables, the tomatoes, sweetcorn, thyme, salt, pepper, celery salt, cayenne and the Worcestershire sauce, if you are using it. Stir well to mix and pour over the stock.

Bring the liquid to the boil, stirring constantly. Reduce the heat to very low, cover the pan and simmer for 20 minutes, or until the rice is cooked and tender and has absorbed all the liquid.

Remove the casserole from the heat. Transfer to a serving dish, sprinkle over the Parmesan and serve.

Chicken, mixed vegetables and rice form the basis of this delicious dish from Belgium, Rizotto Corine. Serve as a sustaining lunch or dinner, accompanied by a mixed salad.

Wild Rice Casserole

 ① ① ⊠

A really delicious, if somewhat extravagant dish, Wild Rice Casserole is super served with a crisp green salad.

6 SERVINGS

2 oz. [¼ cup] butter
1 large onion, finely chopped
1 garlic clove, crushed
1½ lb. boned cooked chicken, cut into ½-inch cubes
8 oz. button mushrooms, wiped clean and sliced
1 teaspoon dried thyme
1 teaspoon salt
½ teaspoon black pepper
1 teaspoon mushroom ketchup
8 oz. [1⅓ cups] wild rice, washed, soaked overnight and drained
16 fl. oz. [2 cups] chicken stock
8 oz. [2 cups] Cheddar cheese, grated

Preheat the oven to moderate 350°F (Gas Mark 4, 180°C).

In a flameproof casserole, melt the butter over moderate heat. When the foam subsides, add the onion and garlic and fry, stirring constantly, for 5 to 7 minutes or until the onion is soft and translucent but not brown. Add the chicken, mushrooms, thyme, salt, pepper and ketchup. Stir in the rice and pour over the stock. Increase the heat to high

A fabulous, informal dish—Wild Rice Meat Loaf with Barbecue Sauce.

and bring the liquid to the boil.

Cover the casserole and transfer it to the oven. Cook the mixture for 20 to 25 minutes or until all the liquid has been absorbed.

Preheat the grill [broiler] to high. Remove the casserole from the oven, remove the lid and sprinkle the cheese over the top. Place the casserole under the grill [broiler] and grill [broil] for 5 minutes or until the cheese has melted and is lightly browned. Remove from the grill [broiler] and serve immediately.

Wild Rice Meat Loaf with Barbecue Sauce

A really unusual meat loaf, Wild Rice Meat Loaf with Barbecue Sauce is ideal for an informal dinner party.

6 SERVINGS

4 oz. [⅔ cup] wild rice, washed, soaked overnight and drained
1 lb. minced [ground] beef
1 lb. minced [ground] veal
4 carrots, scraped and grated
2 onions, finely chopped
1 tablespoon mustard
1½ teaspoons salt

½ teaspoon black pepper
2 eggs, lightly beaten
BARBECUE SAUCE
6 fl. oz. [¾ cup] tomato ketchup
2 tablespoons Worcestershire sauce
2 tablespoons clear honey
1 tablespoon lemon juice
½ teaspoon hot chilli powder
4 fl. oz. [½ cup] water

Preheat the oven to moderate 350°F (Gas Mark 4, 180°C).

In a large mixing bowl, combine all the ingredients for the meat loaf. Mix and knead the ingredients. Spoon the mixture into a 2½-pound loaf tin and smooth the top over with the back of a spoon.

Place the tin in the centre of the oven and bake the loaf for 1¼ to 1½ hours or until the juices run clear when the loaf is pierced with the point of a sharp knife.

Meanwhile, prepare the sauce. In a saucepan, combine all the sauce ingredients. Place the pan over high heat and bring the liquid to the boil, stirring constantly. Boil until the liquid has reduced by one-third. Remove the pan from the heat. Pour the sauce into a warmed sauceboat and keep hot.

Remove the tin from the oven and pour off any fat. Run a knife around the edge of the tin to loosen the sides. Turn the loaf on to a warmed serving dish. Serve immediately, with the sauce.

Yakhni Pulao

LAMB COOKED WITH RICE

This rice pilaff is cooked in a well-flavoured stock called yakhni. Yakhni can be made with any meat or poultry.

4-6 SERVINGS

2 lb. boned leg of lamb, cut into 1-inch cubes, with bones reserved
finely pared rind of 1 lemon
½-inch piece fresh root ginger, peeled and thinly sliced
2 x 2-inch pieces cinnamon stick
¼ teaspoon grated nutmeg
1 green chilli, chopped
12 black peppercorns
5 fl. oz. [⅝ cup] yogurt
½ teaspoon cayenne pepper
juice of ½ lemon
1½ teaspoons salt
4 oz. [½ cup] butter
1 onion, finely chopped
4 cloves, bruised
4 whole cardamom pods, bruised
1 teaspoon whole cumin
12 oz. [2 cups] long-grain rice, washed, soaked in cold water for 30 minutes and drained

GARNISH

2 tablespoons slivered almonds, lightly toasted
1 medium-sized onion, thinly sliced and fried until golden
2 tablespoons raisins, lightly fried
2 hard-boiled eggs, quartered

Put the lamb, the reserved lamb bones, the lemon rind, ginger, cinnamon, nutmeg, chilli and peppercorns in a large saucepan. Add enough water to cover the lamb and bones generously and bring to

the boil. When the water comes to the boil, cover the pan, reduce the heat to low and simmer for 40 minutes or until the lamb cubes are tender.

Using a slotted spoon, remove the lamb cubes from the pan and set them aside in a bowl. Re-cover the pan and continue simmering the stock for 2 hours.

Pour the stock through a strainer into a bowl. Discard the contents of the strainer. Set the stock aside to cool. When the stock is cold, skim off and discard the fat on the surface.

Meanwhile, in a small mixing bowl,

combine the yogurt, cayenne, lemon juice and half the salt. Pour this mixture over the lamb cubes and stir well to mix. Cover the bowl and set aside for 2 hours.

In a large saucepan, melt half the butter over moderate heat. When the foam subsides, add the onion and fry, stirring occasionally, for 8 to 10 minutes or until it is golden. Add the cloves, cardamom and cumin and fry, stirring occasionally, for 2 minutes. Add the rice and fry, stirring frequently, for 6 to 8 minutes or until it becomes translucent.

Preheat the oven to very cool 275°F (Gas Mark 1, 140°C).

Meanwhile, pour the stock into a saucepan and bring to the boil. Remove the pan from the heat and pour enough stock over the rice to cover it by a ½-inch. Add the remaining salt and, when the mixture comes to the boil again, cover the pan, reduce the heat to very low and simmer for 15 to 20 minutes or until the rice is tender and all the stock has been absorbed. Remove the pan from the heat.

Meanwhile, in a large frying-pan, melt the remaining butter over moderate heat. When the foam subsides, add the lamb cubes and the yogurt marinade. Fry the lamb, stirring constantly, for 5 minutes. Reduce the heat to low and continue frying, stirring frequently, for 10 minutes. Remove the pan from the heat.

In a baking dish, layer the rice and lamb, beginning and ending with a layer of rice. Cover the dish tightly with foil.

Place the dish in the oven and cook for 20 minutes.

In a small mixing bowl, combine the almonds, onion and raisins. Set aside.

Remove the dish from the oven. Sprinkle over the garnish and arrange the eggs over the top. Serve immediately.

Yunnan Quick-Fried Prawns or Shrimps on Crackling Rice

☆ ☆   ① ①   ⋈

Serve this adaptation of a Chinese dish as part of a traditional Chinese meal or as a delightfully exotic supper or lunch dish.

4 SERVINGS

8 oz. prawns or shrimps, weighed after shelling
8 oz. boned chicken breast, cut into 2-inch cubes
2 teaspoons salt
1 teaspoon white pepper
1 tablespoon cornflour [cornstarch]
1 lb. [6 cups] cooked rice

Yunnan Quick-Fried Prawns or Shrimps on Crackling Rice is an exotic dish from China.

sufficient vegetable oil for deep-frying
SAUCE
2 tablespoons vegetable oil
1 onion, chopped
5 fl. oz. [⅝ cup] beef stock
2 tablespoons tomato purée
1½ tablespoons soy sauce
1½ tablespoons sugar
1½ tablespoons wine vinegar
2 tablespoons dry sherry
1 teaspoon chilli sauce
4 teaspoons cornflour [cornstarch]

Preheat the oven to very cool 275°F (Gas Mark 1, 140°C).

Sprinkle the prawns or shrimps and chicken cubes with the salt, pepper and cornflour [cornstarch] and, using your fingers, rub them into the shellfish and chicken. Set aside.

Place the rice in an ovenproof dish and put the dish in the oven. Dry out the rice for 15 to 20 minutes or until it is crisp.

Meanwhile, make the sauce. In a large frying-pan, heat the oil over moderate heat. When the oil is hot, add the onion and fry, stirring occasionally, for 3 minutes. Add all the remaining sauce ingredients and mix well to blend. Cook the sauce, stirring constantly, for 2 minutes or until it becomes thick and translucent. Remove the pan from the heat and set aside.

Fill a large, deep-frying pan one-third full with vegetable oil. Set the pan over moderate heat and heat the oil until it reaches 360°F on a deep-fat thermometer or until a small cube of stale bread dropped into the oil turns golden brown in 50 seconds.

Place the prawns or shrimps and chicken cubes in a deep-frying basket and lower them into the oil. Deep-fry them for 1 minute then remove the pan from the heat. Remove the basket from the pan and set it over kitchen paper towels to drain. Transfer the prawns or shrimps and chicken cubes to the sauce in the frying-pan and return the frying-pan to moderate heat. Cook the mixture, stirring constantly, for 2 minutes.

Meanwhile, return the deep-frying pan to moderate heat and reheat the oil until it reaches 350°F on a deep-fat thermometer or until a small cube of stale bread dropped into the oil turns golden brown in 55 seconds.

Remove the rice from the oven, place it in a narrow-meshed deep-frying basket and lower it into the oil. Fry the rice for 1½ minutes, then remove it from the oil and drain on kitchen paper towels.

Arrange the rice on a warmed serving dish and pour over the prawns or shrimps, chicken cubes and sauce. Serve at once.

Pasta

Pasta, a name that is almost synonymous with Italian cuisine, is a farinaceous product made from flour, water and sometimes eggs. The flour used is made from a hard or durum wheat with a high gluten content, which gives the dough its slightly brittle consistency.

Pasta is usually made commercially these days, although some types — most particularly egg noodles, ravioli and gnocchi — are still traditionally made at home. In the factories, machines are used to produce the different shapes and sizes of pasta sold to the public as the familiar cannelloni, farfalle, fettuccine, fusilli, lasagne, macaroni, manicotti, noodles, ravioli, spaghetti, tagliatelli, tortellini, vermicelli, zite. Spinach is sometimes added to the basic pasta dough — thus fettuccine verdi and lasagne verdi.

Pasta is always served with a sauce of some kind — even though it may be as simple as melted butter and grated cheese. In Italy pasta is served as the course before the main, usually meat, course of the meal, although in other parts of Europe and in the United States pasta is more often served as a main course. The lighter, smaller pasta, such as vermicelli, is often used in soups, and the heavier pasta, such as macaroni, can also be made into substantial sweet or savoury puddings.

A selection of some of the more popular types of pasta, including spinach pasta.

Cannelloni Filled with a Savoury Meat and Spinach Mixture with Tomato and Cream Sauces

This famous Italian dish is economical and very tasty. Serve with a tossed mixed salad for a delicious supper.

4 SERVINGS

TOMATO SAUCE

2 tablespoons olive oil
1 small onion, finely chopped
14 oz. canned peeled Italian tomatoes
2½ oz. canned tomato purée
½ tablespoon finely chopped fresh basil or ½ teaspoon dried basil
1 teaspoon chopped fresh oregano or ½ teaspoon dried oregano
1 teaspoon sugar
½ teaspoon salt
½ teaspoon freshly ground black pepper

FILLING

1½ tablespoons olive oil
1 tablespoon butter
1 small onion, finely chopped
2 garlic cloves, finely chopped
8 oz. lean minced [ground] beef
6 oz. fresh spinach, cooked, drained, squeezed and finely chopped or a small packet frozen chopped spinach (thawed)
1 oz. [¼ cup] Parmesan cheese, grated
1½ tablespoons double [heavy] cream
1 egg
1 teaspoon chopped fresh oregano or ½ teaspoon dried oregano
¼ teaspoon salt
½ teaspoon black pepper

CREAM SAUCE

1 oz. [2 tablespoons] butter
4 tablespoons flour
5 fl. oz. [⅝ cup] plus 2 tablespoons milk, warmed
3 tablespoons double [heavy] cream
¼ teaspoon salt
⅛ teaspoon white pepper

PASTA

1 teaspoon salt
8 oz. cannelloni, cut into rectangles 3 inches by 4 inches
3 oz. [¾ cup] Parmesan cheese, grated
1 tablespoon butter, cut into small pieces

Cannelloni Filled with a Savoury Meat and Spinach Mixture with Tomato and Cream Sauces is a filling main dish from Italy.

To make the tomato sauce, in a medium-sized saucepan heat the oil over moderate heat. Add the onion and fry it for 5 to 7 minutes, or until it is soft and translucent but not brown. Stir in the tomatoes with the can juice, tomato purée, basil, oregano, sugar, salt and pepper. Reduce the heat to low, cover and simmer the sauce for 40 minutes, stirring occasionally.

Remove the pan from the heat and set aside.

To make the filling, in a large frying-pan heat the oil with the butter over moderate heat. Add the onion and garlic and fry, stirring occasionally, for 5 to 7 minutes, or until the onion is soft. Add the meat. Cook for 10 minutes or until the meat is browned, stirring occasionally. Add the spinach and, stirring, cook for 3 to 4 minutes or until all the moisture has evaporated.

Transfer the meat and spinach mixture to a medium-sized bowl. Add the Parmesan, cream, egg, oregano, salt and pepper. Mix well with a spoon and set aside.

Now prepare the cream sauce. In a small saucepan, melt the butter over moderate heat. Remove the pan from the heat and, with a wooden spoon, stir in the flour. Gradually stir in 5 fluid ounces [⅝ cup] of the milk and the cream. Return the pan to the heat. Cook,

Elegant Egg Noodles with Pork Sauce is an unusual dish from China and the sauce has a delightfully sweet-sour flavour.

stirring constantly, until the sauce comes to the boil. The sauce will be very thick. Remove the pan from the heat and add the salt and pepper. Pour the 2 tablespoons of milk over the top of the sauce to prevent a skin forming and set the pan aside.

Preheat the oven to fairly hot 375°F (Gas Mark 5, 190°C).

In a large saucepan, bring 3 to 4 pints [2½ quarts] of water to the boil over high heat. Add the teaspoon of salt with the cannelloni pieces and cook them for 8 to 10 minutes or until the cannelloni is 'al dente' or just tender. With a slotted spoon, remove the pasta from the pan and place it on a dampened cloth to drain.

When the cannelloni is cool enough to handle, place a tablespoonful of the filling in the centre of each pasta rectangle and roll them up.

Pour a thin layer of tomato sauce into the bottom of a large shallow ovenproof dish. Place the cannelloni in the dish in a single or double layer.

Stir the milk into the cream sauce and spoon over the cannelloni. Pour the remaining tomato sauce over the top of the mixture. Sprinkle with the grated Parmesan cheese and dot with the tablespoon of butter.

Place the dish in the oven and bake the cannelloni for 30 minutes, or until the

sauce is bubbling and the cheese has melted.

Serve immediately.

Egg Noodles with Pork Sauce

A variation on a traditional Chinese recipe, this dish has an interesting meat sauce with a rather unusual sweet-sour flavour. The garnish has a strong garlic flavour. Thin carrot sticks would make a good accompaniment.

4 SERVINGS

1 large cucumber
3 spring onions [scallions], finely chopped
4 garlic cloves, finely chopped
3 tablespoons vegetable oil
1 lb. minced [ground] pork
2 tablespoons dry sherry
2 tablespoons Worcestershire sauce
1 tablespoon soy sauce
1 large onion, finely chopped
2 teaspoons soft brown sugar
3 fl. oz. [⅜ cup] chicken stock
12 oz. egg noodles

Peel the cucumber and cut it in half lengthways. With the tip of a teaspoon, scoop out the seeds. With a sharp kitchen knife, cut the cucumber lengthways into ¼-inch slices. Cut each of these slices into strips 2 inches long.

Arrange the cucumber and onions [scallions] on a serving plate and sprinkle with the garlic. Set the garnishes aside while you make the sauce.

Warm a large frying-pan over high heat. Add 2 tablespoons of oil and heat for about 1 minute or until the oil is very hot. If the oil begins to smoke, reduce the heat to moderate.

Add the pork and fry it, stirring constantly, for about 5 minutes or until the pork begins to brown.

Stir in the sherry, Worcestershire sauce, soy sauce, onion, sugar and chicken stock.

Bring the liquid to the boil and cook for 10 to 15 minutes, or until all the liquid has evaporated. Cover the pan tightly and remove it from the heat. Set the pan in a warm place to keep the pork sauce warm.

Fill a large saucepan two-thirds full of water and bring it to the boil over high heat. Add the noodles and boil for 6 to 8 minutes or until they are just tender but not mushy. Stir occasionally to prevent the noodles from sticking to each other. Drain the noodles and toss in the remaining tablespoon of oil.

Place the noodles in a large, warmed serving dish and cover with the pork sauce. Sprinkle over some of the spring onions [scallions] and serve with the remaining garnishes.

Fettuccine Alfredo

This delicious mixture of pasta with cheese and cream is especially popular in the United States. Fettuccine Alfredo may be served on its own or accompanied by a mixed green salad.

4 SERVINGS

2 pints [5 cups] water
2 teaspoons salt
1 lb. fettuccine
2 oz. [¼ cup] butter
4 oz. [1 cup] Parmesan cheese, grated
8 fl. oz. double cream [1 cup heavy cream]
½ teaspoon freshly ground white pepper

In a large saucepan, bring the water and salt to the boil over high heat.

Drop the fettuccine into the water. Reduce the heat to moderate and cook the fettuccine for 5 to 7 minutes, or until it is 'al dente' or just tender.

Remove the pan from the heat and drain the fettuccine in a colander.

Transfer the fettuccine to a warmed serving dish.

Add the butter, cheese, cream and pepper to the fettuccine and, using two forks, toss the mixture well.

Serve at once.

Fettuccine alla Romana

A tasty, colourful Italian dish, Fettuccine alla Romana is perfect for a family meal or an informal dinner party.

4 SERVINGS

2 oz. [¼ cup] plus 1 tablespoon
butter
1 medium-sized onion, chopped
1 garlic clove, chopped
14 oz. canned peeled Italian tomatoes
4 oz. mushrooms, wiped clean and
sliced
1½ teaspoons salt
¼ teaspoon freshly ground black
pepper
2 fl. oz. [¼ cup] dry red wine
1 teaspoon sugar
2 pints [5 cups] water
1 lb. fettuccine
2 tablespoons grated Parmesan
cheese

In a large, deep frying-pan, melt 2 ounces [¼ cup] of the butter over moderate heat. When the foam subsides, add the onion and garlic to the pan and fry them, stirring occasionally, for 5 to 7 minutes, or until the onion is soft and translucent but not brown.

Add the tomatoes with the can juice, mushrooms, ½ teaspoon of salt, the pepper, wine and sugar. Stir well and bring the liquid to the boil. Cover the pan, reduce the heat to low and simmer gently for 20 minutes.

Meanwhile, prepare the fettuccine. In a large saucepan bring the water to the boil over high heat. Add the remaining salt and the fettuccine. Reduce the heat

to moderate, boil for 5 to 7 minutes, or until the fettuccine is 'al dente' or just tender.

Remove the pan from the heat and drain the fettuccine in a colander. Transfer it to a warmed serving dish and stir in the remaining butter. Pour over the sauce and sprinkle with the Parmesan cheese.

Serve immediately.

Gnocchi al Forno Napoletana

ITALIAN BAKED DUMPLINGS WITH
TOMATO SAUCE

This tasty dish is popular in the region of Southern Italy around Naples. With its delicious tomato sauce, serve it for a family supper or lunch, accompanied by a tossed mixed salad and lots of crusty bread and butter.

4 SERVINGS

GNOCCHI
4 egg yolks
2 teaspoons sugar
2 oz. [½ cup] flour
2 tablespoons cornflour [cornstarch]
¼ teaspoon salt
2 oz. [¼ cup] plus 1 teaspoon butter,
melted
4 oz. [1 cup] Parmesan cheese,
finely grated
15 fl. oz. [1⅞ cups] milk
SAUCE
1 oz. [2 tablespoons] butter
2 tablespoons olive oil
1 medium-sized onion, finely
chopped
2 garlic cloves, crushed
2 lb. canned peeled Italian tomatoes

2 teaspoons tomato purée
1 bay leaf
1 tablespoon dry vermouth
(optional)
½ teaspoon salt
¼ teaspoon freshly ground black
pepper
1 teaspoon sugar
1 tablespoon finely chopped fresh
parsley

First, make the gnocchi. Place the egg yolks and sugar in a medium-sized saucepan and, using a wire whisk or a rotary beater, beat the mixture until it is creamy and pale.

Carefully sift the flour, cornflour [cornstarch], and salt into a small mixing bowl. Gradually add the flour mixture to the egg yolk mixture, beating constantly with a wooden spoon until the mixture is thick and smooth. Stir in 2 ounces [¼ cup] of the melted butter, then add 3 ounces [¾ cup] of the grated cheese.

Place the saucepan over moderately low heat. Gradually add the milk, stirring constantly with the wooden spoon. Cook the mixture for 3 to 4 minutes or until it is thick and smooth. Remove the pan from the heat.

Rinse a large baking sheet with water. Turn the gnocchi mixture on to the sheet and smooth out the top with a flat-bladed knife. The mixture should be about half an inch thick. Place the baking sheet in the refrigerator and chill the mixture for 30 minutes.

Meanwhile, make the tomato sauce. In a medium-sized saucepan, melt the butter with the olive oil over moderate heat. When the foam subsides, add the onion and garlic to the pan and fry, stirring occasionally, for 5 to 7 minutes or until the onion is soft and translucent but not brown. Add all of the remaining sauce ingredients and bring the mixture to the boil, stirring constantly with a wooden spoon. Reduce the heat to moderately low, cover the pan and simmer the sauce for 30 minutes or until it is rich and thick.

Preheat the oven to fairly hot 375°F (Gas Mark 5, 190°C).

With the remaining teaspoon of butter, lightly grease a medium-sized baking dish. Set the dish aside.

Remove the baking sheet from the refrigerator and cut the gnocchi into squares. Place them, overlapping slightly, in the prepared baking dish. Sprinkle the remaining cheese on top. Put the dish into the oven and bake for 15 to 20 minutes or until the top is golden brown and the cheese has melted.

Remove the baking dish from the oven and serve the gnocchi immediately, either with the sauce poured over the top, or served separately in a warmed sauceboat or jug.

Gnocchi Verdi
SPINACH DUMPLINGS

These tasty Italian dumplings make an unusual first course to an Italian meal. Gnocchi Verdi may also be served as a tasty lunch or supper for the family accompanied by grilled [broiled] bacon and, if liked, a mushroom sauce.

4-6 SERVINGS

1½ lb. spinach, trimmed and washed
3 teaspoons salt
2 oz. [¼ cup] butter
1 medium-sized onion, very finely chopped
8 oz. [1 cup] ricotta cheese
½ teaspoon white pepper
¼ teaspoon grated nutmeg
2 eggs
4 tablespoons grated Parmesan cheese
4 oz. [1 cup] flour
2 oz. [¼ cup] butter, melted

Put the spinach into a large saucepan.

Pour over enough water just to cover the spinach. Add 1 teaspoon of salt and place the pan over moderate heat. Cook the spinach for 7 to 12 minutes, or until it is tender. Remove the pan from the heat and drain the spinach in a colander, pressing down well on the spinach with a wooden spoon to extract all of the excess liquid.

Transfer the spinach to a chopping board. With a sharp knife, finely chop the spinach.

In a large saucepan, melt the butter over moderate heat. When the foam subsides, add the onion to the pan and cook, stirring occasionally, for 5 to 7 minutes, or until it is soft and translucent but not brown. Add the chopped spinach to the pan and, with a wooden spoon, stir in the ricotta cheese, 1 teaspoon of the remaining salt, the pepper and the nutmeg. Beat until the mixture is smooth. Reduce the heat to low and cook for 5 minutes, stirring frequently.

Remove the pan from the heat and beat in the eggs, half the grated Parmesan cheese and the flour. Turn the mixture into a mixing bowl and leave it to cool. Then place the bowl in the refrigerator

Gnocchi dumplings are still widely made at home in Italy—and much enjoyed! You can see why, when you taste delicious Gnocchi al Forno Napoletana.

to chill for 2 to 3 hours or until the mixture is firm and 'set'.

Remove the mixture from the refrigerator and turn it out on to a lightly floured board. Divide the mixture into large walnut-sized pieces and, using the palms of your hands, carefully roll them into balls.

Pour 1 tablespoon of the melted butter into a shallow flameproof dish and sprinkle with 1 tablespoon of the remaining grated Parmesan cheese. Set the dish aside.

Half fill a large saucepan with cold water and add the remaining salt. Place the pan over high heat and bring the water to the boil. Reduce the heat to moderate and, when the water comes to the boil again, drop in the balls, a few at a time. Simmer until they rise to the surface. With a slotted spoon, remove the gnocchi from the pan and drain them on kitchen paper towels. Place them in the flameproof dish and keep them hot while you cook the remaining balls in the same way.

Preheat the grill [broiler] to moderately high.

Pour the remaining melted butter and sprinkle the remaining Parmesan cheese over the gnocchi. Place the dish under the grill [broiler] and grill [broil] the gnocchi for 5 minutes, or until the cheese is golden brown.

Serve immediately, straight from the flameproof dish.

Fusilli Noodles with Tomatoes and Cheese

This simple and absolutely delicious Italian dish is ideal for a quick and filling family meal. Fusilli are a curly, spiral type of spaghetti which go particularly well with this sauce. If they are not available, however, spaghetti may be substituted.

4 SERVINGS

- 2 tablespoons vegetable oil
- 1 medium-sized onion, finely chopped
- 14 oz. canned peeled tomatoes
- 2 tablespoons tomato purée
- 1 teaspoon dried oregano
- 1½ teaspoons salt
- ½ teaspoon black pepper
- 1 lb. fusilli noodles
- 4 oz. Bel Paese cheese, cut into small pieces
- 2 oz. [½ cup] Parmesan cheese, grated

In a medium-sized frying-pan, heat the oil over moderate heat. When the oil is hot, add the onion and fry it, stirring occasionally, for 5 to 7 minutes, or until it is soft and translucent but not brown.

Add the tomatoes with the can juice, the tomato purée, oregano, ½ teaspoon of the salt and the pepper. Stir well and

bring the liquid to the boil over high heat. Reduce the heat to low, cover the pan and simmer for 20 minutes, stirring occasionally.

Meanwhile, half-fill a large saucepan with water. Add the remaining salt and bring the water to the boil over high heat. Reduce the heat to moderate and drop the noodles into the water. Cook for 8 to 10 minutes, depending on whether you like your pasta 'al dente' or just tender.

Remove the pan from the heat. Drain the noodles in a colander and return them to the saucepan.

Add the tomato sauce and cheeses to the pan. Place the pan over low heat and toss the noodles with two forks until the cheeses have melted.

Turn the noodles and sauce into a warmed serving dish and serve the mixture at once.

Macaroni Cheese

Despite its Italian origin, macaroni forms the basis of one of the most typical of English supper dishes, Macaroni Cheese. A simple-to-make economical dish, Macaroni Cheese served with a tossed green salad and crusty bread makes an absolutely delicious meal.

The unusual sauce is what makes Macaroni and Green Pea Sauce really special. Use fresh peas if possible.

2-3 SERVINGS

- 1 oz. [2 tablespoons] plus 1 teaspoon butter
- 1 pint [2½ cups] water
- 1½ teaspoons salt
- 8 oz. macaroni
- 15 fl. oz. [1⅞ cups] béchamel sauce
- ½ teaspoon prepared mustard
- ¼ teaspoon white pepper
- ⅛ teaspoon cayenne pepper
- 4 oz. [1 cup] Cheddar cheese, grated
- 1 oz. [⅓ cup] fine dry breadcrumbs

Preheat the oven to fairly hot 400°F (Gas Mark 6, 200°C). With the teaspoon of butter, lightly grease a medium-sized ovenproof baking dish and set aside.

Pour the water into a medium-sized saucepan and add 1 teaspoon of the salt. Place the pan over high heat and bring the water to the boil. Reduce the heat to moderate and add the macaroni. Cook the macaroni for 8 to 10 minutes, or until it is 'al dente' or just tender. Remove the pan from the heat and drain the macaroni in a colander. Set aside.

In a large mixing bowl, combine the

Macaroni Shells with Mussels makes a delightful informal meal, served with crusty bread and white wine.

remaining salt, béchamel sauce, mustard, the pepper, cayenne and 2 ounces [½ cup] of the cheese, mixing well. Add the macaroni to the mixture and stir well to blend.

Pour the mixture into the prepared dish. In a small bowl, combine the remaining cheese and breadcrumbs and sprinkle the mixture over the macaroni mixture in the dish. Cut the remaining butter into small pieces and dot over the top of the cheese and breadcrumb mixture.

Place the dish in the oven and bake for 15 to 20 minutes, or until the top is crisp and golden brown.

Remove the dish from the oven and serve at once.

Macaroni with Green Pea Sauce

This sauce is only really good when made with fresh green peas and may be served with most boiled pasta. Macaroni with Green Pea Sauce may be served as a supper dish or, in smaller quantities, as a first course to an Italian meal.

4 SERVINGS

2 tablespoons olive oil
1 medium-sized onion, chopped
4 slices lean bacon, chopped
½ teaspoon dried basil
⅛ teaspoon dried dill
1 teaspoon salt
½ teaspoon black pepper
1½ lb. fresh green peas, weighed after shelling
8 fl. oz. [1 cup] water
4 fl. oz. single cream [½ cup light cream]
12 oz. macaroni, cooked for 8 to 10 minutes, drained and kept warm in a colander over a pan of hot water
1 oz. [2 tablespoons] butter
2 oz. [½ cup] Parmesan cheese, grated

In a medium-sized saucepan, heat the oil over moderate heat. When the oil is hot, add the onion and the bacon and fry, stirring occasionally, for 5 to 7 minutes or until the onion is soft and translucent but not brown and the bacon is crisp.

Add the basil, dill, salt, pepper and peas. Pour in the water and bring to the boil. Reduce the heat to low and simmer the mixture for 10 to 12 minutes or until

the peas are tender.

Remove the pan from the heat. Purée the contents of the pan through a food mill or in an electric blender.

Return the puréed sauce to the pan and stir in the cream. Place the pan over low heat and, stirring occasionally, simmer the sauce for 2 minutes or until it is hot. Taste the sauce and add more salt and pepper if necessary. Pour the sauce into a warmed sauceboat. Keep warm.

In a saucepan, combine the macaroni and butter. Place the pan over low heat and toss the pasta in the butter.

Place the buttered macaroni in a warmed serving dish.

Serve immediately with the sauce and cheese handed round separately.

Macaroni Shells with Mussels

Serve this delicious and filling Italian dish with crusty bread and a tossed mixed salad for a family lunch or supper. Chianti would be an excellent accompaniment.

4 SERVINGS

2 fl. oz. [¼ cup] olive oil
2 garlic cloves, finely chopped
1 lb. tomatoes, blanched, peeled

and chopped
8 oz. mushrooms, wiped clean and sliced
1 teaspoon dried basil
½ teaspoon dried oregano
½ teaspoon salt
½ teaspoon black pepper
2 tablespoons tomato purée
1 quart mussels, scrubbed, steamed, removed from their shells and the cooking liquid reserved
8 oz. macaroni shells, cooked for 8 to 10 minutes, drained and kept hot

In a large frying-pan, heat the oil over moderate heat. When the oil is hot, add the garlic and fry, stirring constantly, for 2 minutes. Add the tomatoes, mushrooms, basil, oregano, salt, pepper and tomato purée and fry, stirring occasionally, for 5 minutes or until the mixture begins to boil. Add the mussels, with the reserved cooking liquid, and cook, stirring occasionally, for 2 to 3 minutes or until the mussels are heated through. Remove the pan from the heat.

Place the macaroni in a warmed serving dish. Pour over the mussel sauce and serve at once.

Chow Mein
CHINESE FRIED NOODLES

Chow Mein is surely one of the best known of Chinese dishes — and one which is often badly made in the West. This recipe is easy to prepare and truly delicious.

4 SERVINGS

1 teaspoon salt
1 lb. egg noodles or spaghetti
8 oz. French beans, trimmed and halved
4 tablespoons vegetable oil
1 medium-sized onion, very thinly sliced
1 garlic clove, crushed
4 oz. chicken meat (breast or leg), finely shredded
2 tablespoons soy sauce
1 teaspoon sugar
1 tablespoon sherry
1½ tablespoons butter
3 tablespoons chicken stock
½ chicken stock cube, crumbled

Half-fill a large saucepan with water and bring it to the boil over high heat. Add the salt and noodles or spaghetti. When the water returns to the boil, reduce the heat to moderate and cook the noodles for 5 to 8 minutes, or the spaghetti for 10 to 12 minutes, or until they are 'al dente' or just tender. Remove the pan from the heat and drain the noodles or spaghetti in a colander. Set aside and keep warm.

Half-fill a medium-sized saucepan with water and bring it to the boil over high heat. Add the beans and boil them for 5 minutes. Remove the pan from the heat and drain the beans in a colander. Set aside.

In a large frying-pan, heat the oil over moderate heat. Add the onion and garlic and fry, stirring constantly, for 2 minutes. Add the chicken and stir-fry for 1 minute. Add the beans, soy sauce, sugar and sherry and continue to stir-fry for 1½ minutes.

With a slotted spoon, remove the bean and chicken mixture from the pan and set it aside in a bowl. Keep warm.

Add the butter, chicken stock and stock cube to the oil remaining in the frying-pan. When the butter has melted, add the noodles or spaghetti. Cook, stirring and turning constantly, for 2 minutes or until the pasta is heated through.

Add half of the bean and chicken mixture and mix well. Transfer the mixture

This simple dish of noodles cooked with ham, garlic sausage and tomatoes, makes a tasty supper. Serve Noodles with Ham with salad.

to a warmed serving dish. Set aside and keep warm.

Return the remaining bean and chicken mixture to the frying-pan and increase the heat to high. Fry, stirring constantly, for 1 minute, adding more oil or soy sauce to the pan if necessary.

Remove the pan from the heat and spoon the bean and chicken mixture over the pasta mixture.

Serve immediately.

Noodles with Breadcrumbs and Cheese

An easy-to-prepare supper dish for the family, Noodles with Breadcrumbs and Cheese could be served with French beans and a tomato salad.

6 SERVINGS

1 lb. noodles, cooked for 5 to 8 minutes, drained and kept hot
2 oz. [¼ cup] butter, cut into small pieces
1 oz. [¼ cup] Parmesan cheese, finely grated
2 oz. [½ cup] Gruyère cheese, finely grated
3 tablespoons dry white breadcrumbs
¼ teaspoon freshly ground black pepper

Preheat the grill [broiler] to high.

Place the noodles in a heatproof serving dish. Stir in half the butter. Sprinkle the grated cheeses, breadcrumbs and pepper over the noodles. Dot the top of the dish with the remaining butter.

Place the dish under the grill [broiler] and grill [broil] for 3 to 4 minutes or until the cheeses have melted and the top is a light golden brown.

Remove the dish from under the heat and serve immediately.

Noodles with Ham

A quick supper dish, Noodles with Ham may be sprinkled with grated Parmesan cheese just before serving.

4-6 SERVINGS

1 lb. noodles, cooked for 5 to 8 minutes, drained and kept warm
2 oz. [¼ cup] butter, cut into small pieces
½ teaspoon salt
½ teaspoon freshly ground black pepper
1 teaspoon dried basil
2 oz. prosciutto, cut into thin strips

6 oz. cooked lean ham, cut into thin strips
1 small garlic sausage, cut into thin strips
2 large tomatoes, blanched, peeled, seeded and cut into strips

In a large saucepan, heat the noodles and butter over very low heat. When the butter has melted, using two forks, toss the noodles until they are coated with the butter. Add the salt, pepper, basil, prosciutto, ham, sausage and tomatoes. Increase the heat to moderate and cook the noodle mixture, stirring frequently with a wooden spoon, for 6 to 8 minutes or until it is very hot.

Remove the pan from the heat. Transfer the noodle mixture to a heated large serving dish and serve it immediately.

Noodles with Onions

Noodles with Onions complements the rich taste of a beef pot roast, or goulasch very well.

4 SERVINGS

1 lb. noodles, cooked for 5 to 8 minutes and drained
3 oz. [⅜ cup] butter
½ teaspoon freshly ground black pepper
¼ teaspoon grated nutmeg
2 small onions, thinly sliced and pushed out into rings

Preheat the oven to warm 300°F (Gas Mark 2, 150°C).

Place the noodles in a large shallow ovenproof dish.

Cut 1 ounce [2 tablespoons] of the butter into small pieces and dot the noodles with them. Sprinkle the pepper and nutmeg over the noodles and place the dish in the oven. Bake the mixture for 10 minutes.

Meanwhile, in a small frying-pan, melt the remaining butter over moderate heat. When the foam subsides, add the onions and cook them, stirring occasionally, for 5 to 7 minutes or until they are soft and translucent but not brown. Remove the pan from the heat.

Remove the dish of noodles from the oven and stir well. Pour the onion mixture over the noodles. Increase the oven temperature to moderate 350°F (Gas Mark 4, 180°C). Return the dish to the oven and bake the noodles for a further 15 to 20 minutes or until the onions are crisp.

Remove from the oven and serve immediately.

Peking Noodles with Meat Sauce and Shredded Vegetables

This Chinese peasant dish is gradually becoming a classic. Each diner is given a bowl of noodles to which he adds as much meat sauce and shredded vegetables as he likes.

4 SERVINGS

- 1 teaspoon salt
- 1 lb. noodles or spaghetti
- 3 tablespoons vegetable oil
- 1 onion, thinly sliced
- 2 garlic cloves, crushed
- 2 slices fresh root ginger, peeled and finely chopped, or ½ teaspoon ground ginger
- 12 oz. lean pork or beef, minced [ground]
- 1 tablespoon sesame oil
- 5 tablespoons soy sauce
- 2 tablespoons dry sherry
- 1 tablespoon sugar
- 1 tablespoon cornflour [cornstarch] dissolved in 4 tablespoons chicken stock

SHREDDED VEGETABLES

- 3 to 4 oz. (or a heaped side-dishful) shredded cabbage, blanched for 4 minutes and drained
- 3 to 4 oz. (or a heaped side-dishful) shredded carrots, blanched for 4 minutes and drained
- 3 to 4 oz. (or a heaped side-dishful) bean sprouts, blanched for 1 minute and drained
- 3 to 4 oz. (or a heaped side-dishful) shredded cucumber
- 2 to 3 oz. (or a saucerful) shredded radishes
- 1 to 2 oz. (or a saucerful) mixed pickles
- 1 to 2 oz. (or a saucerful) chutney

Arrange the shredded vegetables, pickles and chutney on individual serving dishes. Set aside.

Half-fill a large saucepan with water and bring it to the boil over high heat. Add the salt and the noodles or spaghetti. When the water returns to the boil, reduce the heat to moderate and cook the noodles for 5 to 8 minutes, or the spaghetti for 10 to 12 minutes, or until they are 'al dente' or just tender. Remove the pan from the heat and drain the pasta in a colander. Set aside and keep warm.

In a large frying-pan, heat the vegetable oil over moderate heat. Add the onion, garlic and ginger and fry, stirring constantly, for 1½ minutes. Add the pork or beef and stir-fry for 5 minutes, or until the meat loses its pinkness.

Stir in the sesame oil, soy sauce, sherry and sugar and continue to stir-fry for 3 minutes. Add the dissolved cornflour [cornstarch] and continue to cook, stirring constantly, until the meat sauce thickens and becomes glossy.

Remove the pan from the heat and transfer the meat sauce to a warmed serving bowl. Keep warm.

Divide the noodles or spaghetti between four serving bowls. Serve immediately, with the meat sauce and vegetables.

Wienerwurst and Noodle Casserole

An unusual dish, Wienerwurst and Noodle Casserole makes a sustaining family supper or lunch. Serve with mixed salad. If wienerwurst sausages are not available, frankfurters may be used instead.

3-4 SERVINGS

- 3 oz. [⅜ cup] butter
- 1 onion, finely chopped
- 1 garlic clove, crushed
- 4 courgettes [zucchini], trimmed and cut into ½-inch lengths
- 1 teaspoon salt
- 2 teaspoons black pepper
- 1 lb. wienerwurst sausages, cooked in hot water for 10 minutes, drained and cut into 1-inch lengths
- 1 oz. [¼ cup] flour
- 10 fl. oz. [1¼ cups] milk
- 4 oz. [1 cup] Gruyère cheese, grated
- ¼ teaspoon red pepper flakes
- 8 oz. egg noodles, cooked for 5 to 8 minutes and drained

In a large frying-pan, melt 2 ounces [¼ cup] of the butter over moderate heat. When the foam subsides, add the onion, garlic and courgettes [zucchini] and fry, stirring and turning occasionally, for 5 to 7 minutes or until the onion is soft and translucent but not brown. Add the salt, 1 teaspoon of pepper and the wienerwurst and continue to cook, turning occasionally, for 5 minutes or until the courgettes [zucchini] are cooked and tender. Remove the pan from the heat.

Preheat the oven to moderate 350°F (Gas Mark 4, 180°C).

In a medium-sized saucepan, melt the remaining butter over moderate heat. Remove the pan from the heat and, using a wooden spoon, stir in the flour to make a smooth paste. Gradually add the milk, stirring constantly to avoid lumps. Return the pan to low heat and cook, stirring constantly, for 2 minutes. Stir in 3 ounces [¾ cup] of the grated cheese, the

remaining pepper and the red pepper flakes and cook, stirring constantly, for a further 1 minute or until the cheese has melted and the sauce is smooth and thick. Stir in the cooked noodles.

Spoon the noodles and the wienerwurst mixture into a large baking dish and, using two large spoons, stir and toss to mix well. Sprinkle over the remaining grated cheese. Place the dish in the oven and bake the mixture for 15 to 20 minutes or until the top is brown and bubbling.

Remove from the oven and serve.

Yangchow Noodles

Yangchow Noodles consist of thinly sliced pork, spring onions [scallions] and celery in a slightly sweet-sour sauce served on a bed of succulent noodles.

3 SERVINGS

- 3 tablespoons vegetable oil
- 1 lb. lean pork, thinly sliced
- 3 tablespoons chopped spring

SAUCE
1 tablespoon olive oil
1 onion, finely chopped
28 oz. canned peeled tomatoes, drained and chopped
½ teaspoon dried basil
½ teaspoon dried oregano
½ teaspoon dried thyme
½ teaspoon salt
½ teaspoon white pepper
1 teaspoon sugar
STUFFING
12 oz. ham, minced [ground]
1 teaspoon chopped fresh parsley
2 garlic cloves, crushed
2 tablespoons olive oil
1 egg, lightly beaten
PASTA
1 teaspoon salt
1¼ lb. rigatoni
1 tablespoon olive oil
4 oz. [1 cup] Parmesan cheese, grated

First make the sauce. In a medium-sized saucepan, heat the olive oil over moderate heat. Add the onion and, stirring frequently, fry for about 5 to 7 minutes or until it is soft and translucent but not brown. Add the tomatoes, basil, oregano, thyme, salt, pepper and sugar. Stir to mix, cover the pan and simmer for 30 minutes or until the sauce is thick. Taste and add more seasoning if necessary.

Meanwhile, make the stuffing. In a medium-sized mixing bowl, combine the ham with the parsley and garlic. In a medium-sized frying-pan, heat the olive oil over moderate heat. Add the ham mixture and fry for 10 minutes, turning constantly with a wooden spoon so that it browns evenly. Put the mixture in a bowl and leave it to cool. When it is cold mix in the egg.

Preheat the oven to warm 325°F (Gas Mark 3, 170°C).

Half-fill a large saucepan with water, add 1 teaspoon of salt and bring to the boil over high heat. Drop in the rigatoni and cook for 10 to 12 minutes or until it is 'al dente' or just tender. Drain and leave to cool for a few minutes. Using a small teaspoon, carefully stuff the rigatoni with the meat mixture.

Grease an ovenproof dish with the tablespoon of olive oil and put the stuffed pasta in it. Cover the dish with aluminium foil and put it in the oven to bake for 30 minutes or until the mixture is cooked.

Reheat the sauce and pour it over the pasta. Sprinkle with the Parmesan cheese and serve immediately.

onions [scallions]
2 celery stalks, thinly sliced
4 fl. oz. [½ cup] chicken stock
1 tablespoon soy sauce
½ teaspoon cayenne pepper
4 oz. button mushrooms, wiped clean and thinly sliced
1 tablespoon soft brown sugar
2 teaspoons cornflour [cornstarch], dissolved in 1 tablespoon water
8 oz. egg noodles

In a large frying-pan, heat 2 tablespoons of the oil over high heat.

Add the pork and fry, stirring constantly, for about 8 minutes or until it is evenly browned. Reduce the heat to moderate and add the spring onions [scallions] and celery. Fry, stirring occasionally, for a further 5 minutes. Stir in the stock, soy sauce, cayenne, mushrooms, sugar and the cornflour [cornstarch] mixture.

Bring the liquid to the boil, stirring constantly, and cook for 10 minutes or until the sauce has thickened. Cover the pan tightly and remove it from the heat. Keep hot while you cook the noodles.

Fill a large saucepan two-thirds full with water and bring it to the boil over high heat. Add the noodles and boil for 5 to 8 minutes or until they are 'al dente' or just tender. Stir occasionally with a fork to prevent the noodles from sticking to each other. Remove the pan from the heat. Drain the noodles in a colander, place them in a large mixing bowl and toss them in the remaining oil.

Place the noodles in a warmed serving dish and spoon the pork mixture over them. Serve immediately.

Stuffed Rigatoni

A surprisingly easy-to-make dish, Stuffed Rigatoni is a tasty way to serve pasta. As both the sauce and stuffing can be made well in advance, the final dish takes a very short time to prepare.

4 SERVINGS

Spaghetti alla Carbonara

SPAGHETTI WITH BACON AND EGG SAUCE

One of the great Italian pasta dishes, Spaghetti alla Carbonara is superb served with a green salad and lots of red wine.

4-6 SERVINGS

1½ oz. [3 tablespoons] butter
 4 oz. lean bacon, rinds removed and chopped
 3 tablespoons double [heavy] cream
 3 eggs
 4 oz. [1 cup] Parmesan cheese, grated
 ½ teaspoon salt
 ¼ teaspoon black pepper
 1 lb. spaghetti, cooked for 10 to 12 minutes, drained and kept hot

In a small frying-pan, melt 1 tablespoon of the butter over moderate heat. When the foam subsides, add the bacon and cook, stirring occasionally, for 5 minutes or until it is crisp. Remove the pan from the heat and stir in the cream. Set aside.

In a medium-sized mixing bowl, beat the eggs and 2 ounces [½ cup] of the Parmesan cheese together with a fork until the mixture is smooth and the ingredients are well blended. Stir in the salt and pepper. Set aside.

Place the spaghetti in a large, deep serving bowl and add the remaining butter. Using two large spoons, toss the spaghetti until the butter has melted. Stir in the bacon mixture, tossing well. Finally, mix in the egg mixture, tossing and stirring until the spaghetti is well coated.

Serve at once, with the remaining grated cheese.

Spaghetti with Fennel Sauce

A fragrant mixture of fresh fennel, pine nuts, sultanas or seedless raisins and sardines combines to make this spaghetti a delicious dish.

4-6 SERVINGS

2 fl. oz. [¼ cup] olive oil
 1 large onion, finely chopped
 1 lb. canned sardines, drained
 1 lb. fresh fennel, cooked, drained and finely chopped
 1 tablespoon sultanas or seedless raisins
 1 tablespoon blanched white pine nuts
 8 fl. oz. [1 cup] dry white wine
 ½ teaspoon salt
 1 teaspoon black pepper
 1 lb. spaghetti, cooked for 10 to 12 minutes, drained and kept hot
 4 oz. [1⅓ cups] dry white breadcrumbs, toasted and kept warm

In a medium-sized frying-pan, heat the olive oil over moderate heat. When the oil is hot, add the onion and sardines and fry, stirring occasionally, for 8 to 10 minutes or until the onion is golden.

Stir in the fennel, sultanas or seedless raisins and pine nuts. Add the wine, salt and pepper and bring the liquid to the boil. Reduce the heat to moderately low and simmer the sauce for 10 minutes, stirring frequently.

Place the spaghetti in a large, deep serving dish and pour over half of the sauce. Sprinkle over half of the breadcrumbs and, using two large spoons, toss the mixture until the spaghetti is thoroughly coated. Pour over the remaining sauce and top with the remaining breadcrumbs. Serve immediately.

Spaghetti with Meatballs and Tomato Sauce

Strictly speaking, Spaghetti with Meatballs and Tomato Sauce is more Italian-American than true Italian, though the Italians do have a passion for meatballs! Nearly every Italian-American cook has her own version of this dish — the main variations being in the composition of the meatballs. This recipe lays no claim to being the one and true original, but it can — and does — lay claim to being absolutely delicious and incredibly easy to eat. Serve as a main course with tossed green salad, garlic bread and lots of red wine.

4 SERVINGS

1 lb. spaghetti, cooked for 10 to 12 minutes, drained and kept hot
 1 oz. [2 tablespoons] butter
 4 oz. [1 cup] Parmesan cheese, grated

MEATBALLS

2 thick slices crusty bread, crusts removed
 2 fl. oz. [¼ cup] milk
 2 lb. lean minced [ground] beef
 1 oz. [⅓ cup] fine dry breadcrumbs
 1 oz. [¼ cup] Parmesan cheese, grated
 1 egg, lightly beaten
 ½ teaspoon salt
 ½ teaspoon black pepper
 1 teaspoon dried thyme
 2 teaspoons grated lemon rind
 1 large garlic clove, crushed
 4 oz. [½ cup] butter

TOMATO SAUCE

2 oz. [¼ cup] butter
 1 large onion, finely chopped
 2 garlic cloves, crushed
 1½ lb. canned Italian plum tomatoes
 2½ oz. tomato purée
 ½ teaspoon salt
 ½ teaspoon freshly ground black pepper
 ½ teaspoon dried oregano

First make the meatballs. In a small bowl, soak the bread in the milk for 5 minutes, or until it has completely absorbed the liquid. Transfer the soaked bread to a large mixing bowl.

Add all the remaining meatball ingredients except the butter to the bowl and, using your hands, mix and knead the ingredients until they are well blended. Shape the mixture into about 30 walnut-sized balls. Place them on a baking sheet or aluminium foil and chill them in the refrigerator for 30 minutes.

Meanwhile, make the tomato sauce. In a large saucepan, melt the butter over moderate heat. When the foam subsides, add the onion and garlic and cook, stirring occasionally, for 5 to 7 minutes or until the onion is soft and translucent but not brown. Stir in the tomatoes with the can juice, the tomato purée, salt, pepper and oregano. Bring the liquid to the boil, stirring occasionally. Reduce the heat to low, cover the pan and simmer the sauce for 35 minutes.

Remove the meatballs from the refrigerator. In a large frying-pan, melt the butter over moderate heat. When the foam subsides, add the meatballs, a few at a time, and cook, carefully turning occasionally, for 6 to 8 minutes or until they are evenly browned. With a slotted spoon, remove the meatballs from the pan as they brown and set aside.

Carefully lower the meatballs into the tomato sauce and re-cover the pan. Continue to simmer for a further 20 to 30 minutes or until the meatballs are cooked.

Place the spaghetti in a large, deep serving dish and add the butter. Using two large spoons, toss the spaghetti until the butter has melted. Remove the pan containing the meatballs and sauce from the heat. Arrange the meatballs over the spaghetti, then pour over the sauce.

Sprinkle over half the Parmesan cheese and serve at once, with the remaining Parmesan cheese.

Serve immediately.

Three marvellous ways with spaghetti – Spaghetti alla Carbonara, Spaghetti with Meatballs and Tomato Sauce and Spaghetti with Fennel Sauce.

Sweet Noodle Pudding with Apples

A delightful but filling pudding, Sweet Noodle Pudding with Apples may be served with custard or cream.

4-6 SERVINGS

2 eggs, lightly beaten with 2
   tablespoons milk
2 tablespoons sugar
¼ teaspoon salt
¼ teaspoon ground cinnamon
¼ teaspoon ground mixed spice or
   allspice
2 large cooking apples, peeled,
   cored and grated
2 oz. [⅓ cup] raisins
12 oz. fine noodles, cooked and
   drained
1 oz. [2 tablespoons] butter, melted

Preheat the oven to moderate 350°F (Gas Mark 4, 180°C).

In a large mixing bowl, combine the egg mixture, sugar, salt, cinnamon, mixed spice or allspice, apples, raisins and noodles. With a wooden spoon, stir the noodle mixture until the ingredients are

Noodles are a very versatile food—as you can see from this warming, filling dessert, Sweet Noodle Pudding with Apples.

well mixed.

Spoon the noodle mixture into a deep ovenproof dish and pour over the melted butter.

Place the dish in the oven and bake for 45 minutes or until the pudding is firm to the touch and lightly browned on top.

Remove the dish from the oven and serve the pudding immediately.

Tagliarini with Chicken Livers

This delightful and economical pasta dish may be served either as a first course or as a main dish, accompanied by a mixed green salad.

4-6 SERVINGS

2 tablespoons olive oil
1 lb. chicken livers, chopped
2 garlic cloves, crushed

1 lb. canned tomatoes, drained
   and with 4 fl. oz. [½ cup] of the
   can juice reserved
1 teaspoon salt
½ teaspoon black pepper
½ teaspoon dried thyme
½ teaspoon dried basil
6 oz. shelled peas
1 lb. tagliarini, cooked for 10 to 12
   minutes and kept hot

In a flameproof casserole, heat the oil over moderate heat. Add the chicken livers and garlic and cook, stirring constantly, for 3 to 4 minutes or until the livers are lightly browned all over.

Add the tomatoes with the can juice, the salt, pepper, thyme and basil and bring the mixture to the boil, stirring. Reduce the heat to low and simmer for 30 minutes, stirring occasionally.

Add the peas and continue cooking, stirring occasionally, for a further 15 minutes. Remove the saucepan from the heat.

Place the tagliarini in a large serving bowl and pour over the sauce. Using two large spoons, toss the mixture until it is blended. Serve immediately.

Venetian Lasagne

☆ ☆　　①　　◫ ◫

This pasta dish is perfect for a family supper. It needs no accompaniment other than a tossed mixed salad and some Chianti wine.

6-8 SERVINGS

- 2 fl. oz. [¼ cup] olive oil
- 1 lb. green lasagne
- 24 fl. oz. [3 cups] béchamel sauce
- 6 oz. [1½ cups] Parmesan cheese, grated

FILLING

- 2 oz. [¼ cup] butter
- 2 medium-sized onions, finely chopped
- 1 lb. uncooked chicken meat, finely minced [ground]
- 1 lb. lean veal, finely minced [ground]
- 1 oz. [¼ cup] flour
- 10 fl. oz. [1¼ cups] home-made chicken stock
- 1 teaspoon grated nutmeg
- 1 teaspoon salt
- 1 teaspoon freshly ground black pepper
- 8 oz. mushrooms, wiped clean and sliced
- 1 lb. leaf spinach, cooked and drained

3 tablespoons single [light] cream

First prepare the filling. In a large saucepan, melt the butter over moderate heat. When the foam subsides, add the onions and fry, stirring occasionally, for 5 to 7 minutes or until they are soft and translucent but not brown. Add the minced [ground] chicken and veal to the pan and fry, stirring occasionally, for 5 to 8 minutes or until the meat is lightly and evenly browned.

Stir in the flour, chicken stock, nutmeg, salt and pepper. Increase the heat to high and bring the liquid to the boil. Reduce the heat to low and simmer for 30 minutes, stirring occasionally. Add the mushrooms and spinach and simmer for another 30 minutes. Stir in the cream and remove the pan from the heat. Set the mixture aside while you cook the pasta.

Meanwhile, half-fill a large saucepan with water and add half of the olive oil. Bring the liquid to the boil over high heat.

Venetian Lasagne is a sustaining mixture of pasta, minced [ground] meat, mushrooms and spinach. Serve, as here, with red wine and salad for a really special family treat.

Reduce the heat to moderately high. Add half the lasagne to the pan, sheet by sheet, and cook it for 12 to 15 minutes or until it is 'al dente' or just tender. When the pasta is cooked, remove it from the pan with a fish slice or tongs, being careful not to tear the sheets. Set the sheets aside.

Add the remaining olive oil to the pan and cook the remaining lasagne in the same way.

Preheat the oven to moderate 350°F (Gas Mark 4, 180°C).

To assemble the lasagne, in a large lightly greased ovenproof casserole, make a layer of pasta. Cover it with a layer of the filling and then with alternating layers of béchamel sauce and Parmesan cheese. Continue making alternate layers of pasta, filling, béchamel sauce and Parmesan cheese, ending with a layer of lasagne sprinkled liberally with Parmesan cheese.

Place the casserole in the centre of the oven and cook the lasagne for 45 minutes to 1 hour. Remove the casserole from the oven.

To serve, cut the lasagne into approximately 3-inch squares and use a fish slice or tongs to remove them from the casserole. Serve the lasagne squares immediately.

Lasagne

A mouth-watering adaptation of the traditional Italian recipe, Lasagne is not for the conscientious weight-watcher! It is, however, quite definitely for those who love the warm rich taste of pasta. Lasagne need be accompanied only by a tossed green salad and a good hearty red wine — Barolo would be particularly appropriate. Cottage cheese may be substituted for the ricotta cheese if liked.

6-8 SERVINGS

2 fl. oz. [¼ cup] olive oil
1 lb. lasagne
1 lb. Mozzarella cheese, thinly sliced
1 lb. ricotta cheese
4 oz. [1 cup] Parmesan cheese, grated

SAUCE

2 fl. oz. [¼ cup] olive oil
2 large onions, finely chopped
2 garlic cloves, finely chopped
2 lb. lean minced [ground] beef
15 fl. oz. [1⅞ cups] tomato sauce (not tomato ketchup)
22 oz. canned peeled Italian tomatoes
2½ oz. tomato purée
4 fl. oz. [½ cup] water
1½ teaspoons salt
1 teaspoon black pepper
2 teaspoons sugar
1 teaspoon dried basil
2 bay leaves
8 oz. mushrooms, wiped clean and sliced

First, prepare the sauce. In a very large saucepan, heat the olive oil over moderate heat. When the oil is hot, add the onions and garlic and fry, stirring occasionally, for 5 to 7 minutes, or until the onions are soft and translucent but not brown. Add the beef to the pan and cook it for 5 to 8 minutes, stirring occasionally with a metal spoon, or until it is lightly and evenly browned.

Stir in the tomato sauce, tomatoes with the can juices, tomato purée, water, salt, pepper, sugar, basil and bay leaves. Bring the sauce to the boil. Reduce the heat to low and simmer the sauce for 2 hours, stirring occasionally.

Add the mushrooms and simmer for another hour.

Remove the pan from the heat and allow the sauce to cool to room temperature. With a metal spoon, skim off the fat from the surface of the sauce and discard the bay leaves. Transfer the sauce to a covered container and place it in the refrigerator overnight or until you are ready to assemble the lasagne.

Half fill a large saucepan with water and add half the olive oil. Bring the water to the boil over high heat. Add half of the lasagne to the pan, sheet by sheet, and cook it for 12 to 15 minutes, or until it is 'al dente' or just tender. When the pasta is cooked, remove it from the pan with a fish slice or tongs, being careful not to tear the sheets.

Add the remaining olive oil to the pan and cook the remaining lasagne in the same way. (The oil prevents the sheets of pasta from sticking together.)

Preheat the oven to moderate 350°F (Gas Mark 4, 180°C).

To assemble the lasagne, in a large ovenproof casserole make a layer of pasta. Cover it with a layer of meat sauce and then with alternating layers of mozzarella, ricotta and Parmesan cheese. Add another layer of pasta, then meat sauce and cheese. Continue adding alternative layers, ending with a layer of pasta sprinkled liberally with the Parmesan cheese.

Place the casserole in the oven and bake the lasagne for 1 hour. Remove the casserole from the oven.

To serve, cut the lasagne into 3-inch squares and use a fish slice to remove the portions from the casserole. Serve the lasagne squares immediately.

Mushroom and Bacon Lasagne

This is a more economical version of lasagne, since it requires only a little meat and omits some of the more expensive Italian cheeses used in the traditional recipe. It is marvellous, nevertheless — make a wonderful informal dinner by serving it with a mixed green salad and lots of smooth Chianti wine.

4 SERVINGS

3 tablespoons olive oil
6 oz. lasagne
15 fl. oz. double cream [1⅞ cups heavy cream], beaten until thick
4 oz. [1 cup] Parmesan cheese, grated

SAUCE

2 fl. oz. [¼ cup] vegetable oil
1 medium-sized onion, thinly sliced
1 garlic clove, crushed
1 carrot, scraped and chopped
1 celery stalk, trimmed and chopped
3 slices streaky bacon, rinds removed and chopped
6 oz. mushrooms, wiped clean and sliced
8 oz. lean beef, minced [ground]
¼ teaspoon dried oregano
¼ teaspoon dried basil

1 teaspoon salt
¼ teaspoon freshly ground black pepper
14 oz. canned peeled Italian tomatoes
3 tablespoons tomato purée
3 tablespoons single [light] cream

To prepare the sauce, in a large saucepan, heat the vegetable oil over moderate heat. When the oil is hot, add the onion, garlic, carrot and celery to the pan and cook, stirring occasionally, for 5 to 7 minutes, or until the onion is soft and translucent but not brown. Add the bacon and mushrooms and cook, stirring occasionally, for 5 minutes.

Add the meat to the pan and cook, stirring constantly, for 8 to 10 minutes, or until the meat is well browned. Stir in the oregano, basil, salt, pepper, tomatoes with the can juice and the tomato purée, mixing until the ingredients are well blended.

Reduce the heat to low, cover the pan and simmer the sauce, stirring occasionally, for 1 hour. If after an hour, the mixture is very liquid, remove the lid from the pan, increase the heat to moderate and cook for a further 15 minutes to evaporate

Lasagne, a rich mixture of pasta, meat, tomato sauce and cheese, makes the perfect dish for informal entertaining.

the excess liquid. Stir the cream into the sauce and remove the pan from the heat. Set aside.

Half fill a large saucepan with water and add 1 tablespoon of the olive oil. Bring the water to the boil over high heat. Add half the lasagne to the pan, sheet by sheet, and cook it for 12 to 15 minutes or until it is 'al dente' or just tender. When the pasta is done, remove it from the pan with a fish slice or tongs, being careful not to tear the sheets.

Add 1 tablespoon of the olive oil to the pan and cook the remaining lasagne in the same way. (The oil prevents the sheets of pasta from sticking together.)

Preheat the oven to moderate 350°F (Gas Mark 4, 180°C) and with a pastry brush, lightly brush a 2½-pound loaf tin with the remaining oil.

Place about one-third of the meat sauce mixture on the bottom of the tin. Pour over about one-third of the cream, then sprinkle over about one-quarter of the Parmesan cheese. Cover the mixture with a layer of one-third of the lasagne. Repeat these layers until all the ingredients are used up, finishing with a layer of Parmesan cheese.

Place the tin in the oven and cook for 40 minutes, or until the top is brown and bubbly. Remove the tin from the oven and cut into squares.

Serve at once.

Spinach Lasagne

With the substitution of spinach for meat, this version of lasagne makes a spicy and rich vegetarian meal. Serve it with a tomato and cucumber salad, lots of crusty bread and some well-chilled light white wine — a Toscano Bianco or a Frascati, for instance.

4-6 SERVINGS

2 tablespoons olive oil
6 oz. lasagne
3 lb. spinach, cooked
12 oz. Mozzarella cheese, thinly sliced
4 oz. [1 cup] Parmesan cheese, grated
SAUCE
2 fl. oz. [¼ cup] olive oil
2 medium-sized onions, thinly sliced
2 garlic cloves, crushed
4 oz. mushrooms, wiped clean and thinly sliced
1½ lb. canned peeled Italian tomatoes
2½ oz. tomato purée
1 teaspoon dried basil
½ teaspoon red pepper flakes
1 teaspoon salt
½ teaspoon freshly ground black pepper

First, prepare the sauce. In a medium-sized saucepan, heat the olive oil over moderate heat. When the oil is hot, add the onions and garlic and cook them, stirring occasionally, for 5 to 7 minutes, or until the onions are soft and translucent but not brown. Add the mushrooms to the pan and cook, stirring occasionally, for 3 to 5 minutes or until they are just tender.

Add the tomatoes with the can juice, the tomato purée, basil, red pepper flakes, salt and pepper and mix well to blend. Bring the liquid to the boil over moderately high heat, reduce the heat to low and simmer the sauce, stirring occasionally, for 40 minutes. Remove the pan from the heat and set aside while you cook the pasta.

Half fill a large saucepan with water and add 1 tablespoon of olive oil. Bring the water to the boil over high heat. Add half the lasagne to the pan, sheet by sheet, and cook it for 12 to 15 minutes or until it is 'al dente' or just tender. When the pasta is cooked, remove it from the pan with a fish slice or tongs, being careful not to tear the sheets.

Add the remaining olive oil to the pan and cook the remaining lasagne in the same way. (The oil prevents the sheets of pasta from sticking together.)

Preheat the oven to fairly hot 375°F (Gas Mark 5, 190°C).

Place one-third of the lasagne on the bottom of a medium-sized ovenproof casserole. Spread over half the cooked spinach and cover with half the mozzarella cheese. Pour over half of the tomato sauce and sprinkle over one-third of the Parmesan cheese. Continue to make layers in the same way until all the ingredients are used up, ending with a layer of lasagne sprinkled over with Parmesan cheese.

Place the casserole in the oven and bake the lasagne for 45 minutes. Remove the casserole from the oven and cut the lasagne into 3-inch squares.

Serve at once.

Paglia e Fieno

PASTA WITH VEAL AND MUSHROOMS

Paglia e Fieno means literally 'straw and hay'. It is a rich dish which needs only a lightly tossed green salad and some garlic bread to make a delicious and sustaining supper for family or guests.

4-6 SERVINGS

2 oz. [¼ cup] plus 1 tablespoon butter
1 small onion, chopped
6 lean bacon slices, chopped
8 oz. veal, finely minced [ground]
½ teaspoon salt
¼ teaspoon black pepper
⅛ teaspoon dried oregano
1 lb. button mushrooms, wiped clean and sliced
8 fl. oz. single cream [1 cup light cream]
2 tablespoons finely chopped fresh parsley
6 oz. egg noodles, cooked for 5 to 8 minutes, drained and kept hot
6 oz. green egg noodles, cooked for 5 to 8 minutes, drained and kept hot
2 oz. [½ cup] Parmesan cheese, grated

In a medium-sized frying-pan, melt the 2 ounces [¼ cup] of butter over moderate heat. When the foam subsides, add the onion and bacon and cook, stirring occasionally, for 5 to 7 minutes or until the onion is soft and translucent but not brown.

Add the veal and cook, stirring constantly, for 5 minutes or until the veal is well browned. Stir in the salt, pepper, oregano and mushrooms and cook, stirring occasionally, for a further 5 minutes or until the mushrooms are tender.

Add the cream and parsley and stir well. Reduce the heat to low and cook the mixture, stirring occasionally, for a further 3 to 5 minutes or until it is hot but not boiling. Remove from the heat.

Colourful Pasta, Sausage and Bean Salad makes a nutritious 'scratch' meal. Serve with lots of red wine and crusty bread.

Place the noodles in a large serving dish. Add the remaining butter and, using two large spoons, toss the noodles.

Pour over the veal and mushroom mixture. Toss well and serve immediately, with the grated Parmesan cheese.

Pasta, Sausage and Bean Salad

An unusual and filling dish, Pasta, Sausage and Bean Salad is ideal to serve if unexpected guests drop in for supper (providing you have a well-stocked larder!) Lots of crusty French bread and butter and a bottle of red wine would be the ideal accompaniments.

6 SERVINGS

14 oz. canned French beans, halved and drained
4 tomatoes, sliced
8 oz. pork luncheon meat, diced
2 medium-sized onions, sliced and pushed out into rings
14 oz. canned red kidney beans, drained

8 frankfurter sausages, cooked,
  drained, cooled and cut into
  ½-inch lengths
4 oz. [1 cup] black olives
8 oz. pasta shells, cooked, drained
  and cooled
1 small chorizo sausage, thinly
  sliced
½ cucumber, peeled and thinly
  sliced
4 oz. beetroots [beets], cooked,
  peeled and sliced
4 tablespoons chopped mustard
  and cress

DRESSING
1 teaspoon sugar
1 teaspoon salt
½ teaspoon black pepper
1 teaspoon prepared French
  mustard
1 garlic clove, crushed
2 fl. oz. [¼ cup] red wine vinegar
8 fl. oz. [1 cup] olive oil

Arrange the French beans in the bottom
of a large salad bowl. Place the sliced
tomatoes around the side of the bowl.
Continue making layers with the luncheon
meat, one of the onions, the kidney
beans, frankfurter sausages, olives and
half of the pasta shells. Cover the pasta
shells with the remaining onion rings, the
chorizo sausage, cucumber and beetroots
[beets]. Cover the beetroots [beets] with
the remaining pasta shells and the
mustard and cress. Set aside.

In a small mixing bowl, combine all
the dressing ingredients. Using a fork,
beat the ingredients together until they
are thoroughly combined.

Pour the dressing over the salad and
serve immediately.

Sweetbreads with Pasta

*This unusual and appetizing dish of sweet-
breads and pasta may be served with
grilled [broiled] tomatoes.*

2-3 SERVINGS

1 lb. sweetbreads, soaked in cold
  water for 3 hours, drained,
  skinned and trimmed
2 oz. [½ cup] seasoned flour, made
  with 2 oz. [½ cup] flour, ½ teaspoon
  salt, ¼ teaspoon freshly ground
  black pepper and ½ teaspoon dried
  marjoram
2 oz. [¼ cup] butter
3 medium-sized carrots, scraped
  and thinly sliced
1 teaspoon dried thyme
1 bay leaf
4 fl. oz. [½ cup] Madeira
8 oz. macaroni, or other pasta,
  cooked and kept hot

Place the sweetbreads in a large saucepan
and cover them with water. Place the pan
over moderately high heat and bring the
water to the boil. Remove the pan from

*The unusual combination of taste
and texture in Sweetbreads with
Pasta makes it an exciting dish.*

the heat and set the sweetbreads aside for
10 minutes.

Using a slotted spoon, remove the
sweetbreads from the pan and drain them
on kitchen paper towels. Discard the
water. Place the sweetbreads on a board
and cut them into ½-inch slices.

Put the seasoned flour on a plate. Dip
the sweetbread slices in the flour, coating
them thoroughly and shaking off any
excess. Set aside.

In a large frying-pan, melt the butter
over moderate heat. When the foam subsides, add the sweetbread slices and fry,
turning occasionally, for 10 to 15 minutes
or until they are lightly and evenly
browned.

Using a slotted spoon, transfer the
sweetbread slices to a plate and keep
them hot.

Add the carrots, thyme, bay leaf and
Madeira to the pan. Cook for 5 minutes,
stirring frequently.

Add the macaroni to the pan, stirring
until it is thoroughly coated with the
sauce.

Remove the pan from the heat. Remove
and discard the bay leaf. Spoon the
mixture into a warmed serving dish.
Arrange the sweetbread slices over the
top and serve at once.

How to fill and cook Ravioli

  ①

Cut the 2 sheets of dough into circles with a 2-inch round, fluted pastry cutter. Using a teaspoon, place a portion of the filling mixture to be used in the centre of half of the dough circles. Using a pastry brush, draw a circle around the edge of each dough circle with a liberal quantity of water. Place the remaining dough circles on top of the filled dough circles and press firmly with your fingers around the edges to seal.

Cut the pasta sheets into rounds with a pastry cutter.

Place 1 teaspoon of the filling over half of the pasta rounds.

Moisten with water, place the remaining pasta rounds on top and seal.

To cook the ravioli, in a large saucepan, bring 3 to 4 pints [7½ to 10 cups] of water to the boil over high heat. Drop the ravioli into the boiling water and cook them, stirring occasionally with a wooden spoon, for 8 to 10 minutes or until the pasta is 'al dente' or just tender. With a slotted spoon, remove the ravioli from the pan and place them on a dampened cloth to drain.

Serve at once.

Ravioli di Manzo e Spinace

RAVIOLI FILLED WITH VEAL AND SPINACH WITH TOMATO SAUCE

 ① ①

This delicious Italian dish is worth the time it takes to prepare. It makes a tasty and filling lunch or supper dish. For special occasions, serve it with a tossed mixed salad and lots of mellow Bardolino wine.

3-4 SERVINGS

SAUCE
2 tablespoons olive oil
1 medium-sized onion, finely chopped
2 lb. fresh tomatoes, blanched, peeled, seeded and chopped
14 oz. canned peeled Italian tomatoes
2½ oz. tomato purée
½ teaspoon dried basil
½ teaspoon dried oregano
1 teaspoon sugar
½ teaspoon salt
½ teaspoon freshly ground black pepper

FILLING
1 tablespoon butter
1½ tablespoons olive oil
1 small onion, finely chopped
2 garlic cloves, crushed
8 oz. lean veal, finely minced [ground]
6 oz. fresh spinach, cooked, drained and finely chopped
1 oz. [¼ cup] Parmesan cheese, finely grated
1 tablespoon double [heavy] cream
2 eggs, well beaten
¼ teaspoon grated nutmeg
¼ teaspoon salt
¼ teaspoon freshly ground black pepper

PASTA
8 oz. bought ravioli pasta, rolled out into 2 thin sheets

GARNISH
2 oz. [½ cup] Pecorino cheese, grated
1 tablespoon finely chopped fresh parsley

First make the tomato sauce. In a

Ravioli di Manzo e Spinace is a marvellous mixture of ravioli pasta filled with veal and spinach in a tomato sauce.

medium-sized saucepan, heat the oil over moderate heat. When the oil is hot, add the onion and fry, stirring occasionally, for 5 to 7 minutes or until it is soft and translucent but not brown. Stir in the fresh and canned tomatoes with the can juice, the tomato purée, basil, oregano,

sugar, salt and pepper, and bring to the boil. Reduce the heat to low, cover the pan and simmer the sauce, stirring occasionally, for 40 minutes or until it is very thick. Set aside.

Meanwhile, make the filling. In a large frying-pan, melt the butter with the oil over moderate heat. When the foam subsides, add the onion and garlic and fry, stirring occasionally, for 5 to 7 minutes or until the onion is soft and translucent but not brown. Add the meat to the pan and cook, stirring occasionally, for 8 to 10 minutes or until it is lightly browned. Add the spinach and, stirring frequently, cook for 5 to 8 minutes or until the juices have evaporated.

Remove the pan from the heat and transfer the meat and spinach mixture to a medium-sized bowl. Add the Parmesan, cream, eggs, nutmeg, salt and pepper and stir well to mix. The filling is now ready to use.

Fill, cook and drain the ravioli according to the instructions given in column one.

Preheat the grill [broiler] to moderately high.

Transfer the cooked ravioli to a warmed, flameproof serving dish and pour over the tomato sauce.

Sprinkle the Pecorino cheese over the tomato sauce and place the dish under the grill [broiler]. Grill [broil] for 5 minutes or until the cheese has melted and is golden.

Remove the dish from the heat, sprinkle over the parsley and serve the ravioli immediately.

119

Ravioli Piedmontese

RAVIOLI FILLED WITH BEEF AND
TOMATOES

*Ravioli Piedmontese is a very popular first
course to an Italian meal.*

6 SERVINGS

FILLING

2 oz. [¼ cup] butter
1 tablespoon vegetable oil
1 large onion, finely chopped
1 garlic clove, crushed
12 oz. lean beef, finely minced
    [ground]
8 fl. oz. [1 cup] beef stock
¼ teaspoon salt
½ teaspoon black pepper
8 oz. canned peeled tomatoes,
    coarsely chopped
1 teaspoon dried rosemary
½ teaspoon dried basil
2 oz. [½ cup] Parmesan cheese,
    finely grated

2 eggs, well beaten
PASTA
8 oz. bought ravioli pasta, rolled out
    into 2 thin sheets

To make the filling, in a large frying-pan,
melt the butter with the oil over moderate
heat. When the foam subsides, add the
onion and garlic and fry, stirring occasionally, for 8 to 10 minutes or until the
onion is golden brown. Add the beef and
fry, stirring occasionally, for 8 minutes
or until the meat is lightly browned.

Pour in the stock, and add the salt,
pepper, tomatoes with the can juice,
rosemary and basil to the beef. Cook the
mixture, stirring frequently, for 10
minutes or until the meat is cooked.

Remove the pan from the heat and
strain the contents through a fine wire
strainer held over a small saucepan. Set
the cooking liquid aside.

Put the contents of the strainer into a
mixing bowl. Add the Parmesan cheese

and eggs and stir the mixture until it is
thoroughly combined. The filling is now
ready to use.

Fill, cook and drain the ravioli according to the instructions given in column
one, page 54. While the ravioli is cooking,
heat the reserved cooking liquid over
moderate heat, stirring occasionally.

Transfer the drained ravioli to a
warmed serving dish, pour over the
cooking liquid and serve immediately.

Ravioli di Pisa

RAVIOLI FILLED WITH CHEESE,
SPINACH AND EGG WITH WALNUT SAUCE

*Ravioli di Pisa is a popular regional dish of
Italy.*

**Ravioli Piedmontese is pasta filled
with a beef and tomato mixture.**

SAUCE

6 oz. [1⅓ cups] walnuts, chopped

2 oz. [½ cup] cashew nuts, chopped

½ teaspoon dried oregano

¼ teaspoon salt

1 tablespoon water

4 oz. ricotta cheese

3 tablespoons olive oil

6 tablespoons single [light] cream

2 oz. [½ cup] Pecorino cheese, finely grated

4 fl. oz. [½ cup] milk

FILLING

2 oz. [¼ cup] butter

4 oz. fresh spinach, cooked, drained and finely chopped or 4 oz. frozen spinach, thawed and chopped

6 oz. ricotta cheese

2 hard-boiled eggs, chopped

¼ teaspoon salt

½ teaspoon black pepper

¼ teaspoon grated nutmeg

⅛ teaspoon ground saffron

PASTA

12 oz. bought ravioli pasta, rolled out into 2 thin sheets

First make the sauce. Place the walnuts, cashew nuts, oregano, salt and water in a mortar or small bowl. Using a pestle or fork, mash the ingredients to a smooth paste. Add the ricotta, olive oil and cream to the mixture and continue to mash until the mixture has a creamy texture. Stir in the Pecorino cheese and milk and transfer the mixture to a medium-sized saucepan.

Alternatively, blend the ingredients together in an electric blender. Place the pan over low heat and gently heat the sauce, stirring occasionally, until it is hot but not boiling. Remove the pan from the heat. Set aside and keep warm.

To make the filling, in a frying-pan melt the butter over moderate heat. When the foam subsides, add the spinach and cook for 4 minutes. Transfer the spinach to a plate. Set aside.

Put the ricotta in a bowl and mash it until it is smooth. Add the reserved spinach, eggs, salt, pepper, nutmeg and saffron and stir well to mix. The filling is now ready to use.

Fill, cook and drain the ravioli according to the instructions given in column one, page 54. Reheat the walnut sauce until it is hot. Transfer the ravioli to a warmed serving dish and pour over the walnut sauce. Stir them gently together and serve.

Ravioli di Pisa is pasta filled with a cheese mixture in walnut sauce.

Polish Ravioli

These little crescent shaped pasta, filled with a variety of sweet and savoury stuffings are the Polish version of ravioli. Serve them with a butter and breadcrumb sauce, as a first course, or with salad as a light meal.

4-6 SERVINGS

PASTA

12 oz. [3 cups] flour

1 teaspoon salt

3 large eggs, lightly beaten

2 to 3 tablespoons lukewarm water

FILLING

1 oz. [2 tablespoons] butter

1 onion, finely grated

1 lb. cream cheese

2 large egg yolks, beaten

½ teaspoon salt

¼ teaspoon black pepper

GLAZE

1 egg, beaten

1 teaspoon lukewarm water

First make the pasta. Sift the flour and salt into a mixing bowl. Make a well in the centre of the flour and pour in the lightly beaten eggs and water. With your fingertips, draw the flour into the liquid, until all the flour has been incorporated and the mixture forms a stiff dough.

Turn the dough out on to a lightly floured board and knead it for 10 minutes or until it is smooth but stiff.

Divide the dough in two and roll each piece out into a very thin sheet, pulling it with your hands into a rectangle.

Cover the sheets with a damp cloth and leave to rest for 30 minutes.

Meanwhile, prepare the filling. In a small frying-pan, melt the butter over moderate heat. When the foam subsides, add the grated onion and fry, stirring constantly, for 5 to 7 minutes, or until it is soft and translucent but not brown. Remove the pan from the heat and tip the contents into a mixing bowl.

Add the cream cheese to the onion and mix the ingredients well. Gradually beat in the egg yolks and salt and pepper until the mixture is smooth and creamy.

Uncover the dough sheets and, with a 3-inch pastry cutter, cut the dough into circles. Place one teaspoon of filling in the centre of each circle.

Combine the egg and the water for the glaze. Moisten the edges of the circles with this mixture. Fold the dough over the fillings to form semi-circles, and seal the edges by pressing them together.

In a large saucepan, bring 4 pints [5 pints] of salted water to the boil over high heat. Drop the circles into the water, cover and cook them for 6 to 15 minutes, depending on the thickness of the pasta, or until they are tender.

Remove the pan from the heat and drain the pasta in a colander. Transfer them to a warmed serving dish and serve.

Ravioli con Pollo

RAVIOLI FILLED WITH CHICKEN

Served with grated Parmesan cheese, this dish makes a delicious first course for an Italian meal or, accompanied by garlic bread and a full-bodied red wine, a filling main course.

2-4 SERVINGS

8 oz. bought ravioli pasta, rolled out into 2 thin sheets

SAUCE

2 tablespoons olive oil

1 small onion, finely chopped

1 garlic clove, finely chopped

1 celery stalk, trimmed and finely chopped

2 lb. canned peeled tomatoes, drained

1 teaspoon dried oregano

2 fl. oz. [¼ cup] red wine

¼ teaspoon salt

¼ teaspoon black pepper

FILLING

8 oz. cooked chicken meat, finely chopped

1 tablespoon grated Parmesan cheese

1 egg yolk, lightly beaten

⅛ teaspoon grated lemon rind

⅛ teaspoon grated nutmeg

⅛ teaspoon salt

⅛ teaspoon black pepper

First, make the sauce. In a medium-sized saucepan, heat the oil over moderate heat. When the oil is hot, add the onion, garlic and celery and fry, stirring occasionally, for 5 to 7 minutes or until the onion is soft and translucent but not brown.

Stir in the tomatoes, oregano, wine, salt and pepper and bring the mixture to the boil, stirring constantly. Reduce the heat to low and simmer the sauce for 40 minutes, stirring occasionally.

Meanwhile, place all the filling ingredients in a large mixing bowl and blend well with a wooden spoon. Set aside.

With a 2-inch round, fluted pastry cutter, cut the pasta dough into circles. Place half a teaspoon of the filling in the centre of each dough circle.

Using a pastry brush, moisten the edge of each dough circle with a liberal quantity of water. Fold the circles over to form semi-circles and press firmly around the edges to seal. Moisten the points of the ends of each semi-circle with a little water and press them together. Set aside.

In a large saucepan, bring about 4 pints

Ravioli con Pollo is pasta filled with chicken in a tomato sauce. Serve as a first or main course.

[5 pints] of water to the boil over high heat. Drop the pasta shapes into the boiling water and cook them, stirring occasionally with a wooden spoon, for 8 to 10 minutes or until the pasta is 'al dente' or just tender and they float to the top of the water.

With a slotted spoon, remove the pasta shapes from the pan and place them on a dampened cloth to drain.

Transfer the ravioli to a warmed serving dish and pour over the sauce. Serve immediately.

Rice Noodles with Pork and Prawns or Shrimps

An adaptation of a Thai dish, Rice Noodles with Pork and Prawns or Shrimps makes a simple one-dish meal or it may be served as part of a Thai meal. Traditionally, fish sauce, a salty mixture of crushed fermenting fish and salt is added to or served with many Thai dishes. Because fish sauce is not

always acceptable to Western taste soy sauce is suggested in its place. Rice noodles are available at Chinese delicatessens.

4-6 SERVINGS

1¼ teaspoons salt
1 lb. rice noodles
6 dried mushrooms, soaked in cold water for 20 minutes
4 tablespoons peanut oil
12 oz. pork fillets, cut into strips
8 oz. prawns or shrimps, shelled and weighed after shelling
6 spring onions [scallions], trimmed and finely sliced
1 garlic clove, crushed
½ teaspoon sugar
2 tablespoons fish sauce or soy sauce
1 tablespoon chopped fresh coriander leaves

Half-fill a large saucepan with water and add 1 teaspoon of salt. Set the pan over moderate heat and bring the water to the boil. Add the noodles and boil for 5 minutes. Drain the noodles and pour over 8 fluid ounces [1 cup] of cold water. Drain again. Place the drained noodles in a warmed serving dish and keep warm.

Remove the mushrooms from the water. Squeeze them dry and remove and discard the stems. Slice the mushrooms and set aside.

In a large frying-pan or wok, heat the oil over high heat. When the oil is very hot, reduce the heat to moderate. Add the pork strips and fry, stirring and turning constantly, for 2 to 3 minutes or until they are tender. Add the prawns or shrimps and fry, stirring constantly, for 2 to 3 minutes or until they turn pink. Add the spring onions [scallions], garlic and mushrooms and fry, stirring constantly, for 2 minutes. Stir in the sugar, fish or soy sauce and the remaining salt. Remove the pan from the heat.

Spoon the pork and prawn or shrimp mixture over the noodles. Garnish with the coriander leaves and serve.

Spaghetti all' Amatriciana
SPAGHETTI WITH BACON IN TOMATO SAUCE

A sumptuous Roman recipe, Spaghetti all' Amatriciana may be served with a mixed salad, crusty bread and wine.

4-6 SERVINGS

2 tablespoons olive oil
1 large onion, thinly sliced
2 garlic cloves, crushed
6 lean bacon slices, diced
2 fl. oz. [¼ cup] dry white wine
1 lb. canned peeled tomatoes, drained
½ teaspoon salt
1 teaspoon black pepper
½ teaspoon dried oregano
1 lb. spaghetti, cooked for 10 to 12 minutes, drained and kept hot
4 oz. [1 cup] Pecorino or Parmesan cheese, grated

In a saucepan, heat the oil over moderate heat. When the oil is hot, add the onion and garlic and fry, stirring occasionally, for 5 to 7 minutes or until the onion is soft and translucent but not brown.

Stir in the bacon and cook for a further 4 minutes, stirring constantly. Add the wine and bring the liquid to the boil. Boil rapidly for 2 minutes, then add the tomatoes. Stir in the salt, pepper and oregano and bring the liquid to the boil again.

Reduce the heat to moderately low and continue cooking for a further 15 minutes, stirring occasionally. Remove the pan from the heat.

Place the spaghetti in a large, deep serving dish and pour over the sauce. Using two large spoons, toss the mixture until the spaghetti is thoroughly coated with the sauce.

Sprinkle over the grated cheese and serve immediately.

Exotic Rice Noodles with Pork and Prawns or Shrimps from Thailand.

Spaghetti with Crabmeat

This is a pasta dish with a difference, since the crabmeat gives the spaghetti a rather exotic flavour. Serve it for a special dinner with a tossed green salad and, to drink, some well-chilled white Vouvray wine.

4 SERVINGS

2 oz. [¼ cup] butter

2 medium-sized onions, finely chopped

8 oz. mushrooms, wiped clean and sliced

8 oz. spaghetti, cooked for 10 to 12 minutes, drained and kept hot

8 oz. crabmeat, shell and cartilage removed

10 oz. canned condensed tomato soup

1 teaspoon salt

½ teaspoon black pepper

6 oz. [1½ cups] Parmesan cheese, grated

10 fl. oz. [1¼ cups] tomato juice

With 2 teaspoons of the butter, grease a

The perfect dish for a hungry family or friends—Tagliatelli Verdi with Bacon and Tomatoes. Serve with salad and crusty bread.

large, ovenproof casserole.

Preheat the oven to moderate 350°F (Gas Mark 4, 180°C).

In a medium-sized frying-pan, melt the remaining butter over moderate heat. When the foam subsides, add the onions and fry, stirring occasionally, for 4 minutes. Add the mushrooms and fry for a further 1 to 3 minutes or until the onions are soft and translucent but not brown. Remove the pan from the heat and set aside.

In a large mixing bowl, combine the mushroom and onion mixture with the spaghetti, crabmeat, soup, salt, pepper and 4 ounces [1 cup] of the cheese. Stir well to mix thoroughly, then pour in the tomato juice. Transfer the mixture to the prepared casserole and sprinkle over the remaining cheese.

Place the casserole in the oven and cook for 35 to 40 minutes or until the cheese is golden and bubbling.

Remove the casserole from the oven and serve at once.

Spaghetti con le Vongole
SPAGHETTI WITH CLAM SAUCE

Spaghetti con le Vongole is a delicious pasta dish from the Naples area. If clams are unobtainable, cockles or mussels may be substituted. Serve Spaghetti con le Vongole as a special light supper dish, accompanied by crusty bread and some well-chilled white wine.

4-6 SERVINGS

3 tablespoons olive oil

2 garlic cloves, crushed

1 tablespoon capers, finely chopped

1 medium-sized onion, finely chopped

1 lb. canned peeled tomatoes, drained

¼ teaspoon salt

½ teaspoon white pepper

1 teaspoon finely chopped fresh basil or ½ teaspoon dried basil

1 lb. canned clams, drained and chopped

1 tablespoon finely chopped fresh
 parsley
1 lb. spaghetti, cooked for 10 to
 12 minutes, drained and kept
 hot
1 lemon, quartered

In a medium-sized saucepan, heat the oil over moderate heat. When the oil is hot, add the garlic, capers and onion and fry, stirring occasionally, for 5 to 7 minutes or until the onion is soft and translucent but not brown.

Stir in the tomatoes, salt, pepper and basil and bring the mixture to the boil, stirring constantly. Reduce the heat to low, cover the pan and simmer, stirring occasionally, for a further 30 minutes. Add the clams and the parsley and cook for a further 5 minutes or until the clams are heated through. Remove the pan from the heat.

Place the spaghetti in a large, deep serving dish and pour over the sauce. Using two large spoons, toss quickly until the spaghetti is thoroughly coated with the sauce.

Garnish with the lemon quarters and serve immediately.

Tagliatelli con Prosciutto

RIBBON PASTA WITH HAM

Tagiatelli con Prosciutto is a simple and delightful dish to serve either as a first or main course. Accompany it with plenty of hot garlic bread, a tossed, mixed green salad and lots of well-chilled white wine such as Soave.

4-6 SERVINGS

6 oz. [¾ cup] butter
12 oz. prosciutto, cut into 2-inch
 strips
1 lb. tagliatelli, cooked for 8 to
 10 minutes, drained and kept
 hot
6 oz. [1½ cups] Parmesan cheese,
 grated

In a medium-sized frying-pan, melt the butter over moderate heat. When the foam subsides, add the prosciutto and cook, stirring constantly, for 5 to 7 minutes or until it has heated through. Remove the pan from the heat and set it aside.

Place the tagliatelli in a large serving bowl and add the prosciutto and the butter remaining in the pan. Using two large spoons, toss the mixture until all the tagliatelli strands are thoroughly coated with the butter.

Sprinkle over the cheese and serve immediately.

Tagliatelli Verdi with Bacon and Tomatoes

This easy-to-make and inexpensive dish may be served as a first course or, with a tossed mixed green salad and crusty bread, as a scrumptious main course for lunch or supper.

4-6 SERVINGS

1 oz. [2 tablespoons] plus 1 teaspoon
 butter
8 streaky bacon slices, rinds
 removed and very coarsely
 chopped
1 medium-sized onion, finely
 chopped
2 large garlic cloves, finely
 crushed
8 oz. small button mushrooms,
 wiped clean and halved
6 medium-sized tomatoes,
 blanched, peeled and coarsely
 chopped
1½ teaspoons salt
1 teaspoon freshly ground black
 pepper
1 tablespoon finely chopped fresh
 tarragon or 1½ teaspoons dried
 tarragon
1 teaspoon chopped fresh oregano
 or ½ teaspoon dried oregano
10 fl. oz. [1¼ cups] béchamel sauce
4 fl. oz. double cream [½ cup heavy
 cream]
4 oz. [1 cup] Parmesan cheese,
 grated
1 lb. tagliatelli verdi, cooked
 for 8 to 10 minutes, drained
 and kept hot
3 tablespoons dry white
 breadcrumbs
1 tablespoon melted butter

Preheat the oven to fairly hot 375°F (Gas Mark 5, 190°C). Using the teaspoon of butter, grease a large, deep-sided baking dish and set it aside.

In a large, heavy-based saucepan, fry the bacon over moderately high heat for 6 to 8 minutes or until it has rendered all of its fat. Scrape the bottom of the pan frequently with a spatula to prevent the bacon from sticking.

Using a slotted spoon, remove the bacon from the pan and set it aside on a plate. Add the remaining butter to the pan and reduce the heat to moderate. When the foam subsides, add the onion and garlic and fry, stirring occasionally, for 8 to 10 minutes or until the onion is golden brown. Add the mushrooms and fry, stirring frequently, for 3 minutes. Stir in the chopped tomatoes, salt, pepper, tarragon, oregano, béchamel sauce, cream, and 3 ounces [¾ cup] of the Parmesan

cheese. Cook the mixture, stirring constantly, for 3 minutes.

Remove the pan from the heat and add the reserved bacon and the tagliatelli to the mixture. Using two large spoons, stir well to coat the mixture thoroughly with the sauce.

Spoon the mixture into the prepared baking dish and set aside.

In a small mixing bowl, combine the remaining cheese with the breadcrumbs and melted butter. Sprinkle the mixture over the tagliatelli mixture and place the dish in the centre of the oven. Bake for 30 minutes or until the top is deep golden brown.

Remove the dish from the oven and serve the tagliatelli immediately, straight from the dish.

Tagliatelli Verdi con Salsa di Tonno

GREEN RIBBON PASTA IN TUNA FISH SAUCE

A simple and colourful pasta dish, Tagliatelli Verdi con Salsa di Tonno is a good 'emergency' meal since most of the ingredients can be kept in the store cupboard. Serve as either a first or main course and accompany it with brown bread and butter and, to drink, some well-chilled white wine, such as Soave.

4-6 SERVINGS

2 fl. oz. [¼ cup] olive oil
12 oz. canned tuna fish, drained and
 flaked
2 tablespoons finely chopped fresh
 parsley
14 fl. oz. [1¾ cups] home-made
 chicken stock
1½ teaspoons freshly ground black
 pepper
1 lb. tagliatelli verdi, cooked
 for 8 to 10 minutes, drained
 and kept hot
1 tablespoon butter

In a medium-sized frying-pan, heat the oil over moderate heat. When the oil is hot, reduce the heat to low and add the tuna fish and 1½ tablespoons of the parsley.

Cook, stirring constantly with a wooden spoon, for 5 minutes, then add the stock and black pepper. Continue cooking for a further 5 minutes, stirring from time to time.

Place the tagliatelli in a large serving bowl and add the butter. Using two large spoons, toss the tagliatelli until all the strands are thoroughly coated with the butter. Pour over the sauce and sprinkle with the remaining parsley.

Serve immediately.

125

Vermicelli Soup

An easily digestible and nourishing soup, Vermicelli Soup is very quick and easy to make once you have prepared the basic chicken stock. This soup is ideal to serve to invalids.

6-8 SERVINGS

3 pints [7½ cups] home-made chicken stock
½ teaspoon salt
1 teaspoon chopped fresh lemon thyme
6 oz. vermicelli
1 tablespoon lemon juice

In a medium-sized saucepan, bring the chicken stock, salt and lemon thyme to the boil over high heat. Add the vermicelli, reduce the heat to moderately low and cook, stirring frequently, for 3 to 5 minutes or until the vermicelli is 'al dente' or just tender. Stir in the lemon juice.

Remove the pan from the heat and pour the soup into a warmed soup tureen. Serve immediately.

Vermicelli and Vegetables Chinese-Style

Quick to make, easy to eat — Vermicelli and Vegetables Chinese-Style is the perfect supper dish for a working wife or mother. Serve with ice-cold lager or some well-chilled Moselle wine.

4 SERVINGS

3 oz. [⅜ cup] butter
1 medium-sized onion, finely chopped
1 garlic clove, crushed
1 large green pepper, white pith removed, seeded and finely chopped
3 celery stalks, trimmed and chopped
2 carrots, scraped and thinly sliced
4 Chinese mushrooms, soaked for 20 minutes in cold water, drained and chopped
8 oz. bean sprouts
4 water chestnuts, sliced
4 oz. canned pineapple chunks, drained and chopped and with 6 fl. oz. [¾ cup] of the can juice reserved
1 tablespoon white wine vinegar

Two superb—and very different—dishes using vermicelli: Vermicelli Soup and Vermicelli and Vegetables Chinese-Style.

½ teaspoon salt
½ teaspoon black pepper
¼ teaspoon cayenne pepper
1½ tablespoons soy sauce
1 lb. vermicelli

In a large saucepan, melt the butter over moderate heat. When the foam subsides, add the onion, garlic, green pepper, celery and carrots and cook, stirring occasionally, for 5 to 7 minutes or until the onion is soft and translucent but not brown. Stir in the mushrooms, bean sprouts, water chestnuts and pineapple chunks and stir to mix well. Pour over the reserved pineapple can juice and vinegar, and add the salt, pepper, cayenne and soy sauce. Bring the liquid to the boil, stirring occasionally. Stir in the vermicelli, reduce the heat to low and simmer the mixture, stirring occasionally, for 3 to 5 minutes or until the vermicelli is 'al dente' or just tender and the vegetables are cooked through.

Remove the pan from the heat and transfer the mixture to a warmed serving dish.

Serve at once.

Wonton Dough

This recipe is for the basic dough used to make wonton wrappers. The dough is rolled out very thinly — not more than $\frac{1}{16}$-inch thick — then cut to the required shapes, filled and cooked.

1 POUND [4 CUPS] DOUGH

1 lb. [4 cups] flour
2 teaspoons salt
2 eggs, lightly beaten with 3 fl. oz. [⅜ cup] water

Sift the flour and salt into a large mixing bowl. Make a well in the centre and pour in the egg mixture. Using your fingers or a spatula, draw the flour into the liquid. When all the flour has been incorporated and the dough comes away from the sides of the bowl, turn the dough on to a lightly floured surface and knead it vigorously for 10 minutes or until it is smooth and elastic.

The dough is now ready to use.

Wontons with Pork and Prawns or Shrimps

These deep-fried wontons are deliciously crunchy and make a marvellous meal served with steamed rice and a salad.

4 SERVINGS

2 tablespoons vegetable oil

8 oz. lean pork, minced [ground]
8 oz. peeled prawns or shrimps, finely chopped
2 tablespoons soy sauce
1 tablespoon dry sherry
½ teaspoon salt
5 canned bamboo shoots, drained and finely chopped
2 Chinese mushrooms, washed, soaked in cold water for 20 minutes, drained and finely chopped
2 spring onions [scallions], trimmed and finely chopped
1 teaspoon cornflour [cornstarch] mixed with 1 tablespoon water or dry sherry
8 oz. wonton dough, thinly rolled and cut into 36 x 3-inch squares, or 36 bought wonton wrappers sufficient vegetable oil for deep frying

In a large frying-pan, heat the oil over high heat. When the oil is hot, reduce the heat to moderately high. Add the pork and fry, stirring constantly, for 1 minute or until the meat begins to brown. Add the prawns or shrimps, soy sauce, sherry, salt, bamboo shoots, mushrooms and spring onions [scallions] and fry, stirring constantly, for a further 1 minute. Add the cornflour [cornstarch] mixture to the pan and stir until the liquid thickens. Remove the pan from the heat and, using a large spoon, transfer the mixture to a bowl. Set aside to cool.

Place the wonton wrappers on a flat working surface. Place a teaspoon of the filling just below the centre of each wrapper. Using a pastry brush dipped in water, wet the edges of the dough. Fold one corner of the dough over the filling to make a triangle and pinch the edges together to seal. Pull the corners at the base of the triangle together and pinch them to seal. As each wonton is ready, place it on a plate. Repeat this process until all the wontons wrappers are filled and sealed.

Fill a large deep-frying pan one-third full with vegetable oil. Set the pan over moderate heat and heat the oil until it reaches 375°F on a deep-fat thermometer or until a small cube of stale bread dropped into the oil turns golden brown in 40 seconds.

Add the wontons to the oil, 8 or 10 at a time, and fry for 2 minutes or until they are golden brown. With a slotted spoon, remove the wontons from the oil and drain them on kitchen paper towels. Keep hot while you fry and drain the remaining wontons in the same way.

Transfer the wontons to a heated serving dish and serve at once.

Zite with Meatballs and Tomato Mushroom Sauce

Serve Zite with Meatballs and Tomato Mushroom Sauce as a main meal with lots of crusty bread, green salad and red wine.

4 SERVINGS

  1 teaspoon salt
  1 lb. zite
MEATBALLS
1½ lb. beef or pork, minced [ground]
  2 slices white bread, soaked in
    4 tablespoons milk for 5 minutes
  2 teaspoons grated lemon rind
  2 oz. [⅔ cup] dried breadcrumbs
  1 large egg
  2 garlic cloves, crushed
  1 teaspoon salt
  1 teaspoon black pepper
1½ teaspoons dried oregano
  2 fl. oz. [¼ cup] olive oil
  8 oz. Italian sausages, chopped
SAUCE
  3 tablespoons olive oil
  1 large onion, thinly sliced
  2 garlic cloves, crushed
  4 oz. mushrooms, sliced
  4 oz. fresh peas
28 oz. canned peeled tomatoes

  6 fl. oz. [¾ cup] red wine
  5 oz. tomato purée
  ½ teaspoon salt
  1 teaspoon black pepper
  1 teaspoon dried oregano
  4 oz. Mozzarella cheese, thinly
    sliced

First make the meatballs. In a mixing bowl, combine all the ingredients except the oil and sausages, beating until they are well mixed. Shape the mixture into walnut-sized balls. Place the balls in a large plate and chill them in the refrigerator for 30 minutes.

Meanwhile, make the sauce. In a saucepan, heat the oil over moderate heat. When the oil is hot, add the onion and garlic and fry, stirring occasionally, for 5 to 7 minutes or until the onion is soft and translucent but not brown. Add the mushrooms and peas and fry for 3 minutes. Add the tomatoes with the can juice, the wine, purée, salt, pepper and oregano and stir to mix. Bring the liquid to the boil over moderate heat. Reduce the heat to low, cover the pan and simmer the sauce for 30 minutes. Remove from the heat.

In a large frying-pan, heat the oil over

Zite with Meatballs and Tomato Mushroom Sauce—fabulous to eat!

moderate heat. When the oil is hot, add the meatballs, a few at a time, and fry, turning occasionally, for 5 to 8 minutes or until they are lightly and evenly browned. Transfer the cooked meatballs to the saucepan containing the sauce. Brown the remaining meatballs and the sausage pieces in the same way. Return the saucepan to low heat and simmer the mixture for a further 30 minutes.

Add the cheese slices to the pan and continue to simmer for a further 10 to 15 minutes or until the cheese has melted.

Meanwhile, half-fill a saucepan with water and add the salt. Set the pan over moderately high heat and bring the water to the boil. When the water boils, add the zite to the pan. Reduce the heat to moderate and cook the zite for 10 to 15 minutes or until it is 'al dente' or just tender. Remove the pan from the heat and drain the zite in a colander.

Transfer the zite to a large serving bowl. Remove the pan of sauce and meatballs from the heat. Pour the mixture over the zite and serve.

Fish and seafood for the family

Fish and Seafood have long formed part of our basic diet. But they are a relatively small part, which is rather surprising when you consider their comparative cheapness and high protein value.

Traditional attitudes to cooking fish are probably partly to blame — all too often, it's dip-it-in-flour-or-batter and fry-it-to-kingdom-come! Some fish can be just as easily poached or baked; and they can form the basis of exotically different (but marvellously tasty!) dishes as well as of flavourful familiar ones. We think you'll agree when you see (and sample) our simple, straightforward recipes like Herrings in Butter Sauce (page 136) and Potted Shrimps or Prawns (page 156). Compare them with 'new' tastes such as Chinese Deep-Fried Prawns

(page 154) and Fillets of Cod with Caper Sauce (pictured below, recipe page 130).

Tasty meals needn't cost the earth, as most of our recipes prove. But, there are occasions in every family when there's a bit extra to spend and when something special is called for. The recipes in **For Special Occasions** are absolutely superb to eat and elegant enough to enhance the finest table.

All of our recipes — the inexpensive, everyday as well as the more special ones — are attractive to look at and good to eat. And, with the busy mum in mind, they have been specially selected so that their preparation won't wear her to a frazzle; food is meant to be enjoyed by ALL who eat it, including the cook!

Cod

Cod Bake

☆ ☆ ① ⧖ ⧖

Tasty and easy to prepare, Cod Bake is an unusual way to serve cod. Accompany with parsley potatoes.

6 SERVINGS

1 tablespoon butter
2 lb. cod fillets, skinned
1 small onion, finely chopped
1 celery stalk, finely chopped
½ green pepper, white pith removed, seeded and finely chopped
3 oz. [½ cup] walnuts, chopped
3 tablespoons chopped fresh parsley
6 tablespoons dry white breadcrumbs
¼ teaspoon black pepper
⅛ teaspoon Tabasco sauce
1 teaspoon Worcestershire sauce
1 teaspoon dried tarragon
2 eggs, separated
4 fl. oz. single cream [½ cup light cream]
4 oz. [½ cup] butter, melted

COURT BOUILLON

16 fl. oz. [2 cups] water
3 parsley sprigs
1 small onion, finely chopped
6 peppercorns
½ teaspoon salt
juice of ½ lemon

SAUCE

2½ oz. [5 tablespoons] butter
3 tablespoons flour
½ teaspoon salt
¼ teaspoon white pepper
2 hard-boiled eggs, chopped
2 tablespoons single [light] cream

This delicious Cod Bake makes a super family dinner.

Preheat the oven to fairly hot 375°F (Gas Mark 5, 190°C).

Grease a medium-sized ovenproof dish with the tablespoon of butter.

To make the court bouillon, pour the water into a large saucepan. Add the parsley, onion, peppercorns, salt and lemon juice and place the pan over high heat. Bring the court bouillon to the boil, reduce the heat to moderately low and add the cod fillets to the pan. Simmer the cod for 12 to 15 minutes, or until it flakes easily.

Transfer the cod to a chopping board. Reserve the court bouillon. Allow the fish to cool slightly, then remove the skin and using a fork, flake the fish.

Strain the court bouillon into a measuring jug and reserve 12 fluid ounces [1½ cups].

In a large bowl, mix together the cod, onion, celery, green pepper, walnuts, parsley, breadcrumbs, pepper, Tabasco, Worcestershire and tarragon.

In a small bowl, beat the egg yolks with a fork until they are pale yellow. Stir the yolks into the cod mixture and then blend in the cream and melted butter.

In a medium-sized bowl, beat the egg whites with a wire whisk or rotary beater until they form stiff peaks. With a metal spoon, carefully fold them into the cod mixture. Turn the mixture into the prepared dish. Place the dish in the oven and bake for 40 minutes or until firm.

While the cod mixture is baking, prepare the sauce. In a small heavy saucepan, melt 1½ ounces [3 tablespoons] of the butter over moderate heat. Remove the pan from the heat, and with a wooden spoon, stir in the flour, salt and pepper. Replace the pan on the heat and, stirring constantly, gradually add the reserved court bouillon. Cook and stir the sauce for 5 minutes or until it has thickened and

is smooth. Remove the pan from the heat.

Stir the remaining butter into the sauce. When the butter has been incorporated, stir in the eggs and cream.

When the cod bake is cooked, remove it from the oven and serve immediately, with the sauce.

Fillets of Cod with Caper Sauce

☆ ① ① ⧖

This attractive dish (pictured on page 129) *makes a superb meal served with croquette potatoes.*

3 SERVINGS

6 small cod fillets, skinned
10 fl. oz. [1¼ cups] fish stock
5 fl. oz. [⅝ cup] dry white wine
¼ teaspoon salt
¼ teaspoon black pepper
¼ teaspoon grated nutmeg
1 teaspoon cornflour [cornstarch] dissolved in 1 tablespoon water

$\frac{1}{8}$ teaspoon cayenne pepper
5 fl. oz. double cream [$\frac{5}{8}$ cup heavy cream]
2 tablespoons capers
6 to 9 large cooked prawns

Roll up each cod fillet and fasten the rolls with thick thread. Lay the rolled fillets in the bottom of a medium-sized heavy saucepan. Pour over the fish stock, wine, salt, pepper and nutmeg. Place the pan over moderate heat and bring the liquid to the boil. Reduce the heat to low, cover the pan and simmer for 20 minutes. Remove the pan from the heat.

Remove the fish fillets from the pan. Remove and discard the thread. Arrange the rolls in a serving dish and keep hot while you finish the sauce.

Return the pan to moderate heat and bring the cooking juices to the boil. Boil for 10 minutes. Stir in the cornflour [cornstarch] and cayenne. Cook the sauce, stirring constantly, for 3 minutes, or until it is thick. Reduce the heat to low and stir in the cream and capers. Continue cooking, stirring constantly, for 3

minutes. Do not allow the sauce to boil.

Remove the pan from the heat and pour the sauce over the fish rolls. Garnish with the prawns and serve.

Cod Steaks with Tomatoes and Anchovies

This is an attractive and exceptionally tasty way of serving cod.

4 SERVINGS

2 fl. oz. [$\frac{1}{4}$ cup] olive oil
1 small onion, thinly sliced
1 garlic clove, chopped
1 green pepper, white pith removed, seeded and thinly sliced
2 oz. canned anchovies, drained and chopped
2 oz. [$\frac{2}{3}$ cup] black olives, stoned
$\frac{1}{8}$ teaspoon fennel seed
8 x 4 oz. cod steaks
3 small tomatoes, thinly sliced
$\frac{1}{2}$ teaspoon salt
$\frac{1}{4}$ teaspoon black pepper
2$\frac{1}{2}$ oz. canned tomato purée

4 fl. oz. [$\frac{1}{2}$ cup] dry red wine

Preheat the oven to fairly hot 400°F (Gas Mark 6, 200°C).

In a medium-sized frying-pan, heat half the olive oil over moderate heat. When the oil is hot, add the onion, garlic and green pepper. Cook them for 5 to 7 minutes, stirring occasionally, or until the onion is soft and translucent but not brown. Remove the pan from the heat and stir in the anchovies, olives and fennel.

Place four of the cod steaks in a greased dish and spread the anchovy mixture over them. Top each steak with another cod steak. Arrange the tomatoes on top. Brush the tomatoes with the remaining oil, salt and pepper.

In a small bowl, combine the tomato purée with the wine. Pour the mixture over the fish. Place the dish in the oven and bake for 30 minutes, basting twice. Serve at once.

Colourful Cod Steaks with Tomatoes and Anchovies.

Haddock with Cider

A pleasant and unusual dish, Haddock with Cider is delicious served for a family lunch or supper with parsley potatoes, buttered carrots and, perhaps, a mixed green salad. Chilled cider would make a good accompanying drink.

4 SERVINGS

8 fl. oz. [1 cup] cider
2 medium-sized onions, thinly sliced
1 green pepper, white pith removed, seeded and coarsely chopped
1½ lb. fresh or frozen and thawed haddock fillets, skinned
3 medium-sized tomatoes, blanched, peeled and coarsely chopped
2 teaspoons chopped fresh marjoram or 1 teaspoon dried marjoram
⅛ teaspoon cayenne pepper
1½ teaspoons salt
½ teaspoon freshly ground white pepper
3 tablespoons fresh white breadcrumbs
1 oz. [¼ cup] Parmesan cheese, grated

Preheat the oven to warm 325°F (Gas

Served with rice, Haddock Croquettes in Hot Sauce make a spicy meal.

Mark 3, 170°C).

In a medium-sized saucepan, bring the cider to the boil over moderate heat. Add the onions and green pepper, reduce the heat to low and simmer the mixture for 5 minutes, or until the cider has reduced by about one-quarter. Remove the pan from the heat.

On a chopping board, cut the fish into 3- or 4-inch pieces and put them into a flameproof casserole. Add the cider mixture and tomatoes and mix well to blend. Sprinkle the marjoram, cayenne, salt and pepper over the mixture. Cover the casserole and place it over moderately high heat. Bring the liquid to the boil. Transfer the casserole to the oven and bake for 20 to 25 minutes, or until the fish flakes very easily when tested with a fork. Remove the casserole from the oven.

Preheat the grill [broiler] to high.

In a small bowl, combine the breadcrumbs and grated cheese together and spread the mixture over the fish. Place the casserole under the grill [broiler] and grill [broil] the mixture for 4 minutes, or until the topping browns and the cheese melts.

Remove the casserole from the heat

and serve at once, straight from the casserole.

Haddock Croquettes in Hot Sauce

Tender Haddock Croquettes, simmered in a spicy sauce, makes an excellent hors d'oeuvre or, served on a bed of rice with a tossed green salad, they are a sustaining meal.

4 SERVINGS

1 lb. haddock, cooked, cooled, skinned, boned and flaked
1 teaspoon salt
½ teaspoon black pepper
1½ oz. [¾ cup] fresh white breadcrumbs
2 tablespoons finely chopped fresh parsley
1 egg, lightly beaten
3 tablespoons flour
SAUCE
1 medium-sized onion, finely chopped
½ teaspoon ground ginger
½ teaspoon ground coriander
¼ teaspoon ground turmeric
⅛ teaspoon hot chilli powder
2 oz. [¼ cup] butter
2 tablespoons vegetable oil
5 fl. oz. [⅝ cup] dry white wine
5 fl. oz. [⅝ cup] fish stock
4 lemon wedges

In a medium-sized mixing bowl, combine the fish, ½ teaspoon of the salt, the pepper, breadcrumbs and 1 tablespoon of the chopped parsley. Add the egg and mix it in thoroughly.

With your hands, shape the mixture into about 10 small croquettes. Put the flour on a board or large plate. Roll the croquettes gently in the flour to coat them on all sides.

Place the croquettes in the refrigerator to chill for at least 45 minutes.

In a small mixing bowl, mix together the onion, ginger, coriander, turmeric, chilli powder, remaining parsley and remaining salt. Set aside.

In a large frying-pan, melt the butter with the oil over moderate heat. When the foam subsides, add the onion and spice mixture. Cook, stirring frequently, for 5 to 7 minutes or until the onion is soft but not brown. Pour in the wine and fish stock. Bring the sauce to the boil, stirring constantly. Reduce the heat to low and simmer the sauce for 2 to 3 minutes.

Gently arrange the croquettes in the pan and baste them with the sauce. Cook the croquettes for 6 to 8 minutes on each side or until they are evenly browned. Baste the croquettes with the sauce frequently during the cooking period.

With a slotted spoon, lift the croquettes out of the pan and arrange them on a warmed serving dish. Pour the sauce over the croquettes and garnish with the lemon wedges.

Serve at once.

Swedish Summer Casserole

A tasty and economical dish suitable for lunch or supper, Swedish Summer Casserole may be served with parsley potatoes and a tossed green salad.

6-8 SERVINGS

3 lb. fresh or frozen and thawed haddock fillets, skinned
1 teaspoon salt
1 tablespoon finely chopped fresh parsley
2 tablespoons finely chopped fresh chives
1 oz. [2 tablespoons] butter blended with 2 tablespoons flour juice of 1 lemon
4 tomatoes, thickly sliced

Sprinkle the fillets with the salt and place them in a flameproof casserole. Sprinkle over the parsley and chives and dot the fish with the butter mixture. Add the lemon juice and pour in just enough water to come about halfway up the sides of the fish.

Place the casserole over moderate heat and bring the liquid to the boil. Reduce the heat to low, cover the casserole and simmer for 10 minutes. Place the sliced tomatoes over the fish and simmer for a further 5 minutes or until the fish flesh flakes easily when tested with a fork.

Remove the casserole from the heat and serve immediately, straight from the casserole.

Swedish Summer Casserole is as good to eat as it is refreshing to look at! Serve with lots of green salad.

Haddock Soufflé is easy to make!

Finnan Haddie

The name Finnan Haddie is derived from Findon haddock. Many centuries ago, there was a glut of haddock in the small Scottish fishing port of Findon, and the housewives discovered the process of smoking the haddock in order to preserve it.

4 SERVINGS

2 lb. smoked haddock
1 large onion, sliced
1 pint [2½ cups] milk
½ teaspoon black pepper
1 oz. [2 tablespoons] butter, cut into
   small pieces

Place the haddock and onion in a medium-sized saucepan. Add enough milk just to cover the fish, the pepper and butter.

Place the pan over moderate heat and bring the milk slowly to the boil.

Cover the pan, reduce the heat to low and simmer gently for 10 minutes, or until the fish flakes easily.

Remove the pan from the heat. To serve, pour a little of the cooking liquid over the fish.

Haddock Soufflé

A souffléd fish dish, Haddock Soufflé is ideal for luncheon or supper when served with a green salad. If you would like to serve this dish as part of a special dinner, as a savoury or fish course, use a medium-sized soufflé dish and allow another 5 minutes cooking time.

3-4 SERVINGS

10 fl. oz. [1¼ cups] water
10 oz. smoked or fresh haddock
1 teaspoon butter
2 tablespoons flour
5 fl. oz. [⅝ cup] milk
2 oz. [½ cup] Cheddar cheese, grated
1 teaspoon grated lemon rind
¼ teaspoon dried or 1 teaspoon
   chopped fresh dill
¼ teaspoon salt
¼ teaspoon black pepper
2 egg yolks
3 egg whites

In a large frying-pan, heat the water and fish over moderate heat. When the water begins to simmer, reduce the heat to low, cover the pan and cook for 12 minutes or until the fish flakes easily when tested with a fork. Remove the pan from the heat and, with a slotted spoon, transfer the fish to a plate. Flake it and discard the skin and any bones. Reserve 5 fluid ounces [⅝ cup] of the cooking liquid.

Preheat the oven to fairly hot 375°F (Gas Mark 5, 190°C).

Using the butter, grease a medium-sized deep pie dish. Set aside.

In a medium-sized saucepan, mix together half the reserved cooking liquid and the flour with a wooden spoon to make a smooth paste. Stir in the remaining cooking liquid and the milk. Place the pan over moderate heat and, stirring constantly bring to the boil. Boil the sauce for 2 minutes.

Remove the pan from the heat and set aside to cool slightly. Stir in the fish, the cheese, lemon rind, dill, salt and pepper. Beat in the egg yolks. Set aside.

In a large mixing bowl, beat the egg whites with a wire whisk or rotary beater until they form stiff peaks.

With a metal spoon, carefully fold the egg whites into the fish mixture. Spoon the mixture into the pie dish.

Place the dish in the oven and bake for 30 minutes or until the soufflé is well risen and a deep golden brown.

Remove the soufflé from the oven and serve immediately.

Hake with Ham and Egg Stuffing

This unusual way of cooking hake originated in Spain, where the fish is known as merluza. Serve it with sautéed potatoes and courgettes [zucchini], and a light white wine such as a good Spanish Chablis.

6 SERVINGS

2 hard-boiled eggs
6 oz. lean cooked ham, finely chopped
4 tablespoons stoned and chopped black olives
2 tablespoons finely chopped fresh parsley
2 teaspoons salt
½ teaspoon freshly ground black pepper
1 x 4 to 5 lb. hake, cleaned, with the backbone removed and the head and tail left on
1 teaspoon olive oil
4 large tomatoes, sliced
1 bay leaf

Preheat the oven to moderate 350°F (Gas Mark 4, 180°C).

In a small bowl, mash the hard-boiled eggs with a fork. Add the ham, olives, parsley, ½ teaspoon salt and ¼ teaspoon of pepper and mix well. Set the stuffing aside.

Wash the fish under cold running water and dry it thoroughly on kitchen paper towels. Place the fish on a wooden board and sprinkle 1 teaspoon of salt over it.

Line a baking dish, large enough to hold the fish, with aluminium foil, overlapping the ends so that they may be used to enclose the fish. With the oil, lightly grease the foil.

Using a metal spoon, fill the fish with the prepared stuffing. Sew or skewer the fish together and place it in the prepared baking dish. Cover the fish with layers of tomatoes, and sprinkle over the remaining salt and pepper. Tuck the bay leaf between the layers and close the foil tightly.

Place the dish in the centre of the oven and bake for 1 hour. Remove the dish from the oven and transfer the whole fish to a warmed serving dish. Unwrap the aluminium foil. Arrange the tomatoes over and around the fish and serve immediately.

Hake with Ham and Egg Stuffing is an economical - and unusual - way of cooking this superb fish.

Herrings in Butter Sauce

A simple yet delicious lunch or supper dish, Herrings in Butter Sauce is very good served with boiled new potatoes.

4 SERVINGS

- 4 large herrings, filleted
- 6½ tablespoons seasoned flour, made with 6 tablespoons flour, 1 teaspoon salt and ½ teaspoon black pepper
- 3 oz. [⅜ cup] butter
- 2 teaspoons lemon juice
- 1 tablespoon chopped fresh parsley

Wash the herring fillets under cold running water and pat them dry with kitchen paper towels.

Place the seasoned flour on a plate and, one by one, dip the herring fillets into it, shaking off any excess flour. Set aside.

In a large frying-pan, melt the butter over moderate heat. When the foam subsides, add the herring fillets to the pan and cook them for 3 minutes on each side, or until they are lightly browned and the flesh flakes easily when tested with a fork.

Remove the pan from the heat and, with a slotted spoon, transfer the herrings from the pan to a warmed serving dish.

So simple to make, so delicious to eat - Herrings in Butter Sauce.

Spoon over the lemon juice, then the pan juices.

Sprinkle over the parsley and serve at once.

Herrings with Mustard Sauce

Sometimes the simple things of life are the best — even in cooking! This recipe for Herrings with Mustard Sauce is an excellent example as it makes an economical family meal that is really delicious.

6 SERVINGS

- 6 large herrings, filleted
- 1 tablespoon lemon juice
- 2 eggs, lightly beaten
- 2 teaspoons dry mustard
- ½ teaspoon salt
- ¼ teaspoon black pepper
- 2 oz. [½ cup] flour
- 3 oz. [⅜ cup] butter
- 6 lemon wedges

MUSTARD SAUCE
- 4 oz. [½ cup] butter
- ½ teaspoon salt
- ¼ teaspoon white pepper
- 1 teaspoon dry mustard

Wash the herring fillets under cold running water and pat them dry with kitchen paper towels. Sprinkle the herrings with the lemon juice and set aside.

In a shallow bowl, combine the eggs,

mustard, salt and pepper, beating with a fork until the ingredients are well blended. Sprinkle the flour on to a plate or a sheet of greaseproof or waxed paper.

Dip the fillets, one at a time, in the egg mixture, then roll them in the flour, coating them on all sides. Set aside.

In a large frying-pan, melt the butter over moderate heat. When the foam subsides, add the fillets and cook them for 3 minutes on each side, or until the flesh flakes easily when tested with a fork. Remove the pan from the heat and transfer the fillets to a warmed serving plate. Keep warm while you make the sauce.

In a small saucepan, melt the butter over low heat. Stir in the salt, pepper and mustard and beat the mixture with a fork or spoon until the ingredients are well blended. Remove the pan from the heat and pour the sauce over the herrings.

Garnish with the lemon wedges and serve at once.

Herrings Stuffed with Rice

Herrings Stuffed with Rice is a superb dish of herrings stuffed with sweetcorn, bacon, rice and cream, baked with wine.

4 SERVINGS

- 2 oz. [¼ cup] butter
- 4 large herrings, cleaned and gutted

1 lemon, quartered
1 teaspoon salt
½ teaspoon black pepper
2 lean bacon slices, diced
1 small onion, finely chopped
3 oz. [1¼ cups] cooked rice
3 tablespoons drained sweetcorn
  kernels
4 tablespoons double [heavy] cream
1 parsley sprig, finely chopped
3 fl. oz. [⅜ cup] dry white wine

Preheat the oven to moderate 350°F (Gas Mark 4, 180°C).

Using 1 tablespoon of the butter, grease a large baking dish and set aside.

Wash the herrings and pat them dry with kitchen paper towels.

Rub the fish all over with the lemon pieces and discard the lemon. Rub ½ teaspoon of salt and ¼ teaspoon of pepper all over the fish.

In a small frying-pan, melt 1 tablespoon of the butter over moderate heat. When the foam subsides, add the bacon and fry, stirring occasionally, for 6 to 8 minutes, or until it is crisp. With a slotted spoon, remove the bacon from the pan and drain it on kitchen paper towels. Transfer the bacon to a medium-sized mixing bowl and set aside.

Add the onion to the frying-pan and cook, stirring occasionally, for 5 to 7 minutes, or until it is soft and translucent but not brown.

Remove the pan from the heat. With a slotted spoon, remove the onion from the pan and add it to the bacon.

Stir the rice, sweetcorn, cream, the remaining salt and pepper and the parsley into the bacon and onion. Combine the mixture thoroughly.

Using a metal spoon, stuff the fish with the rice mixture. Close the cavities with skewers, or a trussing needle and thread.

Arrange the fish in the baking dish. Pour over the wine and dot the fish with the remaining butter, in pieces.

Cover the dish with a lid or aluminium foil and place it in the centre of the oven. Bake for 45 minutes, basting occasionally, or until the fish flakes easily.

Remove the dish from the oven. Remove and discard the trussing thread or skewers and serve immediately.

Herring Roes in Devilled Sauce

These devilled roes make an excellent snack.
2 SERVINGS

2 tablespoons flour
8 oz. soft herring roes
1 oz. [2 tablespoons] butter
1 small onion, finely chopped
1 green pepper, white pith
  removed, seeded and chopped
1 teaspoon curry powder

Herrings Stuffed with Rice makes an economical and nutritious family meal.

¼ teaspoon Worcestershire sauce
½ teaspoon black pepper
⅛ teaspoon cayenne pepper
¼ teaspoon dry mustard
1 tablespoon sweet mango chutney
2 tablespoons chicken stock
2 slices warm buttered toast

Put the flour on a small plate. Dip the roes in the flour and coat them all over.

In a small frying-pan, melt the butter over moderate heat. When the foam subsides, add the roes and fry them for 3 to 4 minutes, turning them frequently, or until they are lightly browned. With a slotted spoon, remove the roes from the pan and set them aside on a plate.

Add the onion to the pan and fry, stirring occasionally, for 5 to 7 minutes or until it is soft and translucent but not brown. Add the green pepper and curry powder and fry, stirring frequently, for 3 minutes. Stir in the Worcestershire, pepper, cayenne, mustard, chutney and stock. Cook the sauce for 1 minute. Return the roes to the pan and turn and toss them in the sauce. Cook for 1 to 2 minutes or until they are heated through.

Turn the roe mixture on to the toast slices, set on warmed plates, and serve.

Kipper

Kipper Kedgeree

Kipper Kedgeree makes a delicious treat for Sunday breakfast. Alternatively, it may be served as an economical supper or lunch dish, accompanied by a tossed mixed salad and lots of brown bread and butter.

4 SERVINGS

1 lb. boned kipper fillets, skinned
2 oz. [¼ cup] butter
8 oz. [3 cups] cooked long-grain rice
2 fl. oz. double cream [¼ cup heavy cream]
4 hard-boiled eggs, finely chopped
¼ teaspoon salt
½ teaspoon freshly ground black pepper
1 teaspoon prepared English mustard

With a sharp knife, cut the kipper fillets into small pieces.

In a large deep frying-pan, melt the butter over moderate heat. When the foam subsides, add the kipper pieces and fry them for 3 to 4 minutes, turning them frequently, or until they are lightly browned.

Add the rice and stir in the cream and chopped eggs. Add the salt, pepper and mustard and cook, stirring constantly, for 3 minutes or until the mixture is heated through.

Remove the pan from the heat and turn the kedgeree into a large warmed serving dish.

Serve at once.

Kipper Paste

This traditional teatime treat is very popular with children. Serve the paste on thickly buttered toast on a cold winter's day. Once the paste has been made and potted, it should be eaten within 2 days.

12 OUNCES PASTE

4 oz. [2 cups] fresh white breadcrumbs
6 fl. oz. [¾ cup] water
4 kippers, cooked, skinned, filleted and flaked
1 garlic clove, crushed
2 oz. [¼ cup] butter, melted
juice of ½ lemon
½ teaspoon freshly ground black pepper
½ teaspoon cayenne pepper

Place the breadcrumbs in a mixing bowl and pour over the water. When the breadcrumbs are thoroughly soaked, squeeze out all the excess water.

This superb Kipper Paste was specially invented to be spread thickly on hot buttered toast!

Place the breadcrumbs, kippers, garlic, butter, lemon juice, pepper and cayenne in a mortar and pound them with a pestle until they form a smooth paste. Alternatively, blend all the ingredients in an electric blender until the paste is very smooth.

Spoon the paste into small pots. Cover the pots with aluminium foil and place in the refrigerator until required.

Kipper Pie

Covered with a golden pastry crust, this tasty Kipper Pie is delicious hot for supper with mashed potatoes and a fresh green vegetable, or cold, with lots of tossed mixed salad.

4 SERVINGS

1 oz. [2 tablespoons] butter
2 tablespoons flour
8 fl. oz. single cream [1 cup light cream]
12 oz. boned kipper fillets, poached, skinned and flaked
¼ teaspoon cayenne pepper
¼ teaspoon salt
½ teaspoon finely grated lemon rind
2 hard-boiled eggs, very thinly sliced

PASTRY
6 oz. [1½ cups] flour
⅛ teaspoon salt

Cool, refreshing Ceviche is an exotic blend of mackerel fillets marinated in lemon juice.

5 oz. [⅝ cup] butter, cut into
   walnut-sized pieces
3 to 4 tablespoons iced water
1 egg, lightly beaten

In a medium-sized saucepan, melt the butter over moderate heat. Remove the pan from the heat and, with a wooden spoon, stir in the flour to make a smooth paste. Gradually add the cream, stirring constantly. Return the pan to the heat and add the flaked kipper, cayenne, salt and lemon rind. Cook, stirring constantly, for 3 minutes, or until the mixture begins to boil.

Remove the pan from the heat and turn the mixture into a medium-sized pie dish. Carefully arrange the egg slices on top of the mixture. Set aside while you prepare the pastry.

Sift the flour and salt into a medium-sized mixing bowl. Add the butter and iced water. With a knife, mix quickly to a firm dough which should be lumpy.

On a lightly floured surface, roll out the dough into an oblong shape. Fold it in three and turn it so that the open edges face you. Roll out again into an oblong shape and proceed as before. Repeat this process once again to make three turns in all.

Wrap the dough in greaseproof or waxed paper and put it in the refrigerator to chill for 30 minutes.

Preheat the oven to fairly hot 400°F (Gas Mark 6, 200°C).

Remove the dough from the refrigerator. If it looks streaky, roll it out into an oblong shape and fold it in three once again. On a floured surface, roll out the dough to a circle 1-inch larger than the top of the pie dish. With a knife, cut a ½-inch strip around the dough. Dampen the rim of the dish with water and press the dough strip on to the rim. With a pastry brush dipped in water, lightly moisten the strip.

Using the rolling pin, lift the dough on to the dish. With a knife, trim the dough and, with your fingers, crimp the edges to seal them to the strip already on the dish. With a sharp knife, cut a 1-inch slit in the centre of the dough. With a pastry brush, coat the surface of the dough with the beaten egg.

Place the pie in the centre of the oven and bake for 50 minutes to 1 hour, or until the pastry is a deep golden brown.

Remove the pie from the oven and serve it at once, or set it aside and serve cold.

Ceviche

MACKEREL FILLETS MARINATED IN LEMON JUICE

This is a traditional Mexican dish, although it is also made in most South American countries with slight variations. The original recipe uses fresh limes but, if these are very difficult to obtain, Ceviche may also be made with fresh lemon juice. If you do use limes, use 8 fluid ounces [1 cup] of lime juice and 8 fluid ounces [1 cup] of lemon juice. Ceviche makes an unusual and delicious hors d'oeuvre or snack meal, accompanied by lots of brown bread and butter.

6 SERVINGS

16 fl. oz. [2 cups] fresh lemon juice
1 teaspoon dried, seeded, hot red chilli pepper, pounded in a mortar
2 medium-sized onions, very thinly sliced and pushed out into rings
½ garlic clove, finely chopped
1 teaspoon salt
½ teaspoon freshly ground black pepper
3 large mackerel, filleted and cut into 1-inch pieces
3 medium-sized sweet potatoes, unpeeled
2 crisp lettuces, washed, separated and chilled
4 ears fresh sweet corn, with outer husks and threads removed and cut across into 2-inch rounds
1 fresh red chilli, washed, split, seeded and cut into very thin pieces

Combine the lemon juice, pounded dried chilli pepper, onion rings, garlic, salt and pepper in a pitcher.

Place the fish pieces in a shallow porcelain dish and pour the lemon juice mixture over them. If the liquid does not cover the fish, add more lemon juice.

Cover the dish with aluminium foil and place it in the refrigerator. Leave the fish for at least 3 hours, or until it is opaque and white.

Thirty minutes before you are ready to serve the dish, bring 3 pints of water to the boil in a large saucepan over high heat. Place the sweet potatoes in the boiling water and cover the pan. Reduce the heat to moderate and cook for about 25 minutes, or until the potatoes are tender when pierced with the point of a sharp knife.

While the potatoes are cooking, arrange a bed of lettuce leaves on 6 individual plates. Set the plates aside.

Remove the pan from the heat and drain the potatoes in a colander. Peel the potatoes and cut each one into 3 slices. Keep the potato slices warm while you cook the corn.

In a medium-sized saucepan, bring 2 pints of water to the boil over high heat. Drop the corn rounds into the boiling water, reduce the heat to moderate and boil them for 4 to 5 minutes, or until the corn turns bright yellow.

Remove the pan from the heat and drain the corn in a colander.

Remove the marinated fish from the refrigerator. Using a slotted spoon, divide the fish between the six plates. Garnish the fish with the onion rings and strips of fresh chilli pepper.

Arrange the sweet potato slices and corn rounds round the fish and serve at once.

Mackerel Kebabs

Mackerel Kebabs are an unusual and tempting way of serving fish. They look especially attractive if served on a bed of watercress and garnished with black olives and slices of lemon.

4 SERVINGS

4 mackerel, cleaned, gutted
   and with backbones removed
6 pickling (pearl) onions
4 small tomatoes
4 button mushrooms, wiped clean
1 large green pepper, white pith
   removed, seeded and cut into
   ½-inch wide strips
2 fl. oz. [¼ cup] white wine vinegar
2 fl. oz. [¼ cup] olive oil
½ teaspoon salt
¼ teaspoon black pepper
1 teaspoon dried oregano

Cut each mackerel into 4 or 5 slices.

Thread the slices of fish on to skewers, alternating with the onions, tomatoes, mushrooms and green pepper strips.

In a large shallow dish, combine the vinegar, olive oil, salt, pepper and oregano. Lay the prepared skewers in the dish and leave to marinate at room temperature for about 2 hours, turning occasionally.

Preheat the grill [broiler] to high.

Remove the kebabs from the marinade and place them under the grill [broiler]. Cook for 8 to 10 minutes, basting the kebabs with the marinade and turning them frequently, or until the fish flakes easily when tested with a fork.

Serve the kebabs immediately, on a warmed serving dish.

140

A fish dish with a difference - Mackerel Kebabs may be served as an elegant first course for dinner or, on a bed of plain boiled rice, for a sustaining family lunch or supper.

Plaice [Flounder] with Artichoke Sauce

Plaice [flounder] fillets, simmered in court bouillon and served with a creamy artichoke sauce, is quick and easy to prepare and tastes delicious. Serve with steamed broccoli or peas, mashed potatoes and, to drink, some light white Burgundy wine, such as Pouilly Fuissé.

6 SERVINGS

2 lb. plaice [flounder] fillets
½ teaspoon salt
¼ teaspoon freshly ground black pepper
1 medium-sized onion, thinly sliced and pushed out into rings
1 celery stalk, trimmed and chopped
1 mace blade
 bouquet garni, consisting of 4 parsley sprigs, 1 thyme spray and 1 bay leaf tied together
6 white peppercorns, finely crushed
10 fl. oz. [1¼ cups] home-made fish stock
6 fl. oz. [¾ cup] dry white wine or water
1 tablespoon lemon juice
1 tablespoon finely chopped fresh parsley

SAUCE

1 oz. [2 tablespoons] butter
1 oz. [¼ cup] flour
¼ teaspoon salt
⅛ teaspoon freshly ground black pepper
⅛ teaspoon cayenne pepper
2 fl. oz. double cream [¼ cup heavy cream]
3 artichoke hearts, simmered in boiling water for 35 minutes, drained and chopped

Put the plaice [flounder] fillets on a working surface and rub them all over with the salt and pepper. Lay the fillets, in one layer if possible, on the bottom of a large flameproof casserole. Add the onion rings, chopped celery, mace blade, bouquet garni and the white peppercorns. Pour over the stock and wine or water and add the lemon juice.

Place the casserole over moderately high heat and bring the liquid to the boil. Reduce the heat to moderately low, cover the casserole and cook for 12 to 15 minutes, or until the fish flakes easily when tested with a fork.

Remove the casserole from the heat.

Using a slotted spoon, carefully transfer the fish to a large warmed serving dish. Set aside and keep hot while you make the sauce.

Pour 10 fluid ounces [1¼ cups] of the cooking liquid through a fine wire strainer set over a medium-sized mixing bowl. Discard the contents of the strainer and set the bowl aside.

In a large frying-pan, melt the butter over moderate heat. Remove the pan from the heat and, with a wooden spoon, stir in the flour to make a smooth paste. Gradually add the strained cooking liquid, stirring constantly. Return the pan to the heat and cook, stirring constantly with a wooden spoon, for 2 to 3 minutes, or until the sauce is thick and smooth and hot but not boiling.

Remove the pan from the heat. Stir in the salt, pepper and cayenne. Stir in the cream, and then the artichoke heart pieces. Taste the sauce for seasoning and add more salt and pepper if necessary. Pour the sauce over the fish fillets and sprinkle them with the chopped fresh parsley.

Serve at once.

Plaice [flounder] is an under-used fish, but we guarantee that you'll want to cook it again and again once you've tasted rich, creamy Plaice [Flounder] with Artichoke Sauce!

Deep-Fried Whitebait

This is a basic recipe for whitebait. Serve with French-fried potatoes, lots of tossed mixed salad and some beer for a tasty light meal.

4 SERVINGS

2 oz. [½ cup] seasoned flour, made with 2 oz. [½ cup] flour, ½ teaspoon salt, ¼ teaspoon freshly ground black pepper and 1 tablespoon very finely chopped fresh parsley
1 lb. whitebait, rinsed and dried on kitchen paper towels
sufficient vegetable oil for deep-frying

Place the seasoned flour on a large plate. Roll the whitebait in the seasoned flour, coating them thoroughly and shaking off any excess. Set aside.

Fill a large, deep-frying pan one-third full with vegetable oil and set it over moderate heat. Heat the oil until it reaches 360°F on a deep-fat thermometer or until a small cube of stale bread dropped into the oil turns golden in 50 seconds. Carefully place the whitebait in the oil and fry them, a handful at a time, for 2 to 3

minutes or until they are crisp and light brown. (If the whitebait stick together during frying, shake the pan gently from time to time.) Using a slotted spoon, transfer the whitebait to kitchen paper towels to drain. Keep hot while you cook and drain the remaining whitebait in the same way.

When all of the fish are cooked, carefully transfer the whitebait to a warmed serving dish and serve at once.

Whiting with Cheese and Breadcrumbs

A simple and relatively economical dish, Whiting with Cheese and Breadcrumbs is perfect for a family supper served with boiled potatoes and fresh minted peas or green beans. For special occasions, accompany this dish by some well-chilled Rhine wine, such as Liebfraumilch.

4 SERVINGS

4 medium-sized whiting fillets, skinned
1 teaspoon salt
½ teaspoon freshly ground black pepper
3 oz. [⅜ cup] butter

1 oz. [¼ cup] flour
8 fl. oz. [1 cup] milk
5 fl. oz. single cream [⅝ cup light cream]
6 oz. [1½ cups] Cheddar cheese, grated
2 oz. [⅔ cup] fine dry white breadcrumbs

Rub the fish all over with the salt and pepper. Set aside.

In a large frying-pan, melt 2 ounces [¼ cup] of the butter over moderate heat. When the foam subsides, add the fish and fry for 5 minutes on each side. Remove the pan from the heat and, using a fish slice or spatula, transfer the fish to a large warmed, flameproof serving dish. Set aside and keep hot while you prepare the sauce.

In a small saucepan, melt the remaining butter over moderate heat. Remove the pan from the heat and, using a wooden spoon, stir in the flour to form a

Deep-Fried Whitebait are easy to make, tasty to eat and economical to buy - serve them with French-fried potatoes and a tossed green salad for a simple but very satisfying meal.

smooth paste. Gradually add the milk and cream, stirring constantly and being careful to avoid lumps. Return the pan to the heat and cook the sauce, stirring constantly with a wooden spoon, for 2 to 3 minutes or until it is smooth and fairly thick and hot but not boiling. Remove the pan from the heat and pour the sauce over the fish.

Preheat the grill [broiler] to moderately high. Sprinkle the cheese and breadcrumbs over the fish. Place the dish under the grill [broiler] and grill [broil] for 3 to 5 minutes or until the top is golden brown and bubbling. Remove the flameproof serving dish from under the grill [broiler].

Serve immediately, straight from the dish.

Whiting Stuffed with Shrimps or Prawns

  ① ①

Whiting Stuffed with Shrimps or Prawns is a delicately flavoured French dish, ideal for lunch or dinner. Serve with croquette potatoes and creamed cauliflower or leeks, and a well-chilled white Burgundy wine such as Puligny-Montrachet or a slightly flinty Loire wine, such as Sancerre.

When you buy the whiting, ask the fish-monger to remove the head, slit the fish open and bone and clean it.

6 SERVINGS

- 6 medium-sized whiting, boned and cleaned
- 1 lemon, quartered
- 1½ teaspoons salt
- 1 teaspoon freshly ground black pepper
- 4 oz. [½ cup] butter
- 10 oz. medium-sized button mushrooms, wiped clean and thinly sliced
- 10 oz. frozen and thawed shrimps or prawns, shelled
- 6 tablespoons finely chopped fresh parsley

Preheat the oven to moderate 350°F (Gas Mark 4, 180°C).

Wash the whiting under cold running water and pat them dry with kitchen paper towels. Squeeze the lemon quarters over the fish and discard the lemon. Rub the fish, inside and out, with 1 teaspoon of the salt and ½ teaspoon of the black pepper. Set the fish aside while you make the stuffing.

In a medium-sized frying-pan, melt 1 ounce [2 tablespoons] of the butter over moderate heat. When the foam subsides, add the sliced mushrooms and the remaining salt and pepper. Fry, stirring

Whiting Stuffed with Shrimps or Prawns is elegant enough to be served at the finest dinner party, inexpensive enough to be served as a sustaining family supper or dinner.

constantly, for 2 to 3 minutes, or until the mushrooms are just tender. Stir in the shrimps or prawns and parsley and cook the mixture, stirring and turning from time to time, for 2 to 3 minutes, or until the shrimps or prawns are thoroughly heated through.

Remove the pan from the heat. With a slotted spoon, remove the prawns or shrimps and mushrooms from the pan and stuff them carefully into the cavities of the fish.

With a sharp knife, cut half the remaining butter into small pieces and dot them over the bottom of a large, shallow baking dish. Place the stuffed fish, side by side, in the prepared dish, in one layer. Cut the remaining butter into small pieces and carefully scatter the pieces all over the fish.

Place the dish in the centre of the oven and bake for 20 to 30 minutes, or until the fish flakes easily when tested with a fork.

Remove the dish from the oven and serve immediately.

Jellied Fish Mould

A striking centrepiece for a summer buffet, Jellied Fish Mould is surprisingly quick and easy to make. Any fish may be used, but cod, haddock or salmon would be especially good.

6 SERVINGS

2 lb. cooked fish, skinned, boned and flaked
½ teaspoon salt
¼ teaspoon black pepper
2 tablespoons chopped fresh chives
1 oz. gelatine
4 fl. oz. [½ cup] hot fish stock
1 crisp lettuce, washed and shredded
8 stuffed olives, sliced

MAYONNAISE

1 egg yolk
¼ teaspoon salt
1 teaspoon paprika
1 teaspoon prepared mustard
5 fl. oz [⅝ cup] olive oil
2 to 3 teaspoons white wine vinegar or lemon juice
5 fl. oz. [⅝ cup] sour cream

First make the mayonnaise. Place the egg

yolk, salt, paprika and mustard in a small mixing bowl. Using a wooden spoon, beat the ingredients until they are thoroughly blended.

Add the oil, a few drops at a time, beating constantly. After the mayonnaise has thickened, the oil may be added a little more rapidly. When all the oil has been added stir in the vinegar or lemon juice and the sour cream.

In a medium-sized mixing bowl, combine the fish, salt, pepper and chives. Beat in the mayonnaise.

In a small mixing bowl, dissolve the gelatine in the fish stock, stirring constantly.

Stir the dissolved gelatine into the fish mixture.

Rinse out a fish or ring mould with cold water and pour the fish mixture into the mould.

Leave the mould in the refrigerator for 2 hours, or until it is set.

To turn the mould out, quickly dip the base of the mould in hot water and turn it out on to a flat serving dish.

Surround the mould with the shredded lettuce and arrange the sliced stuffed olives on top.

Serve at once.

Mixed Fish Casserole

A filling spicy supper dish of Latin American origin, Mixed Fish Casserole may be served hot with a green vegetable and boiled potatoes, or left to cool and served with a salad. Accompany this dish with lots of well-chilled lager or some well-chilled Chilean white wine.

4-6 SERVINGS

2 fl. oz. [¼ cup] olive oil
6 medium-sized onions, finely chopped
3 medium-sized garlic cloves, crushed
1 large green pepper, white pith removed, seeded and cut into strips
1 large red pepper, white pith removed, seeded and cut into strips
1 tablespoon chopped fresh basil or 1½ teaspoons dried basil
1 lb. tomatoes, blanched, peeled

Jellied Fish Mould makes an excitingly different summer lunch or supper for the family.

and sliced
¼ teaspoon hot chilli powder
¼ teaspoon ground cumin
8 oz. halibut steaks, skinned
2 medium-sized mackerel fillets, skinned
8 oz. cod steaks, skinned
½ teaspoon salt
¼ teaspoon freshly ground black pepper
1 tablespoon white wine vinegar

In a large, flameproof casserole, heat the olive oil over moderate heat. When the oil is hot, add the onions and garlic and cook, stirring occasionally, for 5 to 7 minutes, or until the onions are soft and translucent but not brown.

Add the peppers, basil, tomatoes, chilli powder and cumin. Cover the casserole, reduce the heat to low and simmer the mixture for 1½ hours, or until it resembles a thick sauce.

Preheat the oven to warm 325°F (Gas Mark 3, 170°C).

Add the fish, salt and pepper to the casserole and stir well to mix. Place the casserole in the oven and bake for 20 to 30 minutes or until the fish flakes easily when tested with a fork.

Remove the casserole from the oven and stir in the vinegar. Serve immediately, or allow to cool before serving.

Seafood Stew

Seafood Stew should be served with boiled rice and a crisp green salad.

4 SERVINGS

8 fl. oz. [1 cup] dry white wine
1 lb. squid, cleaned thoroughly, skinned and cut into rings
1 tablespoon lemon juice
1 teaspoon salt
½ teaspoon black pepper
2 halibut steaks, bones removed
1 oz. [2 tablespoons] butter
1 tablespoon flour
½ teaspoon dried thyme
½ teaspoon dried rosemary
1 quart mussels, scrubbed, steamed and removed from their shells
8 oz. prawns or shrimps, shelled
2 oz. [½ cup] walnut halves
5 fl. oz. single cream [⅝ cup light cream]
2 tablespoons chopped parsley

Pour 4 fluid ounces [½ cup] of the white wine into a large saucepan. Add the squid, lemon juice, salt and pepper and bring the liquid to the boil over moderate heat. Reduce the heat to low and simmer for 30 minutes. Transfer the squid to a plate. Set aside.

Shrimps or prawns, mussels, halibut and squid combine in this delicately creamy Seafood Stew.

Add the halibut steaks and the remaining wine to the pan and cook the steaks for 5 to 8 minutes or until the flesh is almost tender. Transfer the halibut steaks to the plate. Set aside.

Pour the cooking liquid through a strainer into a bowl and set aside.

In a large flameproof casserole, melt the butter over moderate heat. Remove the casserole from the heat and, with a wooden spoon, stir in the flour to make a smooth paste. Pour the strained cooking liquid into the casserole, stirring constantly. Stir in the thyme and rosemary. Return the pan to moderate heat and bring the sauce to the boil, stirring constantly. Reduce the heat to low and simmer the sauce for 2 minutes.

Add the mussels, the reserved squid and halibut, the prawns or shrimps and walnuts to the sauce and cook for 7 to 10 minutes or until the halibut is tender and the mussels and prawns or shrimps are thoroughly heated through. Stir in the cream and cook the ragoût for a further 1 minute. Do not allow the sauce to boil. Remove the pan from the heat.
Sprinkle over the parsley and serve.

Fish for Special Occasions

Halibut with Bananas

A delicious and unusual dish, Halibut with Bananas makes a very tasty lunch or dinner meal. Serve with creamed potatoes and cauliflower and accompany with a bottle of well-chilled Zeltinger white wine.

4 SERVINGS

3 oz. [1½ cups] fresh white breadcrumbs
1 egg, lightly beaten with 2 tablespoons milk, 1 teaspoon salt and ½ teaspoon white pepper
4 large halibut steaks
3 tablespoons vegetable oil
1 oz. [2 tablespoons] butter
2 oz. [½ cup] flaked almonds
3 tablespoons soft brown sugar
1 tablespoon fresh lemon juice
4 small bananas, peeled and halved lengthways

Place the breadcrumbs on one plate and the seasoned egg and milk mixture in another. Dip the fish steaks first in the egg and milk mixture, and then in the breadcrumbs, coating them thoroughly on both sides and shaking off any excess crumbs. Set the fish aside.

In a large, heavy frying-pan, heat the oil over moderate heat. When the oil is hot, add the fish and cook for 8 to 10 minutes on each side, or until the steaks are browned and flake easily when tested with a fork.

Remove the pan from the heat. Remove the fish steaks from the pan and arrange them on a warmed serving dish. Keep them hot.

Wipe out the frying-pan with kitchen paper towels. Return the pan to moderate heat and add the butter. When the foam subsides, add the flaked almonds and cook them, stirring frequently, for 3 minutes, or until they are lightly browned. Stir in the sugar, lemon juice and bananas and cook, turning the bananas once, for a further 3 minutes, or until the bananas are very tender but not mushy, and the sugar has formed a caramel syrup.

Remove the pan from the heat and arrange the banana mixture around the fish. Serve immediately.

Ocean Rolls

Ocean Rolls are fish fillets stuffed with shrimps or prawns, crabmeat, sweetcorn and dill, poached in white wine. Serve with duchess potatoes and peas for a super meal. For extra-special occasions, some well-chilled white wine would be an excellent accompaniment.

4 SERVINGS

4 white fish fillets, skinned
1 tablespoon lemon juice
1 tablespoon butter
1 shallot, finely chopped
4 oz. frozen and thawed shrimps or prawns, shelled
4 oz. canned or frozen crabmeat, drained or thawed
4 tablespoons canned drained sweetcorn kernels
½ teaspoon dried dill
½ teaspoon salt
½ teaspoon freshly ground black pepper
4 tablespoons double [heavy] cream
12 fl. oz. [1½ cups] dry white wine
1 bay leaf
1 small onion, sliced
1 tablespoon cornflour [cornstarch] mixed with 1 tablespoon white wine

Lay the fish fillets flat on a working surface and sprinkle them with the lemon juice. Set aside.

In a medium-sized frying-pan, melt the butter over moderate heat. When the foam subsides, add the shallot and fry, stirring constantly, for 3 to 4 minutes or until it is soft. Stir in the shrimps or prawns, crabmeat, sweetcorn, dill, salt, pepper and cream. Cook the mixture, stirring constantly, for 3 minutes.

Remove the pan from the heat. Spoon equal amounts of the mixture over each fish fillet. Spread it to the edges of the fillets with your fingertips. Roll up the fillets Swiss [jelly] roll style and secure the rolls with trussing thread or string. Set aside.

In a large, shallow saucepan, bring the wine, bay leaf and onion to the boil over moderately high heat. With a slotted spoon, lower the fish rolls into the liquid, arranging them in one layer. Reduce the heat to low and simmer for 10 minutes.

With the slotted spoon, carefully turn the fish rolls over. Simmer for a further 10 minutes, or until the fish flakes easily when tested with a fork.

Remove the pan from the heat. With the slotted spoon, lift the rolls out of the pan and transfer them to a warmed serving dish. Remove and discard the trussing thread or string. Set aside and keep warm while you finish the sauce.

With the slotted spoon, remove and discard the onion and bay leaf from the cooking liquid. Return the pan to the heat, increase the heat to high and bring the liquid to the boil. Boil for 5 minutes or until the liquid has reduced to one-third of the original quantity.

Reduce the heat to low. Stir in the cornflour [cornstarch] mixture until the sauce is thick and smooth.

Remove the pan from the heat. Pour the sauce over the fish rolls and serve immediately.

Sole Fillets with Tomatoes and Garlic

Quick and easy to make, Sole Fillets with Tomatoes and Garlic is a strongly flavoured dish. It makes an excellent main course accompanied by creamed potatoes and courgettes [zucchini]. Serve with a well chilled white Frascati wine.

4 SERVINGS

2 tablespoons olive oil
1 lb. tomatoes, blanched, peeled, seeded and chopped
4 oz. canned tomato purée
2 large garlic cloves, crushed
1 teaspoon dried oregano
1 teaspoon salt
¼ teaspoon freshly ground black pepper
3 tablespoons flour
2 soles, filleted
1 oz. [2 tablespoons] butter
12 large black olives, stoned

First make the sauce. In a medium-sized saucepan, heat the oil over high heat. Add the tomatoes, tomato purée, garlic, oregano, half the salt and the pepper. Stir to mix. Reduce the heat to low, cover the pan and simmer the sauce for 30 minutes or until it is thick and smooth. If necessary, remove the lid and cook the sauce uncovered, stirring occasionally, until it has the required consistency.

While the sauce is simmering, cook the fish. Mix the flour with the remaining salt on a large plate. Dip the sole fillets in the flour mixture and coat them thoroughly on both sides, shaking off any excess.

Preheat the oven to moderate 350°F (Gas Mark 4, 180°C).

In a large frying-pan, melt the butter over moderately high heat. When the foam subsides, add the fish fillets two at a time. Reduce the heat to moderate and fry the fish for 2 minutes on each side. Transfer the fillets to an ovenproof dish and keep them warm while you cook the remaining fillets in the same way.

When the sauce is ready, stir in the olives. Pour the sauce over the fish. Place the dish in the centre of the oven and bake for 20 minutes. Serve immediately.

Ocean Rolls are guaranteed to make special occasions more special!

Smoked Salmon Quiche

An elegant and easy-to-make dish, Smoked Salmon Quiche may be served as a first course for a dinner party or, with lots of mixed salad and crusty bread, as a light supper or lunch. Accompany it with a bottle of well-chilled Traminer wine.

4-6 SERVINGS

1 x 9-inch flan case made with
    shortcrust pastry
FILLING
4 oz. smoked salmon, cut into
    2-inch pieces
4 fl. oz. single cream [½ cup light
    cream]
3 eggs
2 oz. [½ cup] Gruyère cheese, grated
¼ teaspoon white pepper

Preheat the oven to fairly hot 400°F (Gas Mark 6, 200°C). Place the flan case on a baking sheet.

Arrange the smoked salmon pieces over the bottom of the flan case and set aside.

In a medium-sized mixing bowl, combine the cream, eggs, grated cheese and pepper and beat well to blend. Pour the mixture over the smoked salmon and place the baking sheet in the oven. Bake the quiche for 25 to 30 minutes or until the filling is set and firm and golden brown on top.

Remove the baking sheet from the oven and serve the quiche at once if you are serving it hot.

Grilled [Broiled] Trout

A fragrant Italian way of cooking trout, Grilled [Broiled] Trout makes a sumptuous light lunch when served with fennel and stuffed tomatoes.

4 SERVINGS

4 medium-sized trout, cleaned and
    with the eyes removed
¼ teaspoon salt
½ teaspoon black pepper
2 garlic cloves, halved
4 rosemary sprays
3 tablespoons olive oil
1 lemon, cut into 8 wedges

Preheat the grill [broiler] to moderate.

Place the fish on a wooden board and rub them all over with the salt and pepper. Place half a garlic clove and 1 rosemary spray in the cavity of each fish. With a sharp knife, make 3 shallow cuts on each side of the fish and arrange the trout in the grill [broiler] pan.

With a pastry brush, lightly coat the trout with the oil. Grill [broil] the fish for

5 minutes. Remove the grill [broiler] pan from the heat and, using a fish slice or spatula, turn the fish over. Brush the fish with the remaining oil and return the pan to the heat. Grill [broil] for a further 5 to 6 minutes or until the fish flesh flakes easily when tested with a fork.

Transfer the trout to a warmed serving dish. Remove and discard the garlic and rosemary and garnish the fish with the lemon wedges. Serve immediately.

Tuna Steaks Provençal-Style

Tuna is even more delicious fresh than it is canned, and this superb recipe for Tuna Steaks Provençal-Style really does the fish justice. Serve the dish with sautéed courgettes [zucchini], potatoes and well-chilled white wine.

4 SERVINGS

4 tuna steaks, approximately
    ½-inch thick
½ teaspoon salt
½ teaspoon freshly ground black
    pepper
2 fl. oz. [¼ cup] olive oil
1 large onion, finely chopped
2 garlic cloves, crushed
14 oz. canned peeled tomatoes
8 black olives, stoned and chopped
MARINADE
3 fl. oz. [⅜ cup] olive oil
3 fl. oz. [⅜ cup] dry white wine
2 tablespoons lemon juice
2 garlic cloves, crushed
1 teaspoon freshly ground black
    pepper
1 teaspoon dried basil

First make the marinade. In a large, shallow dish, combine all the marinade ingredients, beating with a fork until they are well mixed. Add the tuna steaks to the dish and baste them well with the marinade. Set aside at room temperature for 2 hours, basting occasionally.

Remove the tuna steaks from the marinade and pat them dry with kitchen paper towels. Reserve the marinade.

Rub the salt and pepper into the tuna steaks and set them aside.

In a large, deep frying-pan, heat the olive oil over moderate heat. When the oil is hot, add the onion and garlic and fry, stirring frequently, for 5 to 7 minutes or until the onion is soft and translucent but not brown. Add the tomatoes with the can juice and olives and cook for a further 3 minutes.

Pour in the reserved marinade and bring the mixture to the boil. Reduce the heat to low and simmer the mixture, uncovered, for 20 minutes or until the

sauce is fairly thick.

Add the tuna steaks to the pan and cook for 8 to 10 minutes on each side, or until the fish flakes easily when tested with a fork. Remove the pan from the heat. Using a slotted spoon, transfer the fish to a warmed serving dish. Pour over the sauce and serve at once.

Yugoslavian Fish Steaks

A delicately flavoured, lightly spiced dish, Yugoslavian Fish Steaks is an unusual way to serve any firm, white-fleshed fish. The dish may be served with plain boiled rice

and spinach.

4 SERVINGS

2 oz. [4 tablespoons] butter
2 tablespoons vegetable oil
2 medium-sized onions, thinly
 sliced
1 lb. tomatoes, blanched, peeled,
 seeded and chopped or 14 oz.
 canned peeled tomatoes, drained
3 fl. oz. [⅜ cup] white wine
1 tablespoon white wine vinegar
¼ teaspoon cayenne pepper
¼ teaspoon freshly ground black
 pepper
1½ teaspoons salt
½ teaspoon dried tarragon
2 tablespoons flour

4 x 8 oz. steaks of any firm white fish

In a medium-sized saucepan, melt 1 ounce [2 tablespoons] of the butter and half of the oil over moderate heat. When the foam subsides, add the onions and fry them for 5 to 7 minutes. Add the tomatoes, wine, wine vinegar, cayenne, pepper, ½ teaspoon salt and tarragon. Bring the liquid to the boil, cover, reduce the heat to moderately low and simmer gently for 30 minutes, stirring occasionally.

While the sauce is simmering, combine the remaining salt and flour together on a plate. Dip the fish steaks in the mixture and coat them well on both sides.

Grilled [Broiled] Trout is a superbly easy way to cook an exceptionally tasty fish. Serve with stuffed tomatoes.

Ten minutes before the end of the sauce's cooking time, melt the remaining butter and oil in a large frying-pan over moderate heat. When the butter foam subsides, add the salted, floured fish to the pan. Cook for 5 to 6 minutes on each side, or until the steaks are lightly browned, adding more butter and oil if necessary. Transfer the fish steaks to a warmed serving dish and spoon the sauce over them. Serve at once.

149

Clam and Corn Bake

Clam and Corn Bake, made with clams, prawns or shrimps, sweetcorn and cream, with a cheese topping, is delicious served hot or cold with a tossed green salad.

4 SERVINGS

10 fl. oz. double cream [1¼ cups heavy cream]
3 eggs
½ teaspoon salt
¼ teaspoon black pepper
⅛ teaspoon cayenne pepper
1 tablespoon finely chopped fresh chives (optional)
10 oz. fresh, frozen or canned and drained sweetcorn
8 oz. prawns or shrimps, shelled
15 clams, steamed, removed from their shells and coarsely chopped
2 oz. [½ cup] Cheddar cheese, grated
1 oz. [⅓ cup] dry breadcrumbs
1 oz. [2 tablespoons] butter

Preheat the oven to moderate 350°F (Gas Mark 4, 180°C).

In a medium-sized mixing bowl, using a wire whisk or rotary beater, lightly beat together the cream, eggs, salt, pepper and cayenne. Stir in the chives, if you are using them, the sweetcorn, prawns or shrimps and clams.

Turn the mixture out into a lightly greased soufflé dish and set aside.

In a small mixing bowl, combine the grated cheese and breadcrumbs and spoon this over the mixture in the soufflé dish. Cut the butter into small pieces and dot over the top.

Place the dish in the oven and bake for 1 hour or until the top is golden.

Remove the dish from the oven and serve immediately, or cool and serve cold.

Japanese Clams

Serve Japanese Clams as an hors d'oeuvre or as part of a Japanese meal.

4 SERVINGS

2 fl. oz. [¼ cup] sake
2 tablespoons sugar
12 clams, removed from their shells
2 tablespoons soy sauce

In a large, heavy frying-pan, combine the sake, sugar and clams. With a wooden spoon, stir the mixture thoroughly. Bring the mixture to the boil over high heat and boil it for 3 minutes, stirring constantly. Stir in the soy sauce and cook for 1 minute, still stirring. Remove the clams from the pan and set aside.

Continue boiling the sauce in the frying-pan for a further 10 minutes or until it becomes thick and syrupy. Return the clams to the pan and stir them gently into the sauce. Cook the mixture, stirring constantly, for 1 minute.

Remove from the heat and serve.

Stuffed Clams

Grilled [broiled] clams flavoured with garlic and parsley, Stuffed Clams may be served as a special hors d'oeuvre, on their own or garnished with lemon wedges, or as a

Clam and Corn Bake is an economical dish from the United States.

light lunch with lots of tomato salad and crusty bread.

4 SERVINGS

24 clams, scrubbed and steamed
3½ oz. [⅜ cup plus 1 tablespoon] butter, melted
2 oz. [⅔ cup] dry white breadcrumbs
2 garlic cloves, crushed
2 tablespoons finely chopped fresh parsley
½ teaspoon salt
½ teaspoon freshly ground black pepper
2 parsley sprigs

Remove and discard the upper clam shell halves, leaving the flesh in the bottom shell halves. Set the clams aside.

Preheat the grill [broiler] to moderately high.

In a small mixing bowl, combine the butter, breadcrumbs, garlic, chopped parsley, salt and pepper.

Sprinkle the mixture evenly over each clam, pressing the mixture down lightly over the clam flesh with your fingertips.

Place the clams, flesh sides up, in a large flameproof dish, in one layer if possible.

Place the dish under the grill [broiler] and grill [broil] the clams for 5 to 6 minutes, or until the topping is golden brown.

Remove the dish from the heat. Garnish with the parsley sprigs and serve immediately.

Clams Baked with Potatoes and Sweetcorn

Easy and quick to make, Clams Baked with Potatoes and Sweetcorn is an inexpensive dish, perfect for a light lunch or dinner.

4 SERVINGS

1 teaspoon butter
2 lb. potatoes, cooked and mashed
2 fl. oz. double cream [¼ cup heavy cream]
2 tablespoons tomato purée
2 teaspoons finely chopped fresh chives
1 teaspoon salt
½ teaspoon black pepper
¼ teaspoon dried thyme
¼ teaspoon grated nutmeg
¼ teaspoon cayenne pepper
1 garlic clove, crushed

These clams are stuffed with parsley, breadcrumbs and garlic.

1 lb. canned clams, drained
10 oz. canned sweetcorn, drained
4 oz. Bel Paese cheese, thinly sliced

Preheat the oven to fairly hot 400°F (Gas Mark 6, 200°C).

With the teaspoon of butter, grease a medium-sized, deep-sided baking dish and set it aside.

In a large mixing bowl, beat the mashed potatoes and cream together with a wooden spoon until the mixture is smooth. Beat in the tomato purée, chives, salt, pepper, thyme, nutmeg, cayenne and garlic. Stir in the clams and sweetcorn and combine the mixture thoroughly.

Spoon the mixture into the prepared baking dish and smooth it down with the back of the spoon. Lay the cheese slices over the mixture to cover it completely.

Place the dish in the centre of the oven and bake for 15 to 20 minutes, or until the cheese has melted and is golden brown.

Remove the dish from the oven and serve immediately.

Mussels Baked with Basil and Tomato Sauce

A delightful dish for a family supper, Mussels Baked with Basil and Tomato Sauce is easy to prepare and fairly economical. It may be served with buttered noodles and a crisp green salad.

4 SERVINGS

1 tablespoon plus 1 teaspoon butter
3 tablespoons olive oil
1 large onion, finely chopped
3 garlic cloves, crushed
1½ lb. canned peeled tomatoes, chopped
½ teaspoon salt
¼ teaspoon black pepper
3 tablespoons chopped fresh basil or 1½ tablespoons dried basil
3 quarts mussels, scrubbed, steamed and removed from their shells
2 tablespoons fresh breadcrumbs
2 oz. [½ cup] Parmesan cheese, grated

Preheat the oven to moderate 350°F (Gas Mark 4, 180°C).

With the teaspoon of butter, lightly grease a medium-sized baking dish.

In a medium-sized saucepan, melt the remaining butter with the olive oil over moderate heat. When the foam subsides, add the onion and garlic and cook, stirring occasionally, for 5 to 7 minutes, or until the onion is soft and translucent but not brown.

Stir in the tomatoes with the can juice, the salt, pepper and basil. Reduce the heat to low and simmer the sauce, stirring occasionally, for 15 minutes. Remove the pan from the heat and stir in the mussels. Pour the mixture into the prepared dish.

In a small bowl, combine the breadcrumbs and grated cheese, mixing until they are well blended. Sprinkle the mixture over the mussel mixture.

Place the dish in the centre of the oven and bake for 20 minutes, or until the top is golden brown and bubbling. Remove the dish from the oven and serve.

Mussel and Beef Pie

A traditional English recipe, Mussel and Beef Pie makes a wonderfully nourishing and sustaining meal.

6 SERVINGS

2 oz. [¼ cup] butter
2 tablespoons vegetable oil
2 lb. lean stewing beef, cut into 1-inch cubes
1 large onion, finely chopped
2 potatoes, peeled and diced
8 oz. mushrooms, wiped clean and sliced
8 fl. oz. [1 cup] dark beer
½ teaspoon dried thyme
½ teaspoon salt
¼ teaspoon black pepper
1 quart mussels, scrubbed, steamed and removed from their shells

PASTRY
6 oz. [1½ cups] flour
¼ teaspoon salt
4 oz. [½ cup] butter
3 to 4 tablespoons iced water
1 egg, lightly beaten

First make the pastry. Sift the flour and salt into a bowl. Cut the butter into small pieces and add them to the flour. Pour in the water and mix quickly into a dough, which should be lumpy.

On a floured surface, roll out the dough into an oblong shape. Fold it in three and turn it so that the open edges face you. Roll again into an oblong shape and fold and turn as before. Repeat once again to make three folds and turns in all. Chill the dough while you make the filling.

Preheat the oven to fairly hot 400°F (Gas Mark 6, 200°C).

Meanwhile, prepare the filling. In a large frying-pan, melt the butter with the oil over moderate heat. When the foam subsides, add the beef cubes, a few at a time, and cook, stirring and turning occasionally, for 8 to 10 minutes or until they are evenly browned. Transfer the cubes to a plate and keep warm while you brown the remaining meat in the same way.

Add the onion and potatoes to the pan and cook, stirring occasionally, for 5 to 7 minutes or until the onion is soft and translucent but not brown. Stir in the mushrooms and cook the mixture for a further 3 minutes.

Pour over the beer and add the thyme, salt and pepper, mixing well to blend. Increase the heat to high and bring the mixture to the boil. Reduce the heat to moderate and return the beef cubes to the pan, stirring well to mix. Simmer the mixture for 15 minutes.

Stir in the mussels and remove the pan from the heat. Pour the mixture into a 9-inch pie dish and set aside.

Remove the dough from the refrigerator. If it looks streaky, roll it out into an oblong shape and fold it in three once again. Roll it out to a piece 1-inch larger than the top of the pie dish. With a sharp knife, cut a ½-inch strip around the dough. Dampen the rim of the dish with water and press the dough strip on to the rim. With a pastry brush dipped in water, lightly moisten the strip.

Using the rolling pin, lift the dough on to the dish. With a knife, trim the dough and, with your fingers, crimp the edges to seal them to the strip already on the dish. With a sharp knife, cut a cross in the centre of the dough. With a pastry brush, coat the surface with the beaten egg.

Place the pie in the oven and bake for 45 to 50 minutes or until the pastry is golden brown.

Remove the pie from the oven and serve.

Mussels with Lemon Sauce

Mussels with Lemon Sauce have a fresh tangy flavour and make a delicious main course for a summer meal.

4 SERVINGS

2½ quarts mussels
2 oz. [¼ cup] butter

2 shallots, finely chopped
  bouquet garni consisting of 4
  parsley sprigs, 1 thyme spray
  and 1 bay leaf tied together
½ teaspoon salt
½ teaspoon black pepper
¼ teaspoon grated nutmeg
  juice of 4 lemons
1 tablespoon flour

Wash the mussels in cold water and, with a stiff brush, scrub them to remove any mud on their shells. Discard any mussels which are not tightly shut or do not close if sharply tapped, and any that float or have broken shells. With a sharp knife, scrape off the tufts of hair, or beards, which protrude from between the closed shell halves. Place the mussels in a large bowl of cold water and soak them for 1 hour. Drain the mussels in a colander and set aside.

In a large saucepan, melt half the butter over moderate heat. When the foam subsides, add the shallots, bouquet garni, salt, pepper and nutmeg. Cook, stirring occasionally, for 2 to 3 minutes, or until the shallots are soft and translucent but not brown. Stir in the lemon juice.

Increase the heat to moderately high and add the mussels to the pan. Cook the mussels, shaking the pan constantly, for 3 minutes or until the shells open.

Remove the pan from the heat. Transfer the mussels and cooking liquid to a large strainer set over a large bowl. Reserve the strained liquid. Set the mussels aside and keep warm.

In a small saucepan, melt the remaining butter over moderate heat. Remove the pan from the heat and, with a wooden spoon, stir in the flour to make a smooth paste. Gradually add the reserved strained cooking liquid, stirring constantly. Return the pan to low heat and, stirring constantly, cook the sauce for 3 to 4 minutes or until it is thick and smooth. Remove the pan from the heat.

Arrange the mussels decoratively in a large warmed serving dish and pour the sauce over them. Serve immediately.

Mussels Mariners' Style

☆

Mussels Mariners' Style make an excellent first course, served in deep soup bowls with a fork to eat the mussels and a soup spoon for the juices.

4 SERVINGS

3 quarts mussels
2 oz. [¼ cup] butter
1 small onion, finely chopped
1 garlic clove, crushed
1 celery stalk, trimmed and finely
  chopped
  bouquet garni consisting of 4
  parsley sprigs, 1 thyme spray
  and 1 bay leaf tied together
16 fl. oz. [2 cups] dry white wine
½ teaspoon salt
¼ teaspoon black pepper
2 tablespoons chopped parsley

Wash the mussels in cold water and, with a stiff brush, scrub them to remove any mud on their shells. Discard any mussels which are not tightly shut or do not close if sharply tapped, and any that float or have broken shells.

With a sharp knife, scrape off the tufts of hair, or beards, which protrude from between the closed shell halves. Place the mussels in a large bowl of cold water and soak them for 1 hour. Drain the mussels in a colander and set aside.

In a large saucepan, melt the butter over moderate heat. When the foam subsides, add the onion and garlic and fry, stirring occasionally, for 5 to 7 minutes or until the onion is soft and translucent but not brown. Add the celery, bouquet garni, wine, salt and pepper and bring the mixture to the boil. Reduce the heat to low, add the mussels and simmer, shaking the pan occasionally, for 5 to 10 minutes, or until the shells open. With a slotted spoon, transfer the mussels to a warmed serving dish. Remove and discard the empty shell halves from the mussels.

Strain the mussel cooking liquid into a bowl, then return it to the saucepan. Place the pan over high heat and bring it to the boil. Boil for 2 minutes. Pour the liquid over the mussels, sprinkle over the parsley and serve.

Mussels Baked with Basil and Tomato Sauce.

Chinese Deep-Fried Prawns

Chinese Deep-Fried Prawns may be served as part of a complete Chinese meal.

4-6 SERVINGS

3 tablespoons tomato purée
2 tablespoons soy sauce
1 teaspoon chilli sauce
1 teaspoon sugar
1½ lb. large prawns or shrimps
1 egg, lightly beaten
3 tablespoons flour
2 teaspoons cornflour [cornstarch]
1 slice root ginger, very finely diced
½ teaspoon salt
3 fl. oz. [⅜ cup] water
sufficient oil for deep-frying

In a small bowl mix together the tomato purée, soy sauce, chilli sauce and sugar until they are thoroughly blended. Put this sauce in a sauceboat and set aside.

To prepare the prawns for cooking, remove the shells leaving the tail shell intact. Under cold running water, remove the black veins from the back flesh. Drain.

To make the batter, put the beaten egg into a medium-sized bowl and, beating continuously with a wire whisk, add the flour, cornflour [cornstarch], ginger, salt and water. Beat until the batter is smooth.

In a deep-frying pan, heat the oil over high heat until it registers 350°F on a deep-fat thermometer, or until a small cube of dry bread dropped into the oil turns golden brown in 55 seconds.

Holding the prawns by the tail, dip each one in the batter. As soon as the oil reaches the correct temperature, put the prawns in a deep-frying basket and put the basket in the oil. Fry the prawns for 2 to 3 minutes, or until they become golden brown. Remove the deep-frying basket from the oil and drain the prawns.

Arrange the prawns on a heated serving dish and serve them with the sauce.

Prawn or Shrimp Cocktail

A very popular first course, Prawn or Shrimp Cocktail is simple to prepare.

4 SERVINGS

4 large lettuce leaves, washed, shaken dry and shredded
6 fl. oz. [¾ cup] mayonnaise
4 tablespoons double [heavy] cream
2 teaspoons Worcestershire sauce
2 teaspoons lemon juice
2 teaspoons tomato ketchup
¼ teaspoon cayenne pepper
½ teaspoon salt
½ teaspoon black pepper
14 oz. prawns or shrimps, shelled
1 teaspoon paprika
4 thin cucumber slices
1 lemon, quartered

Stand 4 individual serving glasses on 4 small plates. Divide the shredded lettuce equally among the glasses and set aside.

In a medium-sized mixing bowl, combine the mayonnaise, cream, Worcestershire sauce, lemon juice, tomato ketchup, cayenne, salt and pepper, beating with a wooden spoon until the mixture is smooth. Stir in the prawns or shrimps.

Spoon the mixture equally over the lettuce and sprinkle over the paprika.

Garnish with the cucumber and lemon quarters and serve immediately.

Creole Shrimps

Serve this tasty dish with plain boiled rice and a mixed salad.

4 SERVINGS

2 tablespoons olive oil
2 celery stalks, finely chopped

Exotic Chinese Deep-Fried Prawns.

2 large onions, finely chopped
8 fl. oz. [1 cup] dry white wine
14 oz. canned peeled tomatoes,
  drained and roughly chopped
1 teaspoon salt
1 tablespoon red wine vinegar
1 tablespoon sugar
1 green pepper, white pith
  removed, seeded and chopped
1 tablespoon cornflour [cornstarch],
  mixed with 2 fl. oz. [¼ cup] water
1½ lb. frozen shelled shrimps, thawed

In a large, deep frying-pan, heat the oil over moderate heat. Add the celery and onions and fry for 5 to 7 minutes, or until the onions are soft and transparent.

Pour the wine into the pan, reduce the heat to low and simmer for 10 minutes, stirring occasionally.

Add the tomatoes, salt, vinegar and sugar to the pan. Continue simmering for a further 10 minutes, stirring occasionally.

Add the green pepper to the pan and simmer for 10 minutes.

Stir in the cornflour [cornstarch] mixture. Raise the heat to moderate, bring the sauce to the boil and cook for 3 minutes.

Add the shrimps to the pan and cook for 4 to 5 minutes longer to heat them through. Remove the pan from the heat and spoon the shrimp mixture on to a bed of rice. Serve immediately.

Prawn or Shrimp and Crabmeat Spread

Prawn or Shrimp and Crabmeat Spread makes an excellent first course, served on thin triangles of toast.

12 OUNCES [1½ CUPS]
4 oz. cooked crabmeat, fresh or
  canned, shell and cartilage
  removed

Serve traditional Creole Shrimps on a bed of plain boiled rice.

2 oz. [¼ cup] butter, softened
2 tablespoons double [heavy] cream
⅛ teaspoon cayenne pepper
¼ teaspoon salt
1 teaspoon fresh lemon juice
8 oz. frozen prawns or shrimps,
  thawed and shelled

Place the crabmeat, butter and cream in a mortar. Using a pestle, pound the mixture until it is smooth. Alternatively, place the ingredients in an electric blender and blend, on and off, for 30 seconds.

Spoon the mixture into a medium-sized mixing bowl. Using a fork, mash in the cayenne, salt and lemon juice. Mix in the prawns or shrimps.

Cover the bowl and chill it in the refrigerator for 1 hour before serving.

155

Prawn or Shrimp Curry

This is a strong curry flavoured with coconut, from South India. If coconuts are not available make the coconut milk with 4 ounces of creamed coconut and 12 fluid ounces [1½ cups] of boiling water.

4-6 SERVINGS

1½-inch piece fresh root ginger, peeled and chopped
3 garlic cloves
4 green chillis, seeded
6 tablespoons chopped fresh coriander leaves (1 bunch)
1 tablespoon whole coriander seeds
juice of 1 lemon
15 fl. oz. [1⅞ cups] thick coconut milk
6 tablespoons vegetable oil
1½ lb. large prawns or shrimps, shelled
2 medium-sized onions, finely chopped
1 teaspoon turmeric
1 teaspoon mustard seed
1 teaspoon salt

Put the ginger, garlic, chillis, coriander leaves and seeds, and the lemon juice in the jar of an electric blender. Pour in 4 tablespoons of the coconut milk. Blend at high speed until the mixture forms a thick paste. Add more coconut milk if the blender sticks. Scrape out the paste and set it aside in a small mixing bowl.

In a large saucepan, heat 4 tablespoons of the oil over moderate heat. When the oil is hot, add the prawns or shrimps and

Potted Shrimps or Prawns is an all-time British favourite.

fry them, turning them frequently, for 5 minutes. With a slotted spoon, transfer the prawns or shrimps to a plate. Set aside.

Add the remaining oil to the pan. When the oil is hot, add the onions and fry them, stirring occasionally, for 8 to 10 minutes or until they are golden brown. Add the turmeric, mustard seed and salt and fry, stirring constantly, for 1 minute. Add the spice paste and fry, stirring constantly, for 5 minutes. Add the prawns or shrimps and remaining coconut milk and cook for 1 minute. When the curry boils, cover the pan, reduce the heat to low and simmer for 30 minutes. Taste the curry and add more salt or lemon juice if necessary.

Remove the pan from the heat. Spoon the curry into a heated serving bowl. Serve immediately.

Greek Prawns or Shrimps with Tomato Sauce

A traditional Greek dish, Greek Prawns or Shrimps with Tomato Sauce is simple to prepare and makes an appetizing and light luncheon dish. Serve with rice and a mixed green salad and a well-chilled Greek white wine, such as Hymmetus.

4-6 SERVINGS

2 oz. [¼ cup] butter
1 medium-sized onion, thinly sliced
2 garlic cloves, crushed
2 lb. fresh tomatoes, blanched peeled, seeded and chopped, or 2 lb. canned peeled tomatoes, drained and chopped
1 teaspoon sugar
1 teaspoon chopped fresh oregano or ½ teaspoon dried oregano
1 teaspoon chopped fresh basil or ½ teaspoon dried basil
1 bay leaf
1 tablespoon chopped fresh parsley
8 fl. oz. [1 cup] dry white wine
1 teaspoon salt
½ teaspoon freshly ground black pepper
1 lb. frozen Dublin Bay prawns [large Gulf shrimps], thawed and shelled
3 oz. feta cheese, cut into small cubes

In a large, heavy frying-pan, melt the butter over moderate heat. When the foam subsides, add the onion and garlic to the pan and cook them, stirring occasionally, for 5 to 7 minutes, or until the onion is soft and translucent but not brown.

Add the tomatoes, sugar, oregano, basil, bay leaf and parsley to the pan and stir well to mix. Reduce the heat to low, cover the pan and simmer the sauce for 15 minutes, stirring occasionally.

Stir in the wine and increase the heat to high. Bring the liquid to the boil. Reduce the heat to low and simmer the sauce, uncovered, for a further 30 minutes, or until it has thickened and reduced somewhat.

Stir in the salt, pepper, prawns and cheese. Cook the mixture for 8 to 10 minutes, or until the prawns are heated through and the cheese has melted.

Remove the pan from the heat and remove and discard the bay leaf. Spoon the mixture into a warmed serving dish and serve at once.

Potted Shrimps or Prawns

A traditional British speciality, Potted Shrimps or Prawns are very easy to prepare. White fish is often added to the shrimps or prawns and the mixture may be put into one big dish rather than small individual pots. Serve with thin slices of brown bread and garnish with watercress. Potted Shrimps or Prawns may be kept for up to 1 week in the refrigerator.

10 SERVINGS

5 oz. [⅝ cup] butter
¼ teaspoon ground mace

$\frac{1}{8}$ teaspoon cayenne pepper
$\frac{1}{2}$ teaspoon salt
$\frac{1}{2}$ teaspoon black pepper
1 lb. shrimps or prawns, cooked and shelled
5 oz. [$\frac{5}{8}$ cup] clarified butter, melted

In a large frying-pan, melt the butter over moderate heat. When the foam subsides, stir in the mace, cayenne, salt and pepper. Add the shrimps or prawns to the pan and coat them thoroughly with the seasoned butter. Remove the pan from the heat.

Spoon equal amounts of the mixture into 10 small pots, leaving a $\frac{1}{4}$-inch space at the top. Pour 1 tablespoon of the clarified butter into each pot. Cover the pots with aluminium foil and put them in the refrigerator to chill for at least 2 hours.

Remove the pots from the refrigerator. Remove and discard the foil and serve at once.

Prawn Savoury

A simple, quickly made dish suitable for lunch or supper, Prawn Savoury may be accompanied by a tomato salad and a baked potato with sour cream.

6 SERVINGS
2 oz. [4 tablespoons] butter
16 oz. canned and drained or frozen and thawed corn kernels
1 green pepper, white pith removed, seeded and finely chopped
12 oz. [1$\frac{1}{2}$ cups] cooked prawns or shrimps, shelled
4 fl. oz. double cream [$\frac{1}{2}$ cup heavy cream]
$\frac{1}{4}$ teaspoon salt
$\frac{1}{4}$ teaspoon black pepper
6 slices toast
$\frac{1}{8}$ teaspoon cayenne pepper

In a large, heavy frying-pan, melt the butter over moderate heat. Add the corn and green pepper to the pan and sauté them gently for 5 minutes, stirring occasionally. Add the prawns and cream and simmer the mixture for 4 more minutes, or until the prawns are thoroughly heated. Add the salt and pepper. Spoon the mixture on to the toast, sprinkle with the cayenne and serve immediately.

Scampi Kebabs

These unusual kebabs, made with prawns [shrimps], peppers and mushrooms and flavoured with lemon, garlic and sage, have a distinctly Mediterranean appearance.

4 SERVINGS
16 Dublin Bay prawns [large Gulf shrimps], shelled
2 green peppers, white pith removed, seeded and cut into 16 pieces
16 medium-sized mushrooms, wiped clean and stalks removed
16 sage leaves
2 lemons, quartered and each quarter cut across in half
MARINADE
2 fl. oz. [$\frac{1}{4}$ cup] olive oil
2 tablespoons lemon juice
3 garlic cloves, crushed
1 teaspoon salt
$\frac{3}{4}$ teaspoon black pepper

In a large, shallow mixing bowl, combine all the marinade ingredients thoroughly. Add the prawns [shrimps] and stir well to coat them with the marinade. Set aside in a cool place to marinate for 1 hour.

Remove the prawns [shrimps] from the marinade and pat them dry with kitchen paper towels. Reserve the marinade.

Preheat the grill [broiler] to moderate.

Thread 1 prawn [shrimp] on to a skewer, then a piece of green pepper, a mushroom, sage leaf and a piece of lemon. Repeat the process 3 more times, then fill 3 more skewers in the same way.

Place the skewers on the rack in the grill [broiler] pan and baste them with a little of the reserved marinade.

Place the pan under the heat and grill [broil] the kebabs for 10 minutes, turning them over occasionally and basting with the reserved marinade.

Remove the kebabs from the heat and place them on a warmed serving dish. Pour over the pan juices and serve.

Prawn Savoury is a mouth-watering mixture of prawns, green pepper and sweetcorn, served on toast.

Crab Patties

A special seafood dish from the eastern part of the United States, Crab Patties are a joy to eat.

4-6 SERVINGS

1 lb. crabmeat, shell and cartilage removed
3 oz. [1½ cups] fresh breadcrumbs
1 egg yolk
2 tablespoons mayonnaise
12 spring onions [scallions], finely chopped
1 hard-boiled egg, finely chopped
½ teaspoon chopped fresh marjoram
2 teaspoons lemon juice
¼ teaspoon salt
¼ teaspoon black pepper
⅛ teaspoon cayenne pepper

4 fl. oz. [½ cup] vegetable oil
½ bunch watercress, trimmed and washed

In a medium-sized mixing bowl, combine the crabmeat, breadcrumbs, egg yolk, mayonnaise, spring onions [scallions], hard-boiled egg, marjoram, lemon juice, salt, pepper and cayenne. Mix and knead the mixture with your hands until it comes away from the sides of the bowl. Shape the crab mixture into 2-inch balls, place them on a board and flatten them with the palm of your hands.

In a large frying-pan, heat the vegetable

A spectacular dish for that special occasion, Dublin Bay Prawns served on a bed of rice.

oil over moderately high heat. When the oil is hot, add the patties, a few at a time, and fry them for 3 to 5 minutes on each side or until they are deep golden brown. Using a slotted spoon, transfer the patties to kitchen paper towels to drain.

Place the patties on a warmed serving dish, garnish with the watercress and serve immediately.

Dublin Bay Prawns

   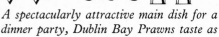

A spectacularly attractive main dish for a dinner party, Dublin Bay Prawns taste as good as they look.

4 SERVINGS

SAUCE
4 teaspoons dark brown sugar

½ teaspoon black pepper
¼ teaspoon salt
½ teaspoon ground ginger
2 teaspoons soy sauce
1 teaspoon Worcestershire sauce
8 fl. oz. [1 cup] dry white wine
1 garlic clove, finely chopped
3 teaspoons cornflour [cornstarch]
   dissolved in 3 teaspoons water
RICE
8 oz. [1⅓ cups] long-grain rice,
   washed, soaked in cold water
   for 30 minutes and drained
19 fl. oz. [2⅜ cups] cold water
1 teaspoon salt
PRAWNS
2 lb. Dublin Bay prawns [large
   Gulf shrimps], shelled
¼ teaspoon cayenne pepper
3 tablespoons olive oil
1 large red pepper, white pith
   removed, seeded and cut into
   ½-inch lengths

To make the sauce, in a medium-sized saucepan, combine the sugar, black pepper, salt and ginger. Add the soy sauce, Worcestershire sauce and wine and mix thoroughly. Add the garlic.

Place the pan over high heat and bring the sauce to the boil. Reduce the heat to low, cover the pan and simmer for 20 minutes.

Remove the pan from the heat and stir in the cornflour [cornstarch]. Return the pan to high heat and bring the mixture to the boil. Reduce the heat to low and simmer for 5 minutes, or until the sauce thickens. Remove the pan from the heat.

Place the rice, water and salt in a large saucepan. Bring to the boil over high heat. Cover the pan, reduce the heat to very low and simmer for 15 minutes. If all the liquid is not absorbed at the end of this time, continue to cook, uncovered, until the rice is dry. Transfer the rice to a warmed serving dish and keep warm.

Meanwhile, sprinkle the prawns with the cayenne. In a large frying-pan, heat the oil over moderate heat. Add the prawns and red pepper to the pan and cook, turning frequently, for 10 minutes.

While the prawns are cooking, reheat the sauce, stirring, over low heat.

Arrange the prawns on top of the rice, pour the hot sauce over them and serve.

Oranges Stuffed with Prawns or Shrimps and Rice

A tangy first course, Oranges Stuffed with Prawns or Shrimps and Rice makes an attractive and tasty dish. Serve on a bed of chopped lettuce.

6 SERVINGS
6 medium-sized oranges, halved
2½ oz. [1 cup] cooked long-grain rice
6 oz. prawns or shrimps, shelled
2 oz. [⅓ cup] raisins
2 oz. [½ cup] slivered almonds
DRESSING
3 tablespoons olive oil
1 tablespoon red wine vinegar
½ teaspoon salt
¼ teaspoon black pepper
½ teaspoon dried thyme

First, prepare the dressing. In a small mixing bowl, beat the oil, vinegar, salt, pepper and thyme together with a fork until they are well combined. Set aside.

Using a serrated-edged knife, carefully cut out the flesh from the oranges, until only the shell is left. Set the shells aside.

Place the orange flesh on a chopping board and cut it into small cubes, discarding any membrane. Transfer the cubes to a medium-sized mixing bowl. Add the rice, prawns or shrimps, raisins and almonds. Spoon over the prepared dressing and mix until all the ingredients are well coated.

Place the bowl in the refrigerator to chill for 30 minutes.

Remove the bowl from the refrigerator. Spoon the orange and rice mixture into the reserved orange shells and serve.

Oysters Kilpatrick - simple to make, beautiful to eat.

Oysters Kilpatrick

Serve this simple but delicious dish with a glass of iced-cold lager and slices of brown bread and butter.

3 SERVINGS
2 oz. [¼ cup] butter, softened
32 fresh oysters, with one shell
   removed
2 teaspoons Worcestershire sauce
12 lean bacon slices, grilled [broiled]
   until crisp and crumbled
2 tablespoons chopped parsley

Preheat the grill [broiler] to moderate.

Using a flat-bladed knife, carefully spread a thin layer of butter over each oyster. Season the oysters with the Worcestershire sauce and sprinkle over the crumbled bacon.

Place the oysters, a few at a time, under the grill [broiler] and grill [broil] for 2 minutes. Remove the oysters from the grill [broiler] and keep warm while you grill [broil] the remaining oysters in the same way.

Sprinkle over the parsley and serve immediately.

Stuffed Squid makes a festive centre-piece to any family meal.

Scallops Sautéed with Garlic and Basil

This simple recipe for scallops is an exquisite first course for a special dinner.
4 SERVINGS

   juice of ½ lemon
¼ teaspoon salt
¼ teaspoon white pepper
1½ lb. scallops, cut into ½-inch pieces
2½ oz. [⅝ cup] flour
 6 tablespoons vegetable oil
 3 shallots, finely chopped
 3 garlic cloves, crushed
¼ teaspoon dried basil
 1 oz. [2 tablespoons] butter
 1 tablespoon chopped parsley

Sprinkle the lemon juice, salt and pepper over the scallops. Put the scallops in a strainer and sprinkle the flour over them.

In a frying-pan heat half the oil over moderate heat. The oil should cover the pan in a thin film, so if necessary add the rest.

Add the scallops and toss lightly. Cook

the scallops for 5 minutes or until they are lightly browned. Add the shallots, garlic and basil to the pan and cook for 2 minutes. Remove the pan from the heat, stir in the butter and parsley and transfer the scallops to individual warmed serving dishes. Serve immediately.

Stuffed Squid

Squid stuffed with a cheese, garlic and parsley mixture and cooked in a wine and tomato sauce is an unusual main dish for a family dinner.

3 SERVINGS

 6 medium-sized squid, cleaned
   and skinned with the tender
   parts of the tentacles reserved
 3 tablespoons fresh breadcrumbs
 2 tablespoons finely chopped parsley
 6 tablespoons grated Parmesan
   cheese
 2 garlic cloves, finely chopped
   plus 4 whole garlic cloves
 1 egg, lightly beaten
 2 fl. oz. [¼ cup] olive oil
⅛ teaspoon cayenne pepper
½ teaspoon salt
¼ teaspoon black pepper

14 oz. canned peeled Italian plum
   tomatoes
½ teaspoon dried rosemary
 2 fl. oz. [¼ cup] dry white wine

Chop the tentacles finely and place them in a mixing bowl. Add the breadcrumbs, parsley, cheese, 1 chopped garlic clove, the egg, 1 tablespoon of olive oil, cayenne, ¼ teaspoon of salt and ⅛ teaspoon of pepper to the bowl. Mix well.

Spoon the mixture into the squid.

With a thick needle and thread, sew up the openings of each squid.

In a large, deep frying-pan, heat the remaining oil over moderate heat. Add the whole garlic cloves to the pan and cook them for 5 minutes, stirring. Remove and discard the garlic cloves.

Add the squid to the pan and brown them on all sides, turning carefully. Add the tomatoes with the can juice, rosemary, the remaining chopped garlic, the wine, and the rest of the salt and pepper.

Reduce the heat to low, cover the pan and simmer gently for 20 to 30 minutes.

Remove the squid from the pan and place them on a plate. Remove and discard the thread. Slice the squid and arrange the slices in a warmed serving dish. Pour over the sauce and serve.

160

Fish and seafood for entertaining

It's not often that people think of entertaining around a fish main course — probably partly a holdover from the formal days of eating when there was a 'fish' course to precede the main or meat offering, but also perhaps partly due to plain ignorance of just how superb, and festive, fish can be. For whatever the reason, prospective guests are the ultimate losers, for fish can provide some of the most nourishing and varied dishes around today.

Fish dishes can be as expensive or as cheap as you care to make them, from the dizzy gourmet heights of Salmon with Dill Mayonnaise (page 170), through elegant Crabmeat and Avocado Mousse (page 182), to delicate, inexpensive Truro Skate with Egg and Lemon Sauce (page 177). And they span the unusual and familiar, too — like exotic Stir-fried Abalone and Chinese Cabbage (pictured below, recipe on page 190), or classic Trout with Almonds (page 174).

For those occasions when there's someone coming to dinner you simply CAN'T put off and coffers are low, there's a whole, colourful **For Budget Occasions** section containing easy-to-make fish and seafood dinners guaranteed to have them coming back for more!

All of them, from the grandest to the more modest, are specially chosen for their ease of preparation and relatively short cooking times — thus giving you time to change your dress, powder your nose, and generally meet and greet your guests the way you want to, feeling relaxed.

Bass with White Butter Sauce

Decorative and easy to prepare, Bass with White Butter Sauce is an ideal main course for a lunch or dinner party, served with new potatoes and courgettes [zucchini] sautéed in butter. A white Burgundy is a good accompaniment.

6 SERVINGS

5 pints [6¼ pints] court bouillon or fish stock
1 x 3 lb. sea bass, cleaned, with the head and tail left on
6 parsley sprigs
SAUCE
2 fl. oz. [¼ cup] white wine vinegar
2 fl. oz. [¼ cup] dry white wine
3 shallots, finely chopped
½ teaspoon salt
¼ teaspoon white pepper
8 oz. [1 cup] unsalted butter, cut into small pieces and chilled

Pour the court bouillon or stock into a large fish kettle and bring it to the boil over high heat.

Meanwhile, wash the fish thoroughly, inside and out, under cold running water. Pat dry with kitchen paper towels and carefully wrap it in a double piece of cheesecloth.

Reduce the heat to low. Place the fish on the rack of the kettle, and lower the rack into the kettle. (The liquid should cover the fish by 2 inches.)

Cover the kettle and simmer the fish very gently for 15 minutes. Remove the kettle from the heat and set aside for 15 minutes.

Lift the fish out of the kettle and transfer it to a large chopping board. Carefully remove and discard the cheesecloth. Carefully remove the skin from the fish with a sharp knife. Arrange the fish on a large serving plate and garnish with the parsley sprigs. Keep warm.

To make the sauce, put the vinegar, wine, shallots, salt and pepper into a medium-sized saucepan. Set the pan over moderate heat and bring the liquid to the boil. Cook, stirring occasionally, until the liquid is reduced to about 1 tablespoon.

Remove the pan from the heat and, with a wire whisk, stir in 4 small pieces of the chilled butter, beating constantly until it is completely absorbed.

Return the pan to very low heat and add the rest of the chilled butter, a small piece at a time, whisking constantly and making sure all the butter is absorbed before adding the next piece. Remove the pan from the heat and pour the sauce into a warmed sauceboat.

Serve the fish at once, accompanied by the sauce.

Easy to prepare, delicious to eat - Bass with White Butter Sauce makes an elegant centrepiece for a special lunch or dinner.

Bream [Porgy] with Fresh Fennel in White Wine

A delicate, aromatic blend of fresh herbs and wine, Bream [Porgy] with Fresh Fennel in White Wine is a simple, yet sophisticated Mediterranean dish. It may be served with boiled new potatoes and petits pois, and accompanied by a well-chilled white Rhine wine, such as Rüdesheimer.

4 SERVINGS

1 x 2 lb. bream [porgy], cleaned and gutted
2 sprigs fresh fennel leaves
2 sprigs fresh thyme
1 oz. [2 tablespoons] butter
½ teaspoon salt
½ teaspoon freshly ground black pepper
5 fl. oz. [⅝ cup] dry white wine
1 tablespoon olive oil
1 fresh fennel, trimmed and sliced
2 tomatoes, sliced
1 lemon, thinly sliced

Preheat the oven to moderate 350°F (Gas Mark 4, 180°C).

With a small, sharp knife, make 2 deep incisions along the back of the fish. Insert the fennel sprigs in the incisions.

Place the thyme and the butter inside the fish. Sprinkle the fish with the salt and pepper.

Place the fish on a rack in a large roasting tin.

Pour the wine and olive oil over the fish, and arrange the fennel, tomatoes and lemon slices on top.

Place the fish in the oven and bake it for about 30 minutes, or until the fish flakes easily when tested with a fork. Baste the fish occasionally with the cooking liquid during cooking.

Carefully transfer the fish to a large shallow serving dish and serve immediately.

Brill with Courgettes [Zucchini]

This delicious dish is surprisingly easy to cook and makes a perfect main course for a dinner party.

4 SERVINGS

3 oz. [⅜ cup] butter
2 lb. brill fillets
1 teaspoon lemon juice

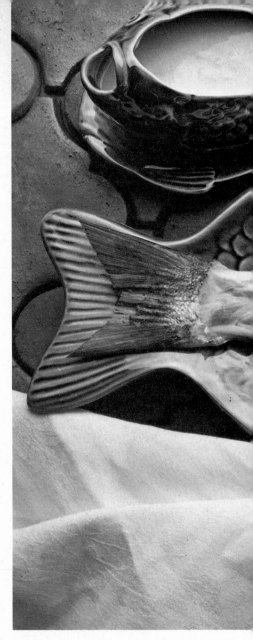

1 lb. courgettes [zucchini], sliced
¾ teaspoon salt
½ teaspoon black pepper
½ teaspoon dried basil
4 tablespoons flour
10 fl. oz. [1¼ cups] milk
1 tablespoon grated cheese

Preheat the oven to moderate 350°F (Gas Mark 4, 180°C).

Grease a shallow baking dish with 1 tablespoon butter. Put the fillets in the baking dish and pour in the lemon juice and just enough water to cover. Poach the fillets in the oven for 15 to 20 minutes, or until the fish flakes easily.

Transfer the fish to a flameproof serving dish and keep warm. Strain the liquid from the baking dish and reserve.

Meanwhile, melt 2 tablespoons of the butter in a saucepan over moderate heat. Add the courgette [zucchini] slices to it. Stir, cover and simmer for about 8 minutes, or until they are just tender. Stir in ½ teaspoon salt, pepper and basil. Place to one side and keep hot.

Preheat the grill [broiler] to moderate.

In another saucepan, melt the remaining butter over moderate heat. Remove the saucepan from the heat and stir in the flour with a wooden spoon. Add the milk and the liquid from the fish, stirring constantly until the mixture is smooth. Replace the pan on the heat and bring the sauce to the boil. Stirring constantly, boil the sauce for 5 minutes. Stir in the remaining salt. Taste the sauce for seasoning and add more salt if necessary.

Pour the sauce over the fish. Sprinkle on the cheese and brown under the grill [broiler]. Surround with the drained courgette [zucchini] slices and serve immediately.

Carp Jewish-Style

Cold carp set in jellied stock is a fine flavoured light dish for the summer. Serve it with a variety of salads and a well chilled Hungarian Riesling. This dish may also be served hot.

6 SERVINGS

3 fish heads
2 pints [5 cups] cold water
1 medium-sized onion, thinly sliced
1 bay leaf
1 teaspoon freshly ground black pepper
1 teaspoon salt
1 clove
2 medium-sized carrots, scraped and diced
1 medium-sized kohlrabi, peeled and diced
2 celery stalks, trimmed and sliced
1 tablespoon lemon juice
1 tablespoon white wine vinegar
1 tablespoon sugar
3 lb. carp, cut into steaks

Put the fish heads and the water in a large saucepan. Add the onion, bay leaf, pepper, salt and clove. Place the pan over high heat and bring the water to the boil. Reduce the heat to moderately low. Cover the pan and simmer the mixture for 30

minutes.

Remove the pan from the heat and strain the stock into a bowl. Discard the fish heads and seasonings. Return the stock to the pan. Add the carrots, kohlrabi and celery and return the pan to moderate heat. Bring to the boil. Cover the pan, reduce the heat to low and simmer for 20 to 30 minutes or until the vegetables are tender.

Stir in the lemon juice, vinegar and sugar. Place the fish steaks on top of the vegetables, cover the pan and simmer for 15 to 20 minutes or until the fish flakes easily when tested with a fork.

Remove the pan from the heat. With a slotted spoon, carefully transfer the fish steaks to a large serving dish. Pour the liquid and the vegetables over the fish and set aside to cool.

Cover the dish and place it in the refrigerator to chill for 1 hour, basting occasionally so that a glaze forms on the fish.

When the cooking liquid has set to a firm jelly, remove the dish from the refrigerator and serve immediately.

Baked Halibut Fillets

Baked Halibut Fillets makes a superb lunch or dinner party dish, served with croquette potatoes and sautéed mushrooms. Accompany with a well-chilled white Moselle wine.

4 SERVINGS

- 4 halibut fillets
- ½ teaspoon salt
- ¼ teaspoon black pepper
- 5 fl. oz. double cream [⅝ cup heavy cream]
- 8 fl. oz. [1 cup] dry white wine
- 1 bay leaf
- 1 tablespoon chopped fresh chives
- ½ teaspoon dried chervil
- 1 tablespoon lemon juice
- 1 tablespoon cornflour [cornstarch] dissolved in 2 tablespoons white wine
- 2 oz. [½ cup] Parmesan cheese, grated

Preheat the oven to fairly hot 375°F (Gas Mark 5, 190°C).

Rub the fish fillets all over with the salt and pepper and arrange them in a large ovenproof dish. Set the dish aside.

In a medium-sized mixing bowl, combine the cream, wine, bay leaf, chives,

Halibut Steaks with Green Peppercorns makes a luxurious dish for special entertaining.

chervil, lemon juice and the cornflour [cornstarch] mixture.

Pour the sauce over the fish in the baking dish. Sprinkle on the grated cheese.

Place the dish in the centre of the oven and bake for 25 to 30 minutes, or until the cheese has melted and the fish flakes easily when tested with a fork.

Remove the dish from the oven. Remove and discard the bay leaf. Serve immediately, straight from the dish.

Halibut Steaks with Green Peppercorns

This luxurious mixture of halibut, green peppercorns, tomatoes, cream and brandy is an unusual dinner party dish. Serve with croquette potatoes, steamed broccoli and, to drink, some well chilled white wine such as Pouilly Fumé.

4 SERVINGS

- 4 halibut steaks
- 1 teaspoon salt

- 1 tablespoon lemon juice
- 1 large garlic clove, crushed
- 1½ oz. [3 tablespoons] butter
- 4 medium-sized tomatoes, blanched, peeled, seeded and finely chopped
- 4 tablespoons canned green peppercorns, drained
- 1 tablespoon French mustard
- 2 fl. oz. [¼ cup] sour cream
- 4 fl. oz. double cream [½ cup heavy cream]
- 2 tablespoons brandy

Rub the fish steaks all over with the salt, lemon juice and garlic and set them aside on a plate.

In a frying-pan large enough to hold all the fish steaks in one layer, melt the butter over moderate heat. When the foam subsides, add the tomatoes, peppercorns and mustard and cook the mixture, stirring frequently, for 6 to 8 minutes or until it is thick.

Stir in the sour cream and place the fish in the pan. Spoon over the tomato mixture and reduce the heat to moderately low. Cook the fish for 8 to 10 minutes on each side or until the flesh flakes easily when tested with a fork.

Using a slotted spoon, remove the fish from the pan and transfer it to a warmed serving dish. Keep hot while you finish the sauce.

Stir the double [heavy] cream and brandy into the sauce and cook, stirring constantly, for 5 minutes.

Remove the pan from the heat, pour the sauce over the fish and serve.

Halibut Steaks with Tomatoes and Cream

This simple dish makes an excellent lunch or dinner. Serve with boiled rice or croquette potatoes.

4 SERVINGS

1 oz. [2 tablespoons] butter
1 large onion, thinly sliced and pushed out into rings
14 oz. canned peeled tomatoes, roughly chopped
1 teaspoon dried marjoram
½ teaspoon salt
¼ teaspoon black pepper
4 halibut steaks
8 oz. small button mushrooms, wiped clean and halved
5 fl. oz. double cream [⅝ cup heavy cream]

In a flameproof casserole, melt the butter over moderate heat. When the foam subsides, add the onion and cook, stirring occasionally, for 5 to 7 minutes, or until it is soft and translucent but not brown.

Stir in the tomatoes and the can juice, marjoram, salt and pepper. Add the fish steaks. Bring the liquid to the boil, stirring occasionally. Reduce the heat to low, cover and simmer for 8 minutes on each side.

Stir the mushrooms and cream into the casserole and cook, stirring occasionally, for a further 2 minutes, or until the sauce is hot but not boiling and the fish flakes easily when tested with a fork.

Remove the casserole from the heat and turn the mixture out into a warmed serving dish. Serve immediately.

Halibut Stuffed with Shrimps and Crabmeat

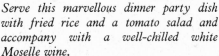

Serve this marvellous dinner party dish with fried rice and a tomato salad and accompany with a well-chilled white Moselle wine.

6 SERVINGS

4 oz. canned crabmeat
2 oz. [¼ cup] plus 1 teaspoon butter
8 oz. shrimps, shelled
2 tablespoons flour
8 fl. oz. [1 cup] fish stock
2 fl. oz. double cream [¼ cup heavy cream]
2 fl. oz. [¼ cup] dry white wine
4 oz. mushrooms, chopped
1 small green pepper, white pith

An unusual and delicate dish - that's Halibut Stuffed with Shrimps and Crabmeat.

removed, seeded and chopped
2 oz. [1 cup] cooked rice
½ teaspoon salt
¼ teaspoon black pepper
1 x 3 lb. tail end of halibut, centre bone removed
2 oz. [¼ cup] butter, melted
    parsley sprigs
    lemon wedges

Remove any shell and cartilage from the crabmeat and set aside.

Preheat the oven to moderate 350°F (Gas Mark 4, 180°C). Lightly grease a large shallow baking dish with the teaspoon of butter. Set aside.

In a large frying-pan, melt the remaining butter over moderate heat. When the foam subsides, reduce the heat to low and add the crabmeat and shrimps to the pan, stirring with a wooden spoon until they are well coated in butter. Stir in the flour.

Pour in the stock, cream and wine, stirring constantly until they are blended. Heat gently until the liquid is hot but not boiling. Stir in the mushrooms, green pepper, rice, salt and pepper. Remove the pan from the heat and spoon the mixture into the pocket of the halibut.

Spread the excess mixture over the bottom of the baking dish. Arrange the stuffed fish on top and pour over the melted butter. Cover and place in the oven. Bake the fish for 50 minutes, or until it is tender but still firm.

Remove the dish from the oven and serve the fish at once, garnished with the parsley and lemon.

Mullets with Bacon and Peas

An unusual combination of fish with the savoury flavour of bacon, Mullets with Bacon and Peas make an attractive and colourful dish. Serve with creamed potatoes and grilled [broiled] tomatoes.

6 SERVINGS

6 streaky bacon slices, finely chopped
1 medium-sized onion, finely chopped
3 oz. [¾ cup] seasoned flour, made with 3 oz. [¾ cup] flour, ½ teaspoon salt, ¼ teaspoon black pepper and ¼ teaspoon paprika
6 medium-sized red mullets, cleaned and with the eyes removed
4 oz. [½ cup] butter
1 tablespoon soft brown sugar
1 lb. fresh peas, weighed after shelling
1 teaspoon salt
½ teaspoon black pepper
½ teaspoon finely chopped fresh thyme or ¼ teaspoon dried thyme
10 fl. oz. [1¼ cups] chicken stock
4 fl. oz. [½ cup] dry white wine
1 tablespoon cornflour [cornstarch] dissolved in 2 tablespoons water

In a medium-sized frying-pan, fry the bacon over moderately high heat, stirring occasionally, for 5 to 8 minutes or until it is crisp and brown and has rendered most of its fat. With a slotted spoon, transfer the bacon from the pan to a plate and keep warm.

Reduce the heat to moderate and add the onion to the frying-pan. Fry, stirring occasionally, for 5 to 7 minutes, or until it is soft and translucent but not brown. Remove the pan from the heat and, with a slotted spoon, transfer the onion to the plate with the bacon.

Place the seasoned flour in a large shallow dish. Dip the fish in the flour mixture, shaking off any excess. Set them aside.

Add half of the butter to the fat in the frying-pan and return it to moderate heat. When the foam subsides, add the fish, three at a time, and fry them for 5 minutes on each side, or until the flesh flakes easily when tested with a fork. Transfer the fish to a warmed serving dish and keep warm while you fry the remaining fish in the same way, using the remaining butter. Keep the fish warm while you prepare the sauce.

Reduce the heat to low and add the onion, bacon and brown sugar to the pan. Cook, stirring constantly with a wooden spoon, for 3 minutes, or until the sugar has completely dissolved.

Add the peas, salt, black pepper, thyme, chicken stock and white wine. Increase the heat to high and bring the mixture to the boil, stirring occasionally.

Reduce the heat to moderately low and simmer for 10 to 12 minutes, or until the peas are tender. Remove the pan from the heat.

Stir in the dissolved cornflour [cornstarch] and return the pan to the heat. Cook the sauce, stirring constantly, for 2 to 3 minutes or until it thickens and is smooth.

Remove the pan from the heat and spoon the sauce over the fish. Serve immediately.

Mullet Baked in Rock Salt

A delectable dish with a special fragrant flavour, Mullet Baked in Rock Salt may be served with green beans and an apple and onion salad for an informal lunch or dinner party.

4 SERVINGS

12 oz. [2 cups] rock salt
1 x 4 lb. grey mullet, cleaned but with the head left on
1 teaspoon chopped fresh chives or ½ teaspoon dried chives
1 teaspoon chopped fresh tarragon or ½ teaspoon dried tarragon
1 rosemary sprig
juice of 1 lemon

Preheat the oven to warm 325°F (Gas Mark 3, 170°C).

Cover the bottom of a large, deep ovenproof dish with approximately one-third of the rock salt. Place the fish on top of the salt. Sprinkle over the chives and tarragon and place the rosemary sprig on top. Sprinkle over the lemon juice. Pour in the remaining rock salt to surround and cover the fish completely. With the back of a wooden spoon carefully pat down the salt.

Place the dish in the centre of the oven and bake the fish for 50 minutes to 1 hour.

Remove the dish from the oven. Using a weight, such as a rolling pin or pestle, break the hardened crust of the salt. With a sharp knife, prise the salt off and discard it.

Serve the fish at once, straight from the dish.

Mullets Baked with Shrimps

A simple, tasty dish originating from West Africa, Red Mullets Baked with Shrimps

may be served with rice or hot crusty bread. Accompany with a light well-chilled Moselle wine, such as Bernkasteler or Moselblumchen for a colourful lunch or supper.

4 SERVINGS

3 fl. oz. [⅜ cup] lemon juice
2 fl. oz. [¼ cup] water
1 tablespoon Worcestershire sauce
3 fl. oz. [⅜ cup] tomato ketchup
1 teaspoon finely chopped fresh rosemary or ½ teaspoon dried rosemary
6 peppercorns
4 red mullets, cleaned and with the eyes removed
1 oz. [2 tablespoons] butter
8 oz. shrimps, shelled and deveined
3 fl. oz. [⅜ cup] olive oil or peanut oil
1 lemon, thinly sliced
1 bunch watercress, washed and shaken dry

In a large mixing bowl, combine the lemon juice, water, Worcestershire sauce, tomato ketchup, rosemary and peppercorns and beat well with a fork until the ingredients are thoroughly combined. Place the fish in the mixture. Cover the bowl and set aside to marinate for at least 30 minutes, at room temperature, basting the fish with the marinade from time to time.

Preheat the oven to moderate 350°F (Gas Mark 4, 180°C).

With 1 tablespoon of the butter, grease an ovenproof dish large enough to take all of the mullets in one layer. Carefully remove the mullets from the marinade. Discard the marinade.

Arrange the fish in the dish, cut the remaining butter into small pieces and dot them over the fish. Scatter the shrimps over the fish, then pour over the oil.

Place the dish in the centre of the oven and bake the fish, basting occasionally with the oil, for 20 to 30 minutes or until the flesh flakes easily when tested with a fork.

Remove the dish from the oven. Transfer the fish to a warmed serving dish and pour over the cooking juices. Garnish the fish with the lemon slices and the watercress.

Serve immediately.

Colourful Mullets Baked with Shrimps is an adaptation of a West African dish. Garnished (as here) with lemon and watercress and served on a bed of rice, it makes an exotic dish for an informal dinner.

Pike Stuffed with Cucumber and Rice

This delightful Scandinavian dish is ideal to serve hot at a dinner party. It can also be eaten cold.

6-8 SERVINGS

1 x 3½ lb. pike, cleaned and gutted, with the head and tail left on and the backbone removed
1 teaspoon salt
½ teaspoon black pepper
4 oz. [½ cup] butter
2 onions, chopped
4 spring onions [scallions], trimmed and finely chopped
3 oz. [½ cup] long-grain rice, washed, soaked in cold water for 30 minutes and drained
1 cucumber, peeled and chopped
1 tablespoon chopped fresh chives
1 teaspoon grated lemon rind
1 tablespoon finely chopped fresh coriander leaves
8 fl. oz. [1 cup] dry white wine

Sprinkle the fish, inside and out, with half of the salt and pepper. Set aside.

Preheat the oven to moderate 350°F (Gas Mark 4, 180°C).

In a large frying-pan, melt half of the butter over moderate heat. When the foam subsides, add the onions and spring onions [scallions] and fry, stirring frequently, for 5 to 7 minutes or until the onions are soft and translucent but not brown. Add the rice, cucumber, chives, lemon rind, coriander leaves and remaining salt and pepper and fry, stirring constantly, for a further 5 minutes.

Remove the frying-pan from the heat and set aside to cool.

Stuff the mixture into the cavity of the fish. Sew up the cavity with a trussing needle and string.

Place the fish in a large baking tin. Cut the remaining butter into small pieces and dot them over the fish. Pour over the wine and place the tin in the centre of the oven. Bake the fish, basting occasionally, for 35 to 45 minutes or until the flesh flakes easily when tested with a fork.

Remove the tin from the oven. Transfer the fish to a warmed serving dish. Pour over the cooking juices and serve at once.

Fluffy and rich and easy to make - that's Plaice [Flounder] Anatole!

Plaice [Flounder] Anatole

A delicious soufflé-like dish, Plaice [Flounder] Anatole is quick and easy to make.

4-6 SERVINGS

2 oz. [¼ cup] plus 1 teaspoon butter
2 lb. plaice [flounder] fillets
1 large green pepper, white pith removed, seeded and sliced
1 pint [2½ cups] mayonnaise
8 oz. [2 cups] Cheddar cheese, grated
½ teaspoon salt
¼ teaspoon white pepper
2 fl. oz. double cream [¼ cup heavy cream]
4 egg whites, stiffly beaten

Preheat the oven to moderate 350°F (Gas Mark 4, 180°C). With the teaspoon of butter, grease a large ovenproof dish.

In a frying-pan, melt the remaining butter over moderate heat. When the foam subsides, add the plaice [flounder] fillets, a few at a time, and fry for 2 minutes on each side. Remove the pan from the heat and remove the skin from the fish fillets. Transfer the fillets to the prepared dish. Arrange the green pepper slices over the fish and set aside.

Place the mayonnaise in a mixing bowl. Stir in the cheese, salt and pepper and then the cream. With a metal spoon, carefully fold in the beaten egg whites until the mixture is thoroughly combined.

Pour the mixture over the fish. Place the dish in the oven and bake for 20 minutes or until the top has turned golden brown.

Remove from the oven and serve.

Red Snapper with Almond and Walnut Sauce

A delicately flavoured dish to tempt everyone, Red Snapper with Almond and Walnut Sauce is surprisingly easy to make.

6 SERVINGS

3 lb. red snapper fillets
2 oz. [½ cup] seasoned flour, made with 2 oz. [½ cup] flour, 1 teaspoon salt and ½ teaspoon white pepper
2 oz. [¼ cup] butter
SAUCE
1½ oz. [3 tablespoons] butter
1½ oz. [6 tablespoons] flour
8 fl. oz. single cream [1 cup light cream]
10 fl. oz. [1¼ cups] dry white wine
1 teaspoon dried marjoram
½ teaspoon salt
½ teaspoon black pepper
2 oz. [½ cup] slivered almonds
2 oz. [½ cup] walnuts, chopped
4 oz. [1 cup] Gruyère cheese, grated

Preheat the oven to moderate 350°F (Gas

Delicately flavoured Red Snapper with Almond and Walnut Sauce.

Mark 4, 180°C).

Dip the fish fillets into the seasoned flour to coat them thoroughly.

In a large frying-pan, melt the butter over moderate heat. When the foam subsides, fry the fillets, a few at a time, for 5 minutes on each side or until they are golden brown all over, adding more butter if necessary. Remove the pan from the heat. With a slotted spoon, remove the fillets from the pan and transfer them to a large, shallow ovenproof dish.

In a medium-sized saucepan, melt the butter over moderate heat. With a wooden spoon, stir in the flour. Remove the pan from the heat and gradually add the cream, stirring constantly and being careful to avoid lumps.

Stir in the wine, marjoram, salt, pepper, almonds and walnuts. Return the pan to the heat and bring the sauce to the boil, stirring constantly. Reduce the heat to low and simmer the sauce for 5 minutes, stirring frequently.

Remove the pan from the heat and pour the sauce over the fish.

Sprinkle the cheese over the sauce and place the dish in the centre of the oven. Bake the fish for 15 to 20 minutes or until the cheese has melted and is golden brown. Serve immediately.

169

Sumptuous Salmon with Dill
Mayonnaise is the ideal party dish.

*Sumptuous Salmon with Dill
Mayonnaise is the ideal party dish.*

While the salmon is cooling, make the sauce. Pour the mayonnaise and cream into a mixing bowl and stir in the reserved cooking liquid, the lemon juice, pepper, salt, cayenne and mustard. Stir until the sauce is smooth and evenly coloured. Fold in the dill and shrimps and set aside.

Place the lettuce, cress, radishes, lemon juice and vinegar in a mixing bowl and toss well with two large spoons.

Line the bottom of a large serving platter with the lettuce mixture. Place the salmon in the centre of the dish and spoon over the sauce to cover the salmon completely.

Arrange the tomatoes, hard-boiled eggs and spring onions [scallions] decoratively around the salmon and serve immediately.

Salmon Roll

Salmon Roll is an ideal dish to eke out fresh salmon flesh taken from the head and tail. Serve as a light luncheon dish with sour cream.

3-4 SERVINGS

2 teaspoons butter
10 oz. cooked fresh salmon, skinned
4 eggs, separated
1 oz. [2 tablespoons] butter, melted
3 tablespoons flour
½ teaspoon salt
½ teaspoon black pepper
2 teaspoons chopped fresh chives
1 teaspoon chopped fresh fennel
½ teaspoon chopped fresh marjoram
2 teaspoons white wine vinegar
2 tablespoons double [heavy] cream

With 1 teaspoon of the butter, grease a 7- x 10-inch baking tin. Line the tin with greaseproof or waxed paper, allowing the paper to stand 1-inch above the sides of the tin. Grease the paper with the remaining butter. Preheat the oven to moderate 350°F (Gas Mark 4, 180°C).

Purée the salmon in a blender or food mill. Set aside.

Place the egg yolks in a mixing bowl and, using a wooden spoon, beat them until they are thick and pale. Gradually beat in the melted butter. Stir in the flour, a tablespoon at a time, and beat until the ingredients are combined.

Stir in the salmon, salt, pepper, chives, fennel, marjoram, vinegar and cream and beat until the mixture is smooth.

In another large mixing bowl, beat the egg whites with a wire whisk or rotary

Salmon with Dill Mayonnaise

This splendid cold dish may be served as a complete summer dinner party meal with crusty French bread and butter and parsley potatoes. A well-chilled Pouilly Fumé would be the ideal accompaniment.

6 SERVINGS

1 x 5 lb. salmon, cleaned
2 lemons, thinly sliced
6 black peppercorns
½ teaspoon dried dill
1½ teaspoons salt
2 small shallots, sliced
2 small bay leaves
10 fl. oz. [1¼ cups] dry white wine
SAUCE
10 fl. oz. [1¼ cups] mayonnaise
2 fl. oz. double cream [¼ cup heavy cream]
2 teaspoons lemon juice
¼ teaspoon black pepper
¼ teaspoon salt
¼ teaspoon cayenne pepper
¼ teaspoon French mustard
1 tablespoon chopped fresh dill
6 oz. small peeled frozen shrimps, thawed and drained
GARNISH
1 medium-sized round [Boston] lettuce, outer leaves removed,
washed and shredded
1 medium-sized bunch mustard and cress, washed and shaken dry
10 small radishes, very thinly sliced
1 teaspoon lemon juice
1 teaspoon tarragon vinegar
6 medium-sized tomatoes, sliced
6 hard-boiled eggs, sliced
6 spring onions [scallions], trimmed

Wash the salmon in cold water and dry with kitchen paper towels.

Line the bottom of a fish kettle or flameproof casserole with the lemon slices. Sprinkle over the peppercorns, dill, salt, shallot slices and bay leaves. Place the salmon in the kettle or casserole and pour over the wine.

Place the kettle or casserole over high heat and bring the wine to the boil. Reduce the heat to low, cover and simmer the salmon for 40 to 50 minutes or until the flesh flakes easily.

Remove the kettle or casserole from the heat. Using two large spoons, remove the salmon from the kettle or casserole and place it on a flat working surface. Strain the cooking liquid and reserve 3 tablespoons, discarding the rest.

Carefully skin the salmon, being careful not to break up the flesh.

Set the salmon aside to cool completely.

beater until they form stiff peaks.

With a large metal spoon, carefully fold the egg whites into the salmon mixture until they are thoroughly combined.

Pour the salmon mixture into the tin and smooth the top with a table knife. Place the tin in the oven and bake the mixture for 15 minutes or until it is just firm to the touch and pale golden brown.

Remove the tin from the oven. Turn the mixture out on to a large piece of greaseproof or waxed paper. Remove the paper from the mixture. With the help of the greaseproof or waxed paper, roll up the mixture Swiss [jelly] roll style. Transfer to a warmed serving dish and serve.

Salmon Steaks Florentine

This superb dish tastes as magnificent as it looks — and it's easy to prepare too!

4 SERVINGS

4 salmon steaks, cut 1-inch thick
2 oz. [¼ cup] unsalted butter, melted
3 lb. spinach, cooked, drained and kept hot
2 fl. oz. double cream [¼ cup heavy cream]
¼ teaspoon salt

¼ teaspoon black pepper
SAUCE
6 oz. [¾ cup] butter, melted
juice of ½ lemon
¼ teaspoon salt
¼ teaspoon white pepper
⅛ teaspoon cayenne pepper

Preheat the grill [broiler] to moderate. Line the pan with aluminium foil.

Place the salmon steaks on the rack and coat them with a little of the melted butter. Place the pan under the grill [broiler] and grill [broil] the steaks for 8 to 10 minutes on each side, basting with the remaining melted butter, or until they are lightly browned and the flesh flakes easily.

Meanwhile, in a large mixing bowl, combine the spinach, cream, salt and pepper, stirring gently until they are blended. Arrange the mixture over the bottom of a warmed, large serving dish.

In a jug, combine all the sauce ingredients, beating until they are well blended.

Remove the steaks from the heat and arrange them on top of the spinach mixture. Pour over the butter sauce and serve at once.

Elegant Smoked Salmon Canapés.

Smoked Salmon Canapés

Luxurious and easy-to-prepare cocktail snacks, Smoked Salmon Canapés may be served as an appetizer before dinner.

24 CANAPES

6 large slices brown bread, crusts removed
4 oz. cream cheese
4 oz. smoked salmon, sliced and cut into 24 pieces
2 tablespoons lemon juice
1 small onion, sliced and pushed out into rings
2 oz. black caviar or lumpfish roe
6 parsley sprigs
1 lemon, cut into wedges

Place the bread slices on a wooden board. Using a sharp knife, cut each slice into 4 diamond shapes. Discard the bread trimmings.

Spread each shape with cream cheese. Cover each one with a piece of smoked salmon. Sprinkle a little lemon juice over the salmon and top with an onion ring. Place a little caviar or lumpfish roe in the centre of each onion ring.

Place the canapés on a decorative serving dish. Garnish with the parsley and lemon wedges and serve at once.

Sole Normande

SOLE FILLETS WITH MUSSELS AND
SHRIMPS

*A classic way to cook sole, Sole Normande
is garnished with shellfish and mushrooms
and has a rich creamy sauce poured over
the top.*

4 SERVINGS

 8 sole fillets, skinned
 1 pint mussels, scrubbed, steamed
    and cooking liquid reserved, or
    4 oz. canned mussels, can juice
    reserved
 1 onion, thinly sliced and pushed
    out into rings
    bouquet garni, consisting of 4
    parsley sprigs, 1 thyme spray and
    1 bay leaf tied together
10 fl. oz. [1¼ cups] dry white wine
 1 oz. [2 tablespoons] butter
 4 shallots, halved
 8 oz. button mushrooms, wiped
    clean and stalks removed
 1 tablespoon lemon juice
 ½ teaspoon salt
 ¼ teaspoon black pepper
 4 oz. frozen shrimps, thawed

SAUCE
 1 tablespoon butter
 2 tablespoons flour
 ¼ teaspoon salt
 ⅛ teaspoon white pepper
 8 fl. oz. double cream [1 cup heavy
    cream]

Roll up the fillets Swiss [jelly] roll style
and secure with thread. Arrange the rolls
in a large ovenproof dish and set aside.

Strain the reserved mussel liquid
through a fine strainer set over a large
saucepan. Add the onion and bouquet
garni and pour over the wine. Set the pan
over high heat and bring the liquid to the
boil. Reduce the heat to low and simmer
the stock for 10 minutes. Remove the pan
from the heat and pour the stock through
a strainer set over a bowl. Discard the
contents of the strainer. Set aside.

Preheat the oven to moderate 350°F
(Gas Mark 4, 180°C).

In a large frying-pan, melt the butter

*Sole Normande, sole fillets garnished
with mussels and shrimps and a
creamy sauce, is a classic recipe.*

over moderate heat. When the foam
subsides, add the shallots, mushrooms,
lemon juice, salt and pepper to the pan.
Fry, stirring occasionally, for 5 minutes.
Transfer the mixture to the dish containing the fish rolls. Set the pan aside.

Add the mussels and shrimps to the
dish and pour over the reserved stock.
Place the dish in the oven and cook for
15 to 20 minutes or until the fish flesh
flakes easily when tested with a fork.
Remove the dish from the oven. Using a
slotted spoon, transfer the fish rolls to a
warmed serving dish. Remove and discard
the thread. Transfer the shallots, mushrooms, mussels and shrimps to the dish
and arrange them decoratively around
the fish. Keep hot.

Pour the cooking liquid through the
strainer into a large bowl. Discard the
contents of the strainer. Add the tablespoon of butter to the butter remaining
in the frying-pan. Place the pan over
moderate heat and melt the butter.
Remove the pan from the heat and, using
a wooden spoon, stir in the flour to make
a smooth paste. Gradually add the
reserved cooking liquid, stirring constantly. Stir in the salt and pepper and

return the pan to the heat. Cook the sauce, stirring constantly, for 2 to 3 minutes or until it is smooth and thick.

Stir in the cream. Pour the sauce over the fish and serve at once.

Sole Spanish-Style

Most of the better known sole recipes are French in origin but the Mediterranean coast of Spain is deservedly noted for its seafood too, and the following method of cooking sole is equal in taste to any of the more complicated French dishes.

4 SERVINGS

4 globe artichokes
1½ teaspoons salt
2 soles, filleted
½ teaspoon white pepper
½ teaspoon lemon juice
8 fl. oz. [1 cup] dry white wine
1 oz. [2 tablespoons] butter
4 oz. mushrooms, thinly sliced
10 fl. oz. [1¼ cups] hot béchamel sauce

Prepare the artichokes for cooking by cutting off the stalks and removing the tough outer leaves. Trim the artichokes by cutting off the top points of the leaves.

Place the artichokes in a large saucepan and add enough water just to cover. Add ½ teaspoon of salt and place the pan over high heat. Bring the water to the boil, reduce the heat to moderate and cook the artichokes for 30 to 35 minutes, or until the bases are tender.

Meanwhile, season the sole fillets with the remaining salt, white pepper and lemon juice. Carefully roll up the fillets Swiss [jelly] roll style, securing them with a skewer or thread.

Place the fillets in a medium-sized saucepan and pour in the white wine. Place the pan over low heat and poach the fillets for 15 minutes, basting occasionally.

About 5 minutes before the artichokes and fish are cooked, prepare the mushrooms. In a frying-pan melt the butter over moderate heat. When the foam subsides, add the mushrooms and cook, stirring occasionally, for 3 minutes. Remove the pan from the heat.

Remove the artichokes from the heat and drain them on kitchen paper towels. Remove the choke and prickly leaves.

Arrange the artichokes on a serving dish. Spoon a little of the mushroom mixture into each cavity and cover with béchamel sauce.

With a slotted spoon, transfer the fish to a plate. Remove the skewers or thread and place one roll on top of each artichoke.

Serve immediately.

Sole Spanish-Style is sole served in succulent artichokes.

Sole Veronique

SOLE FILLETS WITH GRAPES

Sole Veronique, the invention of a sauce chef at the Paris Ritz called Monsieur Malley, is a combination of fresh green grapes, wine sauce and delicately poached fish.

4 SERVINGS

1 oz. [2 tablespoons] plus 1 teaspoon butter
1 lb. Dover sole fillets, skinned and halved
½ teaspoon salt
1 teaspoon black pepper
1 large onion, thinly sliced
1 bay leaf, crumbled
8 fl. oz. [1 cup] dry white wine
2 fl. oz. [¼ cup] water
1 oz. [¼ cup] flour
4 fl. oz. [½ cup] milk
2 fl. oz. double cream [¼ cup heavy cream]
8 oz. green grapes, peeled, halved and seeded

Preheat the oven to moderate 350°F (Gas Mark 4, 180°C). With the teaspoon of butter, grease a large baking dish.

Rub the fish pieces with the salt and pepper and arrange them on the bottom of the baking dish.

Sprinkle over the onion and bay leaf and pour over the wine and water. Place the dish in the oven and cook for 15 to 20 minutes or until the fish flesh flakes easily when tested with a fork.

Remove the dish from the oven and, using a fish slice or slotted spoon, transfer the fish fillets to a warmed serving dish.

Strain the fish cooking liquid into a jug, pressing down on the onion to extract all the liquid. Reserve 4 fluid ounces [½ cup] of the stock.

In a small saucepan, melt the remaining butter over moderate heat. Remove the pan from the heat and, with a wooden spoon, stir in the flour to make a smooth paste. Gradually add the milk and the reserved stock, stirring constantly. Return the pan to the heat and cook, stirring constantly, for 2 to 3 minutes or until the sauce is thick and smooth. Stir in the cream and cook, stirring constantly, for a further 2 minutes.

Remove the pan from the heat and pour the sauce over the fillets. Arrange the grapes around the edge of the dish and serve immediately.

Trout with Almonds

 ① ①

Accompany this elegant dish with buttered French beans, boiled new potatoes and some well chilled Pouilly Fuissé wine.

6 SERVINGS

6 medium-sized trout, cleaned and
    with the eyes removed
1 teaspoon salt
1 teaspoon white pepper
2 tablespoons lemon juice
6 fl. oz. [¾ cup] milk
3 oz. [¾ cup] seasoned flour, made
    with 3 oz. [¾ cup] flour,
    1 teaspoon grated nutmeg and
    ¼ teaspoon dried thyme
5 oz. [⅝ cup] butter
4 oz. [1 cup] slivered almonds
6 lemon quarters

Place the fish on a working surface and rub them all over with the salt, pepper and 1 tablespoon of the lemon juice.

Place the milk in one shallow dish and the seasoned flour in another. Dip the trout, one by one, first in the milk then in the seasoned flour.

In a heavy-based frying-pan large enough to take the fish in one layer, melt 3 ounces [⅜ cup] of the butter over moderate heat. When the foam subsides, add the trout and fry them for 4 to 6 minutes on each side or until the flesh flakes easily. With a fish slice or spatula, transfer the trout to a warmed serving dish. Keep warm.

Add the remaining butter to the frying-pan. When the foam subsides, add the almonds and the remaining lemon juice and cook, stirring frequently, for 3 to 5 minutes or until the almonds are lightly browned. Remove the pan from the heat and pour the mixture over the trout.

Garnish the trout with the lemon quarters and serve at once.

Danish Fried Trout in Sour Cream Sauce

 ① ①

The sour cream and mushroom sauce which accompanies the fried trout in this recipe complements but does not overpower the delicate flavour of the fish. Serve with broccoli and new potatoes and accompany with a well-chilled white Moselle wine.

6 SERVINGS

3 oz. [¾ cup] seasoned flour, made
    with 3 oz. [¾ cup] flour, ½ teaspoon
    salt and ¼ teaspoon black pepper
6 medium-sized trout, cleaned and
    with the eyes removed
4 oz. [½ cup] butter
2 tablespoons vegetable oil

12 small button mushrooms,
    wiped clean and halved
½ teaspoon salt
¼ teaspoon freshly ground
    black pepper
1 teaspoon lemon juice
1 teaspoon paprika
10 fl. oz. [1¼ cups] sour cream
1 tablespoon finely chopped
    fresh parsley

Place the seasoned flour in a large, shallow dish. Dip the fish in the flour mixture, coating them completely and shaking off any excess. Set aside.

In a large saucepan, melt 2 ounces [¼ cup] of the butter with the oil over moderate heat. When the foam subsides, add the fish, 2 at a time, and fry them for 4 to 6 minutes on each side, or until they are lightly browned and the flesh flakes easily. Transfer the fish to a warmed serving dish and keep warm while you prepare the sauce.

Remove the saucepan from the heat and discard the cooking juices. Place the remaining butter in the pan and melt it over moderate heat. When the foam subsides, reduce the heat to low and, using a wooden spoon, scrape any sediment left on the bottom of the pan and incorporate it into the butter.

Add the mushrooms to the pan and cook, stirring occasionally, for 3 minutes. Add the salt, pepper, lemon juice, paprika and sour cream and, stirring constantly, cook for 2 to 3 minutes or until the mixture is hot but not boiling.

Remove the pan from the heat and pour the sauce over the fish. Sprinkle the parsley over the top and serve.

Trout in Tomato Sauce

 ① ①

This Italian method of baking trout makes an interesting alternative to the more traditional methods of cooking this superb fish.

4 SERVINGS

3 fl. oz. [⅜ cup] olive oil
1 garlic clove, crushed
2 lb. tomatoes, blanched, peeled,
    seeded and chopped
2 oz. [½ cup] seasoned flour, made
    with 2 oz. [½ cup] flour, ½ teaspoon
    salt and ¼ teaspoon black pepper
4 medium-sized trout, cleaned and
    with the eyes removed
1 tablespoon finely chopped

A delicious fish cooked in a simply delicious way — Danish Fried Trout in Sour Cream Sauce.

fresh parsley

In a saucepan, heat 2 tablespoons of the oil over moderate heat. When the oil is hot, add the garlic and cook for 2 minutes, stirring constantly. Add the tomatoes, reduce the heat to moderately low and simmer the tomato mixture, stirring occasionally, for 20 minutes.

Meanwhile, preheat the oven to moderate 350°F (Gas Mark 4, 180°C).

Place the seasoned flour in a large, shallow dish. Dip the fish into the flour

mixture, coating them thoroughly.

In a large, flameproof casserole, heat the remaining oil over moderate heat. When the oil is hot, add the fish and cook them for 2 minutes on each side, or until they are lightly browned all over.

Pour the tomato sauce over the trout and place the casserole in the oven. Bake for 10 to 15 minutes or until the fish flesh flakes easily when tested with a fork.

Remove from the oven, sprinkle over the chopped parsley and serve immediately.

Smoked Trout Pâté

Simple and easy-to-make, Smoked Trout Pâté makes the perfect hors d'oeuvre, served with hot toast and butter.

6 SERVINGS

2 lb. smoked trout, skinned, boned and flaked
4 oz. single cream [½ cup light cream]
4 oz. cream cheese
2 tablespoons horseradish sauce
2 tablespoons lemon juice
1 teaspoon black pepper
1 tablespoon chopped fresh parsley

Place the fish and cream in the jar of an electric blender and blend at high speed until the mixture forms a purée.

Spoon the purée into a mixing bowl. Beat in the cream cheese, horseradish sauce, lemon juice, pepper and parsley. Continue beating until it is smooth and creamy. Spoon the pâté into individual ramekin dishes and smooth the top down with the back of a spoon.

Truro Skate with Egg and Lemon Sauce

 ☆ ☆   ①

Refreshing and light, Truro Skate with Egg and Lemon Sauce is delicious served with boiled potatoes and a crisp green salad.

6 SERVINGS

- 2 lb. skate wings, cleaned, trimmed and cut into large strips
- 2 pints [5 cups] fish stock

SAUCE
- 3 eggs, lightly beaten
- juice of 4 lemons
- ½ teaspoon salt
- ¼ teaspoon black pepper
- 1 tablespoon chopped fresh parsley

Place the skate in a shallow saucepan. Pour over the stock and bring to the boil over moderate heat. Reduce the heat to low and simmer the fish for 15 to 20 minutes or until the fish flesh flakes easily.

Remove the pan from the heat and carefully transfer the skate to a warmed serving dish. Keep hot.

Discard all but 2 fluid ounces [¼ cup] of the cooking liquid. Place the eggs, lemon juice, salt, pepper and the reserved cooking liquid in a medium-sized heat-proof mixing bowl. Stir well to mix. Set the bowl in a saucepan half-filled with boiling water and place the saucepan over low heat. Cook the sauce, stirring constantly, for 5 to 6 minutes or until it is fairly thick and smooth.

Remove the pan from the heat and remove the bowl from the pan. Spoon the egg and lemon sauce over the fish, sprinkle over the parsley and serve.

Turbot with Orange

☆   ① ①

The delicacy of turbot is enhanced by marinating it in this mixture of orange and lemon juice. Serve with steamed broccoli and potatoes.

4 SERVINGS

- 4 turbot steaks
- 1 teaspoon salt
- ½ teaspoon black pepper
- grated rind and juice of 2 oranges
- grated rind and juice of 1 lemon
- 2 oz. [¼ cup] butter
- 1 orange, thinly sliced

Place the turbot steaks in a shallow flameproof casserole. Sprinkle over the salt and pepper, orange rind and juice

Two ways with turbot, Turbot with Orange, Turbot with Vegetable Rice.

and lemon rind and juice. Set aside to marinate at room temperature for 1 hour.

Preheat the grill [broiler] to high.

Cut the butter up into small pieces and dot over the fish. Place the dish under the grill [broiler] and grill [broil] for 5 to 8 minutes on each side or until the flesh flakes easily.

Remove the dish from under the heat. Using a fish slice, transfer the turbot steaks to a warmed serving dish. Garnish with the orange slices. Serve at once.

Turbot with Vegetable Rice

☆   ① ①

This classic French way of cooking turbot is a meal in itself.

4 SERVINGS

- 4 turbot steaks
- 1 teaspoon salt
- ½ teaspoon black pepper
- 2 garlic cloves, finely chopped
- 1 teaspoon dried rosemary
- 1 teaspoon dried marjoram
- 2 tablespoons chopped fresh parsley
- 8 fl. oz. [1 cup] fish stock
- 1 oz. [2 tablespoons] butter
- 1 onion, finely chopped
- 2 celery stalks, finely chopped
- 4 oz. mushrooms, sliced
- 12 oz. [2 cups] long-grain rice, washed, soaked in cold water for 30 minutes, drained, cooked and kept hot
- 2 large tomatoes, sliced

Preheat the oven to warm 325°F (Gas Mark 3, 170°C).

Place the turbot steaks on the bottom of a large ovenproof dish. Sprinkle over the salt, pepper, garlic, rosemary, marjoram and parsley. Pour over the stock. Place the dish in the centre of the oven and bake for 15 to 20 minutes or until the fish flesh flakes easily.

Meanwhile, prepare the rice. In a large frying-pan, melt the butter over moderate heat. When the foam subsides, add the onion, celery and mushrooms. Fry, stirring occasionally, for 5 to 7 minutes or until the onion is soft and translucent but not brown. Using a slotted spoon, transfer the vegetables to a large mixing bowl. Stir the rice into the mixture.

Add the tomato slices to the fat in the pan and fry them for 1 minute on each side. Remove the pan from the heat. Remove the turbot from the oven. Using a fish slice, transfer the turbot steaks to a warmed serving dish and arrange them around the edge. Discard the cooking liquid. Pile the rice mixture in the middle and garnish the turbot with the tomato slices. Serve at once.

Chiopino

 ① ① ①

A hearty fish stew from northern California, Chiopino should be served in bowls with hot French or garlic bread.

8-10 SERVINGS

4 fl. oz. [½ cup] olive oil
4 garlic cloves, finely chopped
1 tablespoon chopped parsley
1 celery stalk, chopped
1 green pepper, white pith removed, seeded and chopped
1 lb. tomatoes, blanched, peeled, seeded and coarsely chopped
8 oz. canned tomato purée
1 teaspoon salt
½ teaspoon black pepper
1 teaspoon paprika
8 fl. oz. [1 cup] red wine
½ teaspoon dried oregano
3 lb. white fish fillets, (haddock, cod, whiting, etc), skinned and cut into 1-inch pieces
1 lb. raw shrimps, shelled and deveined
4 oz. freshly cooked or canned crabmeat, shell and cartilage removed
24 mussels or clams, soaked, washed and scrubbed

In a large saucepan, heat the olive oil over moderate heat. Add the garlic, parsley, celery and green pepper and cook until they are lightly browned. Add the tomatoes, tomato purée, salt, pepper, paprika, wine and oregano and stir the ingredients well. Reduce the heat to low and simmer the sauce, covered, for 1 hour.

Add the white fish and shrimps to the sauce and increase the heat to moderate. Cook for 10 minutes, or until the fish and shrimps are tender. Stir in the crabmeat.

Meanwhile, put enough water into a saucepan to make a 1-inch layer on the bottom. Bring the water to the boil over moderate heat and put the mussels or clams in the pan. Cook for 6 to 8 minutes or until the shells open (be sure to discard any that do not open).

Turn the chiopino into a warmed serving dish and place the mussels or clams, in their shells, on top.

Serve immediately, giving each person a bowl for their discarded shells.

Russian Kulebiak

  ① ①

This traditional dish is fish and hard-boiled eggs wrapped in crisp, golden pastry. Accompany the pie with a jug of sour

cream and serve it with creamed potatoes and spinach for a really impressive dinner party dish.

4-6 SERVINGS

PASTRY
6 oz. [1½ cups] flour
⅛ teaspoon salt
5 oz. [⅝ cup] butter, cut into small pieces
1 tablespoon vinegar
1 egg yolk
5 to 6 tablespoons iced water
FILLING
2 lb. cod, haddock or salmon
2 oz. [¼ cup] butter
1 onion, halved
1 carrot, scraped
1 celery stalk, trimmed and halved
   bouquet garni consisting of 4 parsley sprigs, 1 thyme spray and 1 bay leaf tied together
2 fl. oz. [¼ cup] water
1 oz. [2 tablespoons] butter, melted
4 hard-boiled eggs, sliced
1 teaspoon salt
½ teaspoon black pepper
1 tablespoon chopped fresh parsley
1 egg, lightly beaten

First prepare the pastry. Sift the flour and salt into a mixing bowl. Mix the pieces of butter into the flour, using a knife. Add the vinegar, egg yolk and enough water to form the mixture into a firm dough, which should be lumpy.

Roll out the dough into an oblong shape. Fold it in three and turn it so that the open edges face you. Roll out again into an oblong shape and proceed as before. Repeat this once again to make three turns in all. Wrap the dough in greaseproof or waxed paper and put in the refrigerator to chill for 15 minutes.

Meanwhile, prepare the filling. Put the fish, butter, onion, carrot, celery, bouquet garni and water in a medium-sized saucepan. Set the pan over moderate heat and bring to the boil. Reduce the heat to low, cover the pan and simmer for 15 to 20 minutes, or until the fish flakes easily.

Remove the pan from the heat and carefully lift out the fish. Skin and bone the fish and flake it into small pieces.

Preheat the oven to fairly hot 400°F (Gas Mark 6, 200°C).

Remove the dough from the refrigerator and divide it in half. Roll each piece of dough into a rectangle, about 10 inches by 6 inches. Trim the edges and reserve the trimmings.

Carefully lift one piece of dough on to a baking sheet. Arrange the fish on the dough leaving a ¼-inch space around the sides of the dough. Pour the melted butter over the top. Cover with the hard-boiled eggs and sprinkle over the salt,

pepper and parsley.

Place the other piece of dough over the fish and eggs. Turn up the edges of the dough to make a shallow rim round the filling. Using your fingers, pinch the rim to seal the edges.

Cut two slits in the middle of the dough to allow the steam to escape. Roll out the trimmings and use to make a decoration for the top. Brush the dough with the beaten egg.

Place the pie in the oven and bake for 30 minutes, or until the pastry is golden brown.

Remove the sheet from the oven and transfer the fish-filled pastry to a warmed serving dish. Serve at once.

Mediterranean Fish Stew

 ①

This traditional Southern French dish is easy to prepare. It can be made with any type of white or oily fish fillets, or a mixture of the two, and is an excellent lunch or informal dinner party dish. Serve with lots of chilled Provençal white wine.

4-6 SERVINGS

1½ lb. fish fillets, boned
6 medium-sized potatoes, peeled and sliced
1 bay leaf
1 medium-sized onion, finely chopped
1 celery stalk, trimmed and chopped
2 garlic cloves, peeled and crushed plus 1 whole, peeled garlic clove
1 teaspoon salt
½ teaspoon black pepper
1 teaspoon chopped fresh fennel
1 teaspoon chopped fresh parsley
1 teaspoon finely grated orange rind
3 fl. oz. [⅜ cup] olive oil
   boiling water
3 tablespoons alioli (garlic mayonnaise)
4 slices dry toasted French bread

Cut the fish into bite-sized pieces and arrange in the bottom of a large heavy saucepan. Cover with the potatoes. Add the bay leaf, onion, celery and crushed garlic. Sprinkle with salt, pepper, fennel, parsley and grated orange rind. Pour over the olive oil, then add just enough boiling water to cover. Cook the mixture over moderate heat for 20 minutes or until the potatoes are tender.

Strain the broth into another saucepan and put the fish and potatoes on a warmed serving dish. Just before serving the broth, remove the saucepan from the heat and, stirring constantly, very slowly add the alioli.

Place rounds of toast, well rubbed with

the peeled garlic clove, in individual soup bowls and pour the broth over them. Serve the fish and potatoes separately on a warmed serving dish.

White Fish Fondue

 ① ① ① ✕

One of the most pleasurable ways of eating fish, White Fish Fondue is easy to make and fun to eat.

6 SERVINGS

1 lb. hake fillets, cut into 1-inch cubes

1 lb. cod fillets, cut into 1-inch cubes

1 x 1 lb. squid, cleaned, blanched, skinned, beaten and cut into 1-inch cubes

1 lb. large Dublin Bay prawns [large Gulf shrimps], shelled and deveined

8 fl. oz. [1 cup] alioli (garlic mayonnaise)

1 pint [2½ cups] vegetable oil

Divide the hake, cod, squid and prawns or shrimps equally among 6 serving plates. Pour the alioli sauce into a small serving dish.

In a medium-sized saucepan, heat the oil over moderate heat until it reaches 375°F on a deep-fat thermometer or until

This fabulous Mediterranean Fish Stew is a filling meal in itself. Serve the broth (with garlic-flavoured French bread) as a soup, and the fish and potatoes as a main course.

a small cube of stale bread dropped carefully into the oil turns golden brown in 40 seconds.

Carefully pour the oil into a fondue pot. Light the spirit burner and carefully place the fondue pot over it. Cook the fish by spearing it with a fondue fork, and placing it in the hot oil to cook for 5 minutes. Serve with the alioli (garlic mayonnaise).

John Dory in Marsala

A delicate, lovely dish, John Dory in Marsala is both quick and easy to make. Serve it with creamed spinach and a well-chilled Frascati wine.

4 SERVINGS

2 john dory, filleted
3 oz. [¾ cup] seasoned flour, made
 with 3 oz. [¾ cup] flour,
 ½ teaspoon salt and ¼ teaspoon
 black pepper
2 oz. [¼ cup] butter
8 fl. oz. [1 cup] Marsala
8 fl. oz. [1 cup] fish stock
2 tablespoons chopped fresh parsley

Wash the fish fillets and pat them dry with kitchen paper towels. Place the seasoned flour on a plate and coat the fillets with it, shaking off any excess.

In a large, deep frying-pan, melt the butter over moderate heat. When the foam subsides, add the fillets to the pan and fry them for 3 minutes on each side, or until they are very lightly browned. With a slotted spoon, remove the fillets from the pan and set them aside.

Pour in the Marsala and fish stock and bring to the boil over high heat. Boil for 5 to 8 minutes, or until the liquid has reduced by about half.

Reduce the heat to low and return the fish fillets to the pan. Simmer the fish for 5 minutes, or until the flesh flakes easily.

Transfer the mixture to a warmed serving dish, sprinkle over the parsley and serve at once.

Fried Mackerel in Lime Juice

This exotic Indonesian recipe consists of fish marinated in lime juice and fried in peanut oil.

4 SERVINGS

10 fl. oz. [1¼ cups] fresh lime juice
 2 fl. oz. [¼ cup] white wine vinegar
 1 teaspoon salt
 6 black peppercorns
2 x 2 lb. mackerel, filleted
1 teaspoon turmeric
4 tablespoons peanut oil

In a large dish, combine the lime juice, vinegar, ½ teaspoon of salt and the peppercorns. Place the fish in the dish and set aside in a cool place. Leave the fillets to marinate for 1 hour.

Remove the fish from the marinade and dry on kitchen paper towels. Remove and discard the peppercorns from the marinade. Reserve 2 fluid ounces [¼ cup] of the marinade and discard the rest.

Rub the fish all over with the remaining salt and the turmeric. Set aside.

In a large frying-pan, heat the oil over moderate heat. Add the fillets and fry them for 4 to 6 minutes on each side, or until they flake easily.

With a fish slice, transfer the fillets to a serving dish. Pour over the reserved marinade and serve.

Exotic Fried Mackerel in Lime Juice.

Simple Japanese Sardines may be eaten bones and all!

Red Caviar Dip

Red Caviar Dip is an impressive and delicious addition to any buffet spread. Provide thinly buttered rye bread or toast to eat with it.

6-8 SERVINGS

1 lb. cream cheese
2 hard-boiled eggs, finely chopped
1 shallot, finely chopped
1 garlic clove, crushed
4 fl. oz. single cream [½ cup light cream]
3 oz. red caviar
2 teaspoons lemon juice

Place the cream cheese, eggs, shallot and garlic in a bowl. Beat the mixture until it is creamy. Stir in the cream and continue mixing until all the ingredients are thoroughly combined. Stir in the caviar and lemon juice.

Spoon the mixture into a serving bowl and place it in the refrigerator to chill for 30 minutes before serving.

Japanese Sardines

Sardines cooked in the Japanese style, flavoured with ginger and garlic, these can be eaten whole, bones and all. They make a delicious, unusual hors d'oeuvre served with brown bread and butter.

4 SERVINGS

4 fl. oz. [½ cup] soy sauce
2 fl. oz. [¼ cup] vinegar
2 tablespoons lemon juice
1 oz. fresh root ginger, peeled and chopped
2 garlic cloves, crushed
1 lb. fresh sardines, washed thoroughly in cold water and dried

2 tablespoons olive oil

In a small mixing bowl, combine the soy sauce, vinegar, lemon juice, ginger and garlic.

Arrange the sardines in a shallow baking dish and pour the soy sauce mixture over them. Leave the sardines in a cool place to marinate for 2 hours, basting them occasionally.

Preheat the grill [broiler] to high.

Remove the sardines from the marinade. Discard the marinade and dry the fish on kitchen paper towels. Reduce the heat of the grill [broiler] to moderate.

Line the grill [broiler] pan with aluminium foil. Brush the foil with half the oil. Place the sardines on the foil and brush them with the remaining oil.

Cook the sardines for 3 to 5 minutes or longer, depending on the size of the sardines, turning them once so that they are brown on both sides.

Remove the fish from the grill [broiler] and serve immediately.

Crabmeat and Avocado Mousse

This delicately flavoured, attractive mousse makes the perfect fish course for a dinner party. Or serve it as a light summer lunch with a mixed salad and garlic bread.

4-6 SERVINGS

1 teaspoon vegetable oil
3 large avocados, halved, stoned, peeled and chopped
2 tablespoons mayonnaise
1 teaspoon lemon juice
2 hard-boiled eggs, chopped
½ teaspoon salt
¼ teaspoon black pepper
4 spring onions [scallions], trimmed and chopped
¾ oz. gelatine, dissolved in 4 tablespoons hot water
4 oz. canned and drained or frozen and thawed crabmeat, shell and cartilage removed
4 fl. oz. double cream [½ cup heavy cream]
½ teaspoon curry powder

Using the teaspoon of vegetable oil, grease a 1-pint [1-quart] mould and set it aside.

Place the avocados, mayonnaise, lemon juice, eggs, salt, pepper, spring onions [scallions] and 3 tablespoons of the gelatine mixture in the jar of an electric blender. Blend at high speed for 30 seconds or until the mixture forms a smooth purée.

Pour half of the purée into the prepared mould and smooth over the top with the back of a spoon. Chill the mould in the refrigerator for 15 minutes.

Meanwhile, in a medium-sized mixing bowl, combine the remaining gelatine with the crabmeat, cream and curry powder, beating with a wooden spoon until the mixture is well blended and smooth.

Remove the mould from the refrigerator and spoon over the crabmeat mixture, smoothing it over with the back of the spoon. Chill the mould in the refrigerator for 15 minutes. Spoon over the remaining avocado mixture and smooth over the top. Chill the mixture in the refrigerator for a further 4 hours.

To unmould the mousse, run a sharp knife around the edge of the mould to loosen the sides. Quickly dip the bottom of the mould in boiling water. Hold a chilled serving plate, inverted, over the mould and reverse the two, giving the mould a sharp shake. The mousse should slide out easily.

Serve immediately.

Crabmeat Flan

This rich flan may be served hot or cold as an hors d'oeuvre. Accompanied by a tossed salad, it also makes a light but appetizing main dish. A well-chilled white Loire wine, Pouilly Fumé for instance, would go well with it.

6-8 SERVINGS

FILLING
1 lb. crabmeat, fresh or canned
1 teaspoon lemon juice

Creamy, filling Crabmeat Flan makes a perfect dish for informal entertaining.

1 tablespoon chopped fennel leaves
1 small onion, finely chopped
2 tablespoons chopped parsley
2 tablespoons dry sherry
4 eggs, lightly beaten
12 fl. oz. single cream [1½ cups light cream]
¼ teaspoon ground cinnamon
½ teaspoon salt
¼ teaspoon white pepper
PASTRY
6 oz. [1½ cups] flour
2 teaspoons castor sugar
¼ teaspoon salt
1½ oz. [3 tablespoons] butter
1½ oz. [3 tablespoons] vegetable fat
1 to 2 tablespoons iced water

Remove any shell and cartilage from the crabmeat.

In a large mixing bowl, combine the crabmeat, lemon juice, fennel, onion, parsley and sherry together. Cover the bowl and place it in the refrigerator to chill for 1 hour.

Meanwhile to make the pastry, sift the flour, sugar and salt into a medium-sized mixing bowl. Add the butter and vegetable fat and cut them into small pieces with a table knife. With your fingertips, rub the fat into the flour until the mixture resembles fine breadcrumbs.

Add 1 tablespoon of iced water and, using a knife, mix it into the flour mixture. With your hands, mix and knead the

Crabmeat Salad, with its unusual, tangy rémoulade salad dressing, is an ideal summer buffet dish.

dough until it is smooth. Add more water if the dough is too dry. Chill the dough in the refrigerator for 30 minutes.

Preheat the oven to hot 425°F (Gas Mark 7, 220°C).

Roll out the dough ¼-inch thick. Lift the dough on your rolling pin and lay it over a 9-inch pie dish or 12-inch flan ring. Ease the dough into the dish and trim the edges with a sharp knife. Place the pastry shell in the oven and bake 'blind' for 15 minutes.

Remove the pie dish or flan ring from the oven and spoon the crab mixture into the pastry shell, spreading it out evenly.

In a large mixing bowl, combine the eggs, cream, cinnamon, salt and pepper together using a wooden spoon. Strain the mixture over the crab mixture in the pastry shell.

Place the flan in the oven and bake for 10 minutes.

Reduce the heat to moderate 350°F (Gas Mark 4, 180°C) and continue baking for 1 hour, or until a knife inserted into the centre of the flan comes out clean.

Remove the flan from the oven and serve at once if you are serving it hot.

Crabmeat Salad

The tangy rémoulade dressing adds a delicious finishing touch to this colourful and very rich summer salad. Serve as a luxurious lunch or buffet supper with some chilled rosé wine.

4 SERVINGS

MAYONNAISE

2 egg yolks, at room temperature
½ teaspoon salt
¾ teaspoon dry mustard
⅛ teaspoon cayenne pepper
8 fl. oz. [1 cup] olive oil, at room temperature
1 teaspoon white wine vinegar or lemon juice

REMOULADE SAUCE

1 teaspoon anchovy essence
½ teaspoon finely chopped fresh parsley
½ tablespoon capers (optional)
1 hard-boiled egg, chopped
1 garlic clove, crushed
1 teaspoon chopped fresh tarragon or ½ teaspoon dried tarragon

SALAD

1 lb. cooked crabmeat, fresh or canned
1 large Webb [iceberg] lettuce washed, outer leaves removed and separated into leaves
4 firm tomatoes, sliced

1 avocado, peeled, stoned, sliced and gently rubbed with lemon juice
½ cucumber, thinly sliced
9 black olives, stoned

To prepare the mayonnaise, in a medium-sized mixing bowl, combine the egg yolks, salt, mustard and cayenne with a wire whisk. Add the oil, a few drops at a time, whisking constantly. Do not add the oil too quickly or the mayonnaise will curdle. When the mayonnaise is thick, the oil may be added more quickly. As you are adding the oil, beat in a few drops of vinegar or lemon juice from time to time to prevent the mayonnaise from becoming too thick. When all the oil has been added, add the remaining vinegar or lemon juice. Taste for seasoning and add more salt and mustard, if desired.

In a large mixing bowl, combine the mayonnaise with all the other ingredients for the rémoulade sauce and mix thoroughly.

Remove any shell and cartilage from the crabmeat.

Arrange the lettuce leaves on a large serving dish. Put the crabmeat in the centre of the dish and arrange the tomatoes, avocado, cucumber and olives around the crabmeat.

Pour the dressing over the top and serve immediately.

Luxurious Lobster Bouchées are small pastry cases enclosing a rich, creamy lobster, mushrooms, cream and sherry filling. Serve them as a very special appetizer or first course to a fairly light meal.

Homard à l'Americaine

LOBSTER COOKED WITH GARLIC, HERBS, TOMATOES AND WINE

A famous lobster dish, Homard à l'Americaine is said to have originated in France, but it was first served, in its present form, in New York in 1860. It looks most attractive served in a ring of rice, accompanied by a fresh green salad and a well chilled Pouilly Fumé.

4 SERVINGS

2 x 2 lb. cooked lobsters, shells split, claws cracked and grey sac removed
1 oz. [2 tablespoons] butter
2 tablespoons olive oil
2 shallots, peeled and finely chopped
1 garlic clove, chopped
6 tomatoes, blanched, peeled, seeded and chopped
1 tablespoon chopped fresh tarragon or ½ tablespoon dried tarragon
2 tablespoons chopped fresh parsley
2 teaspoons chopped fresh thyme or 1 teaspoon dried thyme
8 fl. oz. [1 cup] dry white wine
½ teaspoon salt
¼ teaspoon freshly ground black pepper
⅛ teaspoon cayenne pepper
2 fl. oz. [¼ cup] brandy

Remove the lobster meat from the shells and claws and cut it into 2-inch pieces. Set aside.

In a large frying-pan, melt the butter with the oil over moderate heat. When the foam subsides, add the shallots and garlic and fry, stirring occasionally, for 3 to 4 minutes, or until the shallots are golden brown.

Add the tomatoes, tarragon, parsley, thyme, wine, salt, pepper and cayenne. Bring to the boil, reduce the heat to moderately low and simmer the mixture for 20 minutes.

Add the lobster pieces to the pan.

In a small saucepan, warm the brandy over low heat until it is hot. Remove the pan from the heat and ignite the brandy. Carefully pour it, still flaming, into the frying-pan.

Cook the mixture for a further 5

minutes, to heat the lobster through thoroughly.

Remove the frying-pan from the heat and transfer the lobster and its sauce to a large, warmed serving dish. Serve at once.

Lobster Bouchées

Lobster Bouchées, with a superb creamy filling, make a delicious hors d'oeuvre or cocktail bites. They are very rich and filling, however, so try not to serve them when you have a rather heavy main course planned to follow.

18 SMALL BOUCHEES

18 small frozen bouchée cases, thawed, baked and kept hot
FILLING
1 x 2 lb. cooked lobster, shell split, claws cracked and grey sac removed
1 oz. [2 tablespoons] butter
8 oz. mushrooms, wiped clean and sliced
2 egg yolks
2 tablespoons double [heavy] cream
10 fl. oz. [1¼ cups] béchamel sauce
½ teaspoon salt
½ teaspoon freshly ground black pepper
⅛ teaspoon cayenne pepper
4 fl. oz. [½ cup] medium-dry sherry

2 teaspoons lemon juice

To make the filling, remove the lobster meat from the shells and claws. Discard the shells and cut the meat into dice. Set aside.

In a medium-sized frying-pan, melt the butter over moderate heat. When the foam subsides, add the mushrooms and cook, stirring occasionally, for 4 to 6 minutes or until they are tender. With a slotted spoon, remove the mushrooms from the pan and set them aside on a plate.

In a small mixing bowl, beat the egg yolks and cream together with a wire whisk or rotary beater until they are blended. Set aside.

In a medium-sized saucepan, heat the béchamel sauce over moderate heat. Add the diced lobster, mushrooms, salt, pepper and cayenne. Stirring carefully, cook the sauce for 2 to 3 minutes. Do not worry if the sauce is quite thick at this stage.

Remove the pan from the heat. Carefully stir in the egg yolk and cream mixture. Return the pan to low heat and, stirring constantly, cook the sauce gently for 2 minutes. Stir in the sherry and lemon juice and cook for 1 minute. Taste the sauce and add more seasoning if necessary.

Spoon a little of the filling into each of the hot bouchée cases, carefully transfer them to an attractive serving dish and serve them at once.

Lobster with Brandy Sauce

This superb dish, flavoured with brandy and cayenne, makes an ideal first course to a lunch or dinner party. Or, alternatively, it may be served as a light luncheon with creamed potatoes.

2-4 SERVINGS

1 x 3 lb. cooked lobster, shell split, claws cracked and grey sac removed
1½ oz. [3 tablespoons] butter
2 teaspoons olive oil
½ teaspoon salt
¼ teaspoon freshly ground black pepper
¼ teaspoon cayenne pepper
6 fl. oz. [¾ cup] brandy
2 teaspoons cornflour [cornstarch] mixed with 2 tablespoons water

Lobster with Brandy Sauce is downright extravagant to make - but the spectacular results are more than worth the initial expense.

Remove the lobster meat from the shell, cut it into small pieces and set aside. Wipe the shell halves clean and place them in a heatproof dish with the claws. Set the dish aside.

In a medium-sized frying-pan, melt the butter with the oil over moderate heat. When the foam subsides, add the lobster meat, salt, pepper and cayenne and fry, stirring occasionally, for 3 to 4 minutes, or until the lobster meat is lightly browned.

Preheat the grill [broiler] to moderate.

In a small saucepan, heat the brandy over low heat until it is hot but not boil-

ing. Remove the pan from the heat and carefully pour the brandy over the lobster meat. Ignite the brandy with a match and leave it until the flames have completely died down.

With a slotted spoon, remove the lobster meat from the pan and place it in the reserved shell halves.

Place the pan over moderate heat and bring the liquid to the boil. Reduce the heat to low and stir in the cornflour [cornstarch] mixture, a little at a time, beating constantly until the ingredients are blended and the sauce has thickened. Remove the pan from the heat and pour the sauce over the lobster meat.

Place the dish under the grill [broiler] and grill [broil] for about 5 minutes or until the lobster is golden brown.

Remove from the grill [broiler] and serve at once.

Oyster Chowder

A warming mixture of oysters, vegetables and cream, Oyster Chowder makes a delicious light lunch or supper served with hot buttered toast.

4-6 SERVINGS

1½ oz. [3 tablespoons] butter
1 large onion, finely chopped
2 celery stalks, trimmed and chopped
1 medium-sized carrot, scraped and chopped
2 medium-sized potatoes, peeled and diced
4 fl. oz. [½ cup] boiling water
1½ teaspoons salt
32 fresh oysters, shelled and with the oyster liquid reserved
½ teaspoon black pepper
10 fl. oz. single cream [1¼ cups light cream]
1 tablespoon chopped fresh parsley

In a large saucepan, melt 1 ounce [2 tablespoons] of the butter over moderate heat. When the foam subsides, add the onion and celery to the pan and fry, stirring occasionally, for 5 to 7 minutes or until the onion is soft and translucent but not brown. Add the carrot and potatoes. Pour over the water and add ½ teaspoon of the salt.

Increase the heat to high and bring the liquid back to the boil. Reduce the heat to low, cover the pan and cook for 15 minutes, or until the potatoes and carrot are tender.

Meanwhile, in a second large saucepan, melt the remaining butter over moderate heat. When the foam subsides, add the oysters and their liquid. Cover the pan and cook the oysters for 2 minutes. Remove the pan from the heat and set aside.

When the potatoes and carrot are cooked, add the remaining salt, the pepper and the cream. Pour in the cooked oysters and their liquid. Cook the chowder, stirring frequently, for a further 2 minutes, or until it is hot but not boiling.

Taste the chowder and add more salt and pepper if necessary.

Remove the pan from the heat. Ladle the chowder into a warmed tureen. Sprinkle with the parsley and serve immediately.

Marinated Oysters is an exquisite dish of fresh oysters marinated in wine, oil and lemon juice.

Oyster Cocktail

Oysters in a piquant sauce resting on a bed of crisp lettuce leaves, Oyster Cocktail makes a tasty start to a meal.

4 SERVINGS

2 tablespoons tomato purée
1 teaspoon Worcestershire sauce
1 tablespoon fresh lemon juice
¼ teaspoon salt
⅛ teaspoon black pepper
5 fl. oz. double cream [⅝ cup heavy cream]
16 fresh oysters, shelled
1 small crisp lettuce, outer leaves removed, washed and separated into leaves
1 lemon, sliced
½ small cucumber, sliced

In a large mixing bowl, combine the tomato purée, Worcestershire sauce, lemon juice, salt and pepper with a fork. Add the cream and beat the mixture well to combine all the ingredients. Stir in the oysters, coating them thoroughly with the sauce.

Line 4 individual serving glasses with the lettuce leaves. Spoon equal amounts of the oyster mixture on to the lettuce

leaves. Garnish each serving with lemon and cucumber slices.

Place the glasses in the refrigerator and chill for 30 minutes before serving.

Oysters with Cream and Cheese

A deliciously tempting first course for a dinner party, Oysters with Cream and Cheese is surprisingly quick and easy to make — and the reward, with this elegant dish, is readily apparent. Canned oysters have been used in this recipe because they are usually more available than fresh. If you do have access to fresh oysters, however, the dish is of course even more superb! Remove them from their shells and cook them first.

4 SERVINGS

2 oz. [¼ cup] plus 1 teaspoon butter, melted
16 canned oysters, drained
6 fl. oz. double cream [¾ cup heavy cream]
2 oz. [½ cup] Parmesan cheese, grated

Preheat the grill [broiler] to moderately high. With the teaspoon of butter, lightly grease a medium-sized shallow, flame-proof baking dish.

Place the oysters, in one layer, in the baking dish. Spoon a little of the cream over each one, then sprinkle generously with grated cheese. Spoon a little of the remaining melted butter on top of each oyster and place the dish under the grill [broiler]. Cook the oysters for 3 to 5 minutes, or until the topping bubbles slightly and has browned.

Remove the dish from the grill [broiler] and serve the oysters at once.

Marinated Oysters

This exquisitely simple first course is a delectable combination of fresh oysters, white wine, lemon juice and herbs, served cold. It makes an elegant start to a dinner party although, since it is quite rich and filling, it is best followed by a light main course. Serve with small squares of brown bread and butter and a well-chilled white Chablis wine.

4 SERVINGS

16 fresh oysters
MARINADE
6 fl. oz. [¾ cup] dry white wine
2 fl. oz. [¼ cup] olive oil
2 fl. oz. [¼ cup] lemon juice
¼ teaspoon salt

¼ teaspoon black pepper
¼ teaspoon dried thyme
¼ teaspoon dried chervil
1 teaspoon chopped fresh parsley
1 garlic clove, crushed

First, prepare the marinade. In a large mixing bowl, combine all the marinade ingredients, stirring with a fork or spoon to blend well. Set aside for 15 minutes.

Meanwhile, detach the oysters from their shells and place them in a medium-sized saucepan. Discard the shells.

Add the marinade to the oysters and place the pan over moderate heat. Bring the liquid to the boil, then remove the pan from the heat.

Transfer the oysters and liquid to a medium-sized serving bowl and set aside to cool to room temperature.

Serve the oysters cold, in their marinade.

Oysters Rockefeller

A delicious appetizer, Oysters Rockefeller is an adaptation of a well-known American

Oysters Rockefeller is a classic American hors d'oeuvre.

recipe which originated in New Orleans.

4 SERVINGS

sufficient rock salt to cover the bottom of 2 large baking dishes in a layer about ½-inch thick
4 spring onions [scallions], chopped
2 celery stalks, finely chopped
8 oz. cooked spinach
3 parsley sprigs
1 teaspoon salt
¼ teaspoon black pepper
¼ teaspoon cayenne pepper
2 fl. oz. single cream [¼ cup light cream]
1 tablespoon Pernod
36 fresh oysters, one shell removed

Preheat the oven to very hot 450°F (Gas Mark 8, 230°C).

Cover the bottom of two large baking dishes with the rock salt. Set aside.

Place the spring onions [scallions], celery, spinach, parsley, salt, pepper, cayenne and cream in an electric blender and blend, off and on, for 2 minutes or until the ingredients are puréed. Transfer the purée to a mixing bowl. Add the Pernod and stir well. Divide the oysters equally between the baking dishes. Cover each one with a teaspoonful of the purée. Place the baking dishes in the oven and bake for 4 minutes.

Remove the baking dishes from the oven and serve immediately.

187

Coquilles St.-Jacques à la Crème

SCALLOPS IN CREAM SAUCE

A superbly elegant first course to serve for a dinner party, Coquilles St.-Jacques à la Crème takes very little time to prepare.

4 SERVINGS

4 fl. oz. [½ cup] white wine
½ teaspoon lemon juice
1 lb. scallops
1 tablespoon butter
2 tablespoons flour
5 fl. oz. single cream [⅝ cup light cream]
¼ teaspoon salt
¼ teaspoon black pepper
⅛ teaspoon cayenne pepper
red food colouring
1 oz. [¼ cup] Gruyère cheese, grated

In a heavy, medium-sized saucepan heat the wine and lemon juice over moderate heat. When the liquid boils, reduce the heat to moderately low and drop the scallops into the pan. Simmer them gently for 8 to 10 minutes or until they are firm. Remove the pan from the heat and place to one side to cool.

When the liquid has cooled, strain it into a bowl or jug. With a sharp knife, slice the scallops in half and set them aside. In a medium-sized heavy saucepan, melt the butter over low heat. Remove the pan from the heat and, with a wooden spoon, stir in the flour. Gradually add the liquid from cooking the scallops to the pan, stirring constantly. Return the pan to moderate heat and bring the sauce to the boil. Stirring constantly, cook the sauce for 3 minutes. Stir in the cream, salt, pepper, cayenne and a few drops of red food colouring as liked, and cook for a further 2 minutes. Fold the scallops into the sauce.

Preheat the grill [broiler] to moderate.

Spoon the scallops and sauce into four large scallop shells or individual cocotte dishes. Sprinkle the grated cheese over the tops and brown under the grill [broiler] for 4 to 5 minutes. Serve.

Coquilles St-Jacques Gratinées

SCALLOPS AND MUSHROOMS IN WHITE WINE SAUCE AND CHEESE

This mouthwatering main dish may be served with puréed potatoes, buttered peas or broccoli.

4 SERVINGS

1 tablespoon butter
1½ lb. scallops, sliced

6 fl. oz. [¾ cup] dry white wine
4 oz. mushrooms, sliced
½ teaspoon salt
6 peppercorns
1 bay leaf
3 parsley sprigs
2 shallots, finely minced
2 fl. oz. [¼ cup] water
SAUCE
2½ oz. [¼ cup plus 1 tablespoon] butter
4 tablespoons flour
6 fl. oz. [¾ cup] milk
2 egg yolks
4 fl. oz. double cream [½ cup heavy cream]
¼ teaspoon salt
⅛ teaspoon white pepper
¼ teaspoon grated nutmeg
1 teaspoon lemon juice
2 oz. [½ cup] Gruyère cheese, grated
1 tablespoon melted butter

With the butter, grease 4 shallop shells or a medium-sized flameproof serving dish.

Put the scallops in a medium-sized saucepan and add the wine, mushrooms, salt, peppercorns, bay leaf, parsley and shallots. The scallops should be almost covered so if necessary, add the water. Heat the liquid to boiling point over moderate heat, cover and cook the scallops for 5 minutes. Remove the scallops and mushrooms from the liquid and put them in a bowl to one side.

Increase the heat to high and boil the liquid in the saucepan until it is reduced by about one-third. Pour the liquid through a strainer into a jug.

Preheat the grill [broiler] to moderate.

To make the sauce, in a small saucepan, melt the butter over low heat. Remove the pan from the heat and, with a wooden spoon, stir in the flour. Gradually stir in 6 fluid ounces [¾ cup] of the reduced scallop cooking liquid. Return the pan to the heat and bring to the boil. Cook, stirring constantly, for 5 minutes or until the sauce is thick and smooth. Lightly beat in the milk and cook, stirring, for a further 1 minute. Remove the pan from the heat and place to one side.

Put the egg yolks in a small bowl with the cream and beat with a fork to mix. Stirring constantly, add a little hot sauce to the beaten egg yolks and cream. Stir the mixture into the remaining sauce in the pan and return the pan to the heat. Heat the sauce gently, stirring, and remove the pan from the heat. Add the salt, pepper, nutmeg and lemon juice. Fold the scallops and mushrooms into the sauce.

Spoon the scallop mixture into the shells or dish. Sprinkle the grated cheese and the melted butter over the tops of

each shell or over the dish. Brown under the grill [broiler] for 6 minutes or until the cheese has melted and is brown and sizzling. Serve immediately.

Scallop Salad

A colourful and appetizing dish, Scallop Salad makes a delightful meal to serve at an informal dinner party. Serve with garlic bread and a well-chilled white wine, such as Graves.

4-6 SERVINGS

16 scallops, poached, drained and halved
12 mussels, scrubbed, steamed and removed from their shells
6 oz. prawns or shrimps, shelled and deveined
1 small head of fennel, trimmed and thinly sliced
2 medium-sized green peppers, white pith removed, seeded and sliced
8 oz. green beans, cooked, drained and cut into 1-inch lengths
6 medium-sized tomatoes, quartered
12 small new potatoes, boiled, drained and peeled
6 spring onions [scallions], trimmed and cut into 1-inch lengths
1 medium-sized cucumber, roughly diced
12 stoned black olives
DRESSING
2 garlic cloves, crushed
1 teaspoon prepared French mustard
2 teaspoons sugar
½ teaspoon salt
½ teaspoon black pepper
2 teaspoons chopped fresh basil or 1 teaspoon dried basil
6 fl. oz. [¾ cup] olive oil
2 fl. oz. [¼ cup] white wine vinegar

First prepare the dressing. In a medium-sized bowl, combine the garlic, mustard, sugar, salt, pepper and basil. Gradually beat in the olive oil and vinegar until the mixture is thoroughly combined. Set aside.

In a large salad bowl, combine the scallops, mussels, prawns or shrimps, fennel, peppers, beans, tomatoes, potatoes, spring onions [scallions], cucumber and black olives. Pour the dressing over the salad and, using two large spoons, toss the salad until the ingredients are coated with the dressing. Serve immediately.

Refreshing Scallop Salad.

Stir-fried Abalone and Chinese Cabbage

This unusual dish of Chinese cabbage, abalone and leek, flavoured with soy sauce, ginger and lemon juice (pictured on page 161) may be served as part of a Chinese meal, or as a light lunch with boiled rice or noodles.

4 SERVINGS

3 tablespoons peanut oil
½-inch piece fresh root ginger, peeled and very thinly sliced
1 small leek, white part only, thinly sliced and pushed out into rings
1 small Chinese cabbage, coarse outer leaves removed, washed and shredded
⅛ teaspoon monosodium glutamate (optional)
½ teaspoon salt
¼ teaspoon white pepper
2 teaspoons soy sauce
1½ tablespoons fresh lemon juice
14 oz. canned abalone, drained and sliced

In a large frying-pan, heat the oil over moderate heat. When the oil is hot, add the ginger and leek and stir-fry for 2 minutes. Add the cabbage and stir-fry for 4 minutes, or until the cabbage is cooked but still crisp.

Sprinkle over the monosodium glutamate (if you are using it), salt, pepper, soy sauce and lemon juice. Stir in the sliced abalone and cook the mixture, stirring constantly, for 5 minutes.

Remove the pan from the heat. Turn the mixture into a warmed serving dish and serve immediately.

Clams Marinara

Clams Marinara is clams steamed in white wine and covered with a sauce of tomatoes, onion and garlic. If clams are not available small oysters or cockles can be substituted. This dish may be served as a main course with buttered rice, and a mixed salad. Serve with crusty rolls or French bread.

4 SERVINGS

2 hard-boiled eggs
3 tablespoons olive oil
1 large onion, chopped
2 garlic cloves, crushed
1½ oz. [¾ cup] fresh white breadcrumbs
1½ lb. tomatoes, blanched, peeled and chopped
½ teaspoon salt
¼ teaspoon black pepper

4 dozen small fresh clams, in shells
15 fl. oz. [1⅞ cups] white wine
2 tablespoons chopped fresh parsley
2 lemons, cut in wedges

Separate the egg whites from the yolks. Chop the whites into small pieces. Press the yolks through a strainer or, if you have one, a garlic crusher. Set aside.

In a medium-sized frying-pan, heat the oil over moderate heat. Add the onion and garlic and fry, stirring occasionally, for 5 to 7 minutes or until the onion is soft and translucent but not brown. Add the breadcrumbs, tomatoes, egg yolks, salt and pepper. Stir and mash with the back of a wooden spoon until the mixture becomes a smooth, thick purée. Set aside.

Place the clams in a heavy pot. Pour the wine over them and bring to the boil. Cover, reduce the heat and simmer for 10 minutes or until the clams open. Throw away any clams that have remained closed.

Place the clams in a deep, heated serving dish. Strain the liquid from the pan and add to the purée. Taste and adjust seasoning by adding more salt and pepper if necessary. Pour the sauce over the clams. Sprinkle with parsley and the egg whites and serve immediately. The lemon wedges should be served on a separate dish.

Paella

You may vary the ingredients in Paella using tiny eels and prawns or shrimps instead of the combination suggested here. Rabbit may be substituted for the chicken.

6-8 SERVINGS

1 lobster, shell split, claws cracked and grey sac removed
3 fl. oz. [⅜ cup] olive oil
1 x 3 lb. chicken, cut into 12 serving pieces
6 lean bacon slices, chopped
2 large tomatoes, blanched, peeled, seeded and chopped
2 garlic cloves, finely chopped
8 oz. mange-tout, washed
1 lb. [2⅔ cups] long-grain rice, washed, soaked in cold water for 30 minutes and drained
2 teaspoons paprika
2 pints [5 cups] water
2 teaspoons salt
¼ teaspoon ground saffron
12 small clams, steamed
6 snails
8 oz. baby squid, cleaned
6 lemon wedges

Remove the lobster meat from the shell

and claws and cut it into 1-inch pieces.

In a large flameproof casserole, heat the olive oil over moderate heat. When it is hot, add the chicken pieces and the bacon and fry, turning occasionally, for 5 to 8 minutes or until the chicken pieces are lightly browned. Add the tomatoes, garlic and mange-tout and fry for a further 5 minutes, stirring frequently.

Using a slotted spoon, remove the mixture from the casserole. Set aside.

Add the rice and paprika to the casserole and, shaking it frequently, cook for 3 minutes or until the rice is well coated with the oil. Add the water, salt and saffron, stir and bring to the boil. Reduce the heat to low, add the chicken and vegetable mixture and cook for 10 minutes, stirring occasionally. Add the clams, snails, squid and lobster and cook for a further 5 to 10 minutes or until the chicken is cooked through and all the liquid has been absorbed by the rice.

Remove the casserole from the heat. Serve, garnished with the lemon wedges.

Shrimp and Avocado Surprise

An unusual appetizing dish which is both easy to make and impressive to serve, Shrimp and Avocado Surprise may be accompanied by melba toast and butter.

6 SERVINGS

3 ripe avocados, halved and stoned
10 oz. frozen peeled shrimps, thawed and drained
5 fl. oz. [⅝ cup] mayonnaise
2 garlic cloves, crushed
1 teaspoon ground coriander
¼ teaspoon grated nutmeg
1 teaspoon salt
½ teaspoon black pepper
juice of ½ lemon
6 slices streaky bacon, rinds removed, grilled [broiled] until very crisp and crumbled

Using a teaspoon, scoop out the avocado flesh, leaving the skins intact. Set the skins aside.

Place the avocado flesh in a medium-sized mixing bowl. Mash the flesh with a fork until it is smooth and creamy. Add the shrimps, mayonnaise, garlic, coriander, nutmeg, salt, pepper and lemon juice. With a wooden spoon, stir the ingredients until they are well blended.

Spoon the avocado mixture back into the reserved avocado skins. Sprinkle over the crumbled bacon and serve.

Classic Paella from Spain.

Shrimp Egg Foo Yung

This Chinese omelet makes a delightful first course for a dinner party, or it may be served as part of a Chinese meal.

4 SERVINGS

3 tablespoons vegetable oil
8 oz. shrimps, chopped
4 oz. mushrooms, sliced
4 oz. bean sprouts, washed
4 eggs, lightly beaten
SAUCE
8 fl. oz. [1 cup] chicken stock
2 teaspoons soy sauce
¼ teaspoon salt
1 tablespoon cornflour [cornstarch]
    mixed with 1 tablespoon water

In a frying-pan, heat 1 tablespoon of the oil over moderate heat. When the oil is hot, add the shrimps to the pan and stir-fry for 3 minutes or until they are heated through. Remove from the heat and set aside.

To make the sauce, in a small saucepan, bring the stock, soy sauce, salt and corn-flour [cornstarch] mixture to the boil over moderate heat, stirring constantly. Cook the sauce for 1 minute, or until it has thickened slightly. Set aside.

In a mixing bowl, combine the mush-rooms, bean sprouts, eggs and shrimps and beat them together with a fork.

Return the frying-pan to moderate heat. Add the remaining oil to the pan. When the oil is hot, add a quarter of the egg mixture and cook it for 1 minute or until the bottom is set and golden brown. Using a spatula or palette knife, turn the omelet over and cook for a further 1 minute or until it is just set. Transfer the omelet to a serving dish and keep warm. Cook the remaining egg mixture in the same way, to make 3 more omelets.

Return the pan to moderate heat and bring the sauce to the boil, stirring. Remove the pan from the heat and pour a little of the sauce over the omelets. Serve immediately.

Squid in Red Wine

This economical recipe makes an unusual but festive supper dish.

4 SERVINGS

2½ lb. squid, cleaned and skinned
4 tablespoons olive oil
2 medium-sized onions, sliced
2 garlic cloves, crushed
5 fl. oz. [⅝ cup] red wine
½ teaspoon salt

Delicate Shrimp Egg Foo Yung.

½ teaspoon black pepper
1 teaspoon dried oregano
½ teaspoon fennel seeds
¼ teaspoon dried marjoram
6 large tomatoes, blanched, peeled,
    seeded and chopped
1 teaspoon dried basil

Cut the squid into ¼-inch slices and chop the tentacles.

In a flameproof casserole, heat half the oil over moderate heat. When the oil is hot, add the onions and garlic and fry stirring, for 5 to 7 minutes, or until the onions are soft and translucent.

Add the squid and fry, stirring occa-sionally, for 4 minutes. Stir in the wine, salt, pepper, oregano, fennel seeds and marjoram. Cover, reduce the heat to low and simmer for 1 hour, or until tender.

Meanwhile, make the tomato sauce. In a frying-pan, heat the remaining oil over moderate heat. When the oil is hot, add the tomatoes and basil and, stirring occasionally, cook for 20 minutes or until the tomatoes are pulpy.

Add the tomato pulp to the casserole, stir well, and bring the stew to the boil. Remove from the heat and serve.

Vegetables and salads for the family

Vegetables and Salads were traditionally served as accompaniments to meat, fish or other 'main' dishes. Now, however, with the cost of meat and fish escalating, they are coming into their own. And variety has never been better — vegetables once considered 'exotic' and 'foreign' (and sometimes suspect!) are rapidly becoming more available, more familiar and less expensive, with beneficial effects upon our diet.

The difficulty was to decide what to include and, in the end, a compromise was reached.

You will find familiar recipes, such as Bubble and Squeak (page 196) and Salmagundy (page 223), old favourites with a new slant, such as Potatoes Stuffed and Baked (page 204) and the classic Russian Salad (pictured below, recipe page 222),

and also 'new' tastes, such as Broccoli with Black Olives (page 194) and Korean Vegetable Salad (page 217). Plus lots of exciting dressings to cheer up the dullest salads, including a fail-safe method of making your own mayonnaise.

Most of our recipes are not only simple and quick to make, they are inexpensive too. But of course there are times (birthdays, anniversaries and so on) when the unusual and the slightly more expensive are desired and we have therefore selected some extra-special dishes **For Special Occasions.** All are guaranteed fit for a king.

There is no healthier way to live than to eat lots of vegetables and salads — and just because they're good for you doesn't mean they have to be dull and uninspired.

Asparagus with Butter Sauce

As well as making a simple but elegant hors d'oeuvre, asparagus is a delicious vegetable accompaniment to meat and fish dishes. The season for fresh asparagus is a short one so frozen asparagus may be used instead.

4 SERVINGS

2 pints [5 cups] water
1 tablespoon plus ¼ teaspoon salt
1 lb. frozen asparagus, thawed
    and drained
6 tablespoons hot, melted butter
¼ teaspoon freshly ground black
    pepper

Pour the water into a large saucepan and add 1 tablespoon of the salt. Place the pan over moderate heat and bring the water to the boil. Drop the asparagus into the water. When the water returns to the boil, boil rapidly for 4 to 6 minutes, or until the asparagus is almost tender but still firm.

If the asparagus is not to be served immediately, put in a colander and run cold water through it to prevent it from cooking further and to retain the colour and texture.

Just before serving, put the asparagus in a warmed serving dish and pour the butter over it. Taking care not to break the asparagus, gently toss it in the hot butter to finish the cooking and to coat it with butter. Sprinkle with the remaining salt and the black pepper, and serve at once.

Broccoli with Black Olives

Try this unusual way of serving broccoli — with black olives, garlic and Parmesan cheese. Green olives may be used instead of black, but the colour of the dish will not be as interesting. Serve Broccoli with Black Olives as an accompaniment to grilled [broiled] steaks or pork chops.

4 SERVINGS

1½ lb. broccoli
10 fl. oz. [1¼ cups] water
 2 teaspoons salt
 3 tablespoons olive oil
 1 garlic clove, finely chopped
 ½ teaspoon freshly ground black
    pepper
 2 oz. [¾ cup] stoned black olives,
    halved
 4 tablespoons finely grated

Parmesan cheese

Wash the broccoli, remove the leaves and break the flowerets into fairly large bunches.

In a large saucepan, bring the water to the boil. Add 1 teaspoon of salt and the broccoli. Cover the pan and cook the broccoli for 10 minutes over moderately high heat. Drain the broccoli. Reserve the water in which the broccoli was cooked.

In a large frying-pan, heat the oil over low heat. Add the garlic and fry for 2 minutes. Add the broccoli and season with the remaining salt and the pepper. Cook the broccoli for 10 minutes, stirring frequently. Add some of the water in which the broccoli was cooked if the pan gets too dry.

Add the olives to the pan and cook for another 2 minutes. Turn the broccoli and olives into a warmed serving dish. Sprinkle with the Parmesan cheese and serve at once.

Asparagus with Butter Sauce is simple enough to be served to the family, elegant enough for a special dinner party.

Brussels Sprouts with Chestnuts

An interesting vegetable dish, Brussels Sprouts with Chestnuts goes well with roast chicken, turkey, goose or duck. In this recipe the Brussels sprouts are blanched, plunged in cold water and drained to prevent them from losing their flavour and colour.

6 SERVINGS

1½ lb. fresh or frozen Brussels
    sprouts
2 teaspoons salt
24 chestnuts
2 tablespoons arrowroot
1 tablespoon port or water
15 fl. oz. [1⅞ cups] home-made beef
    stock
2 oz. [¼ cup] butter
½ teaspoon freshly ground black
    pepper
2 oz. [¼ cup] butter, melted

Preheat the oven to warm 325°F (Gas Mark 3, 170°C).

With a sharp knife, trim the base of each Brussels sprout and cut a cross in it. Wash and drain the sprouts, and remove any yellow or wilted leaves.

Fill a large saucepan with water and add 1 teaspoon of salt. Set the pan over moderately high heat and bring the water to the boil. When the water is boiling, drop in the Brussels sprouts and bring the water back to the boil.

Reduce the heat to moderately low and simmer the sprouts slowly for 6 to 8 minutes, or until they are almost tender. Drain off the water and place the saucepan full of sprouts under cold, running water for 3 minutes. Drain the sprouts again

Broccoli with Black Olives makes an unusual vegetable for the family. Serve with steaks or chops.

and place to one side.

Using a sharp knife, split the skins of the chestnuts at the pointed end. Put the chestnuts in a medium-sized saucepan, cover with water and bring them to the boil over moderate heat. Boil for 30 seconds, then drain and peel the chestnuts with a sharp knife.

Put the peeled chestnuts in a large flameproof casserole or baking dish. In a small bowl, mix the arrowroot with the port or water. Then pour in the stock and mix well. Pour this liquid over the chestnuts. Add 1½ ounces [3 tablespoons] of butter. The chestnuts should be well covered with the liquid. If there is not enough liquid to cover, add a little more water.

Place the casserole over moderate heat and bring to the boil. Then cover the casserole and place it in the lower part of the oven. Cook for 45 to 60 minutes or until the chestnuts are tender. (Test them for tenderness by piercing with a sharp pointed knife.)

Take the casserole out of the oven and raise the heat to moderate 350°F (Gas Mark 4, 180°C). Lift the chestnuts out of the casserole with a slotted spoon and discard the cooking liquid. Replace the chestnuts in the casserole and add the Brussels sprouts. Sprinkle with the remaining salt, the black pepper and the melted butter.

With the remaining butter, grease a sheet of greaseproof or waxed paper and carefully cover the casserole with it. Bake in the oven for a further 20 minutes, then

turn the vegetables into a warmed serving dish.

Serve immediately.

Brussels Sprouts Creole

This simple recipe makes a colourful change from plain, boiled Brussels sprouts. It may be served with any savoury dish from an omelet to the Sunday roast.

4 SERVINGS

1½ lb. fresh or frozen Brussels
    sprouts
1½ oz. [3 tablespoons] butter
1 large onion, finely chopped
1 garlic clove, crushed
1 green pepper, white pith removed,
    seeded and chopped
1 lb. tomatoes, blanched, peeled
    and chopped
½ teaspoon freshly ground black
    pepper
¼ teaspoon dried basil
1 teaspoon salt

With a sharp knife, trim any tough or discoloured outer leaves from the sprouts, and wash them thoroughly. Cut a cross in the base of each sprout.

In a heavy, medium-sized saucepan, melt the butter over moderate heat. Add the onion, garlic and green pepper. Cook them, stirring occasionally, for 8 minutes. Add the tomatoes, sprouts, black pepper, basil and salt. Taste the mixture and add more salt and pepper if necessary.

Reduce the heat to low, cover the pan and cook for 15 to 20 minutes, or until the sprouts are tender. Turn the mixture into a warmed serving dish.

Serve at once.

Exotic Carrots Algerian-Style is easy to make and tastes delicious hot or cold.

Put the carrot slices into a medium-sized saucepan. Add enough water just to cover the carrots and bring it to the boil over moderate heat. Cover the pan and cook the carrots for 15 minutes, or until they are firm but tender when pierced with a skewer. Using a slotted spoon, remove the carrots from the pan and transfer them to a bowl. Reserve 5 fluid ounces [⅝ cup] of the cooking liquid.

In a medium-sized saucepan, mix together the oil, salt, pepper, cinnamon, cumin seeds, garlic and thyme over very low heat. Simmer for 10 minutes. Add the reserved cooking liquid and the bay leaf, cover the pan and simmer for a further 15 to 20 minutes.

Add the carrots to the saucepan. Toss them in the sauce and cook for 2 to 3 minutes to heat the carrots thoroughly. Sprinkle over the lemon juice, remove the bay leaf and serve immediately, if the dish is to be eaten hot.

Carrots with Mushrooms

A delicious way of serving carrots, Carrots with Mushrooms is excellent with grilled [broiled] steak or fish.

4 SERVINGS

1 lb. carrots, scraped and sliced
½ teaspoon salt
10 fl. oz. [1¼ cups] water
1 tablespoon sugar
2 oz. [¼ cup] butter
4 oz. mushrooms, wiped clean and quartered
1 tablespoon finely chopped onion

In a medium-sized saucepan, place the carrots, salt, water, sugar and half of the butter over moderate heat. Bring the water to the boil and cover the pan. Reduce the heat to low and simmer the carrots for about 30 minutes, or until they are tender and most of the liquid has been absorbed.

While the carrots are cooking, prepare the mushrooms.

In a small frying-pan, melt the remaining butter over moderate heat. Add the mushrooms and fry them gently for about 3 minutes, or until they are softened. Mix in the onion with a wooden spoon and cook gently for another 3 to 4 minutes.

Add the mushroom mixture to the carrots. Taste and add more salt and pepper if necessary. Turn into a hot serving dish and serve immediately.

Bubble and Squeak

This traditional English dish was originally made from leftover boiled beef, mixed with cold mashed potatoes and greens and then fried. Its name comes from the noise it makes when frying. Today, however, the meat is usually omitted and Bubble and Squeak consists only of leftover mashed potatoes and cabbage. The quantities of each should be approximately equal, but it really depends on how much you have left over.

4 SERVINGS

8 oz. cold mashed potatoes
8 oz. cooked cold cabbage
½ teaspoon salt
¼ teaspoon black pepper
2 oz. [¼ cup] butter
1 teaspoon vinegar

In a large mixing bowl, mix the potatoes and cabbage together. Season with the salt and pepper.

In a large, deep frying-pan, melt the butter over moderately high heat. Add the potato-and-cabbage mixture. Cook for 5 to 6 minutes, or until the potato and cabbage mixture is thoroughly hot, stirring frequently.

Sprinkle the vinegar on top of the mixture. Remove the pan from the heat and turn the Bubble and Squeak into a warmed serving dish. Serve at once.

Cabbage in Sour Cream

Quick and easy to prepare, Cabbage in Sour Cream goes well with lamb dishes.

6 SERVINGS

3 oz. [⅜ cup] butter
1 small green cabbage, coarse
outer leaves removed, washed and finely sliced
1 egg, lightly beaten
8 fl. oz. [1 cup] sour cream
2 tablespoons sugar
1 tablespoon white wine vinegar
2 teaspoons caraway seeds
½ teaspoon salt
¼ teaspoon black pepper

In a large saucepan, melt the butter over moderate heat. Add the cabbage and cook for 10 minutes, or until the cabbage is tender but not coloured. Stir occasionally to prevent the cabbage sticking to the pan.

In a medium-sized mixing bowl, combine the egg, sour cream, sugar, vinegar, caraway seeds, salt and pepper. Pour the mixture into the saucepan and stir to coat the cabbage completely with the sauce. Cook for 2 to 3 minutes, stirring constantly. Do not allow the sauce to boil. Transfer it to a warmed serving dish and serve immediately.

Carrots Algerian-Style

Carrots Algerian-Style is equally delicious hot or cold. Serve with boiled beef, roasted pork or lamb.

4 SERVINGS

2 lb. carrots, scraped and cut into ½-inch slices
5 tablespoons olive oil
1 teaspoon salt
½ teaspoon white pepper
½ teaspoon ground cinnamon
½ teaspoon cumin seeds
3 garlic cloves, crushed
½ teaspoon dried thyme
1 bay leaf
1 teaspoon lemon juice

Spicy Cauliflower

An exotic dish of cauliflower flavoured with mustard seed, Spicy Cauliflower may be served as part of an Indian meal.

4 SERVINGS

3 tablespoons vegetable oil
1 teaspoon mustard seed
1-inch piece fresh root ginger, peeled and cut into strips
1 onion, sliced
1 teaspoon turmeric
1 green chilli, chopped
1 large cauliflower, trimmed, washed and separated into flowerets
1 teaspoon salt
juice of ½ lemon
3 tablespoons water
1 tablespoon finely chopped fresh coriander leaves

In a large saucepan, heat the oil over moderately high heat. Add the mustard seed, reduce the heat to moderate and cover the pan. When the seeds stop spattering, remove the lid and add the ginger, onion, turmeric and green chilli. Fry, stirring occasionally, for 3 minutes.

Add the cauliflower and salt and stir well. Sprinkle over the lemon juice and water, cover the pan, reduce the heat to low and cook the cauliflower for 20 minutes, or until the flowerets are tender.

Turn the contents of the pan into a warmed serving dish. Sprinkle over the chopped coriander leaves and serve.

Cauliflower with Tomatoes and Cheese

An elegant dish requiring minimal preparation, Cauliflower with Tomatoes and Cheese may be served with chops or omelets.

4-6 SERVINGS

1 tablespoon butter
1 large cauliflower, trimmed, washed and separated into flowerets
6 tomatoes, blanched, peeled, seeded and roughly chopped

Cauliflower with Tomatoes and Cheese is a hearty dish, absolutely guaranteed to satisfy the hungriest family!

½ teaspoon salt
¼ teaspoon black pepper
4 oz. [½ cup] butter, melted
2 tablespoons dry breadcrumbs
2 tablespoons grated Parmesan cheese
2 tablespoons grated Emmenthal cheese

Preheat the oven to fairly hot 375°F (Gas Mark 5, 190°C).

Lightly grease a large shallow casserole with the tablespoon of butter.

In a large saucepan, cook the cauliflower flowerets in boiling salted water over moderate heat for 9 to 12 minutes, or until they are tender. Drain the flowerets.

Place the flowerets in the buttered casserole. Arrange the chopped tomatoes on top and sprinkle with salt, pepper and half of the melted butter.

In a small bowl, combine the breadcrumbs with the Parmesan and Emmenthal cheeses and sprinkle the mixture over the vegetable pieces. Spoon the remaining melted butter over the mixture and bake in the oven for about 30 minutes, or until the top is golden brown. Remove the dish from the oven and serve immediately.

Grilled Courgettes [Broiled Zucchini]

Grilled Courgettes [Broiled Zucchini] makes an unusual accompaniment to grilled [broiled] chops, roasts or steaks, or it may be served on its own as a light luncheon or supper dish. If you serve it on its own, accompany it with lots of crusty bread, a baked potato and, to drink, some well-chilled white wine.

4 SERVINGS

1 tablespoon butter
8 courgettes [zucchini], trimmed, cleaned and blanched
2 garlic cloves, crushed
2 teaspoons sugar
1 teaspoon salt
1 tablespoon chopped fresh dill or 1½ teaspoons dried dill
1 medium-sized onion, sliced and pushed out into rings
3 oz. [¾ cup] Parmesan cheese, grated

Preheat the oven to moderate 350°F (Gas Mark 4, 180°C). Grease a shallow flame-proof baking dish with the tablespoon of butter.

With a sharp knife, slice the courgettes [zucchini] in half, lengthways, and arrange them in the bottom of the baking dish, skin side down. Sprinkle them with the

Serve Courgettes [Zucchini] Provencal-Style as a delicious accompaniment to omelets or chops.

garlic, sugar, salt and dill and arrange the onion rings over the top. Spread the grated cheese on top of the mixture and bake in the upper part of the oven for 15 minutes.

Preheat the grill [broiler] to moderately high.

Remove the courgettes [zucchini] from the oven and place them under the grill [broiler] for 4 minutes, or until the cheese is bubbly and brown.

Serve immediately.

Courgettes [Zucchini] Provençal-Style

A delicious vegetable dish, Courgettes [Zucchini] Provençal-Style is a must for garlic lovers. Serve it with grilled [broiled] steak or omelets, or by itself with crusty bread for a light but sustaining luncheon dish.

4 SERVINGS

8 courgettes [zucchini], trimmed, cleaned and blanched
4 tablespoons olive oil
½ teaspoon salt

½ teaspoon freshly ground black pepper
3 garlic cloves, crushed
2 oz. [⅔ cup] fine dry breadcrumbs
2 tablespoons finely chopped fresh parsley

Cut the courgettes [zucchini] into ½-inch slices, crosswise, and dry them thoroughly on kitchen paper towels.

In a large frying-pan, heat the olive oil over moderate heat. When the oil is hot, add the courgettes [zucchini] to the pan and cook them for 8 to 10 minutes, stirring occasionally with a wooden spoon to prevent them from sticking to the bottom of the pan.

Raise the heat to fairly high and stir in the salt, pepper, garlic, breadcrumbs and parsley. Remove the pan from the heat and toss the ingredients gently together until they are well mixed. Transfer the mixture to a warmed serving dish and serve immediately.

French Beans, Hungarian-Style

A colourful and unusual vegetable dish, French Beans, Hungarian-Style goes particularly well with grilled [broiled] pork or lamb chops or steaks or fried or grilled

[broiled] *fish.*

4 SERVINGS

1½ pints [3¾ cups] water
1 teaspoon salt
1 lb. French beans, trimmed and washed
2 tablespoons vegetable oil or olive oil
2 medium-sized onions, finely chopped
1 tablespoon paprika
1 tablespoon tomato purée
5 fl. oz. [⅝ cup] sour cream

In a large saucepan, bring the water to the boil over high heat. Add the salt and the French beans to the pan. Reduce the heat to moderately low and simmer the beans for 5 to 15 minutes, or until they are just tender.

Remove the pan from the heat and drain the beans in a large colander. Set aside.

In a large frying-pan, heat the oil over moderate heat. When the oil is hot, add the onions to the pan. Fry them, stirring occasionally, for 5 to 7 minutes, or until they are soft and translucent but not brown.

Remove the pan from the heat. With a wooden spoon, stir the paprika, tomato purée and sour cream into the onion

mixture.

Return the pan to low heat and mix in the drained beans. Cook, stirring occasionally, for 5 minutes or until the beans and sauce are heated through.

Remove the pan from the heat and turn the mixture into a large, warmed serving dish.

Serve at once.

French Beans with Apples and Almonds

An unusual accompaniment, French Beans with Apples and Almonds goes marvellously well with venison, grilled [broiled] or fried beef steaks, or any of the other darker meats, such as hare.

4 SERVINGS

1½ pints [3¾ cups] water
1 teaspoon salt
1 lb. French beans, trimmed, washed and halved
3 oz. [⅜ cup] butter

A tasty way of cooking a delicious vegetable, French Beans, Hungarian-Style combines beans, onions, paprika and sour cream.

1 medium-sized onion, very thinly sliced and pushed out into rings
2 medium-sized cooking apples, peeled, cored and very roughly chopped
1 oz. [¼ cup] flaked blanched almonds

In a large saucepan, bring the water to the boil over high heat. Add the salt and French beans to the pan. Reduce the heat to moderately low and simmer the beans for 5 to 15 minutes, or until they are just tender.

Remove the pan from the heat and drain the beans in a large colander. Set the beans aside.

In a large frying-pan, melt the butter over moderate heat. When the foam subsides, add the onion and apples to the pan. Cook them, stirring occasionally, for 8 to 10 minutes, or until the onion is golden brown and the apples are tender but still firm.

Stir in the beans and almonds and reduce the heat to low. Cook the mixture, stirring frequently, for 5 minutes or until the beans are heated through.

Remove the pan from the heat and transfer the mixture to a warmed serving dish.

Serve at once.

Lettuces Baked with Shrimps

☆　　①　①　　

Lettuces Baked with Shrimps can either be served as a light lunch or, baked in individual ramekin dishes (as pictured below), as a first course to an informal lunch or dinner.

4 SERVINGS

8 fl. oz. double cream [1 cup heavy cream]
2 teaspoons prepared French mustard
1 teaspoon Worcestershire sauce
⅛ teaspoon cayenne pepper
⅛ teaspoon grated nutmeg
½ teaspoon salt
¼ teaspoon freshly ground black pepper
¼ teaspoon Tabasco sauce
1 teaspoon cornflour [cornstarch] dissolved in 1 tablespoon double [heavy] cream
2 medium-sized lettuces, coarse outer leaves removed, washed, shaken dry and very finely shredded
1 tablespoon butter
8 oz. frozen and thawed shrimps, shelled
4 medium-sized tomatoes, blanched, peeled, seeded and chopped
2 teaspoons lemon juice
2 oz. [½ cup] Parmesan cheese, grated

Preheat the oven to fairly hot 375°F (Gas Mark 5, 190°C).

In a medium-sized saucepan, combine the cream, mustard, Worcestershire sauce, cayenne pepper, nutmeg, salt, black pepper, Tabasco sauce and the cornflour [cornstarch] mixture. Set the saucepan over moderately low heat and cook the sauce for 3 to 4 minutes, or until it is thick and smooth. Remove the pan from the heat and stir in the shredded lettuces. Stir well to coat them thoroughly. Set the mixture aside.

Using the tablespoon of butter, generously grease a large baking dish. Spread half the lettuce mixture in the bottom of the dish. Cover with the shrimps and cover the shrimps with the chopped tomatoes.

Spread the remaining lettuce mixture over the tomatoes. Sprinkle over the lemon juice and cover with the grated Parmesan cheese.

Place the dish in the centre of the oven and bake for 35 to 40 minutes, or until the lettuce is tender and the top lightly browned.

Remove the dish from the oven and serve the mixture immediately, straight from the dish.

Marrow [Summer Squash] with Savoury Stuffing

☆　　①　　

An inexpensive dish, Marrow [Summer Squash] with Savoury Stuffing makes the ideal winter family meal. Serve with mashed potatoes, hot tomato sauce and lots of sautéed or steamed French beans.

6 SERVINGS

2 oz. [¼ cup] plus 1 tablespoon butter
1 x 3 lb. vegetable marrow [summer squash]
2 medium-sized onions, coarsely chopped
1 large green pepper, white pith removed, seeded and coarsely

Lettuces Baked with Shrimps—a delightfully different and elegant dish to serve for a light family supper or lunch.

Serve Marrow [Summer Squash] with Savoury Stuffing as an inexpensive but filling lunch or supper, guaranteed to satisfy the whole family.

chopped
1 lb. lean beef, finely minced [ground]
4 medium-sized tomatoes, blanched, peeled, seeded and coarsely chopped
2 small carrots, scraped, cooked and diced
1½ teaspoons salt
½ teaspoon freshly ground black pepper
1 teaspoon paprika
1 teaspoon chopped fresh thyme or ½ teaspoon dried thyme
2 oz. [1 cup] fresh white breadcrumbs
2 medium-sized egg yolks, well beaten with 2 fl. oz. single cream [¼ cup light cream]
4 oz. [1 cup] Parmesan cheese, finely grated

Preheat the oven to moderate 350°F (Gas Mark 4, 180°C).

With the tablespoon of butter, generously grease a large, oblong baking dish and set it aside.

With a long, sharp knife (a bread knife is ideal), cut the marrow [summer squash] in half, lengthways. With a sharp-edged metal spoon, scoop out and discard the seeds, making a cavity in the centre of each marrow [summer squash] half. Place the marrow [summer squash] halves, side by side and with the cut sides upwards, in the prepared baking dish and set aside.

In a medium-sized saucepan, melt 1 ounce [2 tablespoons] of the remaining butter over moderate heat. When the foam subsides, add the onions and green pepper and fry, stirring occasionally, for 8 to 10 minutes, or until the onions are golden brown and the green pepper is translucent.

Add the minced [ground] beef and tomatoes to the pan and cook, stirring and turning occasionally to break up the meat, for 6 to 8 minutes, or until it loses its pinkness.

Remove the pan from the heat. Stir in the diced carrots, salt, black pepper, paprika and fresh or dried thyme. Set the mixture aside.

In a small mixing bowl, combine the breadcrumbs with the egg yolks and cream mixture. Stir the mixture into the meat mixture in the saucepan and beat briskly to combine the stuffing as thoroughly as possible.

Pile the stuffing into the cavities of the marrow [summer squash] halves. Lightly pat the stuffing down with the back of a wooden spoon so that the centres are domed slightly.

Sprinkle the Parmesan cheese over the stuffing. Cut the remaining butter into small pieces and dot them over the cheese. Place the dish in the centre of the oven and bake for 1 to 1¼ hours or until the marrow [summer squash] is very tender when pierced with the point of a sharp knife, and the filling is cooked and well browned.

Remove the marrow [summer squash] from the oven and transfer the halves to a deep, warmed serving dish.

Serve at once.

Stuffed Mushrooms

These mushrooms, filled with a cream and parsley mixture and topped with cheese, are delicious and easy to prepare. They may be served either as an appetizing hors d'oeuvre, as an attractive garnish to a roast or as a simple, after-school snack for hungry children.

4 SERVINGS

12 large mushrooms, wiped clean
1 teaspoon salt
½ teaspoon freshly ground black pepper
1 teaspoon melted butter
1 oz. [2 tablespoons] butter
2 shallots or spring onions [scallions], finely chopped
1 tablespoon flour
4 fl. oz. single cream [½ cup light cream]
3 tablespoons finely chopped fresh parsley
1½ tablespoons grated Parmesan cheese

Preheat the oven to fairly hot 375°F (Gas Mark 5, 190°C).

Remove the stems from the mushrooms and set them aside. Season the mushroom caps with ½ teaspoon of the salt and ¼ teaspoon of the black pepper and, using a pastry brush, coat them with the melted butter. Arrange them, hollow side up, in a lightly greased shallow baking dish. Set the dish aside while you prepare the stuffing.

With a sharp knife, chop the mushroom stems finely. Wrap them in kitchen paper towels and twist the towels to extract as much juice from the mushroom stems as possible.

In a medium-sized frying-pan, melt the 1 ounce [2 tablespoons] of butter over moderate heat.

When the foam subsides, add the chopped mushroom stems and shallots or spring onions [scallions]. Sauté them together for 3 to 4 minutes, or until the shallots or spring onions [scallions] are soft and translucent but not brown. Reduce the heat to low and, stirring constantly, add the flour to the pan. Cook for 1 minute.

Remove the pan from the heat and stir in the cream, a little at a time. When the sauce is smooth and all the ingredients are thoroughly blended, return the pan to the heat and simmer the sauce for 2 to 3 minutes, or until it has thickened and is smooth.

Stir in the parsley and the remaining salt and pepper and mix well.

Remove the pan from the heat and spoon a little of the mixture into each of the prepared mushroom caps.

Top each mushroom with a little grated cheese. Place the dish in the oven and bake the mushrooms for 15 minutes or until they are tender and the stuffing is lightly browned on top.

Remove from the oven and serve.

Onion Pie

This Onion Pie makes a perfect main course for a vegetarian meal or it may be served as a first course. Serve either hot or cold, with a tossed green salad, lots of crusty bread and, to drink, some well-chilled lager or cider.

4-6 SERVINGS

1 x 9-inch flan case, made with frozen and thawed shortcrust pastry, baked blind
1 oz. [2 tablespoons] butter
4 medium-sized onions, thinly sliced
5 spring onions [scallions], finely chopped
2 eggs, lightly beaten
6 fl. oz. single cream [¾ cup light cream]
4 oz. [1 cup] Cheddar cheese, finely grated
1 tablespoon chopped fresh basil or 1½ teaspoons dried basil
1 tablespoon finely chopped fresh parsley
1 teaspoon salt
½ teaspoon freshly ground black pepper

Preheat the oven to fairly hot 375°F (Gas Mark 5, 190°C).

Place the flan case on a large baking sheet. Set aside.

In a large frying-pan, melt the butter over moderate heat. When the foam subsides, add the onions and spring onions [scallions]. Cook, stirring occasionally, for 5 to 7 minutes, or until all of the onions are soft and translucent but not brown.

Remove the pan from the heat and set aside.

In a medium-sized mixing bowl, lightly beat the eggs, cream and cheese together with a fork. Stir in the basil, parsley, salt and pepper. Add the onion mixture and mix well.

Pour the mixture into the flan case and place the baking sheet in the centre of the oven. Bake the pie for 35 to 40 minutes, or until the filling has risen and the top is lightly browned.

Remove the baking sheet from the oven. Serve immediately, or allow to cool before serving.

Small Garden Peas with Bacon and Onions

Small Garden Peas with Bacon and Onions is a classic French way of preparing garden peas. Serve with grilled [broiled] steaks, roast beef or roast lamb.

4-6 SERVINGS

4 streaky bacon slices, rinds removed and diced
1 tablespoon butter
5 small white onions, peeled and finely chopped
2 tablespoons flour
½ teaspoon salt

½ teaspoon freshly ground black pepper
8 fl. oz. [1 cup] veal or chicken stock
bouquet garni, consisting of 4 parsley sprigs, 1 thyme spray and 1 bay leaf tied together
1½ lb. small fresh garden peas, weighed after shelling or 1½ lb. frozen petits pois, thawed

In a medium-sized saucepan, fry the bacon over moderately high heat, stirring occasionally, for 6 to 8 minutes or until it is crisp and has rendered most of its fat.

With a slotted spoon, remove the bacon from the pan and set it aside to drain on kitchen paper towels.

Reduce the heat to moderate and add the butter to the pan. When the foam subsides, add the onions and fry them, stirring occasionally, for 8 to 10 minutes or until they are golden brown.

Remove the pan from the heat. With a slotted spoon, remove the onions from the pan and add them to the bacon. Using a wooden spoon, stir in the flour, salt and pepper into the pan to make a smooth paste. Gradually add the stock, stirring constantly and being careful to avoid lumps. Add the bouquet garni and the reserved onions and bacon. Return the pan to the heat.

Bring the liquid to the boil, stirring constantly. Stir in the peas and reduce the heat to low. Cover the pan and simmer for 6 to 8 minutes, stirring occasionally, or until the peas are tender.

Remove the pan from the heat and remove and discard the bouquet garni. Spoon the mixture into a warmed serving dish.

Serve immediately.

Delightful Small Garden Peas with Bacon and Onions are a very special family treat.

with oil. Heat the oil in one pan over moderate heat until it reaches 325°F on a deep-fat thermometer or until a piece of stale bread dropped into the oil turns golden brown in 65 seconds.

Heat the oil in the other pan over moderate heat until it reaches 375°F on a deep-fat thermometer or until a piece of stale bread dropped into the oil turns golden brown in 40 seconds.

Drop the potato slices into the first pan and fry them for 4 minutes.

Using a slotted spoon, transfer the slices to the second pan and fry them for 2 to 3 minutes or until they puff up. Immediately the slices puff up, remove them from the oil and drain them on kitchen paper towels.

Sprinkle with the salt and serve.

Potatoes Stuffed and Baked

Baked potatoes are doubly delicious when the flesh is scooped out, mixed with savoury ingredients, returned to the shell and reheated in the oven until the top is golden.

First bake the potatoes in their jackets, remove them from the oven and place them on a board. Remove a ½-inch slice from the top flat side of the potato. Scoop out the inside of each potato to within ¼-inch of the shell, being careful not to pierce the skin. Place the flesh in a mixing bowl and arrange the shells in a roasting tin. Prepare the filling and spoon it into the potato shells, piling it up and rounding the top. Place the potatoes in an oven preheated to fairly hot 375°F (Gas Mark 5, 190°C) and bake them for 10 to 12 minutes or until the top of the filling is golden brown.

FILLING 1
 the flesh from 4 potatoes baked
  in their jackets
2 oz. Brie cheese
½ teaspoon dried chives
½ teaspoon salt
1 egg yolk
2 oz. [¼ cup] butter, softened
In a medium-sized mixing bowl, combine the potato flesh, Brie, chives, salt, egg yolk and butter. Beat them with a wooden spoon until they are all thoroughly mixed.

FILLING 2
 the flesh from 4 potatoes baked
  in their jackets
2 oz. Gorgonzola cheese, crumbled
1 tablespoon single [light] cream

Potatoes Dauphinoise

One of the classic French potato dishes, Potatoes Dauphinoise goes magnificently with roast lamb.

6 SERVINGS

1 garlic clove, halved
1 oz. [2 tablespoons] butter
2 lb. potatoes, peeled and cut into
 ¼-inch slices
1 teaspoon salt
1 teaspoon black pepper
6 oz. [1½ cups] Cheddar cheese,
 grated
1 egg, lightly beaten
10 fl. oz. [1¼ cups] milk, scalded
⅛ teaspoon grated nutmeg

Preheat the oven to fairly hot 375°F (Gas Mark 5, 190°C).

Rub the garlic over the bottom and sides of a medium-sized baking dish. Grease the dish with half the butter.

Place about one-third of the potato slices in the baking dish and sprinkle over ½ teaspoon of the salt, ½ teaspoon of the pepper and 1 ounce [¼ cup] of the grated cheese. Top with another one-third of the potatoes. Sprinkle on the remaining salt and pepper and a further 1 ounce [¼ cup] of cheese and top with the remaining potato slices.

In a small saucepan, beat the egg, milk and nutmeg together with a fork until they are well blended. Place the pan over moderate heat and bring to the boil. Remove the pan from the heat and pour the mixture into the baking dish.

Sprinkle the remaining grated cheese over the top. Cut the remaining butter into small pieces and dot them on top.

Place the dish in the oven and bake for 45 to 50 minutes, or until the potatoes are tender but still firm.

Remove from the oven and serve.

Potato Puffs

Potato Puffs are thinly sliced potatoes fried in two lots of oil — the first at a low temperature, the second at a high temperature. This method of frying makes the potatoes puff up. Serve with grilled [broiled] meat or fish.

2-4 SERVINGS

1 lb. potatoes, peeled and cut into
 ⅛-inch thick slices
 sufficient vegetable oil for
  deep-frying
1 teaspoon salt

Place the potato slices in a large bowl of cold water for 30 minutes. Drain them and dry thoroughly with a clean cloth.

Fill two large saucepans one-third full

2 teaspoons tomato purée
½ teaspoon black pepper
½ teaspoon dried basil
2 oz. [¼ cup] butter, softened

In a medium-sized mixing bowl, combine the potato flesh, Gorgonzola, cream, tomato purée, pepper, basil and butter. Beat them with a wooden spoon until they are thoroughly mixed.

FILLING 3
the flesh from 4 potatoes baked in their jackets
4 oz. Cheshire cheese, crumbled
1 small eating apple, peeled, cored and finely chopped
1 teaspoon prepared mustard
½ teaspoon salt
2 oz. [¼ cup] butter, softened

Potatoes Stuffed and Baked six ways to make marvellous snacks for hungry children and fabulous accompaniments to meat dishes.

In a medium-sized mixing bowl, combine the potato flesh, Cheshire, apple, mustard, salt and butter. Beat them with a wooden spoon until they are thoroughly mixed.

FILLING 4
the flesh from 4 potatoes baked in their jackets
4 oz. [1 cup] Cheddar cheese, grated
2 teaspoons sour-sweet chutney
1 small celery stalk, finely chopped
2 oz. [¼ cup] butter, softened

In a medium-sized mixing bowl, combine the potato flesh, Cheddar, chutney, celery and butter. Beat them with a wooden spoon until they are thoroughly mixed.

FILLING 5
the flesh from 4 potatoes baked in their jackets
4 slices bacon, grilled [broiled] until golden and crumbled
1 oz. [2 tablespoons] butter
4 oz. mushrooms, chopped
½ teaspoon salt
¼ teaspoon black pepper

In a medium-sized mixing bowl, combine the potato flesh and the bacon. Set aside.

In a small frying-pan, melt the butter over moderate heat. When the foam subsides, add the mushrooms and fry, stirring constantly, for 3 minutes. Remove the pan from the heat and pour the contents of the pan into the mixing bowl. Add the salt and pepper. Beat the ingredients with a wooden spoon until they are mixed.

FILLING 6
the flesh from 4 potatoes baked in their jackets
4 oz. shrimps, shelled
4 spring onions [scallions], chopped
½ teaspoon grated lemon rind
½ teaspoon chopped fresh parsley
¼ teaspoon cayenne pepper
2 oz. [¼ cup] butter, softened

In a medium-sized mixing bowl, combine the potato flesh, shrimps, spring onions [scallions], lemon rind, parsley, cayenne and butter. Beat with a wooden spoon until they are thoroughly mixed.

Creamed Spinach

This rich, smooth vegetable dish goes beautifully with baked ham, liver, sweetbreads, chicken or veal. It may be garnished with two chopped hard-boiled eggs.

4 SERVINGS

4 pints [5 pints] water
2 teaspoons salt
2 lb. frozen and thawed
    spinach, washed and chopped
1 tablespoon butter
1 tablespoon flour
10 fl. oz. single cream [1¼ cups light
    cream]
¼ teaspoon black pepper

In a large saucepan, bring the water and salt to the boil over high heat. Add the spinach and when the water boils again reduce the heat to moderate and cook gently for 10 minutes, or until the spinach is tender.

Drain off the liquid leaving the spinach in the saucepan.

In a small heavy saucepan, melt the butter over low heat. Remove the pan from the heat and, with a wooden spoon, stir in the flour. Gradually add the cream, stirring constantly. Return the pan to moderate heat and bring the sauce to the boil. Stirring constantly, cook for 5 minutes. Add the pepper.

Pour the sauce over the spinach in the large saucepan and return to moderate heat. Stir to mix. Cook for 2 minutes to reheat the spinach and remove the pan from the heat. Serve at once.

Spinach with Cheese

An excellent and simple-to-make vegetable dish, Spinach with Cheese makes a delicious accompaniment to cold meats.

4 SERVINGS

2 lb. frozen and thawed spinach,
    washed and chopped
1½ teaspoons salt
4 oz. [½ cup] butter
4 oz. [1 cup] Cheddar cheese,
    finely grated
½ teaspoon black pepper

Put the spinach in a large saucepan. Pour over enough water just to cover the spinach. Add 1 teaspoon of the salt and place the pan over moderately high heat. Bring the water to the boil. Reduce the heat to moderate and cook the spinach for 10 minutes. Drain the spinach in a colander, pressing it well down with a wooden spoon to remove all excess liquid.

In a large frying-pan, melt the butter

over moderate heat. When the foam subsides, add the spinach to the pan. Gradually stir in three-quarters of the cheese with a wooden spoon and cook, still stirring, for 3 minutes, or until the ingredients are well blended. Add the pepper and remaining salt.

Preheat the grill [broiler] to high.

Remove the pan from the heat and transfer the spinach mixture to a flameproof casserole. Sprinkle the remaining cheese on top of the spinach and place it under the grill [broiler]. Cook for 7 to 10 minutes, or until the cheese is golden and melted.

Remove the casserole from the heat and serve immediately.

Sweetcorn Moulds

Creamy sweetcorn custards garnished with watercress and crispy bacon make these moulds a really unusual first course.

6 SERVINGS

1 teaspoon vegetable oil
10 oz. canned creamed sweetcorn
4 oz. [1 cup] Gruyère cheese, grated
5 fl. oz. double cream [⅝ cup heavy
    cream]
1 teaspoon salt
½ teaspoon black pepper
2 teaspoons prepared mustard
4 eggs, lightly beaten
GARNISH
2 bunches watercress, washed and
    shaken dry
8 oz. streaky bacon, rinds removed,
    grilled [broiled] until crisp and
    crumbled

Preheat the oven to warm 325°F (Gas Mark 3, 170°C).

Using the teaspoon of oil, lightly grease 6 dariole moulds. Set aside.

In a medium-sized mixing bowl, combine the sweetcorn, cheese, cream, salt, pepper and mustard, beating well until the ingredients are thoroughly combined. Gradually beat in the eggs. Spoon the mixture into the prepared dariole moulds. Place the moulds in a large roasting tin and pour in enough boiling water to come half way up the sides of the moulds. Place the tin in the oven and bake for 45 minutes or until a knife inserted into the centre of each mould comes out clean.

Remove the tin from the oven and take out the moulds. Set aside for 5 minutes.

Run a knife around the edge of the moulds to loosen the sides. Hold individual serving plates, inverted, over each of the moulds and reverse the two. The moulds should slide out easily. Garnish with the watercress and crumbled bacon

and serve at once.

Tomato Pie

An economical supper dish, Tomato Pie is ideal for vegetarians. A green salad and lots of lightly buttered brown bread are all that are needed to accompany this dish.

4-6 SERVINGS

1 teaspoon butter
12 oz. [3 cups] frozen and thawed
    shortcrust pastry
1 lb. firm tomatoes, thinly sliced
1 medium-sized onion, very thinly
    sliced and pushed out into rings
4 oz. button mushrooms, wiped
    clean and coarsely chopped
½ teaspoon salt
½ teaspoon freshly ground black
    pepper
1 teaspoon dried oregano
1 teaspoon dry mustard
4 oz. [1 cup] Cheddar cheese,
    grated
1 egg, lightly beaten

Preheat the oven to fairly hot 400°F (Gas Mark 6, 200°C). With the teaspoon of butter, grease a 9-inch pie plate and set aside.

On a lightly floured board, roll out half the dough to a 10-inch circle. Using the rolling pin, lift the dough on to the plate and press it down with your fingertips. Trim off any excess with a table knife. Reserve the trimmings.

Arrange half the tomatoes, onion and mushrooms in the centre of the plate, leaving the rim clear. Sprinkle over half the salt, pepper, oregano, mustard and cheese. Continue making layers in this way until all the ingredients have been used. Dampen the edges of the dough with water.

Roll out the remaining dough to a 10-inch circle. Using the rolling pin, lift the dough over the filling and press the edges together. Trim off any excess, and reserve it. Crimp the edges together to seal them. Roll out the trimmings, cut them into fancy shapes and use them to decorate the pie. With a pastry brush, brush the dough with the beaten egg. Cut a small cross in the centre of the pie.

Place the plate on a baking sheet and place the baking sheet in the oven. Bake for 20 to 25 minutes or until the pastry is golden brown and crisp.

Remove the baking sheet from the oven and serve the pie at once.

Serve Tomato Pie as a light lunch or supper dish for the family.

Tomatoes Stuffed with Anchovies, Breadcrumbs and Garlic

These classic stuffed tomatoes are simply delicious as a first course for a dinner party. They may be served either hot or cold.

6 SERVINGS

2 tablespoons olive oil
10 tomatoes, 6 halved and seeded and 4 peeled, seeded and roughly chopped
2 teaspoons finely chopped fresh parsley
2 garlic cloves, crushed
3 oz. [1½ cups] fresh breadcrumbs, 2 oz. [1 cup] soaked in 2 fl. oz. [¼ cup] home-made beef stock for 10 minutes
4 anchovy fillets, very finely chopped
2 tablespoons grated Parmesan cheese

Preheat the oven to moderate 350°F (Gas Mark 4, 180°C).

In a medium-sized flameproof casserole, heat half of the oil over moderate heat. When the oil is hot, add the halved tomatoes, cut sides up, and fry for 1 minute. With a slotted spoon, transfer the tomatoes to an ovenproof baking dish and set aside.

Add ½ tablespoon of the remaining oil to the casserole. Add the chopped tomatoes, the parsley and garlic and cover the casserole. Cook, stirring occasionally, for 5 minutes.

Meanwhile, using the back of a wooden spoon, rub the soaked breadcrumbs through a fine wire strainer into a small bowl. Set aside.

Stir the puréed breadcrumbs and the anchovies into the mixture in the casserole and cook for a further 2 minutes, stirring occasionally.

Remove the casserole from the heat and, using a teaspoon, spoon equal quantities of the stuffing mixture into each tomato half.

In a small bowl, mix together the remaining breadcrumbs and the cheese. Sprinkle this mixture over each tomato half and dribble over the remaining oil.

Place the baking dish in the centre of the oven and bake for 15 to 20 minutes. Remove the dish from the oven and serve immediately, straight from the baking dish.

Alternatively, set the baking dish aside and allow the tomatoes to cool completely before serving.

Turnip, Potato and Carrot Hash

A very economical and tasty dish, Turnip, Potato and Carrot Hash makes an excellent accompaniment to boiled beef or grilled [broiled] sausages.

6 SERVINGS

1 large turnip, peeled and coarsely chopped
3 medium-sized carrots, scraped and coarsely chopped
1 large onion, coarsely chopped
3 medium-sized potatoes, peeled and coarsely chopped
8 fl. oz. [1 cup] canned beef consommé
½ teaspoon salt
1½ teaspoons freshly ground black pepper
1 tablespoon butter, cut into small pieces

Place the turnip, carrots, onion and potatoes in a medium-sized saucepan and add the consommé and salt. Place the saucepan over high heat and bring the liquid to the boil. Reduce the heat to moderately low and simmer the mixture, uncovered, for 20 to 30 minutes or until the vegetables are very tender and most of the liquid has been absorbed.

Preheat the oven to fairly hot 400°F (Gas Mark 6, 200°C).

Remove the pan from the heat and pour off any excess liquid. Add the pepper to the pan and, using a potato masher or fork, mash the vegetables until they form a thick purée.

Transfer the mixture to a medium-sized baking dish, smoothing over the surface with the back of a fork. Dot the surface with the butter.

Place the baking dish in the oven and bake for 10 to 15 minutes or until the top of the mixture is golden brown.

Remove the dish from the oven and serve immediately, straight from the dish.

Vegetable Curry

This is a simple curry which can be made with almost any combination of vegetables. Serve with boiled rice, chutneys and poppadums.

4-6 SERVINGS

3 tablespoons vegetable oil
2 medium-sized onions, finely chopped
1½-inch piece fresh root ginger, peeled and very finely chopped
2 garlic cloves, crushed
2 green chillis, seeded and finely chopped
1 teaspoon turmeric
1 tablespoon ground coriander
1 tablespoon paprika
½ teaspoon cayenne pepper
¼ teaspoon ground fenugreek
¼ teaspoon freshly ground black pepper
2 tablespoons lemon juice
1 lb. potatoes, peeled and cut into 1-inch cubes
8 oz. turnips, peeled and cut into 1-inch cubes
8 oz. carrots, scraped and cut into ¼-inch slices
4 oz. French beans, trimmed and sliced
4 oz. fresh peas, weighed after shelling
1 teaspoon salt

This colourful and nutritious Vegetable Curry is very easy and quick to make and has an authentically hot Indian taste.

14 oz. canned peeled tomatoes, rubbed through a strainer with the can juice

In a large saucepan, heat the oil over moderate heat. When the oil is hot, add the onions, ginger, garlic and chillis and fry, stirring occasionally, for 8 to 10 minutes or until the onions are golden.

Meanwhile, in a small bowl, combine the turmeric, coriander, paprika, cayenne pepper, fenugreek and pepper. Add the lemon juice and a little water, if necessary, to make a smooth paste. Add the spice paste to the onion mixture and fry, stirring constantly, for 5 minutes. Add a spoonful of water if the mixture gets too dry. Add the vegetables to the pan and fry, stirring constantly, for 5 minutes. Stir in the salt and the strained tomatoes and bring the mixture to the boil. Cover the pan, reduce the heat to low and simmer the curry for 20 to 25 minutes or until the vegetables are cooked. Taste the curry and add more salt if necessary. Remove the pan from the heat.

Transfer the curry to a deep serving dish and serve immediately.

Vegetable Rissoles

Filling and nourishing, Vegetable Rissoles make an ideal vegetarian lunch or supper dish, and the children will love them. Serve with mashed potatoes and brown bread.

4 SERVINGS

4 oz. [½ cup] red lentils, soaked overnight, cooked and drained
1 large onion, finely chopped
1 celery stalk, trimmed and finely chopped
2 small carrots, scraped and grated
2 oz. French beans, cooked and finely chopped
2 oz. [1 cup] fresh white bread-crumbs
3 eggs
1½ teaspoons salt
1 teaspoon freshly ground black pepper
1 teaspoon dried mixed herbs
3 oz. [1 cup] dry white breadcrumbs
2 fl. oz. [¼ cup] vegetable oil

Place the lentils, onion, celery, carrots, beans, fresh white breadcrumbs, 2 of the eggs, the salt and pepper and mixed

Children will love these filling Vegetable Rissoles—and they're good for them too!

herbs in a medium-sized mixing bowl. Using a wooden spoon, mix well until the ingredients are thoroughly combined. Set the mixture aside at room temperature for 30 minutes.

Using your hands, shape the mixture into 8 equal-sized balls and flatten the balls between the palms of your hands to make small cakes. Set aside.

Using a fork, beat the remaining egg in a small shallow dish. Place the dry breadcrumbs on a plate. Dip each rissole first in the egg and then into the bread-crumbs, coating the rissoles thoroughly and shaking off any excess crumbs.

In a medium-sized frying-pan, heat the vegetable oil over moderate heat. When the oil is hot, add the rissoles and fry them for 10 minutes on each side or until they are golden brown.

Remove the pan from the heat. Using a fish slice, transfer the rissoles to kitchen paper towels and drain. Place the rissoles on a warmed serving dish and serve immediately.

Braised Carrots and Bacon

A rich vegetable accompaniment with a difference, Braised Carrots and Bacon is not difficult or expensive to make. It goes well with omelets or grilled [broiled] meats.

2-3 SERVINGS

1 lb. carrots, scraped and cut into 1-inch slices
1 tablespoon butter
8 oz. lean bacon, coarsely chopped
2 fl. oz. double cream [¼ cup heavy cream]
1 teaspoon grated nutmeg
½ teaspoon salt
½ teaspoon black pepper
2 oz. [½ cup] Gruyère cheese, grated
parsley sprigs (to garnish)

Place the carrot slices in a medium-sized saucepan. Add enough salted water to cover, and bring to the boil over moderate heat. Cook the carrots for 10 minutes. Remove the pan from the heat and drain the carrots thoroughly in a colander.

In a medium-sized frying-pan, melt the butter over moderate heat. When the foam subsides, add the bacon. Reduce the heat to low. Add the carrots to the pan and cook the bacon and carrots together for 5 to 8 minutes, turning both the carrots and the bacon constantly with a slotted spoon. Stir in the cream, nutmeg, salt and pepper. Continue cooking for a further 3 minutes. Remove the pan from the heat.

Preheat the grill [broiler] to hot.

Arrange the carrot and bacon mixture in a medium-sized shallow, flameproof casserole or, if you prefer, in small individual ramekins. Sprinkle the cheese over the top of the mixture and place the casserole or ramekins under the grill [broiler] for 2 to 3 minutes or until the cheese melts and turns a very light golden colour. Remove from the heat, garnish with the parsley sprigs and serve.

Brussels Sprouts Polonaise

Brussels sprouts served in this way are a tasty accompaniment to roast lamb or beef or grilled [broiled] steaks.

4 SERVINGS

1½ lb. Brussels sprouts
1¼ teaspoons salt
2 hard-boiled eggs, finely chopped
2 tablespoons chopped fresh parsley
¼ teaspoon freshly ground black pepper
1½ oz. [3 tablespoons] butter
2 oz. [1 cup] fresh white breadcrumbs

With a sharp knife, trim any old or dis-

Braised Carrots and Bacon are absolutely superb.

coloured leaves from the sprouts and wash them thoroughly. Cut a cross in the base of each sprout.

Half-fill a medium-sized saucepan with water and add 1 teaspoon of the salt. Bring the water to a boil over moderately high heat. Add the sprouts. Bring the water back to the boil and cook the sprouts uncovered for 5 minutes. Cover the pan and cook the sprouts for 10 minutes longer or until they are tender but still crisp.

Drain the sprouts and transfer them to a heated serving dish. Sprinkle them with the eggs, parsley, pepper and remaining salt. Set the dish aside.

In a small saucepan, melt the butter over moderate heat. Add the breadcrumbs. Cook the mixture for 10 minutes, or until the breadcrumbs are golden, stirring occasionally with a wooden spoon.

Sprinkle the browned breadcrumbs over the sprouts and serve at once.

Mushroom Purée

A spectacularly tasty accompaniment to roast poultry, Mushroom Purée is well worth the effort required to make it.

6 SERVINGS

2½ oz. [¼ cup plus 1 tablespoon] butter
2 lb. mushrooms, wiped clean and sliced
3 fl. oz. [⅜ cup] water

2 teaspoons salt
2 tablespoons lemon juice
1 teaspoon grated nutmeg
½ teaspoon black pepper
2 tablespoons flour
3 fl. oz. [⅜ cup] milk
1 tablespoon chopped fresh parsley
4 to 6 croûtons

In a medium-sized frying-pan, melt 1½ ounces [3 tablespoons] of the butter over moderate heat. When the foam subsides, add the mushrooms and mix well. Pour in the water and add 1 teaspoon of the salt, the lemon juice, nutmeg and black pepper. Bring the mixture to the boil, stirring frequently. Simmer, stirring occasionally, for 8 minutes.

Remove the pan from the heat and strain the mushrooms and cooking liquid into a large mixing bowl. Reserve the cooking liquid and set aside.

Purée the mushrooms in a blender or food mill, or, alternatively, mash them with a fork. Set aside.

Add the remaining butter to the frying-pan and melt it over moderate heat. Remove the pan from the heat and, with a wooden spoon, stir in the flour to make a smooth paste. Gradually add the reserved cooking liquid and the milk, stirring constantly. Return the pan to the heat. Simmer the mixture, stirring constantly, for 2 minutes or until it is thick.

Succulent Brussels Sprouts Polonaise is a festive mixture of sprouts, eggs, parsley and breadcrumbs, cooked to perfection.

Stir the puréed mushrooms into the sauce and cook, stirring, for 2 minutes. Add the remaining salt if required.

Remove the pan from the heat and transfer the purée to a warmed serving dish. Sprinkle over the parsley and arrange the croûtons decoratively around the purée. Serve at once.

Ratatouille

A classic French vegetable casserole, Ratatouille is a beautifully simple, yet delicious dish to prepare and serve. It can be eaten with steamed rice as a complete meal, as a first course, or as a vegetable accompaniment to meat or fish.

4-6 SERVINGS

1 oz. [2 tablespoons] butter
2 fl. oz. [¼ cup] olive oil
2 large onions, thinly sliced
2 garlic cloves, crushed
3 medium-sized aubergines [eggplants], thinly sliced and dégorged
1 large green pepper, white pith removed, seeded and chopped
1 large red pepper, white pith removed, seeded and chopped
5 medium-sized courgettes [zucchini], trimmed and sliced
14 oz. canned peeled tomatoes
1 teaspoon dried basil
1 teaspoon dried rosemary
1½ teaspoons salt
¾ teaspoon freshly ground black pepper
2 tablespoons chopped fresh parsley

In a large flameproof casserole, melt the butter with the oil over moderate heat. When the foam subsides, add the onions and garlic and fry, stirring occasionally, for 5 to 7 minutes or until the onions are soft and translucent but not brown.

Add the aubergine [eggplant] slices, green and red peppers and courgette [zucchini] slices to the casserole. Fry for 5 minutes, shaking the casserole frequently. Add the tomatoes with the can juice, the basil, rosemary, salt and pepper. Sprinkle over the parsley.

Increase the heat to high and bring to the boil. Reduce the heat to low, cover the casserole and simmer for 40 to 45 minutes or until the vegetables are tender but still quite firm.

Remove the casserole from the heat and serve at once, straight from the casserole.

Salad Dressings

Coleslaw Dressing

Yogurt enlivens the flavour of this creamy salad dressing, which is particularly good with coleslaw, but can accompany any green salad.

12 FLUID OUNCES [1½ CUPS]

10 fl. oz. [1¼ cups] mayonnaise
4 tablespoons yogurt
1 teapoon sugar
½ teaspoon salt
1 tablespoon finely grated onion or spring onion [scallion]
1 tablespoon finely chopped celery

Blend the mayonnaise with the yogurt, mixing well with a wooden spoon. Add the remaining dressing ingredients and beat for 1 minute.

Use immediately.

Fines Herbes Vinaigrette

HERB DRESSING

A delicately flavoured herb dressing, Fines Herbes Vinaigrette can be made well in advance and will keep for up to a month if stored in a cool place or in the refrigerator. Serve the dressing with a tossed green salad or a tomato salad.

8 FLUID OUNCES [1 CUP]

½ teaspoon finely chopped fresh chervil
1 teaspoon finely chopped fresh chives
1 tablespoon finely chopped fresh parsley
1 teaspoon prepared French mustard
½ teaspoon salt
¼ teaspoon freshly ground black pepper
1 garlic clove, crushed
12 tablespoons olive oil
4 tablespoons tarragon vinegar
2 teaspoons lemon juice

In a small mixing bowl, combine the chervil, chives, parsley, mustard, salt, pepper and garlic with a small wooden spoon. Gradually stir in 3 tablespoons of the olive oil. Pour the contents of the bowl into a clean screw-top jar. Pour in the remaining oil, the tarragon vinegar and lemon juice.

Firmly screw on the lid. Shake the jar vigorously for 1 minute.

Unscrew the lid and pour as much of the vinaigrette as you require over your ingredients.

Replace the lid and store the remainder in a cool place or in the refrigerator until needed.

French Dressing

The classic French dressing consists of olive oil, wine vinegar, salt and pepper. Crushed garlic, mustard and/or chopped herbs may also be added, in which case the dressing becomes sauce vinaigrette, or vinaigrette dressing. The dressing may be beaten with a fork as suggested or, more conveniently, all the ingredients may be placed in a screw-top jar and then shaken thoroughly. The advantage of this method is that any extra dressing may be kept in the jar indefinitely in a cool place.

Home-made Mayonnaise—it will cheer up the dullest salad or the stodgiest sandwich.

ABOUT 4 FLUID OUNCES [½ CUP]

6 tablespoons olive oil
1 teaspoon salt
1 teaspoon freshly ground black pepper
2 tablespoons wine vinegar

In a small mixing bowl, beat the oil, salt and pepper together with a fork. Gradually beat in the vinegar. Use as required.

Honey and Vinegar Dressing

This delightfully sweet-sour dressing is excellent for serving with a plain green salad or with a chicory [French or Belgian endive] and apple salad. Any good quality wine or cider vinegar may be used.

ABOUT 6 FLUID OUNCES [¾ CUP]

1 tablespoon clear honey
5 fl. oz. [⅝ cup] vinegar
½ teaspoon salt
¼ teaspoon freshly ground black pepper
1 teaspoon finely chopped fresh chives

Place all the ingredients in a screw-top jar and shake well. Use the dressing as required.

Mayonnaise

Mayonnaise is a cold sauce made from egg yolks and oil which are beaten together to form an emulsion. The sauce is used to coat and combine cold vegetables, fish and eggs, and as a dressing with all types of salads. Once the making of the sauce is mastered, a great variety of flavourings and colourings may be added to increase its versatility (see Mayonnaise Aurore below).

If the oil is added to the egg yolks too quickly initially, and the mixture curdles, reconstitute the mixture by placing another egg yolk and the given seasonings in another bowl and beating well. Gradually add the curdled mixture to the fresh egg yolk, beating constantly until the mixture thickens, then add the mixture a little more quickly until it is all absorbed.

When making mayonnaise it is important to use fresh, unrefrigerated eggs as they have a greater ability to hold the oil in a stable emulsion.

If you wish a lighter, less rich mayonnaise, use whole eggs instead of just egg yolks.

10 FLUID OUNCES [1¼ CUPS]

2 egg yolks, at room temperature
½ teaspoon salt
¾ teaspoon dry mustard
⅛ teaspoon freshly ground white pepper
10 fl. oz. [1¼ cups] olive oil, at room temperature
1 tablespoon white wine vinegar or lemon juice

Place the egg yolks, salt, mustard and pepper in a medium-sized mixing bowl. Using a wire whisk, beat the ingredients until they are thoroughly blended and have thickened. Add the oil, a few drops at a time, whisking constantly. Do not add the oil too quickly or the mayonnaise will curdle.

After the mayonnaise has thickened the oil may be added a little more rapidly.

Beat in a few drops of vinegar or lemon juice from time to time to prevent the mayonnaise from becoming too thick. When all of the oil has been added, stir in the remaining wine vinegar or lemon juice.

Taste the sauce for seasoning and add more salt, mustard and wine vinegar if desired.

MAYONNAISE AURORE
Add 2 tablespoons of tomato purée, 1 tablespoon of single [light] cream and 2 drops of Worcestershire sauce to the mayonnaise.

Mint Dressing

A cool, refreshing, slightly tart dressing, Mint Dressing is perfect spooned over cold cooked lamb, roast beef or on a tomato or potato salad.

ABOUT 2 FLUID OUNCES [¼ CUP]

3 tablespoons olive oil
1 tablespoon lemon juice
½ teaspoon salt
½ teaspoon freshly ground black pepper
1 tablespoon finely chopped fresh mint
2 teaspoons sugar

In a small mixing bowl, combine the olive oil, lemon juice, salt, black pepper, mint and sugar and mix well with a wooden spoon. Alternatively place all the ingredients in a screw-top jar and shake well to blend.

Place the dressing in the refrigerator to chill for at least 30 minutes before serving.

Roquefort Dressing

Serve this deliciously different salad dressing with a mixed green salad, or with a cold fish dish.

ABOUT 8 FLUID OUNCES [1 CUP]

6 fl. oz. [¾ cup] olive oil
2 teaspoons salt
2 teaspoons freshly ground black pepper
2 fl. oz. [¼ cup] wine vinegar
2 oz. Roquefort cheese, finely crumbled
1 tablespoon chopped fresh chives

In a medium-sized mixing bowl, beat the oil, salt and pepper together with a fork. Gradually beat in the vinegar, then mash in the cheese until the mixture is thoroughly combined. Stir in the chives.

Either use the dressing immediately or pour it into a screw-top jar and chill in the refrigerator until required.

Thousand Island Dressing

A salad dressing with a mayonnaise base, Thousand Island Dressing is thought to have originated in the United States. It is particularly excellent served with mixed vegetable salads, and of course, with hamburgers.

ABOUT 1 PINT [2½ CUPS]

16 fl. oz. [2 cups] mayonnaise
1¼ teaspoons Tabasco sauce
2 tablespoons chopped pimientos or sweet pickle
10 stuffed green olives, finely chopped
2 hard-boiled eggs, very finely chopped
1 medium-sized shallot, very finely chopped
3 tablespoons olive oil
½ teaspoon salt
½ teaspoon freshly ground black pepper
1 tablespoon wine vinegar

In a large bowl, combine the mayonnaise, Tabasco, chopped pimientos or pickle, green olives, chopped eggs, shallot, olive oil, salt, black pepper and wine vinegar and beat them together with a wooden spoon, until they are thoroughly blended.

Pour the dressing into a serving bowl and chill in the refrigerator for at least 1 hour before serving.

Yogurt Dressing

Serve Yogurt Dressing with salads as an interesting alternative to mayonnaise or vinaigrette, or as an accompaniment to fried vegetables or kebabs.

ABOUT 12 FLUID OUNCES [1½ CUPS]

12 fl. oz. [1½ cups] yogurt
juice of 1 lemon
1 garlic clove, crushed
1 teaspoon salt
1 teaspoon black pepper

Place all the ingredients in a medium-sized mixing bowl and beat them together with a fork until they are thoroughly combined.

The dressing is now ready to use.

Cabbage, Pepper and Onion Salad

This tasty and attractive Cabbage, Pepper and Onion Salad is ideal to serve with meat or chicken when salad greens are not available.

8 SERVINGS

1 large red pepper, white pith removed, seeded and finely sliced
1 large green pepper, white pith removed, seeded and finely sliced
6 to 8 spring onions [scallions], finely chopped
1 cucumber, cut into ½-inch cubes
1 lb. tomatoes, finely sliced
½ white cabbage, coarse outer leaves removed, washed and finely sliced
2 tablespoons clear honey
juice of 1 lemon
10 tablespoons olive or vegetable oil
4 tablespoons vinegar
2 teaspoons salt
1 teaspoon freshly ground black pepper

Combine the peppers, spring onions [scallions], cucumber, tomatoes and cabbage in a large salad bowl.

Put the honey, lemon juice, oil, vinegar, salt and pepper into a screw-top jar and shake it until the dressing is well mixed.

Pour the dressing over the salad just before serving and toss well.

Chef's Salad

An excellent way to use leftover meats and vegetables, Chef's Salad makes an appetizing supper or luncheon entrée. Turkey and ham may be substituted for the meats suggested in the recipe below, and vegetables such as asparagus tips, cold cooked peas, cooked French beans or beetroot [beet] may be used rather than cheese and egg as in this recipe.

4 SERVINGS

1 medium-sized lettuce, outer leaves removed, washed and chilled
3 oz. cold, cooked chicken, cut in strips about 4 inches by ½ inch
3 oz. cold, cooked tongue, cut in strips about 4 inches by ½ inch
3 oz. Gruyère cheese, cut into pieces
1 hard-boiled egg, very thinly sliced
1 tablespoon finely chopped onion
3 tablespoons stoned, chopped black olives
6 tablespoons olive oil
2 tablespoons red wine vinegar
½ teaspoon lemon juice
¼ teaspoon prepared French mustard
1 teaspoon salt
½ teaspoon freshly ground black pepper

Place the lettuce leaves in a large salad bowl. Add the chicken, tongue, cheese, egg, onion and olives.

In a screw-top jar, combine the olive oil, vinegar, lemon juice, mustard, salt and pepper, and shake the jar vigorously until all of the ingredients are well blended.

Pour the dressing over the salad, and place the bowl in the refrigerator to chill for 10 minutes. Just before serving, toss the salad well.

Cucumber and Grape Salad

Cucumber and grapes set in a tangy lemon-flavoured jelly [gelatin] is a refreshing salad

Cabbage, Pepper and Onion Salad is economical and super to eat.

and makes an attractive addition to a summer buffet.

6 SERVINGS

1 large cucumber, peeled and thinly sliced
1 lb. green grapes, washed, halved and seeded
15 fl. oz. [1⅞ cups] water
5 oz. packet lemon jelly [gelatin]
3 tablespoons orange juice
5 tablespoons lemon juice
1 tablespoon very finely chopped onion
⅛ teaspoon cayenne pepper
½ teaspoon salt
¼ teaspoon freshly ground black pepper
1 Webb [iceberg] lettuce, outer leaves removed, washed and shredded

MARINADE

3 tablespoons olive oil
1 tablespoon wine vinegar
¼ teaspoon salt
¼ teaspoon freshly ground black pepper
¼ teaspoon dry mustard

To prepare the marinade, in a medium-sized bowl, combine the oil, vinegar, salt, pepper and mustard, beating with a fork until all the ingredients are blended.

Place the cucumber slices and grapes in the bowl and marinate them for at least 30 minutes or until you are ready to use them.

In a small saucepan, bring 5 fluid ounces [⅝ cup] of the water to the boil over moderate heat. Remove the pan from the heat and add the jelly [gelatin]. Stir until the jelly [gelatin] has dissolved. Stir in the remaining water. Stir in the orange and lemon juice, onion, cayenne, salt and pepper. Cool the jelly [gelatin] until it is almost set. With a slotted spoon, remove the grapes and cucumber slices from the

Cucumber and Grape Salad makes a refreshing buffet centrepiece.

marinade. Drain them thoroughly on kitchen paper towels and then add most of them to the jelly [gelatin]. Reserve the marinade and the remaining grapes and cucumber slices for the garnish.

Spoon the jelly [gelatin] into a 2½-pint [1½-quart] mould. Cover the mould with plastic wrap or aluminium foil and put it in the refrigerator to chill for 3 to 4 hours or until the jelly [gelatin] is completely set.

Arrange the lettuce on a serving dish. Quickly dip the mould into hot water and turn the jelly [gelatin] out on to the lettuce. Arrange the reserved grapes and cucumber slices around the salad and pour a little of the reserved marinade over them.

Serve at once.

215

Fennel, Watercress, Cucumber and Tomato Salad

Delicious Fennel, Watercress, Cucumber and Tomato Salad is a meal in itself — try it for lunch with lots of crusty bread and a glass of milk.

4 SERVINGS

1 bunch watercress, washed and shaken dry

½ fennel, trimmed and sliced

½ small cucumber, thinly sliced

4 tomatoes, quartered

6 anchovy fillets, halved

1 spring onion [scallion], trimmed and finely chopped

2 tablespoons finely chopped pimiento

3 fl. oz. [⅜ cup] French dressing

In a large, deep serving platter or salad bowl, combine all the ingredients except the French dressing, tossing with two spoons until they are well mixed.

Pour the French dressing into the mixture and, using the spoons, gently toss until all the ingredients are well coated. Serve at once.

Fruit and Vegetable Salad

This beautiful salad is ideal to serve at a summer buffet. Alternatively, it may be eaten as a light meal on its own.

4-6 SERVINGS

4 oz. canned pineapple chunks, drained

8 oz. small seedless green grapes

2 fresh peaches, peeled, stoned and sliced

2 carrots, scraped and grated

1 small green pepper, white pith removed, seeded and thinly sliced

2 spring onions [scallions], finely chopped

6 radishes, sliced

5 fl. oz. [⅝ cup] French dressing, made with lemon juice instead of

Delicious Fennel, Watercress, Cucumber and Tomato Salad tastes even better than it looks!

vinegar

1 cos [romaine] lettuce, outer leaves removed, washed and shredded

In a medium-sized mixing bowl, carefully combine the pineapple, grapes, peaches, carrots, green pepper, spring onions [scallions], radishes and French dressing.

Arrange the shredded lettuce leaves around the outer edge of a shallow serving dish and pile the fruit and vegetable mixture in the centre. Serve immediately.

Greek Salad

A simple dish using Greek feta cheese, this salad is very colourful and can be served on its own for lunch or as an accompaniment to a cold savoury flan or pie. The dressing

216

should not be added to the salad until just before serving.

4-6 SERVINGS

1 cos [romaine] lettuce, outer leaves removed, washed and separated into leaves
1 bunch radishes, cleaned and sliced
8 oz. feta cheese, cut into cubes
¼ teaspoon dried marjoram
4 tomatoes, blanched, peeled and sliced
6 anchovies, drained and finely chopped
6 large black olives, halved and stoned
1 tablespoon chopped fresh parsley
½ teaspoon freshly ground black pepper

DRESSING
4 tablespoons olive oil
1½ tablespoons white wine vinegar
1 tablespoon chopped mixed fresh herbs, such as marjoram, chives or lemon thyme
4 spring onions [scallions], chopped
1 teaspoon sugar
¼ teaspoon salt
½ teaspoon freshly ground black pepper

Tear the lettuce leaves into pieces and arrange them on a large dish. Scatter the radish slices over the lettuce. Arrange the cheese in the centre of the dish and sprinkle it with the marjoram. Place the tomatoes in a circle around the cheese and put the anchovies on top of the tomatoes, alternating with the olives. Sprinkle the parsley and pepper on top.

In a small bowl, mix together the oil, vinegar, fresh herbs, spring onions [scallions], sugar, salt and pepper.

Pour the dressing over the salad and serve.

Gruyère and Mushroom Salad

Light and refreshing, Gruyère and Mushroom Salad perfectly complements roasts and grilled [broiled] meats, especially the lighter meats such as veal and lamb.

4 SERVINGS

8 oz. Gruyère cheese, cut into small cubes
4 oz. button mushrooms, wiped clean and quartered
4 large lettuce leaves, washed and shaken dry
1 tablespoon chopped fresh parsley

DRESSING
6 tablespoons olive oil
2 tablespoons red wine vinegar

1 garlic clove, crushed
½ teaspoon salt
¼ teaspoon freshly ground black pepper

First, make the dressing. In a medium-sized mixing bowl, combine all the dressing ingredients, beating with a fork until they are well blended. Set aside.

In a medium-sized bowl, combine the cheese and mushrooms. Pour over the dressing and, using two large spoons, toss the cheese and mushrooms until they are well coated. Set aside to marinate for 20 minutes.

Line the bottom of a shallow salad bowl or four individual serving plates with the lettuce leaves. Spoon the cheese and mushroom mixture on top and sprinkle over the parsley. Serve immediately.

Korean Vegetable Salad

This attractive crunchy salad may be served as a delicious accompaniment to roast pork or as an unusual first course.

4 SERVINGS

1 small turnip, peeled
1 teaspoon salt
2 to 4 tablespoons vegetable oil
1 small onion, finely chopped
4 oz. mushrooms, wiped clean and thinly sliced
2 celery stalks, thinly sliced

Tasty Gruyère and Mushroom Salad.

3 spring onions [scallions], chopped
1 carrot, scraped and sliced
1 tablespoon chopped pine nuts

DRESSING
3 tablespoons soy sauce
1 tablespoon soft brown sugar
1 tablespoon vinegar
¼ teaspoon black pepper
¼ teaspoon ground ginger

With a sharp knife, cut the turnip into long, thin strips. Sprinkle the strips with the salt and set aside for 15 minutes.

In a small frying-pan, heat 2 tablespoons of the oil over moderate heat. When the oil is hot, add the turnip strips. Fry for 3 to 4 minutes, turning occasionally or until they are crisp. Transfer the strips to kitchen paper towels to drain.

Add the onion to the pan and fry, stirring occasionally, for 8 to 10 minutes, or until it is golden brown. Transfer the onion to kitchen paper towels to drain.

Add the mushrooms to the pan, with more oil if necessary, and fry, stirring frequently, for 4 minutes. Transfer the mushrooms to kitchen paper towels to drain.

Fry the celery for 2 to 3 minutes, or until it is gold. Transfer the celery to kitchen paper towels to drain.

When the fried vegetables are cold, combine them with the spring onions [scallions] and carrot in a serving dish. Sprinkle the pine nuts on top.

In a screw-top jar, combine the soy sauce, sugar, vinegar, pepper and ginger. Shake well and pour the dressing over the vegetables. Serve at once.

Melon and Avocado Salad

Melon and Avocado Salad is an unusual combination for a savoury salad. It is the perfect accompaniment to grilled [broiled] lamb chops or steak. This dish can also be served as a first course.

4 SERVINGS

2 medium-sized avocados, halved and stoned
1 tablespoon lemon juice
½ medium-sized honeydew melon, seeded
½ teaspoon finely chopped fresh tarragon or ¼ teaspoon dried tarragon

DRESSING

6 tablespoons olive oil
½ teaspoon salt
¼ teaspoon black pepper
2 tablespoons lemon juice

With a small melon baller, scoop out the avocado flesh to within ⅛-inch of the skin. Reserve the avocado shells. Place the avocado balls in a medium-sized mixing bowl and sprinkle over the tablespoon of lemon juice. Set aside.

Scoop out the melon flesh in the same way and add the melon balls to the avocado balls. Place the bowl in the refrigerator to chill while you make the dressing.

In a small mixing bowl, beat the oil, salt and pepper together with a fork. Gradually add the lemon juice.

Remove the melon and avocado from the refrigerator and pour over the dressing. With a wooden spoon carefully toss the ingredients together until the balls are well coated. Serve at once.

Mushroom and Bacon Salad

Mushroom and Bacon Salad may be served as part of an hors d'oeuvre, as an accompaniment to grilled [broiled] meat or as part of a large mixed salad.

4 SERVINGS

8 oz. button mushrooms, wiped clean and thinly sliced
4 streaky bacon slices, rinds removed
1 celery stalk, trimmed and finely chopped
1 tablespoon chopped fresh parsley
1 tablespoon chopped fresh chives

DRESSING

6 tablespoons olive oil
2 tablespoons white wine vinegar
½ teaspoon salt
¼ teaspoon freshly ground black pepper

First make the dressing. In a medium-sized mixing bowl, combine all the dressing ingredients, beating with a fork until they are well blended. Add the sliced mushrooms and set aside to marinate for 30 minutes.

Meanwhile, preheat the grill [broiler] to high.

Place the bacon slices on a rack in the grill [broiler] pan and grill [broil] the bacon, turning once, for 5 minutes, or until it is crisp. Remove the bacon from the grill [broiler] and set aside to drain and cool on kitchen paper towels.

Crumble the bacon into the mushroom mixture and add the celery, parsley and

Unusual Mussel, Hake and Vegetable Salad is served hot.

chives. Mix well. Transfer to a serving dish and serve immediately.

Mussel, Hake and Vegetable Salad

A delightful hot salad Mussel, Hake and Vegetable Salad may be served with crusty bread and butter for an hors d'oeuvre or light meal.

4-6 SERVINGS

4 fl. oz. [½ cup] olive oil
¼ teaspoon hot chilli powder
2 tablespoons chopped fresh parsley
¼ teaspoon dried thyme
1 bay leaf
2 garlic cloves, crushed
1½ lb. hake, cut into 6 x 1-inch slices
4 oz. frozen petits pois, thawed, cooked until tender and drained
3 canned red pimientos, drained and cut into strips
24 mussels, scrubbed and steamed
GARNISH
8 croûtons, kept hot
2 hard-boiled eggs, quartered

In a shallow ovenproof dish large enough to hold the fish slices in one layer, combine the olive oil, chilli powder, parsley, thyme, bay leaf and garlic. Place the fish in the dish and marinate at room temperature for 1 hour, basting occasionally.

Preheat the oven to fairly hot 375°F (Gas Mark 5, 190°C).

Cover the dish tightly and place it in the oven. Bake for 15 minutes.

Remove the dish from the oven. Uncover and place the petits pois, pimientos and mussels in the dish. Return it to the oven and bake for a further 5 to 10 minutes or until the fish flakes easily when tested with a fork.

Remove the dish from the oven. Remove and discard the bay leaf.

Garnish with the croûtons and hard-boiled eggs and serve immediately.

Nun's Salad

A simple dish, Nun's Salad is so called because of the use of black and white ingredients. Serve it as a light supper dish or as a first course.

4 SERVINGS

1 lb. cooked chicken, diced
12 spring onions [scallions], white part only, chopped
1 lb. potatoes, peeled, cooked and diced
2 oz. [⅓ cup] seedless raisins
8 oz. large black grapes, halved and seeded
2 oz. [⅔ cup] large black olives, halved and stoned
½ teaspoon salt
¼ teaspoon freshly ground black pepper
1 large apple, peeled, cored and diced
6 fl. oz. [¾ cup] mayonnaise

In a large salad bowl, combine the chicken, spring onions [scallions], potatoes, raisins, half the grapes, the olives, salt, pepper and apple. Pour over the mayonnaise and, using two large spoons, toss the salad, mixing the ingredients together thoroughly.

Arrange the remaining grape halves decoratively over the top. Place the bowl in the refrigerator and chill the salad for 30 minutes before serving.

Good to look at, satisfying to eat, Nun's Salad makes an excellent summer supper for the family.

219

Potato Salad

This simple Potato Salad with mayonnaise dressing may be served with cold meat or as one of a selection of salads. Use the green part of the leeks for this recipe and save the white parts for future use.

4 SERVINGS

1 lb. potatoes, cooked, peeled and sliced
4 fl. oz. [½ cup] mayonnaise
1 tablespoon lemon juice
1 tablespoon olive oil
½ teaspoon salt
½ teaspoon freshly ground black pepper
2 tablespoons finely chopped fresh chives
4 tablespoons finely chopped leeks

Place three-quarters of the potatoes in a medium-sized mixing bowl. Pour over the mayonnaise and sprinkle with the lemon juice, oil, salt, pepper and 1 tablespoon of chives. Using two large spoons, carefully toss the potatoes until they are thoroughly coated with the mayonnaise mixture.

Spoon the mixture into a serving bowl. Arrange the remaining potato slices over the top of the salad. Sprinkle with the remaining chives and scatter the leeks around the edge of the bowl.

Cover the bowl and place it in the refrigerator to chill for 30 minutes before serving.

Potato, Beef and Tomato Salad

Potato, Beef and Tomato Salad is a delicious salad with a sour cream and horseradish sauce. Serve with crusty bread and a chilled Tavel Rosé wine for a perfect spring supper or lunch.

4 SERVINGS

1 small lettuce, outer leaves removed, washed and separated into leaves
2 lb. cold roast beef, cubed
4 medium-sized cold cooked potatoes, cubed
4 medium-sized tomatoes, blanched, peeled, seeded and quartered
4 pickled gherkins, sliced
2 hard-boiled eggs, thinly sliced
¼ teaspoon paprika
SAUCE
12 fl. oz. [1½ cups] sour cream
3 tablespoons cold horseradish sauce
½ teaspoon salt

½ teaspoon white pepper

Arrange the lettuce leaves decoratively on a large, shallow serving plate and set aside.

In a large mixing bowl, combine the meat, potatoes, tomatoes and gherkins. Set aside.

In a small bowl, mix the sour cream, horseradish sauce, salt and pepper together, beating until they are well blended.

Spoon the sauce over the meat mixture and, using two spoons, carefully toss to coat well.

Arrange the meat mixture on the lettuce leaves. Garnish with the egg slices and sprinkle over the paprika. Serve at once.

Rice and Ham Salad

Rice and Ham Salad is a delicious ham, fruit, vegetable and rice salad which makes a refreshingly different summer lunch or dinner. Made in a smaller quantity, the salad can be used as a superb stuffing for avocados or large fresh tomatoes.

4 SERVINGS

8 oz. [1⅓ cups] long-grain rice, washed, soaked in cold water for 30 minutes and drained
1 teaspoon salt
4 very thick slices cooked, lean ham, diced
4 canned pineapple rings, drained and chopped
2 medium-sized green peppers, white pith removed, seeded and coarsely chopped
1 red eating apple, cored and chopped
DRESSING
1 egg yolk, at room temperature
¼ teaspoon salt
½ teaspoon dry mustard
⅛ teaspoon white pepper
4 fl. oz. [½ cup] olive oil, at room temperature
1 tablespoon lemon juice
2 fl. oz. double cream [¼ cup heavy cream]
¼ teaspoon cayenne pepper
1 tablespoon finely chopped fresh chives

Place the rice, salt and enough water just to cover the rice in a medium-sized saucepan. Set the pan over high heat and bring the water to the boil. Reduce the heat to very low, cover the pan and simmer for 15 minutes, or until all the water has been absorbed and the rice is tender.

Remove the pan from the heat and set the rice aside to cool completely.

To make the dressing, place the egg yolk, salt, mustard and pepper in a

medium-sized mixing bowl. Using a wire whisk, beat the ingredients until they are thoroughly blended. Add the oil, a few drops at a time, whisking constantly. Do not add the oil too quickly or the mayonnaise will curdle. After the mayonnaise has thickened the oil may be added a little more rapidly. Beat in a few drops of the lemon juice from time to time to prevent the mayonnaise from becoming too thick. When all the oil has been added, stir in the remaining lemon juice. Taste for seasoning and add more salt, mustard or lemon juice if desired.

Stir in the cream, cayenne and chives and blend well.

Add the ham, pineapple, green peppers, apple and the rice to the dressing. Toss the ingredients thoroughly. Turn the salad out into a medium-sized serving bowl. Place it in the refrigerator to chill for 30 minutes before serving.

Tomato and French Bean Salad

The combination of red and green in Tomato and French Bean Salad makes it colourful as well as delicious. This salad is very good with cold meats and has the advantage that it may be prepared well in advance of serving.

6-8 SERVINGS

1 lb. tomatoes, very thinly sliced and seeded
1 lb. French beans, trimmed, cooked and drained
DRESSING
3 tablespoons wine vinegar
6 tablespoons olive oil
¼ teaspoon salt
¼ teaspoon freshly ground black pepper
½ teaspoon prepared French mustard
½ teaspoon sugar
1 garlic clove, crushed

Place all the dressing ingredients in a screw-top jar and shake vigorously until they are well mixed. Set the dressing aside.

Place the tomatoes and beans in a large serving dish and pour over the dressing. Using two large spoons, toss the salad until the vegetables are thoroughly coated with the dressing.

Chill the salad in the refrigerator before serving.

Easy to make, even easier to eat, Potato Salad is a favourite dish throughout the world.

Salads for Special Occasions

Caesar Salad

This unusual salad comes from the United States where it is eaten on its own as a light lunch dish, or served with grilled [broiled] steak, or fish.

4 SERVINGS

5 fl. oz. [⅝ cup] olive oil
4 thick slices white bread, crusts removed and cut into cubes
1 garlic clove
1½ teaspoons salt
2 tablespoons wine vinegar
1 teaspoon lemon juice
½ teaspoon Worcestershire sauce
¼ teaspoon prepared mustard
⅛ teaspoon sugar
¼ teaspoon black pepper
2 heads cos [romaine] lettuce, washed and dried
6 anchovy fillets, cut in small pieces
1 egg, cooked in boiling water for 1 minute
2 oz. [½ cup] Parmesan cheese, grated

Heat 2 fluid ounces [¼ cup] of the olive oil in a large, heavy frying-pan over moderately high heat. Fry the bread cubes in the oil for 10 to 15 minutes or until crisp, turning frequently with a spoon. Remove the croûtons from the pan and drain them on kitchen paper towels.

Mash the garlic together with the salt in the bottom of a large salad bowl. Add the remaining olive oil, the vinegar, lemon juice, Worcestershire sauce, mustard, sugar and the pepper and mix well.

Tear the lettuce into bite-sized pieces and add to the salad bowl with the anchovies. Toss well with the dressing.

Break the egg over the top of the salad, add the croûtons and Parmesan cheese and toss the salad again. Serve immediately.

Russian Salad

Russian Salad (pictured on page 193) is a selection of cooked vegetables and meat coated in mayonnaise. Served with meat as suggested here, Russian Salad makes an excellent main course with crusty bread and a well-chilled white wine. Alternatively, the meat is often omitted and the salad served as a substantial side dish.

4-8 SERVINGS

3 large cooked potatoes, diced
4 medium-sized cooked carrots, diced
4 oz. cooked French beans, halved
1 small onion, very finely chopped

4 oz. cooked fresh peas, weighed after shelling
2 oz. cooked tongue, diced
4 oz. cooked chicken, diced
2 oz. garlic sausage, diced
8 fl. oz. [1 cup] mayonnaise
¼ teaspoon cayenne pepper
GARNISH
2 hard-boiled eggs, sliced
1 cooked beetroot [beet], sliced
2 gherkins, thinly sliced

In a large salad bowl, combine all of the salad ingredients except the mayonnaise and cayenne. Set aside.

In a small bowl, beat the mayonnaise and cayenne together with a fork until they are well blended. Spoon the mayonnaise into the salad bowl and toss well.

Garnish the salad with the eggs, beetroot [beet] and gherkins and chill in the refrigerator for 15 to 20 minutes before serving.

Salade Niçoise

POTATO, FRENCH BEAN AND TOMATO SALAD

Salade Niçoise is one of the great classic dishes of regional France and its succulent mixture of potatoes, French beans, tomatoes, anchovies and capers in a spicy French dressing evokes the warmth of its city of origin. Tuna fish is often added to the salad, both in France and outside, although strictly speaking this is not traditional. With the addition of tuna fish, however, and accompanied by crusty bread and lots of well-chilled Provençal white wine, it makes a delightful meal.

3-6 SERVINGS

1 small lettuce, outer leaves removed, washed and separated into leaves
6 medium-sized cold cooked potatoes, diced
10 oz. cold cooked French beans, cut into ½-inch lengths
6 tomatoes, blanched, peeled and quartered
4 fl. oz. [½ cup] French dressing
GARNISH
6 anchovy fillets, halved
10 black olives, stoned
2 tablespoons capers

A classic Salad from France, Salade Niçoise is a blend of potatoes, French beans and tomatoes, garnished with anchovies and olives.

Arrange the lettuce leaves decoratively on a large, shallow serving plate and set aside.

In a large mixing bowl, combine the potatoes, beans and tomatoes. Pour over the French dressing and, using two spoons, carefully toss the vegetables until they are thoroughly coated.

Spoon the vegetables on to the lettuce leaves and garnish with the anchovy fillets, olives and capers. Serve at once.

Salmagundy

Salmagundy is a traditional British salad, popular in the seventeenth and eighteenth centuries, which is built up like a small pyramid, with different, brightly coloured ingredients. The salad can be garnished with parsley, tomatoes and lemon and orange segments. A very large round plate is required on which to serve the salad, and a shallow pudding basin or large saucer is inverted and placed on the plate, to give a base upon which to build the salad. The butter 'statue' is traditional to the dish, but it may be omitted, if preferred.

8-10 SERVINGS

1 teaspoon vegetable oil
½ medium-sized curly endive [chicory], coarse outer leaves removed, washed, shaken dry and shredded
1 lb. cooked chicken meat, sliced
1 lb. lean cooked tongue, sliced
6 hard-boiled eggs, separated and finely chopped
8 rollmops or pickled herrings, drained
2 large tomatoes, quartered
1 large lemon, quartered
1 large orange, quartered
1 small cooked beetroot [beet], finely chopped
8 black olives, stoned
1 small dill pickle, finely chopped
8 tablespoons chopped fresh watercress
8 oz. [1 cup] butter, frozen in 1 piece

With the oil, lightly grease the outside of a shallow pudding basin or large saucer and place it, inverted, on a large round serving plate.

Sprinkle the endive [chicory] over the saucer.

Salmagundy makes an extra special treat for the family.

Arrange the chicken slices around the edge of the serving plate and then, inside, make another slightly smaller circle with the tongue. Make a circle with the chopped egg yolks. Arrange the herrings inside the egg yolk circle and place a tomato quarter between each herring. Make a circle with the egg whites. Make a circle with the lemon and orange quarters, arranging them alternately.

Sprinkle the beetroot [beet], olives and dill pickle around the edge of the endive [chicory] on the basin or saucer. Make a circle around the outer edge of the plate with the watercress. Place the plate in the refrigerator and chill for at least 30 minutes.

Place the butter on a wooden board. Using a small sharp knife, carve the butter into a decorative shape, such as a flower, fruit or bird.

Remove the plate from the refrigerator. Place the butter decoration in the centre of the endive [chicory].

Serve at once.

Sour Cream Chicken Salad

The secret of Sour Cream Chicken Salad is in the attractive presentation. The colourful ingredients make it look pretty as well as tasty to eat. Serve for a special family meal with lots of crusty bread and some well-chilled white wine such as Hungarian Riesling.

4-6 SERVINGS

1 x 4 lb. cooked chicken, cold
6 medium-sized hard-boiled eggs
2 green peppers, white pith removed, seeded and finely shredded
4 tablespoons stuffed green olives, sliced
1 lb. green grapes, peeled and seeded
4 oz. [1 cup] blanched sliced almonds
½ teaspoon freshly ground black pepper

FRENCH DRESSING

3 tablespoons white wine vinegar
2 teaspoons prepared French mustard
½ teaspoon salt
½ teaspoon freshly ground black pepper
6 tablespoons olive oil

SOUR CREAM DRESSING

6 tablespoons white wine vinegar
10 fl. oz. [1¼ cups] sour cream
2 teaspoons sugar
½ teaspoon salt
½ teaspoon freshly ground white pepper

On a wooden board, carve the chicken into pieces and, with a small, sharp knife, detach the meat from the skin and bones. Discard the skin and bones. Cut the meat into thin strips and put them into a salad bowl.

Separate the yolks from the whites of the hard-boiled eggs. Finely chop the whites and add to the chicken. Keep the egg yolks aside on a plate. Add the green peppers, olives, grapes and almonds. Do not mix or toss the ingredients. Set the salad bowl aside.

Prepare the French dressing. In a small mixing bowl, combine the vinegar,

Sour Cream Chicken Salad makes an especially delightful summer meal, served with crusty bread and well chilled white wine.

mustard, salt and pepper. With a large spoon, beat the ingredients together to mix well, then stir in the olive oil. Pour the dressing over the ingredients in the salad bowl.

Press the egg yolks through a fine strainer or push them through a garlic press over the chicken mixture. Toss the salad to mix the ingredients well. Sprinkle the black pepper over the top. Cover the salad bowl and keep it in the refrigerator until you are ready to serve it.

Lastly prepare the sour cream dressing. In a small mixing bowl, slowly beat the vinegar into the sour cream. Add the sugar, salt and pepper and mix well. Taste the dressing and add more salt, sugar, vinegar or white pepper, if necessary. Pour the dressing into a sauce boat or small serving bowl.

Serve the salad, accompanied by the sour cream dressing.

Vegetables and salads for entertaining

Vegetables and salads tend to be a bit neglected when you're planning a 'special' meal; with all that energy about to be expended on a fancier meat or fish dish, perhaps a dessert as well, there usually isn't much time (or inclination) for anything else. Which is a pity because a well-chosen accompaniment or two can make the difference between a merely acceptable meal and a spectacularly successful one — and just in case you need convincing of this, we recommend that you check (and preferably try) our fabulous recipes for Celery with Almonds (page 233), Légumes Nouveaux Flambés (pictured below, page 241) and Cabbage and Sesame Seed Salad (page 254).

Vegetables and salads can also make more than palatable meals on their own — and are in fact often much more suitable for informal entertaining than heavier, more conventional meals centred around meat. For light but elegant occasions, for instance, you could serve Artichokes Stuffed with Pork and Almonds (page 226); Boston Baked Beans (page 242), on the other hand, is probably the ultimate — and perfect — special dish to serve to any guest under the age of 12, and Rice Salad with Garlic Sausage (page 250) makes a perfect offering for a summer supper.

Most of the recipes which follow have been specially chosen for their ease of preparation, always a consideration since it's a dire fate indeed to be too tired to sit down and enjoy your own dinner parties. Nor will any of them break the bank, especially if the ingredients are bought (as all fresh vegetables and fruit should be for the best results) on a seasonal basis.

So — lots of luck, lots of happy experimenting and, most especially, lots of very good eating!

Artichokes Stuffed with Pork and Almonds

This is an unusual and rather expensive way to serve artichokes although it may be served as a main course rather than as a vegetable accompaniment. Serve with some melted butter, into which the artichoke leaves and hearts can be dipped.

4 SERVINGS

4 large artichokes
2 fl. oz. [¼ cup] lemon juice
　enough boiling water to cover the artichokes
1 tablespoon salt
STUFFING
2 oz. [¼ cup] vegetable fat
8 oz. minced [ground] pork
1 medium-sized onion, chopped
2 oz. [1 cup] fresh white breadcrumbs
2 tablespoons chopped fresh parsley
½ teaspoon salt
¼ teaspoon black pepper
½ teaspoon celery salt
2½ oz. [½ cup] blanched almonds, finely chopped
1 egg, lightly beaten
1 tablespoon vegetable oil

Wash and prepare the artichokes for boiling. Pour a little lemon juice over the cut areas to prevent them from dis-colouring. Using a sharp knife, cut off the top third of each artichoke. Pull open the centre leaves carefully and pull out the yellow and purple leaves from the centre. Using a teaspoon, scrape and pull off all the fuzzy chokes to expose the heart. Pour a little lemon into the hollows. Push the leaves back together again.

Stand the artichokes in a large sauce-pan. If they do not fit snugly into the saucepan, tie a piece of string around each one so they will keep their shape while boiling.

Pour the boiling water and the remaining lemon juice over the artichokes so that they are completely covered. Add the salt. Cover the saucepan and simmer the artichokes over moderately low heat for 25 minutes, or until the bases are tender when pierced with a sharp knife. When the artichokes are cooked, with a slotted spoon remove them from the water and turn them upside down in a colander to drain.

While the artichokes are boiling, pre-heat the oven to moderate 350°F (Gas Mark 4, 180°C) To make the stuffing, in a large, heavy frying-pan, melt the fat over moderate heat. When the foam sub-sides, add the pork and onion and fry, stirring occasionally, for 5 to 7 minutes

or until the onion is soft and translucent but not brown. Remove the frying-pan from the heat and add the breadcrumbs, parsley, salt, pepper, celery salt, almonds and beaten egg. Stir the mixture thor-oughly with a wooden spoon.

Place the artichokes in a baking dish and fill the centres with the stuffing.

Pour a little water around the artichokes and brush them generously with the oil. Cover the dish with aluminium foil and bake in the oven for 30 to 40 minutes or until the artichokes and fillings are cooked and tender.

Serve hot.

Artichoke Hearts in Butter

This simple, well-flavoured dish may be served either as a first course or as an accompaniment to lighter meats, such as chicken, lamb or veal.

4 SERVINGS

2 tablespoons lemon juice
12 artichoke hearts
4 oz. [½ cup] butter
4 tablespoons chopped shallots or spring onions [scallions]
½ teaspoon salt
½ teaspoon freshly ground white pepper
1½ tablespoons chopped fresh parsley

Half-fill a large saucepan with water and add the lemon juice. Place the pan over moderately high heat and bring the water to the boil. Reduce the heat to low, add the artichoke hearts and simmer them for 10 minutes or until they are tender. Remove the artichoke hearts from the pan and drain them in a colander. Cut them into quarters, then set the quarters aside.

Meanwhile, preheat the oven to warm 325°F (Gas Mark 3, 170°C).

In a medium-sized flameproof cas-serole, melt the butter over moderate heat. When the foam subsides, add the shallots or spring onions [scallions] and artichoke hearts, and cook, stirring, for 1 or 2 minutes or until the hearts are well coated with the butter. Sprinkle over the salt and pepper.

Cover the casserole and cook in the oven for 15 minutes. Remove the cas-serole from the oven, sprinkle over the parsley and serve at once.

Artichokes Stuffed with Pork and Almonds – elegant to look at, mar-vellous to eat – makes a festive lunch or supper dish.

Artichoke Hearts with Cream

This smooth vegetable dish is particularly delicious served with roast leg of lamb or pork.

4 SERVINGS

2 oz. [¼ cup] butter
12 artichoke hearts, cooked as in the previous recipe and cut into quarters
1 teaspoon salt
½ teaspoon white pepper
8 fl. oz. double cream [1 cup heavy cream]
1 tablespoon lemon juice
½ teaspoon grated nutmeg

In a medium-sized saucepan, melt the

butter over moderate heat. When the foam subsides, add the artichoke hearts and, with a wooden spoon, baste them thoroughly in the melted butter. Stir in half of the salt and pepper. Reduce the heat to low, cover the pan and simmer the artichoke hearts for 10 minutes or until they are thoroughly heated through.

Meanwhile, in a small, heavy saucepan, scald the cream over low heat (bring it to just below boiling point). Add the remaining salt and pepper and stir in the lemon juice. Simmer the cream sauce for 3 minutes, stirring constantly with a wooden spoon.

Remove the artichokes from the heat and transfer them to a warmed serving dish. Pour over the cream sauce and sprinkle with the nutmeg. Serve the

artichokes immediately.

Asparagus with Eggs

This delicately-flavoured dish is easy and quick to make and is an elegant start to a dinner, or, accompanied by salad and brown bread and butter, a light snack lunch.

6 SERVINGS
3 lb. frozen asparagus, thawed and drained
3 hard-boiled eggs, shells removed and chopped
2 tablespoons finely chopped fresh parsley
½ teaspoon salt

¼ teaspoon freshly ground black pepper
6 oz. [¾ cup] butter, melted
2 tablespoons lemon juice

Cook the asparagus for 4 to 6 minutes according to the method indicated on page 2 (under Asparagus with Butter Sauce).

Meanwhile, using a fork, thoroughly blend the eggs, parsley, salt and black pepper in a medium-sized mixing bowl. Stirring constantly, add the melted butter, a little at a time. Continue stirring until the sauce is smooth, then stir in the lemon juice.

Drain the asparagus and transfer it to a large, heated serving dish. Pour over the sauce and serve the asparagus at once.

Aubergines Gratinées

This excellent vegetarian dish can be served either as a main course on its own, or as an accompaniment to meat or chicken.

4 SERVINGS

4 aubergines [eggplants], sliced and dégorged
3 oz. [¾ cup] flour
3 fl. oz. [⅜ cup] vegetable oil
5 oz. [1¼ cups] Parmesan cheese, grated
1 oz. [⅓ cup] dry white breadcrumbs
1 oz. [2 tablespoons] butter, cut into small pieces
SAUCE
1½ oz. [3 tablespoons] butter
1 small onion, finely chopped
3 tablespoons flour
14 oz. canned peeled tomatoes
1 teaspoon tomato purée
½ teaspoon dried basil
¼ teaspoon black pepper
½ teaspoon salt

To make the sauce, in a saucepan, melt the butter over moderate heat. When the foam subsides, add the onion and fry for 5 minutes or until it is soft. Stir in the flour and cook for 1 minute.

Strain the liquid from the tomatoes and stir it into the onion mixture. Add the tomatoes, tomato purée, basil, pepper and salt. Bring to the boil, stirring constantly. Reduce the heat to low, cover and simmer the sauce for 15 minutes.

Preheat the oven to moderate 350°F (Gas Mark 4, 180°C).

Dry the aubergine [eggplant] slices with kitchen paper towels. Dip the slices into the flour to coat. In a large frying-pan, heat half the oil over moderately

high heat. When the oil is hot, add the aubergine slices, a few at a time. Fry, turning occasionally with tongs, until they are well browned. Remove and drain on kitchen paper towels. Keep hot while you fry the remaining slices in the same way, adding more oil if necessary.

Pour a layer of the sauce into an oven-proof casserole. Sprinkle over some of the cheese, then put in a layer of aubergines [eggplants]. Continue making layers until all the ingredients are used up, finishing with a layer of sauce. Sprinkle over the remaining cheese and all the breadcrumbs. Dot with the butter. Bake in the oven for 25 minutes or until golden brown. Serve at once.

Caponata

A tangy vegetable dish, Caponata may be served as an appetizer to a dinner or as an extra-special accompaniment to cold roasted meat.

4-6 SERVINGS

4 small aubergines [eggplants], peeled, diced and dégorged
4 fl. oz. [½ cup] olive oil
4 celery stalks, thinly sliced
2 large onions, thinly sliced
4 oz. tomato purée diluted in 2 fl. oz. [¼ cup] water
1 tablespoon capers
2 oz. green olives, chopped
3 fl. oz. [⅜ cup] red wine vinegar
1 tablespoon sugar

Rinse the aubergines [eggplants] with cold water and pat them dry with kitchen paper towels.

In a large frying-pan, heat 3 fluid ounces [⅜ cup] of oil over moderate heat.

Versatile Aubergines Gratinées is delicious with meat or on its own.

Add the diced aubergines [eggplants] and cook for 8 to 10 minutes, or until they are soft and brown. Remove them from the pan and drain them in a colander. Dry them slightly on kitchen paper towels and set aside.

Pour the remaining oil into the pan and add the celery and onions. Cook for 8 minutes, or until they are lightly coloured. Pour in the tomato purée mixture and stir to coat the vegetables. Reduce the heat to low and simmer the mixture, covered, for 15 minutes.

Stir in the capers, olives, vinegar and sugar. Return the aubergines [eggplants] to the pan and coat with the sauce. Cook over low heat for 20 minutes.

Remove the caponata from the heat and transfer it to a serving dish. Chill in the refrigerator for at least 2 hours, or until you are ready to serve.

Imam Bayeldi

A classic Turkish dish of aubergines [eggplants] stuffed with tomatoes, raisins and onions, Imam Bayeldi means, literally, 'the priest has fainted'.

4-6 SERVINGS

4 aubergines [eggplants]
1½ teaspoons salt
2 oz. [¼ cup] butter
4 onions, thinly sliced
2 garlic cloves, crushed
6 large tomatoes, blanched, peeled, seeded and chopped
2 oz. [⅓ cup] raisins
1 teaspoon black pepper

½ teaspoon dried thyme
1 tablespoon chopped fresh parsley
10 fl. oz. [1¼ cups] olive oil

Halve the aubergines [eggplants] and hollow out four deep slits, ¼-inch wide, crosswise in each half, reserving the scooped out flesh. Sprinkle with 1 teaspoon of the salt and dégorge for 30 minutes. Drain the aubergines [eggplants] and set aside.

Meanwhile, in a large frying-pan, melt the butter over moderate heat. When the foam subsides, add the onions and garlic and cook them, stirring occasionally, for 5 to 7 minutes, or until they are soft and translucent but not brown.

Add the tomatoes, raisins, reserved aubergine [eggplant] flesh, the remaining salt, the pepper, thyme and parsley. Reduce the heat to low and simmer the mixture, stirring occasionally, for 10 to 12 minutes, or until it has pulped. Remove the pan from the heat and allow the mixture to cool.

Preheat the oven to cool 300°F (Gas Mark 2, 150°C).

When the mixture is cool, spoon it into the slits in the reserved aubergine [eggplant] halves. Spread the remaining mixture over the top of each half.

Place the aubergines [eggplants] in an ovenproof dish large enough to hold them in one layer. Spoon 1 tablespoon of olive oil over the top of each aubergine [eggplant] half, then pour the remaining oil carefully around them. The oil should come about one-quarter of the way up the sides of the aubergines [eggplants].

Bake the mixture for 1¾ hours, or until the aubergines [eggplants] are very soft and there is a slightly sticky residue on the bottom of the dish.

Remove the dish from the oven and cool to room temperature. Chill the aubergines [eggplants] in the refrigerator for 1 hour, or until they are very cold.

Remove the dish from the refrigerator, carefully transfer the aubergines [eggplants] to a serving dish and serve.

Guacamole

☆   ① ①   ⧖

A piquant dish from Latin America, Guacamole is equally good as a dip or a dressing.

12 FLUID OUNCES [1½ CUPS]
3 medium-sized avocados
3 teaspoons lemon juice
2 teaspoons olive oil
½ teaspoon salt
½ teaspoon black pepper
½ teaspoon ground coriander
1 hard-boiled egg, finely chopped
½ small green pepper, white pith removed, seeded and chopped
1½ chillis, blanched and chopped
2 spring onions [scallions], chopped
1 tomato, blanched, peeled, seeded and chopped

Halve the avocados. Slice off the skins and cut out the stones. Discard the stones and skin. Place the flesh in a mixing bowl and mash it with a fork.

Add the lemon juice, oil, salt, pepper and coriander, and stir to blend. Still stirring, add the egg, green pepper, chillis, spring onions [scallions] and tomato. The dip should be fairly thick. It is best used immediately, but if it is to be kept, cover the bowl with foil and store in the refrigerator. Stir well before serving.

The perfect start to any festive meal – colourful Guacamole!

Harvard Beets

One of the most famous of all American vegetable dishes, Harvard Beets makes a delicious and unusual accompaniment to fried calf's or lamb's liver or tender boiled beef.

4 SERVINGS

2 oz. [¼ cup] sugar
1 teaspoon cornflour [cornstarch]
2 fl. oz. [¼ cup] vinegar
4 fl. oz. [½ cup] water
1 lb. cooked beetroots [beets],
    thinly sliced

In a small mixing bowl, combine the sugar and cornflour [cornstarch] and set the bowl aside.

In a medium-sized saucepan, heat the vinegar and water together over low heat. When the mixture is lukewarm, gradually add the sugar mixture, stirring constantly with a wooden spoon until it is completely absorbed. Bring the mixture to the boil and cook, stirring constantly, for 2 minutes, or until the sauce is fairly thick and smooth.

Add the beetroots [beets] to the pan and stir to baste well. Simmer the beetroots [beets] for 5 to 8 minutes, or until they are heated through.

Remove the pan from the heat and serve at once.

Broccoli Soufflé, filled with tiny new potatoes, makes a delicious vegetable accompaniment to roasts or fish.

Broccoli Soufflé

A tasty and attractive dish, Broccoli Soufflé may be filled with tiny, new boiled potatoes and served with almost any meat or fish dish.

6 SERVINGS

1½ oz. [3 tablespoons] butter
1 oz. [¼ cup] plus 1 tablespoon flour
10 fl. oz. [1¼ cups] water
1½ teaspoons salt
1½ lb. broccoli, trimmed, washed
    and cut into small pieces
1 garlic clove
8 fl. oz. double cream [1 cup heavy
    cream]
4 eggs, separated and the yolks
    lightly beaten
¼ teaspoon black pepper
2 oz. [½ cup] Parmesan cheese,
    grated

Grease a 2-pint [1¼-quart] ring mould with 1 tablespoon of butter and lightly coat the mould with 1 tablespoon of flour. Knock out any excess flour and set the mould aside.

In a large saucepan bring the water, with 1 teaspoon salt, to the boil. Place the broccoli and garlic in the water, bring the water back to the boil, cover the pan and cook the broccoli over moderate heat for 15 minutes. Discard the garlic.

Drain the broccoli, chop it finely and set it aside in a large bowl.

Preheat the oven to moderate 350°F (Gas Mark 4, 180°C).

In a medium-sized saucepan melt the remaining butter over low heat. Stir in the remaining flour. Cook for 1 minute, stirring constantly. Slowly add the cream, stirring constantly with a wooden spoon. When the sauce is thick and smooth, stir in the broccoli. Remove the pan from the heat and stir in the beaten egg yolks, the remaining ½ teaspoon of salt and the pepper.

In a medium-sized mixing bowl, using a wire whisk, beat the egg whites until they form stiff peaks. With a metal spoon, carefully fold the egg whites into the broccoli mixture. Turn the mixture into the buttered mould. Stand the mould in a pan of boiling water and bake it in the oven for 35 to 40 minutes, or until the soufflé has risen and is set.

Remove the mould from the oven and loosen the soufflé with a knife. Place a serving platter, inverted, over the mould and reverse the two. The soufflé should slide out easily. Sprinkle over the Parmesan cheese and serve at once.

Carrot Cake

This unusual American Jewish cake is made with eggs, carrots and ground almonds. The finished cake has a moist consistency rather like cheesecake. Serve with tea or coffee as a morning or afternoon snack.

ONE 9-INCH CAKE

1 teaspoon butter
6 eggs, separated
8 oz. [1 cup] sugar
12 oz. carrots, cooked and puréed
1 tablespoon finely grated orange rind
1 tablespoon brandy
12 oz. [2 cups] ground almonds

Preheat the oven to warm 325°F (Gas Mark 3, 170°C). With the teaspoon of butter, lightly grease a 9-inch loose-bottomed cake tin.

In a medium-sized bowl, beat the egg yolks with a wire whisk until they begin to thicken. Gradually add the sugar and continue beating until the mixture is thick and creamy. Add the carrot purée, orange rind, brandy and almonds and stir to mix thoroughly.

In a large bowl, beat the egg whites with a wire whisk or a rotary beater until they form stiff peaks. With a metal spoon or rubber spatula, carefully fold the egg whites into the carrot mixture.

Pour the mixture into the cake tin and bake in the centre of the oven for about 50 minutes, or until a skewer inserted into the centre of the cake comes out clean.

Remove the cake from the oven and leave it to cool in the tin for 15 minutes. Turn the cake out on to a wire rack to cool completely.

Serve cold.

Carrots and Onions with Raisins in Wine Sauce

A fascinating and exotic-tasting blend of vegetables and herbs, Carrots and Onions with Raisins in Wine Sauce makes a most impressive accompaniment to meat at a dinner party.

4 SERVINGS

2 oz. [¼ cup] butter
1 lb. carrots, scraped and cut into 1-inch slices
8 oz. small white onions, peeled and left whole
4 oz. [⅔ cup] sultanas or seedless raisins

1 teaspoon salt
1 teaspoon black pepper
½ teaspoon cayenne pepper
1 teaspoon dried thyme
1 bay leaf
4 fl. oz. [½ cup] medium-dry white wine
2 fl. oz. double cream [¼ cup heavy cream]

In a large saucepan, melt the butter over moderate heat. When the foam subsides, add the carrots, onions and sultanas or raisins. Cook them, stirring constantly, for 4 minutes. Add the salt, pepper, cayenne, thyme and bay leaf to the pan. Pour in the wine, mixing well to blend. Cover the pan, reduce the heat to very low and simmer for 45 to 50 minutes, or until the carrots and onions are tender but still firm.

Remove the pan from the heat and remove and discard the bay leaf. Stir in the cream. Return the pan to very low heat for 1 to 2 minutes to warm the sauce slightly. Turn into a warmed serving dish and serve the mixture immediately.

Carrots and Onions with Raisins in Wine Sauce makes an interesting and 'different' vegetable accompaniment to plain meat dishes.

Pain de Chou Fleur

CAULIFLOWER LOAF

This beautifully elegant supper party dish makes a spectacular accompaniment to grilled [broiled] steak or to a roast. Served with a tossed mixed salad and brown bread, it is a complete and light spring luncheon in itself.

4-6 SERVINGS

2 medium-sized cauliflowers, broken into flowerets
1 tablespoon plus 1 teaspoon butter
1½ lb. potatoes, cooked and quartered
2 teaspoons salt
1 teaspoon white pepper
¼ teaspoon cayenne pepper
6 eggs
5 oz. [1¼ cups] Gruyère cheese, grated

Place the cauliflowers in a large saucepan and add enough water just to cover. Place the pan over moderately high heat and bring the water to the boil. Reduce the heat to moderate and cook the cauliflowers for 12 to 15 minutes or until the flowerets are very tender. Drain the flowerets in a colander and set aside.

Preheat the oven to moderate 350°F (Gas Mark 4, 180°C). Lightly grease a 4-pint [2½-quart] mould with the teaspoon of butter. Set aside.

Place the cauliflower, potatoes, the remaining butter, the salt, pepper and cayenne in a large mixing bowl. With a potato masher or fork, mash the ingredients together to form a purée. Add the eggs, one by one, beating well between each addition. Alternatively, purée the cauliflower and potatoes with the butter, seasoning and eggs in an electric blender.

Add 4½ ounces [1 cup plus 2 tablespoons] of the grated cheese and stir until it blends into the mixture.

Spoon the purée into the mould. Cover it tightly with aluminium foil and place the mould in a roasting tin one-third full of boiling water. Place the tin in the centre of the oven and bake the mixture for 1 hour.

Remove the roasting tin from the oven and remove the mould from the tin. Remove the aluminium foil. Place a heat-proof serving dish, inverted, over the top of the mould and turn the loaf out. Sprinkle the top of the loaf with the remaining grated cheese and put the dish

Walnut Cauliflower is warming, filling and so good to eat. Serve on its own or as an accompaniment.

back into the oven. Bake for a further 5 minutes to melt the cheese.

Remove the loaf from the oven and serve immediately.

Walnut Cauliflower

Cooked cauliflower covered in a creamy, mustard-flavoured walnut sauce, Walnut Cauliflower may be served as a vegetable accompaniment to plain meat dishes or as a vegetarian meal.

4-6 SERVINGS

1 oz. [2 tablespoons] butter
1 oz. [¼ cup] flour
12 fl. oz. [1½ cups] milk
6 fl. oz. single cream [¾ cup light cream]
1 egg, lightly beaten
2 fl. oz. [¼ cup] cider vinegar
2 tablespoons soft brown sugar
2 tablespoons prepared French mustard
4 oz. [⅔ cup] walnuts, coarsely chopped and toasted
1 medium-sized cauliflower, cooked until tender and kept hot

In a medium-sized saucepan, melt the butter over moderate heat. Remove the pan from the heat and, using a wooden spoon, stir in the flour to make a smooth paste. A little at a time, add the milk and cream, stirring constantly and being careful to avoid lumps. Add the egg, vinegar, sugar and mustard. Return the pan to low heat and cook, stirring constantly, for a further 2 to 3 minutes or until the sauce is thick and smooth. Do not allow the sauce to come to the boil or the egg will scramble. Stir in the walnuts and cook for a further 1 minute, stirring constantly.

Remove the pan from the heat. Place the cauliflower on a warmed serving dish and pour over the sauce.

Serve at once.

Celery with Almonds

The almonds in this celery dish give it a crisp and unusual texture. Celery with Almonds makes an excellent accompaniment to roast pork.

4 SERVINGS

2 medium-sized heads of celery, washed and the stalks cut into 2-inch lengths
2 oz. [¼ cup] butter
1 small onion, chopped
½ teaspoon salt
¼ teaspoon black pepper
1 tablespoon flour

8 fl. oz. single cream [1 cup light cream]
5 fl. oz. [⅝ cup] chicken stock
6 oz. [1½ cups] almonds, toasted and shredded

Prepare, parboil and drain the celery. In a medium-sized saucepan, melt the butter over moderate heat. Add the celery, onion, salt and pepper. Tightly cover the pan and reduce the heat to low. Cook for 15 minutes. Stir occasionally and, if the celery shows signs of sticking to the pan, add a little water.

Remove the pan from the heat. Sprinkle the flour into the pan and mix well. Gradually add the cream and stock, stirring constantly. Replace over moderate heat and cook, stirring constantly, until the sauce boils and thickens. Remove from the heat, stir in the almonds, and serve.

Endive Farcie

CHICORY [FRENCH OR BELGIAN ENDIVE] LEAVES STUFFED WITH CREAM CHEESE

Endive Farcie is a delectable dish of chicory [French or Belgian endive] leaves stuffed with a mixture of cream cheese, cream, mustard and mixed nuts. The leaves are rolled and fastened, and served cold as an appetizer or as a snack with drinks.

6-8 SERVINGS

6 oz. cream cheese
3 fl. oz. double cream [⅜ cup heavy cream]
⅛ teaspoon cayenne pepper
¼ teaspoon salt
¼ teaspoon black pepper
½ teaspoon French mustard
1 teaspoon Worcestershire sauce
2½ oz. [½ cup] walnuts, finely chopped
2½ oz. [½ cup] hazelnuts, finely chopped
20 medium-sized to large chicory [French or Belgian endive] leaves, washed and shaken dry

In a medium-sized mixing bowl, mash the cream cheese with a fork until it is soft and smooth. Add the cream, cayenne, salt, pepper, mustard and Worcestershire sauce and beat well to blend the ingredients thoroughly. Stir in the nuts.

Lay the chicory [endive] leaves on a clean, flat surface. Put about 1 tablespoon of the cheese mixture on the base end of each leaf. Roll the leaves up and fasten each roll with a cocktail stick.

Arrange the stuffed leaves on a serving platter and place it in the refrigerator to chill for at least 30 minutes before serving.

233

Courgettes Gratinées à la Milanaise

COURGETTES [ZUCCHINI] BAKED WITH CHEESE

A light and subtle blend of tastes, Courgettes Gratinées à la Milanaise makes an excellent accompaniment to grilled [broiled] or roasted meats. Or serve with a tossed salad and brown bread and butter for an informal lunch.

4 SERVINGS

8 medium-sized courgettes [zucchini], trimmed, cleaned and blanched
2 oz. [¼ cup] butter
2 tablespoons olive oil
½ teaspoon salt
½ teaspoon white pepper
4 oz. [1 cup] Parmesan cheese, grated
1 oz. [2 tablespoons] melted butter

Using a sharp knife, cut the courgettes [zucchini] into ½-inch slices, crosswise, and dry them thoroughly on kitchen paper towels.

Preheat the oven to hot 425°F (Gas Mark 7, 220°C). Grease a large, ovenproof baking dish with a teaspoon of the butter.

In a large frying-pan, melt the remaining butter with the olive oil over moderate heat. When the foam subsides, add the courgette [zucchini] slices to the pan and cook them for 3 minutes, stirring occasionally to prevent them from sticking to the bottom of the pan. Add the salt and pepper. Remove the frying-pan from the heat.

Sprinkle the bottom of the baking dish with one-quarter of the grated cheese. Cover the cheese with a layer of courgette [zucchini] slices and on top of them spread a second layer of about 1 ounce [¼ cup] of grated cheese. Sprinkle 1 tablespoon of the melted butter over the cheese. Repeat the layers until all the courgettes [zucchini] and cheese have been used, then pour over the remaining melted butter.

Bake in the top part of the oven for 15 minutes, or until the courgettes [zucchini] are cooked and tender.

Serve immediately.

Zucchini Ripieni

STUFFED COURGETTES

These tasty stuffed courgettes [zucchini] are a regional speciality from Liguria in the north of Italy. Serve Zucchini Ripieni as a vegetable accompaniment to a plain

meat dish, especially grilled [broiled] steaks or fried calf's liver.

6 SERVINGS

½ oz. dried mushrooms
12 medium-sized courgettes [zucchini], trimmed and cleaned
2 oz. [1 cup] fresh white breadcrumbs, soaked in 4 tablespoons milk
2 eggs, lightly beaten
½ teaspoon salt
1 teaspoon freshly ground black pepper
2 teaspoons finely chopped fresh oregano or 1 teaspoon dried oregano
6 oz. [1½ cups] Parmesan cheese, finely grated
2 oz. prosciutto, chopped
2 fl. oz. [¼ cup] olive oil

Place the dried mushrooms in a medium-sized mixing bowl, pour over enough water to cover and set aside to soak for 30 minutes. Drain the mushrooms, chop them finely and set aside.

Bring a large saucepan of salted water to the boil over high heat. Add the courgettes [zucchini] and boil for 7 to 8 minutes or until they are just tender when pierced with the point of a sharp knife. Remove the pan from the heat and drain the courgettes [zucchini] in a colander. With a sharp knife, slice the vegetables, lengthways, in half and, using a teaspoon, scoop out the flesh from each half, taking care not to break the skins. Set aside.

With your hands, squeeze any excess moisture out of the breadcrumbs and place them in a medium-sized mixing bowl. Add the reserved courgette [zucchini] flesh, the eggs, salt, pepper, oregano, half the cheese, the prosciutto and the reserved mushrooms. Using your hands or a wooden spoon, mix all the ingredients together until they are thoroughly combined.

Preheat the oven to fairly hot 400°F (Gas Mark 6, 200°C). Using a pastry brush, coat a shallow ovenproof casserole, large enough to take all the vegetables in one layer, with a little of the oil. Set the casserole aside.

Using a teaspoon, spoon a little of the stuffing into each courgette [zucchini] half and sprinkle the remaining cheese over the tops. Place the courgettes [zucchini] in the casserole and sprinkle with the remaining oil.

Place the casserole in the centre of the oven and cook for 15 minutes or until the cheese has melted and the courgettes [zucchini] are golden on top. Remove the casserole from the oven and transfer the

courgettes [zucchini] to a warmed serving dish.

Serve immediately.

Fenouils à la Grecque

FENNELS GREEK-STYLE

An extremely aromatic dish, Fenouils à la Grecque is usually eaten — either hot or cold — as an hors d'oeuvre. If fennel is not available, artichoke hearts can be substituted.

4 SERVINGS

2 heads of fennel
4 tablespoons olive oil
8 oz. small white onions, peeled and left whole
1 teaspoon salt
½ teaspoon white pepper
½ teaspoon cayenne pepper
½ teaspoon ground coriander
½ teaspoon finely chopped fresh thyme or ¼ teaspoon dried thyme
1 bay leaf
2 tablespoons tomato purée
3 fl. oz. [⅜ cup] dry white wine
2 oz. [⅓ cup] sultanas or raisins

Wash and trim the fennel and discard any withered outer leaves. Cut the heads into quarters and set side.

In a large frying-pan, heat the olive oil over moderate heat. When the oil is hot, add the fennel pieces and small onions. Fry them, stirring occasionally, for 4 to 5 minutes. Add the salt, pepper, cayenne, coriander, thyme, bay leaf and tomato purée to the pan and mix to blend thoroughly.

Add the wine, cover the pan and reduce the heat to very low. Simmer for 30 minutes, or until the vegetables are tender. Halfway through the cooking period, add the sultanas or raisins.

When the vegetables are cooked, remove the pan from the heat and remove and discard the bay leaf.

Serve at once, if you are serving the dish hot.

Jerusalem Artichoke Soufflé

This delicious and unusual soufflé can be served as a light lunch dish with lots of melba toast or crusty bread and butter, or on its own as a first course for a lunch or dinner party.

4-6 SERVINGS

2 oz. [¼ cup] plus 1 teaspoon butter
2 oz. [½ cup] flour
10 fl. oz. [1¼ cups] milk
½ teaspoon salt

Fenouils à la Grecque is usually eaten as an aromatic hors d'oeuvre.

¼ teaspoon freshly ground black pepper

⅛ teaspoon cayenne pepper

¼ teaspoon finely chopped fresh oregano or ⅛ teaspoon dried oregano

2 oz. [½ cup] Parmesan cheese, grated

8 oz. Jerusalem artichokes, peeled, simmered for about 30 minutes or until tender and drained

2 tablespoons double [heavy] cream

4 egg yolks

5 egg whites

Preheat the oven to fairly hot 375°F (Gas Mark 5, 190°C).

Using 1 teaspoon of the butter, grease a 3-pint [1½-quart] soufflé dish. Tie a strip of greaseproof or waxed paper around the rim of the soufflé dish so that it projects about 2 inches over the top. Set the soufflé dish aside.

In a large, heavy saucepan, melt the remaining butter over moderate heat. Remove the pan from the heat and, with a wooden spoon, stir in the flour to make a smooth paste. Gradually stir in the milk, being careful to avoid lumps.

Return the pan to the heat and cook the sauce for 2 to 3 minutes, stirring constantly, or until it becomes very thick and smooth.

Remove the pan from the heat. Stir in the salt, pepper, cayenne, oregano and cheese. Set aside to cool slightly.

Meanwhile, place a fine strainer over a medium-sized mixing bowl. Using the back of a wooden spoon, rub the cooked artichokes through the strainer to make a purée.

Stir the puréed artichokes and the cream into the sauce mixture. Stir in the egg yolks and combine the mixture thoroughly. Set aside.

In a medium-sized mixing bowl, beat the egg whites with a wire whisk or rotary beater until they form stiff peaks.

Using a metal spoon, carefully fold the egg whites into the artichoke mixture.

Spoon the mixture into the prepared soufflé dish. Place the dish in the centre of the oven and bake for 35 to 40 minutes, or until the soufflé has risen and is golden brown on top.

Remove the dish from the oven. Quickly remove and discard the paper collar.

Serve the soufflé immediately.

235

Mushrooms Baked with Cream and Sherry

This unusual dinner party hors d'oeuvre is a luscious concoction of mushrooms flavoured with cream and sherry.

4 SERVINGS

1 oz. [2 tablespoons] butter
1 teaspoon lemon juice
1 teaspoon salt
3 slices of buttered toast, cut about
½ inch thick and with crusts
removed
1 lb. mushrooms, wiped clean and
with the stems removed
½ teaspoon black pepper
4 fl. oz. double cream [½ cup heavy
cream]
1 tablespoon sherry

Preheat the oven to fairly hot 375°F (Gas Mark 5, 190°C).

In a small mixing bowl, combine the butter with ½ teaspoon lemon juice and ½ teaspoon salt, beating with a wooden spoon until the mixture becomes light and creamy.

Coat the bottom and sides of a deep, round ovenproof dish with the mixture and arrange the toast slices on the bottom. Pile the mushroom caps, pyramid-style, on the toast. Season the pyramid with the remaining salt, pepper and lemon juice and cover it with 3

Mushrooms Baked with Cream and Sherry is an unusual hors d'oeuvre.

fluid ounces [⅜ cup] of cream.

Cover the dish and bake in the oven for 15 to 20 minutes. Five minutes before the end of the cooking period, add the remaining cream to the mixture.

Remove the dish from the oven and sprinkle the mushrooms with the sherry.

Onions in Sweet and Sour Sauce

An adaptation of a famous Italian recipe, Onions in Sweet and Sour Sauce may be eaten hot as a vegetable accompaniment, or cold as part of a cold buffet or hors d'oeuvre.

6 SERVINGS

3 fl. oz. [⅜ cup] olive oil
1 lb. pickling (pearl) onions, peeled
and blanched for 5 minutes
2 fl. oz. [¼ cup] malt vinegar
2 tablespoons soft brown sugar
3 oz. [½ cup] walnuts, chopped
3 oz. [½ cup] raisins (optional)

In a medium-sized saucepan, heat the oil over moderate heat. When the oil is hot, add the onions and cook, stirring occasionally, for 8 to 10 minutes, or until they are lightly browned. With a slotted spoon,

transfer the onions to a plate.

Add the vinegar and sugar to the pan and cook, stirring frequently, for 5 minutes, or until the sugar has dissolved and the mixture is hot. Return the onions to the pan and cook for 3 minutes, basting frequently.

Stir in the walnuts and raisins, if you are using them, and cook for 2 minutes.

Remove the pan from the heat and transfer the onion mixture to a warmed serving dish. Serve immediately if you are serving the dish hot. Or set aside to cool, if you are serving cold.

Stuffed Green Peppers

Peppers stuffed with scrambled eggs, onion and cheese, Stuffed Green Peppers make a light and colourful first course or a vegetable accompaniment to a main course. Serve them hot on their own or cold with French dressing with chopped parsley.

6 SERVINGS

1 teaspoon olive oil
6 medium-sized green peppers,
wiped clean
4 eggs
½ teaspoon salt
½ teaspoon black pepper
2 teaspoons flour
2 tablespoons milk
1 large onion, finely chopped

1 garlic clove, crushed
2 oz. [½ cup] Parmesan cheese,
    grated
2 tablespoons chopped fresh
    parsley
2 egg yolks
2 egg whites, stiffly beaten

With the teaspoon of olive oil, lightly grease a medium-sized baking dish and set it aside.

With a sharp knife, slice off a 1-inch strip from the wider end of each pepper. Chop each pepper strip into small dice. Carefully remove and discard the white pith and seeds from the inside of each pepper. Set aside.

Half-fill a large saucepan with water and bring it to the boil over moderately high heat. Add the peppers and blanch them for 5 minutes. Remove the saucepan from the heat. Using a slotted spoon, remove the peppers from the water and pat them dry with kitchen paper towels. Set aside.

Preheat the oven to moderate 350°F (Gas Mark 4, 180°C).

In a medium-sized heatproof mixing bowl, set over a saucepan half-filled with hot water, combine the eggs, salt, pepper, flour and milk. Beating constantly with a wire whisk or rotary beater, cook the mixture over low heat until it thickens.

Remove the pan from the heat and stir in the onion, garlic, chopped pepper, cheese and parsley. When these are thoroughly incorporated, fold in the egg yolks and then the egg whites with a metal spoon.

Spoon equal quantities of the egg mixture into each pepper.

Stand the peppers upright in the prepared baking dish and place the dish in the centre of the oven. Bake for 20 to 25 minutes or until the tops are golden brown.

Remove the dish from the oven and transfer the peppers to a warmed serving dish. Either serve them immediately or leave them to cool.

Peperonata

Peperonata is equally good hot or cold and will keep for several days if stored in a screw-top jar.

4-6 SERVINGS

1 oz. [2 tablespoons] butter
2 tablespoons olive oil
1 large onion, thinly sliced
1 garlic clove, crushed
1 lb. red peppers, white pith
    removed, seeded and cut into
    strips

1 lb. tomatoes, blanched, peeled and
    chopped
½ teaspoon salt
¼ teaspoon black pepper
1 bay leaf

In a large saucepan, heat the butter with the oil over moderate heat. When the foam subsides, add the onion and garlic and fry, stirring occasionally, for 5 to 7 minutes or until the onion is soft and translucent but not brown.

Add the red peppers. Cover, reduce the heat to low and cook for 15 minutes. Add the tomatoes, salt, pepper and bay leaf and simmer for 25 minutes.

Remove the pan from the heat and remove and discard the bay leaf. Serve at once, if you are serving hot.

Petits Pois à la Française

One of the classic vegetable dishes of French cuisine, Petits Pois à la Française is easy both to prepare and to eat! Serve it with

Petits Pois à la Française is one of the classics of French cuisine.

omelets, or with grilled [broiled] chops or steaks.

4-6 SERVINGS

1½ lb. small fresh garden peas,
    weighed after shelling or 1½ lb.
    frozen petits pois
1 teaspoon salt
½ teaspoon black pepper
1 teaspoon sugar
1 onion, thinly sliced
4 lettuce leaves, washed, shaken dry
    and shredded
1 tablespoon butter blended into a
    paste with 1 tablespoon flour

Place the peas, salt, pepper, sugar, onion and lettuce in a large saucepan. Pour over enough hot water to cover the peas and set the pan over moderately high heat. Bring the water to the boil.

Reduce the heat to very low, cover the pan and simmer the pea mixture for 20 to 30 minutes or until the onion is soft and translucent and the peas are very tender. Stir in the butter mixture, a little at a time, stirring constantly. Simmer the mixture for 2 minutes or until it has thickened.

Remove the pan from the heat. Spoon the mixture into a warmed serving dish and serve immediately.

Pommes de Terre Galette

A golden, crisp potato cake, Pommes de Terre Galette is excellent served with grilled [broiled] fish or meat.

4 SERVINGS

2 lb. potatoes, peeled and cooked
1 small onion, finely chopped
2 teaspoons salt
¼ teaspoon black pepper
1 tablespoon chopped fresh parsley
2 oz. [¼ cup] butter, softened
2 eggs, lightly beaten
½ teaspoon paprika

Preheat the oven to fairly hot 375°F (Gas Mark 5, 190°C).

With a potato masher or fork, mash the potatoes and place them in a medium-sized mixing bowl. Add the onion, salt, pepper and parsley and mix well.

Beat in 1½ ounces [3 tablespoons] of the butter and the eggs and stir until the ingredients are well blended.

Using the remaining butter, generously grease a medium-sized baking dish. Spoon the mixture into the dish, flattening the top with a palette knife. Sprinkle over the paprika.

Place the dish in the oven and bake the mixture for 20 to 30 minutes or until it is golden brown and crisp.

Remove the dish from the oven and cut the galette into wedges. Serve immediately.

Potatoes Country-Style

This sustaining mixture of fried potato cubes, onion, bread croûtons and eggs, makes a filling accompaniment to lamb chops or ham. Or, served with lots of cold beer and crusty bread, it may be served as a snack lunch.

4-6 SERVINGS

1½ lb. potatoes, weighed after peeling
2 teaspoons salt
2 oz. [¼ cup] butter
2 medium-sized onions, finely chopped
1 garlic clove, crushed
2 thick slices day-old white bread, crusts removed and cut into cubes
3 eggs
3 fl. oz. [⅜ cup] milk
½ teaspoon black pepper
¼ teaspoon dried thyme
1 tablespoon chopped fresh parsley

Place the potatoes in a large saucepan and pour over enough water just to cover. Add 1 teaspoon of the salt and place the pan over high heat. Bring the water to the

boil, reduce the heat to moderate and cook the potatoes for 8 minutes. Remove the pan from the heat and drain the potatoes. Set aside to cool slightly.

When the potatoes are cool enough to handle, transfer them to a chopping board. With a sharp knife, cut them into cubes and set aside.

Meanwhile, in a large, deep frying-pan, melt the butter over moderate heat. When the foam subsides, add the onions, garlic and bread cubes and cook, stirring occasionally, for 8 to 10 minutes or until the onions are golden brown.

Add the potato cubes to the pan and cook them, turning occasionally, for 5 to 8 minutes or until the potatoes are tender when pierced with the point of a sharp knife.

Meanwhile, in a small mixing bowl, beat the eggs, milk, the remaining salt, the pepper and thyme together until they are well blended.

Pour the egg mixture over the potato mixture and cook, stirring and turning constantly, for 3 minutes or until the eggs are cooked and the mixture is still moist.

Remove the pan from the heat and transfer the mixture to a warmed serving dish. Sprinkle over the parsley and serve at once.

Duchess Potatoes

This elegant potato purée can be piped around a meat entrée and served as it is, or it can be browned in the oven. It makes an excellent accompaniment to roast meats or steaks.

4-6 SERVINGS

1 lb. potatoes, thickly sliced
2 teaspoons salt
1 teaspoon vegetable oil
2 oz. [¼ cup] butter, softened
2 egg yolks
1 teaspoon white pepper
½ teaspoon grated nutmeg

Place the potatoes in a saucepan. Pour over enough water to cover the potatoes and add 1 teaspoon of the salt. Bring the water to the boil over high heat. Reduce the heat to low, cover the pan and simmer for 20 to 25 minutes, or until the potatoes are soft. Drain well.

Preheat the oven to fairly hot 400°F (Gas Mark 6, 200°C). With the vegetable oil, grease a baking sheet. Set it aside.

With a potato masher, mash the

potatoes until they are completely smooth. Add the butter, egg yolks, pepper, nutmeg and the remaining salt to the purée and mix well.

If you wish to pipe the purée into decorative shapes, fill a forcing bag with the mixture. Pipe the potato on to the baking sheet in the shapes you wish. Place the sheet in the centre of the oven and bake for 10 minutes, or until the potato purée is golden-brown. Remove

A filling mixture of potato cubes, onion, croûtons and eggs, that's Potatoes Country-Style.

the purée from the sheet and serve.

Potatoes Provençal-Style

This rustic, hearty dish of potatoes cooked in oil, garlic and anchovies is an excellent accompaniment to stews and casseroles.

4 SERVINGS

2 fl. oz. [¼ cup] olive oil

2 garlic cloves, crushed
2 lb. potatoes, parboiled in their skins for 10 minutes
½ teaspoon salt
¼ teaspoon black pepper
6 anchovy fillets, halved
1 tablespoon chopped fresh parsley

In a large frying-pan, heat the oil over moderate heat. When the oil is hot, add the garlic and cook, stirring constantly,

for 3 minutes.

Peel the potatoes and cut them into ½-inch slices. Add the potatoes to the pan, sprinkle over the salt and pepper and cook them, turning once, for 10 to 12 minutes or until they are golden brown.

Just before serving, add the anchovy fillets and cook for a further 2 minutes.

Using a slotted spoon, transfer the potatoes to a warmed serving dish. Sprinkle with the parsley and serve.

Dulma

STUFFED AUBERGINES [EGGPLANTS],
COURGETTES [ZUCCHINI] AND TOMATOES

A colourful Middle Eastern dish of mixed vegetables stuffed with a tasty mixture of lamb and rice, Dulma may be served with saffron rice and salad.

6 SERVINGS

4 small aubergines [eggplants]
2 teaspoons salt
6 small courgettes [zucchini]
6 large tomatoes
2 tablespoons olive oil
1 large onion, finely chopped
2 garlic cloves, crushed
1½ lb. minced [ground] lamb
6 tablespoons cooked rice
3 tablespoons chopped fresh parsley
2 tablespoons coriander seeds, crushed
½ teaspoon ground cumin
1 teaspoon turmeric
½ teaspoon black pepper
2 eggs
1 oz. [2 tablespoons] melted butter

With a small, sharp knife, score the skin

Exotic Dulma makes an excitingly different lunch for special guests.

of the aubergines [eggplants] and cut them in half, lengthways. Sprinkle the halves with 1 teaspoon of salt and leave them to dégorge on kitchen paper towels for 30 minutes.

Wash the courgettes [zucchini] under cold running water and dry them thoroughly on kitchen paper towels. Cut about ½-inch off both ends of each courgette [zucchini]. With a teaspoon or apple corer, carefully scoop out the centre from each courgette [zucchini]. Discard the centre.

Cut the tops off the tomatoes and hollow out the centres. Discard the centres.

Wipe the moisture from the aubergines [eggplants] with kitchen paper towels. With a spoon, hollow out the centres, leaving a ½-inch shell. Discard the centres.

Preheat the oven to moderate 350°F (Gas Mark 4, 180°C).

In a large frying-pan, heat the oil over moderate heat. When the oil is hot, add the onion and garlic and fry for 8 to 10

minutes, or until the onion is browned.

Stir in the lamb and cook, stirring occasionally, for 10 minutes, or until the meat loses its pinkness.

Remove the pan from the heat and turn the mixture into a large mixing bowl.

Add the rice, parsley, coriander, cumin, turmeric, pepper and the remaining salt. With a wooden spoon, stir the eggs into the mixture. Beat the mixture vigorously until it is well blended.

Spoon the mixture into the courgettes [zucchini], tomatoes and aubergines [eggplants]. Replace the tomato lids.

Place the stuffed vegetables in a shallow ovenproof dish. Spoon the melted butter over the stuffed vegetables and place the dish in the oven.

Bake for 45 to 50 minutes, or until the vegetables are tender.

Remove the dish from the oven and serve at once.

Fried Mixed Vegetables

Fried Mixed Vegetables is a classic and very popular Chinese dish, which may be

served as part of a Chinese meal, or on its own as a vegetarian lunch or dinner.

2-4 SERVINGS

3 tablespoons vegetable oil
1 garlic clove, crushed
1-inch piece fresh root ginger,
  peeled and sliced
½ teaspoon salt
¼ teaspoon white pepper
2 carrots, scraped and thinly sliced
1 small green pepper, white pith
  removed, and shredded
1 very small cauliflower, trimmed
  washed and broken into flowerets
2 oz. bean sprouts, washed and
  shaken dry
5 fl. oz. [⅝ cup] chicken stock
2 teaspoons soy sauce
1 teaspoon soft brown sugar

In a large frying-pan, heat the oil over moderate heat. When it is hot, add the garlic, ginger, salt and pepper. Fry, stirring constantly, for 1 minute. Add the carrots and fry for a further minute, still stirring. Add the green pepper and cauliflower and stir-fry for 3 minutes. Add the bean sprouts and fry, stirring, for a further 1 minute. Stir in the stock, soy sauce and sugar. Cover the pan and cook for a further 4 minutes.

Remove the pan from the heat. Turn the vegetables into a warmed serving dish and serve immediately.

Légumes Nouveaux Flambés
MIXED FRESH VEGETABLES WITH BRANDY

Légumes Nouveaux Flambés (pictured on page 225) is a delicious way of cooking ordinary vegetables. Serve with braised lamb or pork chops.

8 SERVINGS

3 oz. [⅜ cup] butter
2 lb. carrots, scraped and cut into
  1-inch lengths
1 lb. turnips, peeled and chopped
1 lb. small white onions, peeled
1 teaspoon salt
1 teaspoon black pepper
2 tablespoons soft brown sugar
3 fl. oz. [⅜ cup] brandy
2 tablespoons chopped fresh parsley

In a large frying-pan, melt the butter over moderate heat. When the foam subsides, add the carrots, turnips and onions and coat them thoroughly with the butter. Add the salt, pepper and brown sugar, and stir to blend. Reduce the heat to low, cover the pan and cook the vegetables for 35 minutes, basting occasionally.

In a small saucepan, gently heat the brandy over low heat until it is hot but not boiling. Remove the pan from the heat and ignite the brandy with a match. While it is still flaming, pour it into the frying-pan. When the flames die down, re-cover the pan and cook the mixture for a further 10 minutes, or until the vegetables are tender but still firm.

Remove the pan from the heat and transfer the mixture to a warmed serving dish. Sprinkle over the chopped parsley and serve at once.

Vegetable Paella

A colourful version of a Spanish national dish, Vegetable Paella is delicious.

4-6 SERVINGS

4 fl. oz. [½ cup] olive oil
2 large onions, thinly sliced
2 garlic cloves, crushed
1 large red pepper, white pith
  removed, seeded and sliced
12 oz. [2 cups] long-grain rice,
  washed, soaked in cold water for
  30 minutes and drained
1 pint [2½ cups] vegetable stock
4 large tomatoes, blanched, peeled,
  seeded and chopped

This Chinese dish of Fried Mixed Vegetables is easy and quick to cook.

3 oz. frozen petits pois
2 celery stalks, chopped
18 black olives, halved and stoned
1 teaspoon salt
1 teaspoon black pepper
¼ teaspoon crushed saffron threads
  dissolved in 2 teaspoons hot water
2 oz. [½ cup] slivered almonds

In a saucepan, heat the oil over moderate heat. When the oil is hot, add the onions, garlic and red pepper. Cook, stirring occasionally, for 5 to 7 minutes or until the onions are soft and translucent but not brown. Stir in the rice, coating it well with the oil, and continue cooking, stirring occasionally, for 5 minutes. Pour in the stock and increase the heat to high. Bring the liquid to the boil. Reduce the heat to low and stir in the tomatoes, petits pois, celery, olives, salt, pepper and saffron. Cover and simmer the mixture for 35 minutes or until the rice is tender.

Remove the pan from the heat and turn the paella into a warmed dish. Sprinkle over the almonds and serve.

Boston Baked Beans

Flavoured with molasses and baked to a dark, rich brown, Boston Baked Beans is a traditional American dish. In colonial New England, this nourishing combination of beans, salt pork and molasses was often baked in the oven with the week's bread and then eaten with thick slices of the steaming hot, brown bread. Today, Boston Baked Beans are usually served with roast pork or ham.

6-8 SERVINGS

- 8 oz. salt pork
- 2 lb. dried haricot, pea or kidney beans, washed, soaked in cold water overnight and drained
- 2 teaspoons salt
- 1 large onion
- 3 oz. [½ cup] soft brown sugar
- 6 tablespoons molasses or black treacle
- 3 teaspoons dry mustard
- 1 teaspoon black pepper

Put the salt pork in a large bowl. Add cold water to cover. Soak the salt pork for 3 hours and drain well.

Place the beans in a saucepan and add enough cold water to cover. Add 1 teaspoon of salt. Bring the water to the boil over high heat. Boil the beans for 2 minutes. Remove the pan from the heat and let the beans soak in the water for 1 hour.

Return the pan to the heat and bring the beans to the boil again. Reduce the heat to very low, partially cover the pan and slowly simmer the beans for 30 minutes. Drain the beans and discard the liquid.

Preheat the oven to very cool 250°F (Gas Mark ½, 130°C).

Place the onion in the bottom of a flameproof casserole. Add a layer of the cooked, drained beans to the casserole.

Thickly slice the drained salt pork and cut each slice into small chunks. Arrange a layer of salt pork over the beans in the casserole. Add another layer of beans and finish with a layer of salt pork.

In a small mixing bowl, with a wooden spoon, mix together the brown sugar, molasses or treacle, mustard, black pepper and the remaining 1 teaspoon of salt. Spoon the mixture over the beans and pork. Add enough boiling water to cover the beans.

Cover the casserole and place it in the oven. Bake for 5 hours, adding boiling water from time to time so that the beans are always just covered.

Remove the lid of the casserole and bake uncovered for 45 minutes. Serve straight from the casserole.

Red Cabbage and Bacon Casserole

A hearty winter dish from Czechoslovakia, Red Cabbage and Bacon Casserole makes an economical and filling special lunch or supper. Accompany the casserole with fresh rye bread and butter and some well-chilled lager.

4 SERVINGS

- 1½ tablespoons vegetable oil
- 1 large onion, finely sliced
- 6 streaky bacon slices, chopped
- 1 large cooking apple, peeled, cored and sliced
- 2 large potatoes, sliced
- 1 medium-sized red cabbage, washed, coarse outer leaves removed and shredded
- 1½ teaspoons caraway seeds
- 2 tablespoons lemon juice
- 1 tablespoon wine vinegar
- 1 teaspoon salt
- ½ teaspoon black pepper
- 10 fl. oz. [1¼ cups] chicken stock
- 1 tablespoon soft brown sugar

In a large flameproof casserole, heat the oil over moderate heat. Add the onion and cook, stirring occasionally, for 8 minutes, or until it is browned. Add the bacon to the pan and, stirring occasionally, cook until the pieces become brown.

Preheat the oven to moderate 350°F (Gas Mark 4, 180°C).

Stir the apple, potatoes, red cabbage, caraway seeds, lemon juice, vinegar, salt, pepper, stock and brown sugar into the pan and bring the liquid to the boil, stirring occasionally.

Cover the casserole and transfer it to the oven. Braise for 2 hours, or until the cabbage is very tender.

Remove from the oven and serve.

Spinach Ring

A tempting cold dish, Spinach Ring may be served on its own or as an edible container for egg mayonnaise, shrimps in cream sauce or ham in sour cream. The filled Spinach Ring makes an attractive hors d'oeuvre or a light luncheon or buffet dish. It is important to squeeze as much moisture as possible from the spinach when draining it.

4-6 SERVINGS

- 1½ lb. spinach, cooked, drained and chopped
- ½ cucumber, finely chopped
- 6 spring onions [scallions], chopped
- ½ teaspoon dried marjoram
- ¼ teaspoon salt
- ½ teaspoon black pepper
- ¼ teaspoon dry mustard
- ½ oz. gelatine, dissolved in 3 tablespoons hot water
- 14 fl. oz. [1¾ cups] chicken stock
- 2 tablespoons cider vinegar

In a large mixing bowl, combine the spinach, cucumber, spring onions [scallions], marjoram, salt, pepper and mustard. Rinse a 2-pint [1¼-quart] ring mould with cold water. Spoon the spinach mixture into the prepared mould and mix thoroughly.

Pour the dissolved gelatine, stock and vinegar into the bowl and stir well. Pour the mixture into the ring mould.

Chill the ring mould in the refrigerator for 4 hours or until the mixture has set. Remove the ring mould from the refrigerator. Quickly dip the bottom of the mould into hot water, place a chilled serving dish over the top and invert the two, giving the mould a sharp shake. The spinach ring should slide out easily.

Serve immediately.

Sweetcorn Bake

Serve as a sustaining accompaniment to steaks or chops or with crusty bread and salad as a light lunch or supper dish.

4-6 SERVINGS

- 1 oz. [2 tablespoons] butter
- 1½ lb. sweetcorn kernels
- 14 oz. canned peeled tomatoes
- 5 oz. tomato purée
- 2 tablespoons flour
- 2 tablespoons treacle or molasses
- ½ teaspoon salt
- 1 teaspoon black pepper
- ½ teaspoon cayenne pepper
- ½ teaspoon dry mustard
- 4 oz. [1 cup] Cheddar cheese, grated

Preheat the oven to moderate 350°F (Gas Mark 4, 180°C). With a little butter, lightly grease a medium-sized baking dish and set aside.

In a mixing bowl, combine the sweetcorn, tomatoes with the can juice, tomato purée, flour, treacle or molasses, salt, pepper, cayenne and mustard and beat well. Spoon the mixture into the dish.

Sprinkle over the cheese. Cut the remaining butter into small pieces and dot them over the cheese. Place the dish in the oven and bake for 30 minutes or until the top of the mixture is brown.

Remove from the oven and serve.

Serve Boston Baked Beans with brown bread for a super supper.

Artichoke Heart Salad

This delicately flavoured hors d'oeuvre may be served with thinly sliced brown bread and butter.

4 SERVINGS

12 canned artichoke hearts, drained and quartered
2 shallots, finely chopped
½ teaspoon finely grated lemon rind
6 small new potatoes, scrubbed, cooked and quartered

DRESSING

3 fl. oz. [⅜ cup] olive oil
1 tablespoon white wine vinegar
1 tablespoon lemon juice
½ teaspoon salt
½ teaspoon black pepper
½ teaspoon chopped fresh tarragon or ¼ teaspoon dried tarragon
½ teaspoon chopped fresh basil or ¼ teaspoon dried basil

GARNISH

2 small tomatoes, quartered
8 black olives, halved and stoned

In a medium-sized glass serving bowl, combine the artichoke hearts, shallots, lemon rind and potatoes. Set aside.

In a small mixing bowl, combine all the dressing ingredients and beat well with a fork until they are thoroughly combined. Alternatively, place all the dressing ingredients in a small screw-top jar, screw on the lid and shake vigorously until they are thoroughly combined.

Pour the dressing over the artichoke heart mixture and toss well with two large spoons. Garnish with the tomatoes and olives.

Either serve the salad immediately or cover and chill in the refrigerator until required.

Bean Sprout Salad

This fresh, crunchy salad is ideal to serve with or after grilled [broiled] fish or chicken, or with other salads.

4 SERVINGS

1 lb. fresh or canned and drained bean sprouts
2 oz. canned pimiento, chopped
1 pickled cucumber, chopped
1 tablespoon finely chopped fresh chives

DRESSING

2 tablespoons olive oil
1 tablespoon wine vinegar
½ teaspoon prepared mustard
2 teaspoons soy sauce
½ teaspoon sugar
½ teaspoon salt

Put the bean sprouts in a salad bowl with the pimiento, pickled cucumber and chives.

Mix all the ingredients for the dressing together, making sure the salt and sugar are dissolved. Pour the dressing over the salad. Toss the salad well and put in a refrigerator or a cool place for 1 hour before serving.

Beetroot and Orange Salad

This is a delicious salad of contrasting flavours, textures and colours.

4 SERVINGS

6 beetroots [beets], cooked
2 large oranges
2 bunches watercress

DRESSING

4 tablespoons olive oil
1½ tablespoons wine vinegar
1 teaspoon prepared mustard
¼ teaspoon dried tarragon
½ teaspoon salt
½ teaspoon sugar

Peel and slice the beetroots [beets] into rounds. Grate the rind of 1 orange and set aside. Peel the oranges, removing the white pith, and slice them into rounds.

Wash the watercress and cut off the stalks. Arrange the watercress on a shallow serving dish.

Arrange the beetroot [beet] and orange slices alternately, overlapping, on the bed of watercress.

Mix all the dressing ingredients in a cup and add the reserved orange rind.

Spoon the dressing over the overlapping slices just before serving.

Coleslaw with Caraway

Caraway seeds provide the interesting variation in this crisp coleslaw salad. It is a perfect accompaniment to cold meat and cold roast chicken.

Beetroot and Orange Salad provides an unusual blend of taste and texture.

1 large white cabbage, coarse outer leaves removed, washed, cored and shredded

1 medium-sized onion, finely chopped

½ green pepper, white pith removed, seeded and finely chopped

½ teaspoon lemon juice

1 tablespoon caraway seeds

DRESSING

6 fl. oz. double cream [¾ cup heavy cream]

3 fl. oz. [⅜ cup] sour cream

1 tablespoon prepared French mustard

3 tablespoons lemon juice

1 tablespoon sugar

½ teaspoon salt

¼ teaspoon white pepper

Arrange the shredded cabbage in a large serving dish and sprinkle with the onion, green pepper and lemon juice. Set aside.

In a medium-sized mixing bowl, combine the double [heavy] cream, sour cream, mustard and lemon juice, beating vigorously with a wooden spoon until the ingredients are thoroughly blended. Add the sugar, salt and white pepper and mix well.

Pour the dressing over the shredded

Crunchy, nutritious Coleslaw with Caraway tastes even better than it looks. Serve with cold meat or pâté.

cabbage and add the caraway seeds to the mixture. Using two large spoons or forks, toss the cabbage mixture until it is completely saturated with dressing. Chill in the refrigerator for at least 1 hour and serve cold.

Cucumber and Yogurt Salad

Cucumber and Yogurt Salad is both crunchy and creamy. Serve it as an accompaniment to cold meat dishes or with hot dishes such as curries or goulasches.

6 SERVINGS

1 cucumber, peeled and finely chopped

2 tablespoons malt vinegar

1 teaspoon sugar

6 spring onions [scallions], trimmed and finely chopped

1 green pepper, white pith removed, seeded and finely chopped

8 fl. oz. [1 cup] yogurt

2 fl. oz. [¼ cup] sour cream

1 teaspoon salt

½ teaspoon black pepper

3 teaspoons chopped fresh dill or 1½ teaspoons dried dill

1 round [Boston] lettuce, outer leaves removed, washed and separated into leaves

Place the cucumber in a small mixing bowl and add the vinegar and sugar. Set aside for 10 minutes to dégorge.

Place the cucumber in a wire strainer held over a small mixing bowl. With the back of a wooden spoon, gently press the cucumber until most of the liquid is extracted. Discard the liquid.

Place the cucumber in a medium-sized mixing bowl and add the spring onions [scallions] and green pepper. Mix them together with the wooden spoon and set aside.

In another medium-sized mixing bowl, mix the yogurt, sour cream, salt, pepper and two-thirds of the dill. Pour the yogurt mixture over the cucumber mixture and toss them together with two large spoons until all the ingredients are thoroughly coated.

Arrange the lettuce leaves around the edges of a large serving platter and spoon the yogurt and cucumber mixture into the centre. Sprinkle the remaining dill over the mixture and serve immediately.

Danish Blue Salad

This fresh, colourful cheese salad may be served with cold ham, or on its own as a light snack.

2 SERVINGS

2 oz. Danish blue cheese, cut into small pieces
2 oz. Cheddar cheese, cut into small pieces
1 medium-sized red pepper, white pith removed, seeded and thinly sliced
3 spring onions [scallions], trimmed and finely chopped
1 teaspoon dried dill

DRESSING

½ teaspoon prepared French mustard
6 tablespoons olive oil
2 tablespoons white wine vinegar
½ teaspoon paprika
½ teaspoon salt
¼ teaspoon black pepper

To prepare the dressing, in a small mixing bowl beat the mustard into the olive oil with a fork. Gradually beat in the vinegar and add the paprika, salt and pepper.

In a medium-sized serving bowl, combine the Danish blue and Cheddar cheeses, the red pepper, spring onions [scallions] and the dill.

Pour the dressing over the mixture and, using two large spoons, toss well to blend. Serve at once.

Egg and Spinach Salad

This fresh green salad makes an ideal light meal — and will taste even better if it is accompanied by thick slices of French bread and butter.

4 SERVINGS

¼ teaspoon black pepper
½ teaspoon salt
⅛ teaspoon cayenne pepper
1 teaspoon prepared mustard
5 hard-boiled eggs
1 large garlic clove, crushed
2 fl. oz. [¼ cup] tarragon vinegar
4 fl. oz. [½ cup] olive oil
1 tablespoon lemon juice
1 small lettuce, washed, trimmed and the leaves separated
12 oz. fresh leaf spinach, washed, trimmed and drained
8 large radishes, washed, trimmed and thinly sliced
1 tablespoon finely chopped fresh chives
1 small green pepper, white pith removed, seeded and very

finely chopped

In a small bowl, combine the pepper, salt, cayenne and mustard. Slice the eggs in half and scoop out the yolks. Rub the yolks through a strainer into the mustard mixture and stir in the garlic. Chop the egg whites and set them aside.

In a small bowl, beat the vinegar, oil and lemon juice together. Gradually pour into the egg yolk mixture, stirring constantly until the dressing is blended.

Arrange the lettuce, spinach, radishes, chives, green pepper and egg whites in a large salad bowl. Pour the dressing on top and, using two large spoons, toss the salad thoroughly.

Chill the salad in the refrigerator for 30 minutes before serving.

Fagioli con Tonno

WHITE BEAN AND TUNA SALAD

An attractive Italian salad, Fagioli con Tonno may be served as a refreshing first course on its own, or as part of a colourful antipasto.

4 SERVINGS

1 lb. canned white haricot beans, drained
1 medium-sized onion, finely chopped
½ tablespoon white wine vinegar
2 tablespoons olive oil
1 teaspoon lemon juice
1 garlic clove, crushed
1 teaspoon salt
½ teaspoon black pepper
2 tablespoons chopped fresh basil or 1 tablespoon dried basil
7 oz. canned tuna fish, drained and coarsely flaked
6 black olives, stoned

Put the beans and onion in a medium-sized serving dish. In a small bowl, beat the vinegar, olive oil, lemon juice, garlic, salt, black pepper and basil together with a fork.

Pour the mixture over the beans and onion and toss well together.

Arrange the tuna fish and olives on top of the bean mixture and serve the salad at once.

Garlic Salad

An easy-to-make and strongly flavoured dish, Garlic Salad may be served as a first course or, accompanied by lots of bread and butter, for a light but satisfying summer lunch.

4 SERVINGS

6 large lettuce leaves, washed and shaken dry
8 medium-sized hard-boiled eggs, sliced
4 medium-sized tomatoes, washed and sliced
1 small green pepper, white pith removed, seeded and finely chopped
8 anchovy fillets

DRESSING

1 tablespoon finely chopped fresh parsley
¼ teaspoon dry mustard
¼ teaspoon salt

Garlic Salad is an enticing mixture of lettuce, eggs, tomatoes, green pepper and anchovies, covered with a strong garlic dressing. Serve with crusty bread for a special summer meal.

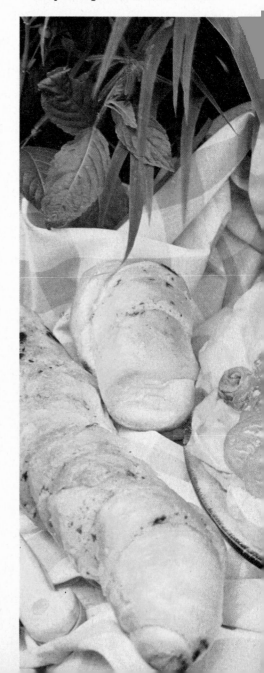

¼ teaspoon freshly ground black
pepper
3 garlic cloves, crushed
4 tablespoons olive oil
1 tablespoon tarragon or red wine
vinegar
1 tablespoon lemon juice

Arrange the lettuce leaves on a large
serving plate.

Place the egg and tomato slices on the
lettuce leaves, in alternating layers, beginning from the centre of the dish. Sprinkle
on the chopped green pepper. Roll up the
anchovy fillets and arrange them on the
outer edge of the dish.

To make the dressing, in a medium-
sized mixing bowl, combine the parsley,
mustard, salt, black pepper and garlic
cloves. Slowly beat in the olive oil,
vinegar and lemon juice. Combine the
mixture thoroughly and pour it carefully
over the salad so that all the ingredients
are thoroughly coated.

Place the salad in the refrigerator to
chill for 15 minutes before serving.

Grapefruit and Avocado Salad

*A delightfully fresh-tasting dish, Grapefruit
and Avocado Salad may be served as an
elegant and unusual first course to a summer
dinner party, or as part of a summer
buffet.*

4 SERVINGS

2 large ripe avocados, halved and
stoned
2 teaspoons lemon juice
1 large grapefruit, peeled, white
pith removed and roughly
chopped
1 head of chicory [French or Belgian
endive], trimmed, washed and
chopped
2 teaspoons sugar
3 tablespoons French dressing

Using a teaspoon, carefully scoop out the
avocado flesh and place it in a medium-
sized mixing bowl. Reserve the avocado
shells.

Add 1 teaspoon of the lemon juice, the
chopped grapefruit, chicory [French or
Belgian endive] and sugar and, using a
fork, mash the ingredients carefully
together until they form a relatively
smooth mixture.

Stir the dressing into the avocado mixture. Spoon the mixture into the avocado
shells and sprinkle over the remaining
lemon juice. Place the filled avocados in
the refrigerator and chill them for 30
minutes.

Remove the filled avocado shells
from the refrigerator and serve them
immediately.

Jellied Veal

☆ ☆ ① ① ① ✄ ✄ ✄

This dish should be prepared the day before it is to be served to allow the stock to set to a firm jelly which can be turned out easily.

6-8 SERVINGS

2 lb. lean leg of veal, boned
8 streaky bacon slices
1 small onion, thinly sliced
1 celery stalk, chopped
1 carrot, scraped and chopped
  bouquet garni, consisting of 4
  parsley sprigs, 1 thyme spray and
  1 bay leaf tied together
¼ teaspoon salt
½ teaspoon black pepper
1 pint [2½ cups] water
5 fl. oz. [⅝ cup] white wine
½ oz. gelatine
6 artichoke hearts, cooked and
  thinly sliced
½ large cucumber, trimmed and cut
  into ¼-inch slices

Tie the veal into a neat shape, if necessary. Tie the bacon slices neatly around the meat. Place the veal, onion, celery, carrot, bouquet garni, salt and pepper in a large saucepan. Pour the water and wine into the pan and bring to the boil over high heat. Cover the pan, reduce the heat to low and simmer for 1¼ hours, or until the veal is very tender.

Remove the pan from the heat and allow the veal to cool slightly in the cooking liquid. Remove the veal from the pan and set it aside on a board.

Strain the cooking liquid into a saucepan and bring it to the boil. Remove the pan from the heat and sprinkle the gelatine over the liquid, stirring until it has dissolved. Set aside to cool.

Rinse a 3-pint [1½-quart] soufflé dish with water. Set aside.

Cut the veal into 1-inch cubes and arrange one-quarter of them in the soufflé dish. Arrange a layer of one-third of the artichoke heart slices on top. Then place one-third of the cucumber slices over the artichokes. Repeat the layers until all the ingredients are used up, ending with a layer of veal.

Pour the cooled cooking liquid over the mixture and place the dish in the refrigerator. Chill for at least 4 hours, or until the jelly [gelatin] is very firmly set.

Remove the dish from the refrigerator. Dip the base quickly in hot water and place a serving dish, inverted, over the top. Reverse the two — the jellied veal should slide out easily. Serve cold.

Beautiful Jellied Veal makes the perfect centrepiece for that special summer buffet. Make it the day before for worry-free entertaining.

Kokonda

☆ ① ① ① ✄ ✄

Kokonda is a spicy fish dish, ideal for a summer meal. Serve with a tossed green salad, and a well-chilled white wine.

6-8 SERVINGS

1½ lb. white fish fillets, cooked,
  skinned and roughly chopped
4 tablespoons lime juice
4 tablespoons fresh lemon juice
4 oz. fresh coconut, grated
1 red pepper, white pith removed,
  seeded and shredded
1 green pepper, white pith removed,
  seeded and shredded
2 bananas, thinly sliced
4 medium-sized tomatoes, chopped
1 cucumber, peeled and diced
4 oz. canned pineapple, drained and
  chopped
DRESSING
1 teaspoon salt
½ teaspoon black pepper
⅛ teaspoon ground cumin

1 green chilli, finely minced
1 garlic clove, crushed
5 fl. oz. [⅝ cup] sour cream
2 tablespoons single [light] cream

In a medium-sized dish, mix together the fish and lime and lemon juices. Set the mixture aside to marinate in a cool place for 1 hour, basting occasionally.

Drain the fish, reserving 1 tablespoon of the marinade. Place the fish in a serving bowl and add the remaining salad ingredients. Toss well and set aside.

To make the dressing, place the reserved marinade and the dressing ingredients in a small mixing bowl.

Blend the dressing thoroughly and pour it over the salad. Toss well and chill in the refrigerator for 1 hour.

Remove the salad from the refrigerator and toss well before serving.

Macaroni and Herring Salad

A deliciously different salad, Macaroni and Herring Salad makes a tasty meal served with crusty bread, or it may be served as part of a summer buffet.

4-6 SERVINGS

4 oz. cooked macaroni
2 celery stalks, chopped
2 oz. mushrooms, sliced
3 pickled herring fillets, drained and chopped

2 hard-boiled eggs, sliced
1 medium-sized potato, cooked and chopped
2 tablespoons olive oil
1 tablespoon red wine vinegar
1 teaspoon salt
½ teaspoon black pepper
½ teaspoon dried dill
¼ teaspoon cayenne pepper
¼ teaspoon turmeric
½ teaspoon ground cumin
1 teaspoon ground coriander
4 fl. oz. [½ cup] mayonnaise
5 fl. oz. [⅝ cup] sour cream

Arrange the macaroni, celery, mushrooms, herrings, eggs and potato in a large salad bowl and set aside. In a small bowl, combine the olive oil, vinegar, salt, pepper and dill, beating until they are well blended. Pour the dressing over the salad mixture, tossing with two large spoons until the mixture is coated. Place the bowl in the refrigerator to chill for 1 hour.

Just before serving, remove the salad from the refrigerator.

With a wire whisk, beat the cayenne, turmeric, cumin and coriander into the mayonnaise, whisking until the ingredients are well blended. Stir in the sour cream. Spoon the mayonnaise mixture over the salad ingredients and, using two large spoons, mix well until the salad mixture is thoroughly coated. Serve at once.

Mushroom and Asparagus Mayonnaise

Mushroom and Asparagus Mayonnaise makes an excellent accompaniment to cold roast meat.

4-6 SERVINGS

8 oz. button mushrooms, wiped clean and thinly sliced
1 lb. asparagus, cooked and sliced into 1-inch pieces
8 fl. oz. [1 cup] mayonnaise
1 tablespoon chopped fresh chives
2 hard-boiled eggs, thinly sliced
DRESSING
6 tablespoons olive oil
2 tablespoons white wine vinegar
¼ teaspoon salt
¼ teaspoon black pepper

First prepare the dressing. In a medium-sized mixing bowl, combine all the dressing ingredients, beating until they are blended. Add the mushrooms and set aside to marinate for 30 minutes.

Add the asparagus, mayonnaise and chives to the mixture and mix well, being careful not to mash the asparagus.

Transfer to a large serving dish. Garnish with the egg slices and serve.

Kokonda is a spicy fish salad from Africa. Serve with lots of bread and salad for a summer lunch.

Pork and Vegetable Salad

This fresh-tasting, colourful salad makes an ideal summer lunch, served with crusty rolls and butter. A lightly chilled rosé wine, such as Rosé d'Anjou, would be a good accompaniment.

4-6 SERVINGS

14 oz. green beans, cooked, drained and halved
4 medium-sized tomatoes, roughly chopped
2 medium-sized potatoes, cooked and chopped
1 large green pepper, white pith removed, seeded and thinly sliced
4 spring onions [scallions], trimmed and chopped
1 garlic clove, crushed
4 cooked beetroots [beets], sliced
6 black olives, halved and stoned
2 courgettes [zucchini], cooked and sliced
1 lb. lean cooked pork, cut into ½-inch cubes

DRESSING

5 fl. oz. [⅝ cup] sour cream
2 tablespoons lemon juice
4 tablespoons mayonnaise
1 teaspoon salt
1 teaspoon black pepper
2 teaspoons paprika
2 teaspoons prepared French mustard
2 tablespoons finely chopped fresh chives

Place all the salad ingredients in a large salad bowl and set aside.

In a small mixing bowl, beat all the dressing ingredients together with a wooden spoon until the mixture is smooth.

Pour the dressing over the salad and, using two large spoons, toss the salad until it is thoroughly combined. Chill the salad in the refrigerator for 1 hour before serving.

Potato, Egg and Anchovy Salad

This strongly flavoured salad may be served with cold roast poultry, such as chicken or turkey.

4 SERVINGS

1 lb. new potatoes, cooked, peeled and sliced
½ head of fennel, trimmed and thinly sliced
1 tablespoon finely chopped fresh chives

2 hard-boiled eggs, chopped
10 anchovy fillets, chopped
1 tablespoon red wine vinegar
2 tablespoons olive oil
½ teaspoon salt
½ teaspoon freshly ground black pepper
4 fl. oz. [½ cup] mayonnaise
1 tablespoon capers

In a medium-sized mixing bowl, combine the potatoes, fennel, chives, eggs and anchovies together.

In a small mixing bowl, beat the vinegar, oil, salt and pepper together with a kitchen fork. Stir the mayonnaise into the dressing. Pour the mayonnaise mixture over the potato mixture and toss well with two forks until the ingredients are well mixed. Transfer the salad to a glass salad bowl. Sprinkle the capers over the salad.

Serve immediately or chill the salad until it is required.

Radish, Celery and Cucumber Salad

This crispy, crunchy salad makes a palate-tingling hors d'oeuvre, which may precede almost any main course. Since the radishes are left whole, small ones would be best; if you have large ones, either cut them in half or quarter them.

3-4 SERVINGS

8 oz. radishes, trimmed
4 celery stalks, trimmed and cut into ¼-inch lengths
½ small cucumber, peeled and diced
3 oz. [½ cup] cashew nuts
½ teaspoon chopped fresh chervil or ¼ teaspoon dried chervil
½ teaspoon chopped fresh tarragon or ¼ teaspoon dried tarragon
¼ teaspoon salt
½ teaspoon black pepper
4 fl. oz. [½ cup] sour cream
1 tablespoon mayonnaise
1 tablespoon cider vinegar

In a medium-sized serving bowl, combine the radishes, celery, cucumber, cashew nuts, chervil and tarragon. Set the bowl aside.

In a small mixing bowl, combine the salt, pepper, sour cream, mayonnaise and vinegar, beating well with a fork until they are well blended. Pour the dressing over the vegetables and, using two large spoons, toss well until they are thoroughly coated.

Serve immediately or chill until it is required.

Rice Salad with Garlic Sausage

A tasty dish from southern France, this Rice Salad with Garlic Sausage makes a colourful addition to any table. Serve with crusty bread and chilled white Provençal wine.

4-6 SERVINGS

4 oz. [⅔ cup] long-grain rice, washed, soaked in cold water for 30 minutes and drained
1½ teaspoons salt
½ teaspoon black pepper
3 fl. oz. [⅜ cup] mayonnaise
2 teaspoons chopped fresh chervil or 1 teaspoon dried chervil
½ red pepper, white pith removed, seeded and chopped
2 hard-boiled eggs
1 small lettuce, outer leaves removed, washed, separated into leaves and shaken dry
1 x 8-inch garlic sausage, cut into ¼-inch slices

Put the rice in a saucepan. Pour over enough water to cover the rice and add 1 teaspoon of the salt. Bring the water to the boil over moderately high heat and cover the pan. Reduce the heat to very low and simmer for 15 to 20 minutes or until all the liquid has been absorbed and the rice is cooked and tender. Remove the pan from the heat. Transfer the rice to a large mixing bowl and set it aside to cool for 5 minutes.

Meanwhile, in a small mixing bowl, combine the remaining salt, the pepper, mayonnaise and chervil.

Pour half the mayonnaise mixture over the rice and add the red pepper. Using two large spoons, toss the rice mixture until it is well coated with the mayonnaise. Set the mixture aside to cool completely.

Meanwhile, cut the eggs in half, remove the yolks and add them to the remaining mayonnaise mixture. Mash the yolks into the mayonnaise mixture with a wooden spoon and beat well. Spoon the mayonnaise mixture into the cavities in the egg whites.

Arrange the lettuce leaves in a salad bowl. Pile the rice mixture on top of the leaves, then arrange the sausage slices and filled egg whites around the rice.

Serve immediately.

This sumptuous Rice Salad with Garlic Sausage makes an ideal centrepiece for informal summer entertaining.

4 tablespoons finely chopped fresh
   parsley
2 tablespoons finely chopped fresh
   mint
1 medium-sized onion, finely
   chopped
3 spring onions [scallions], trimmed
   and finely chopped
1 lb. tomatoes, coarsely chopped
1 teaspoon salt
2 teaspoons black pepper
2 fl. oz. [¼ cup] lemon juice
3 fl. oz. [⅜ cup] olive oil
10 lettuce leaves, washed and
   shaken dry
4 tomatoes, quartered

In a medium-sized mixing bowl, mix together the wheat, 3 tablespoons of the parsley, the mint, onion, spring onions [scallions] and chopped tomatoes until they are thoroughly combined. Set the bowl aside.

In a small mixing bowl, combine the salt, pepper, lemon juice and oil, beating well with a kitchen fork. Pour the dressing over the salad and toss well, using two large spoons.

Line a medium-sized salad bowl with the lettuce leaves and arrange the salad in the middle. Garnish with the tomato quarters and remaining parsley before serving.

Sweetcorn Salad

Piquant Sweetcorn Salad is an imaginative yet easily made accompaniment to hamburgers or grilled [broiled] *steaks.*

4 SERVINGS

1 lb. canned sweetcorn, drained
1 small green pepper, white pith
   removed, seeded and finely
   chopped
3 canned pimientos, drained and
   finely chopped
4 spring onions [scallions], trimmed
   and finely chopped
2 fl. oz. [¼ cup] olive oil
1 tablespoon white wine vinegar
1 bay leaf
2 teaspoons soft brown sugar
½ teaspoon salt
½ teaspoon black pepper
⅛ teaspoon Tabasco sauce
1 teaspoon dry mustard
1 garlic clove, crushed

Place the sweetcorn, green pepper, pimientos and spring onions [scallions] in a decorative salad bowl and toss well with two forks until they are thoroughly combined.

Colourful Sweetcorn Salad makes a delicious accompaniment to grilled [broiled] hamburgers.

In a small mixing bowl, mix together the olive oil, wine vinegar, bay leaf, sugar, salt, pepper, Tabasco sauce, mustard and garlic until they are well blended.

Pour the dressing over the sweetcorn mixture and stir well to mix. Set aside at room temperature for at least 2 hours. Remove and discard the bay leaf before serving.

Tomato and Wheat Salad

This tasty tomato salad with wheat and fresh mint is an adaptation of a traditional Arab dish. It may be served as an hors d'oeuvre or as an accompaniment to spiced meat or chicken. Cracked wheat is available from most health food stores.

6 SERVINGS

8 oz. [1⅓ cups] cracked wheat,
   soaked in cold water for 20
   minutes and drained

Turnip and Date Salad

A really unusual combination of flavours, Turnip and Date Salad is an ideal accompaniment to cold roast poultry, such as duck or chicken.

2 SERVINGS

2 tart eating apples, peeled, cored
   and diced
2 teaspoons lemon juice
1 medium-sized turnip, peeled and
   finely grated
14 fresh or dried dates, stoned and
   coarsely chopped
2 teaspoons sugar
2 fl. oz. single cream [¼ cup light
   cream]
1 small carrot, scraped and finely
   grated

Place the apples in a medium-sized salad bowl and sprinkle over the lemon. Add the grated turnip and the chopped dates and sprinkle over 1½ teaspoons of the sugar. Stir carefully with a wooden spoon until the ingredients are thoroughly combined.

Pour in the cream and, using two large spoons, toss the salad until the ingredients are thoroughly coated. Garnish the salad with the grated carrot and sprinkle over the remaining sugar.

Serve immediately.

Wurstsalat

GERMAN SAUSAGE SALAD

One of the classic German first courses, Wurstsalat may be made with any combination of cooked German sausages — we would suggest a combination of garlic sausage, salami, cooked frankfurters or bratwurst *and ham sausage but it's up to you! Serve with a well-chilled white wine and rye or pumpernickel bread.*

4-6 SERVINGS

1 lb. mixed cooked German wurst, sliced
1 medium-sized green pepper, white pith removed, seeded and sliced

The unusual combination of ingredients in Turnip and Date Salad makes a nutritious and tasty dish.

1 medium-sized red pepper, white pith removed, seeded and sliced
1 onion, thinly sliced and pushed out into rings
4 fl. oz. [½ cup] French dressing
2 small gherkins, halved

Arrange the wurst, green pepper and red pepper decoratively on a serving plate. Scatter over the onion rings. Pour over the French dressing and garnish with the gherkin halves.

Place the plate in the refrigerator to chill for 30 minutes before serving.

Cabbage and Sesame Seed Salad

A salad with an unusual flavour, Cabbage and Sesame Seed Salad is particularly good served as a side dish with cold beef or ham.

4 SERVINGS

12 oz. white cabbage, coarse outer leaves removed, cleaned and finely shredded
4 oz. bean sprouts, washed and drained
4 tomatoes, quartered
2 medium-sized carrots, scraped and finely grated
1 medium-sized avocado, peeled, stoned and chopped
1 tablespoon butter
2 tablespoons sesame seeds
6 fl. oz. [¾ cup] French dressing

Place the cabbage, bean sprouts, tomatoes, carrots and avocado in a medium-sized serving bowl and set aside.

In a small saucepan, melt the butter over moderate heat. When the foam subsides, add the sesame seeds and cook, stirring frequently with a wooden spoon, for 3 to 5 minutes or until the seeds are golden brown. Remove the pan from the heat and transfer the seeds and cooking juices to the salad.

Pour the French dressing over the salad and, using two large spoons, toss well. Serve immediately.

Mange-tout Salad

An adaptation of a Chinese recipe, crunchy Mange-tout Salad may be served as an accompaniment to cold meats, or as part of a Chinese meal.

4 SERVINGS

4 dried Chinese mushrooms, soaked for 30 minutes in cold water
1 tablespoon vegetable oil
6 oz. canned bamboo shoots, drained and thinly sliced
12 oz. mange-tout [snow peas], trimmed
1 celery stalk, trimmed and cut into 2-inch pieces
1 teaspoon salt
½ teaspoon sugar
1 teaspoon white wine vinegar

Drain the mushrooms. Strain the soaking liquid and reserve 1 tablespoonful. With a sharp knife, cut the mushrooms into thin slices.

In a large frying-pan heat the oil over moderately high heat. When the oil is hot, add the mushrooms and bamboo shoots and cook them, stirring constantly, for 2 minutes.

Add the mange-tout [snow peas] and celery to the pan and cook, still stirring, for 2 minutes. Sprinkle the salt, sugar, vinegar and reserved soaking liquid over the vegetables. Cook the mixture for a further 2 minutes or until the liquid has evaporated.

Remove the pan from the heat. Pour the vegetable mixture into a medium-sized serving dish and set aside to cool. Cover the dish with plastic wrap and place it in the refrigerator to chill for at least 1 hour before serving.

Picnic Salad

This fabulous salad makes a filling picnic meal served with either French bread or rolls and butter. Or serve it at home on its own as a first course to a main meal. To take the salad on your picnic, place it in a plastic bowl and cover with an airtight lid — it is preferable to chill the salad in the refrigerator for at least one hour before the journey.

6 SERVINGS

1 lb. lean cooked chicken meat, diced
6 oz. canned or frozen sweetcorn, drained or thawed
4 oz. small button mushrooms, wiped clean and thinly sliced
1 medium-sized avocado, peeled, stoned and coarsely chopped
2 medium-sized peaches, blanched, peeled, stoned and coarsely chopped
5 oz. [2 cups] cooked long-grain rice, or 6 oz. cooked diced potatoes, cold
2 shallots, finely chopped
2 tablespoons finely chopped fresh chives
1 tablespoon finely chopped fresh parsley
DRESSING
6 fl. oz. [¾ cup] mayonnaise
2 fl. oz. double cream [¼ cup heavy cream], whipped until thick but not stiff
1 tablespoon lemon juice
2 teaspoons curry powder
1 teaspoon salt
½ teaspoon freshly ground black pepper
⅛ teaspoon cayenne pepper

First make the dressing. In a large mixing bowl, beat the mayonnaise, cream and lemon juice together with a wooden spoon. Add the curry powder, salt, black pepper and cayenne pepper, and stir well to blend.

Add all of the salad ingredients and, using two large spoons, toss the salad thoroughly. Cover the bowl with aluminium foil and chill the salad in the refrigerator for at least 1 hour before serving, tossing it occasionally.

Salade Mimosa
LETTUCE HEART, CELERY AND WATERCRESS SALAD

An attractive French composite salad, Salade Mimosa makes a lovely hors d'oeuvre. It may also be served as an accompaniment to grilled [broiled] steaks or lamb chops.

4 SERVINGS

2 lettuce hearts, washed and shredded
½ bunch watercress, washed, shaken dry and roughly chopped
2 celery stalks, trimmed and chopped
3 fl. oz. [⅜ cup] French dressing
2 hard-boiled egg yolks, roughly chopped
GARNISH
2 oranges, peeled, white pith removed and segmented
2 teaspoons olive oil
1 teaspoon white wine vinegar
1 banana, peeled and thinly sliced
1 tablespoon lemon juice
10 green grapes, halved and seeded
1 tablespoon single [light] cream

In a medium-sized mixing bowl, combine the lettuce hearts, watercress, celery, French dressing and egg yolks. Using two large forks or spoons, toss the ingredients until they are well mixed. Transfer the lettuce mixture to a glass serving dish.

In a small mixing bowl, combine the orange segments, oil and vinegar. In another small mixing bowl, combine the banana and lemon juice and in a third small mixing bowl, combine the grape halves and cream.

Arrange the fruits and their dressings decoratively over the top of the lettuce mixture.

Serve immediately.

Cabbage and Sesame Seed Salad is a refreshing mixture of cabbage, bean sprouts, tomatoes, carrots, avocado and sesame seeds.

Sweet Pepper Salad may be served as an attractive hors d'oeuvre.

Wilted Lettuce Salad

In this American salad, the crispness of the bacon contrasts well with the texture of the lettuce.

4 SERVINGS

1 round [Boston] lettuce, outer leaves removed, washed and shaken dry
6 streaky bacon slices, chopped
2 fl. oz. [¼ cup] white wine vinegar
1 teaspoon sugar
½ teaspoon black pepper
6 spring onions [scallions], trimmed and chopped

Tear the lettuce leaves into medium-sized pieces and place them in a large bowl.

In a frying-pan, fry the bacon over moderate heat for 6 to 8 minutes or until the bacon is crisp. Scrape the bottom of the pan frequently to prevent the bacon from sticking. Using a slotted spoon, remove the bacon from the pan and drain it on kitchen paper towels.

Stir the vinegar, sugar, pepper and spring onions [scallions] into the frying-pan. Bring the liquid to the boil. Remove the pan from the heat and pour the contents over the lettuce.

Toss the salad to coat it with the dressing. Sprinkle over the bacon and serve.

Yorkshire Ploughboy

This traditional English salad should be eaten as an accompaniment to cold meat.

4-6 SERVINGS

1 small red cabbage, coarse outer leaves removed, washed and very finely shredded
1 onion, thinly sliced
1 tablespoon dark treacle or molasses
2 tablespoons white wine vinegar
½ teaspoon prepared mustard
½ teaspoon salt
½ teaspoon black pepper

Place the cabbage and onion in a large serving dish.

Place the treacle or molasses, vinegar, mustard, salt and pepper in a small bowl and stir with a metal spoon until the ingredients are well blended. Pour the dressing over the cabbage mixture and, using two forks, toss the salad until it is thoroughly combined. Serve at once.

Sweet Pepper Salad

This Romanian salad can be served as an hors d'oeuvre, as a salad course or as an accompaniment to a meat dish.

4 SERVINGS

4 green peppers
4 red peppers
6 tablespoons white wine vinegar
2 tablespoons medium-dry sherry
1 tablespoon Worcestershire sauce
6 tablespoons olive oil
1 teaspoon salt
¼ teaspoon black pepper
2 teaspoons sugar
1 teaspoon paprika
12 stoned black olives
8 oz. cream cheese, cut into cubes

Wash and dry the peppers. Halve and remove the white pith and seeds. Cut the peppers into quarters. Half-fill a saucepan with water and bring to the boil. Add the peppers and blanch for 3 minutes. Drain and dry on kitchen paper towels. Cool.

In a large mixing bowl, combine the vinegar, sherry, Worcestershire sauce, oil, salt, pepper, sugar and paprika. Taste and add more seasoning if necessary.

Put the peppers into the marinade and turn and mix until they are coated with the dressing. Cover and marinate for 24 hours in the refrigerator.

To serve, place the peppers in a shallow bowl or dish. Spoon a little of the marinade over them. Place the olives and cheese over the top and serve.

Tomato and Fish Salad

This adaptation of a classic South American recipe makes an unusual and refreshing first course.

4-6 SERVINGS

2 lb. mackerel fillets, skinned, cooked and cut into 1-inch pieces
juice of 4 lemons
1 teaspoon salt
1 teaspoon black peppercorns, crushed
4 fl. oz. [½ cup] olive oil
6 tomatoes, blanched, peeled and chopped
2 large onions, thinly sliced and pushed out into rings
4 oz. [1⅓ cups] stoned green olives
½ teaspoon dried oregano
2 green chillis, finely chopped
6 fl. oz. [¾ cup] dry white wine
1 avocado, halved, stoned, peeled and thinly sliced

Place the mackerel in a shallow serving dish and pour over the lemon juice. Sprinkle over the salt and pepper and set aside for at least 4 hours.

In a medium-sized mixing bowl, combine the oil, tomatoes, onions, olives, oregano, chillis and wine and stir well.

Drain off and discard the lemon juice from the fish and pour over the oil and wine mixture. Chill the salad in the refrigerator for 30 minutes. Remove the dish from the refrigerator and garnish with the avocado slices. Serve at once.

Cheese and eggs

Eggs and cheese were, until recently, thought of primarily as 'fillers' — in the case of eggs, the perfect thing to go to work on, for cheese a great thing for a snack with beer. Few people thought of them as a possible basis for dishes in their own right, so that it's only now that their true versatility is becoming apparent.

For if it's diversity you want, from casual nibbles to sumptuous desserts or cakes, then eggs and cheese are for you. You can catch up on a fabulous selection of basic (and not-so-basic) omelets and soufflés; or if it's inexpensive nourishing snacks that take your fancy, well, there are whole pages crammed full of mouth-watering rarebits and scrambles.

And you needn't restrict eggs and cheese to those end-of-the-week suppers for the family — they can be festive too, and there are whole sections in the book to prove it. If you need convincing, a quick glance at Cheese Fondue (pictured above, page 306) or Eggs Benedict (page 277) should do the trick; elegant dishes, both, guaranteed to make your dinner party swing.

For whatever the occasion, the recipes in this book will provide you with lots of easy-to-cook, practical dishes, at modest budget prices.

Eggs have always been symbols of birth, rebirth, fertility and even witchcraft through the ages. Nowadays, however, they are chiefly valued as food in themselves and as an ingredient in cooking. Eggs are high in protein and fat, calcium, iron and vitamins.

Eggs should be eaten as fresh as possible; if you must store eggs, store them in a cool, airy place. If you store them in the refrigerator, allow them to warm to room temperature before using. To test the freshness of an egg, lay it, horizontally, in a bowl of cold water. If it stays horizontal it is fresh, but if it stands vertical it is too stale to eat.

PREPARING EGGS

Separating eggs: To separate eggs, crack them sharply then open them carefully just enough to let the white slip out. Tip the yolk carefully from one half of the shell to the other to let out all the white.

Beating egg whites: Whichever type of bowl you use, it must be without a trace of grease. To ensure this, rub the inside of the bowl with a piece of lemon.

Begin by beating slowly. When the whites begin to foam, add a pinch of salt (if you are using a stainless steel bowl add a pinch of cream of tartar instead) and quicken the pace of beating gradually until you are beating vigorously and the whites resemble stiff snow.

Beaten egg whites will not remain firm for long unless sugar has been added, and even then it will be for a short time only.

COOKING EGGS

In cooking, eggs may be prepared in many ways. The basic methods are: boiling, scrambling, frying, poaching and baking. Eggs can also be made into omelets or soufflés.

Boiled eggs: Boiled eggs should not, in fact, be boiled, but simmered gently to prevent them from cracking. There are two chief ways of soft boiling.

1. Place the egg in a pan of boiling water. Boil for 1 minute. Turn off the heat, cover the pan and leave for 5 minutes. (This is also known as coddling.)

2. Place the egg in a pan of boiling water and simmer for 3 to 4 minutes according to the size of the egg. At the end of this time the egg white will be lightly set and the yolk runny.

For a hard-boiled egg, put the egg in a pan of boiling water and bring the water back to the boil. Cook over moderate heat for 10 minutes. With a slotted spoon, remove the egg from the pan and place it at once under cold running water to prevent the yolk from discolouring.

Scrambled eggs: In a small bowl, beat 2 eggs together with $\frac{1}{2}$ teaspoon of salt, $\frac{1}{4}$ teaspoon of black pepper and, if liked, 2 tablespoons of milk, cream or water, until the mixture is frothy. In a medium-sized saucepan, melt 1 tablespoon of butter over moderate heat. Pour the egg mixture into the pan and cook for 3 to 4 minutes, stirring constantly with a wooden spoon until it thickens. Remove the pan from the heat and continue stirring until the mixture is creamy. Serve at once.

Fried eggs: In a small frying-pan, heat 1 tablespoon of olive oil or butter or bacon fat over moderate heat. When the oil or fat is sizzling, break an egg carefully into the pan. Reduce the heat to low and cook gently, basting frequently with the hot fat, until the white is set and the yolk is firm. Remove the fried egg from the pan with a spatula or fish slice.

Poached eggs: Poached eggs may either be cooked in boiling water or steamed in a poaching pan.

For the first method, half-fill a small saucepan with water. Add $\frac{1}{2}$ teaspoon of salt and 1 teaspoon of vinegar. Place the pan over moderate heat and bring the water to the boil. Break an egg into a cup. When the water is boiling, carefully tip the egg into the centre of the bubbling water. Reduce the heat to moderately low and simmer gently for 3 minutes. Remove the egg with a slotted spoon.

To use an egg-poaching pan, half-fill the bottom of the pan with water. Place $\frac{1}{4}$ teaspoon of butter in the centre of each cup, unless you are using a non-stick pan. Place the pan, with the cups in place, over the heat. When the water boils, break the eggs into the cups. Cover

and simmer for 3 to 5 minutes or until the eggs are lightly set. Loosen the eggs with a knife and slide them out on to a plate.

Baked eggs: One of the oldest methods of cooking eggs, baked eggs are usually prepared in individual cocotte dishes, although several may be baked together in a small ovenproof dish. Place the dishes or dish on a baking sheet. Put ½ teaspoon of butter in each dish and place the baking sheet in the oven preheated to fairly hot 400°F (Gas Mark 6, 200°C) for 2 minutes. Break an egg into each dish, season with a little salt and pepper and return the dishes to the oven. Bake for 4 to 5 minutes or until the eggs are lightly set. Serve at once.

Omelet: To make good omelets, you will require a special omelet pan. The pan should be thick with a good smooth surface and should never be used for cooking anything else.

Never make too large an omelet. The best size is with 4 eggs and the limit should be 6 eggs. A medium-sized pan, one with a base 7 inches in diameter, will

do for the smaller omelet and a pan with a 9-inch base for the larger.

To make an omelet for 3 people, break 6 eggs into a bowl. Add ¼ teaspoon of salt and pepper (or more if you like) and 2 tablespoons of cold water. Beat well to mix with either a fork or a wire whisk.

Heat the pan over moderate heat for 10 seconds or until it is quite hot. Add ½ tablespoon of butter and when the foam subsides, pour in the beaten eggs. Stir the eggs, then leave them for a few seconds until the bottom sets. Reduce the heat to low. Using a palette knife or spatula, lift the edge of the omelet and at the same time tilt the pan away from you so that the liquid egg escapes from the top and runs into the pan. Put the pan down flat again over the heat and leave until the omelet begins to set. Tilt the pan away from you again and, with the help of the palette knife, flip one half of the omelet over to make a semi-circle. Slide the omelet quickly on to a heated plate and serve it immediately.

Soufflé: To make a cheese soufflé for four people, first grease a medium-sized soufflé dish with butter. Sprinkle 4 tablespoons of grated cheese (preferably a hard cheese, such as Cheddar) around the inside of the dish and press it on to the bottom and sides.

In a large saucepan, melt 2 ounces [¼ cup] of butter over moderate heat. With a wooden spoon, stir 4 tablespoons of flour into the butter and cook, stirring constantly, for 1 minute. Remove the pan from the heat and add 10 fluid ounces [1¼ cups] of milk, stirring constantly. Return the pan to the heat and cook the mixture, stirring constantly, for 1 minute or until it is thick and smooth.

Remove the pan from the heat and add salt, pepper and spices to taste. Beat 5 egg yolks, one at a time, into the hot sauce. Set aside to cool slightly.

Meanwhile, in a mixing bowl, beat 6 egg whites with a wire whisk or rotary beater until they form stiff peaks.

Stir 4 ounces [1 cup] of grated cheese (again preferably a hard cheese, such as Cheddar) into the cooling egg yolk mixture. When the cheese is blended, using a metal spoon, spoon the egg whites on top of the yolk mixture, then quickly fold them in.

Spoon the mixture into the prepared soufflé dish and cook in a fairly hot oven 400°F (Gas Mark 6, 200°C) for 25 to 30 minutes or until the soufflé has risen and is golden brown on top, and a skewer inserted into the middle comes out clean.

Remove the soufflé from the oven and serve it immediately.

Eggs Baked with Chicken Livers and Mushrooms

 ①

This is a light, tasty and nourishing dish which may be served as a first course or, if the quantities are doubled, as a main dish.

4 SERVINGS

1 oz. [2 tablespoons] butter
1 onion, finely chopped
4 slices lean bacon, diced
8 oz. chicken livers, roughly chopped
4 oz. button mushrooms, wiped clean and halved
2 tablespoons tomato purée
½ teaspoon salt
¼ teaspoon black pepper
4 eggs
2 oz. [½ cup] Cheddar or Parmesan cheese, finely grated

Preheat the oven to fairly hot 375°F (Gas Mark 5, 190°C). Grease four ramekin dishes or small individual baking dishes with half the butter.

In a small frying-pan, melt the remaining butter over moderate heat. When the foam subsides, add the onion and bacon and fry them for 5 minutes. Add the chicken livers and mushrooms and fry for a further 5 minutes or until the livers are lightly browned, the bacon crisp and the onion and mushrooms cooked. Remove the pan from the heat and drain off the excess fat.

Stir in the tomato purée, salt and pepper.

Put equal amounts of the liver mixture into each dish. Break an egg on top and sprinkle the cheese on top of the eggs. Bake in the centre of the oven for 15 to 20 minutes, or until the eggs are set and the tops lightly browned. Remove the dishes from the oven and serve immediately.

Egg and Corn Savoury

 ①

This delicious dish is simple, cheap and quick to prepare. It makes a tasty supper served with brown bread and butter.

4 SERVINGS

1 oz. [2 tablespoons] butter
1 garlic clove, crushed
1 medium-sized onion, thinly sliced
4 slices of stale white bread, crusts removed, cut into small squares
10 oz. canned condensed celery soup
2 tablespoons tomato purée
12 oz. frozen sweetcorn, thawed
15 oz. canned celery hearts, drained
½ teaspoon salt
¼ teaspoon black pepper
1 teaspoon paprika
1 tablespoon Worcestershire sauce
6 eggs
4 tablespoons milk
⅛ teaspoon grated nutmeg

In a large saucepan, melt the butter over moderate heat. When the foam subsides, add the garlic, onion and bread squares to the pan. Cook the mixture, stirring occasionally, for 5 to 7 minutes, or until the onion is soft and translucent and the bread squares are crisp.

Stir in the soup, tomato purée, corn, celery hearts, salt, pepper, paprika and Worcestershire sauce. Reduce the heat to

Egg and Corn Savoury is marvellously easy to prepare - and even easier to eat!

low, and simmer, stirring constantly, for 15 minutes.

In a small mixing bowl, beat the eggs, milk and nutmeg together. Stir the mixture into the pan.

Simmer for a further 10 minutes, stirring constantly, or until the mixture is thick and creamy. Remove the pan from heat and turn the savoury into a warmed serving dish. Serve at once.

Egg Croquettes

A tasty lunch or supper dish, Egg Croquettes are delicious with tomato sauce and thick slices of wholemeal bread.

2 SERVINGS

3 oz. [⅜ cup] butter
2 oz. [½ cup] flour
8 fl. oz. [1 cup] milk
½ teaspoon salt
¼ teaspoon cayenne pepper
2 hard-boiled eggs, finely chopped
1 egg yolk
2 oz. [½ cup] seasoned flour, made with 2 oz. [½ cup] flour, 1 teaspoon salt and ½ teaspoon black pepper
1 egg, lightly beaten
2 oz. [⅔ cup] dry breadcrumbs

In a small saucepan, melt 1 ounce [2 tablespoons] of the butter over moderate heat. Remove the pan from the heat and, with a wooden spoon, stir in the flour to make a smooth paste. Gradually add the milk, stirring constantly.

Return the pan to the heat. Add the salt and cayenne and cook, stirring constantly, for 2 to 3 minutes or until the mixture is very thick and smooth.

Remove the pan from the heat and stir in the chopped eggs and egg yolk.

Spoon the mixture into a shallow bowl and cover. Place the bowl in the refrigerator to chill for 1 hour.

With well-floured hands, shape the mixture into balls.

Place the seasoned flour, beaten egg and breadcrumbs on three separate plates. Roll the balls first in the seasoned flour, then in the beaten egg and finally in the breadcrumbs, coating them on all sides.

In a medium-sized frying-pan, melt the remaining butter over moderate heat. When the foam subsides, add the croquettes and fry, turning occasionally, for 5 minutes, or until they are golden brown.

With a slotted spoon, remove the croquettes from the pan and serve at once.

Curried Eggs

Curried Eggs are ideal for an impromptu supper since they are quick and easy to prepare and very economical.

2-3 SERVINGS

2 oz. [⅓ cup] raisins
2 oz. [¼ cup] butter
2 onions, finely chopped
1 garlic clove, crushed
1 small tart apple, cored and diced
2 tablespoons flour

A filling, spicy supper dish – that's Curried Eggs.

2 teaspoons curry powder
8 fl. oz. [1 cup] milk
2 fl. oz. double cream [¼ cup heavy cream]
½ teaspoon salt
¼ teaspoon black pepper
4 hard-boiled eggs, halved
3 tablespoons slivered almonds, toasted

Place the raisins in a small bowl and cover with boiling water. Soak them for 10 minutes, then drain. Set aside.

Meanwhile, in a medium-sized saucepan, melt the butter over moderate heat. When the foam subsides, add the onions, garlic and apple to the pan. Cook, stirring occasionally, for 7 minutes, or until the onions and apple are soft but not brown.

With a wooden spoon, stir the flour and curry powder into the pan. Cook, stirring, for 3 minutes.

Remove the pan from the heat and stir in the milk. Return the pan to the heat. Cook, stirring, for 3 to 4 minutes or until the sauce has thickened. Stir in the cream, salt and pepper.

Carefully fold the egg halves into the sauce. Simmer the sauce for 4 to 5 minutes, or until the eggs are thoroughly heated.

Remove the pan from the heat. Serve the curry at once on a bed of rice with the raisins and almonds sprinkled on top.

Eggs Flamenco

A quite delicious way of serving eggs, Eggs Flamenco can be served as a first course, as a light snack lunch or, accompanied by lots of crusty bread, for a family supper.

4 SERVINGS

4 tablespoons olive oil
1 medium-sized onion, thinly sliced
2 garlic cloves, crushed
8 oz. lean bacon, diced
2 small red peppers, white pith removed, seeded and chopped
6 medium-sized tomatoes, blanched, peeled and finely sliced
4 oz. mushrooms, wiped clean and finely sliced
½ teaspoon salt
¼ teaspoon freshly ground black pepper
⅛ teaspoon cayenne pepper
1 tablespoon chopped fresh parsley
8 oz. canned sweetcorn, drained
4 large eggs

Preheat the oven to moderate 350°F (Gas

Eggs Flamenco is a tasty mixture of bacon, red peppers, tomatoes, mushrooms, sweetcorn and eggs.

Mark 4, 180°C).

In a large frying-pan, heat the oil over moderate heat. Add the onion and garlic and cook, stirring occasionally, for 5 to 7 minutes, or until the onion is soft and translucent but not brown. Add the bacon and the red peppers to the pan and fry, stirring, for 10 to 12 minutes or until the peppers are soft. Stir in the tomatoes, mushrooms, salt, pepper, cayenne and parsley and continue cooking for 5 minutes, or until the tomatoes begin to pulp. Stir in the sweetcorn and remove the frying-pan from the heat.

Pour the mixture into an ovenproof baking dish. Using the back of a spoon, make four small depressions in the vegetable mixture. Break an egg into each depression.

Place the dish in the centre of the oven and bake for 25 to 30 minutes or until the eggs have set. Serve hot.

Egg Flan

A quick and nourishing supper dish, Egg Flan is a tasty way to use up leftover vegetables. It may be served either hot or cold, for lunch or supper.

4 SERVINGS

PASTRY
6 oz. [1½ cups] flour
⅛ teaspoon salt
1½ oz. [3 tablespoons] butter
1½ oz. [3 tablespoons] vegetable fat
1 to 2 tablespoons iced water
FILLING
1½ oz. [3 tablespoons] butter
1 medium-sized onion, finely chopped
2 tablespoons flour
10 fl. oz. [1¼ cups] milk
1 large potato, cooked and sliced
1 large carrot, scraped, cooked and diced
2 tablespoons cooked peas
½ teaspoon salt
¼ teaspoon white pepper
4 hard-boiled eggs, sliced

2 oz. [½ cup] Cheddar cheese,
grated

To make the pastry, sift the flour and
salt into a medium-sized mixing bowl.
Add the butter and vegetable fat and cut
them into small pieces with a table knife.
With your fingertips, rub the fat into the
flour until the mixture resembles fine
breadcrumbs.

Add 1 tablespoon of iced water and,
using the knife, mix it into the flour
mixture. With your hands, mix and knead
the dough until it is smooth. Add more
water if the dough is too dry. Chill the
dough in the refrigerator for 30 minutes.

Preheat the oven to fairly hot 400°F
(Gas Mark 6, 200°C).

Roll out the dough to ¼-inch thick. Lift
the dough on your rolling pin and lay it
over an 8-inch flan or pie dish. Ease the
dough into the dish and trim the edges
with a knife. Cover the dough with
aluminium foil and a layer of dried beans.
Place the dish in the oven and bake the
dough blind for 15 minutes. Remove the
dish from the oven. Remove the aluminium foil and dried beans. Return to the
oven for 10 minutes or until the pastry is
golden brown.

To make the filling, in a small saucepan, melt the butter over moderate heat.
When the foam subsides, add the onion
and cook for 5 to 7 minutes, or until it
is soft and translucent but not brown.

Remove the pan from the heat. With a
wooden spoon, stir in the flour to make a
smooth paste. Gradually add the milk,

stirring constantly.

Return the pan to the heat and, still
stirring, bring the sauce to the boil. Simmer for 2 to 3 minutes or until the sauce
is thick and smooth. Stir in the potato,
carrot, peas, salt and pepper.

Preheat the grill [broiler] to high.

Line the bottom of the pastry case
with the hard-boiled eggs. Pour the sauce
over the eggs. Sprinkle the top with the
grated cheese and place the flan under the
grill [broiler]. Grill [broil] for 3 to 4
minutes, or until the top is lightly brown.
Serve at once, if you wish to eat the flan
hot. Otherwise, allow the flan to cool to
room temperature and then chill it for
30 minutes before serving.

Egg Flip I

*This non-alcoholic Egg Flip is an ideal way
to start the day.*

1 SERVING

1 egg
½ teaspoon castor sugar
5 fl. oz. [⅝ cup] orange juice

In a small bowl, lightly beat the egg and
sugar together with a fork. Gradually
beat in the orange juice.

Serve at once.

*Serve Egg Flan, hot or cold, as a
nutritious lunch or supper dish,
accompanied by salad and bread.*

Egg Flip II

*This warming drink is an alcoholic version
of the basic egg flip and is ideal for a quick
pick-me-up or nightcap.*

1 SERVING

1 egg yolk
1 teaspoon sugar
1 tablespoon brandy
10 fl. oz. [1¼ cups] hot milk
¼ teaspoon grated nutmeg

In a small bowl, lightly beat the egg yolk
and sugar together with a fork. Gradually
beat in the brandy and hot milk. Pour the
flip into a tumbler. Sprinkle over the
nutmeg and serve.

Eggs with Mushrooms

*A delicious dish of poached eggs, baked
with cream, cheese and mushrooms, Eggs
with Mushrooms makes an excellent light
snack or appetizer for a main meal.*

4 SERVINGS

1 tablespoon plus ½ teaspoon butter
4 eggs, lightly poached
8 oz. mushrooms, wiped clean and
sliced
½ teaspoon salt
¼ teaspoon freshly ground black
pepper
⅛ teaspoon cayenne pepper
3 fl. oz. single cream [⅜ cup light
cream]
1 tablespoon finely chopped fresh
parsley
2 tablespoons grated Parmesan
cheese

Preheat the oven to moderate 350°F (Gas
Mark 4, 180°C).

With the ½ teaspoon of butter, grease a
medium-sized baking dish. Arrange the
poached eggs in the baking dish and set
aside.

In a small saucepan, melt the remaining
butter over moderate heat. When the
foam subsides, add the mushrooms, salt,
pepper and cayenne to the pan. Cook,
stirring occasionally, for 4 to 5 minutes
or until the mushrooms are cooked.
Remove the pan from the heat.

Stir the cream into the saucepan, mixing well with the mushrooms and their
juices. Stir in the parsley.

Pour the creamed mushrooms over the
eggs. Sprinkle the grated Parmesan on
top and bake at the top of the oven for
15 minutes, or until the cheese is lightly
browned.

Remove from the oven and serve
immediately.

Ranchers Eggs

A relatively inexpensive supper dish, Ranchers Eggs is delicious served with crusty French bread and butter.

6 SERVINGS

1 tablespoon olive oil
2 garlic cloves, crushed
2 onions, finely chopped
6 large tomatoes, peeled, seeded and chopped
2 oz. canned pimientos, chopped
1 green chilli, seeded and finely chopped
1 teaspoon sugar
1 teaspoon salt
½ teaspoon black pepper
½ teaspoon ground coriander
12 eggs
6 oz. [1½ cups] Cheddar cheese, grated
1 tablespoon butter, cut into small pieces
¼ teaspoon chilli powder

In a large frying-pan, heat the oil over moderate heat. Add the garlic and onions and fry, stirring occasionally, for 5 to 7 minutes, or until the onions are soft and translucent but not brown. Add the tomatoes, pimientos, chilli, sugar, salt, pepper and coriander to the pan.

Reduce the heat to low and simmer the mixture, stirring frequently, for 15 to 20 minutes or until it is soft and pulpy.

Preheat the oven to very hot 450°F (Gas Mark 8, 230°C).

Remove the pan from the heat and transfer the mixture to a large ovenproof baking dish. With the back of a tablespoon make 12 hollows in the mixture. Place one egg in each hollow. Sprinkle the cheese over the eggs. Dot the butter over the cheese and sprinkle on the chilli powder.

Place the dish in the centre of the oven and bake the eggs for 6 to 8 minutes or until the cheese is golden brown and the eggs have set. Remove the dish from the oven. Serve immediately.

Scandinavian Bacon and Egg Cake

This traditional egg cake is cooked on top of the stove until it is set. Serve for brunch or a light supper.

Ranchers Eggs makes a spicy impromptu supper for the family. Serve with lots of crusty bread.

8 oz. streaky bacon, sliced
6 eggs
4 fl. oz. double cream [½ cup heavy cream]
2 teaspoons flour
½ teaspoon salt
¼ teaspoon black pepper
2 tablespoons chopped chives

Cut each slice of bacon in half, crosswise. In a medium-sized frying-pan, fry the bacon over moderate heat for 4 to 6 minutes, or until it is golden brown.

With tongs, remove the bacon pieces from the pan and set them aside on kitchen paper towels to drain.

Pour out all but 1 tablespoon of bacon fat from the pan.

In a large mixing bowl, beat the eggs, cream, flour, salt and pepper together with a wire whisk.

Pour the egg mixture into the pan. Reduce the heat to very low.

As the mixture begins to set, lift the set edges to allow the liquid egg mixture to run on to the pan. Place the bacon on top and sprinkle over the chives. Cook for about 20 minutes, or until the underside is golden brown.

Slide the cake on to a warmed serving dish. Serve at once, cut into wedges.

Spanish-Style Eggs

Easy and quick to prepare, Spanish-Style Eggs is a tempting combination of green peppers, onions and tomatoes topped with fried eggs.

4 SERVINGS

- 3 tablespoons vegetable oil
- 2 medium-sized onions, sliced and pushed out into rings
- 1 garlic clove, chopped
- 2 small green peppers, white pith removed, seeded and sliced
- 6 tomatoes, blanched, peeled and sliced
- 4 black olives, stoned
- ½ teaspoon salt
- ¼ teaspoon black pepper
- 4 fried eggs, kept hot

In a medium-sized frying-pan, heat the oil over moderate heat. When the oil is hot, add the onions, garlic and green peppers. Cook, stirring frequently, for 5

Spanish-Style Eggs is fried eggs, served on a bed of tomatoes, onions, green peppers and black olives. Serve for a snack or supper, with lots of toast.

to 7 minutes or until the onions are soft and translucent but not brown.

Add the tomatoes, olives, salt and pepper and cook for a further 5 minutes, stirring frequently.

Remove the pan from the heat. Turn the mixture into a warmed serving dish and place the eggs on top.

Serve at once.

Eggs with Spinach

A classic dish, Eggs with Spinach is poached eggs on a bed of creamy spinach sauce. It makes a superb luncheon dish.

4 SERVINGS

- 12 fl. oz. [1½ cups] béchamel sauce
- ¼ teaspoon grated nutmeg
- 1½ lb. spinach, cooked, drained and puréed
- 8 poached eggs, kept warm
- 2 oz. [½ cup] Parmesan cheese, grated

In a medium-sized saucepan, combine one-quarter of the béchamel sauce with the nutmeg and spinach. Place the pan over moderate heat and cook, stirring constantly, for 3 to 4 minutes or until the sauce is hot and smooth.

Preheat the grill [broiler] to high.

Pour the spinach sauce into a medium-sized shallow flameproof serving dish. Place the poached eggs on top. Spoon the remaining béchamel sauce over the eggs, and sprinkle the top with the cheese. Place the dish under the grill [broiler] and grill [broil] for 3 to 4 minutes or until the top is brown and bubbly.

Remove the dish from the heat and serve immediately.

Cheese Omelet

One of the simplest of supper dishes, Cheese Omelet is also one of the tastiest and quickest to prepare. Serve with a tossed mixed green salad, sautéed potatoes and brown bread liberally spread with butter for a really satisfying informal meal.

2-3 SERVINGS

6 eggs
¼ teaspoon salt
¼ teaspoon freshly ground black pepper
2 tablespoons cold water
1 tablespoon butter
3 tablespoons grated cheese (either Parmesan or Cheddar or a mixture of Gruyère and Parmesan)

In a medium-sized mixing bowl, beat the eggs, salt, freshly ground pepper and water together with a kitchen fork until they are well mixed.

In a large omelet pan, melt the butter over moderate heat. When the foam subsides, pour in the egg mixture. Stir the eggs, then leave them for a few seconds until the bottom sets. Reduce the heat to low. Using a palette knife or spatula, lift the edges of the omelet and, at the same time, tilt the pan away from you so that the liquid egg escapes from the top and runs on to the pan. Put the pan down flat over the heat and sprinkle over the grated cheese. Leave until the omelet begins to set again. Tilt the pan away from you again and, with the help of the palette knife, flip one half of the omelet over to make a semi-circle.

Remove the pan from the heat and slide the omelet quickly on to a heated serving dish.

Cut into two or three and serve it at once.

Green Pea Omelet

A deliciously different omelet, Green Pea Omelet may be served with fried potatoes

and buttered carrots.

2-3 SERVINGS

4 oz. peas, weighed after shelling
1¼ teaspoons salt
1 oz. [2 tablespoons] butter
6 eggs
¼ teaspoon freshly ground black pepper
2 tablespoons cold water

Place the peas in a medium-sized saucepan and sprinkle over 1 teaspoon of the salt. Add enough water just to cover the peas. Place the pan over moderately high heat and bring the water to the boil. Reduce the heat to moderate and cook the peas for 8 to 10 minutes or until they are tender.

Remove the pan from the heat and drain the peas in a colander.

Purée the peas in a food mill or in an electric blender. Place the purée in a small bowl. Add half of the butter and stir until the butter has melted. Set aside and keep warm.

In a medium-sized mixing bowl, beat the eggs, the remaining salt, the freshly ground pepper and water together with a kitchen fork until they are well mixed.

In a large omelet pan, melt the remaining butter over moderate heat. When the foam subsides, pour in the egg mixture. Stir the eggs, then leave them for a few seconds until the bottom sets. Reduce the heat to low. Using a palette knife or spatula, lift the edges of the omelet and, at the same time, tilt the pan away from you so that the liquid egg escapes from the top and runs on to the pan. Put the pan down flat over the heat and leave until the omelet begins to set again.

Spoon over the pea purée. Tilt the pan away from you again and, with the help of the palette knife, flip one half of the omelet over to make a semi-circle.

Remove the pan from the heat and slide the omelet quickly on to a warmed serving dish.

Cut into two or three and serve it at once.

Omelet with Haddock, Cream and Cheese

This omelet is different from the classic French omelet in that the eggs are separated and the omelet finished cooking under the grill [broiler]. Serve with puréed spinach for a light but satisfying meal.

2-3 SERVINGS

1½ oz. [3 tablespoons] butter
4 oz. cooked, flaked smoked haddock
5 fl. oz. double cream [⅝ cup heavy cream]
6 eggs, separated
3 tablespoons grated Parmesan cheese
½ teaspoon salt
¼ teaspoon black pepper
1 tablespoon chopped fresh parsley

In a small frying-pan, melt 1 ounce [2 tablespoons] of the butter over moderate heat. When the foam subsides, add the smoked haddock and 2 tablespoons of cream, stirring well to mix. When the cream is hot, remove the pan from the heat and set aside to cool.

In a large mixing bowl, beat the egg yolks with half of the cheese and the salt, pepper and parsley. Add the fish mixture.

In another large mixing bowl, beat the egg whites with a wire whisk or rotary beater until they form stiff peaks. With a metal spoon, fold the egg whites into the haddock mixture.

Preheat the grill [broiler] to high.

In a large omelet pan, melt the remaining butter over moderate heat. When the foam subsides, pour in the egg mixture.

Leave it for 2 minutes or until the bottom sets and becomes brown.

Sprinkle over the remaining cheese and pour over the remaining cream. Remove the pan from the heat and place it under the grill [broiler]. Grill [broil] for 30 seconds.

Remove the pan from the grill [broiler]

and transfer the omelet to a warmed serving dish. Cut into two or three and serve at once.

Ham Omelet

A nourishing yet delicate dish, Ham Omelet makes an excellent supper dish, served with a tomato salad and a green vegetable.

2-3 SERVINGS

1 oz. [2 tablespoons] butter
2 oz. lean cooked ham, diced
6 eggs
¼ teaspoon salt
¼ teaspoon black pepper
2 tablespoons cold water

In a small frying-pan, melt half of the butter over moderate heat. When the foam subsides, add the ham and cook, stirring occasionally, for 5 minutes or until the ham is heated through and very lightly browned. Remove the pan from the heat and set aside. Keep warm.

In a medium-sized mixing bowl, beat the eggs, salt, pepper and water together with a fork until they are well mixed.

In a large omelet pan, melt the remaining butter over moderate heat. When the foam subsides, pour in the egg mixture. Stir the eggs, then leave them for a few seconds until the bottom sets. Reduce the heat to low. Using a palette knife or spatula, lift the edges of the omelet and, at the same time, tilt the pan away from you so that the liquid egg escapes from the top and runs on to the pan. Put the pan down flat over the heat and leave until the omelet begins to set again. Spoon over the ham. Tilt the pan away from you again and, with the help of the palette knife, flip one half of the omelet over to make a semi-circle.

Remove the pan from the heat and slide the omelet quickly on to a warmed serving dish. Cut into two or three and serve at once.

Herb Omelet

One of the great classic French omelets, Herb Omelet makes a delicious and elegant lunch dish. Serve with buttered asparagus tips and a green salad and, to drink, a well-chilled white Chablis wine.

2-3 SERVINGS

6 eggs
¼ teaspoon salt
¼ teaspoon freshly ground black pepper
2 tablespoons cold water
1½ tablespoons chopped fresh mixed herbs
1 tablespoon butter

In a medium-sized mixing bowl, beat the eggs, salt, pepper, water and mixed herbs together with a fork until they are well mixed.

In a large omelet pan, melt the butter over moderate heat. When the foam subsides, pour in the egg mixture. Stir the eggs, then leave them for a few seconds until the bottom sets. Reduce the heat to low. Using a palette knife or spatula, lift the edges of the omelet and, at the same time, tilt the pan away from you so that the liquid egg escapes from the top and runs on to the pan. Put the pan down flat over the heat and leave until the omelet begins to set again. Tilt the pan away from you again and, with the help of the palette knife, flip one half of the omelet over to make a semi-circle.

Remove the pan from the heat and slide the omelet quickly on to a heated serving dish.

Cut into two or three and serve it at once.

Onion, Mushroom and Bacon Omelet

This sustaining dish may be served with grilled [broiled] tomatoes and a mixed

salad, for supper or lunch.

2 SERVINGS

1 oz. [2 tablespoons] butter
1 medium-sized onion, finely chopped
2 lean bacon slices, rinds removed and diced
4 medium-sized mushrooms, wiped clean and thinly sliced
4 eggs
¼ teaspoon salt
¼ teaspoon freshly ground black pepper
1½ tablespoons cold water

In a small frying-pan, melt half of the butter over moderate heat. When the foam subsides, add the onion and bacon and cook, stirring occasionally, for 5 minutes. Add the mushrooms and cook for a further 3 minutes, or until the mushrooms are lightly cooked and the bacon is crisp. Remove the pan from the heat and, with a slotted spoon, transfer the mixture to a plate. Set aside and keep the mixture warm.

In a medium-sized mixing bowl, beat the eggs, salt, pepper and water together with a fork. Add the onion mixture and beat briskly until the ingredients are well mixed.

In a medium-sized omelet pan, melt the remaining butter over moderate heat. When the foam subsides, pour in the egg mixture. Stir the eggs, then leave them for a few seconds until the bottom sets. Reduce the heat to low. Using a palette knife or spatula, lift the edges of the omelet and, at the same time, tilt the pan away from you so that the liquid egg escapes from the top and runs on to the pan. Put the pan down flat over the heat and leave until the omelet begins to set again. Tilt the pan away from you again and, with the help of the palette knife, flip one half of the omelet over to make a semi-circle.

Remove the pan from the heat and slide the omelet quickly on to a warmed serving dish. Cut into two and serve at once.

Algerian Scrambled Eggs with Sausage and Green Peppers

This spicy dish is easy to prepare and can be served as a snack lunch or as an informal supper. Accompany with lots of crusty bread and lager.

4 SERVINGS

½ teaspoon cayenne pepper
¼ teaspoon ground cumin
⅛ teaspoon salt
2 tablespoons olive oil
1 lb. spicy sausage, such as hot Italian sausage or Spanish chorizos, cut into 1-inch rounds
1 garlic clove, crushed
14 oz. canned peeled Italian tomatoes, drained and chopped
¼ teaspoon freshly ground black pepper
2 medium-sized green peppers, white pith removed, seeded and cut into strips
6 eggs, lightly beaten

In a small dish, mix the cayenne, cumin and salt together. Set aside.

In a large, heavy frying-pan, heat the oil over moderate heat. When the oil is hot, add the sausage and fry, turning from time to time, for 4 minutes or until the slices are evenly browned and cooked through.

Stir in the garlic, cayenne mixture, the tomatoes and black pepper. Cook, stirring occasionally, for 3 minutes or until the mixture is thick. Add the pepper strips, cover and cook, stirring occasionally, for 8 minutes.

Pour the beaten eggs, a little at a time, over the sausage mixture, stirring constantly. Cook over low heat, stirring constantly, for 3 to 5 minutes or until the eggs are just scrambled.

Remove the pan from the heat, transfer the scrambled egg mixture to a warmed dish and serve at once.

Egg and Bacon Scramble

This tasty dish of eggs cooked with bacon and vegetables may be served as a light lunch or supper dish. Accompany with lots of hot buttered toast.

4 SERVINGS

1 tablespoon vegetable oil
1 medium-sized onion, finely chopped
8 slices streaky bacon,

Courgettes [zucchini], bacon, tomatoes, mushrooms and eggs form the basis of Egg and Bacon Scramble. It makes a filling, tasty and inexpensive dish.

coarsely chopped
4 courgettes [zucchini], trimmed and chopped
2 large tomatoes, blanched, peeled and chopped
4 oz. button mushrooms, wiped clean and halved
½ teaspoon salt
¼ teaspoon freshly ground black pepper
6 eggs
4 tablespoons milk
⅛ teaspoon grated nutmeg
2 oz. [1 cup] coarse fresh white breadcrumbs
1 tablespoon butter, cut into small pieces

In a shallow, flameproof casserole, heat the oil over moderate heat. When the oil is hot, add the onion and bacon and cook, stirring occasionally, for 7 minutes or until the onion is soft but not brown and the bacon pieces are cooked through and crisp.

Add the courgettes [zucchini], tomatoes, mushrooms, salt and pepper to the casserole. Reduce the heat to low and cook, stirring occasionally, for 15 minutes or until the courgettes [zucchini] are tender. Remove the casserole from the heat and set aside.

Preheat the grill [broiler] to moderately high.

In a medium-sized mixing bowl, beat

mixture. Cook for 5 to 7 minutes, stirring constantly, or until the eggs are firm and only slightly moist.

Remove the pan from the heat and transfer the mixture to a warmed serving dish.

Serve immediately.

Savoury Scramble

A delicious, spicy lunch or supper dish, Savoury Scramble is very quick to make and may be served on hot buttered toast.

4 SERVINGS

1 oz. [2 tablespoons] butter
1 medium-sized onion, finely chopped
10 lambs' kidneys, cleaned, prepared and quartered
2 oz. mushrooms, wiped clean and chopped
1 tablespoon flour
5 fl. oz. [⅝ cup] home-made beef stock
½ teaspoon Tabasco sauce
1 tablespoon tomato purée
2 tablespoons finely chopped fresh parsley
1 teaspoon salt
½ teaspoon freshly ground black pepper
8 eggs, lightly beaten

In a large saucepan, melt the butter over moderate heat. When the foam subsides, add the onion and fry, stirring occasionally, for 5 to 7 minutes or until it is soft and translucent but not brown. Add the kidneys and mushrooms and fry, stirring occasionally, for 3 minutes. Stir in the flour and cook for 1 minute. Remove the pan from the heat and gradually stir in the stock, Tabasco sauce and tomato purée. Return the pan to the heat and cook, stirring constantly, for 2 minutes. Reduce the heat to low and simmer for 20 minutes.

Stir in the parsley, salt and pepper. Remove the pan from the heat and stir in the eggs, beating with a wooden spoon until the ingredients are thoroughly combined. Return the pan to low heat. Stir for 3 to 5 minutes or until the eggs are set.

Remove the pan from the heat and serve at once.

---

the eggs, milk and nutmeg together. Stir the egg-and-milk mixture into the casserole. Return the casserole to the heat and cook gently, stirring constantly, until the eggs are nearly scrambled. Remove the casserole from the heat.

Sprinkle the breadcrumbs on top of the mixture and carefully dot with the butter pieces.

Place the casserole under the grill [broiler] and grill [broil] the mixture for 3 minutes or until the top is lightly browned.

Remove the casserole from the heat and serve immediately, straight from the casserole.

Matzo Brei

SCRAMBLED EGGS AND MATZO

A traditional Jewish breakfast dish served during Passover, Matzo Brei may also be served as an after-dinner savoury. Fried onions may be added if liked.

2 SERVINGS

2 matzos, broken into 2-inch pieces
4 fl. oz. [½ cup] milk
2 eggs, lightly beaten
½ teaspoon salt
⅛ teaspoon grated nutmeg
1 tablespoon butter

Place the matzo pieces in a large mixing bowl and pour over the milk.

Leave to soak for about 5 minutes. With a slotted spoon, transfer the matzos to a medium-sized mixing bowl. Discard any leftover milk.

Pour the eggs on to the matzos. Add the salt and nutmeg and mix well with a wooden spoon.

In a medium-sized saucepan, melt the butter over moderate heat. When the foam subsides, pour in the matzo and egg

Cheese and Sour Cream Soufflé

Adapted from an old Romanian recipe, Cheese and Sour Cream Soufflé may be served with salad as an unusual lunch or light supper dish.

4 SERVINGS

1 tablespoon butter, softened
3 teaspoons flour
8 oz. cream cheese
3 fl. oz. [⅜ cup] sour cream
3 egg yolks
3 fl. oz. [⅜ cup] milk
½ teaspoon salt
4 egg whites

Preheat the oven to fairly hot 400°F (Gas Mark 6, 200°C).

Using your fingertips or a piece of paper, spread the softened butter over the bottom and sides of a 7-inch soufflé dish. Sprinkle about 1 teaspoon of flour into the soufflé dish and shake it so that it evenly coats the insides. Knock out any excess flour and set the dish aside.

In a mixing bowl, beat the cream cheese with a wooden spoon until it is soft and creamy. Using a whisk, beat in the sour cream, a spoonful at a time. Continue to beat until the mixture is smooth.

Add the egg yolks, one at a time, beating well after each addition. Stir in the milk, salt and the remaining flour, beating briskly until the mixture is smooth.

In a large bowl, beat the egg whites with a wire whisk or rotary beater until they form stiff peaks. Using a metal spoon, fold the whites into the egg yolk and sour cream mixture.

Reduce the oven temperature to fairly hot 375°F (Gas Mark 5, 190°C) and pour the mixture into the prepared soufflé dish. Bake the soufflé in the centre of the oven for 25 to 35 minutes or until it has risen and is golden brown on top, and a skewer inserted into the middle comes out clean.

Remove the soufflé from the oven and serve immediately.

Parsnip Soufflé

Parsnip Soufflé makes an unusual and deliciously flavoured lunch or supper dish.

Soufflés are relatively simple to make yet always seem somehow 'special' to eat - this Cheese and Sour Cream Soufflé is inexpensive enough to serve for a family supper, yet elegant enough for a party.

Serve with parsley potatoes and tomato salad.

4 SERVINGS

2 oz. [¼ cup] butter
3 medium-sized parsnips, peeled, cooked and drained
1 large onion, boiled, drained and chopped
½ teaspoon salt
1 teaspoon freshly ground black pepper
¼ teaspoon ground cloves
2 fl. oz. single cream [¼ cup light cream]
2 oz. [½ cup] flour
6 fl. oz. [¾ cup] milk
4 egg yolks
5 egg whites

Preheat the oven to fairly hot 400°F (Gas Mark 6, 200°C).

Using 1 tablespoon of the butter, grease a 3-pint [2-quart] soufflé dish and set it aside.

Using the back of a wooden spoon, rub the parsnips and onion through a large, fine strainer into a medium-sized mixing bowl. Add the salt, pepper and cloves and stir in the cream. Set aside.

In a medium-sized saucepan, melt the remaining butter over moderate heat. Remove the pan from the heat and, with the wooden spoon, stir in the flour to make a smooth paste. Gradually add the milk, stirring constantly.

Return the pan to the heat and cook, stirring constantly, for 2 to 3 minutes or until the sauce is thick and smooth. Add the parsnip mixture, stirring constantly, and continue cooking for a further 4 minutes.

Remove the pan from the heat and set aside to cool to lukewarm. Stir in the egg yolks and mix well until the ingredients are thoroughly combined.

In a medium-sized mixing bowl, beat the egg whites with a wire whisk or rotary beater until they form stiff peaks. Using a large metal spoon, carefully fold the egg whites into the sauce.

Pour the mixture into the prepared soufflé dish. Place the dish in the centre of the oven and reduce the heat to fairly hot 375°F (Gas Mark 5, 190°C). Bake for 20 to 30 minutes or until the soufflé has risen and is golden brown on top, and a skewer inserted into the centre comes out clean.

Remove the soufflé from the oven and serve immediately.

Spinach Soufflé with Ham

A tasty mixture of spinach, ham and cheese

combines to make Spinach Soufflé with Ham a satisfying dish to serve for a light lunch.

4 SERVINGS

3 oz. [⅜ cup] butter
2 shallots, finely chopped
4 oz. lean cooked ham, finely chopped
2 oz. [½ cup] flour
4 fl. oz. [½ cup] milk
4 tablespoons spinach purée
½ teaspoon salt
1 teaspoon freshly ground black pepper
1 teaspoon paprika
2 oz. [½ cup] Emmenthal cheese, grated
2 tablespoons single [light] cream
4 egg yolks
5 egg whites

Preheat the oven to fairly hot 400°F (Gas Mark 6, 200°C). Grease a 2½-pint [1½-quart] soufflé dish with a tablespoon of the butter. Set aside.

In a medium-sized saucepan, melt 1 ounce [2 tablespoons] of the remaining butter over moderate heat. When the foam subsides, add the shallots and ham and cook, stirring frequently, for 3 to 4 minutes or until the shallots are soft and translucent but not brown. With a slotted spoon, remove the shallots and ham from the pan and keep warm.

Add the remaining butter to the pan and melt it over moderate heat. Remove the pan from the heat and, with a wooden spoon, stir in the flour to make a smooth paste. Gradually add the milk, stirring constantly. Stir in the spinach.

Return the pan to the heat and cook, stirring constantly, for 2 to 3 minutes or until the sauce is thick and smooth. Stir in the salt, pepper, paprika and cheese and cook, stirring constantly, for a further 2 minutes or until the cheese has melted. Remove the pan from the heat and stir in the cream. Add the reserved shallot and ham mixture and stir well to mix. Set aside to cool to lukewarm, then beat in the egg yolks, one at a time.

In a mixing bowl, beat the egg whites with a wire whisk or rotary beater until they form stiff peaks. With a metal spoon, carefully fold the beaten egg whites into the sauce. Pour the mixture into the soufflé dish.

Place the dish in the centre of the oven and reduce the temperature to fairly hot 375°F (Gas Mark 5, 190°C). Bake for 25 to 30 minutes or until the soufflé has risen and is golden brown on top, and a skewer inserted into the centre comes out clean.

Remove from the oven and serve the soufflé immediately.

Eggs Stuffed with Ham and Herbs

Hard-boiled eggs stuffed with a delicious ham and herb mixture and then fried, Eggs Stuffed with Ham and Herbs may be served with a thick tomato and onion sauce for a superbly sustaining family lunch or supper.

2 SERVINGS

4 hard-boiled eggs
2 oz. cooked ham, very finely chopped
4 oz. [½ cup] butter
1 tablespoon finely chopped chives
2 teaspoons chopped fresh thyme or 1 teaspoon dried thyme
1 teaspoon Worcestershire sauce
2 eggs
½ teaspoon salt
¼ teaspoon freshly ground black pepper
4 tablespoons dry white breadcrumbs

Cut the eggs in half, lengthways. Remove the yolks and place them in a medium-sized mixing bowl. Set the whites aside. Add the ham, half of the butter, the chives, thyme, Worcestershire sauce, one egg, salt and pepper.

With a wooden spoon, cream the mixture thoroughly until it is well blended and smooth.

Spoon the mixture into the egg white halves. Sandwich the halves together to form a whole egg. The halves should not fit tightly together.

In a small bowl, lightly beat the second egg with a fork. Roll the stuffed eggs in the beaten egg and then in the breadcrumbs.

In a medium-sized frying-pan, melt the remaining butter over moderate heat. When the foam subsides, place the stuffed eggs in the pan and fry them, turning occasionally, for 5 minutes, or until they are golden brown all over.

With a slotted spoon, carefully transfer the stuffed eggs from the pan to a warmed serving dish.

Serve at once.

Mexican Stuffed Eggs

An unusual combination of egg, green pepper, avocado and prawns or shrimps, Mexican Stuffed Eggs may be served as a refreshing appetizer to dinner or as part of a cold buffet. Serve on a bed of lettuce leaves, garnished with sliced tomatoes and stuffed green olives.

6 SERVINGS

6 hard-boiled eggs
1 medium-sized avocado, peeled, stoned and chopped
1 medium-sized onion, finely minced
1 small green pepper, white pith removed, seeded and finely minced
4 oz. small prawns or shrimps, shelled, deveined and finely chopped
1 teaspoon lemon juice
1 teaspoon wine vinegar
½ teaspoon salt
½ teaspoon freshly ground black pepper
⅛ teaspoon cayenne pepper
1 tablespoon finely chopped fresh parsley

Slice the eggs in half, lengthways, and scoop out the yolks. Set the egg whites

Eggs Stuffed with Ham and Herbs are very versatile - serve them with tomato sauce, crusty bread and salad for a satisfying lunch or supper, or as a filling between-meals snack.

Mexican Stuffed Eggs are a spicy mixture of avocado, onion, green pepper and prawns or shrimps stuffed into hard-boiled egg halves.

aside. Using the back of a wooden spoon, rub the yolks and the avocado flesh through a fine nylon strainer into a medium-sized mixing bowl. Carefully stir in the onion, green pepper and chopped prawns or shrimps.

Add the lemon juice, vinegar, salt, pepper and cayenne, mixing well to blend. With a teaspoon, generously stuff the egg white halves with the mixture. Arrange the stuffed eggs on a serving dish. Sprinkle with the parsley and chill the eggs in the refrigerator for 30 minutes before serving.

Scotch Eggs

A very old favourite in the British Isles, Scotch Eggs are a delicious and nourishing snack or meal, with some tossed mixed salad and lots of liberally buttered brown bread. Served hot with a tomato sauce, or cold with a salad, they are ideal for the busy housewife to prepare. In past centuries, Scotch Eggs were sometimes called birds' nests.

4 SERVINGS

1 lb. pork sausage meat
2 teaspoons Worcestershire sauce
1 tablespoon seasoned flour, made with 1 tablespoon flour, ⅛ teaspoon salt, ⅛ teaspoon black pepper and ⅛ teaspoon dried thyme
4 medium-sized hard-boiled eggs
1 large egg, well beaten
2 oz. [⅔ cup] fine dry breadcrumbs sufficient vegetable oil for deep-frying

Place the sausage meat and Worcestershire sauce in a medium-sized mixing bowl. Add the seasoned flour mixture and blend the ingredients together with your hands. Divide the mixture into four equal pieces.

Mould each piece of meat around an egg and carefully roll each egg between your hands to shape the sausage meat coating.

Place the beaten egg and breadcrumbs in two separate, shallow dishes. Dip the eggs first in the beaten egg, and then in the breadcrumbs, coating them thoroughly and shaking off any excess crumbs. Set aside.

Fill a large saucepan or deep-frying pan one-third full with vegetable oil.

Place the pan over moderate heat and heat the oil until it reaches 350°F on a deep-fat thermometer or until a small cube of stale bread dropped into the oil turns light brown in 55 seconds.

Using tongs or a slotted spoon, carefully lower the eggs into the oil. Fry them for 5 minutes, or until they are deep golden brown.

Remove the pan from the heat. Using the tongs or slotted spoon, transfer the eggs to kitchen paper towels to drain.

Place the eggs on a warmed serving plate and serve at once, if they are to be eaten hot.

Eggs Stuffed with Tuna

Stuffed with a mixture of tuna fish, pickled gherkins and mayonnaise, these eggs make an attractive hors d'oeuvre or part of a cold buffet. Or serve them with lots of brown bread and butter for a light summer lunch or supper.

6-12 SERVINGS

2 oz. [¼ cup] butter
4 oz. canned tuna fish, drained and flaked
1 tablespoon lemon juice
4 tablespoons mayonnaise
¼ teaspoon freshly ground black pepper

½ teaspoon paprika
3 small, sweet pickled gherkins, finely chopped
12 hard-boiled eggs
1 bunch of watercress, washed and shaken dry

In a medium-sized mixing bowl, mash the butter and tuna fish together with a kitchen fork until they are thoroughly combined. Add the lemon juice, mayonnaise, black pepper, paprika and chopped pickled gherkins. Combine the ingredients thoroughly and set the bowl aside.

Cut off about 1 inch of the rounded end of each of the eggs. Retain these 'lids'. Slice a thin strip from the pointed ends of each of the eggs so that they will sit flat. Using a teaspoon, carefully remove the egg yolks from the whites, being careful to keep the whites intact. Set the whites aside.

Mash the egg yolks into the tuna fish mixture with a fork, mixing them in thoroughly. Carefully stuff the egg whites with the tuna and egg yolk mixture. Replace the 'lids' on top of the stuffed eggs.

Arrange the watercress on a large shallow serving dish. Place the eggs, standing upright, on the cress.

Place the serving dish in the refrigerator and allow the eggs to chill for 20 minutes before serving.

Eggs in Artichokes

These unusual stuffed artichokes make an ideal appetizer for a dinner or lunch party, being both decorative and delicious. They can also be served as a vegetable accompaniment to grilled [broiled] steak or chops.

4 SERVINGS

4 medium-sized artichokes, cooked and cooled
4 hard-boiled eggs
½ teaspoon salt
¼ teaspoon black pepper
⅛ teaspoon cayenne pepper
4 oz. canned sweetcorn, drained
2 tablespoons chopped fresh chives
2 tablespoons double [heavy] cream
1 oz. [2 tablespoons] butter, melted
3 oz. [¾ cup] Parmesan cheese, grated

Preheat the oven to moderate 350°F (Gas Mark 4, 180°C).

Gently pull the leaves of each artichoke apart and remove the yellow inner core. With a fork or spoon, scrape out the choke and discard it. Trim the base of each artichoke so that it stands upright. Place the artichokes in a baking dish.

Slice the eggs in half and scoop out the yolks. Rub the yolks through a fine strainer into a medium-sized mixing bowl. Finely chop the egg whites and add them to the bowl. Mix in the salt, pepper, cayenne, sweetcorn, chives and cream.

Fill the centre of each artichoke with the egg mixture. Using a pastry brush, coat the leaves of the artichoke with the melted butter. Top each filling with a liberal sprinkling of cheese.

Pour a little water around the artichokes and place the dish in the oven. Bake for 10 minutes or until the filling is melted and brown. Serve at once.

Eggs in Baked Potatoes

A delicious and filling dish suitable for a light informal lunch or dinner, these baked potatoes are stuffed with a mixture of eggs, butter, cream and chives.

4 SERVINGS

4 large potatoes, scrubbed
1 tablespoon butter
1 tablespoon chopped chives
1 teaspoon salt
¼ teaspoon black pepper
⅛ teaspoon grated nutmeg
4 tablespoons double [heavy] cream
4 eggs

Preheat the oven to fairly hot 375°F (Gas Mark 5, 190°C).

Prick the potatoes lightly with a fork. Place the potatoes on the centre shelf in the oven and bake them for 1½ hours.

Remove the potatoes from the oven and cut off an inch from the top of each one. Scoop out the inside of each potato, taking care not to break the skin.

In a mixing bowl, mash the potato

Eggs in Baked Potatoes is a satisfying snack lunch.

flesh and butter together using a fork. Add the chives, salt, pepper and nutmeg. Stir in the cream and beat until the ingredients are thoroughly combined. Gradually beat in the eggs.

Stuff equal amounts of the egg and cream filling into each potato. Place the potatoes in a baking dish and return them to the oven. Bake for 10 to 12 minutes, or until the top of the filling is lightly browned. Serve immediately.

Eggs Benedict

Crumpets [English muffins] topped with ham, poached eggs and hollandaise sauce, Eggs Benedict is a famous American dish.

4 SERVINGS

8 thick slices cooked ham
8 crumpets [English muffins]
1 oz. [2 tablespoons] butter
8 hot poached eggs
HOLLANDAISE SAUCE
3 egg yolks
1 tablespoon cold water
4 oz. [½ cup] butter, softened
¼ teaspoon salt
⅛ teaspoon cayenne pepper
1 teaspoon lemon juice
1 tablespoon single [light] cream

Preheat the oven to very cool 275°F (Gas Mark 1, 140°C).

Preheat the grill [broiler] to high.

Place the ham slices on the grill [broiler] pan and grill [broil] them for 2 to 3 minutes on each side. Transfer the ham slices to an ovenproof dish and put it in the oven to keep warm.

To prepare the sauce, in a heatproof bowl set over a pan of hot water, beat the egg yolks and the water together with a wire whisk until the mixture is pale.

Gradually beat in the butter, in small pieces. Continue beating until the sauce begins to thicken.

Add the salt, cayenne and lemon juice. Beat in the cream. Remove the pan from the heat and set it aside. Keep warm.

Toast the crumpets [muffins] and spread them with the butter. Arrange the crumpets [muffins] on warmed plates. Place a slice of ham on each crumpet [muffin] and top with a poached egg.

Spoon a little of the sauce over each crumpet [muffin] and serve at once.

Egg Bread

This beautifully light Egg Bread, or Challah, is plaited [braided] and sprinkled with poppy seeds. It is traditionally baked

for Hebrew Sabbaths and festivals.

ONE 2-POUND LOAF

½ oz. fresh yeast
1½ tablespoons sugar
6 fl. oz. [¾ cup] milk, lukewarm
1 lb. [4 cups] flour
1½ teaspoons salt
2 eggs, beaten
1 tablespoon vegetable oil
½ teaspoon butter

GLAZE
1 egg yolk, beaten with 1 tablespoon
   cold water
2 tablespoons poppy seeds

Crumble the yeast into a small bowl and mash in ½ teaspoon of the sugar with a fork. Add 2 teaspoons of the warm milk and cream the milk and yeast together to form a smooth paste. Cover the bowl with a clean cloth and set it aside in a warm, draught-free place for 15 to 20 minutes, or until the yeast mixture has risen and is puffed up and frothy.

Sift the flour, remaining sugar and the salt into a large, warmed mixing bowl. Make a well in the centre of the flour and pour in the yeast mixture. Add the remaining milk, eggs and oil and, using a spatula, gradually draw the flour into the liquid. Continue mixing until all the flour is incorporated and the dough

Eggs Benedict, an American classic.

comes away from the sides of the bowl.

Cover the bowl with a clean damp cloth. Set the bowl in a warm, draught-free place and leave it for 1½ to 2 hours, or until the dough has risen and has almost doubled in bulk.

Grease a baking sheet with the butter.

Turn the risen dough out of the bowl on to a lightly floured surface and knead it for about 5 to 8 minutes. Divide the dough into three ropes, each about 12 inches long. Fasten the ropes together at one end and loosely plait [braid] the three pieces together, fastening again at the end.

Place the loaf on the greased baking sheet and cover it again with a clean cloth. Set it aside in a warm place for 2 to 2½ hours, or until the loaf has risen and expanded across the baking sheet.

Preheat the oven to hot 425°F (Gas Mark 7, 220°C).

Paint the top of the loaf with the egg yolk glaze and sprinkle the poppy seeds over the top. Place the baking sheet in the centre of the oven and bake for 10 minutes. Then reduce the temperature to fairly hot 375°F (Gas Mark 5, 190°C) and bake for a further 25 to 30 minutes or until the loaf is golden brown.

After removing the bread from the oven, tip the loaf off the baking sheet and rap the underside with your knuckles. If the bread sounds hollow, like a drum, it is cooked. If it does not sound hollow, return it to the oven for a further 5 to 10 minutes. Cool the loaf on a wire rack.

Eggs Caviar

☆   ① ①   ⊠

These stuffed eggs make an extravagant and tempting hors d'oeuvre.

6 SERVINGS

6 hard-boiled eggs
1 tablespoon black or red caviar
1 teaspoon lemon juice
¼ teaspoon cayenne pepper
1 bunch watercress

Cut the eggs in half, lengthways. Cut a thin slice off the bottom of each half so that the stuffed eggs will have a flat bottom. Remove the yolks and press them through a strainer into a bowl.

With a fork, beat the caviar, lemon juice and cayenne into the yolks.

Spoon the mixture into the egg whites. Arrange on a serving dish and chill for 30 minutes.

Garnish with the watercress and serve.

Egg-Drop Soup

A light, delicate first course, this classic Egg-Drop Soup is adapted from a Cantonese recipe.

6 SERVINGS

1 tablespoon vegetable oil
1 medium-sized onion, thinly sliced
1 small cucumber, finely diced
3 pints [7½ cups] hot chicken stock
4 tomatoes, quartered
1 egg, lightly beaten

In a large saucepan, heat the oil over moderate heat. When it is hot, add the onion and cook, stirring constantly, for 1 minute. Add the cucumber to the pan and cook, still stirring, for 1 minute.

Stir in the chicken stock and bring it to the boil. Reduce the heat to low and simmer, stirring occasionally, for 10 minutes. Add the tomatoes to the soup and simmer for a further 5 minutes.

Remove the pan from the heat and beat the egg into the soup. Serve at once.

Eggs Mornay

Poached eggs and ham on toast with a creamy cheese sauce, Eggs Mornay is the ideal dish for a quick supper snack.

4 SERVINGS

4 slices hot, buttered toast
1 tablespoon butter
4 thick slices cooked lean ham
4 poached eggs, kept warm
SAUCE
1½ oz. [3 tablespoons] butter
3 tablespoons flour
8 fl. oz. [1 cup] milk
5 fl. oz. single cream [⅝ cup light cream]
½ teaspoon salt
¼ teaspoon black pepper
⅛ teaspoon cayenne pepper
1 teaspoon Worcestershire sauce
1 teaspoon paprika
2 oz. [½ cup] Cheddar cheese, grated

First make the sauce. In a saucepan, melt the butter over moderate heat. Remove the pan from the heat and, with a wooden spoon, stir in the flour to make a smooth paste. Gradually add the milk and cream, stirring constantly. Add the salt, pepper, cayenne, Worcestershire sauce and paprika, and stir well.

Return the pan to the heat and, stirring constantly, bring the sauce to the boil. Boil for 1 minute, stirring, or until the sauce is thick. Stir in the cheese. Remove from the heat and keep hot.

Preheat the grill [broiler] to high.

Line the grill [broiler] pan with aluminium foil. Place the toast slices on the foil. Set aside.

In a frying-pan, melt the butter over moderate heat. Add the ham to the pan and heat it for 2 minutes on each side.

Remove the slices of ham from the pan and place them on the slices of toast.

Top each slice of ham with a poached egg and spoon the hot sauce over the eggs. Place the grill [broiler] pan under the heat and grill [broil] for 1 to 2 minutes or until the sauce is golden and bubbling.

Remove the pan from the heat and serve immediately.

Egg Mousse

A delightful dish for a summer buffet lunch, this Egg Mousse is surprisingly easy to prepare.

8-10 SERVINGS

1 teaspoon vegetable oil
½ oz. gelatine
3 fl. oz. [⅜ cup] white wine
2 egg yolks, at room temperature
1 teaspoon salt
¾ teaspoon dry mustard
⅛ teaspoon white pepper
8 fl. oz. [1 cup] olive oil, at room temperature
1 tablespoon lemon juice or white wine vinegar
6 to 8 anchovies, soaked in milk for 10 minutes, drained and finely chopped
1 large onion, finely chopped
1 tablespoon chopped fresh parsley
1 tablespoon chopped fresh chives
10 hard-boiled eggs, chopped
8 fl. oz. [1 cup] béchamel sauce
8 fl. oz. double cream [1 cup heavy cream], lightly beaten
¼ teaspoon cayenne pepper
½ teaspoon paprika
10 stuffed olives, sliced

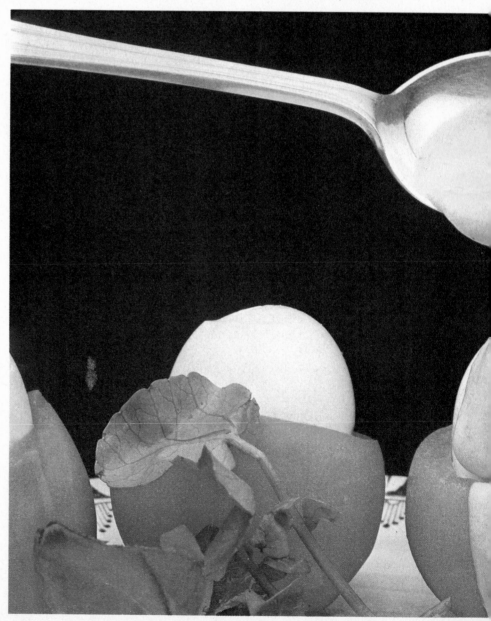

Using the oil, grease a 2½-pint [1½-quart] mould. Turn the mould upside down on kitchen paper towels to drain out any excess oil.

Place the gelatine in a heatproof mixing bowl. Add the wine and place the bowl over a pan of simmering water. Stir constantly to dissolve the gelatine. Remove from the heat.

Place the egg yolks, ½ teaspoon salt, the mustard and pepper in a mixing bowl. Using a wire whisk, beat the ingredients until they are thoroughly blended. Add the oil, a few drops at a time, whisking constantly. Do not add the oil too quickly or the mayonnaise will curdle. After the mayonnaise has thickened the oil may be added a little more rapidly.

Beat in a few drops of lemon juice or

Elegant Portuguese Eggs in Tomato Shells may be served cold, as a first course to a special dinner.

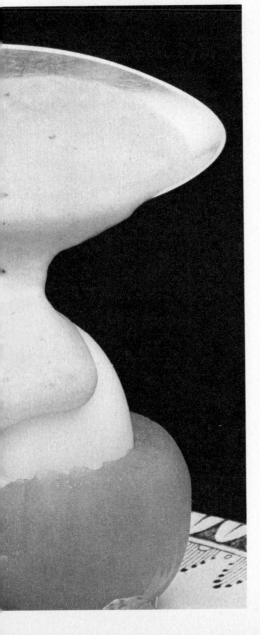

vinegar from time to time to prevent the mayonnaise from becoming too thick. When all the oil has been added, stir in the remaining lemon juice or vinegar. Taste for seasoning and add more salt, mustard and vinegar if desired.

Stir the anchovies, onion, parsley, chives, eggs and dissolved gelatine into the mayonnaise. Fold in the béchamel sauce with the cream, cayenne, paprika and the remaining salt.

Pour the mixture into the mould and place it in the refrigerator. Leave to chill for at least 2 hours or until it is completely set.

Run a knife round the edge of the mould and dip it quickly into hot water. Reverse the mould on to a serving dish, giving a sharp shake. The mousse should then slide out easily.

Garnish with the olives and serve.

Portuguese Eggs in Tomato Shells

Portuguese Eggs in Tomato Shells are eaten cold as a first course, or with a mixed green salad as a light lunch.

6 SERVINGS
6 large firm tomatoes, blanched and peeled
1 teaspoon salt
½ teaspoon black pepper
2 tablespoons olive oil
1 small onion, finely chopped
2 teaspoons chopped fresh basil
1 tablespoon tomato purée
6 hard-boiled eggs
4 tablespoons mayonnaise
watercress

Cut a circle out of the stalk end of each tomato so that there will be an opening big enough to insert an egg. With a teaspoon, scoop out the pulp and seeds. Reserve the pulp, seeds and lids. Sprinkle the insides of the scooped-out tomatoes with half the salt and pepper.

In a saucepan, heat the oil over moderate heat. When the oil is hot, add the onion and fry, stirring occasionally, for 5 to 7 minutes or until the onion is soft and translucent but not brown. Add the reserved tomato pulp and seeds, tomato lids, basil, tomato purée and the remaining salt and pepper. Reduce the heat to low, cover and simmer for 20 minutes or until the mixture is thick.

Remove the pan from the heat and set the sauce aside to cool.

Place the tomato shells on a serving dish. Place a hard-boiled egg in each shell. Place the dish in the refrigerator and chill for at least 20 minutes.

When the sauce is cold, stir in the mayonnaise. Transfer the sauce to a small mixing bowl and place it in the refrigerator to chill.

Remove the tomato shells and sauce from the refrigerator. Spoon the sauce over the eggs, garnish with watercress and serve.

Egg Ratatouille

An unusual dish to serve for a light supper, Egg Ratatouille needs no accompaniment other than crusty bread and butter.

4 SERVINGS
2 large aubergines [eggplants], washed and sliced
2½ teaspoons salt
1 lb. courgettes [zucchini], washed and sliced
2 fl. oz. [¼ cup] olive oil
1 large onion, sliced and pushed out into rings
1 large garlic clove, crushed
1 green pepper, white pith removed, seeded and sliced
4 tomatoes, blanched, peeled and chopped
4 oz. mushrooms, sliced
¼ teaspoon black pepper
¼ teaspoon dried basil
1 oz. [2 tablespoons] butter
4 eggs

Place the aubergine [eggplant] slices in a colander and sprinkle over 1 teaspoon of salt. Leave them to dégorge for 30 minutes. Place the courgette [zucchini] slices on a plate and sprinkle over 1 teaspoon salt. Set aside for 30 minutes to dégorge.

Dry the slices on kitchen paper towels.

In a very large saucepan, heat the olive oil over moderate heat. When the oil is hot, add the onion and garlic and fry for 5 to 7 minutes or until the onion is soft and translucent but not brown. Add the courgettes [zucchini], aubergines [eggplants] and pepper to the pan and cook for 10 minutes. Stir in the tomatoes and mushrooms and sprinkle over the remaining salt, the pepper and basil. Half cover the pan with the lid on a slant, reduce the heat to low and simmer the ratatouille, stirring occasionally, for 45 minutes.

Five minutes before the ratatouille is ready, in a large frying-pan, melt the butter over moderate heat. Break the eggs into the pan and fry them for 4 to 5 minutes or until the whites are set.

Turn the ratatouille into a warmed serving dish. Top the mixture with the fried eggs and serve at once.

Quick-Fried Eggs with Petits Pois and Shrimps

An adaptation of a traditional Chinese dish, Quick-Fried Eggs with Petits Pois and Shrimps may be served as part of a Chinese meal, or accompanied by ice-cold lager and green salad, as a light lunch or supper.

2-3 SERVINGS

5 eggs
1 teaspoon salt
1 oz. [2 tablespoons] butter
1-inch piece fresh root ginger, peeled and chopped
1 medium-sized onion, thinly sliced
4 oz. small frozen shrimps, thawed
8 oz. frozen petits pois, thawed
1 tablespoon soy sauce
½ teaspoon sugar
2 tablespoons vegetable oil

In a medium-sized mixing bowl, beat the eggs and salt together until they are well blended. Set aside.

In a medium-sized saucepan, melt the butter over moderate heat. When the foam subsides, add the ginger and onion and stir-fry for 30 seconds. Add the shrimps, petits pois, soy sauce and sugar and stir-fry the mixture for 1½ minutes. Remove the pan from the heat and set the mixture

aside.

In a large frying-pan, heat the oil over moderate heat. When the oil is hot, pour the egg mixture into the pan. Stir the eggs, then leave for a few seconds until the bottom sets. Remove the pan from the heat and pour in the shrimps and petits pois. Turn, mix and toss the mixture a few times. Return the pan to the heat and cook, stirring occasionally, for 1 minute. Remove the pan from the heat.

Transfer the mixture to a warmed serving dish and serve at once.

Ricotta and Olive Mix

A quick and relatively inexpensive way of brightening up scrambled eggs, Ricotta and Olive Mix may be served for breakfast or, with crusty bread, for a light lunch.

2-3 SERVINGS

3 tablespoons olive oil
4 oz. [1 cup] green olives, stoned and quartered
1 red pepper, white pith removed, seeded and chopped
4 oz. ricotta cheese, crumbled
6 eggs
4 tablespoons milk
½ teaspoon freshly ground black pepper

Ricotta and Olive Mix is a nutritious mixture of eggs, green olives, red pepper and ricotta cheese. Serve with lots of hot toast.

½ teaspoon dried basil
2 oz. [½ cup] Parmesan cheese, grated

Preheat the grill [broiler] to moderately high.

In a shallow, flameproof casserole, heat the olive oil over moderate heat. When the oil is hot, add the olives and red pepper and cook, stirring frequently, for 3 minutes. Add the ricotta cheese and, stirring constantly, cook for a further 2 minutes.

Meanwhile, in a medium-sized mixing bowl, lightly beat the eggs, milk, pepper and basil together.

Reduce the heat to low. Add the egg mixture and cook, stirring constantly, until the eggs are nearly scrambled.

Remove the casserole from the heat. Sprinkle over the Parmesan cheese and place the casserole under the grill [broiler] and grill [broil] for 3 minutes or until the cheese has melted and the top is lightly browned.

Remove the casserole from the grill [broiler] and serve at once.

Russian Coloured Eggs

Exchanging eggs at Easter is a world-wide custom dating back to pre-Christian times. It became very fashionable in Imperialist Russia when Tzar Alexander III presented his wife with an expensive jewelled egg, designed and made by the court jeweller, Karl Fabergé. On a more humble level, ordinary Russians, particularly Ukrainians, adopted the fashion and, over the years, attained a high standard of artistic skill in decorating and dyeing ordinary egg shells.

To make Russian Coloured Eggs natural vegetable dye or food colouring should be used. Place only white-shelled eggs in a saucepan containing the chosen dye (see the colour guide which follows for further information on this) and bring the liquid to the boil. Simmer the eggs

These traditional Russian Coloured Eggs are so pretty to look at, yet so easy to decorate.

over low heat for 10 minutes. Remove the pan from the heat and, using a slotted spoon, remove the eggs from the pan. Pat the eggs dry with kitchen paper towels and set aside to cool.

If they are to remain a plain colour, rub the eggs with vegetable oil. If they are to be further hand painted, rub them with vegetable oil when decoration is complete.

COLOUR GUIDE FOR NATURAL VEGETABLE DYES

The outer skins of
onions boiled in water . . . . . . deep yellow
Raw beetroots [beets]
boiled in water . . . . red, pink
Birch leaves boiled
in water . . . . green
Moss-down boiled in water . . light green

Alternatively, a few drops of edible food colouring can be added to the water.

DECORATING THE EGGS

Onion skins wrapped around the eggs and tied on with cotton thread develop a marbled effect when the skins are removed.

Eggs wrapped in silk material and tied with cotton take on a 'tie-dye' effect when the material is removed.

Thin strips of masking tape stuck on to the eggs in varying geometric and flower patterns, before boiling, will reveal patterns in white when the tape is removed.

Flower petals stuck to damp, uncooked eggs and then covered with onion or shallot skins, tied with cotton thread, produce yellow flower-patterned eggs.

Dental floss or cotton thread rubbed in beeswax and wound around the eggs, then removed when the egg is cold, produces a myriad of lined patterns. Alternatively, unwaxed cotton thread wound around the eggs produces a myriad of deeper coloured patterned lines.

Eggs which are simply simmered gently in an edible food colour may be hand-painted with other edible food colours to any design imaginable.

The eggs should be eaten within 48 hours of decoration.

Egg Salad

This unusual and attractive salad may be served either as an addition to a light fish dish or by itself with hot crusty bread as an interesting summer lunch.

2-4 SERVINGS

6 hard-boiled eggs, sliced
2 small green peppers, white pith removed, seeded and roughly chopped
1 pimiento, cut into strips
3 button mushrooms, wiped clean and thinly sliced
6 black olives, stoned
1 tablespoon finely chopped walnuts

DRESSING

1 small garlic clove, crushed
1 teaspoon paprika
2 tablespoons white wine vinegar
6 tablespoons olive oil
¼ teaspoon salt
⅛ teaspoon black pepper
½ teaspoon sugar

Arrange the eggs, peppers, pimiento, mushrooms and olives in a medium-sized serving dish. Sprinkle the walnuts over the ingredients.

This colourful Egg Salad, with its spicy garlic-flavoured dressing, makes an inexpensive, satisfying lunch or supper.

In a screw-top jar, combine all the ingredients for the dressing. Shake briskly and pour the dressing over the salad. Toss to coat the ingredients well with the dressing.

Chill for at least 30 minutes before serving.

Egg, Sausage and Pepper Casserole

This piquant and filling casserole, flavoured with spices and herbs, makes an interesting supper dish.

4 SERVINGS

1 teaspoon butter
3 tablespoons vegetable oil
2 medium-sized onions, thinly sliced
1 medium-sized red pepper, white pith removed, seeded and finely sliced
1 medium-sized green pepper, white pith removed, seeded and finely sliced
2 large tomatoes, blanched, peeled and sliced
1 teaspoon paprika
½ teaspoon dried thyme
½ teaspoon salt
¼ teaspoon black pepper
8 beef or pork sausages
8 eggs
½ teaspoon prepared English mustard

1 tablespoon tomato purée
4 fl. oz. [½ cup] tomato juice
3 tablespoons grated Parmesan cheese

Preheat the oven to moderate 350°F (Gas Mark 4, 180°C).

Grease a large baking dish with the butter.

In a medium-sized frying-pan heat 2 tablespoons of the oil over moderate heat. When the oil is hot, add the onions, red and green peppers, tomatoes, paprika, thyme, salt and black pepper. Fry, stirring occasionally, for 8 to 10 minutes or until the onions and peppers are soft and golden and the tomatoes are pulpy. Turn the mixture into the greased baking dish and set aside.

Heat the remaining oil in the frying-pan. When the oil is hot, place the sausages in the pan and fry them for 5 minutes or until they are browned all over. Remove the pan from the heat and arrange the sausages on top of the vegetables, leaving a gap between each one. Carefully break one egg into each of the gaps.

In a small mixing bowl, combine the mustard and tomato purée. Stir in the tomato juice and pour the mixture over the ingredients in the baking dish. Sprinkle the cheese on top.

Bake in the centre of the oven for 20 to 30 minutes, or until the eggs are set and the sausages cooked. Remove from the oven and serve hot.

Shirred Eggs

 ①

Shirred Eggs are eggs which are broken into a buttered flameproof dish and baked, fried or grilled [broiled] quickly.

Shirred Eggs make an excellent light, nourishing snack, first course, or breakfast dish.

4 SERVINGS

1½ oz. [3 tablespoons] butter
8 large eggs
½ teaspoon salt
¼ teaspoon freshly ground black
   pepper

Preheat the grill [broiler] to high.

In a large flameproof dish or shallow flameproof casserole, melt the butter over moderately low heat. When the foam subsides, break in the eggs, being careful not to break the yolks. Tilt the dish or casserole so that the butter runs over the eggs. Cook for 1 minute.

Remove the dish or casserole from the heat and place it under the grill [broiler]. Grill [broil] for 3 minutes, basting occasionally with the butter, or until the whites have set and a thin film covers the yolks.

Remove the dish or casserole from the heat. Season with the salt and pepper and serve at once.

Egg Tartlets

 ①

These delicious little tartlets are made with shortcrust pastry and are filled with chopped eggs and topped with a garlic, basil and mayonnaise sauce. They make an ideal hors d'oeuvre or first course, and are especially suitable for a dinner party as the pastry cases and mayonnaise can be made well in advance then filled just before serving.

6 SERVINGS

PASTRY
  6 oz. [1½ cups] flour
  ⅛ teaspoon salt
1½ oz. [3 tablespoons] plus 2
   teaspoons butter
1½ oz. [3 tablespoons] vegetable fat
  1 to 2 tablespoons iced water
FILLING
10 fl. oz. [1¼ cups] mayonnaise
  1 large garlic clove, crushed
  4 tablespoons coarsely chopped
   fresh basil
  4 hard-boiled eggs, finely chopped
GARNISH
  6 slices hard-boiled egg
  6 small basil sprigs

Preheat the oven to fairly hot 400°F

(Gas Mark 6, 200°C).

First make the pastry. Sift the flour and salt into a medium-sized mixing bowl. Add 1½ ounces [3 tablespoons] of the butter and the vegetable fat and cut them into small pieces with a table knife. With your fingertips, rub the fat into the flour until the mixture resembles fine breadcrumbs.

Add 1 tablespoon of iced water and, using the knife, mix it into the flour mixture. With your hands, mix and knead the dough until it is smooth. Add more water if the dough is too dry. Chill the dough in the refrigerator for 30 minutes.

Using the remaining butter, grease 6 3-inch fluted tartlet tins. Set aside.

To make the filling, blend the mayonnaise, garlic and chopped basil together. Set aside.

On a lightly floured surface roll out the dough to ¼ inch thick. Using a 4-inch round pastry cutter, cut the dough into 6 circles. Line the tartlet tins with the dough circles, easing the dough in carefully. With a knife, trim off the excess dough. Fill the pastry cases with crumpled greaseproof or waxed paper and place them in the oven. Bake blind for 15 minutes, removing the paper 5 minutes before the baking time is completed to allow the pastry to brown.

Remove the tins from the oven and leave to cool for 30 minutes. Turn the pastry cases out of the tins.

Half-fill the pastry cases with chopped hard-boiled eggs. Pour enough of the mayonnaise mixture over the eggs just to fill the pastry cases.

Decorate each tartlet with 1 slice of hard-boiled egg and a sprig of basil. Serve cold.

These pretty little Egg Tartlets contain a creamy mixture of eggs with garlic and basil in a mayonnaise sauce. Serve them as a filling first course to a formal dinner.

Weston Eggs

 ① ①

A delicious, mousse-like first course, Weston Eggs are very simple to make. Serve with croûtons or melba toast.

4-6 SERVINGS

  8 oz. spaghetti, cooked for 8 to 10
   minutes and thoroughly
   drained
  4 hard-boiled eggs
  2 tablespoons mayonnaise
  1 tablespoon tomato purée
  ½ teaspoon salt
  ½ teaspoon freshly ground black
   pepper
  8 fl. oz. double cream [1 cup
   heavy cream]
  1 hard-boiled egg yolk

Push the spaghetti and the eggs through a food mill or, alternatively, purée them in a blender.

Place the mixture in a medium-sized mixing bowl and, using a wooden spoon, gradually stir in the mayonnaise, tomato purée, salt, black pepper and cream, beating until all the ingredients are thoroughly combined.

Transfer the mixture to a small soufflé dish and place the dish in the refrigerator to chill for 1 hour.

Remove the dish from the refrigerator and crumble the remaining egg yolk over the top.

Serve at once.

Frittata di Carne e Vegetali

VEGETABLE AND MEAT OMELET

An economical and easy supper dish, Frittata de Carne e Vegetali may be served at an informal dinner. It is a firm omelet and should be cut like a cake. The vegetables used here are typically Italian, but any other chopped vegetables may be used.

4 SERVINGS

1 oz. [2 tablespoons] butter
1 tablespoon olive oil
1 onion, finely chopped
2 courgettes [zucchini], trimmed, washed and sliced
2 large tomatoes, blanched, peeled, seeded and finely chopped
6 oz. cooked ham, finely chopped
6 eggs
¼ teaspoon salt
¼ teaspoon dried oregano
¼ teaspoon dried marjoram
½ teaspoon black pepper
2 oz. [½ cup] Provolone cheese, grated

In a large omelet pan, melt the butter with the oil over moderate heat. When the foam subsides, add the onion and fry it for 8 to 10 minutes, or until it is golden. Add the courgettes [zucchini] to the pan and fry for 4 minutes, turning occasional-

ly. Add the tomatoes and ham and cook the mixture for a further 4 minutes.

Meanwhile, break the eggs into a small bowl. Add the salt, oregano, marjoram and pepper and beat to blend.

Preheat the grill [broiler] to high.

Increase the heat under the omelet pan to moderately high. Pour the beaten eggs over the vegetables in the pan. Allow the base to set, reduce the heat to low and continue cooking the omelet until the eggs are just about to set on top. Sprinkle over the cheese and remove the pan from the heat. Place it under the grill [broiler] and cook for 2 minutes, or until the cheese has melted. Cut the omelet into quarters and serve.

Javanese Omelet

Unlike the traditional light fluffy French omelets, Javanese Omelet is a spicy version, cooked until it is completely set and golden brown. It may be served on its own as a light supper snack.

2-4 SERVINGS

6 eggs
1 tablespoon cold water
½ teaspoon salt
1 tablespoon soy sauce
1 teaspoon soft brown sugar

Frittata di Carne e Vegetali.

2 tablespoons vegetable oil
1 small onion, finely chopped
2 green chillis, seeds removed and finely sliced

In a mixing bowl, beat the eggs, water, salt, soy sauce and sugar together with a wire whisk or rotary beater until the mixture is light and foamy.

In an omelet pan, heat the oil over moderate heat. Add the onion and chillis. Cook, stirring occasionally, until they are soft but not brown.

Onion and Aubergine [Eggplant] Omelet

An unusual supper dish, Onion and Aubergine [Eggplant] Omelet is adapted from an Iranian recipe. Serve with a tomato salad.

2-3 SERVINGS

3 tablespoons vegetable oil
1 onion, finely chopped
1 medium-sized aubergine [eggplant], cut into ¾-inch cubes and dégorged
½ teaspoon turmeric
¼ teaspoon ground cumin
¾ teaspoon salt
½ teaspoon black pepper
4 eggs
1½ tablespoons cold water
1 tablespoon butter

In a medium-sized frying-pan, heat the oil over moderate heat. When the oil is hot, add the onion and fry, stirring occasionally, for 8 to 10 minutes or until it is golden brown.

Add the aubergine [eggplant] cubes and cook them, stirring constantly, for 3 minutes. Stir in the turmeric, cumin, ½ teaspoon of the salt and ¼ teaspoon of the pepper. Reduce the heat to low and simmer the aubergine [eggplant] mixture for 10 minutes or until the aubergine [eggplant] cubes are tender. Set aside.

In a medium-sized mixing bowl, beat the eggs, the remaining salt and pepper and the water together with a fork. Add the aubergine [eggplant] mixture and beat until the ingredients are well mixed.

In a medium-sized omelet pan, melt the butter over moderate heat. When the foam subsides, pour in the egg mixture. Stir the eggs, then leave them for a few seconds until the bottom sets. Reduce the heat to low. Using a palette knife or spatula, lift the edge of the omelet and, at the same time, tilt the pan away from you so that the liquid egg escapes from the top and runs into the pan. Put the pan down flat over the heat and leave until the omelet begins to set.

Invert a medium-sized plate over the omelet pan and reverse the two. The omelet should fall on to the plate. Slide the omelet back into the pan, so that the browned side is uppermost, and continue cooking for 1 minute or until the omelet is completely set.

Slide the omelet on to a heated serving dish. Cut into wedges and serve immediately.

Tilt the pan and pour in the beaten egg mixture. Cook until the eggs are almost set. With a flat-bladed knife, lift the edges of the setting omelet and tilt the pan so that the remaining liquid seeps to the bottom.

When the omelet is completely set, continue cooking it for 3 to 5 minutes, or until it is golden brown on the bottom.

Remove the pan from the heat and slide the omelet on to a warmed serving plate. Serve at once.

Pipérade
PEPPER AND TOMATO OMELET

One of the great classic French regional dishes, Pipérade originated in the Basque country near Béarn. Serve Pipérade with some crusty French bread, a tossed lettuce salad and some vin ordinaire.

2 SERVINGS

2 fl. oz. [¼ cup] olive oil
1 small onion, finely chopped
2 garlic cloves, crushed
1 green pepper, white pith removed, seeded and chopped
1 red pepper, white pith removed, seeded and chopped
3 tomatoes, blanched, peeled, seeded and chopped
6 eggs
¼ teaspoon salt
¼ teaspoon black pepper
2 tablespoons water

In a large omelet pan or frying-pan, heat the oil over moderate heat. When the oil is hot, add the onion, garlic and peppers and cook, stirring occasionally, for 5 to 7 minutes or until the onion is soft and translucent but not brown. Stir in the tomatoes and cook, stirring occasionally, for 5 minutes.

Meanwhile, in a large mixing bowl, beat the eggs, salt, pepper and water together until they are well mixed.

Pour the egg mixture into the pan. Stir the eggs, then leave them for a few seconds until the bottom sets. Reduce the heat to low. Using a palette knife or spatula, lift the edges of the omelet and, at the same time, tilt the pan away from you so that the liquid egg escapes from the top and runs on to the pan. Put the pan down flat over the heat and leave until the omelet begins to set again.

Remove the pan from the heat and, with the help of the palette knife, slide the pipérade quickly on to a warmed serving dish. Cut into two and serve at once.

Classic French Pipérade.

Courgette [Zucchini] Soufflé

Like most soufflés, Courgette [Zucchini] Soufflé is an extremely light and fluffy main course dish. Serve with a vegetable salad and some well-chilled white wine, such as Muscadet or Chablis.

4 SERVINGS

1½ oz. [3 tablespoons] butter
4 tablespoons olive oil
8 medium-sized courgettes [zucchini], trimmed, blanched and sliced
½ teaspoon salt
1 teaspoon freshly ground black pepper
1 garlic clove, crushed
2 oz. [⅔ cup] fine dry breadcrumbs
4 egg yolks
3 oz. [¾ cup] plus 1 tablespoon Parmesan cheese, grated
1 tablespoon prepared French mustard
2 tablespoons flour
4 fl. oz. single cream [½ cup light cream]
6 egg whites, stiffly beaten
1 tablespoon finely chopped fresh parsley

Using 1 tablespoon of the butter, grease a 2½-pint [1½-quart] soufflé dish and set aside.

In a large frying-pan, heat the olive oil over moderate heat. When the oil is hot, add the courgettes [zucchini] to the pan and fry them, stirring occasionally, for 10 minutes.

Raise the heat to moderately high and stir in the salt, half the black pepper, the garlic and dry breadcrumbs. Remove the pan from the heat and toss the courgette [zucchini] slices gently. Transfer the mixture to a fine wire strainer held over a medium-sized mixing bowl. Using the back of a wooden spoon, rub the ingredients through the strainer. Discard any pulp remaining in the strainer. Alternatively, place the courgette [zucchini] mixture in the jar of an electric blender and blend on and off until the mixture forms a fine purée.

Place the purée in the refrigerator to chill for 1 hour.

Preheat the oven to very hot 450°F (Gas Mark 8, 230°C).

Meanwhile, in a medium-sized mixing bowl, beat the egg yolks, 3 ounces [¾ cup] of the cheese, the remaining pepper and the mustard together with a wooden spoon until the ingredients are thoroughly combined. Set aside.

In a medium-sized saucepan, melt the remaining butter over moderate heat. Remove the pan from the heat and, using

a wooden spoon, stir in the flour to form a smooth paste. Gradually add the cream, stirring constantly and being careful to avoid lumps. Return the pan to moderately low heat and cook, stirring constantly, for 2 to 3 minutes or until the mixture thickens. Remove the pan from the heat and set aside to cool.

When the mixture is cool, stir in the egg yolk mixture. Remove the purée from the refrigerator and stir 8 fluid ounces [1 cup] of the purée into the sauce. Discard any remaining purée or set aside for future use. With a metal spoon, gently fold in the beaten egg whites. Transfer the mixture to the prepared soufflé dish and sprinkle the top with the remaining cheese. Place the dish in the centre of the oven and cook for 10 minutes.

Reduce the heat to fairly hot 400°F (Gas Mark 6, 200°C) and continue to

The unusual combination of pears and carrots give this Pear and Carrot Soufflé its unusual flavour. Serve with salad for a delicious meal.

cook for 20 minutes or until the soufflé has risen and is golden brown, and a skewer inserted into the centre comes out clean.

Remove the soufflé dish from the oven. Sprinkle over the chopped parsley and serve immediately.

Pear and Carrot Soufflé

Pear and Carrot Soufflé is a superb light and fluffy main course dish, with special appeal for vegetarians. Serve with lots of

tossed mixed salad and crusty bread and a chilled sparkling wine such as Blanc de Blancs or vinho verde.

4 SERVINGS

5 medium-sized carrots, scraped and grated

4 soft pears, peeled, cored and chopped

2 fl. oz. [¼ cup] water

1½ oz. [3 tablespoons] butter

4 egg yolks

4 oz. [1 cup] plus 1 teaspoon Parmesan cheese, grated

½ teaspoon freshly ground black pepper

1 tablespoon prepared French mustard

2 tablespoons flour

4 fl. oz. single cream [½ cup light cream]

6 egg whites, stiffly beaten

Place the carrots, pears and water in a medium-sized saucepan. Set the pan over moderate heat and bring the liquid to the boil. Cover the pan, reduce the heat to low and simmer for 20 minutes. Remove the pan from the heat and set the mixture aside to cool.

Place the mixture in a fine wire strainer held over a medium-sized mixing bowl. Using the back of a wooden spoon, rub the ingredients through the strainer, discarding any pulp remaining in the strainer. Alternatively, place the carrot and pear mixture in the jar of an electric blender and blend on and off until the mixture forms a fine purée.

Place the purée in the refrigerator to chill for 1 hour.

Preheat the oven to very hot 450°F (Gas Mark 8, 230°C). Using 1 tablespoon of the butter, grease a 4-pint [2½-quart] soufflé dish and set aside.

Meanwhile, in a medium-sized mixing bowl, beat the egg yolks, 4 ounces [1 cup] of the cheese, the pepper and mustard together with a wooden spoon until all the ingredients are thoroughly combined. Set aside.

In a medium-sized saucepan, melt the remaining butter over moderate heat. Remove the pan from the heat and, using a wooden spoon, stir in the flour to make a smooth paste. Gradually add the cream, stirring constantly and being careful to avoid lumps. Return the pan to moderately low heat and cook, stirring constantly, for 2 to 3 minutes or until the mixture thickens. Remove the pan from the heat and set the mixture aside to cool.

When the mixture is cool, stir in the egg yolk mixture. Remove the purée from the refrigerator and add 8 fluid ounces [1 cup] of the purée to the sauce. Blend the mixture together. With a metal spoon, gently fold in the beaten egg whites. Transfer the mixture to the prepared soufflé dish and sprinkle the top with the remaining cheese.

Place the dish in the centre of the oven and cook for 10 minutes.

Reduce the heat to fairly hot 400°F (Gas Mark 6, 200°C) and continue to cook for 20 minutes or until the soufflé has risen and is golden brown, and a skewer inserted into the centre comes out clean. Remove the soufflé dish from the oven.

Pour the remaining purée into a sauceboat and serve immediately, with the soufflé.

Salmon Soufflé

A delightful way to use up leftover cooked fresh salmon, if you happen to be lucky enough to have it (canned salmon is nearly as delicious if you aren't), Salmon Soufflé may be served as a light supper dish accompanied by a mixed salad, brown bread and butter and some well-chilled white wine, such as Chablis.

4 SERVINGS

1½ oz. [3 tablespoons] butter

10 oz. cooked fresh salmon, skinned, boned and flaked
   or 12 oz. canned salmon, drained

3 fl. oz. single cream [⅜ cup light cream]

1 oz. [¼ cup] flour

10 fl. oz. [1¼ cups] milk

2 oz. [½ cup] Gruyère cheese, finely grated

½ teaspoon salt

½ teaspoon freshly ground black pepper

¼ teaspoon Tabasco sauce

4 egg yolks

5 egg whites

Preheat the oven to fairly hot 375°F (Gas Mark 5, 190°C). Using 1 tablespoon of butter, grease a 2½-pint [1½-quart] soufflé dish. Set aside.

Using the back of a wooden spoon, rub the salmon through a fine wire strainer into a medium-sized mixing bowl. Gradually beat the cream into the salmon purée. Set aside.

Alternatively, put the salmon and cream in an electric blender and blend on and off at high speed until the mixture forms a purée. Set aside.

In a medium-sized saucepan, melt the remaining butter over moderate heat. Remove the pan from the heat and, using a wooden spoon, stir in the flour to make a smooth paste. Gradually add the milk, stirring constantly. Return the pan to moderately low heat and cook the sauce, stirring constantly with the spoon, until it is thick and smooth. Remove the pan from the heat and add the salmon purée, the cheese, salt, black pepper and Tabasco sauce. Set the mixture aside to cool to lukewarm, then beat in the egg yolks, one by one.

In a large mixing bowl, beat the egg whites with a wire whisk or rotary beater until they form stiff peaks. With a metal spoon, carefully fold the beaten egg whites into the mixture.

Spoon the mixture into the prepared soufflé dish.

Place the dish in the centre of the oven and bake for 25 to 30 minutes or until the soufflé has risen and is golden brown, and a skewer inserted into the centre comes out clean.

Remove the soufflé from the oven and serve immediately.

Icicles

Attractive meringue biscuits [cookies], Icicles make a delicious coffee-break snack.

15 BISCUITS [COOKIES]

2 oz. [¼ cup] plus 1 teaspoon butter
2 oz. [¼ cup] sugar
3 oz. [¾ cup] flour
1 oz. cornflour [¼ cup cornstarch]
3 teaspoons water
½ teaspoon vanilla essence
2 oz. apricot jam
1 teaspoon lemon juice
MERINGUE
2 egg whites
4 oz. [½ cup] castor sugar

Preheat the oven to moderate 350°F (Gas Mark 4, 180°C).

Using the teaspoon of butter, grease two large baking sheets.

In a medium-sized mixing bowl, cream the remaining butter with a wooden spoon until it is soft. Add the sugar and beat until the mixture is light and fluffy. Sift the flour and cornflour [cornstarch] on to the mixture, and mix it in with a metal spoon. Mix in the water and the vanilla essence. Lightly knead the dough.

On a lightly floured surface, roll out the dough to a circle about ¼-inch thick. Using a 1½-inch pastry cutter, cut out circles of the dough and place them on the baking sheets. Place the baking sheets in the oven and bake for 8 minutes or until the biscuits [cookies] are a light golden brown.

While the biscuits [cookies] are baking, prepare the meringue. In a large mixing bowl, beat the egg whites with a wire whisk or rotary beater until they form stiff peaks. Add 1 tablespoon of the sugar and continue beating for 1 minute. Using a metal spoon, carefully fold in the remaining sugar.

Remove the biscuits [cookies] from the oven and set them aside to cool slightly.

In a small mixing bowl, mix together the apricot jam and lemon juice. Place a small teaspoonful of the jam mixture in the centre of each biscuit [cookie].

Place a ½-inch star nozzle in a large forcing bag and fill the bag with the meringue mixture. Pipe swirls of meringue on to the biscuits [cookies], covering them completely and pulling the last squeeze up into a point.

Return the baking sheets to the oven and bake for 8 minutes or until the meringue is set and lightly browned.

Remove the baking sheets from the oven and allow the icicles to cool slightly. Transfer the icicles to a wire rack and allow them to cool completely before serving.

Pavlova

Pavlova is a famous meringue-based dessert, named after the Russian ballerina, Anna Pavlova. It was created in honour of her performance of the Dying Swan in Swan Lake which she danced while touring Australia, and the dessert is now considered to be traditionally Australian.

ONE 9-INCH CAKE

5 egg whites
10 oz. [1¼ cups] plus 1 tablespoon castor sugar
2 teaspoons cornflour [cornstarch], sifted
½ teaspoon vanilla essence
1 teaspoon malt vinegar
1 teaspoon orange-flavoured liqueur
10 fl. oz. double cream [1¼ cups heavy cream], stiffly whipped
1 lb. fresh or canned and drained fruit

Preheat the oven to cool 300°F (Gas Mark 2, 150°C). With a pencil draw a 9-inch circle on a piece of non-stick silicone paper and place this on a baking sheet.

In a large mixing bowl, beat the egg whites with a wire whisk or rotary beater until they form stiff peaks. Beat in 4 ounces [½ cup] of the sugar and continue beating until the mixture is very stiff and glossy. Fold in all but 1 tablespoon of the remaining sugar, the cornflour [cornstarch], vanilla essence and vinegar.

Spoon one-third of the mixture on to the circle of paper to make a base about ¼-inch thick. Fill a forcing bag, fitted with a 1-inch nozzle, with the remaining mixture and pipe it round the edge of the circle in decorative swirls, to form a case.

Place the baking sheet in the oven and bake for 1 hour. Turn off the oven and leave the meringue in the oven for a further 30 minutes, or until it is crisp on the outside but still soft in the centre.

Remove the baking sheet from the oven. Leave the meringue to cool completely. When it is cold, lift it off the baking sheet and carefully remove and discard the paper from the bottom.

Place the meringue case on a serving plate. Fold the orange-flavoured liqueur and the remaining tablespoon of sugar into the cream. Spoon the cream into the centre of the meringue case and pile the fruit on top of the cream. Serve at once.

Pineapple and Meringue Soufflé

This delicately flavoured dish makes a

To make Pavlova, draw a 9-inch circle on non-stick silicone paper (use a plate or board as guide).

When the meringue mixture is stiff, spread one-third over the circle to make a base about ¼-inch thick.

Using a forcing bag with a 1-inch nozzle, pipe the remaining mixture around the edge of the circle.

When the meringue case has cooked and cooled completely, transfer it to a serving plate.

decorative dessert for a formal dinner.

4 SERVINGS

1 pint [2½ cups] milk
4 egg yolks
4 oz. [½ cup] castor sugar
¼ teaspoon vanilla essence
2 teaspoons grated lemon rind
2 tablespoons kirsch
5 oz. canned pineapple rings, drained and chopped
3 egg whites
1 tablespoon sifted icing [confectioners'] sugar

Preheat the oven to warm 325°F (Gas Mark 3, 170°C).

In a medium-sized saucepan, scald the milk over moderate heat. Set aside.

In a medium-sized mixing bowl, beat the egg yolks with a wire whisk or rotary beater until they are pale and thick. Beat in the sugar, vanilla essence, lemon rind and kirsch. Continue beating until the mixture is smooth. Very gradually, beating constantly, pour in the milk.

Place the pineapple in a 2-pint [1½-quart] baking dish. Pour the custard through a strainer over the pineapple. Cover the dish with foil. Put the dish in a roasting tin and pour in enough boiling

Stunning Pavlova - a meringue case filled with fruit.

water to come halfway up the sides of the dish. Place the tin in the centre of the oven. Bake the custard for 60 to 70 minutes or until it is just set.

Ten minutes before the custard is ready, prepare the meringue. In a medium-sized mixing bowl, beat the egg whites with a wire whisk or rotary beater until they form soft peaks. Add the icing [confectioners'] sugar and continue beating until the mixture forms stiff peaks.

Remove the tin from the oven. Spread the egg white mixture on top of the custard.

Replace the dish in the oven and bake for 15 to 20 minutes, or until the meringue is brown. Serve immediately.

Zabaglione Orientale

Zabaglione Orientale is a piquant variation of the traditional zabaglione. The distinctive orange flavour helps to counteract the richness of the eggs and sugar.

6 SERVINGS

6 ratafia biscuits [cookies]
4 fl. oz. [½ cup] orange-flavoured liqueur
2 tablespoons gin
1 tablespoon grated orange rind
4 egg yolks
4 tablespoons castor sugar

Place one ratafia biscuit [cookie] on the bottom of each of 6 serving glasses and distribute 2 fluid ounces [¼ cup] of orange liqueur evenly over them.

Pour the remaining orange liqueur and the gin into a cup. Add the orange rind and beat well with a fork.

In a heatproof mixing bowl, beat the egg yolks and sugar with a wire whisk or rotary beater until they thicken and become pale yellow. Put the bowl over a saucepan one-third full of boiling water and place the pan over moderate heat. Pour in the orange rind and gin mixture and continue beating until the mixture stiffens and rises slightly.

Remove the pan from the heat and remove the bowl from the pan. Pour equal quantities of the mixture into the serving glasses and serve the zabaglione immediately.

Cheese

The making of cheese was originally a method of preserving milk, but became popular for its own sake early in history. Cheese has kept its popularity ever since, being a relatively inexpensive, and very versatile and nourishing food. Cheese is a very valuable protein food, containing as it does high proportions of both protein and fat.

Cheese is made by curdling milk by adding a preparation of rennet or a particular starter culture which changes the milk into lactic acid during the cheese-making process. The curds are separated from the liquid whey and are then ripened in various ways. The milk used in Europe and America is usually that of cows, goats or ewes.

The processes used in the cheese-making and the climate and vegetation that produced the milk vary so greatly that many cheeses cannot be reproduced successfully outside their original districts. Others are more easily reproduced and are made commercially in large quantities.

THE COUNTRIES THAT PRODUCE CHEESE
The United States is the world's largest producer of cheese, making twice as much as France, its nearest rival. There are, however, only two well-known American

A wonderful and delicious variety of cheeses from England, Scotland, Wales, France, Holland, Switzerland, Denmark and Italy - choose a colourful selection of them to serve after your next dinner party.
1 Edam 2 Gouda 3 Danish Blue 4 Havarti 5 Samsoe 6 Esrom 7 Gruyère 8 Emmenthal 9 Caerphilly 10 Lancashire 11 Cheshire 12 Sage Derby 13 Caboc 14 Stilton 15 Dunlop 16 Cheddar 17 Derby 18 Roquefort 19 Port Salut 20 Camembert 21 Brie 22 Marc de Raisin 23 Parmesan 24 Mozzarella 25 Gorgonzola 26 Bel Paese.

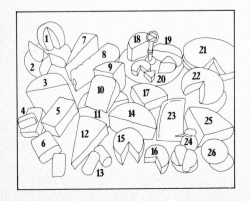

cheeses, the rest being either processed cheeses, or imitations of foreign varieties, although some of these are considered to be as good as, or even better than, their originals.

Liederkranz and Brick are the only well-known originally American cheeses. Liederkranz, aromatic and acid, was invented accidentally by Emil Frey, a New York cheese-maker. He was trying to duplicate a German cheese, but produced Liederkranz instead. He named his invention after a local singing society (the word means 'wreath of song').

Brick is little known outside the Middle West — it originated in Wisconsin, the leading American dairy state. When new it is mild in flavour, but it strengthens as it ages. A mature Brick is excellent with a glass of beer.

Great Britain produces several fine cheeses, of which the best-known are Cheddar, Cheshire and Stilton — one of the world's finest blue-veined cheeses. Cheddar — perhaps the most famous and versatile cheese in the world — is now produced commercially in large quantities all the year round and all over the world. Cheshire, the oldest English cheese, has a nutty, slightly salty flavour, and is rarely imitated successfully. Stilton, traditionally eaten with port and walnuts after a meal, is mellow and rich and has a dark, wrinkled skin.

There are several other well-known British cheeses. Caerphilly is one of these — a very soft, easily digested cheese, now made in the West of England, although it was originally Welsh. Derby, a white, mild, open-textured cheese, is sometimes found in the form of Sage Derby, a variety with the white cheese layered or mottled with green coloured cheese that is flavoured with sage. Lancashire cheese is white and crumbly, excellent for toasting or sprinkling over soups. Leicester is a bright orange coloured cheese, with a creamy and tangy flavour and is very good for adding colour to cheese dishes, particularly in Welsh rarebit and cheese sauces.

Dunlop is one of the Scottish cheeses, although it is said to have been originally Irish, introduced during the seventeenth century by a fugitive from religious persecution. It is similar in texture to Cheddar but milder in flavour.

Denmark produces several copies of foreign cheeses, such as Brie, Camembert, Emmenthal and Gorgonzola, but the best-known of its original cheeses are Danish Blue, a blue-veined, salty but creamy cheese, Samsoe which has a slightly sweet flavour and Havarti which is a mild cheese.

Of the Dutch cheeses the best-known are Gouda and Edam. Gouda is strong, with a few small holes and a yellow rind. It is wheel-shaped, while Edam is round with a red skin when the cheese is exported.

Emmenthal and Gruyère are the best-known of the Swiss cheeses, and are both used in cookery, particularly in the making of *fondue*, the traditional Swiss dish of melted cheese (see page 50 for the recipe). Emmenthal has large holes and is creamy in taste while Gruyère has smaller holes and is tangier in flavour. A third well-known Swiss cheese is Appenzeller, a firm cheese with a spicy flavour and tiny holes.

France produces the widest range of cheeses in the world — nearly every village has its own speciality — of every shape, taste and texture. One of the most popular is Camembert, a pale yellow cheese of soft, creamy texture which originated in Normandy. Its rind is orange-yellow with a powdery white crust. Next in popularity is Brie, very similar to Camembert in texture, but with its own distinctive flavour.

Roquefort, a salty cheese made from ewes' milk, has a greyish crust and is flecked inside with green-blue, from the action of a mould similar to penicillin which is found in the caves where the cheese is stored.

Port Salut was originally made by Trappist monks, and is a semi-hard cheese, mild and fresh in flavour and in texture rather like butter. It is one of the best all round French cheeses. Fromage au Marc de Raisin is a sweet, cream cheese rolled in a crust of grape seeds. These are only a very few of the 400 to 500 cheeses of France, most of which are local specialities.

Cheese is a fundamental ingredient in Italian cooking, and may be classified according to its use — grating, cooking and for the table.

The hard Italian cheeses, used mostly in their grated form, are Parmigiano Reggiano, the original Parmesan, and Pecorino Romano, a sharp cheese made from fresh ewes' milk.

The most important cooking cheese in northern Italy is *grana*, of which Parmesan is the best-known variety. In the south, Mozzarella is the chief cooking cheese, very often used in pizzas. Mozzarella is ideally made from buffalo milk but most often from cows' milk. Ricotta is a fresh, moist, unsalted cottage cheese much used in Italian cooking and is the traditional ingredient in classic Italian cheesecake.

Of the eating cheeses, the best-known are Gorgonzola and Bel Paese. Gorgonzola is a blue-veined cheese, spiced and

sharp in flavour. Bel Paese is rubbery, mild and soft.

USES FOR CHEESE

Cheese is one of the most versatile of foods, and can be eaten both cooked and uncooked, depending on the variety in question. Serve it, for instance, as a snack with milk for children, as a savoury course at the end of a special meal, or with French bread and butter, as the delicious adjunct to a wine party! Its cooking uses are equally numerous: it may be served in soups, savoury dishes (particularly Italian pasta sauces), and in desserts.

TYPES OF CHEESE FOR COOKING

Wherever cheeses are produced, they can generally be classified under three types: cream, soft and hard. All cheeses are suitable for eating on their own and some are more suitable for use in cooking than others.

Soft and semi-soft cheeses can be used in cooking but tend to be sticky. Hard cheeses — Cheddar, Edam, Gruyère, Emmenthal, Cheshire, Parmesan, Lancashire, Leicester and Derby — are ideal for cookery. Very hard cheeses, such as Parmesan and Pecorino are generally grated before using.

Whatever type of cheese is used in cooking, it should never receive more heat than is necessary to melt and if necessary brown it, because overcooking makes it tough and indigestible. When cheese is being grated prior to cooking, a fine grater should be used for hard cheese, while a soft cheese should be shredded. Very soft cheese can simply be sliced thinly.

STORING CHEESE

Once cut, cheese deteriorates fairly rapidly, and it is advisable to buy only enough for a few days or for a week at most, and to store it in a cool place, such as a cold larder. It should be covered loosely, but not so as to make it airtight. If it is airtight it may become mouldy, while if it is entirely exposed to the air it will become hard and dry. Cheese can be stored in the refrigerator for about one week but should be wrapped in waxed paper or aluminium foil, otherwise it will dry too rapidly.

Cheese can be hardened and dried by hanging it in a cheesecloth bag where the air can circulate around it. Dried, grated cheese can be stored in a screw-top jar for several weeks. If you have a home freezer, freshly grated cheese, packed in polythene bags, is a useful standby to have to add to pasta sauces and savoury dishes.

Cheese Bakes

Easy and quick to prepare, Cheese Bakes make a tasty first course, or a light lunch dish.

2-4 SERVINGS

- 1 oz. [2 tablespoons] butter
- 4 oz. mushrooms, wiped clean and sliced
- 10 fl. oz. double cream [1¼ cups heavy cream], whipped until thick
- 4 oz. [1 cup] Cheddar cheese, grated
- ¼ teaspoon grated nutmeg
- ½ teaspoon salt
- ¼ teaspoon black pepper
- 8 oz. cooked smoked haddock, skinned, boned and flaked

Preheat the oven to fairly hot 375°F (Gas Mark 5, 190°C). Using half of the butter, grease 4 ramekins, individual baking dishes or one medium-sized baking dish, and set aside.

In a small saucepan, melt the remaining butter over moderate heat. When the foam subsides, add the mushrooms and cook, stirring occasionally, for 5 minutes.

Remove the pan from the heat and drain the mushrooms, discarding the juice. Set the mushrooms aside.

In a medium-sized mixing bowl, combine the whipped cream, half of the cheese, the nutmeg, salt and pepper. Stir in the haddock and mushrooms.

Pour equal amounts of the mixture into the ramekins or baking dish. Sprinkle over the remaining cheese.

Place the dishes or dish in the oven and bake for 20 to 30 minutes, or until the tops are lightly browned.

Remove the dishes or dish from the oven and serve immediately.

Cheese and Bread Bake

This savoury bake makes a light and tasty supper dish, and is delicious garnished with crisply fried bacon and parsley.

4 SERVINGS

- 1 thick slice white bread, cubed
- 7 fl. oz. [⅞ cup] milk
- 8 slices of white bread, crusts removed
- 1½ oz. [3 tablespoons] butter
- 3 eggs, separated
- 1½ tablespoons flour
- 8 oz. [2 cups] Cheddar cheese, grated

Garnish this delicious Cheese and Bread Bake with bacon and parsley, as here, and serve as a filling lunch or supper dish.

- ½ teaspoon salt
- ¼ teaspoon grated nutmeg
- 4 fl. oz. single cream [½ cup light cream]

Preheat the oven to moderate 350°F (Gas Mark 4, 180°C).

Put the bread cubes in a shallow dish and sprinkle over half of the milk. In another dish, spread out the bread slices and sprinkle them with the remaining milk. Leave the cubes and slices to soak.

In a large bowl, cream the butter with a wooden spoon and mix in the egg yolks, one at a time. Stir in the flour. Add the soaked bread cubes, cheese, salt and nutmeg. Blend well and stir in the cream.

In a medium-sized bowl, beat the egg whites with a wire whisk until they are stiff. Fold them into the cheese mixture.

Line a greased straight-sided, oven-proof dish or casserole with the soaked bread slices. Pour the cheese mixture into the dish. Bake in the oven for 35 to 40 minutes. Serve immediately.

293

Beef and Cheese Roll

Served with a green vegetable and buttered noodles, this is a tasty and easy-to-prepare main dish for a family lunch or supper. The tomato sauce is served separately and may be made a day or two in advance, stored in the refrigerator in a covered jar, and reheated before serving.

4 SERVINGS

3 thick slices white bread,
  crusts removed
4 tablespoons milk
1½ lb. minced [ground] beef
2 eggs, lightly beaten
2 teaspoons dry mustard
1 teaspoon salt
⅛ teaspoon black pepper
½ teaspoon dried basil
1 onion, finely chopped
2 tablespoons finely chopped fresh
  parsley
1 tablespoon flour
8 oz. Mozzarella cheese,
  thinly sliced
1 oz. [2 tablespoons] butter, melted
SAUCE
1½ oz. [3 tablespoons] butter
2 medium-sized onions, finely
  chopped
1 garlic clove, crushed
1 lb. ripe tomatoes, blanched,
  peeled and chopped
1 teaspoon dried thyme
⅛ teaspoon salt
2 fl. oz. [¼ cup] red wine
⅛ teaspoon black pepper

Put the bread into a large bowl and pour the milk over it. Gently squeeze the bread and pour off the excess milk. Add the meat, eggs, mustard, salt, pepper, basil, onion and parsley. With your hands, knead the ingredients together until they are thoroughly blended.

Lightly dust a piece of waxed paper or aluminium foil with the flour. Put the meat mixture on it. With floured hands, press the meat into a thin rectangle. Cover lightly with aluminium foil and place the meat in the refrigerator for 1 hour or until it is thoroughly chilled.

Preheat the oven to moderate 350°F (Gas Mark 4, 180°C).

When the meat is cold, cover the top of it evenly with the sliced cheese.

Roll the meat, beginning at a narrow end, using the paper to lift it.

Place the beef roll carefully in a shallow baking tin, with the joined edges underneath. Brush the meat with the melted butter. Bake in the oven for 50 minutes.

Meanwhile, make the tomato sauce. In a medium-sized saucepan, melt the butter

Beef and Cheese Roll is creamy slices of Mozzarella cheese enclosed by a minced [ground] beef mixture.

over moderate heat. When the foam subsides, add the onions and garlic and fry, stirring occasionally, for 5 to 7 minutes or until the onions are soft and translucent but not brown.

Add the tomatoes, thyme, salt, red wine and pepper, and reduce the heat to low. Simmer the sauce for 40 minutes, stirring occasionally. Pour into a warmed sauceboat and serve with the beef roll.

Crowdie

This traditional Scottish cheese takes only a few hours to prepare, and can be varied by mixing it with chopped nuts, herbs or other seasonings.

4 SERVINGS

2 pints [5 cups] unpasteurized milk,
  fresh or sour
½ teaspoon rennet
1 tablespoon single [light] cream
½ teaspoon salt
½ teaspoon white pepper

Pour the milk into a medium-sized saucepan. Place the pan over moderate heat and heat the milk to blood heat. Remove the pan from the heat and pour the milk into a large bowl. Stir in the rennet. Set the bowl aside in a warm place for 10 minutes or until the milk separates into curds and whey.

Line a colander with two or three layers of cheesecloth or muslin and place it over a large bowl. Pour the curds and whey into the colander. Leave the curds to drain for 1½ to 2 hours. When the whey no longer drains out, turn the curds into a medium-sized serving bowl. Discard the whey.

With a wooden spoon, stir the cream, salt and pepper into the curds. Mix to a smooth consistency. Taste the crowdie and add more seasoning if desired. Leave in a cool place until it is set.

Devilled Cheese

A variant on Welsh Rarebit, Devilled Cheese makes an excellent quick and tasty supper dish.

6 SERVINGS

8 oz. [2 cups] Cheddar cheese, finely
  grated
4 teaspoons chutney
3 teaspoons curry powder
6 slices white bread, toasted,
  buttered and kept hot

Preheat the grill [broiler] to moderately high.

In a medium-sized mixing bowl, mix the cheese, chutney and curry powder together with a fork. With a knife, spread the mixture on one side of each slice of toast. Place the toast on the grill [broiler] rack and grill [broil] for 4 minutes or until the mixture is bubbling.

Remove the toast from the heat and serve at once.

Glamorgan Sausages

A marvellous family lunch or supper dish, Glamorgan Sausages are made from a tasty and economical mixture of cheese, onion and herbs. Accompany with French fried potatoes and peas.

2 SERVINGS

1 large onion, finely chopped
3 oz. [¾ cup] Cheddar cheese, finely grated
2 oz. [1 cup] fresh white breadcrumbs
1 tablespoon finely chopped fresh parsley
½ teaspoon dried thyme
1 teaspoon salt
½ teaspoon black pepper
¼ teaspoon dry mustard
1 egg yolk
2 tablespoons flour
1 egg white, lightly beaten
3 oz. [1 cup] dry white breadcrumbs
2 oz. [¼ cup] butter
2 tablespoons vegetable oil

In a medium-sized mixing bowl, combine the onion, cheese, fresh breadcrumbs, parsley, thyme, salt, pepper, mustard and egg yolk with a fork.

With your hands, shape the mixture into eight sausages. Dip each sausage in the flour, then in the egg white and then roll it in the dry breadcrumbs.

In a large frying-pan, melt the butter with the oil over moderate heat. When the foam subsides, add the sausages and fry, turning occasionally, for 5 to 8 minutes, or until they are well browned on all sides.

Remove the pan from the heat and transfer the sausages to a warmed serving dish. Serve at once.

Gougère

CHEESE PASTRY

A classic French pastry, said to have originated at Sens, Gougère may be served hot or cold, as an hors d'oeuvre or a delicious light lunch or supper dish.

4 SERVINGS

4 oz. [½ cup] plus 1 teaspoon butter
8 fl. oz. [1 cup] water
1 teaspoon salt
6 oz. [1½ cups] flour
4 eggs

Glamorgan Sausages — inexpensive and traditionally Welsh.

4 oz. Gruyère cheese, finely diced

Preheat the oven to hot 425°F (Gas Mark 7, 220°C).

Using the teaspoon of butter, lightly grease a large baking sheet. Set aside.

Put the remaining butter, the water and salt in a large saucepan. Place the pan over moderate heat and cook, stirring frequently, until the butter has melted and the mixture comes to the boil.

Remove the pan from the heat and stir in the flour. Return the pan to the heat and cook, stirring constantly, for 3 to 4 minutes, or until the mixture forms a dough and comes away easily from the sides of the pan.

Remove the pan from the heat and beat in the eggs, one at a time. Then beat in all but 2 tablespoons of the cheese.

Place heaped tablespoonfuls of the mixture, one against the other, in the shape of a ring, on the greased baking sheet.

Sprinkle the remaining cheese over the top of the dough ring and place it in the oven.

Bake for 40 to 45 minutes, or until the gougère is puffed and brown.

Remove from the oven and serve immediately or allow to cool before serving.

Cottage Cheese and Grapefruit Cups

This dish makes either a refreshing (and slimming!) first course or, served with crispbread and fresh fruit, a tasty light lunch.

4 SERVINGS

2 large grapefruit, halved
8 lettuce leaves, washed
12 oz. cottage cheese
4-inch piece of cucumber, cut into cubes

With a sharp knife, carefully cut around the grapefruit halves between the skin and flesh. Remove the flesh, discarding membrane and pith, and chop into bite-sized pieces.

Line each grapefruit shell with two lettuce leaves.

In a mixing bowl, combine the cottage cheese, cucumber and grapefruit flesh, beating to mix well. Pile the mixture back into the shells and serve at once.

Cheese and Ham Rolls

Cheese and Ham Rolls may either be served as a light luncheon, accompanied by new potatoes and French beans or, in greater quantities, as part of a buffet table at a party.

2 SERVINGS

4 oz. [½ cup] ricotta cheese
2 tablespoons mayonnaise
2 tablespoons chopped walnuts
1 celery stalk, trimmed and finely chopped
¼ teaspoon salt
¼ teaspoon black pepper
4 thin slices Gruyère cheese, about 4- x 6-inches
4 thin slices cooked ham
1 teaspoon prepared French mustard

Place the ricotta cheese, mayonnaise, walnuts, chopped celery, salt and pepper in a medium-sized mixing bowl. Using a wooden spoon, mix all the ingredients together until they are well blended. Set the bowl aside.

Place the slices of cheese on a flat working surface and lay the ham slices on top of them. Spread the mustard thinly over the ham. Spoon a quarter of the ricotta cheese mixture on to each slice of ham. Carefully roll the ham and

Cottage Cheese and Grapefruit Cup - a perfectly delicious lunch for would-be slimmers!

cheese up around the cheese mixture to form a cylinder and secure with cocktail sticks.

Place the rolls on a serving plate and serve immediately.

Mozzarella Chicken

Delightfully different, Mozzarella Chicken makes a delicious family dinner dish. Serve it with plain boiled rice and a crisp salad.

6 SERVINGS

2 tablespoons vegetable oil
1 medium-sized onion, finely chopped
14 oz. canned peeled tomatoes
2 tablespoons tomato purée
1 teaspoon dried oregano
1 teaspoon salt
½ teaspoon black pepper
6 streaky bacon slices
1 oz. [2 tablespoons] butter
1 teaspoon finely chopped fresh tarragon
6 chicken breasts, skinned and boned
4 oz. Mozzarella cheese, cut into slices

In a medium-sized saucepan, heat the oil over moderate heat. When the oil is hot, add the onion and fry, stirring occasionally, for 5 to 7 minutes, or until it is soft and translucent but not brown.

Add the tomatoes with the can juice, the tomato purée, oregano, salt and pepper. Stir well and bring the liquid to the boil over high heat. Reduce the heat to very low and simmer the tomato sauce for 20 minutes, stirring occasionally.

Meanwhile, in a large frying-pan, fry the bacon over moderate heat for 5 minutes or until it is crisp and has rendered most of its fat. Remove the bacon from the pan and set aside to drain on kitchen paper towels. Keep warm.

Add the butter to the bacon fat in the frying-pan. When the foam subsides, stir in the tarragon. Add the chicken breasts and fry, turning occasionally, for 15 to 20 minutes, or until they are tender.

Preheat the grill [broiler] to high.

Remove the frying-pan from the heat. With a slotted spoon, transfer the chicken breasts to a warmed flameproof serving dish. Place a slice of bacon over each breast and pour over the tomato sauce.

Place the slices of cheese over the top and place the dish under the grill [broiler]. Grill [broil] for 4 to 5 minutes or until the cheese has melted and is lightly browned.

Remove the dish from the heat and serve at once, straight from the dish.

Cheese and Onion Pie

This economical pie can be served as a light supper dish with a mixed salad.

4 SERVINGS

8 oz. [2 cups] flour
1 teaspoon salt
2 oz. [¼ cup] plus 3 tablespoons butter
2 oz. [¼ cup] vegetable fat
2 tablespoons iced water
3 onions, finely chopped
2 garlic cloves, crushed
8 oz. [2 cups] Cheddar cheese, grated
1 egg, lightly beaten
½ teaspoon white pepper

Make the pastry by sifting the flour and half the salt into a mixing bowl. Put in 2 ounces [¼ cup] of the butter and the vegetable fat and cut it into small pieces with a table knife. With your fingertips, rub the fat into the flour until the mixture resembles fine breadcrumbs. Add 2 tablespoons of iced water and, using the knife, mix it into the flour. With your hands, mix until a smooth dough is formed. Add more water if the dough is too dry. Form the dough into a ball and wrap it in greaseproof or waxed paper. Chill for 20 minutes.

Preheat the oven to fairly hot 400°F (Gas Mark 6, 200°C). Grease a medium-sized pie dish with 1 tablespoon of the remaining butter and set it aside.

In a frying-pan, melt the remaining 2 tablespoons of butter over moderate heat. Add the chopped onions and garlic, reduce the heat to low and cook the mixture gently for 10 minutes, stirring occasionally. Set aside.

In a mixing bowl, combine the onion mixture with the grated cheese. Add most of the beaten egg (keep a little to glaze the pie crust), remaining salt and the pepper and beat to blend well. Set aside.

Divide the dough ball into two portions, one slightly larger than the other. Roll out the larger portion of dough until it is quite thin and is large enough to overlap the sides of the pie dish. Line the pie dish, and trim off the excess dough with a knife. Spoon the cheese-and-onion mixture into the dish.

Roll out the other portion of dough to a circle slightly larger than the pie dish. Place the circle of dough on top of the filling. Fold under the overhanging dough and press the edges together with your fingertips to seal. Coat the surface of the pie with the remaining beaten egg. Bake in the centre of the oven for about 35 minutes, or until the pastry is deep golden. Serve either hot or cold.

Neapolitan Pizzas

A traditional Italian dish from Naples, Neapolitan Pizzas make a delicious meal, which is both inexpensive and filling. Serve Neapolitan Pizzas with a crisp green salad and a bottle of dry white Italian wine.

2 SERVINGS

½ oz. fresh yeast
¼ teaspoon sugar
4 fl. oz. [½ cup] plus 1 tablespoon
    lukewarm water
8 oz. [2 cups] flour
1 teaspoon salt
2 teaspoons olive oil
FILLING
2 tablespoons tomato purée
4 medium-sized tomatoes,
    blanched, peeled, seeded and
    coarsely chopped
8 oz. Mozzarella cheese, sliced
8 anchovy fillets, cut in half
¼ teaspoon black pepper
2 teaspoons chopped fresh oregano

Crumble the yeast into a small bowl. Add the sugar and 1 tablespoon of the water and cream the water and yeast together. Set the bowl aside in a warm, draught-free place for 15 to 20 minutes, or until the yeast mixture is puffed up and frothy.

Sift the flour and salt into a warmed,

Crisp pastry topped with tomatoes, anchovies and Mozzarella cheese - that's Neapolitan Pizzas. Serve with mellow red wine.

large mixing bowl. Make a well in the centre and pour in the yeast mixture and the remaining water.

Using your fingers or a spatula, gradually draw the flour into the liquids. Continue mixing until all the flour is incorporated and the dough comes away from the sides of the bowl.

Turn the dough out on to a lightly floured board or marble slab and knead it for about 10 minutes, reflouring the surface if the dough becomes sticky. The dough should be elastic and smooth.

Rinse, thoroughly dry and lightly grease the large mixing bowl. Shape the dough into a ball and return it to the bowl. Dust the top of the dough with a little flour and cover the bowl with a clean, damp cloth. Set the bowl in a warm, draught-free place and leave it for 45 minutes to 1 hour, or until the dough has risen and has almost doubled in bulk.

Preheat the oven to very hot 450°F (Gas Mark 8, 230°C). With a teaspoon of the olive oil, lightly grease a large baking sheet and set aside.

Turn the risen dough out of the bowl

on to a floured surface and knead it for 3 minutes. Cut the dough in half. With a lightly floured rolling pin, roll out each dough half to a circle about ¼-inch thick. Carefully arrange the dough circles, well apart, on the prepared baking sheet.

Spoon a tablespoon of tomato purée on to each circle and spread it out with a table knife. Decorate each circle with half of the tomatoes, cheese and anchovy fillets and sprinkle over the black pepper and oregano Moisten each pizza with the remaining olive oil.

Place the pizzas in the centre of the oven and bake for 15 to 20 minutes, or until the dough is cooked and the cheese has melted. Remove from the oven and transfer the pizzas to a warmed serving dish. Serve immediately.

Gruyère Puffs

These light and savoury puffs are a favourite for children's tea-parties.

4 SERVINGS

2 egg whites
4 oz. [1 cup] Gruyère cheese, grated
2 oz. [⅔ cup] fine dry white
    breadcrumbs
    sufficient vegetable oil for
    deep-frying

In a medium-sized mixing bowl, beat the egg whites with a wire whisk or rotary beater until they are frothy. Add the grated cheese and, with your fingers, work the mixture into a soft paste. Form the paste into small balls by rolling teaspoonfuls between the palms of your hands.

Sprinkle the breadcrumbs on to a sheet of greaseproof or waxed paper. Roll each ball in the breadcrumbs so that they are coated on all sides.

Place the crumbed cheese balls on a plate and put them in the refrigerator to chill for 2½ hours.

Fill a large deep-frying pan one-third full with vegetable oil. Place the pan over moderate heat and heat the oil until it reaches 350°F on a deep-fat thermometer, or until a cube of stale bread dropped into the oil turns golden in 55 seconds.

Carefully drop a few of the balls into the oil and cook them for 2 minutes, or until they are puffed and lightly browned. With a slotted spoon, transfer the balls to kitchen paper towels to drain. Keep them warm while you fry the remaining balls in the same way.

Serve hot.

Grated Cheddar cheese and fish combine to make Cheese and Sardine Fritters a wholesome yet inexpensive supper dish for the family.

Cheese and Sardine Fritters

Cheese and Sardine Fritters may be served with sweet potatoes, lots of mixed, tossed salad and some ice-cold lager.

4 SERVINGS

2 lb. fresh sardines, cleaned and with the eyes removed
10 oz. [2½ cups] Cheddar cheese, grated
½ garlic clove, crushed
2 eggs, lightly beaten
juice of 1 lime
6 oz. [1½ cups] flour
½ teaspoon freshly ground black pepper
2 oz. [⅔ cup] fine dry white breadcrumbs
sufficient vegetable oil for deep-frying
3 limes, quartered

Preheat the grill [broiler] to moderately high.

Wash the sardines under cold running water and pat them dry with kitchen paper towels.

Place the sardines on the rack in the grill [broiler] pan and place the pan under the grill [broiler]. Grill [broil] for 6 minutes, turning the fish occasionally. Remove the grill [broiler] pan from the heat.

Place the sardines on a flat surface. Remove and discard the head, tail and spine from each sardine. Place the flesh in a medium-sized mixing bowl. Add the cheese, garlic, 1 egg and the lime juice. Using a wooden spoon, blend the mixture well.

On a plate, combine the flour, pepper and the breadcrumbs. Place the remaining egg on a second plate.

Roll the sardine mixture into small patties and dip each patty first in the beaten egg, then in the flour mixture, coating them thoroughly and shaking off any excess.

Fill a large deep-frying pan one-third full with vegetable oil. Set the pan over moderate heat and heat the oil until it registers 375°F on a deep-fat thermometer or until a small cube of stale bread dropped into the oil turns golden brown in 40 seconds. Place the patties, a few at a time, in a deep-frying basket and carefully lower the basket into the vegetable oil. Fry the patties for 3 to 5 minutes or until they are golden brown all over. Remove the basket from the oil and transfer the fritters to kitchen paper towels to drain. Keep warm while you fry and drain the remaining patties in the same way.

Place the fritters on a heated serving dish, garnish with the lime quarters and serve immediately.

Cheese Soufflé

Serve Cheese Soufflé with a crisp green salad, or a green vegetable such as courgettes [zucchini], and French bread.

6-8 SERVINGS

2 oz. [¼ cup] plus 1 tablespoon butter
5 oz. [1¼ cups] cheese, coarsely grated (preferably a mixture of Gruyère and Parmesan)
4 tablespoons flour
10 fl. oz. [1¼ cups] milk, scalded
1 teaspoon salt
⅛ teaspoon white pepper
⅛ teaspoon ground mace
⅛ teaspoon paprika

5 egg yolks
6 egg whites
¼ teaspoon cream of tartar

Preheat the oven to moderate 350°F (Gas Mark 4, 180°C).

With the tablespoon of butter, grease a 2½-pint [1½-quart] soufflé dish. Sprinkle 4 tablespoons of the grated cheese around the inside of the dish and, with a table knife, press it on to the bottom and sides. Set the soufflé dish aside.

In a large saucepan, melt the remaining butter over moderate heat. With a wooden spoon, stir the flour into the butter and cook, stirring constantly, for 1 minute. Do not let this roux brown.

Remove the pan from the heat. Grad-

Elegant to look at, easy to prepare and super to eat - that's creamy Cheese Soufflé!

ually add the milk, stirring constantly.

Return the pan to the heat and cook the mixture, stirring constantly, for 1 minute or until it is thick and smooth.

Remove the pan from the heat and add ½ teaspoon salt, the pepper, mace and paprika. Beat the egg yolks, a little at a time, into the hot sauce. Set the pan aside to allow the egg yolk mixture to cool slightly.

In a mixing bowl, beat the egg whites with a rotary beater or wire whisk until they are foamy. Add the remaining salt and the cream of tartar. Continue beating until the egg whites form stiff peaks.

Stir the remaining cheese into the hot sauce. When the cheese is thoroughly mixed in, spoon the egg whites on top of the sauce and gently, but quickly, fold them in with a metal spoon.

Spoon the mixture into the prepared soufflé dish. With a table knife, carefully mark a deep circle in the centre of the soufflé.

Place the soufflé in the centre of the oven and bake for 40 to 45 minutes, or until it is lightly browned on top and it has risen ½-inch above the top of the dish.

Remove the soufflé dish from the oven and serve at once.

Cheese Soup

This unusual and warming winter soup is especially good with hot crusty bread and lots of butter.

4 SERVINGS

2 oz. [¼ cup] butter
2 medium-sized onions, chopped
2 tablespoons flour
4 fl. oz. [½ cup] chicken stock
1½ pints [3¾ cups] milk
12 oz. [3 cups] Cheddar cheese, grated
3 oz. [¾ cup] Gruyère cheese, grated
½ teaspoon prepared mustard
½ teaspoon salt
¼ teaspoon black pepper
1½ teaspoons paprika
1 teaspoon Worcestershire sauce

In a large heavy saucepan, melt the butter over moderate heat. When the foam subsides, add the onions and cook for 8 to 10 minutes or until they are golden. Stir in the flour and cook, stirring, for 2 to 3 minutes. Remove the pan from the heat and gradually stir in the stock. When the mixture is smooth, stir in the milk.

Add the cheese and the mustard. Return the pan to low heat. Cook, stirring, until the cheese melts. Do not allow the soup to reach boiling point. Remove the pan from the heat. Season with salt, pepper and paprika. The amount of seasoning depends on the strength of the cheese, and it is advisable to taste and season as the soup requires. Add the Worcestershire sauce and serve.

Tuna Cheese with Dill

This delicious dish makes a perfect, inexpensive supper dish for the family. Serve with baked potatoes and some salad.

The ideal snack meal, Tuna Cheese with Dill can be made from the contents of your store cupboard.

4 SERVINGS

1½ oz. [3 tablespoons] butter
1 medium-sized onion, finely chopped
10 oz. condensed cream of mushroom soup
½ teaspoon white pepper
¼ teaspoon salt
1 teaspoon dried dill
10 oz. canned tuna fish, drained and flaked
4 oz. canned sweetcorn, drained
3 oz. [¾ cup] Gruyère cheese, grated
6 thin slices of Gruyère cheese
1½ oz. [¾ cup] fresh breadcrumbs

Preheat the grill [broiler] to moderately high.

In a medium-sized frying-pan, melt the butter over moderate heat. When the foam subsides, add the onion and fry, stirring occasionally, for 5 to 7 minutes or until it is soft and translucent but not brown.

Stir in the soup, pepper, salt and dill and mix well. Bring the mixture to the boil. Stir in the tuna fish, sweetcorn and half of the grated cheese. Heat the mixture, stirring occasionally, for 3 minutes or until it is heated through.

Remove the pan from the heat and spoon the mixture into a medium-sized baking dish. Lay the cheese slices over the mixture.

In a small bowl, combine the remaining grated cheese and the breadcrumbs. Sprinkle them over the cheese slices, to cover completely.

Place the dish under the grill [broiler] and grill [broil] for 5 to 8 minutes or until the top is brown and bubbly. Remove the dish from the heat and serve at once.

Asparagus Quiche

A delicately flavoured and coloured dish, Asparagus Quiche may be served with a lettuce salad.

4-6 SERVINGS

1 x 9-inch flan case made with shortcrust pastry

FILLING

6 oz. lean cooked ham, chopped
4 fl. oz. single cream [½ cup light cream]
3 fl. oz. [⅜ cup] milk
3 eggs
1 oz. [¼ cup] Cheddar cheese, grated
¼ teaspoon salt
½ teaspoon white pepper

12 asparagus tips, cooked and drained

Preheat the oven to fairly hot 400°F (Gas Mark 6, 200°C). Place the flan case on a baking sheet.

Cover the bottom of the flan case with the chopped ham and set aside.

In a medium-sized mixing bowl, combine the cream, milk, eggs, grated cheese, salt and pepper and beat well to blend.

Pour the mixture over the ham. Arrange the asparagus tips around the edge of the filling.

The perfect dish for impressive entertaining - Asparagus Quiche.

Place the baking sheet in the centre of the oven. Bake the quiche for 35 to 40 minutes or until the filling is set and firm and golden brown on top.

Remove the baking sheet from the oven and serve the quiche at once, if you are serving it hot.

Quiche Lorraine
CHEESE AND BACON QUICHE

Quiche Lorraine makes a beautifully elegant light lunch or supper dish served with a tossed mixed salad and crusty bread. There are, by the way, almost as many 'original' recipes for this dish as

there are villages in Lorraine — this is merely one of the basic ones and lays no claim to being the one true version!

4-6 SERVINGS

1 x 9-inch flan case made with shortcrust pastry

FILLING

4 oz. Gruyère cheese, thinly sliced

6 oz. lean bacon, grilled [broiled] until crisp and crumbled

5 fl. oz. single cream [⅝ cup light cream]

3 eggs

½ teaspoon salt

½ teaspoon white pepper

Preheat the oven to fairly hot 400°F (Gas Mark 6, 200°C). Place the flan case on a baking sheet.

Cover the bottom of the flan case with the cheese slices, then cover with the crumbled bacon. Set aside.

In a bowl, combine the cream, eggs, salt and pepper and beat well to blend. Pour the mixture over the cheese.

Place the baking sheet in the centre of the oven and bake the quiche for 25 to 30 minutes or until the filling is set and firm and golden brown on top.

Remove the baking sheet from the oven and serve the quiche at once, if you are serving it hot.

Mushroom Quiche

A ·marvellously tasty dish, Mushroom Quiche may be served either hot or cold.

4-6 SERVINGS

1 x 9-inch flan case made with shortcrust pastry

FILLING

2 oz. [¼ cup] butter

2 shallots, finely chopped

1 lb. button mushrooms, wiped clean and thinly sliced

¼ teaspoon salt

¼ teaspoon white pepper

¼ teaspoon grated nutmeg

4 fl. oz. single cream [½ cup light cream]

3 eggs

2 oz. [½ cup] Cheddar cheese, grated

Preheat the oven to fairly hot 400°F (Gas Mark 6, 200°C). Place the flan case on a baking sheet and set aside.

In a large frying-pan, melt the butter over moderate heat. When the foam subsides, add the shallots and cook, stirring occasionally, for 3 to 4 minutes or until they are soft and translucent but not brown. Add the mushrooms to the pan and cook, stirring occasionally, for 3

minutes. Remove the pan from the heat and stir in the salt, pepper and nutmeg.

In a medium-sized mixing bowl, combine the cream, eggs and grated cheese and beat well to blend.

Add the mixture to the mushrooms, stirring until they are blended.

Pour the mixture into the flan case and place the baking sheet in the centre of the oven. Bake the quiche for 25 to 30 minutes or until the filling is set and firm and golden brown on top.

Remove the baking sheet from the oven and serve the quiche at once, if you are serving it hot.

Three-Cheese Quiche

A subtle mixture of Roquefort, Camembert and cream cheese gives a special rich taste to Three-Cheese Quiche. Serve as an elegant first course to a dinner or, with lots of salad and crusty bread, as a light lunch or supper. Served cold, this quiche makes an excellent picnic food. Serve with a selection of salads.

4-6 SERVINGS

1 x 9-inch flan case made with shortcrust pastry

FILLING

3 oz. Roquefort cheese, crumbled

3 oz. Camembert cheese, rind removed

3 oz. cream cheese

1 tablespoon softened butter

1 shallot, finely chopped

2 fl. oz. single cream [¼ cup light cream]

3 eggs

¼ teaspoon salt

⅛ teaspoon white pepper

⅛ teaspoon cayenne pepper

Preheat the oven to fairly hot 400°F (Gas Mark 6, 200°C). Place the flan case on a baking sheet and set aside.

In a medium-sized mixing bowl, mash the Roquefort, Camembert, cream cheese and butter together with a fork until the mixture is smooth and the ingredients well blended. (If the mixture is a little lumpy, put the cheese through a strainer, lined with a piece of cheesecloth, pressing down hard with the back of a wooden spoon.)

Stir in the shallot and beat well to mix.

In a second medium-sized mixing bowl, combine the cream, eggs, salt, pepper and cayenne and beat well to blend.

Add the cream mixture to the cheese, stirring constantly until they are well blended.

Pour the mixture into the flan case and place the baking sheet in the centre of the oven. Bake the quiche for 30 to 35 minutes or until the filling is set and firm and golden brown on top.

Remove the baking sheet from the oven and serve the quiche at once, if you are serving it hot.

Tuna Fish Quiche

A delightfully satisfying light lunch or supper dish, Tuna Fish Quiche may be served with tomato and green pepper salad.

4-6 SERVINGS

1 x 9-inch flan case made with shortcrust pastry

FILLING

1 oz. [2 tablespoons] butter

2 small onions, finely chopped

1 large garlic clove, crushed

2 tablespoons chopped pimientos

7 oz. canned tuna fish, drained and flaked

2 oz. [⅔ cup] stoned black olives

¼ teaspoon salt

¾ teaspoon black pepper

⅛ teaspoon cayenne pepper

4 fl. oz. single cream [½ cup light cream]

3 eggs

2 oz. [½ cup] Cheddar cheese, grated

Preheat the oven to fairly hot 400°F (Gas Mark 6, 200°C). Place the flan case on a baking sheet and set aside.

In a large frying-pan, melt the butter over moderate heat. When the foam subsides, add the onions and garlic and cook, stirring occasionally, for 5 to 7 minutes or until the onions are soft and translucent but not brown.

Stir in the pimientos, tuna fish, olives, salt, pepper and cayenne and mix well to blend. Reduce the heat to low and simmer the mixture, stirring occasionally, for 5 minutes or until the tuna fish is heated through. Remove the pan from the heat and set aside.

In a medium-sized mixing bowl, combine the cream, eggs and grated cheese and beat well to blend.

Add the cream mixture to the tuna fish, stirring constantly until they are well blended.

Pour the mixture into the flan case and place the baking sheet in the centre of the oven. Bake the quiche for 35 to 40 minutes or until the filling is set and firm and golden brown on top.

Remove the baking sheet from the oven and serve the quiche at once, if you are serving it hot.

Bean Rarebit

This delicious, easy-to-make dish is a typical snack from the Southwestern United States. Serve for a snack lunch or supper.

4 SERVINGS

1 oz. [2 tablespoons] butter
1 medium-sized onion, finely chopped
1 garlic clove, crushed
1 green pepper, white pith removed, seeded and finely chopped
14 oz. canned kidney beans, drained
14 oz. canned baked beans
4 tablespoons tomato ketchup
1 tablespoon Worcestershire sauce
½ teaspoon salt
1 teaspoon black pepper
2 teaspoons mild chilli powder
6 oz. [1½ cups] Cheddar cheese, grated
4 large slices hot buttered toast

In a medium-sized frying-pan, melt the butter over moderate heat. When the foam subsides, add the onion, garlic and green pepper and fry, stirring occasionally, for 5 to 7 minutes or until the onion is soft and translucent but not brown. Stir in the kidney beans, baked beans with the can juice, ketchup, Worcestershire sauce, salt, pepper and chilli powder and stir well to mix. Cook the mixture, stirring occasionally, for a further 5 minutes.

Stir in the cheese and cook, stirring constantly, for a further 3 minutes or until the cheese has melted and the mixture is hot and thick.

Remove the pan from the heat. Place the toast slices on individual serving plates and spoon the bean mixture over them. Serve at once.

Bean Rarebit is a warming mixture of beans, cheese and spices on toast.

Sweetcorn Rarebit

Sweetcorn Rarebit makes a delightful snack lunch, accompanied by a tomato and lettuce salad.

4 SERVINGS

1 oz. [2 tablespoons] butter
1 small green pepper, white pith removed, seeded and finely chopped
1 medium-sized onion, finely chopped
4 eggs
½ teaspoon salt
½ teaspoon freshly ground black pepper
3 drops Tabasco sauce
4 tablespoons tomato purée
6 oz. canned sweetcorn, drained
8 oz. [2 cups] Cheddar cheese, grated
4 slices toast, crusts removed and kept hot

the cheese has melted.

Remove the pan from the heat and divide the mixture among the slices of toast. Place the toast in the grill [broiler] pan and place the pan under the heat. Grill [broil] for 3 to 4 minutes or until the mixture is golden brown. Remove the pan from under the heat.

Transfer the toast slices to individual warmed plates and serve the rarebit immediately.

Yorkshire Rarebit

This is a northern version of the traditional Welsh Rarebit, and makes a very nourishing and tasty lunch or supper dish. Serve Yorkshire Rarebit with a mixed salad and grilled [broiled] mushrooms or fried tomatoes.

2 SERVINGS

1 tablespoon butter
1 tablespoon flour
2 tablespoons milk
2 tablespoons brown ale or dark beer
½ teaspoon prepared French mustard
¼ teaspoon salt
½ teaspoon freshly ground black pepper
4 oz. [1 cup] Cheddar cheese, grated
2 slices hot buttered toast
2 thick slices lean cooked ham
2 poached eggs, kept hot

Preheat the grill [broiler] to moderately high.

In a small saucepan, melt the butter over moderate heat. Remove the pan from the heat and, with a wooden spoon, stir in the flour to make a smooth paste. Gradually add the milk, brown ale or beer, mustard, salt and pepper, stirring constantly and being careful to avoid lumps. Return the pan to low heat and cook, stirring constantly, for 2 to 3 minutes or until the mixture is thick and smooth. Add the cheese to the mixture and cook, stirring constantly, for a further 2 minutes or until the cheese has completely melted.

Remove the pan from the heat and divide the mixture between the 2 slices of toast. Place a slice of ham on each slice and place the toast on the rack in the grill [broiler] pan. Place the pan under the heat and grill [broil] for 3 to 4 minutes or until the ham has turned golden brown. Remove the pan from under the heat. Place a poached egg on each slice of toast.

Place each slice on a plate and serve at once.

In a small frying-pan, melt the butter over moderate heat. When the foam subsides, add the green pepper and onion and fry, stirring occasionally, for 5 to 7 minutes or until the onion is soft and translucent but not brown.

Meanwhile, in a medium-sized mixing bowl, using a wire whisk or rotary beater, lightly beat together the eggs, salt, pepper and Tabasco sauce. Set aside.

Add the tomato purée, sweetcorn and grated cheese to the frying-pan and cook, stirring constantly, until the cheese has melted. Pour the beaten egg mixture into the pan and cook, stirring constantly, for 5 to 7 minutes or until the mixture thickens slightly. Remove the pan from the heat.

Place the slices of toast on warmed, individual serving plates and carefully spoon equal quantities of the mixture on to the toast. Serve immediately.

Welsh Rarebit

Welsh Rarebit is a quickly made traditional British dish, which is both tasty and satisfying. Serve with grilled [broiled] tomatoes and a green salad for a light luncheon or supper.

4 SERVINGS

1 tablespoon butter

Welsh Rarebit, a satisfying mixture of cheese, flavourings and ale or beer on toast, is almost the British national snack dish!

1 tablespoon flour
2 tablespoons milk
2 fl. oz. [¼ cup] brown ale or dark beer
2 teaspoons Worcestershire sauce
1 teaspoon prepared English mustard
½ teaspoon salt
½ teaspoon freshly ground black pepper
8 oz. [2 cups] Cheddar cheese, grated
4 slices toast, buttered and kept hot

Preheat the grill [broiler] to moderately high.

In a medium-sized saucepan, melt the butter over moderate heat. Remove the pan from the heat and, with a wooden spoon, stir in the flour to make a smooth paste. Gradually add the milk, ale or beer, Worcestershire sauce, mustard, salt and pepper, stirring constantly. Return the pan to low heat and cook, stirring constantly, for 2 to 3 minutes or until the mixture is thick and smooth. Add the cheese to the mixture and cook, stirring constantly, for a further 1 minute or until

Georgian Cheese Bread

A savoury cheese bread from one of the southern republics of the U.S.S.R., Georgian Cheese Bread is so popular that small individual versions of the bread are made and sold by hawkers in the streets.

ONE 2-POUND LOAF

½ oz. fresh yeast
½ teaspoon sugar
4 to 5 fl. oz. [½ to ⅝ cup] lukewarm milk
1 lb. [4 cups] flour
1 teaspoon salt
3 oz. [⅜ cup] plus 1 teaspoon butter, melted

FILLING

1¾ lb. Caerphilly or any crumbly white cheese, crumbled
2 oz. [¼ cup] butter, softened
1 egg
1 egg yolk
1 teaspoon chopped fresh parsley

Crumble the yeast into a small bowl and mash in the sugar with a fork. Add 4 tablespoons of the milk and cream the milk and yeast together. Set the bowl aside in a warm, draught-free place for 15 to 20 minutes or until the yeast mixture is puffed up and frothy.

Sift the flour and salt into a warmed large mixing bowl. Make a well in the centre and pour in the yeast mixture, the remaining milk and 3 ounces [⅜ cup] of the butter. Using your fingers or a spatula, gradually draw the flour mixture into the liquids. Continue mixing until all the flour is incorporated and the dough comes away from the sides of the bowl.

Turn the dough out on to a lightly floured board or marble slab and knead it for 8 minutes, reflouring the surface if the dough becomes sticky. The dough should be elastic and smooth.

Rinse, thoroughly dry and lightly grease the large mixing bowl. Shape the dough into a ball and return it to the bowl. Cover the bowl with a clean damp cloth and set it in a warm, draught-free place. Leave it for 1 hour, or until the dough has risen and almost doubled in bulk.

Turn the risen dough out of the bowl on to a floured surface and knead it for about 3 minutes. Shape the dough into a ball and return it to the bowl. Cover and leave for 1 hour, or until it has risen and almost doubled in bulk.

Meanwhile, prepare the filling. In a medium-sized mixing bowl, mash the cheese, butter, egg, egg yolk and parsley together, beating until the ingredients are well blended. Place the bowl in the refrigerator and chill the mixture until it is required.

With the remaining teaspoon of butter, lightly grease an 8-inch loose-bottomed cake tin and set it aside.

Turn the risen dough out of the bowl on to a floured surface and, with a rolling pin, roll it out into a circle, approximately 21 inches in diameter. Lift the dough circle carefully on the rolling pin and place it over the cake tin so that there is an even amount of dough hanging all around the tin. Gently ease the dough into the tin, leaving the excess dough hanging over the sides.

Remove the filling from the refrigerator and spoon it into the centre of the lined tin. With your fingers, draw the excess dough up and over the filling, pleating it into loose folds. Gather the dough in the centre and twist it into a small knob.

Set the dough aside in a warm, draught-free place for 20 minutes, or until the dough has risen and increased in bulk.

Meanwhile, preheat the oven to fairly hot 400°F (Gas Mark 6, 200°C).

Place the tin in the oven and bake the bread for 30 minutes. Reduce the oven temperature to moderate 350°F (Gas Mark 4, 180°C) and bake for a further 20 minutes, or until the bread is well risen and deep golden in colour.

Remove the bread from the oven and leave it to cool in the tin for 30 minutes. Remove the sides and place the bread, still on the base of the tin, on a wire rack to cool completely. Serve cold.

Broccoli with Cheese Sauce

This is a novel way to prepare broccoli. Serve it with steak, chicken or fish.

6 SERVINGS

1½ to 2 lb. broccoli, washed and trimmed
1 teaspoon salt

SAUCE

1 oz. [2 tablespoons] butter
4 tablespoons flour
10 fl. oz. [1¼ cups] milk
¼ teaspoon white pepper
2 oz. [½ cup] Parmesan cheese, grated
6 anchovies, chopped, plus 4 anchovies for garnish

Break the broccoli flowerets into medium-sized clusters. Place them in a pan with the salt and about 10 fluid ounces [1¼ cups] of boiling water. Bring the water back to the boil over moderately high heat and cook the broccoli, uncovered, for 5 minutes. Then cover the pan and cook for 10 to 15 minutes more.

Fabulous Georgian Cheese Bread from the USSR.

While the broccoli is cooking, prepare the sauce. In a small saucepan, melt the butter over moderate heat. Stir in the flour with a wooden spoon. Cook for 1 minute, stirring constantly. Remove the pan from the heat and add the milk, a little at a time, stirring constantly. Return the pan to the heat and cook until the sauce is thick. Add the pepper, cheese and chopped anchovies and continue stirring until the cheese has melted.

Drain the broccoli in a colander and arrange it on a warmed serving dish. Pour the sauce over the broccoli, garnish with the remaining anchovies and serve at once.

Cheese Fondue

A wonderfully sociable dish that is ideal for informal entertaining, Cheese Fondue (pictured on page 257) is best served with a well-chilled dry white wine, such as Fendant or Neuchâtel. When the fondue is ready, it is eaten by spearing the bread pieces on a fondue fork or skewer and dipping it into the pot.

4 SERVINGS

1 garlic clove, cut in half
8 fl. oz. [1 cup] dry white wine
1 teaspoon lemon juice
8 oz. Gruyère cheese, cut into small cubes
8 oz. Emmenthal cheese, cut into small cubes
2 teaspoons cornflour [cornstarch], dissolved in 1 tablespoon wine
¼ teaspoon black pepper
⅛ teaspoon cayenne pepper
2 tablespoons kirsch
1 long thin French loaf (*baguette*), cut into quarters, lengthways, then into 1-inch slices, crosswise

Rub the garlic halves around a saucepan and discard. Pour the wine and lemon juice into the pan and place it over low heat. When the liquid is hot, add the cheese cubes and stir until they melt and the mixture is blended. Add the cornflour [cornstarch] mixture, pepper and cayenne and cook, stirring constantly, for 2 minutes, or until the mixture thickens. Do not allow to boil.

Stir in the kirsch and beat for 1 minute. Then pour the cheese mixture into the fondue pot. Light the spirit burner and place the fondue pot over the heat. The fondue is now ready to serve with the bread.

Mozzarella Savoury

A simple dish to prepare and a filling one to eat, Mozzarella Savoury may be served with lots of green salad and a well-chilled white wine.

6 SERVINGS

2 oz. [¼ cup] butter
1 medium-sized onion, finely
   chopped
¼ teaspoon salt
¼ teaspoon black pepper
2 teaspoons dried basil
1 lb. tomatoes, blanched, peeled,
   seeded and chopped
2 oz. cream cheese
15 oz. [6 cups] cooked Italian rice
3 tablespoons olive oil
4 oz. [1 cup] Parmesan cheese,
   finely grated
6 x 4 oz. Mozzarella cheeses
12 black olives, stoned

In a medium-sized saucepan, melt the butter over moderate heat. When the foam subsides, add the onion and fry, stirring occasionally, for 5 to 7 minutes or until it is soft and translucent but not brown. Add the salt, pepper, 1 teaspoon of the basil and the tomatoes. Reduce the heat to low, cover the pan and simmer for 1 hour. Remove the pan from the heat and set aside to cool to room temperature.

Place the vegetable mixture in the jar of an electric blender and blend until the mixture forms a purée. Scrape the purée into a medium-sized mixing bowl. Add the cream cheese and beat the mixture until it is well blended.

Place the cooked rice, oil, the remaining basil and the Parmesan in a large mixing bowl. Stir well to mix.

Mozzarella Savoury is blend of cheese, rice, olives and sauce.

Spoon the rice mixture on to a large, flat serving dish. Pour half the purée mixture into the centre of the rice, and pour the remainder into a sauceboat. Place the Mozzarella cheeses down the centre of the dish and garnish with the olives.

Serve cold.

Cheese Pancakes

Serve these light and tasty Cheese Pancakes with grilled [broiled] bacon and tomatoes for a delicious lunch.

4 SERVINGS

4 oz. [1 cup] flour
½ teaspoon salt
4 eggs
12 fl. oz. double cream [1½ cups
   heavy cream]
3 tablespoons vegetable oil

Classic Quenelles de Fromage.

4 oz. [1 cup] Gruyère cheese, grated

Sift the flour and salt into a medium-sized mixing bowl. Make a well in the centre of the flour mixture and break the eggs into it. Add 1 tablespoon of the cream and stir the eggs and cream together with a wooden spoon, mixing well. Slowly incorporate the flour.

Add the remaining cream, a little at a time. Continue mixing until all the flour and half the cream is blended to make a thick batter. With a wire whisk or rotary beater, beat in the rest of the cream and 1 tablespoon of the oil. Continue beating until the batter is smooth. Stir in the cheese. Cover and set aside for 30 minutes.

With a pastry brush, grease a medium-sized, heavy frying-pan with a little of the remaining oil. Place the pan over moderate heat and heat the pan for 30 seconds or until it is very hot. Drop spoonfuls of the batter into the hot pan, well spaced. Cook for 2 minutes or until the pancakes are brown on the underside. Turn them over and brown the other sides. Transfer the pancakes to a warmed serving plate and keep them warm while you make the rest of the pancakes in the same way, adding more oil when necessary. Serve piping hot.

Quenelles de Fromage

CHEESE QUENELLES

These little crusty-topped Quenelles de Fromage have soft, melting centres. Serve them with creamed spinach garnished with croûtons as a light luncheon dish, or on their own as part of a hot buffet. A well-chilled white wine, such as Meursault or Pouilly Fuissé, would complement this dish nicely.

4 SERVINGS

6 oz. Brie or Camembert cheese
2 egg yolks
1 oz. [½ cup] fresh white breadcrumbs
1 teaspoon flour
½ teaspoon black pepper
2 tablespoons double [heavy] cream
2 tablespoons milk
1 teaspoon salt
1 tablespoon grated Parmesan cheese

In a medium-sized mixing bowl, mash the Brie or Camembert and the egg yolks together with a kitchen fork until they form a fairly smooth paste. Rub the cheese mixture through a fine wire strainer into another medium-sized mixing bowl. Discard any pulp remaining in the strainer. Stir the fresh breadcrumbs, reserving 1 tablespoon, the flour, black pepper, cream and milk into the cheese mixture.

Cover the bowl with a clean cloth and chill the mixture in the refrigerator for 30 minutes.

Preheat the oven to hot 425°F (Gas Mark 7, 220°C).

Half-fill a large saucepan with water and add the salt. Place the pan over moderately high heat and bring the water to the boil.

Remove the bowl from the refrigerator. Cut the cheese mixture into approximately 2- by 1-inch pieces and roll the pieces, between the hands, to form small sausage shapes.

Drop the sausage shapes into the boiling water, a few at a time. Cook for 30 seconds. As the quenelles rise to the surface, remove them from the pan with a slotted spoon and place them on a plate. Set aside and keep warm while the remaining shapes are cooked in the same way.

Arrange the quenelles in a shallow ovenproof dish.

In a small bowl, mix together the reserved breadcrumbs and the Parmesan cheese. Sprinkle the breadcrumb mixture over the quenelles and place the dish in the centre of the oven. Bake the quenelles for 10 minutes or until the cheese mixture has melted and become golden brown.

Remove the dish from the oven and serve the quenelles immediately, straight from the dish.

Four Cheeses with Italian Rice

 ① ①

This delicious snack dish may be prepared in advance and chilled until it is baked.

4-6 SERVINGS

12 oz. [4⅔ cups] cooked Italian rice, such as avorio
1 small onion, finely chopped
1 celery stalk, trimmed and finely chopped
2 oz. [½ cup] Provolone cheese, grated
1½ oz. Bel Paese cheese, thinly sliced
3 oz. Fontina cheese, thinly sliced
3 oz. prosciutto, chopped
3 oz. [¾ cup] Parmesan cheese, finely grated
1½ oz. [3 tablespoons] butter, cut into small pieces

Preheat the oven to fairly hot 375°F (Gas Mark 5, 190°C).

Arrange one-quarter of the rice on the bottom of a large ovenproof dish. Sprinkle over one-third of the onion and celery. Cover with one-third of the Provolone, Bel Paese and Fontina. Cover with one-third of the prosciutto and one-quarter of the Parmesan cheese. Continue making layers in this way until all the ingredients are used up, ending with a layer of rice covered with Parmesan cheese.

Dot the butter pieces on top of the mixture and place the dish in a baking tin half-filled with boiling water.

Place the tin in the oven and bake for 30 minutes or until the top is bubbling.

Remove the tin from the oven and the dish from the tin. Serve immediately.

Roquefort and Cream Cheese Ring

Roquefort and Cream Cheese Ring makes an impressive centrepiece for a summer buffet party.

6-8 SERVINGS

2 teaspoons vegetable oil
6 oz. Roquefort cheese, crumbled
8 oz. cream cheese
¼ teaspoon cayenne pepper
1 teaspoon anchovy essence
2 tablespoons finely chopped spring onions [scallions], green part only
½ oz. gelatine dissolved in 2 fl. oz. [¼ cup] hot water
6 fl. oz. [¾ cup] mayonnaise
6 fl. oz. double cream [¾ cup heavy cream]
8 lettuce leaves
12 tomato slices
8 stuffed olives, halved

With the 2 teaspoons of oil, grease a 1½-pint [1-quart] ring mould. Place the mould, upside-down, on kitchen paper towels to drain.

Using the back of a wooden spoon, rub the cheese through a fine strainer into a medium-sized mixing bowl. Beat in the cream cheese, cayenne, anchovy essence and spring onions [scallions].

Quickly stir the dissolved gelatine into the cheese mixture and continue stirring until all the ingredients are blended.

With a metal spoon, fold the mayonnaise and cream into the mixture. Pour the mixture into the ring mould. Place the mould in the refrigerator and leave to chill for 1 hour or until the mould has set.

Remove the ring mould from the refrigerator and quickly dip the bottom into hot water. Invert a serving plate over the mould, reverse the two and turn the cheese ring out on to the plate. The ring should slide out easily.

Garnish the ring with the lettuce leaves, tomato slices and halved olives. Serve immediately, or chill in the refrigerator until required.

Roquefort Mousse

Serve Roquefort Mousse on toast or crusty bread as a first course for a special dinner.

4-6 SERVINGS

2 teaspoons vegetable oil
1 lb. Roquefort cheese, crumbled
8 fl. oz. single cream [1 cup light cream]
½ teaspoon ground cinnamon
12 fl. oz. double cream [1½ cups heavy cream], beaten until thick
½ oz. gelatine dissolved in 4 tablespoons hot water
small bunch mustard and cress, washed and shaken dry

With the oil, grease dariole moulds or individual dishes. Place them, upside-down, on kitchen paper towels to drain.

With the back of a wooden spoon, rub the cheese through a fine strainer into a large heatproof mixing bowl. Gradually pour the single [light] cream on to the cheese, beating constantly. Place the bowl over a saucepan half-filled with hot water. Add the cinnamon and stir constantly until the mixture becomes smooth.

Remove the pan from the heat and the bowl from the pan and allow to cool for 10 minutes. Place the bowl in the refrigerator and chill for 1 hour.

Remove the bowl from the refrigerator. Fold in the double [heavy] cream and the dissolved gelatine. Spoon the cheese mixture into the moulds or dishes and

place in the refrigerator to chill for 1 hour or until the mousse is firm.

Remove the moulds or dishes from the refrigerator and run a knife around the edge of each one. Turn the mousse out on to individual plates and garnish with the mustard and cress. Serve immediately.

Sage and Cheese Bake

A tasty dish to serve for a snack lunch or supper, Sage and Cheese Bake may be served with grilled [broiled] tomatoes.

4 SERVINGS

1 teaspoon butter
16 fl. oz. [2 cups] milk
8 oz. [2 cups] Cheddar cheese, finely grated
6 oz. [3 cups] fresh white breadcrumbs
2 teaspoons dried sage
½ small onion, finely chopped
½ teaspoon salt
¼ teaspoon black pepper
4 eggs, separated

Preheat the oven to moderate 350°F (Gas Mark 4, 180°C). Using the butter, grease a medium-sized ovenproof dish.

Pour the milk into a small saucepan set over moderate heat. Scald the milk. Remove the pan from the heat and set the milk aside to cool to lukewarm.

In a large mixing bowl, combine the cheese, breadcrumbs, sage, onion, salt, pepper and egg yolks.

Gradually stir in the milk. Set the breadcrumb mixture aside for 30 minutes to soak.

In a large mixing bowl, beat the egg whites with a wire whisk or rotary beater until they form stiff peaks. Using a large metal spoon, carefully fold the egg whites

This glorious Roquefort and Cream Cheese Ring makes the ideal centrepiece for a summer buffet. Serve with well-chilled white wine and thin slivers of toast.

into the cheese mixture. Spoon the mixture into the prepared dish. Place the dish in the oven and bake for 50 to 55 minutes or until the top is golden brown and firmly set.

Remove the dish from the oven and serve the bake at once, straight from the dish.

311

Shrimp and Cheese Mould

Shrimp and Cheese Mould makes an appetizing first course for any dinner party, served with brown bread.

8-10 SERVINGS

1 teaspoon vegetable oil
½ cucumber, peeled and diced
1 tablespoon salt
3 tablespoons white wine vinegar
12 oz. cream cheese
4 fl. oz. double cream [½ cup heavy cream]
6 fl. oz. [¾ cup] mayonnaise
1 tablespoon paprika
½ teaspoon black pepper
2 tablespoons chopped fresh chives
½ oz. gelatine, dissolved in 2 fl. oz. [¼ cup] hot water
8 oz. frozen peeled shrimps, thawed and drained
1 bunch watercress, washed and shaken dry
5 tomatoes, quartered
9 black olives, stoned

With the teaspoon of oil, grease a 1½-pint [1-quart] ring mould. Place upside-down on kitchen paper towels and drain.

Place the cucumber in a colander and sprinkle over the salt and vinegar. Set aside for 1 hour to dégorge. Drain off any liquid and set aside.

In a medium-sized mixing bowl, beat the cheese with a wooden spoon until it is soft and creamy. Fold in the cream and mayonnaise. Stir in the paprika, pepper and chives. Add the dissolved gelatine mixture and continue stirring until all the ingredients are thoroughly blended.

Fold in the shrimps and cucumber. Pour the mixture into the prepared mould and place in the refrigerator. Chill for 1 hour or until the filling has set. Remove the mould from the refrigerator and quickly dip the bottom into hot water. Invert a serving dish over the mould and reverse the two, giving the mould a sharp shake. The mixture should slide out easily.

Garnish the ring with the watercress, tomato quarters and olives and serve.

Stilton Pâté

A creamy, sharp-tasting pâté, adapted from an old English recipe, Stilton Pâté is an unusual first course. Serve with toast.

8-10 SERVINGS

24 fl. oz. [3 cups] milk

Rich and creamy Stilton Pâté – serve it with hot buttered toast.

1 large onion, coarsely chopped
1 carrot, scraped and chopped
2 celery stalks, chopped
  bouquet garni, consisting of 4 parsley sprigs, 1 thyme spray and 1 bay leaf tied together
3 oz. [⅜ cup] butter
3 oz. [¾ cup] flour
3 tablespoons mayonnaise
2 teaspoons lemon juice
3 garlic cloves, crushed
10 stuffed olives, finely chopped
½ teaspoon salt
½ teaspoon black pepper
⅛ teaspoon cayenne pepper
12 oz. Stilton cheese, rind removed, and crumbled

Pour the milk into a saucepan set over high heat. Bring the milk to the boil. Reduce the heat to low and add the onion, carrot, celery and bouquet garni. Cover and simmer for 15 minutes.

Remove the pan from the heat. Set the milk aside until it has cooled to room temperature. Pour the milk through a strainer into a large bowl, pressing on the vegetables with the back of a spoon to extract any juices. Discard the contents of the strainer and set the milk aside.

In a medium-sized saucepan, melt the butter over moderate heat. When the foam subsides, remove the pan from the heat and, using a wooden spoon, stir in the flour to make a smooth paste. Gradually add the milk, stirring constantly. Return the pan to the heat and cook, stirring constantly, for 2 to 3 minutes or until the sauce is very thick and smooth. Remove from the heat and set the sauce aside to cool to room temperature.

When the sauce is cool, beat in the mayonnaise, lemon juice, garlic and olives and season with the salt, pepper and cayenne. Place the cheese in a strainer set over a bowl. Using the back of a wooden spoon, rub the cheese through the strainer. Beat the cheese into the sauce until the mixture is smooth.

Spoon the mixture into a serving dish and smooth the surface with the back of the spoon. Place the pâté in the refrigerator to chill for 1 hour. Serve.

Tomato-Filled Cheese Choux Pastry Ring

Tomato-Filled Cheese Choux Pastry Ring is an adaptation of the classic French gougère. Serve with a green salad.

6 SERVINGS

1 oz. [2 tablespoons] plus 1 teaspoon butter
1 medium-sized onion, thinly sliced

1 oz. [¼ cup] flour
4 fl. oz. [½ cup] chicken stock
3 tablespoons tomato chutney
3 large tomatoes, blanched, peeled and chopped
4 oz. prawns or shrimps, shelled
¼ teaspoon salt
¼ teaspoon black pepper
2 oz. [½ cup] Cheddar chesse, grated

PASTRY

5 fl. oz. [⅝ cup] water
1½ oz. [3 tablespoons] butter, cut into small pieces
½ teaspoon salt
½ teaspoon cayenne pepper
½ teaspoon dry mustard
5 oz. [1¼ cups] flour
2 large eggs
1 egg white
2 oz. [½ cup] Cheddar cheese, grated
½ teaspoon black pepper

Using the teaspoon of butter, grease a 12-inch ovenproof flan dish.

First make the pastry. In a saucepan, bring the water to the boil over moderate heat. Add the butter, salt, cayenne and mustard. When the butter has melted, remove the pan from the heat and beat in the flour. Beat until the mixture pulls away from the sides of the pan.

Beat the eggs and the egg white into the mixture, beating each one until it is blended before adding the next. When the eggs and the egg white have been absorbed, the mixture should be thick and smooth. Stir in the cheese and pepper.

Preheat the oven to fairly hot 400°F (Gas Mark 6, 200°C).

In a large saucepan, melt the remaining butter over moderate heat. When the foam subsides, add the onion to the pan and cook, stirring occasionally, for 5 to 7 minutes or until the onion is soft and translucent but not brown. Remove the pan from the heat and, with a wooden spoon, stir in the flour to make a smooth paste. Gradually add the stock, stirring constantly. Return the pan to the heat and cook, stirring constantly, for 2 to 3 minutes or until the sauce is thick and smooth. Remove the pan from the heat and stir in the chutney, tomatoes, prawns or shrimps, salt and pepper.

Spoon the reserved dough mixture in large mounds, ½-inch apart, around the edge of the flan dish. Using another large spoon, spoon the tomato and prawn or shrimp mixture into the centre. Sprinkle the grated cheese over the top and place the dish in the oven. Cook for 30 to 35 minutes or until the pastry has doubled in size and is light brown in colour.

Remove the dish from the oven and pierce the pastry with a knife to allow the steam to escape. Serve immediately.

Brie Cheese Croquettes

These delicious Brie Cheese Croquettes may be served with drinks.

25 CROQUETTES

10 oz. Brie cheese, rind removed
1½ oz. [3 tablespoons] butter
6 tablespoons flour
10 fl. oz. [1¼ cups] milk
¼ teaspoon white pepper
¼ teaspoon cayenne pepper
1 egg yolk
1 egg, lightly beaten
2 oz. [⅔ cup] dry breadcrumbs
    sufficient vegetable oil for
    deep-frying

With a wooden spoon, press the cheese through a strainer and set aside.

In a medium-sized saucepan, melt the butter over moderate heat. Remove the pan from the heat and stir in the flour to make a smooth paste. Gradually add the milk, stirring constantly. Return the pan to the heat and cook, stirring constantly, for 2 to 3 minutes or until the sauce is thick and smooth. Remove the pan from the heat and stir in the pepper and cayenne. Allow the mixture to cool.

When the mixture is lukewarm, stir in the egg yolk and strained cheese. Turn the mixture on to a plate and place it in the refrigerator to chill.

Remove the mixture from the refrigerator and, with floured hands, shape the mixture into walnut-sized balls. Dip the balls in the beaten egg, then roll them in the breadcrumbs.

Fill a deep-frying pan one-third full with vegetable oil. Place the pan over moderate heat and heat the oil until it registers 350°F on a deep-fat thermometer or until a small cube of stale bread dropped into the oil becomes golden in 55 seconds. Carefully lower the croquettes, a few at a time, into the oil. Cook for 1 minute or until they are crisp and golden.

Remove the croquettes from the oil and drain on kitchen paper towels. Serve.

Creamed Camembert

A superb cheese-wine spread, Creamed Camembert is delicious on cocktail biscuits as an hors d'oeuvre.

4 SERVINGS

5 oz. Camembert cheese
2 fl. oz. [¼ cup] dry white wine
2 oz. [¼ cup] unsalted butter,
    softened

With a small, sharp knife, cut the rind off

These spicy, crisp little Brie Cheese Croquettes are a mixture of cheese, breadcrumbs, milk and cayenne pepper. Serve as an unusual appetizer with cocktails.

the cheese and discard it. Put the cheese in a china bowl. Spread the cheese out so that it covers the bottom of the bowl. Pour over the wine to cover the cheese. Cover the bowl and leave, at room temperature, for at least 12 hours.

Drain off any excess wine and, using a wooden spoon, beat in the butter until the mixture is a smooth, creamy paste.

With your hands, reshape the cheese mixture into a round and allow it to harden a little. Do not chill it.

Cheese and Chive Spread

This quick and easy-to-make cream cheese spread is delicious served in baked potatoes or sandwiches, or as an accompaniment to charcoal grilled [broiled] steak. It may also be served as a cocktail party dip with celery stalks and carrot sticks.

ABOUT 8 OUNCE [1 CUP] SPREAD

8 oz. cream cheese
3 tablespoons finely chopped fresh
    chives
2 tablespoons single [light] cream
⅛ teaspoon salt
¼ teaspoon black pepper
⅛ teaspoon cayenne pepper

Combine all the ingredients together in a medium-sized mixing bowl, and using a wooden spoon, mix them to a soft cream.

Chill slightly before serving.

Creamy Cheese Dip

Quick and easy to prepare, this Creamy Cheese Dip is ideal to serve with crudités for a party or buffet.

2 POUNDS

16 oz. cottage cheese
8 fl. oz. [1 cup] sour cream
5 oz. Roquefort cheese
8 spring onions [scallions], chopped
4 tablespoons mayonnaise
½ teaspoon salt
1 teaspoon black pepper

In a large bowl, mix the cottage cheese and sour cream together with a wooden spoon until the mixture is creamy. Put the Roquefort cheese in a small bowl and mash it well with a fork.

Mix the Roquefort into the cream cheese mixture and stir well.

Stir in the spring onions [scallions], mayonnaise, salt and pepper. Taste and add more salt and pepper if necessary. Chill in the refrigerator before serving.

Gorgonzola Biscuits

Flavourful savoury biscuits which use a fine Italian cheese, these Gorgonzola Biscuits may be served on their own with drinks or after the main course of a meal with cheese.

40 BISCUITS

2 oz. [¼ cup] butter
6 oz. Gorgonzola cheese
8 oz. [2 cups] flour, sifted
1 egg
¼ teaspoon salt
¼ teaspoon black pepper

1 tablespoon water (optional)

In a medium-sized mixing bowl, cream the butter with a wooden spoon until it is soft. Add the cheese and mash it into the butter. Cream well. Blend in the flour, egg, salt and pepper. Knead the mixture lightly to form a smooth dough. If the dough is too dry, add the water. Cover the dough and place it in the refrigerator to chill for 30 minutes.

Preheat the oven to hot 425°F (Gas Mark 7, 220°C).

On a lightly floured surface, roll out the dough into a rectangular shape ¼-inch thick. Trim the edges of the dough and cut into 1-inch squares with a sharp knife. Transfer the squares to a large baking sheet and place it in the oven. Bake the biscuits for 12 to 15 minutes or until they are golden brown.

Remove the baking sheet from the oven and cool the biscuits on a wire rack.

These delicious savoury Gorgonzola Biscuits may be served as a strongly-flavoured snack with drinks.

Cheese and Spinach Canapés

An unusual and tempting mixture of spinach and cheese on crisp croûtes, Cheese and Spinach Canapés may be served with cocktails. The canapés may be prepared well in advance and reheated by grilling [broiling], just before serving.

24 CANAPES

1 teaspoon salt
1½ lb. spinach, washed and stalks removed
2 oz. [¼ cup] butter
½ teaspoon freshly ground black pepper
3 oz. [¾ cup] Cheddar cheese, grated
1 tablespoon olive oil
24 triangles of white bread
1 oz. [⅓ cup] fine dry white breadcrumbs
1 oz. [2 tablespoons] butter, melted

Half-fill a large saucepan with cold water. Add the salt and bring the water to the boil over high heat. Put the spinach in the pan and reduce the heat to moderate.

Cook the spinach for 7 to 12 minutes or until it is tender.

Drain the spinach in a colander and squeeze it dry between two plates. Chop it finely and return it to the saucepan. Add 1 ounce [2 tablespoons] of the butter, the pepper and two-thirds of the cheese and stir to mix. Cover the pan and set it aside in a warm place.

In a large frying-pan, melt the remaining butter with the oil over moderately high heat. When the foam subsides, add the triangles of bread.

Fry for 10 minutes on each side, or until browned.

Remove the croûtes from the pan with a slotted spoon and place them on kitchen paper towels to drain.

Preheat the grill [broiler] to high.

Place a tablespoon of the spinach and cheese mixture on each croûte and top with the remaining cheese, breadcrumbs and melted butter.

Place the canapés under the grill [broiler] and cook for 2 to 3 minutes or until they are hot and the cheese lightly browned.

Serve at once.

Cheesecake

This popular sweet-sour confection probably originated in Greece and is now world famous. There are hundreds of variations, but the basic ingredients are similar, cottage, curd or cream cheese, eggs and a thickening such as flour, cornflour [cornstarch], semolina or ground nuts. Extra ingredients are added for flavour; fresh or dried fruits, essences and spices being the most usual. Cheesecake generally has a pastry or biscuit [cookie] crust as a base and some recipes require baking and others are just chilled in the refrigerator.

ONE 9-INCH CAKE

3 oz. [⅜ cup] plus 1 teaspoon butter, melted

6 oz. digestive biscuits [3 cups graham crackers], crushed

2 tablespoons sugar

FILLING

1½ lb. full fat cream cheese

3 oz. [⅜ cup] sugar

3 eggs, separated

1 teaspoon grated lemon rind

1 tablespoon cornflour [cornstarch] mixed with 2 tablespoons lemon juice

2 oz. [⅓ cup] currants

1½ oz. [¼ cup] glacé cherries, chopped

5 fl. oz. [⅝ cup] sour cream

2 teaspoons castor sugar

½ teaspoon vanilla essence

Preheat the oven to moderate 350°F (Gas Mark 4, 180°C).

With the teaspoon of butter, grease a 9-inch loose-bottomed cake tin.

In a medium-sized mixing bowl combine the crushed digestive biscuits [graham crackers], sugar and remaining butter with a wooden spoon. Spoon the mixture into the cake tin and press it firmly, covering the bottom of the tin.

This rich Cheesecake is guaranteed to have them coming back for more!

In a large mixing bowl, combine the cream cheese and sugar with a wooden spoon. Add the egg yolks and beat the mixture until it is smooth. Stir in the lemon rind, cornflour [cornstarch] mixture, currants and glacé cherries.

In another large mixing bowl, beat the egg whites with a wire whisk or rotary beater until they form stiff peaks. Fold the egg whites into the cheese mixture.

Spoon the mixture into the prepared tin. Bake in the centre of the oven for 20 minutes or until the centre is firm when pressed with a fingertip.

In a mixing bowl, combine the sour cream, castor sugar and vanilla essence.

Remove the tin from the oven and, using a palette knife, spread the sour cream mixture over the top of the cake. Return the cake to the oven and bake for a further 5 minutes.

Remove the tin from the oven and set aside to cool. When cool remove the cake from the tin and chill it in the refrigerator before serving.

Crostata di Ricotta

CHEESE PIE

☆ ☆ ① ① ① ⊠ ⊠ ⊠

This rich, creamy cheese pie is one of the most famous of all Italian cheesecakes. If you are unable to buy ricotta, any whole-curd cottage cheese may be substituted.

ONE 9-INCH PIE

PASTRY

6 oz. [¾ cup] plus 1 teaspoon butter, cut into small pieces
8 oz. [2 cups] flour
¼ teaspoon salt
4 egg yolks, lightly beaten
2 tablespoons sugar
5 tablespoons Marsala
grated rind of 1 lemon

FILLING

2½ lb. ricotta cheese, strained
4 oz. [½ cup] sugar
2 tablespoons flour
¼ teaspoon salt
½ teaspoon vanilla essence
grated rind of 1 orange
grated rind and juice of 2 lemons
4 egg yolks
3 tablespoons raisins
2 tablespoons finely chopped candied peel
2 tablespoons slivered, blanched almonds
1 egg white, lightly beaten

Moist Crostata di Ricotta is Italian in origin and absolutely irresistable to taste.

With the teaspoon of butter, grease a 9-inch springform pan and set aside.

To make the pastry, sift the flour and salt into a large mixing bowl. Make a well in the centre of the flour and into it drop the remaining butter, the egg yolks, sugar, Marsala and lemon rind.

With your fingertips, combine all of the ingredients and lightly knead the dough until it is smooth and can be formed into a ball. Do not over handle it.

Cover the dough and refrigerate it for about 1 hour, or until it is fairly firm.

Break off about one-quarter of the dough. Dust it with flour, cover it and put it back in the refrigerator.

Reshape the rest of the dough into a ball. On a floured board, flatten the ball into a circle.

Sprinkle flour over the top of the dough circle and roll it out into a circle 2 inches wider in diameter than the spring-form pan.

Lift the dough on the rolling pin and lay it over the pan. Gently ease the dough into the pan.

With a knife, trim off the excess dough round the rim of the pan. Set the dough case aside.

Preheat the oven to moderate 350°F (Gas Mark 4, 180°C).

In a medium-sized mixing bowl, beat the ricotta cheese, sugar, flour, salt, vanilla essence, grated orange and lemon rind, lemon juice and egg yolks together with a wooden spoon until they are well combined. Stir in the raisins and candied peel.

Spoon the mixture into the pastry case, spreading it out evenly with a spatula. Sprinkle the top with the almonds.

Remove the reserved dough from the refrigerator and roll it out into a rectangle, at least 10 inches long. With a sharp knife, cut the dough into long strips. Arrange the dough strips over the filling to make a lattice pattern.

Using a pastry brush, brush the strips with the beaten egg white.

Place the pie in the oven and bake for 1 hour, or until the crust is golden brown and the filling is firm to the touch.

Remove the pie from the oven and place it on a wire cake rack.

Carefully undo the spring and remove the outside rim of the pan. Leave the pie to cool.

When the pie is cool, carefully slide a knife between the crust and the pan bottom and slide the pie carefully on to a dish.

Coeur à la Crème

This is an attractive, light classic French dessert. Coeur à la Crème is traditionally served with wild strawberries and sprinkled with sugar.

6 SERVINGS

1 lb. cream cheese
⅛ teaspoon salt
10 fl. oz. double cream [1¼ cups heavy cream]
2 egg whites
2 tablespoons soft brown sugar

Gently rub the cream cheese and salt through a strainer into a large mixing bowl. Using a wooden spoon, beat in the cream until it is thoroughly blended and the mixture is smooth.

In a mixing bowl, beat the egg whites with a wire whisk or rotary beater until they form stiff peaks. With a metal spoon, fold them into the cheese mixture.

With a layer of cheesecloth, line 6 *coeur à la crème* moulds if you have them. If not, use 6 small moulds with perforated bottoms. Spoon the cheese mixture into the moulds.

Stand the moulds in a large soup dish or plate to catch the liquid that will drain out of the cheese mixture and put both the moulds and dish into the refrigerator

Coeur à la Crème, a classic French confection, is a mixture of cream cheese and cream with brown sugar.

for 12 hours or overnight.

Invert the moulds on to a serving platter and remove the cheesecloth lining. Place a teaspoon of brown sugar on top of each coeur à la crème and serve them accompanied by a jug of cream.

Cream Cheese Delight

This scrumptious mixture of mandarin oranges, cream, cream cheese and apple sauce may be served as an elegant end to a dinner party.

6 SERVINGS

8 oz. cream cheese
10 fl. oz. double cream [1¼ cups heavy cream]
4 fl. oz. [½ cup] thick apple sauce
2 tablespoons castor sugar
22 oz. canned mandarin oranges, drained and with the can juice reserved
1 teaspoon grated orange rind
2 tablespoons medium sherry
juice of 1 lemon
½ oz. gelatine, dissolved in 4

tablespoons hot water
2 tablespoons slivered almonds, toasted

In a bowl, beat the cream cheese with a wooden spoon until it is soft and fluffy. Using a metal spoon, gradually fold the cream into the cheese so that they are thoroughly combined. Stir in the apple sauce, sugar and about three-quarters of the mandarin oranges. Set aside.

Pour the reserved can juice into a medium-sized mixing bowl and stir in the orange rind, sherry and lemon juice. Add the gelatine and beat well to blend.

Gradually pour the gelatine mixture into the cream mixture, beating constantly. When the ingredients are combined, pour the mixture into a large mould. Place the mould in the refrigerator to chill for 2 hours or until it is set.

Remove the mould from the refrigerator and dip the bottom quickly into hot water. Run a knife around the edge of the mould to loosen the mixture. Place a serving plate, inverted, over the mould and reverse the two, giving the mould a sharp shake. The mixture should slide out easily.

Arrange the remaining mandarin oranges decoratively over the top of the mixture and scatter over the toasted almonds. Serve at once.

Maids of Honour

These little cakes originated in Richmond, Surrey. The story goes that when Henry VIII lived in Richmond Palace, he was inspecting the kitchens and saw someone trying a new recipe for cakes. He liked them so much that he asked the maid of honour to continue making the cakes.

Eventually, the secret recipe was given to a baker who had a shop in Richmond and so Maids of Honour cakes became famous. Although the old shop was destroyed, the recipe was passed on to another baker and this shop is now in Kew, Surrey.

12 CAKES

PASTRY
8 oz. [1 cup] plus 2 teaspoons
    unsalted butter
8 oz. [2 cups] flour
¼ teaspoon salt
5 fl. oz. [⅝ cup] iced water
FILLING
4 oz. [½ cup] curd cheese
4 oz. [½ cup] butter
4 oz. [½ cup] sugar
4 egg yolks
1 medium-sized potato, cooked
    and mashed
2 oz. [⅓ cup] ground almonds
    grated rind of 1 lemon

¼ teaspoon grated nutmeg
3 fl. oz. [⅜ cup] brandy

With the 2 teaspoons of butter, grease 12 patty tins. Set aside.

To make the pastry, sift the flour and salt into a medium-sized mixing bowl. With a knife, cut 2 ounces [¼ cup] of the butter into the flour.

With your fingertips, rub the butter into the flour until the mixture resembles fine breadcrumbs. Add the water and mix to a firm dough. Cover the dough with greaseproof or waxed paper and put it in the refrigerator to chill for 15 minutes.

Put the remaining butter between two pieces of greaseproof or waxed paper. Beat it with the back of a wooden spoon or mallet into a flat oblong about ¾-inch thick.

On a floured board, roll out the dough into a rectangular shape ¼-inch thick. Place the oblong of butter in the centre of the dough. Fold the dough over it to make a parcel. Cover the dough and put it in the refrigerator for 10 minutes.

Place the dough, with the folds downwards, on the board and roll it out away from you into a rectangle. Fold the rectangle in three. Turn so that the open end is facing you and roll out again. Cover the dough and put it in the refrigerator to chill for 15 minutes. Repeat this rolling and folding twice more.

Preheat the oven to fairly hot 400°F (Gas Mark 6, 200°C).

To prepare the filling, in a medium-sized mixing bowl, combine the cheese, butter and sugar with a wooden spoon.

In a small mixing bowl, beat the egg yolks with a wire whisk or rotary beater until they are thick and creamy. Pour the egg yolks into the cheese mixture and mix well. Add the potato, ground almonds, lemon rind, nutmeg and brandy. Stir well until all the ingredients are thoroughly mixed. Set the filling aside.

On a floured board, roll out the dough until it is about ¼-inch thick. With a 4-inch pastry cutter, cut the dough into twelve circles. Line the bottoms and sides of the prepared patty tins with the dough circles. Fill each dough case with a spoonful of the filling.

Place the patty tins on a baking sheet and put it in the oven. Bake for 20 to 25 minutes or until the pastry is golden.

Carefully remove the cakes from their tins and set aside on a wire rack to cool completely before serving.

Maids of Honour are little cheese cakes first popularized by Henry VIII.

10 oz. [2½ cups] flour
½ teaspoon salt
1 egg, lightly beaten
7 fl. oz. [⅞ cup] tepid water
1 oz. [2 tablespoons] butter, melted
FILLING
1½ lb. cottage cheese
2 oz. [¼ cup] sugar
2 eggs, lightly beaten
¼ teaspoon salt
  grated rind of 1 lemon
4 oz. [⅔ cup] sultanas or raisins
4 oz. [½ cup] butter, melted
2 oz. [1 cup] fresh breadcrumbs

Sift the flour and salt into a large bowl. Beat the egg, water and butter together until they are well blended. Stir the egg and water mixture into the flour and mix well. Knead with your hands until a firm dough is formed.

Place the dough on a floured board and continue kneading for about 10 minutes until it is smooth and elastic. Place the dough in a warmed, large mixing bowl. Cover the bowl and set it in a warm, draught-free place for 30 minutes.

Meanwhile, prepare the filling. In a bowl, combine the cheese, sugar, eggs, salt, lemon rind and sultanas or raisins, beating until they are well blended.

Spread out a large, clean cloth on a table. Sprinkle with flour. Place the dough on the cloth and roll out the dough as thinly as possible.

Lift and stretch the dough, pulling the dough until it is paper thin. This should be done as carefully as possible. Do not worry if a few small holes appear. With scissors, trim the outer edges of the dough so that the sides are straight.

Preheat the oven to very hot 450°F (Gas Mark 8, 230°C). Grease two baking sheets with half the melted butter.

Brush the dough with half the remaining melted butter and sprinkle with nearly all the breadcrumbs. Spoon the cheese in a long strip on to the dough, 3 inches away from the edges of the sides.

Using the cloth, lift the dough over the filling and roll it up Swiss [jelly] roll style. Tuck in the ends. Brush the top with the remaining melted butter and cover with the rest of the breadcrumbs.

With a sharp knife, divide the strudel into pieces long enough to fit the baking sheets. Place the strudels on the baking sheets with the seams underneath. Put the baking sheets in the oven and bake for 10 minutes. Reduce the oven temperature to fairly hot 400°F (Gas Mark 6, 200°C) and bake for a further 20 minutes, or until the strudels are golden brown.

Mexican Cheese Squares

Pastry, filled with cottage cheese mixed with egg and fruit, then cut into little squares, Mexican Cheese Squares are delicious.

8 SQUARES

12 oz. [3 cups] flour
¼ teaspoon salt
6 oz. [¾ cup] butter, chilled
2 small eggs, lightly beaten
3 to 4 tablespoons iced water
2 tablespoons milk
FILLING
8 oz. cottage cheese, strained
1 egg, beaten with 2 egg yolks
4 oz. [½ cup] castor sugar
3 oz. [½ cup] currants
1 teaspoon lemon juice
¼ teaspoon vanilla essence

Sift the flour and salt into a large mixing bowl. Add the butter and cut it into small pieces with a table knife. With your fingertips, rub the butter into the flour until the mixture resembles breadcrumbs.

Add the eggs with 2 tablespoons of the water and mix into the flour with the knife.

Knead the dough gently and form it into a ball. Chill in the refrigerator for 30 minutes.

Preheat the oven to fairly hot 400°F (Gas Mark 6, 200°C).

To make the filling, place all the ingredients in a bowl and beat together until they are mixed.

Remove the dough from the refrigerator and divide it in half. On a lightly floured board, roll out half of the dough to a rectangle large enough to line a 7- x 11-inch baking sheet. Lift the dough on to the rolling pin and place it on the baking sheet. Spoon the filling on to the dough, spreading it out evenly to within ¼-inch of the edges. Moisten the edges of the dough with a little water.

Roll the remaining dough out to a rectangle large enough to cover the filling. Lift the dough on to the filling, pressing the edges together to seal. Cut a slit in the centre of the dough and trim the edges. Brush the top of the dough with the milk.

Place the baking sheet in the oven and bake the dough for 20 to 25 minutes or until it is golden brown.

Remove the sheet from the oven and set it aside to cool. Cut the pastry into 8 squares and serve.

Cheese Strudel

Cheese Strudel takes a long time to make, but the finished dish is delicious.

6-8 SERVINGS

Sweets and puddings for the family

Desserts are the gilt on the gingerbread — not essential, exactly, but often the thing that makes cooking meals worthwhile. And when you've a young family to cater for, they are often the only food (with the possible exception of baked beans and fish fingers) for which enthusiasm is shown!

Desserts cover a whole range of eating experience, and this has been our prime consideration in selecting recipes for this book. So you will find filling, familiar dishes such as Apple Pie (page 322), lighter traditional dishes such as Fruit Fool (page 332), as well as elegant ones such as Chestnut Pudding (pictured below, recipe page 348). All are

guaranteed to satisfy your most demanding family gourmet AND not to shatter your budget!

But of course there are times (birthdays, anniversaries and so on) when economy is not the order of the day and when you're quite prepared to stay in the kitchen for longer than usual. For times like these, something extra-special is called for, and these recipes are included in **For Special Occasions.** They MAY cost a bit more, they may take a bit more time to prepare, but they **will** make the most glorious finale to that special meal.

If it is the little luxuries that make life really worth living, you can't afford to ignore desserts.

321

Apple Fritters

 ①

This inexpensive and easy-to-make dessert is a favourite with children. Bananas, apricots and pineapple rings may also be used.

4 SERVINGS

4 oz. [1 cup] flour
⅛ teaspoon salt
2 egg yolks, plus 1 egg white
1 tablespoon cooking oil
5 fl. oz. [⅝ cup] milk
1 lb. cooking apples
   juice of 1 lemon
   castor sugar
4 oz. [½ cup] butter

Sift the flour and salt into a medium-sized mixing bowl. Make a well in the centre of the flour and put in the egg yolks, white and oil. With a wooden spoon, mix them, slowly incorporating the flour and gradually adding the milk. Mix to a smooth batter, then beat well. Cover and keep in a cool place for 30 minutes.

Peel and core the apples and slice into rings ¼-inch thick. Lay the rings on a plate and sprinkle with lemon juice and sugar.

In a large frying-pan, melt the butter over high heat. Using a skewer, dip the apple rings into the batter and drop them one by one into the hot butter. Cook the rings on both sides until they are golden brown. Arrange on a plate and dredge with castor sugar. Serve at once.

Apple Pie

 ①

Traditional Apple Pie differs from other pies in several ways. First, the pastry is made with a greater proportion of fat to flour than are other pie crusts. In the filling, the apples are cut in rather thick slices. The filling is spiced with cinnamon, allspice and nutmeg and thickened with cornflour [cornstarch]. In the United States, Apple Pie is frequently served warm with vanilla ice cream.

6 SERVINGS

PASTRY
10 oz. [2½ cups] flour
¼ teaspoon salt
4 oz. [½ cup] vegetable shortening
   or lard
2 oz. [¼ cup] butter
6 tablespoons iced water
1 tablespoon single [light] cream

FILLING
6 oz. [¾ cup] sugar
1 teaspoon ground cinnamon
¼ teaspoon ground allspice
¼ teaspoon grated nutmeg
1 tablespoon cornflour [cornstarch]

2 lb. cooking apples, peeled, cored
   and quartered and each quarter
   cut into 3 slices
1 tablespoon lemon juice
1 oz. [2 tablespoons] butter, cut into
   small pieces

Sift the flour and salt into a large mixing bowl. Add the vegetable shortening or lard and the butter. With your fingertips, rub the fats into the flour until the mixture resembles fine breadcrumbs. Add the water a little at a time, and stir the dough, using a knife, until it is firm and not sticky. Knead the dough gently until it is smooth. Wrap the dough in aluminium foil and place it in the refrigerator for 30 minutes, or until it is well chilled.

Grease the bottom and sides of a 9-inch deep pie dish with a little butter.

Divide the dough in half. On a floured board, roll out one half in a circle large enough to line the pie dish. Lift the dough on to the rolling pin and unroll it over the pie dish. With your fingers gently ease the dough into the dish without pulling or stretching the dough. Using a sharp knife trim the dough so that it is even with the outer rim of the pie dish.

Preheat the oven to fairly hot 375°F (Gas Mark 5, 190°C).

For the filling, blend the sugar, cinnamon, allspice, nutmeg and cornflour [cornstarch] in a large mixing bowl. Add the sliced apples and lemon juice and toss together thoroughly.

Fill the pie shell with the apple mixture, piling it higher in the centre. Although the filling may seem to be quite high it will shrink when it bakes. Dot the top of the filling with the remaining butter.

For the top crust, roll out the remaining half of the dough into a circle which is about ⅛-inch thick and about 12-inches in diameter.

Lift it up on the rolling pin and over the filling. With scissors, trim the top crust to within ¼-inch of the dish. Tuck the overhanging dough under the edge of the bottom crust all around the rim and then press down with your fingers to seal the two crusts and make a design.

Brush the dough with the cream. With the scissors, cut two small gashes in the centre of the top.

Bake the pie in the middle of the oven for 40 minutes or until the crust is golden brown. Serve at once.

Serve this traditional Apple Pie the way the Americans do—with dollops of delicious vanilla ice-cream for lunch or dinner.

Porridge Apples

   ①

This warming Scottish dessert is easy to make and very economical. Serve it with plenty of whipped cream or thick, hot custard.

6 SERVINGS

8 oz. [1 cup] plus 1 teaspoon butter, melted

8 oz. [2 cups] rolled oats

6 oz. [1 cup] soft brown sugar

¼ teaspoon salt

8 medium-sized cooking apples, peeled, cored and thinly sliced

5 fl. oz. [⅝ cup] water

1 large cooking apple, cored and thinly sliced

2 tablespoons strained apricot jam, warmed

Preheat the oven to moderate 350°F (Gas Mark 4, 180°C).

Using the teaspoon of butter, grease a large baking dish and set aside.

In a medium-sized mixing bowl, combine the oats, sugar, salt and the remaining butter, stirring well with a wooden spoon to blend.

Layer the oat mixture and apple slices in the prepared baking dish, beginning and ending with a layer of oat mixture. Carefully pour the water over the mixture.

Porridge Apples makes a nutritious and filling dessert.

Place the unpeeled apple slices decoratively over the top of the pudding and, using a pastry brush, brush them with the apricot jam.

Place the dish in the centre of the oven and bake for 40 to 50 minutes or until the top of the pudding is deep golden brown.

Remove the dish from the oven and serve immediately.

Apple Charlotte

 ①

This delicious hot pudding is perfect for family lunches or dinners.

4-6 SERVINGS

FILLING

2 oz. [¼ cup] plus 1 teaspoon butter

2 lb. cooking apples, peeled, cored and cut into quarters

2 oz. [¼ cup] sugar
the rind of 1 lemon

1 small loaf of bread, a day or two old, crusts removed and cut into as many thin slices as required

4 oz. [½ cup] butter, melted
castor sugar

SAUCE

5 tablespoons apricot jam

3 tablespoons water

2 tablespoons medium sherry

Preheat the oven to moderate 350°F (Gas Mark 4, 180°C). Lightly grease a charlotte mould or ovenproof dish with the teaspoon of butter.

Put the apples, sugar, lemon rind and remaining butter in a medium-sized saucepan and, stirring occasionally with a wooden spoon, simmer over low heat for 10 minutes or until the apples are very soft. (They should neither be completely whole nor completely mashed.) Discard the lemon rind.

Cut the bread slices in halves. Dip the halved slices in the melted butter and line the bottom and sides of the mould or dish, overlapping the slices slightly. Fill with the apple mixture and cover with a layer of bread slices dipped in melted butter. Sprinkle the pudding with castor sugar and bake in the oven for 40 minutes, or until the top is golden brown.

While the charlotte is baking, put the jam and water in a small saucepan. Stir and bring to the boil. Reduce the heat to low and simmer for 3 minutes. Remove from the heat and stir in the sherry.

After taking the apple charlotte from the oven, let it stand for a minute or two before turning it out on to a warmed serving dish. Pour the warm, but not hot, jam sauce over it and serve immediately.

Apricot Bourdaloue Tart

The sharp taste of the apricots in this dessert tart contrasts pleasantly with the sweet cream.

4-6 SERVINGS

PASTRY
4 oz. [1 cup] flour
⅛ teaspoon salt
2 teaspoons castor sugar
1 oz. [2 tablespoons] butter
2 tablespoons vegetable fat
1 egg yolk
½ to 1 tablespoon iced water

FILLING
2 egg yolks
2 oz. [¼ cup] castor sugar
grated rind of 1 orange
1½ tablespoons each cornflour [corn-
   starch] and flour mixed
10 fl. oz. [1¼ cups] milk
1 egg white
14 oz. canned halved apricots
   or 1 lb. fresh apricots, halved,
   stoned and poached in syrup
1 oz. [¼ cup] roasted almonds, flaked

Preheat the oven to moderate 350°F (Gas Mark 4, 180°C).

Sift the flour and salt into a medium-sized mixing bowl. Add the sugar and mix. Using a table knife, cut the butter and vegetable fat into the flour. Using your fingertips, rub the fat into the flour until the mixture resembles fine breadcrumbs. Make a well in the centre of the mixture and add the egg yolk mixed with ½ tablespoon of iced water. To begin with, use the knife to mix the flour mixture with the egg yolk, then use your hands to knead the dough until it is smooth. Add more iced water if the dough is too dry. Pat the dough into a ball, cover and refrigerate for 15 minutes.

Roll out the dough to line a 7½-inch flan tin. Refrigerate for 10 minutes. Bake blind, covering the bottom with foil weighed down with dried beans, for 30 minutes.

To make the crème bourdaloue, in a medium-sized mixing bowl beat the egg yolks with half the sugar. Add the grated orange rind and the cornflour [cornstarch] and flour mixture and beat until smooth. Put the milk in a pan on moderate heat and bring to the boil. Just as it comes to the boil, pour it slowly, stirring all the time, over the egg mixture. Stir until smooth. Return the mixture to the pan and, stirring constantly, bring to the boil. Remove from the heat and cool.

In a small mixing bowl, beat the egg white with the remaining sugar until stiff. Fold it into the cooked mixture.

Drain the apricot halves. Put the syrup into a small pan and boil rapidly until it thickens. Cool and set aside.

Remove the pastry shell from the tin and place it on a serving dish. Put the crème bourdaloue into the middle of the pastry shell and smooth with a knife. Cover completely with the apricots, sprinkle with the almonds and brush with the reduced syrup. Serve.

Apricot Pudding

Apricot Pudding is a delightful blend of apricots and cream.

6 SERVINGS

1½ lb. apricots, halved and stoned
4 fl. oz. [½ cup] water
5 tablespoons sugar
¾ oz. gelatine
1 x 7-inch sponge cake
4 tablespoons apricot jam
4 tablespoons medium sherry
1 teaspoon vegetable oil
3 oz. [½ cup] pistachios, chopped
15 fl. oz. double cream [1⅞ cups
   heavy cream]
6 fl. oz. [¾ cup] milk

Preheat the oven to warm 325°F (Gas Mark 3, 170°C).

Place the apricots in an ovenproof dish and pour over the water. Sprinkle 4 tablespoons of the sugar over the apricots and place the dish in the oven. Cook the apricots for 40 minutes or until they are

Super Apricot Bourdaloue Tart.

tender. Remove the dish from the oven. Transfer the apricots to a plate.

Pour the apricot cooking juices into a small saucepan and add the gelatine. Place the pan over low heat and cook, stirring constantly, for 2 to 3 minutes or until the gelatine has dissolved. Do not allow the liquid to boil. Remove the pan from the heat. Add the remaining sugar to the pan and stir until the sugar has dissolved. Set aside to cool.

Slice the sponge cake in half, horizontally, and spread the jam over the bottom half. Sandwich together again. Cut into 1-inch squares and place the squares in a mixing bowl. Pour over the sherry and set aside for 5 minutes.

With the oil, grease a 3-pint [2-quart] mould. Arrange the apricot halves and pistachios in the mould.

In a medium-sized mixing bowl, beat the cream with a wire whisk or rotary beater until it is thick but not stiff. Carefully fold in the milk and the apricot jelly [gelatin] mixture.

Pour half the cream mixture into the mould and chill in the refrigerator for 30 minutes or until it is set.

Remove the mould from the refrigerator. Place the sponge in the centre of the mould and pour the remaining cream mixture on top. Chill the mould in the refrigerator for 2 hours or until it has set completely.

Remove the mould from the refrigerator. Dip the mould quickly in hot water. Invert a serving dish over the mould and, grasping the two firmly together, reverse them. The mould should slide out easily. Serve immediately.

Black Bottom Parfait

These two-tiered chocolate and vanilla parfaits make a mouth-watering dessert for lunch or dinner. They are easy to make and most attractive.

6 SERVINGS

2 teaspoons cornflour [cornstarch]
16 fl. oz. [2 cups] milk
4 egg yolks
4 oz. [½ cup] plus 1 tablespoon castor sugar
8 oz. dark [semi-sweet] chocolate, melted in 3 tablespoons dark rum or coffee

1 teaspoon vanilla essence
½ oz. gelatine
2 fl. oz. [¼ cup] boiling water
5 fl. oz. double cream [⅝ cup heavy cream], chilled
2 egg whites
¼ teaspoon salt
¼ teaspoon cream of tartar
2 oz. plain dark chocolate caraque curls

In a heavy medium-sized saucepan, mix the cornflour [cornstarch] and the milk together and, stirring continuously, bring to the boil over moderate heat.

Reduce the heat to low and cook, stirring constantly, for 5 minutes. Remove from the heat and allow to cool.

In a small bowl, beat the egg yolks and 4 ounces [½ cup] of sugar with a whisk until the egg yolks have thickened and become pale yellow. When the milk mixture has cooled, gradually stir the beaten eggs into it. Replace the pan on low heat and cook, stirring continuously, for 5 minutes, or until the mixture is thick. Do not boil or it will curdle.

Pour about half this custard into a medium-sized bowl. Add the melted chocolate and ½ teaspoon of vanilla essence and stir until well blended. Taste the chocolate custard and, if it is not sweet enough, add a little more sugar. Spoon the chocolate custard into 4 parfait or sundae glasses. Put them in the refrigerator to chill.

Put the gelatine in a small saucepan. Add the boiling water and stir over low heat until the gelatine has completely dissolved. Add it, with the remaining vanilla, to the custard in the saucepan.

Pour the cream into a medium-sized bowl and beat it with a whisk or rotary beater until it thickens slightly. Fold this into the custard mixture.

Put the egg whites, salt and cream of tartar in a medium-sized bowl and, with a balloon whisk or rotary beater, beat the egg whites until they are foamy. Gradually add the tablespoon of castor sugar and continue beating until the egg whites are stiff.

With a metal spoon, fold the beaten egg whites into the custard mixture in the saucepan.

Pour this mixture on top of the chocolate custard in the parfait or sundae glasses. Put the glasses back in the refrigerator to chill for at least 4 hours.

When the parfaits are quite firm, decorate the tops with chocolate caraque and serve immediately.

Black Bottom Parfait—a rich dessert for any occasion.

Chocolate Mousse

A mouthwatering, rich dish, Chocolate Mousse makes a superb dinner dessert. You could use the egg whites to make chocolate meringues and serve them with the mousse.

4 SERVINGS

4 oz. dark [semi-sweet] cooking
   chocolate, broken into pieces
2 oz. [¼ cup] castor sugar
10 fl. oz. [1¼ cups] milk
4 egg yolks
3 tablespoons dark rum or brandy
10 fl. oz. double cream [1¼ cups
   heavy cream]

Place the chocolate, sugar and milk in a medium-sized heavy saucepan. Set the pan over moderately low heat and cook, stirring frequently, for 3 to 5 minutes, or until the chocolate has melted.

Remove the pan from the heat and set it aside. In a heatproof mixing bowl, beat the egg yolks together with a wire whisk or rotary beater. Gradually add the milk mixture, beating constantly.

Set the bowl in a pan half-filled with hot water. Set the pan over low heat and cook the mixture, stirring constantly with a wooden spoon, until it coats the back of the spoon.

Remove the pan from the heat. Lift the bowl out of the pan. Stir in the rum or brandy and set the custard aside to cool completely, stirring occasionally.

Pour the cream into a medium-sized mixing bowl. Using a wire whisk or rotary beater, beat the cream until it forms stiff peaks. Fold the cream into the cooled chocolate custard, blending it in thoroughly.

Pour the mixture into a chilled glass serving bowl or individual glasses and chill in the refrigerator for 4 hours before serving.

Chocolate and Rum Fondue

This is a very unusual dessert to serve for dinner. The fondue should be served with a selection of fruit such as pears and bananas or cake cut into small pieces. The fruit or cake is speared on dessert forks and dipped into the hot chocolate.

6-8 SERVINGS

8 oz. dark [semi-sweet] chocolate,
   broken into small pieces

This unusual Chocolate and Rum Fondue is guaranteed to make any meal extra-special!

6 tablespoons double [heavy] cream
2 tablespoons rum
2 oz. icing sugar [½ cup
   confectioners' sugar], sifted

In a small bowl set over a pan of hot water, melt the chocolate with the cream, stirring constantly with a wooden spoon. As soon as the chocolate has melted, remove the bowl from the heat. Stir in the rum and the sugar.

Pour the mixture into a fondue pot set over a small spirit lamp.

Ignite the spirit lamp and serve the fondue with the fruit or pieces of cake.

Easy to make, even easier to eat— that's creamy, mouth-watering Chocolate Mousse.

Clafoutis

FRENCH CHERRY PUDDING

This is the basic — and traditional — version of clafoutis. Clafoutis may be served on its own or with whipped cream or a light custard sauce.

6 SERVINGS

1 teaspoon margarine or butter

1¼ lb. fresh black cherries, washed and stoned or 1¼ lb. canned black cherries, stoned and drained

6 fl. oz. [¾ cup] milk

2 eggs

2 teaspoons vanilla essence

5 tablespoons icing [confectioners'] sugar

7 tablespoons flour

⅛ teaspoon salt

Preheat the oven to moderate 350°F (Gas Mark 4, 180°C). Grease a medium-sized baking dish with the teaspoon of margarine or butter.

Dry the black cherries thoroughly on kitchen paper towels and set aside.

In a large mixing bowl, blend the milk, eggs and vanilla essence, beating with a wire whisk until the liquid is smooth. Add 4 tablespoons of the sugar, 1 tablespoon at a time, whisking constantly, and make sure that each tablespoon has been

This traditional French Clafoutis is black cherries baked in batter. Serve with lots of custard or cream for a warming dessert.

absorbed before the next one is added. Add the flour, tablespoonful by tablespoonful in the same way, adding the salt with the final tablespoonful. When all the sugar and flour has been beaten in, the batter should be very smooth and of a very light pancake batter consistency.

Pour the batter into the greased baking dish and add the cherries, spreading them evenly throughout the batter. Bake in the centre of the oven for 50 minutes to 1 hour, or until a sharp knife inserted in the middle of the clafoutis comes out clean.

Remove the clafoutis from the oven, sprinkle the top of the pudding with the remaining icing [confectioners'] sugar and serve immediately.

Coriander Fruit Crumble

This unusual aromatic dessert is inexpensive, simple to make and has a very interesting flavour. Serve it for a family supper either hot or cold, with whipped cream or lots of custard.

4-6 SERVINGS

1 teaspoon butter

1½ lb. cooking apples, peeled, cored and thinly sliced

8 oz. fresh or frozen and thawed blackberries, washed

2 tablespoons soft brown sugar

1 teaspoon ground cinnamon

TOPPING

4 oz. [1 cup] flour

4 oz. [½ cup] sugar

4 oz. [½ cup] butter

2 teaspoons ground coriander

Preheat the oven to moderate 350°F (Gas Mark 4, 180°C). Lightly grease a 3-pint [2-quart] baking dish with the teaspoon of butter.

Put the apples and blackberries in the baking dish and sprinkle with the brown sugar and cinnamon.

To make the crumble topping, put the flour and sugar in a medium-sized mixing bowl. Add the butter and cut it into the flour with a table knife. Then using your fingertips, rub the butter into the flour and sugar until the mixture resembles coarse breadcrumbs. Mix in the ground coriander.

Sprinkle the crumble on top of the fruit and bake in the centre of the oven for 45 minutes.

Remove the baking dish from the oven and serve the crumble at once, if you are eating it hot.

Crème Caramel
BAKED CARAMEL CUSTARD

☆ ☆ ☆ ① ① ⊠ ⊠

Crème Caramel is an exquisitely light dessert and, as it may be made in advance and chilled in the refrigerator, it is ideal to serve for a family dinner.

6 SERVINGS

CARAMEL
4 oz. [½ cup] sugar
2½ fl. oz. [¼ cup plus 1 tablespoon] water

CREME
1 pint [2½ cups] milk
3½ oz. [⅜ cup plus 1 tablespoon] sugar
½ vanilla pod or 1 teaspoon vanilla essence
2 eggs
2 egg yolks

To make the caramel, in a heavy, medium-sized saucepan, heat the sugar and water over low heat, stirring until the sugar dissolves completely. Increase the heat to moderately high and allow the syrup to come to the boil. Cook for 3 to 4 minutes, or until it turns a light golden brown in colour.

Be careful not to overcook the syrup or it will darken too much and become bitter. Immediately the caramel has reached the right colour, remove the pan from the heat and pour it into six individual ramekins or one heatproof dish. Do not allow the caramel to cool before pouring it into the ramekins or dish.

In a heavy, medium-sized saucepan bring the milk and sugar to the boil over moderate heat, stirring occasionally to dissolve the sugar. When the sugar has dissolved, add the vanilla pod to the milk. Cover the pan, remove from the heat and leave the vanilla to infuse with the milk for 20 minutes.

In a medium-sized mixing bowl, beat the eggs and the egg yolks with a wire whisk until they thicken and become pale yellow.

Beating continuously, gradually add the milk to the beaten eggs, pouring it in through a strainer. Discard the vanilla pod. If you have not used the vanilla pod, stir in the vanilla essence at this point. Stir well and pour the mixture into a large jug.

Preheat the oven to warm 325°F (Gas Mark 3, 170°C).

Pour the milk mixture through a silk tammy or a very fine strainer into the six ramekins or the dish. Spoon off any froth which appears on the surface.

Place the dishes in a deep baking tin or bain marie and add enough boiling water to reach about half way up the sides of the dishes.

Place the baking tin or bain marie in the lower part of the oven and bake for 40 minutes, or until the centre of the crème is firm when pressed with your finger. Do not allow the water to simmer during the baking because if it does the custard will have a grainy texture. (If the water does begin to simmer, lower the oven heat immediately).

Remove the dish from the water and allow to cool thoroughly. Chill in the refrigerator for 1 hour. Then run a knife around the edge of the ramekins or dish and place a serving plate on top. Reverse the crème caramel on to it and serve immediately.

Cream Cheese Cake

☆ ① ① ⊠ ⊠

A delicious cheesecake with an excitingly different spice flavour, Cream Cheese Cake is very easy to make and will be a great favourite with all the family! Serve as a special dessert for lunch and dinner or as a rich after-school or tea-time snack for the children.

ONE 9-INCH CAKE

2 oz. [¼ cup] plus 1 teaspoon butter, melted
6 oz. crushed digestive biscuits [1½ cups crushed graham crackers]
12 oz. cream cheese
6 oz. [¾ cup] sugar
1 egg, well beaten
1½ teaspoons ground ginger
12 fl. oz. [1½ cups] sour cream
4 tablespoons canned pineapple, drained and crushed

Preheat the oven to moderate 350°F (Gas Mark 4, 180°C). Lightly grease a 9-inch cake tin with the teaspoon of butter and set aside.

In a medium-sized mixing bowl, combine the digestive biscuits [graham crackers] and the remaining melted butter, beating until they are well blended. Spoon the mixture into the prepared cake tin and, using your fingers or a metal spoon, line the tin evenly with the mixture. Set aside.

In a medium-sized mixing bowl, combine the cream cheese, half of the sugar and the egg, beating with a fork until the mixture is smooth. Stir in 1 teaspoon of the ginger and mix well. Pour the mixture into the lined cake tin and place it in the centre of the oven. Bake for 25 to 30 minutes, or until the filling is set and firm to touch.

Meanwhile, in a large mixing bowl, combine the sour cream, the remaining sugar and the remaining ginger, beating briskly until the sugar has dissolved. Set aside.

Remove the cake from the oven and turn off the heat.

Spread the sour cream mixture evenly over the top of the cake and arrange the crushed pineapple on top. Return the tin to the oven and leave it there, with the door closed, for 5 minutes.

Remove the tin from the oven and place it in the refrigerator to chill for at least 1 hour.

Remove the tin from the refrigerator and serve cold, in small wedges.

Exquisite Creme Caramel is one of the shining glories of French cuisine —and its delicate taste is absolutely guaranteed to delight the entire family.

Flemish Strawberry and Almond Cake

A lovely dessert for a summer lunch or dinner, Flemish Strawberry and Almond Cake is surprisingly easy and economical to prepare.

6-8 SERVINGS

CAKE
3 oz. [⅜ cup] plus 1 teaspoon butter, softened
2 oz. [½ cup] plus 2 teaspoons self-raising flour
3 oz. [⅜ cup] castor sugar
3 eggs
3 oz. [½ cup] ground almonds

FILLING
12 oz. strawberries, washed, hulled and puréed
2½ oz. icing sugar [½ cup plus 2 tablespoons confectioners' sugar]
5 fl. oz. double cream [⅝ cup heavy cream], whipped until stiff
¼ oz. gelatine dissolved in 1 tablespoon hot water
4 oz. strawberries, washed, hulled and halved

Preheat the oven to fairly hot 375°F (Gas

Scrumptious Flemish Strawberry and Almond Cake.

Mark 5, 190°C).

Lightly grease a round 7-inch cake tin with the teaspoon of butter. Sprinkle in the 2 teaspoons flour and tip and rotate the tin to distribute the flour evenly. Knock out any excess flour and set the tin aside.

In a medium-sized mixing bowl, cream the remaining butter and the sugar together with a wooden spoon until the mixture is fluffy. Beat in the eggs.

With a metal spoon, fold in the remaining flour and the ground almonds.

Turn the mixture into the prepared cake tin and place it in the centre of the oven.

Bake for 30 to 40 minutes, or until a skewer inserted into the centre of the cake comes out clean.

Remove the cake from the oven. Run a knife round the edge of the cake and reverse it onto a wire rack. Leave to cool.

Wash and thoroughly rinse out the cake tin.

To make the filling, in a medium-sized mixing bowl, combine the strawberry purée and 2 ounces [½ cup] of the sugar. Fold in the cream and then the dissolved gelatine. Turn the mixture into the dampened cake tin and place it in the refrigerator. Chill for 1 to 1½ hours or until the filling is set.

With a long sharp knife, slice the cake into two layers. Place one layer on a serving platter and turn out the strawberry filling on to it. Place the other cake layer on top.

Sift the remaining icing [confectioners'] sugar over the top of the cake and decorate

Traditional English Flummery has been a favourite all over Britain for centuries.

with the strawberry halves.

Flummery

A traditional English sweet dish, Flummery makes a delicious family lunch or dinner dessert. Serve with lots of stiffly whipped cream or a mixed fresh fruit compôte.

4 SERVINGS

4 oz. [⅔ cup] round-grain rice, washed, soaked in cold water for 30 minutes and drained
10 fl. oz. [1¼ cups] milk
10 fl. oz. double cream [1¼ cups heavy cream]
2 oz. [¼ cup] sugar
1 tablespoon finely grated lemon rind
1 teaspoon ground cinnamon

Combine all the ingredients in the top part of a double saucepan. Half fill the bottom part with boiling water and place the double saucepan over moderately low heat. Cover the saucepan and cook the mixture, stirring occasionally, for 50 minutes to 1 hour, or until the rice is soft and tender and has absorbed most of the liquid.

Remove the pan from the heat and pour the mixture into a 1-pint [1½-pint] soufflé

or other decorative serving dish. Allow the mixture to cool to room temperature, then place the dish in the refrigerator to chill for 3 hours, or until the flummery is set and firm.

Serve cold.

Ginger Pear Sauce

This is a sweet fruit sauce to serve with ice-cream or hot gingerbread for a super luncheon treat.

12 FLUID OUNCES [1½ CUPS]

14 oz. canned pear halves, drained, chopped and the syrup reserved
4 tablespoons evaporated milk
2 tablespoons finely chopped preserved ginger
1 tablespoon rum (optional)

Measure 8 fluid ounces [1 cup] of the pear syrup and pour it into a small saucepan. Add the evaporated milk and stir well. Place the pan over moderate heat and bring the liquid to the boil. Boil the syrup for 10 minutes or until it has reduced by one-third the original quantity.

Remove the pan from the heat and stir in the chopped pears, ginger and the rum if you are using it.

Serve the sauce immediately.

Fruit Fool

A fruit fool is one of the simplest and most delicious of all summer desserts. The two ingredients are simply fruit and cream. Custard may be substituted for the cream but the result is not nearly so good. Strawberries, gooseberries, raspberries, blackcurrants and apricots make the best fools — and of these, gooseberries, blackcurrants and apricots should be poached in a little water first until they are tender. The fruit should then be drained since the purée should be thick. Fruit fools may be served with sponge finger biscuits [cookies] or digestive biscuits [graham crackers].

4 SERVINGS

2 lb. fresh fruit, washed and hulled
  if necessary
10 fl. oz. double cream [1¼ cups
  heavy cream], lightly whipped

If necessary, poach the fruit first, then drain it. With a wooden spoon, mash the fruit through a strainer or purée it through a food mill into a large mixing bowl. Set the bowl aside and allow the purée to cool.

Lightly fold the whipped cream into the purée. Place the bowl in the refrigerator and chill for at least 2 hours.

Pour the fool into a serving dish and serve cold.

Hasty Pudding

Hasty Pudding, made from milk, flour, butter and spices, is an old English dessert, so named because it could be quickly prepared from the staple contents of the larder. Serve it with strawberry jam or golden [light corn] syrup for a family lunch or supper.

2-3 SERVINGS

2 oz. [¼ cup] plus 1 teaspoon butter
2 tablespoons flour
16 fl. oz. [2 cups] milk
½ teaspoon finely grated nutmeg
4 tablespoons soft brown sugar
½ teaspoon ground cinnamon

Preheat the grill [broiler] to high.

Lightly grease a medium-sized flame-proof baking dish with the teaspoon of butter.

In a medium-sized saucepan, melt half of the remaining butter over moderate heat. Remove the pan from the heat and, with a wooden spoon, stir in the flour to make a smooth paste. Gradually add the milk, stirring constantly. Return the pan to the heat and cook, stirring constantly,

This fabulous Ice-Cream Roll is a guaranteed 'hit' at any children's party!

for 2 to 3 minutes, or until the mixture is thick and smooth. Add the nutmeg and 2 tablespoons of the sugar. Reduce the heat to low and simmer for 3 minutes. Remove the pan from the heat.

Pour the mixture into the baking dish and dot the surface with the remaining butter, cut into small pieces. Sprinkle the remaining sugar and the cinnamon thickly on top of the butter. Place the dish under the grill [broiler] and cook for 3 to 5 minutes or until the top is golden brown.

Serve hot or cold.

Ice-Cream Roll

Ideal to serve at a children's tea party or as a simple dessert, Ice-Cream Roll is cool and delicious. It may be decorated with glacé cherries and candied angelica before serving.

ONE ICE-CREAM ROLL

1 teaspoon vegetable oil
3 eggs
3 oz. [⅜ cup] castor sugar
3 oz. [¾ cup] flour, sifted
¼ teaspoon vanilla essence
1 tablespoon sifted cornflour
  [cornstarch]
FILLING
4 oz. strawberry jam

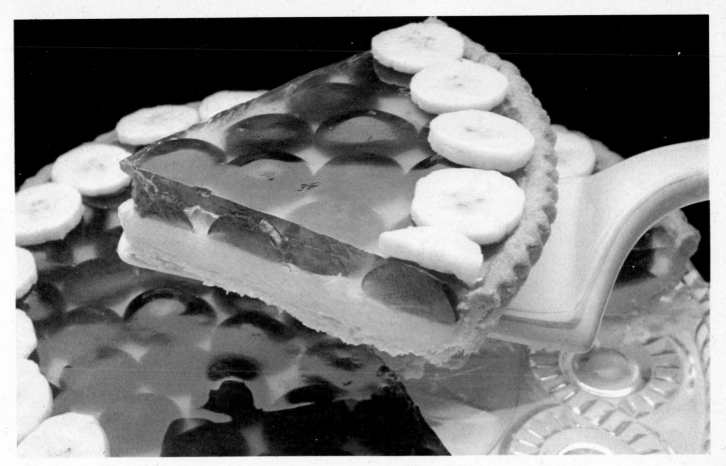

16 fl. oz. [2 cups] vanilla ice-cream

Preheat the oven to hot 425°F (Gas Mark 7, 220°C).

Line an 8- x 12-inch Swiss [jelly] roll tin with non-stick silicone paper or aluminium foil. If you use aluminium foil, grease it with the vegetable oil. Set the tin aside.

Put the eggs and sugar in a medium-sized heatproof mixing bowl. Place the bowl in a saucepan half-filled with hot water. Set the saucepan over moderately low heat.

Using a wire whisk or rotary beater, beat the eggs and sugar together until the mixture is very thick and will make a ribbon trail on itself when the whisk is lifted.

Remove the bowl from the saucepan. Using a metal spoon or spatula, fold in the flour and the vanilla essence.

Pour the batter into the prepared tin and smooth it down with a flat-bladed knife.

Place the tin in the centre of the oven and bake for 8 minutes, or until a skewer inserted into the centre of the sponge comes out clean.

Remove the tin from the oven.

Lay a piece of greaseproof or waxed paper flat on the working surface and dust it with the cornflour [cornstarch]. Turn the sponge out on to the paper. Carefully remove the silicone paper or

Pretty to look at, satisfying to eat Jelly Tart is the perfect—and economical—dessert for a family lunch or dinner.

foil from the sponge.

With a sharp knife, make a shallow cut across the sponge about 2½ inches from the end, to make the rolling easier. With the help of the greaseproof or waxed paper, carefully roll up the sponge, Swiss [jelly] roll style, with the paper inside. Set the cake aside to cool completely.

When the cake is cold, carefully unroll it. Discard the greaseproof or waxed paper and, using a flat-bladed knife, spread the jam evenly over the surface of the cake. Spread the ice-cream thickly on top of the jam.

Roll up the Swiss [jelly] roll and place it on a serving plate. Serve the roll immediately.

Jelly Tart

☆ ☆ ① ⊠ ⊠ ⊠

This is not an easy dessert to make, since it requires great care in handling, but the final result is well worth the trouble! Any fruit in season may be used, but grapes, bananas and mandarin oranges are perhaps the most attractive. Serve for a family lunch or dinner with lots of stiffly whipped double

[heavy] *cream.*

4-6 SERVINGS

1 x 9-inch flan case, made with shortcrust pastry, baked blind and cooled
12 fl. oz. [1½ cups] thick custard
10 fl. oz. [1¼ cups] lemon jelly [gelatin], cool and on the point of setting
6 oz. black grapes, seeded, or 4 bananas, thinly sliced, or 4 mandarin oranges, separated into segments
1 banana, thinly sliced and sprinkled with 1 tablespoon lemon juice

Half-fill the flan case with the thick custard. Place the flan in the refrigerator and chill the custard for at least 30 minutes.

Remove the flan from the refrigerator and pour over half of the lemon jelly [gelatin]. Return the flan to the refrigerator for 30 minutes to allow the jelly [gelatin] to set.

When the jelly [gelatin] is set, cover it with a layer of fruit and pour over the remaining jelly [gelatin]. Place the flan in the refrigerator and leave until the jelly [gelatin] is completely set.

Remove the flan from the refrigerator. Place the banana slices decoratively around the edge of the flan case and serve at once.

Junket

This is the basic recipe for Junket. If you like, you can add 1 tablespoon of brandy to the milk just before you stir in the rennet. Or sprinkle grated nutmeg on top and serve with whipped cream.

4-6 SERVINGS

1 pint [2½ cups] milk
1 tablespoon sugar
1 teaspoon rennet

In a medium-sized saucepan, heat the milk and sugar to blood heat (98°F or 37°C) over moderate heat, stirring to dissolve the sugar.

Remove the pan from the heat and stir in the rennet. Pour the mixture into a serving dish and leave it to set at room temperature. Junket should not be put in the refrigerator.

Krammerhuse

GINGER CREAM-FILLED HORNS

Krammerhuse are Danish cones filled with whipped cream, served for a delicious dessert or afternoon tea. This variation of the basic recipe has the addition of ginger and Madeira to make it all the more superb.

38 CONES

3 oz. [⅜ cup] plus 4 teaspoons butter, melted
2 oz. [¼ cup] sugar
2 oz. [½ cup] flour, sifted
1 teaspoon ground ginger
4 large egg whites
8 fl. oz. double cream [1 cup heavy cream]
1 tablespoon Madeira
2 tablespoons chopped preserved ginger

Preheat the oven to fairly hot 400°F (Gas Mark 6, 200°C).

With 1 teaspoon of the butter, grease a large baking sheet. Set aside while you make the biscuit [cookie] mixture.

In a medium-sized bowl, combine 3 ounces [⅜ cup] of the remaining melted butter, the sugar, flour and ground ginger. Beat well with a wooden spoon to make a smooth paste.

In a medium-sized bowl, beat the egg whites with a wire whisk or rotary beater until they form stiff peaks.

With a metal spoon, carefully fold the egg whites into the batter.

Drop about eight teaspoonfuls of the

This elegant Lemon and Almond Flan is smooth and creamy to taste.

batter on to the baking sheet, leaving plenty of space between each spoonful. Gently flatten them with the spoon. Place the baking sheet in the oven and bake for 3 to 5 minutes or until the biscuits [cookies] are light golden.

Remove the baking sheet from the oven and loosen the biscuits [cookies] with a spatula. While they are still hot, form them quickly into cones by shaping them with your fingers.

Continue baking and shaping the biscuits, greasing the baking sheet with more melted butter when necessary. If the biscuits [cookies] become too cool and stiff to shape, return them to the oven for a few seconds to soften.

When all the biscuits [cookies] have been baked and shaped, allow them to cool.

In a small mixing bowl, beat the cream with a wire whisk or rotary beater until it is stiff. Stir in the Madeira and preserved ginger.

When the cones are completely cool, fill them with the cream and ginger mixture. Arrange the cones on a serving dish and serve.

Lemon and Almond Flan

Lemon and Almond Flan has a smooth and creamy filling thickly sprinkled with toasted almonds. It should be served cold with cream for lunch or dinner.

6-8 SERVINGS

1 x 9-inch flan case made from frozen and thawed shortcrust pastry, baked blind and cooled

FILLING
½ oz. gelatine
2 fl. oz. [¼ cup] hot water
3 egg yolks
4 oz. [½ cup] sugar
⅛ teaspoon salt
finely grated rind of 1 lemon

6 fl. oz. [¾ cup] hot milk
½ teaspoon lemon essence
5 fl. oz. double cream [⅝ cup heavy cream]
3 egg whites
2 tablespoons slivered almonds, toasted

In a cup, soften the gelatine in the water. Place the cup in a pan of simmering water to dissolve the gelatine completely. Set aside.

In a medium-sized mixing bowl, beat the egg yolks, half the sugar, the salt and the lemon rind together with a wire whisk until they are pale and thick. Gradually add the hot milk, stirring constantly. Pour the mixture into a medium-sized saucepan and set it over low heat. Cook the custard gently, stirring constantly with a wooden spoon, for 6 to 8 minutes, or until it coats the back of the spoon. Be careful not to boil the custard or it will curdle.

Remove the pan from the heat and pour the custard through a strainer back into the bowl. Stir in the gelatine and the lemon essence. Allow the custard to cool to room temperature, then place it in the refrigerator to chill for about 45 minutes or until it is beginning to set.

Meanwhile, in a small mixing bowl, beat the cream with a wire whisk or rotary beater until it is thick but not stiff. Set aside.

In another bowl, beat the egg whites with a wire whisk or rotary beater until they are frothy. Add the remaining sugar and continue beating until they form stiff peaks.

With a metal spoon, fold the whipped cream into the almost setting custard. When it is completely mixed in, fold in the egg whites.

Pour the mixture into the pastry case. Place the flan in the refrigerator and chill it for at least 2 hours, or until the filling is firm and very cold. Sprinkle over the toasted almonds and serve.

Lemon Bread Pudding

Easy and inexpensive to make, Lemon Bread Pudding is made with candied peel, almonds, lemon rind and white bread. Serve for a warming and filling winter or autumn dessert.

3-4 SERVINGS

1 teaspoon butter
6 large slices white bread, crusts removed and very generously buttered
2 tablespoons flaked blanched almonds
2 oz. [⅓ cup] chopped mixed candied peel
¼ teaspoon ground mixed spice or allspice
finely grated rind of 2 lemons
2 tablespoons soft brown sugar

CUSTARD
2 eggs
¼ teaspoon vanilla essence
⅛ teaspoon almond essence
15 fl. oz. [1⅞ cups] milk
1 tablespoon sugar

Preheat the oven to fairly hot 375°F (Gas Mark 5, 190°C).

Using the teaspoon of butter, lightly grease a medium-sized shallow baking dish.

Cut the bread slices into quarters. Place a third of the bread quarters, buttered sides up, in the bottom of the prepared baking dish. Sprinkle over half the flaked almonds, candied peel, mixed spice or allspice, grated lemon rind and brown sugar.

Cover with a second layer of bread quarters. Sprinkle over the remaining almonds, candied peel, mixed spice or allspice, lemon rind and sugar. Cover with the remaining bread quarters, buttered sides up. Set aside.

To make the custard, beat the eggs, vanilla essence and almond essence together in a medium-sized mixing bowl. Set the bowl aside.

In a medium-sized saucepan, heat the milk and sugar over moderate heat. When the sugar has dissolved and the milk is hot, remove the pan from the heat. Beating constantly, gradually pour the hot milk into the beaten egg mixture.

Pour the custard through a fine wire strainer on to the bread layers in the dish. Set aside for 15 minutes, or until the bread has absorbed most of the liquid.

Place the dish in the centre of the oven and bake the pudding for 35 to 40 minutes, or until the top is golden and crisp.

Remove the pudding from the oven and serve immediately, straight from the dish.

Morello Cherries with Yogurt

A simple pudding with a very fresh flavour, Morello Cherries with Yogurt may be served for breakfast with cereal sprinkled on top, or as a simple lunch or dinner dessert for the family.

4 SERVINGS

1 lb. canned stoned Morello
   cherries, drained
3 oz. [½ cup] soft brown sugar
½ teaspoon ground ginger
½ teaspoon vanilla essence
15 fl. oz. [1⅞ cups] yogurt

In a large saucepan, heat the cherries and sugar over low heat, stirring frequently until the sugar has dissolved. Add the ginger and vanilla essence and stir well. Cover the pan and simmer the mixture for 5 to 8 minutes or until the cherries are very soft but not pulpy. Remove the pan from the heat.

Pour the cherry mixture into a heat-proof serving dish and allow to cool for 30 minutes. Then place the dish in the refrigerator to chill for 1 hour.

Remove the dish from the refrigerator and stir in the yogurt.

Serve immediately.

Pears Poached in Red Wine

Simple to make and absolutely delicious, Pears Poached in Red Wine may be served with whipped cream for a super family lunch or dinner.

6 SERVINGS

6 large firm pears
6 oz. [¾ cup] sugar
4 fl. oz. [½ cup] water
2-inch piece cinnamon stick
   pared rind of 1 lemon
4 fl. oz. [½ cup] red wine

With a sharp knife, peel the pears.

Place the pears, sugar, water, cinnamon stick and lemon rind in a large saucepan. Place the pan over moderate heat, cover and cook the pears for 10 minutes. Add the wine, reduce the heat to very low and simmer, turning occasionally, for a further 20 to 25 minutes or until the pears are tender but still firm when pierced with a sharp knife.

Using a slotted spoon, transfer the

This tempting Pineapple Upside-down Cake was originally American but is now a popular dessert cake all over the world.

pears to a serving dish and set aside.

Increase the heat to high and boil the cooking liquid for 8 minutes or until it has thickened slightly.

Remove the pan from the heat and strain the liquid over the pears. Set the dish aside at room temperature until the pears are cool, then chill them in the refrigerator for at least 1 to 1½ hours before serving.

Peach Flan

Sweet and melting Peach Flan is best made when fresh peaches are plentiful and cheap. Serve the flan with single [light] cream or, if you like really sweet desserts, brandy butter.

4-6 SERVINGS

1 x 9-inch flan case made with
   frozen and thawed shortcrust
   pastry, baked blind and cooled
4 large peaches, blanched, peeled,
   stoned and sliced
1 tablespoon peach brandy
   (optional)
TOPPING
2 tablespoons ground almonds
1 tablespoon chopped blanched
   almonds
1 tablespoon finely chopped
   walnuts
3 tablespoons soft brown sugar
1 teaspoon finely grated orange
   rind
1 tablespoon butter, cut into small
   pieces

Place the flan case on a flameproof serving dish. Arrange the peach slices in the flan case. Sprinkle over the peach brandy, if you are using it. Set the flan case aside.

Preheat the grill [broiler] to high.

To make the topping, in a small mixing bowl, combine the ground and chopped almonds, the walnuts, sugar and orange rind.

Sprinkle the topping over the peach slices and dot the top with the butter pieces.

Place the dish under the grill [broiler] and grill [broil] for 4 minutes or until the topping is crisp and bubbling.

Remove the dish from under the grill [broiler] and serve immediately, straight from the dish, or allow to cool completely before serving.

Pineapple Upside-down Cake

This is a well-known American cake in

which the fruit is arranged decoratively on the bottom of the cake tin and the batter is poured over the top. When the cake is baked it is turned out, upside-down, to display the fruit. Serve it with whipped cream or lots of cold, thick custard for a scrumptious family dessert. Or serve as a rich after-school snack.

9 SERVINGS

5 oz. [⅝ cup] plus 1 teaspoon
   butter, softened
2 tablespoons soft brown sugar
1 medium-sized fresh pineapple,
   peeled, cored and cut into 9 rings
   or 14 oz. canned pineapple rings,
   drained
9 glacé cherries
4 oz. [½ cup] sugar
2 eggs
6 oz. [1½ cups] self-raising flour,
   sifted
3 tablespoons milk
1-inch piece angelica cut into 18
   leaves (optional)

Preheat the oven to moderate 350°F (Gas Mark 4, 180°C).

With the teaspoon of the butter, lightly grease the sides of an 8- x 8-inch cake tin. Cut 1 ounce [2 tablespoons] of the remaining butter into small pieces and dot them over the base of the tin. Sprinkle the brown sugar carefully over the top. Arrange the pineapple slices decoratively on top of the sugar, and place a glacé cherry in the centre of each ring. Set the cake tin aside.

In a medium-sized mixing bowl, beat the remaining butter with a wooden spoon until it is soft and creamy. Add the sugar and cream it with the butter until the mixture is light and fluffy. Add the eggs, one at a time, beating well until they are thoroughly blended. Using a large metal spoon, fold in the flour. Stir in enough of the milk to give the batter a dropping consistency.

Spoon the batter into the cake tin, being careful not to dislodge the glacé cherries. Smooth down the top of the batter with a flat-bladed knife. Place the cake tin in the centre of the oven and bake the cake for 50 minutes to 1 hour or until the cake is golden brown and a skewer inserted into the centre of the cake comes out clean.

Remove the tin from the oven and allow the cake to cool for 5 minutes. Run a knife around the sides of the cake. Invert a serving dish over the cake tin and reverse the two. The cake should slide out easily. Decorate each cherry with two angelica leaves, if desired.

Serve the cake immediately or set it aside to cool completely before serving, cut into small portions.

Plum Compôte

Plum Compôte is a simple but delicious dessert which may be served cold, with whipped cream.

4 SERVINGS

10 fl. oz. [1¼ cups] water
 6 oz. [¾ cup] sugar
   finely grated rind of ½ lemon
1½ lb. plums, halved and stoned

In a medium-sized saucepan, combine the water, sugar and lemon rind together. Set the pan over low heat and cook the mixture, stirring occasionally, until the sugar has dissolved. Increase the heat to moderate and boil the syrup for 5 minutes, without stirring, or until it has reduced and thickened slightly.

Add the plums to the pan, reduce the heat to low and simmer, stirring occasionally, for 3 to 5 minutes or until the plums are cooked but still retain their shape.

Remove the pan from the heat and set the compôte aside for 30 minutes. Turn the compôte into a serving dish and set aside to cool completely or chill in the refrigerator before serving.

Prune and Apple Meringue Flan

A delicious combination of prunes, apples and meringue makes this pie an ideal dessert.

6-8 SERVINGS

1 x 9-inch flan case made with
   shortcrust pastry, uncooked
FILLING
6 oz. prunes, soaked overnight,
   drained, stoned and halved
8 oz. cooking apples, weighed after
   peeling, coring and slicing
1 teaspoon lemon juice
2 oz. [⅓ cup] sultanas or seedless
   raisins
½ teaspoon ground cinnamon
2 tablespoons sugar
MERINGUE
3 egg whites
6 oz. [¾ cup] castor sugar

Preheat the oven to fairly hot 400°F (Gas Mark 6, 200°C).

Place the flan case on a baking sheet.

In a medium-sized mixing bowl, combine the prunes, apples, lemon juice, sultanas or seedless raisins, cinnamon and 1 tablespoon of the sugar. Transfer the mixture to the flan case, smoothing it out evenly with a knife. Sprinkle over the remaining sugar. Place the sheet in the oven and bake the flan for 15 minutes.

Meanwhile, in a large mixing bowl,

beat the egg whites with a wire whisk or rotary beater until they form stiff peaks. Beat in 1 tablespoon of the castor sugar and continue beating until the meringue is stiff and glossy. With a metal spoon, fold in the remaining sugar.

Remove the baking sheet from the oven. Reduce the oven temperature to moderate 350°F (Gas Mark 4, 180°C).

Spoon the meringue over the filling to cover it completely. Pull the meringue, using the back of the spoon, into decorative peaks.

Return the flan to the oven and continue baking for 20 to 25 minutes or until the meringue has set and is golden brown.

Remove the baking sheet from the oven. Transfer the flan to a serving dish and serve immediately.

Queen of Puddings

A traditional British pudding, Queen of Puddings is delicious and filling and is sure to be a great favourite with all the family.

4 SERVINGS

2 oz. [¼ cup] plus 1 teaspoon butter,
   softened
2 oz. [¼ cup] sugar
   finely grated rind of 2 lemons

338

4 oz. [2 cups] fresh white
  breadcrumbs
1 pint [2½ cups] milk
2 eggs, separated
3 tablespoons strawberry jam
4 oz. [½ cup] castor sugar

Preheat the oven to moderate 350°F (Gas Mark 4, 180°C).

Using the teaspoon of butter, grease an ovenproof dish and set aside.

Place the remaining butter, the sugar and lemon rind in a medium-sized mixing bowl. Beat well with a wooden spoon until the mixture is smooth and creamy. Stir in the breadcrumbs. In a small saucepan,

scald the milk over moderate heat. Pour the milk over the breadcrumb mixture in the bowl, stirring constantly with the wooden spoon. Set aside and leave to cool for 10 minutes.

With the spoon, beat the egg yolks into the mixture, one at a time. Pour the mixture into the prepared dish and place the dish in the oven. Bake for 35 to 45 minutes or until the pudding is firm to the touch. Remove the dish from the oven and set aside to cool slightly. Spread the jam over the pudding and set aside.

Reduce the oven temperature to very cool 275°F (Gas Mark 1, 140°C).

In a medium-sized mixing bowl, beat the egg whites with a wire whisk or rotary beater until they form stiff peaks. Add 1 tablespoon of the castor sugar and continue beating until the mixture is stiff and glossy.

With a large metal spoon, fold in the remaining castor sugar. Using a spatula spread the meringue over the pudding.

Return the dish to the oven and continue baking for 20 to 25 minutes or until the meringue has set and is golden brown.

Remove the pudding from the oven and serve immediately.

Railway Pudding

A delicious sweet cherry pudding, Railway Pudding can be served with warmed custard sauce.

6 SERVINGS

4 oz. [½ cup] plus 3 teaspoons butter
4 oz. [½ cup] sugar
2 eggs
2 tablespoons double [heavy] cream
  grated rind of 1 small lemon
½ teaspoon vanilla essence
6 oz. [1½ cups] flour
1 teaspoon baking powder
8 oz. sweet red cherries, halved
  and stoned

Grease a 2-pint [1½-quart] pudding basin with 2 teaspoons of the butter. Set the basin aside.

In a medium-sized mixing bowl, cream 4 ounces [½ cup] of the butter with a wooden spoon until it is light and fluffy. Add the sugar and beat the mixture until it is smooth and creamy. Beat the eggs in one at a time. Stir in the cream, lemon rind and vanilla essence. Sift the flour and baking powder on to the creamed mixture

A marvellous mixture of custard, strawberry jam and meringue— that's Queen of Puddings.

and, using a metal spoon, fold in until it is combined. Stir in the cherries.

Fill a large saucepan one-third full of water and bring it to the boil over high heat.

Meanwhile, spoon the pudding mixture into the basin, smoothing the top over. Cut out a circle of greaseproof or waxed paper 4-inches wider than the basin. Using the remaining teaspoon of butter, grease the paper circle. Cut out a circle of aluminium foil, the same size as the paper circle, and place the two circles together, the buttered side of the paper away from the foil. Holding them firmly together, make a 1-inch pleat across the centre. Place the circles, buttered side down, over the pudding basin. With a piece of string, securely tie the foil and paper circles around the rim of the basin.

Place the basin in the saucepan. Cover the pan, reduce the heat to moderately low and steam the pudding for 2 hours. Add more boiling water to the pan during cooking if necessary.

Remove the pan from the heat and lift the basin out of the pan. Remove and discard the paper and foil. Place a serving dish, inverted, over the pudding basin and reverse the two. The pudding should slide out easily.

Serve immediately.

Raspberry Sauce

This delicious sauce is an excellent accompaniment to sponge puddings, and adds that special something to vanilla ice-cream. For a more luxurious sauce, add 1 or 2 tablespoons of kirsch.

ABOUT 10 FLUID OUNCES [1¼ CUPS]

1 lb. fresh raspberries, washed and
  hulled
2 oz. [¼ cup] sugar
2 teaspoons lemon juice
1 teaspoon arrowroot dissolved in
  1 tablespoon water

Place the raspberries in a medium-sized bowl and sprinkle over half the sugar. Set aside for 2 hours.

Using the back of a wooden spoon, rub the raspberries and any liquid from the bowl through a fine strainer held over a medium-sized saucepan. Discard the pulp remaining in the strainer.

Add the remaining sugar and the lemon juice and place the saucepan over high heat. Bring the purée to the boil, reduce the heat to low and stir in the dissolved arrowroot. Simmer the sauce for 2 to 3 minutes or until it is smooth and thick.

Remove the pan from the heat and pour the sauce into a sauceboat.

Rhubarb Brown Betty

A wholesome and scrumptious family dessert, Rhubarb Brown Betty is even more delicious when served with whipped cream.

4-6 SERVINGS

6 oz. [¾ cup] plus 1 tablespoon
    butter, melted
4 oz. [2 cups] fresh brown
    breadcrumbs
6 oz. crushed digestive biscuits
    [1½ cups crushed graham crackers]
4 oz. [⅔ cup] soft brown sugar
1 teaspoon ground cinnamon
¼ teaspoon grated nutmeg
    grated rind of 1 lemon
    grated rind of 1 orange
1½ lb. cooked rhubarb
4 oz. [⅔ cup] sultanas or seedless

A sustaining dessert to delight the whole family — that's Rhubarb Cream Flan.

    raisins

Preheat the oven to fairly hot 375°F (Gas Mark 5, 190°C). Using the tablespoon of butter, generously grease a medium-sized ovenproof dish. Set aside.

In a large bowl, combine the breadcrumbs, biscuits [crackers], sugar, cinnamon, nutmeg, lemon and orange rind and the remaining melted butter.

Place one-third of the mixture on the bottom of the prepared dish, smoothing it down with the back of the spoon. Cover with half of the rhubarb and sprinkle over half of the sultanas or raisins. Continue

making layers in this way until all the ingredients are used up, ending with a layer of the breadcrumb mixture.

Place the dish in the oven and bake for 30 minutes or until the top is golden.

Remove the dish from the oven and serve immediately.

Rhubarb Cream Flan

Serve Rhubarb Cream Flan warm, with cream.

4-6 SERVINGS

8 oz. [2 cups] shortcrust pastry
3 tablespoons water
2 lb. fresh rhubarb, trimmed,
    washed and cut into ½-inch lengths
6 oz. [¾ cup] sugar

1 oz. [2 tablespoons] butter
1 oz. [¼ cup] flour
12 fl. oz. single cream [1½ cups light cream]
¼ teaspoon vanilla essence
2 eggs, separated

Using a floured rolling pin, roll the dough out into a circle approximately ⅛-inch thick. Lift the dough on the rolling pin and lay it over an 8-inch cake tin with a removable base. Ease the dough into the tin. Trim the dough so that it comes halfway up the sides. Discard any leftover dough. Place the tin in the refrigerator.

In a large pan, combine the water, rhubarb and 4 ounces [½ cup] of the sugar. Set the pan over low heat and cook, stirring occasionally, for 25 minutes or until the rhubarb is tender. Remove the pan from the heat, pour off any excess liquid and set the rhubarb aside to cool.

Remove the tin from the refrigerator and spoon in the rhubarb. Set aside.

Preheat the oven to moderate 350°F (Gas Mark 4, 180°C).

In a medium-sized saucepan, melt the butter over moderate heat. Remove the pan from the heat and stir in the flour to make a smooth paste. Gradually add the cream, stirring constantly and being careful to avoid lumps. Stir in the remaining sugar and the vanilla essence.

Return the pan to the heat and cook the sauce, stirring constantly, until it is thick and the sugar has dissolved. Remove the pan from the heat, cool the sauce to lukewarm and then beat in the egg yolks.

In a small mixing bowl, beat the egg whites with a wire whisk or rotary beater until they form stiff peaks. Using a metal spoon, fold the egg whites into the sauce.

Spoon the sauce over the rhubarb in the tin and place the tin in the centre of the oven. Bake the flan for 45 to 50 minutes or until the top is deep golden.

Remove the flan from the oven and set it aside to cool for 10 minutes. Carefully lift the sides of the tin and slide the flan on to a serving plate. Serve immediately.

Roly-Poly

☆ ① ✕ ✕ ✕

Roly-Poly is an old-fashioned English steamed pudding which can be made with any kind of jam. Serve with custard or plenty of cream.

4-6 SERVINGS

8 oz. [2 cups] flour
1 teaspoon salt
2 tablespoons sugar
2 teaspoons baking powder
3 oz. [⅜ cup] shredded suet
10 to 12 tablespoons water

6 oz. raspberry jam
1 tablespoon milk

Sift the flour, salt, sugar and baking powder into a large mixing bowl. Stir in the suet. Gradually add 6 tablespoons of water to the mixture and knead lightly until the dough is light and pliable. Add more water if necessary, spoonful by spoonful, if the dough is too stiff.

Roll out the dough to a rectangle ¼-inch thick. Spread the jam evenly over the surface, leaving a margin of about ¼-inch all around the edge. With a pastry brush, brush the edges with the milk.

Roll up the dough Swiss [jelly] roll style, pressing the edges together to secure them. Wrap the roll loosely in greased aluminium foil, making a pleat in the foil to allow for expansion.

Half-fill a large saucepan with water and place it over high heat. When the water comes to the boil, put in the pudding, reduce the heat to moderate and steam for 2½ hours, replenishing the water when necessary. Unwrap the pudding and serve.

Russian Blackberry Cream

☆ ① ✕ ✕ ✕

This delicately flavoured blackberry jelly [gelatin], topped with cream, makes a refreshing dessert to end a dinner.

6 SERVINGS

2 lb. blackberries, hulled
2 fl. oz. [¼ cup] water
8 oz. [1 cup] sugar
1 oz. gelatine, dissolved in 4 tablespoons hot water
10 fl. oz. double cream [1¼ cups heavy cream], whipped until thick
2 oz. [½ cup] flaked almonds

Put the blackberries, water and sugar in a saucepan. Bring the mixture to the boil, stirring constantly. Cover the pan and simmer over low heat for 20 minutes or until the blackberries are pulpy.

Remove the pan from the heat and pour the mixture into a strainer held over a bowl. Using the back of a wooden spoon, rub the berries through the strainer into the bowl. Stir in the dissolved gelatine.

Pour the mixture into a serving dish and set aside to cool, then chill in the refrigerator for 2 hours.

When the jelly [gelatin] has set, spread over the whipped cream and, using the back of a fork, make decorative swirls. Sprinkle over the almonds and serve.

Cool and refreshing to eat, Russian Blackberry Cream makes a perfect light summer dessert for the entire family.

Sago Pudding

Sago Pudding makes an excellent family dessert. Serve it either hot or cold accompanied by stewed fruit and whipped cream. Or stir in lots of strawberry jam.

2-3 SERVINGS

16 fl. oz. [2 cups] milk
2 oz. [⅓ cup] sago
½ teaspoon salt
1 tablespoon butter
2 oz. [¼ cup] sugar
½ teaspoon ground cinnamon
2 teaspoons grated lemon rind
2 egg yolks

Pour the milk into a medium-sized, heavy-based saucepan and set the pan over moderate heat. When the milk is hot but not boiling, sprinkle over the sago and salt. Bring the milk to the boil and cook, stirring constantly, for 10 minutes or until the mixture thickens and the sago becomes clear.

Meanwhile, preheat the oven to moderate 350°F (Gas Mark 4, 180°C). Grease a 3-pint [2-quart] soufflé or straight-sided ovenproof dish with the butter and set aside.

Reduce the heat to low and add the sugar, cinnamon and lemon rind to the saucepan containing the sago. Cook, stirring constantly, for 2 to 3 minutes or until the sugar dissolves. Remove the pan from the heat and stir in the egg yolks.

Pour the contents of the saucepan into the prepared dish and bake for 30 to 35 minutes or until the pudding is brown on top and of a thick creamy consistency. The pudding is now ready to serve if it is to be eaten hot.

Scandinavian Whipped Berry Pudding

Scandinavian Whipped Berry Pudding is simply delicious served with chilled whipped cream.

6 SERVINGS

1½ lb. canned raspberries
4 oz. [½ cup] castor sugar
2 oz. [½ cup] semolina
⅛ teaspoon almond essence

Pour the raspberries with the can juice into a medium-sized fine wire strainer

A delicious old-fashiond milk pudding, Sago Pudding makes a warming winter dessert.

held over a medium-sized mixing bowl. Using the back of a wooden spoon, rub the fruit through the strainer to form a purée. Discard the pips in the strainer. Alternatively, blend the fruit and juice in an electric blender.

Pour the fruit into a medium-sized saucepan and bring to the boil over moderate heat. Gradually add the sugar and the semolina, stirring constantly. Reduce the heat to low and simmer the mixture for 10 minutes, stirring occasionally.

Remove the pan from the heat and transfer the mixture to a large mixing bowl. Stir in the almond essence. Using a wire whisk or rotary beater, beat the mixture for 15 minutes or until it has doubled in volume and is light and fluffy.

Spoon the pudding into 6 individual serving dishes and serve immediately.

Soufflé Omelet

Soufflé Omelet is cooked in the oven rather than on the top of the stove — and the result is correspondingly different. Serve Soufflé Omelet plain or with whipped cream as an elegant dessert.

4-6 SERVINGS

1 teaspoon butter

1 tablespoon icing [confectioners']
  sugar
4 oz. [½ cup] sugar
6 egg yolks
1 tablespoon finely grated lemon
  rind
8 egg whites

Preheat the oven to hot 425°F (Gas Mark 7, 220°C). With the teaspoon of butter, lightly grease a 9- x 12-inch baking dish. Sprinkle over the icing [confectioners'] sugar, shaking out any excess. Set the dish aside.

In a large mixing bowl, beat the sugar, egg yolks and lemon rind together with a fork until the mixture is well mixed.

In another large mixing bowl, beat the egg whites with a wire whisk or rotary beater until they form stiff peaks. With a metal spoon, carefully fold the egg whites into the egg yolk mixture.

Pour the mixture into the prepared baking dish, shaping it into a dome shape with a flat-bladed knife. Place the dish in the oven and bake for 8 to 10 minutes or until the omelet is lightly browned.

Remove the dish from the oven and serve at once.

Strawberry Sponge Roll

A light, thin sponge filled with chopped fresh strawberries, Strawberry Sponge Roll makes a delicious dessert served on its own or with whipped cream or cold custard sauce.

4-6 SERVINGS

4 eggs
6 oz. [¾ cup] plus 6 tablespoons
  castor sugar
  finely grated rind of 1 large
  orange
1 lb. fresh strawberries, washed
  and hulled

Preheat the oven to fairly hot 400°F (Gas Mark 6, 200°C).

Line a 10- x 18-inch Swiss [jelly] roll tin with non-stick silicone paper or greaseproof or waxed paper and set the tin aside.

In a large mixing bowl, beat the eggs together with a wire whisk or rotary beater until they are well mixed. Add 6 ounces [¾ cup] of the castor sugar and the finely grated orange rind and continue beating until the mixture is fluffy.

Tasty Strawberry Sponge Roll.

Spoon the egg mixture into the prepared Swiss [jelly] roll tin and smooth it to the edges with the back of a metal spoon.

Place the tin in the centre of the oven and bake for 10 to 12 minutes or until the top of the sponge is golden brown and springs back when lightly pressed with a fingertip.

Meanwhile, chop half of the strawberries coarsely and place them in a medium-sized mixing bowl. Add 3 tablespoons of the remaining castor sugar and, using a metal spoon, stir well to mix.

Remove the tin from the oven. Spoon the chopped strawberries evenly over the sponge and, carefully lifting up one end of the silicone or greaseproof or waxed paper, carefully roll up the sponge Swiss [jelly] roll style.

Carefully transfer the roll to a large serving dish. Arrange the remaining whole strawberries over and around the roll and sprinkle over the remaining sugar. Set the roll aside to cool completely before serving.

Summer Pudding

This traditional British pudding does not require any cooking but it must be made the day before it is required. Summer Pudding is also good made with ripe blackberries or blackcurrants or a mixture of the two.

4-6 SERVINGS

1 teaspoon butter
2 lb. raspberries, hulled
4 oz. [½ cup] castor sugar
4 fl. oz. [½ cup] milk
8 slices stale white bread, crusts removed
10 fl. oz. double cream [1¼ cups heavy cream]

Using the teaspoon of butter, grease a deep pie dish or pudding basin.

Place the raspberries in a large mixing bowl and sprinkle over the sugar. Set aside. Using a teaspoon, sprinkle a little of the milk over each slice of bread to moisten it.

Line the dish or basin with two-thirds of the bread slices, overlapping the edges slightly. Pour the raspberries into the dish or basin and arrange the remaining bread slices on top to cover the raspberries.

Place a sheet of greaseproof or waxed

This traditional British Summer Pudding tastes even better than it looks!

paper on top of the dish or basin and put a plate, which is slightly smaller in diameter than the dish or basin, on top. Place a heavy weight on the plate and put the pudding in the refrigerator to chill for at least 8 hours or overnight.

Remove the pudding from the refrigerator and lift off the weight and the plate. Remove and discard the grease-proof or waxed paper. Invert a serving plate over the top of the dish or basin and, holding the two firmly together, reverse them giving a sharp shake. The pudding should slide out easily.

In a medium-sized serving bowl, using a wire whisk or rotary beater, beat the cream until it is thick but not stiff. Serve the pudding immediately, with the cream.

Swedish Custard Pie

A delicious pie, Swedish Custard Pie may be served hot or cold.

4-6 SERVINGS

8 oz. [1⅓ cups] soft brown sugar
8 oz. [1 cup] sugar
6 oz. [¾ cup] butter, melted
6 fl. oz. double cream [¾ cup heavy cream]
3 eggs
¾ teaspoon almond essence
1 x 9-inch flan case made with shortcrust pastry
1 teaspoon grated nutmeg

Preheat the oven to very hot 450°F (Gas Mark 8, 230°C).

Place the sugars, butter and cream in a medium-sized heatproof bowl and place the bowl over a medium-sized saucepan half-filled with boiling water. Set the pan over moderate heat. Cook the mixture, stirring constantly with a wooden spoon, until the sugar has dissolved and the mixture is thick enough to leave a ribbon trail on itself when the spoon is lifted.

Meanwhile, in a large mixing bowl, using a wire whisk or rotary beater, beat the eggs until they are pale and thick.

Remove the saucepan from the heat and the bowl from the saucepan. Gradually beat the sugar mixture into the eggs until they are thoroughly combined. Stir in the almond essence.

Place the flan case on a baking sheet and pour the filling into the flan case. Sprinkle over the nutmeg and place the baking sheet in the centre of the oven. Bake for 10 minutes.

Reduce the oven temperature to warm 325°F (Gas Mark 3, 170°C) and continue baking the pie for 30 minutes or until a skewer inserted into the centre of the filling comes out clean.

Remove the pie from the oven and carefully transfer it to a serving plate. Serve immediately, or allow to cool completely before serving.

Syllabub

☆　　①①　⊠

A delightful dish that can be made in a moment, Syllabub is a traditional English dessert. Serve on its own or with poached fruit.

4-6 SERVINGS

2 oz. [¼ cup] sugar
  juice of 1 large lemon
  rind and juice of ½ orange
6 tablespoons medium-dry sherry
2 tablespoons brandy

10 fl. oz. double cream [1¼ cups heavy cream], beaten until thick

In a medium-sized mixing bowl, combine the sugar, lemon juice, orange rind and juice, sherry and brandy. Gradually pour the cream into the bowl, beating constantly with a kitchen fork until the ingredients are thoroughly combined.

Cover the bowl and chill it in the refrigerator for at least 30 minutes or until ready to serve.

Remove the bowl from the refrigerator and pour the syllabub into chilled individual serving dishes. Serve immediately.

Trifle

☆☆　　①①　⊠⊠

A marvellous concoction of cake, jelly [gelatin], fruit and custard, Trifle is a rich dessert to serve at dinner.

6 SERVINGS

1 x 7-inch stale sponge cake
2 fl. oz. [¼ cup] sweet sherry
12 fl. oz. [1½ cups] thick custard
15 oz. canned fruit cocktail, drained
12 fl. oz. [1½ cups] strawberry jelly

[gelatin], cool and on the point of setting
10 fl. oz. double cream [1¼ cups heavy cream], stiffly whipped
4 oz. fresh strawberries, hulled, washed and halved
2 tablespoons slivered almonds

Break the sponge into small pieces and place it on the bottom of a large glass serving bowl. Pour over the sherry and set aside for 20 minutes. Stir in the custard and refrigerate for 30 minutes.

Stir the fruit cocktail into the jelly [gelatin] mixture, then pour it over the sponge mixture. Place the bowl in the refrigerator for 45 minutes to 1 hour or until the jelly [gelatin] has set.

Meanwhile, in a medium-sized mixing bowl, beat the cream with a wire whisk or rotary beater until it forms stiff peaks. Fold in half of the strawberries.

Spoon the cream mixture over the jelly [gelatin], decorate with the remaining strawberries and almonds and serve.

Swedish Custard Pie tastes equally delicious hot or cold.

Vanilla Soufflé

Vanilla Soufflé is quick and economical to make and may be served as a treat for the family or as a dinner party dessert.

6 SERVINGS

1½ oz. [3 tablespoons] butter
2 tablespoons icing [confectioners']
  sugar
8 fl. oz. [1 cup] milk
1 vanilla pod
1 oz. [¼ cup] flour
3 egg yolks
1 tablespoon sugar
5 egg whites

Preheat the oven to moderate 350°F (Gas Mark 4, 180°C). Using 1 tablespoon of the butter, grease a 2½-pint [1½-quart] soufflé dish. Sprinkle the bottom and sides of the dish with the icing [confectioners'] sugar, knocking out any excess.

Cool and refreshing, Watermelon and Banana Salad is a perfect summer dessert.

In a medium-sized saucepan, scald the milk and vanilla pod over moderate heat. Remove the pan from the heat, cover and set aside for 20 minutes. Remove the vanilla pod from the milk.

In a large saucepan, melt the remaining butter over moderate heat. Remove the pan from the heat and, with a wooden spoon, stir in the flour to make a smooth paste. Gradually add the hot milk, stirring constantly. Return the pan to the heat and cook the mixture, stirring constantly, for 2 minutes or until it is thick and smooth. Remove the pan from the heat and let the sauce cool slightly.

In a small mixing bowl, beat the egg yolks with the sugar and mix them into the cool sauce, a little at a time.

In a large mixing bowl, beat the egg whites with a wire whisk or rotary beater until they form stiff peaks.

With a metal spoon, carefully fold the egg whites into the sauce.

Spoon the mixture into the prepared soufflé dish. Place the dish in the oven and bake the soufflé for 20 to 30 minutes or until it is lightly browned on top and is well risen.

Remove the soufflé from the oven and serve at once.

Watermelon and Banana Salad

The exotic combination of watermelon, banana and rum gives Watermelon and Banana Salad a delightful contrast of colour, flavour and texture.

6 SERVINGS

1 large watermelon, cut in half
  lengthways
6 bananas, peeled and sliced
  juice of 1 lemon
  juice of 2 limes
4 fl. oz. [½ cup] white rum
2 oz. [¼ cup] plus 2 tablespoons
  sugar

Using a sharp knife, carefully scoop out the flesh of the watermelon and cut it into cubes, removing and discarding as many seeds as possible. Place the watermelon cubes in a medium-sized mixing bowl and gently combine them with the

White Grape and Ginger Syllabub is an unusual yet delicious dessert for dinner.

banana slices. Set aside.

In a small bowl, combine the lemon and lime juice with the rum. Add the 2 ounces [¼ cup] of sugar and stir the mixture until the sugar has dissolved.

Spoon the watermelon and banana mixture into the melon halves and pour the rum mixture equally over the two halves. Place the melon in the refrigerator to chill for 30 minutes or until ready to serve.

Remove the melon from the refrigerator and place the halves on a serving dish. Sprinkle over the remaining 2 tablespoons of sugar and serve immediately.

Wheat and Fruit Dessert

A delicious dish from Israel, Wheat and Fruit Dessert may be served for dessert or breakfast. Almost any fruit purée may be substituted for the one suggested in this recipe.

6 SERVINGS

  3 tablespoons wheat germ soaked for 1 hour in the juice of 2 oranges
  4 medium-sized eating apples, cooked and puréed
  4 tablespoons chopped walnuts
  2 tablespoons slivered almonds
  1 large orange, peeled, white pith removed and cut into segments grated rind of ½ orange
10 fl. oz. [1¼ cups] yogurt
  2 tablespoons soft brown sugar

Put the soaked wheat germ into a large serving bowl. Mix in the apple purée, walnuts, almonds, orange segments and rind. Using a large metal spoon, stir gently to blend.

Place the bowl in the refrigerator to chill for 30 minutes. Spoon over the yogurt, sprinkle over the sugar and serve at once.

White Grape and Ginger Syllabub

An unusual and refreshing dessert, White Grape and Ginger Syllabub is the perfect dish to serve at dinner.

6 SERVINGS

  2 lb. seedless white grapes, with 6 grapes reserved, halved
  8 oz. crushed ginger biscuits [2 cups crushed ginger cookies]
  4 egg whites, stiffly beaten
  8 oz. [1 cup] castor sugar
10 fl. oz. [1¼ cups] white wine juice of ½ lemon
15 fl. oz. double cream [1⅞ cups heavy cream]
  4 oz. [1 cup] slivered almonds, toasted

Arrange one-quarter of the grapes on the bottom of a medium-sized serving bowl. Cover with one-quarter of the ginger biscuit [cookie] crumbs. Continue making layers in this way until the grapes and the ginger crumbs are used up. Set aside.

Place the beaten egg whites in a medium-sized mixing bowl. Beat in one-quarter of the sugar. Using a metal spoon, fold in the remaining sugar. Pour over the wine and lemon juice and stir the ingredients carefully until they are thoroughly combined. Set aside.

Pour the cream into a large mixing bowl and, using a wire whisk or rotary beater, beat the cream until it is thick but not stiff. Using a metal spoon, fold the egg white mixture into the cream. Pour the cream mixture over the fruit and biscuit [cookie] mixture and place in the refrigerator to chill for 2 hours.

Remove the bowl from the refrigerator.

Arrange the reserved grapes on top and sprinkle over the almonds. Serve.

White Peaches with Caramelized Sugar

White Peaches with Caramelized Sugar is a rich dessert which takes little time to prepare and tastes superb.

6 SERVINGS

  6 white peaches, blanched, peeled, halved and stoned
  3 fl. oz. [⅜ cup] brandy
  1 pint double cream [2½ cups heavy cream], stiffly beaten
  4 tablespoons soft brown sugar

Preheat the grill [broiler] to high.

Place the peaches in a flameproof serving dish. Sprinkle over the brandy and set aside for 10 minutes.

Using a flat-bladed knife, spread the cream over the peaches, making sure the surface is flat. Sprinkle over the sugar.

Place the dish under the grill [broiler]. Grill [broil] for 1 to 2 minutes or until the sugar has melted and formed a very dark brown crust.

Remove the dish from under the grill [broiler] and serve immediately.

Bananas Baked in Rum and Cream

  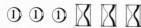

A rich dessert, Bananas Baked with Rum and Cream is excellent for lunch or dinner.

4 SERVINGS

6 bananas
1 tablespoon castor sugar
6 tablespoons white rum
4 oz. [½ cup] crushed macaroons
4 tablespoons melted butter
10 fl. oz. double cream [1¼ cups heavy cream]

Preheat the oven to moderate 350°F (Gas Mark 4, 180°C).

Peel the bananas and put them in a greased baking dish. Sprinkle over the sugar and rum. Bake for 15 minutes.

Remove the dish from the oven and allow to cool for 10 minutes.

Reduce the oven to warm 325°F (Gas Mark 3, 170°C).

Mix the crushed macaroons with the melted butter. Pour the cream over the bananas. Sprinkle the macaroon mixture on top of the cream. Return the dish to the oven and bake for another 20 minutes. Serve hot, straight from the dish.

Bombe Coppelia

  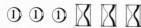

A rich and unusual dessert, Bombe Coppelia is a mouth-watering combination of coffee ice-cream and praline. To make this dessert you will require a large frozen food compartment in your refrigerator.

10-12 SERVINGS

3 pints [7½ cups] coffee-flavoured ice-cream, slightly softened in the refrigerator
8 egg yolks
4 oz. [½ cup] sugar
3 tablespoons dark rum
1 tablespoon water
10 fl. oz. double cream [1¼ cups heavy cream]
PRALINE
1 tablespoon vegetable oil
3 oz. [⅜ cup] castor sugar
3 oz. [½ cup] blanched almonds

Prepare a chilled 3-pint [2-quart] bombe mould by spooning a little of the ice-cream into the base. Working quickly, so that the ice-cream does not thaw too much, spoon scoops of the ice-cream into the mould and, with the back of a metal spoon, pat the ice-cream firmly against the sides. Press a chilled glass bowl, 1-inch smaller than the mould, inside the mould so that the ice-cream forms a solid wall between the bowl and the mould. Cut out more slices of ice-cream to fill up any gaps in the walls.

Place the mould in the freezer and chill for 1 hour or until the ice-cream is completely firm. Chill the remaining ice-cream in a separate bowl for later use.

While the ice-cream is freezing, prepare the praline filling. Using a pastry brush, coat a baking sheet with the vegetable oil.

In a small saucepan, dissolve the castor sugar over very low heat. Add the almonds and cook, turning the nuts constantly, until they are browned. Remove the pan from the heat. Pour the mixture on to the greased baking sheet. Leave the mixture to cool for 10 minutes, or until it is firm.

Place the pieces of praline mixture between greaseproof or waxed paper. Pound them to a coarse powder with a wooden mallet or a rolling pin.

Set the praline aside while you prepare the bombe mixture. In a large bowl, beat the egg yolks with a wire whisk until they are pale and form a ribbon trail on themselves when the whisk is lifted.

Place the sugar, rum and water in a large saucepan and cook over moderate heat, stirring continuously with a wooden spoon. When the sugar has dissolved, bring the liquid to the boil. As soon as the syrup reaches a temperature of 230°F on a sugar thermometer, or a few drops of the syrup spooned into cold water immediately form a soft ball, remove the pan from the heat.

Slowly pour the hot syrup into the egg yolks, beating continuously with a wooden spoon. Continue to beat the mixture as it cools. Beat in the praline.

In a mixing bowl, beat the cream with a wire whisk until it forms stiff peaks. Gently fold the cream into the praline mixture. Continue folding until all the cream is blended.

Remove the ice-cream mould from the freezer and pour the praline mixture into the centre of the ice-cream shell. Return the mould to the freezer for 2 to 3 hours or until the praline is firm.

Remove the remaining ice-cream from the freezer, and allow to thaw for a few minutes, until it is soft enough to spread. With a rubber spatula, smooth the ice-cream slices over the praline filling and ice-cream shell in the mould. Cover the mould with foil. Return the bombe to the freezer for 8 hours or overnight.

Chill a serving plate for 15 minutes.

When you are ready to serve the bombe, unmould it by dipping the mould in hot water for about 30 seconds. Place the chilled plate upside-down on top of the mould. Pressing the plate down firmly on to the mould, turn the mould and plate over quickly. The bombe should slip out smoothly. Serve at once.

Chestnut Pudding

    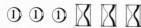

A subtle blend of chestnuts, chocolate and brandy makes this dessert (pictured on page 321) something really special. If at all possible use a good-quality Cognac rather than a cooking brandy for this recipe.

8-10 SERVINGS

1 teaspoon vegetable oil
2 lb. unsweetened chestnut purée
7 oz. [⅞ cup] unsalted butter
7 oz. [⅞ cup] sugar
10 oz. dark [semi-sweet] cooking chocolate, broken into small pieces
3 fl. oz. [⅜ cup] Cognac
DECORATION
10 fl. oz. double cream [1¼ cups heavy cream], whipped until stiff
6 oz. strawberries, hulled and washed

Using half the oil, grease a 2-pound loaf tin. Line the tin with a sheet of greaseproof or waxed paper and grease the paper with the remaining oil. Set the tin aside.

Using the back of a wooden spoon, rub the chestnut purée through a fine wire strainer into a medium-sized mixing bowl. Set aside.

In a large mixing bowl, cream the butter with a wooden spoon until it is smooth and creamy. Gradually add the sugar, beating constantly until the mixture is light and fluffy. Set the mixture aside.

In a small, heavy-based saucepan, melt the chocolate over low heat. Remove the pan from the heat and set aside to cool for 5 minutes.

Stir the chocolate and chestnut purée into the butter and sugar mixture. Pour in the Cognac. Beat the ingredients together until they are thoroughly combined.

Turn the mixture into the prepared tin and place the tin in the refrigerator to chill overnight.

To serve, remove the tin from the refrigerator and turn the mixture out on to a serving dish. Remove and discard the greaseproof or waxed paper.

Spoon the cream into a forcing bag fitted with ½-inch star-shaped nozzle. Pipe the cream over and around the chestnut mixture. Decorate the cream with the strawberries and serve the dessert at once.

Bombe Coppelia—cool, rich, elegant and delicious—the perfect special-occasion dessert.

Ginger Ale Fruit Jelly
[Gelatin]

Quick and easy to prepare, this attractive, refreshing fruit jelly [gelatin] is an ideal dessert for lunch. Canned oranges, cherries and apricots are better in this recipe as fresh ones may retard the setting process.

4 SERVINGS

½ oz. gelatine
2 tablespoons hot water
2 fl. oz. [¼ cup] boiling water
2 fl. oz. [¼ cup] lemon juice
8 fl. oz. [1 cup] ginger ale
1 tablespoon sugar
4 oz. canned mandarin oranges, drained
4 oz. canned morello cherries, drained
1 eating apple, cored and diced
1 banana, thinly sliced
6 oz. canned apricot halves, drained

Pretty and colourful, Ginger Ale Fruit Jelly [Gelatin] is a great family favourite!

In a small bowl, soften the gelatine in the hot water for 5 minutes.

Pour the boiling water into a medium-sized mixing bowl. Stir in the softened gelatine and continue stirring until the gelatine dissolves.

Stir in the lemon juice, ginger ale and sugar. Set the bowl aside for 1 hour, or until the jelly [gelatin] is just beginning to set.

Fold in the oranges, cherries, apple, banana and apricots. Pour the mixture into a 2-pint [1½-quart] mould and place it in the refrigerator.

Leave for 3 to 4 hours, or until the jelly [gelatin] is completely set.

Remove the mould from the refrigerator and dip the base quickly into hot water. Place a serving dish over the top

of the mould and reverse the two. Serve at once.

Norwegian Rhubarb Dessert

Deliciously cool and refreshing, Norwegian Rhubarb Dessert is an easy to prepare dessert for a summer dinner. The rhubarb should be young as it has a better colour and a sharper flavour.

6 SERVINGS

2 lb. rhubarb, washed and cut into 1-inch pieces
8 oz. [1 cup] sugar
2 fl. oz. [¼ cup] water
2 bananas, mashed
8 fl. oz. double cream [1 cup heavy cream]
2 egg whites

In a medium-sized saucepan, simmer the rhubarb, sugar and water over moderate heat, stirring occasionally, for 15 minutes, or until the rhubarb is soft.

Remove the pan from the heat. Drain the rhubarb and transfer it to a large mixing bowl. Discard the juice. Set the rhubarb aside to cool. When it is cool, stir in the mashed bananas and the double [heavy] cream.

In a small mixing bowl, beat the egg whites with a wire whisk or rotary beater until they form stiff peaks.

With a metal spoon, fold the egg whites into the rhubarb mixture. Spoon the mixture into a decorative medium-sized serving dish and place the dish in the refrigerator.

Leave to chill for at least 4 hours before serving.

Orange and Chocolate Mousse

This version of Orange and Chocolate Mousse is made with the zest of oranges, orange-flavoured liqueur, chocolate, cream and eggs. As the mousse is so rich, it should be served after a light meal.

4 SERVINGS

2 large firm, bright-skinned oranges
4 large sugar cubes
10 fl. oz. single cream [1¼ cups light cream]
1 small vanilla pod
4 egg yolks
6 oz. dark [semi-sweet] cooking chocolate, melted
2 tablespoons orange-flavoured liqueur
4 egg whites

Rub each orange all over with the sugar cubes to extract all the zest from the rind. Place the sugar in a small mixing bowl and crush the cubes with a wooden spoon. Set aside. Reserve the oranges for future use.

In a small saucepan, scald the cream (bring to just under boiling point) with the vanilla pod over moderate heat. Remove the pan from the heat. Remove the vanilla pod, wipe it dry and store it for future use.

Gradually add the hot cream to the sugar cubes, stirring constantly, and continue stirring until the sugar has completely dissolved. Set aside.

In a medium-sized heatproof mixing bowl, beat the egg yolks with a wire whisk or rotary beater until they are pale and frothy. Gradually beat in the sugar and cream mixture and combine them thoroughly.

Place the bowl in a large saucepan half-filled with hot water. Set the pan over low heat and cook the mixture, stirring constantly with a wooden spoon, for 5 to 6 minutes, or until it is thick enough to coat the spoon. Do not let the mixture boil or the eggs will scramble.

Remove the pan from the heat. Gradually beat in the melted chocolate. Stir in the orange-flavoured liqueur. Lift the bowl out of the pan and set it aside to cool completely.

In a medium-sized mixing bowl, beat the egg whites with a wire whisk or rotary beater until they form stiff peaks. With a metal spoon, carefully fold the beaten egg whites into the orange and chocolate mixture.

Spoon the mousse into a chilled glass serving dish and chill in the refrigerator for at least 2 hours before serving.

Peaches with Macaroon Cream Filling

A simple but rich dessert, Peaches with Macaroon Cream Filling may also be served in a pre-cooked flan case for lunch or dinner.

6 SERVINGS

6 peaches, blanched, peeled, halved and the stones removed
6 tablespoons redcurrant jelly dissolved in 1 tablespoon brandy
FILLING
10 fl. oz. [1¼ cups] milk
1 vanilla pod
2 eggs
2 egg yolks
2 oz. [¼ cup] sugar
1 tablespoon flour
1 oz. [2 tablespoons] unsalted butter
6 oz. [¾ cup] crushed macaroons
¼ teaspoon almond essence

First make the filling. In a medium-sized saucepan, scald the milk with the vanilla pod over moderate heat (bring to just below boiling point). Remove the pan from the heat. Set aside to cool slightly. Remove the vanilla pod, wipe it dry and store it for future use.

In a medium-sized mixing bowl, beat the eggs, egg yolks and sugar together with a wooden spoon until the mixture is pale and thick. Stir in the flour.

Gradually pour the cooled milk into the egg mixture, stirring constantly with the wooden spoon. Return the custard to the saucepan and bring to just under boiling point, stirring constantly.

Remove the pan from the heat and beat the thickened custard until it is smooth. Beat in the butter, crushed macaroons and almond essence. Spoon the custard mixture into a bowl and set aside to cool. When the mixture is cool, cover the bowl with aluminium foil and put it in the refrigerator for 30 minutes.

Place the peach halves in the refrigerator and chill them for 30 minutes.

Arrange the peach halves, cut sides up, on a chilled serving dish and spoon equal quantities of the filling into them. Pour equal amounts of the redcurrant jelly mixture over each filled peach.

Serve immediately.

Cooling Norwegian Rhubarb Dessert.

Pecan Pie

A delectable pie, one of the glories of American cuisine, Pecan Pie is so rich that it is best served in small wedges.

6-8 SERVINGS

1 x 9-inch flan case made with frozen and thawed shortcrust pastry
2 oz. [⅓ cup] whole pecans
3 eggs
8 fl. oz. golden syrup [1 cup light corn syrup]
3 oz. [½ cup] soft brown sugar
½ teaspoon vanilla essence
¼ teaspoon salt

Preheat the oven to fairly hot 375°F (Gas Mark 5, 190°C).

Place the flan case in the oven and bake blind for 10 minutes. Remove the flan case from the oven and remove the foil or paper and beans. Set aside for 10 minutes.

Increase the oven temperature to hot 425°F (Gas Mark 7, 220°C).

When the flan case has cooled, arrange the pecans, in concentric circles, on the bottom. Set aside.

In a medium-sized mixing bowl, beat the eggs with a wire whisk or rotary beater until they are light and frothy. Beat in the syrup, then the sugar, and continue beating until it has dissolved. Add the vanilla essence and salt and beat the mixture until it is smooth.

Carefully pour the mixture into the flan case, taking care not to disturb the pecan circles — the pecans will rise to the top but will keep their pattern.

Place the pie in the oven and bake for 10 minutes. Reduce the oven temperature to moderate 350°F (Gas Mark 4, 180°C) and continue to bake the pie for a further 30 minutes.

Remove the pie from the oven and set it aside to cool completely before serving. As the pie cools, the filling will set and become firm.

Zabaglione

Sometimes called Coupe Siciliana, Zabaglione is a light egg and Marsala custard chilled until very cold and served in wine glasses.

4-6 SERVINGS

3 oz. [⅜ cup] sugar
2 fl. oz. [¼ cup] water
2 egg whites
6 egg yolks
3 tablespoons Marsala

In a small saucepan, dissolve the sugar in the water over low heat, stirring constantly. When the sugar has dissolved, increase the heat to high and boil the syrup until the temperature registers 240°F on a sugar thermometer or until a little of the syrup dropped into cold water forms a soft ball. Remove the pan from the heat.

In a medium-sized mixing bowl, quickly whisk the egg whites with a wire whisk or rotary beater until they form stiff peaks. Pour on the syrup and continue whisking until the egg whites and syrup are well mixed. Set the mixing bowl aside.

In a medium-sized heatproof mixing bowl, combine the egg yolks with the Marsala. Place the bowl over a saucepan of barely simmering water.

Beat the egg yolks and Marsala with a wire whisk or rotary beater for 5 to 8 minutes or until the mixture is very thick and pale in colour.

When the mixture is thick, remove the bowl from the heat and fold the egg yolk mixture into the egg white mixture. Spoon the custard into wine glasses. Cover the glasses with plastic wrap and put them into the refrigerator to chill for at least 1 hour before serving.

This rich and filling Pecan Pie is traditionally served, in small wedges, at American Thanksgiving Day festivities.

Sweets and puddings for entertaining

Most people consider a spectacular finish essential to any special meal — especially when there are favoured guests around willing to be impressed! And it's with this in mind that the dishes included in this section have been selected; and they're show-stoppers every one, from the intriguing combination of cold ice-cream and hot meringue in Baked Alaska (page 354), through the cool elegance of Cherries with Marsala (page 355) and classic Diplomate Pudding (pictured above, page 359), to the most famous cake of them all the Viennese Sachertorte (page 372).

And we haven't forgotten those occasions when you have to impress on a strict budget, as a quick glance at (and some judicious testing from) the **For Budget Occasions** section will confirm — serve dishes like Apple Pudding (page 380) or Yeast Buckwheat Pancakes with Blackberries and Sour Cream (page 384) and you're sure to please.

While most of the recipes do take a bit of time to prepare, almost all of them can be made well in advance, even the day before — an invaluable help to even the most experienced hostess, especially since every one is absolutely guaranteed to more than repay any care and attention required to make it. Each and every one fulfills the criteria that desserts not only look absolutely fabulous but taste superb as well.

Apricot Condé

A classic French dessert, Apricot Condé makes an elegant end to a special dinner.

6 SERVINGS

1 teaspoon vegetable oil
4 oz. [⅔ cup] round-grain rice
1½ pints [3¾ cups] milk
12 oz. [1½ cups] sugar
1 oz. [2 tablespoons] butter
⅛ teaspoon salt
1 teaspoon vanilla essence
6 egg yolks, lightly beaten
2 lb. apricots, peeled and halved
8 fl. oz. [1 cup] water
2 tablespoons kirsch
1 oz. [¼ cup] flaked almonds

Preheat the oven to cool 300°F (Gas Mark 2, 150°C). Lightly grease an 8-inch soufflé dish with the oil. Set aside.

In a flameproof casserole, bring the rice, milk, 4 ounces [½ cup] of sugar, the butter, salt and vanilla essence to the boil over moderate heat, stirring constantly.

Cover the casserole and transfer it to the oven. Bake for 1 hour, or until all the liquid has been absorbed. Remove the casserole from the oven. Stir in the egg yolks and place the casserole over low heat. Cook, stirring constantly, for 3 minutes. Remove the casserole from the heat and set it aside to cool.

Slice half a pound of the apricots.

When the rice is cool, spoon one-third of it into the soufflé dish. Place half the apricot slices on top. Continue making layers, ending with the rice. Cover the dish and place it in the refrigerator to chill for 2 hours or until the rice is firm.

Meanwhile, in a saucepan, dissolve the remaining sugar in the water over moderate heat, stirring constantly. Add the

Baked Alaska is simply superb.

remaining apricot halves. Reduce the heat to low and simmer for 10 minutes or until the apricots are tender but firm. Remove the pan from the heat.

With a slotted spoon, remove 12 apricot halves from the pan and set them aside. Purée the remaining halves with the syrup in a blender and return the purée to the saucepan. Return the pan to high heat. Boil for 3 minutes. Remove from the heat.

Stir in the kirsch and almonds. Set the sauce aside to cool. Then chill it in the refrigerator.

Unmould the pudding on to a serving dish. Arrange the reserved apricot halves on the top and around the sides. Spoon over the sauce and serve immediately.

Baked Alaska

An impressive dessert, Baked Alaska is

sponge cake topped with ice-cream and covered with meringue.

6 SERVINGS

1 tablespoon butter
3 oz. [¾ cup] plus 1 tablespoon flour
6 oz. [¾ cup] castor sugar
4 egg yolks, at room temperature
1 teaspoon vanilla essence
4 egg whites, at room temperature
1 teaspoon baking powder
¼ teaspoon salt
5 oz. apricot jam
2 pints [5 cups] vanilla ice-cream, softened

MERINGUE

6 egg whites
⅛ teaspoon salt
6 oz. [¾ cup] castor sugar

Preheat the oven to moderate 350°F (Gas Mark 4, 180°C). Grease two 8-inch sandwich tins with the butter.

Mix the 1 tablespoon of flour with 1 tablespoon of castor sugar and dust the sandwich tins with the mixture. Shake out any excess flour and sugar.

Put the egg yolks in a mixing bowl. Add the vanilla essence and beat with a wire whisk or rotary beater until the mixture is pale. Add the remaining sugar, reserving 4 tablespoons, and beat to mix.

In another mixing bowl beat the egg whites with a wire whisk or rotary beater until they form soft peaks. Add the reserved sugar and continue beating until the whites form stiff peaks.

Fold the beaten egg whites into the egg yolk mixture until they are mixed.

Sift the remaining flour with the baking powder and salt into the egg mixture.

Pour the mixture evenly into the two cake tins and bake in the oven for 25 minutes or until a skewer inserted into the cakes comes out clean. Turn the cakes out on to a rack to cool.

When the cakes have cooled, spread one cake with the apricot jam. Put the second cake on top. Trim off the corners to make an oval shape.

Put the ice-cream on a sheet of aluminium foil and mould it gently to the size of the cake. Cover with foil and place in the frozen food storage compartment of the refrigerator to become hard.

Preheat the oven to very hot 450°F (Gas Mark 8, 230°C).

In a medium-sized bowl, using a whisk or rotary beater, whip the egg whites and salt until they form stiff peaks. Add the sugar a little at a time and continue beating until the whites are glossy. Do not overbeat or the whites will begin to collapse.

Put the cake on a baking sheet. Remove the ice-cream from the refrigerator, take off the foil and place the ice-cream on top

of the cake. Cover the outside of the cake and the ice-cream with the meringue mixture, making sure there is no cake or ice-cream showing. (This must be done very quickly and the meringue must cover the ice-cream and cake completely or the ice-cream will melt.)

Put the baking sheet in the centre of the oven and bake it for 3 to 4 minutes, until the meringue turns a pale golden colour. Serve at once.

Cherries with Marsala

☆　①①　✕✕

Cool and refreshing, Cherries with Marsala makes a luscious end to a rich meal.

4 SERVINGS

2 lb. canned stoned Morello cherries, drained
5 fl. oz. [⅝ cup] Marsala

Cool, refreshing and elegant – that's Cherries with Marsala.

1 tablespoon sugar
5 fl. oz. double cream [⅝ cup heavy cream], stiffly whipped

In a saucepan, bring the cherries, Marsala and sugar to the boil over moderate heat. Reduce the heat to low and simmer gently for 10 minutes.

Remove the pan from the heat. Transfer the cherries from the pan to a serving dish. Return the pan to the heat and boil the liquid for 3 to 4 minutes, or until it is thick and syrupy. Remove the pan from the heat and pour the syrup over the cherries.

Place the dish in the refrigerator and chill for at least 1 hour. Top the cherries with the whipped cream and serve.

Chestnut Dessert

This delectable French dessert of Madeira-soaked sponges, covered with chestnut purée and cream, is easy and quick to make. It makes a perfect dinner party dessert, as it can be made in advance.

4 SERVINGS

4 trifle sponge squares [4 small stale sponge cakes]
4 fl. oz. [½ cup] Madeira
8 oz. canned sweetened chestnut purée
5 fl. oz. double cream [⅝ cup heavy cream], stiffly whipped

Place the sponge cakes in four individual serving glasses, trimming them to fit the shape of the glass if necessary. Pour equal amounts of the Madeira over each sponge and set aside for 10 to 15 minutes, or until the sponges have absorbed all the Madeira.

Spoon the chestnut purée on top of the soaked sponges and smooth it down.

Fill a small forcing bag, fitted with a medium-sized star-shaped nozzle, with the whipped cream. Pipe the cream decoratively over the chestnut purée in the glasses.

Place the glasses in the refrigerator and chill the mixture for 30 to 40 minutes before serving.

Chocolate Chiffon Pie

A tempting American pie with a nutty pie crust and a chocolate cream filling, Chocolate Chiffon Pie will be a special treat for those people who love rich creamy desserts.

4-6 SERVINGS

PIE CRUST
5 oz. [1 cup] Brazil nuts
2 tablespoons sugar
FILLING
½ oz. gelatine
4 oz. [½ cup] sugar
¼ teaspoon salt
6 fl. oz. [¾ cup] milk
2 eggs, separated
6 oz. dark [semi-sweet] cooking chocolate, broken into pieces
1 teaspoon vanilla essence
6 fl. oz. double cream [¾ cup heavy cream], stiffly whipped
2 tablespoons chopped Brazil nuts

Preheat the oven to fairly hot 400°F (Gas Mark 6, 200°C).

To make the crust, grind the Brazil nuts either with a food mill or in an electric blender.

Put the ground nuts in a medium-sized bowl with the sugar and blend them together thoroughly, using the back of a spoon. If you prefer, the sugar may be blended into the nuts in the blender.

With your fingers, press the mixture into the bottom and around the sides of a 9-inch pie dish.

Place the dish in the oven and bake for 8 to 10 minutes, or until the crust is lightly browned. Remove the dish from the oven and leave to cool.

To make the filling, put the gelatine, half the sugar and the salt in the top part of a double saucepan or in a bowl placed over boiling water. With a wooden spoon, stir in the milk, egg yolks and chocolate.

Stirring constantly, cook for 6 minutes or until the gelatine has dissolved and the chocolate has melted. Remove the pan or bowl from the heat and beat the mixture until it is thoroughly blended. Stir in the vanilla essence and set aside to cool. Place in the refrigerator to chill for about 45 minutes.

Remove the chocolate mixture from the refrigerator. It should be just on the point of setting. With a metal spoon, fold 4 fluid ounces [½ cup] of the whipped cream into the chocolate mixture.

With a rotary beater or wire whisk, beat the egg whites until they are almost stiff. Add 2 teaspoons of the remaining sugar and continue to beat until the egg whites form stiff peaks. Using a metal spoon, fold the remaining sugar into the egg whites. Carefully fold the beaten egg whites into the chilled chocolate mixture. Pour the filling into the pie shell and place it in the refrigerator to chill for 3 hours or until it is firm. Decorate with the remaining whipped cream and the chopped Brazil nuts just before serving the pie.

Coupe Jacques

This classic French dessert is made of lemon and raspberry sorbet, served in individual shallow glass bowls, and moulded so that each half of the bowl is a different colour. The ice is topped with fresh fruit, steeped in kirsch, and decorated with blanched almonds. Any fruits suitable for fresh fruit salad may be used.

6 SERVINGS

1 pint assorted fresh fruit, cut into small pieces
2 tablespoons castor sugar
2 teaspoons lemon juice
7 tablespoons kirsch
1 pint [2½ cups] raspberry sorbet
1 pint [2½ cups] lemon sorbet

2 oz. [½ cup] blanched almonds, halved

In a medium-sized bowl, combine the fruit, sugar, lemon juice and 6 tablespoons of kirsch. Toss and mix the fruit well with a spoon. Cover the bowl and chill in the refrigerator for 1 hour.

Rinse 6 shallow glass bowls in cold water.

Put a large tablespoonful of raspberry sorbet and another of lemon sorbet side by side in each bowl, leaving a small space between the two sorbets.

Remove the fruit from the refrigerator and put a large tablespoonful of fruit on top of and in between the two sorbets.

Sprinkle the Coupe Jacques with the remaining kirsch and decorate with blanched almonds. Serve the Coupe immediately.

Crème Brulée

GLAZED BAKED CUSTARD

A rich, delicious dessert, with a topping of crisp caramelized brown sugar, Crème Brulée makes an impressive end to a dinner party.

4 SERVINGS

2 oz. [¼ cup] castor sugar
5 egg yolks
16 fl. oz. double cream [2 cups heavy cream], scalded
1 teaspoon vanilla essence
2 oz. [⅓ cup] light brown sugar

In a large mixing bowl, beat the sugar and egg yolks with a wire whisk until they are pale and smooth, or until the mixture will form a ribbon trail on itself when the whisk is lifted. Gradually beat in the scalded cream.

Pour the mixture into a large, heavy saucepan. Place the pan over low heat and stir constantly with a wooden spoon until the crème is thick enough to coat the spoon. Do not allow the crème to boil. Remove the pan from the heat and beat the crème for 1 to 2 minutes. Stir in the vanilla essence.

Strain the crème into individual ramekins or a deep flameproof serving dish. Allow to cool and then place the crème in the refrigerator to chill for 2 hours.

Preheat the grill [broiler] to high.

Remove the ramekins or dish from the refrigerator and sprinkle the surface of the crème with a thick layer of light brown sugar. Place the dish on a baking sheet and put it under the grill [broiler]. Cook until the sugar melts and caramelizes, taking care to remove it before it burns. Serve at once.

Small Custard Creams

This rich version of traditional small cups of custard is flavoured with coffee and brandy. Serve this filling dessert after a light main course.

6 SERVINGS

1 pint single cream [2½ cups light cream]
5 egg yolks
1 egg
3 tablespoons sugar
2 tablespoons coffee essence
2 tablespoons brandy

These rich Small Custard Creams are flavoured with coffee and brandy.

Preheat the oven to warm 325°F (Gas Mark 3, 170°C).

In a small saucepan, heat the cream over low heat. When the cream is hot but not boiling, remove the pan from the heat and set aside.

In a mixing bowl, beat the egg yolks, egg, sugar, coffee essence and brandy together with a wooden spoon until they are just combined. Stirring constantly with the spoon, gradually pour the cream on to the egg mixture, beating until they are well blended. Strain the mixture into another bowl.

Pour the mixture into 6 small ramekins or ovenproof custard cups. Place the filled dishes in a baking tin and pour in enough boiling water to come half way up the sides. Cover each dish with aluminium foil.

Place the tin in the oven and bake for 25 to 30 minutes or until the custards are lightly set.

Remove the tin from the oven and leave to cool, then chill in the refrigerator before serving.

357

Diplomate Pudding

This classic dessert (pictured on page 353) is rich with fruit soaked in kirsch. It may be served surrounded by fresh apricots.

6 SERVINGS

12 sponge finger biscuits [cookies], finely crushed
2 oz. [⅓ cup] sultanas or raisins
2 oz. [⅓ cup] raisins
4 fl. oz. [½ cup] kirsch
1 teaspoon vegetable oil
1¼ pints [3⅛ cups] milk
1 vanilla pod
5 tablespoons sugar
5 egg yolks
½ oz. gelatine, dissolved in 3 tablespoons boiling water
5 fl. oz. double cream [⅝ cup heavy cream]
4 glacé cherries, halved
4 fresh apricots, blanched, peeled, stoned and sliced

Place the sponge finger biscuit [cookie] crumbs, sultanas and raisins in a shallow dish. Pour over the kirsch. Leave the crumbs and fruit to soak for 1 hour.

Using a pastry brush, grease a 2½-pint [1½-quart] mould with the vegetable oil. Place the mould upside down on kitchen paper towels to drain off the excess oil.

In a medium-sized saucepan, warm the milk with the vanilla pod over moderate heat. When the milk is hot, but not boiling, remove it from the heat.

Put the sugar in a heatproof bowl. Make a well in the centre of the sugar. Drop the egg yolks, one at a time, into the well and, with a wooden spoon, beat the yolks, slowly incorporating the sugar. Continue this process until all the egg yolks and sugar are well mixed.

Remove the vanilla pod from the milk and, beating all the time, pour the milk on to the egg-and-sugar mixture.

Place a large pan, one-third full of water, over high heat. When the water is about to boil, reduce the heat to low. (The water must be hot, but not simmering.) Place the bowl in the water and, stirring slowly with the spoon, cook until the custard is thick enough to coat the spoon. Be careful not to overheat the custard as it will curdle. Remove the pan from the heat.

Stir the gelatine into the custard. Strain the custard into a large mixing bowl. Place the bowl over ice and stir until the custard thickens.

Two classic French cakes, fit to grace the finest table—Gâteau Noisette and Gâteau à l'Orange.

In a small bowl, whip the cream with a wire whisk until it is thick but not stiff. Lightly fold the cream into the thickening custard.

Cover the bottom of the mould with the cherries. Place the slices of apricot between the cherries, forming a wheel. Cover with a layer of one-quarter of the biscuit [cookie] mixture.

Pour one-quarter of the custard into the mould. Cover with another layer of the biscuit mixture. Repeat the layers until all the custard and biscuit mixture have been used up, finishing with a layer of the custard.

Cover the mould with foil and place in the refrigerator to chill for 6 hours, or until the pudding is completely set.

To serve, dip the bottom of the mould in hot water for 1 second. Run a knife around the edge of the pudding and turn it out on to a chilled serving dish.

Gâteau Noisette

Layers of meringue sandwiched together with a rich chocolate buttercream and covered with hazelnuts, Gâteau Noisette is a superb dessert for a dinner party.

8 SERVINGS

6 egg whites
12 oz. [1½ cups] castor sugar
FILLING
2 egg whites
4 oz. icing sugar [1 cup confectioners' sugar]
8 oz. [1 cup] unsalted butter
4 oz. dark [semi-sweet] cooking chocolate
1 teaspoon lemon juice
5 oz. [1 cup] chopped hazelnuts

Preheat the oven to cool 300°F (Gas Mark 2, 150°C). Line two large baking sheets with non-stick silicone paper.

In a mixing bowl, beat the egg whites with a wire whisk or rotary beater until they are light and frothy. Beat in 2 ounces [¼ cup] of the sugar and continue beating until the whites form stiff peaks. Carefully fold in the remaining sugar.

Spread the mixture into four circles, each about ¼-inch thick, two on each of the prepared baking sheets.

Place the baking sheets in the oven and bake for about 1 hour. Turn the circles over and bake for a further 15 minutes.

Remove the meringue circles from the oven and leave them to cool.

Meanwhile prepare the filling. In a mixing bowl set over a pan of simmering water, beat the egg whites with the icing [confectioners'] sugar until the mixture is thick. Remove the bowl from the heat.

In a second mixing bowl, cream the butter with a wooden spoon until it is fluffy. Beat in the egg white mixture.

In a small saucepan, melt the chocolate over low heat. As soon as it has melted, remove the pan from the heat.

Beat the melted chocolate into the egg white and butter mixture. Then beat in the lemon juice and half of the hazelnuts, beating until the mixture is well blended.

Carefully remove the meringue circles from the baking sheets.

Sandwich the circles together with the filling, covering the top as well.

Cover the top of the cake with the remaining hazelnuts. Leave the cake in a cool place for about a day before serving.

Gâteau à l'Orange

When Gâteau à l'Orange is to be served as a dessert, fill it with whipped cream and brush the sides and top with apricot glaze. Coat the sides with slivered almonds and decorate the top with glazed orange slices.

6-8 SERVINGS

1 teaspoon butter
4 oz. [1 cup] plus 1 tablespoon flour
4 eggs
4 oz. [½ cup] sugar
grated rind of 1 orange
4 tablespoons orange juice
4 oz. [½ cup] butter, melted

Preheat the oven to fairly hot 375°F (Gas Mark 5, 190°C). With the butter, grease a loose-bottomed 7-inch cake tin. Sprinkle in the tablespoon of flour and tip and rotate to distribute the flour evenly.

In a heatproof bowl, combine the eggs and sugar. Place the bowl in a pan of hot water, and put over low heat.

Whisk the eggs and sugar with a wire whisk or rotary beater until the mixture is light and pale and will make a ribbon trail on itself when the whisk is lifted. Remove the bowl from the heat and continue beating until the mixture is cool.

Using a metal spoon fold in the orange rind and juice.

Sift the remaining flour on to the surface of the egg mixture and gently fold it in. Pour the melted butter gradually into the mixture and fold and cut it in gently until it is all absorbed. Pour the mixture into the cake tin. Set the tin on a baking sheet and place it in the centre of the oven. Bake for 20 to 30 minutes, or until the cake will spring back when lightly pressed.

Remove the cake from the oven and allow it to cool for 5 minutes. Turn the cake out on to a wire rack to cool.

Serve cold, decorated as above.

Hazelnut Cream

Quick and easy to make, Hazelnut Cream is a delicious dinner party dessert of crushed hazelnuts and cream with a subtle flavouring of coffee. If you like, the cream may be decorated with a few hazelnuts just before serving.

4-6 SERVINGS

4 oz. [1 cup] whole hazelnuts, shelled and peeled
¼ oz. gelatine
2 tablespoons hot water
10 fl. oz. [1¼ cups] milk
4 egg yolks
4 oz. [½ cup] sugar
2 tablespoons coffee essence
10 fl. oz. double cream [1¼ cups heavy cream]

Using a blender or pestle and mortar, blend or pound the hazelnuts until they are coarsely crushed. Set the hazelnuts aside.

In a small saucepan, dissolve the gelatine in the water over low heat. Set aside.

In a medium-sized saucepan, bring the nuts and milk to the boil over moderately low heat, stirring constantly with a wooden spoon. Remove the pan from the heat.

In a medium-sized mixing bowl, beat the egg yolks and sugar together with a wire whisk or rotary beater until the mixture is pale and thick.

Pour the hot milk and nut mixture on to the egg yolk and sugar mixture, stirring constantly. Return the mixture to the saucepan and replace the saucepan over low heat.

Cook, stirring constantly, for 2 to 3 minutes, or until the mixture thickens and is smooth. Do not boil or the custard will curdle.

Remove the saucepan from the heat and stir in the dissolved gelatine and the coffee essence.

Pour the mixture into a medium-sized mixing bowl and set it aside to cool.

In another mixing bowl, beat the cream with a wire whisk or rotary beater until it is thick but not stiff.

When the hazelnut mixture is quite cold but not yet set, lightly but thoroughly fold in the beaten cream with a metal spoon.

Pour the mixture into a 2-pint [1½-quart] soufflé dish or bowl, or into individual dishes.

Cover the dish and place it in the refrigerator. Leave for at least 4 hours, or until the cream is completely set and firm.

Remove the dish from the refrigerator and serve at once.

Ile Flottante

FLOATING ISLAND

A classic French dessert, Ile Flottante is a rich mixture of kirsch and maraschino-soaked sponge cake 'floating' in a fresh fruit sauce. While a thin, creamy custard is often recommended rather than the raspberry or strawberry sauce suggested below, the latter is now a commonly accepted alternative. Serve after a light main course.

6-8 SERVINGS

1 x 8-inch round sponge cake, slightly stale
3 fl. oz. [⅜ cup] kirsch
3 fl. oz. [⅜ cup] maraschino liqueur
6 oz. apricot jam
2 tablespoons blanched slivered almonds
2 tablespoons chopped pistachio nuts
2 oz. [⅓ cup] raisins or currants, soaked in cold water for 2 hours and drained
10 fl. oz. double cream [1¼ cups heavy cream], very stiffly whipped

SAUCE

1 lb. fresh raspberries or hulled strawberries, washed
2 oz. [¼ cup] sugar
2 tablespoons lemon juice

With a sharp knife, slice the cake into four equal layers. Place the bottom layer in a large, wide serving dish and sprinkle it generously with about one-quarter of the kirsch and one-quarter of the maraschino liqueur. Spread the slice with about one-quarter of the apricot jam, then sprinkle on some almonds, pistachios and raisins or currants. Continue to make layers as above until all of the ingredients have been used up, reserving a few almonds, pistachios and raisins or currants for decoration. Place the dish in the refrigerator and chill for 15 minutes.

Remove the cake from the refrigerator and, using a flat-bladed knife, generously spread the top and sides with the beaten cream. Return the cake to the refrigerator to chill while you make the fruit sauce.

To make the sauce, rub the raspberries or strawberries through a fine strainer into a medium-sized mixing bowl, using the back of a wooden spoon to extract all the juices from the fruit. Discard the pulp remaining in the strainer. Alternatively, purée the fruit in an electric blender or in a food mill.

Stir the sugar and lemon juice into the fruit, beating with a fork until the mixture is well blended.

Remove the cake from the refrigerator

and spoon the sauce around it. Sprinkle the reserved almonds, pistachios and raisins or currants decoratively over the top.

Chill the mixture in the refrigerator for 15 minutes, then remove and serve cold.

Lemon Posset

A posset is an old-fashioned English dessert which, traditionally, would have been served in a china posset dish with a cover. The diarist Samuel Pepys' favourite

Ile Flottante is a sumptuous mixture of sponge cake, kirsch, maraschino, apricot jam and cream, 'floating' in a delightfully refreshing raspberry or strawberry sauce. Serve after a light main course.

posset was made with cream, sherry, egg yolks, sugar and spices and this version, although simpler, is equally rich, delicious and easy to make. Serve Lemon Posset with some sponge finger biscuits [cookies] or langues de chats.

4 SERVINGS

2 sugar cubes
1 lemon
10 fl. oz. double cream [1¼ cups heavy cream]
3 tablespoons dry white wine
2 tablespoons dry white vermouth
1 tablespoon sugar
2 egg whites

Rub the cubes of sugar over the surface of the lemon until they have absorbed all of the oil.

In a medium-sized mixing bowl, crush the sugar cubes using a wooden spoon or a fork. Using a wire whisk or rotary beater, beat in the cream. Continue beating until the cream forms stiff peaks. Squeeze out the juice of half the lemon and carefully stir it into the cream with the wine and white vermouth. Stir in the sugar.

In another medium-sized mixing bowl, using a wire whisk or rotary beater, whisk the egg whites until they form stiff peaks. With a large metal spoon, carefully fold the beaten egg whites into the cream mixture.

Spoon the mixture into four individual serving glasses. Place the glasses in the refrigerator to chill for 1 hour.

Remove the dishes from the refrigerator and serve at once.

Macaroon and Apricot Whip

Macaroon and Apricot Whip is a delightful mixture of apricots, brown sugar, brandy, macaroons and ground almonds.

4-6 SERVINGS

8 oz. dried apricots, soaked
   overnight and drained
10 fl. oz. [1¼ cups] water
1 tablespoon lemon juice
2 tablespoons soft brown sugar
2 fl. oz. [¼ cup] brandy
16 macaroons, finely crushed
2 oz. [⅓ cup] ground almonds
1 teaspoon butter
4 egg whites

In a saucepan, bring the apricots and the water to the boil over moderate heat. Reduce the heat to low, cover the pan and simmer the apricots for 10 to 15 minutes or until they are tender. With a slotted spoon, lift out the apricots and put them in a blender. Blend at high speed until they are puréed.

Put the purée into a medium-sized mixing bowl. Stir in the lemon juice,

sugar, brandy, macaroons and almonds.

Preheat the oven to moderate 350°F (Gas Mark 4, 180°C). With the butter grease a 2-pint [1½-quart] baking dish.

In a large bowl, beat the egg whites with a wire whisk or rotary beater until they form stiff peaks.

Using a metal spoon, fold the egg whites into the apricot mixture. Pour the mixture into the baking dish. Put the dish in a deep baking tin. Pour in enough boiling water to come half way up the side of the dish. Put the baking tin in the oven and bake for 25 to 30 minutes or until the top is lightly browned.

Remove the dish from the oven and set it aside to cool. When it is cool put the whip in the refrigerator to chill for 1 to 1½ hours before serving.

Marmalade Chocolate Cake

A sumptuous chocolate cake with a tangy flavour, Marmalade Chocolate Cake makes an ideal festive cake. The cake can be decorated with crystallized flowers —

This rich, moist Marmalade Chocolate Cake makes a superb dessert, or it may be served for tea.

roses, violets, etc. as in the picture.

6-8 SERVINGS

CAKE

6 oz. [¾ cup] plus 1 teaspoon butter
6 oz. dark [semi-sweet] chocolate,
   broken into small pieces
8 oz. [1 cup] castor sugar
3 tablespoons orange marmalade
5 eggs, separated
8 oz. [2 cups] flour, sifted
2 teaspoons baking powder
2 oz. [⅓ cup] ground almonds

FILLING

8 oz. dark [semi-sweet] chocolate,
   broken into small pieces
2 oz. [¼ cup] butter, cut into pieces
2 eggs, well beaten

ICING

4 oz. dark [semi-sweet] chocolate,
   broken into small pieces
4 oz. [½ cup] butter, softened
10 oz. icing sugar [2½ cups
   confectioners' sugar]

362

1 tablespoon strong black coffee

Preheat the oven to warm 325°F (Gas Mark 3, 170°C).

With the teaspoon of butter, grease a 9-inch round cake tin and set it aside.

In a small saucepan, melt the chocolate over low heat, stirring occasionally. As soon as the chocolate has melted, remove the pan from the heat and set it aside.

In a mixing bowl, cream the remaining butter with a wooden spoon until it is soft. Beat in the sugar and continue beating until the mixture is fluffy. Cream in the melted chocolate and the marmalade.

Beat the egg yolks into the mixture, one at a time, adding a tablespoon of the flour with each yolk. Fold in the remaining flour, the baking powder and the almonds, and combine the batter thoroughly.

In a large mixing bowl, beat the egg whites with a wire whisk or rotary beater until they form stiff peaks. With a metal spoon, fold the whites into the batter.

Turn the batter into the prepared cake tin, smoothing it out with a knife.

Place the tin in the oven and bake for 1½ hours or until a skewer inserted into the centre of the cake comes out clean.

Remove the cake from the oven and set it aside to cool for 30 minutes. Turn the cake out of the tin on to a wire rack and set it aside to cool completely.

Meanwhile, make the filling. Place the chocolate pieces in a heatproof mixing bowl set in a pan half filled with hot water. Set the pan over low heat and cook, stirring occasionally, until the chocolate has melted. With a wooden spoon, beat in the butter, a few pieces at a time, beating until it is well blended.

Using a small wire whisk or rotary beater, beat in the eggs. Cook the mixture, beating constantly, for 5 minutes, never letting the water come to the boil or the eggs will scramble. The mixture should have the consistency of custard.

Remove the pan from the heat. Lift the bowl out of the pan. Place it in the refrigerator to cool completely, stirring occasionally to prevent lumps from forming as the mixture thickens.

To make the icing, in a small saucepan, melt the chocolate over low heat, stirring occasionally. As soon as the chocolate has melted, remove the pan from the heat and set it aside.

In a medium-sized mixing bowl, cream the butter with a wooden spoon until it is soft. Sift in half of the icing [confectioners'] sugar and cream the mixture thoroughly. Beat in the melted chocolate and the coffee. Sift in the remaining icing [confectioners'] sugar and beat the mixture until it is smooth and creamy. Set

aside in a cool place.

When the cake is completely cold, slice it into four equal layers.

Set the top of the cake aside and place the three remaining layers flat on a working surface.

Spoon equal amounts of the filling on to each of the three layers. Spread the filling evenly over the layers to the edges. Sandwich the layers together, placing the reserved layer on top.

With a flat-bladed knife, spread the icing over the top and sides of the cake, bringing it up into decorative peaks.

Place the cake on a serving plate and set it aside in a cool place for 1 hour before slicing and serving.

Nectarine Cream Mould

☆ ① ① ╳ ╳

A delicately flavoured cream, nectarine and brandy mixture, Nectarine Cream Mould makes a refreshing dessert.

4 SERVINGS

2 teaspoons vegetable oil
6 medium-sized nectarines, peeled, stoned and finely chopped
⅛ teaspoon ground allspice

3 oz. icing sugar [¾ cup confectioners' sugar]
2 tablespoons brandy
½ oz. gelatine dissolved in 4 tablespoons hot water
10 fl. oz. double cream [1¼ cups heavy cream]

Grease a 2-pint [1½-quart] mould with the oil. Place the mould, upside down, on kitchen paper towels to drain.

In a mixing bowl, combine the nectarines, allspice, sugar, brandy and gelatine.

In a small mixing bowl, beat the cream with a wire whisk or rotary beater until it forms stiff peaks. Fold the cream into the fruit mixture. Spoon the mixture into the prepared mould. Place the mould in the refrigerator to chill for 2 hours or until the dessert has set and is firm.

To unmould the dessert, run a knife around the edge to loosen the sides. Place a serving plate, inverted, over the mould and reverse the two, giving a sharp shake. The cream should slide out easily.

Nectarine Cream Mould makes a spectacular ending to dinner.

An exotic mixture of fresh and dried fruit makes Oriental Fruit Salad a very different dessert.

honey and kirsch dressing, Oriental Fruit Salad may be served on its own or with cream.

6 SERVINGS

4 fl. oz. [½ cup] clear honey
3 fl. oz. [⅜ cup] kirsch
10 dried figs, stalks removed and coarsely chopped
20 dried dates, halved and stoned
2½ oz. [½ cup] whole unblanched hazelnuts
2½ oz. [½ cup] whole unblanched almonds
1 medium-sized musk melon (honeydew, cantaloup, ogen, etc.)

In a medium-sized shallow dish, combine the honey and kirsch. Add the figs, dates, hazelnuts and almonds. Stir well to coat the fruit and nuts with the liquid. Cover the dish and set aside to soak at room temperature for 4 hours, stirring occasionally.

Using a sharp knife, cut the melon in half. With a sharp-edged metal spoon, scoop out and discard the seeds. Peel the melon and discard the skin. Chop the flesh into cubes.

Stir the melon cubes into the fruit and nut mixture. Place the dish in the refrigerator and chill the fruit salad for at least 1 hour.

Remove the fruit salad from the refrigerator and stir well. Divide the fruit, nuts and liquid equally among 6 individual serving glasses and serve immediately.

Parisian Fruit Tart

Succulent fruit encased in a rich walnut pastry and topped with whipped cream and nuts, Parisian Fruit Tart is usually served cold. It makes an absolutely delicious dessert for a summer or autumn dinner party.

4-6 SERVINGS

PASTRY
10 oz. [2½ cups] flour
½ teaspoon salt
3 oz. [⅜ cup] butter, cut into walnut-sized pieces
2 oz. [¼ cup] vegetable fat
4 oz. [½ cup] plus 2 tablespoons castor sugar
1½ oz. [¼ cup] walnuts, finely chopped
2 egg yolks, lightly beaten
3 tablespoons iced water

Orange Soufflés

These piping hot, pretty Orange Soufflés may be served with cream for a very special dessert.

6 SERVINGS

6 large oranges
1 oz. [2 tablespoons] butter
1 oz. [¼ cup] flour
10 fl. oz. [1¼ cups] hot milk
grated rind and juice of 1 orange
4 egg yolks
2 tablespoons sugar
5 egg whites

Cut about a ½-inch slice from the top of each orange so that the flesh and membranes may be extracted easily with a teaspoon. Discard the flesh and membranes. Cut out six pieces of aluminium foil large enough to cover the orange shells.

Place each orange shell in the centre of an aluminium foil square and draw up the edges of the foil until the orange shells are completely enclosed. Trim the edges of the aluminium foil with scissors so that they are level with the edge of the shell. Place the covered orange shells in a shallow ovenproof dish. Set aside.

Preheat the oven to moderate 350°F (Gas Mark 4, 180°C).

In a large saucepan, melt the butter over moderate heat. Remove the pan from

the heat and, with a wooden spoon, stir in the flour to make a smooth paste. Gradually add the hot milk, stirring constantly.

Return the pan to the heat and cook the mixture, stirring constantly, for 2 minutes or until it is thick and smooth. Mix in the grated orange rind and juice. Remove the pan from the heat and let the mixture cool slightly.

In a small mixing bowl, beat the egg yolks and sugar together with a fork. Gradually mix them into the hot orange mixture.

In a large mixing bowl, beat the egg whites with a wire whisk or rotary beater until they form stiff peaks.

With a metal spoon, carefully fold the egg whites into the orange mixture.

Spoon the mixture into the prepared orange shells in the dish. Place the dish in the oven and bake the soufflés for 15 to 20 minutes or until they are lightly browned on top and have risen ½-inch above the tops of the shells.

Remove the dish from the oven. Peel the aluminium foil off the orange shells and serve immediately.

Oriental Fruit Salad

An unusual fruit salad made with dried figs, dates, nuts and melon cubes with a

1 egg white, lightly beaten

FILLING

2 oz. [¼ cup] sugar

5 fl. oz. [⅝ cup] water

4 large peaches, apples or pears, peeled, halved and cored

5 fl. oz. double cream [⅝ cup heavy cream], stiffly whipped

2 tablespoons chopped walnuts

First make the pastry. Sift the flour and salt into a large mixing bowl. Add the butter and the vegetable fat and cut them into small pieces with a table knife. Rub the fats into the flour with your fingertips until the mixture resembles coarse bread-crumbs. Mix in 4 ounces [½ cup] of the sugar and the finely chopped walnuts.

Add the egg yolks with a spoonful of the water and mix it in with the knife. With your hands, mix and knead the dough until it is smooth. Add more water if the dough is too dry. Wrap the dough in greaseproof or waxed paper and place it in the refrigerator to chill for 30 minutes.

Meanwhile make the filling. In a medium-sized saucepan, dissolve the sugar in the water over low heat, stirring constantly. When the sugar has dissolved, increase the heat to high and boil the syrup for 4 minutes.

Add the fruit halves, reduce the heat to low and simmer the fruit halves for 10 to 15 minutes or until they are tender but still firm. Remove the pan from the heat. Set aside to cool.

Preheat the oven to fairly hot 375°F (Gas Mark 5, 190°C).

On a lightly floured board, roll out two-thirds of the dough into a circle large enough to line a 9-inch flan ring. Lift the dough on the rolling pin and lay it over the flan ring. Gently ease the dough into the ring. Trim off any excess.

With a slotted spoon, remove the fruit from the pan. Arrange the fruit halves in a circle and cut sides down, in the dough case. Dampen the edges of the dough.

On a lightly floured board, roll out the remaining dough into a circle large enough to fit over the top of the tart.

Rich walnut pastry enclosing fresh fruit, makes Parisian Fruit Tart a special treat.

Using a 3-inch pastry cutter, cut a hole in the centre of the dough circle. Discard the small circle of dough. Lift the dough on the rolling pin and lay it over the tart. Using your fingers, gently press the dough edges together. Trim off any excess dough.

With a pastry brush, brush the top of the dough with the egg white and dust with the remaining 2 tablespoons of castor sugar.

Place the tart in the top of the oven and bake for 30 to 35 minutes or until the pastry is firm to the touch.

Remove the tart from the oven and set it aside to cool completely. When it is cold, carefully remove the tart from the flan ring.

Spoon the whipped cream into the centre of the tart and sprinkle with the chopped walnuts. Serve at once.

Paskha

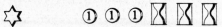

Easter is the main festival of the Russian Orthodox church, a time when families come together, when a great deal of food is consumed, when rejoicing is general. Paskha, a luscious dessert made from cream cheese, sour cream, almonds and fruit, is an integral part of the feasting. A special pyramid-shaped perforated mould, called a paskha mould, is traditionally used to make this dish, but a flower pot or colander with suitable perforations may be substituted.

6-8 SERVINGS

2 lb. cream cheese
4 oz. [½ cup] butter, softened
4 fl. oz. [½ cup] sour cream
4 oz. [½ cup] sugar
1 egg yolk
¼ teaspoon vanilla essence
grated rind of 1 lemon
3 tablespoons sultanas or seedless raisins
2 tablespoons raisins
2 tablespoons slivered almonds
1 tablespoon slivered almonds, toasted
1 tablespoon chopped glacé cherries

Place the cream cheese in a large wire strainer set over a small mixing bowl. Cover the cheese with a clean cloth and place a heavy weight on top. Leave the cheese to drain for at least 1½ hours.

Discard any liquid in the bowl. Transfer the cheese to a large bowl. With a wooden spoon, beat the butter into the cheese, a little at a time, and continue beating until the mixture is blended.

In a medium-sized mixing bowl, combine the sour cream, sugar and egg yolk with a fork or spoon, beating until the sugar has dissolved. Gradually add the sour cream mixture to the cream cheese mixture, beating constantly. Beat in the vanilla essence and grated lemon rind. Fold in the sultanas or seedless raisins, the raisins, almonds, toasted almonds and glacé cherries. Set aside.

Line a paskha mould, if you have one, or some similar perforated mould, with cheesecloth. Spoon in the cream cheese mixture and smooth the top with a knife. Cover the mould with a damp cloth and place a heavy weight on top. Place the mould, on a large plate, in the refrigerator to chill for 8 hours or overnight.

To serve, remove the weight and cloth from the mould. Place a serving dish,

Pears in Chocolate Sauce is inexpensive, easy to make — and even easier to eat!

inverted, over the mould and reverse the two, giving the mould a sharp shake. The dessert should slide out easily. Remove and discard the cheesecloth. The paskha is now ready to decorate and serve.

Peach and Blackberry Dessert

Serve this delicious Peach and Blackberry Dessert on its own or with whipped cream for a super dessert.

4 SERVINGS

6 oz. [¾ cup] sugar
10 fl. oz. [1¼ cups] water
4 large peaches, blanched, peeled, halved and stoned
8 oz. blackberries
2 tablespoons brandy
DECORATION
12 large blackberries

In a medium-sized saucepan, dissolve the sugar in the water over low heat, stirring constantly. When the sugar has dissolved, increase the heat to moderate and boil the syrup for 3 minutes, without stirring.

Add the peach halves to the pan, cut sides down, and poach them for 3 to 5 minutes, or until they are just tender.

Remove the pan from the heat. Using a slotted spoon, transfer the peach halves to 4 individual serving glasses, allowing 2 peach halves for each glass. Set aside.

Pour off all but 2 fluid ounces [¼ cup] of the poaching syrup from the pan. Stir the blackberries and brandy into the reserved syrup and return the pan to moderately low heat. Cook the blackberries, stirring constantly, for 5 minutes, or until they are beginning to pulp.

Remove the pan from the heat. Strain the mixture into a small mixing bowl. Using the back of a wooden spoon, rub the blackberries through the strainer into the bowl. Discard any dry pulp remaining in the strainer.

Spoon the blackberry purée over the peaches. Decorate each glass with three of the whole blackberries.

Place the glasses in the refrigerator and chill the dessert for 1 hour before serving.

Pears Baked with Cardamom

Pears baked in liqueur and cardamom, Pears Baked with Cardamom makes a light dessert after a rich main course.

4-6 SERVINGS

3 large pears, peeled, halved and cored
2 tablespoons soft brown sugar

4 fl. oz. [½ cup] orange-flavoured liqueur
2 teaspoons ground cardamom
8 fl. oz. double cream [1 cup heavy cream], stiffly whipped

Preheat the oven to moderate 350°F (Gas Mark 4, 180°C).

Cut the pears into slices. Arrange them in a shallow ovenproof dish and sprinkle over the sugar. Pour the liqueur over the top, then sprinkle over the cardamom.

Place the dish in the oven and bake for 40 minutes or until the pear slices are tender. Transfer the pear mixture to individual serving dishes and set aside to cool completely.

When the pears are cold, spoon equal amounts of the cream into each dish and serve at once.

Pears with Chocolate Sauce

This delicious dessert is easy to make, inexpensive and will make a spectacular dinner party dish.

6 SERVINGS

1½ pints [3¾ cups] water
6 oz. [¾ cup] castor sugar
2 vanilla pods
4 cloves
6 ripe dessert pears
CHOCOLATE SAUCE
12 oz. dark [semi-sweet] cooking chocolate, broken into pieces
6 tablespoons water
1½ oz. [3 tablespoons] butter
3 tablespoons double [heavy] cream

In a medium-sized saucepan, combine the water, sugar, vanilla pods and cloves. Place the pan over moderate heat and bring the water to the boil, stirring constantly until the sugar has dissolved. Boil rapidly for 1 minute.

Peel the pears, leaving the stalks on. Slice about ¼-inch from the larger ends so that they can stand upright.

Place the pears upright in the syrup, reduce the heat to low and poach them for 15 to 20 minutes or until they are tender but still firm. Remove the pears from the pan and place them on a serving dish. Set aside to cool completely.

Meanwhile, make the chocolate sauce. In a heatproof bowl, combine the chocolate and water. Place the bowl in a pan of simmering water over low heat and cook, stirring constantly, until the mixture is smooth. Gradually beat in the butter and cream.

Remove the pan from the heat and the bowl from the pan. Pour the sauce over the pears and serve at once.

Pineapple with Kirsch

This very simple dessert is an ideal light and refreshing end to a rich meal.

4 SERVINGS

1 medium-sized fresh pineapple, peeled, cored and thinly sliced into rings
1 tablespoon castor sugar
2 fl. oz. [¼ cup] kirsch

Lay the pineapple rings in a medium-sized, shallow serving dish. Sprinkle on the sugar and pour over the kirsch.

Place the dish in the refrigerator and marinate the pineapple for 3 hours, basting and turning the slices frequently.

Remove the dish from the refrigerator and serve immediately.

Pistachio Ice-Cream

Pistachio Ice-Cream may be served sprinkled with toasted almonds or pistachios. For this ice-cream, an ice-cream container equipped with paddles or a hand-propelled ice-cream churn is essential.

1 PINT [2½ CUPS]

8 fl. oz. single cream [1 cup light cream]
4 oz. [1 cup] pistachios, shelled, blanched and chopped
8 fl. oz. double cream [1 cup heavy cream]
½ teaspoon almond essence
3 egg yolks
2 oz. [¼ cup] sugar
3 fl. oz. [⅜ cup] water
3 egg whites, stiffly beaten

Place the single [light] cream and the nuts in an electric blender. Blend, on and off, for 30 seconds or until the nuts are puréed within the cream.

Spoon the mixture into a small saucepan and, using a wooden spoon, stir in the double [heavy] cream. Place the pan over low heat and cook until the mixture is hot. Remove the pan from the heat. Cover the pan and leave it to cool.

Pour the cream mixture into a small mixing bowl. Beat in the almond essence and set aside.

In a medium-sized mixing bowl, beat

Pineapple with Kirsch is light and refreshing, and takes about 5 minutes to prepare.

the egg yolks with a wire whisk or rotary beater until they are well blended.

In a small saucepan, dissolve the sugar in the water over low heat, stirring constantly. When the sugar has dissolved, increase the heat to moderate and boil the syrup until the temperature reaches 220°F on a sugar thermometer or until a little of the syrup spooned out of the pan and cooled, will form a short thread when drawn out between your index finger and thumb. Remove the pan from the heat and let the syrup stand for 1 minute.

Pour the syrup over the egg yolks, whisking constantly with a wire whisk or rotary beater. Continue whisking until the mixture is thick and fluffy. Mix in the cooled cream mixture. With a metal spoon, fold in the egg whites.

Pour the mixture into an ice-cream container equipped with paddles or into a hand-propelled ice-cream churn, and freeze. Serve as required.

Raspberry Charlotte

This impressive dessert takes a surprisingly short time to prepare. If fresh raspberries are not in season, frozen ones are equally

good to use.

8-10 SERVINGS

25-30 sponge finger biscuits [cookies]
4 oz. [½ cup] castor sugar
8 egg yolks
½ oz. gelatine, dissolved in 2
    tablespoons hot water
1½ lb. fresh raspberries, hulled and
    washed
1¼ pints double cream [3⅛ cups
    heavy cream], stiffly whipped

Line the sides of a 3-pint [2-quart] mould with dampened greaseproof or waxed paper. Place a row of sponge fingers upright all around the inside of the mould, with the curved sides against the side. Do not line the bottom of the mould with biscuits [cookies].

In a heatproof bowl, beat the sugar into the egg yolks with a wire whisk. Continue beating until the mixture is pale yellow and will form a ribbon trail on itself when the whisk is lifted.

Place the mixing bowl over a saucepan of just-simmering water and continue beating, over moderate heat, until the mixture is thick and hot.

Remove the mixing bowl from the heat and stand it in a basin of cold water. Add the dissolved gelatine. Continue to beat the mixture until it is cold. Place the bowl in the refrigerator and leave it to chill for at least 30 minutes.

Strain 1 pound of the berries into a small bowl and measure out 16 fluid ounces [2 cups] of purée. Place the purée in the refrigerator to chill.

With a metal spoon, fold the chilled berry purée into the chilled egg yolk mixture. Add 1 pint [2½ cups] of the cream and stir until well blended.

Pour the mixture into the lined mould and arrange the remaining sponge fingers over the top to cover completely. Trim off any protruding sponge fingers.

Cover the mould with greaseproof or waxed paper and refrigerate for at least 6 hours or overnight.

To unmould the charlotte, remove the paper from the top and run a knife around the edge of the mould. Place a serving dish over the mould and reverse the two, giving a sharp shake. The charlotte should slide out easily. Decorate with the remaining berries and cream.

Raspberry and Redcurrant Compôte

A refreshing way to end a meal, Raspberry and Redcurrant Compôte should be served with vanilla ice-cream or whipped cream.

4-6 SERVINGS

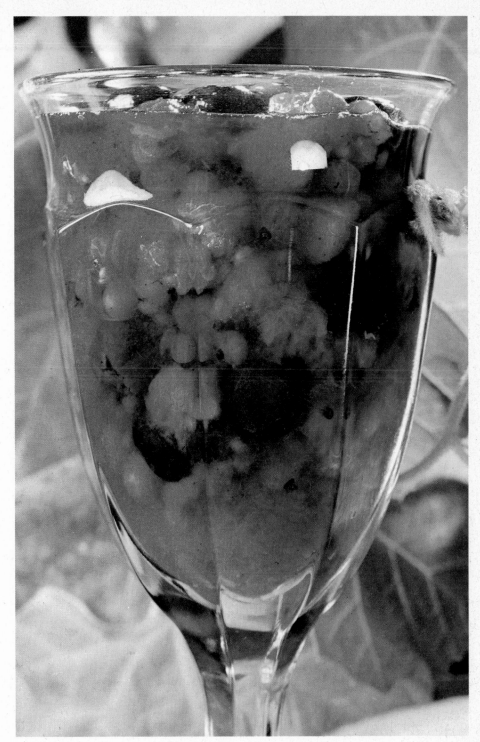

This beautifully elegant Raspberry and Redcurrant Compôte makes a delightful dinner party dessert.

1 lb. redcurrants, trimmed
8 oz. cooking plums, halved and
    stoned
8 oz. canned stoned Morello
    cherries, drained
1 lb. [2 cups] sugar
6 fl. oz. [¾ cup] water
1 lb. raspberries, hulled and washed
2 tablespoons medium sherry

Place the redcurrants, plums, cherries and sugar in a large saucepan. Pour over the water. Place the pan over low heat and stir constantly until the sugar has dissolved. Increase the heat to moderately low and cook the fruit for 20 to 25 minutes, stirring frequently, or until the mixture is soft and pulpy. Stir in the raspberries and continue cooking for a further 5 minutes. Set aside to cool to room temperature.

Stir in the sherry and pour the compôte into a glass serving bowl. Place the bowl in the refrigerator to chill for at least 1 hour.

Remove the dish from the refrigerator and serve immediately.

Redcurrant Cheesecake

☆ ① ① ① ⌛ ⌛

Redcurrant Cheesecake is a delicious combination of tart redcurrants mixed with cream cheese on a crunchy biscuit [cracker] base. The cheesecake is not cooked and is therefore simple and quick to make.

6 SERVINGS

4 oz. [½ cup] plus 1 teaspoon butter, melted

8 oz. crushed digestive biscuits [2 cups crushed graham crackers]

1 teaspoon ground cinnamon

1 lb. cream cheese

2 oz. [¼ cup] castor sugar

4 fl. oz. single cream [½ cup light cream]

1¼ lb. redcurrants, trimmed

½ oz. gelatine, dissolved in 2 tablespoons hot water

15 fl. oz. double cream [1⅞ cups heavy cream]

1 egg white, stiffly beaten

This filling, delicious Redcurrant Cheesecake tastes even better than it looks!

Lightly grease a 9-inch loose-bottomed cake tin with the teaspoon of butter.

In a medium-sized mixing bowl, combine the crushed biscuits [crackers], the remaining melted butter and the cinnamon together with a wooden spoon. Line the base of the cake tin with the biscuit [cracker] mixture, pressing it firmly against the bottom of the tin with your fingers. Set aside.

In a medium-sized mixing bowl, beat the cream cheese and sugar together with the wooden spoon until the mixture is smooth and creamy. Stir in the single [light] cream and 1 pound of the redcurrants. Beat in the dissolved gelatine mixture and spoon the mixture on to the biscuit [cracker] base. Place the tin in the refrigerator to chill for 30 minutes or until

the mixture has set.

Meanwhile, in a large mixing bowl, beat the double [heavy] cream with a wire whisk or rotary beater until it forms stiff peaks. With a large metal spoon, fold the egg white into the cream.

Remove the cake tin from the refrigerator. Spoon the cream mixture on to the cheesecake, making swirling patterns with the back of the spoon.

Sprinkle the remaining redcurrants over the cream. Serve immediately, or return to the refrigerator until required.

Rhubarb and Ginger Compôte

☆ ① ① ① ⌛

Rhubarb and Ginger Compôte illustrates how well gin complements the flavour of rhubarb. It makes an ideal dessert for a summer dinner party. Serve with cream.

4 SERVINGS

8 oz. [1 cup] sugar
4 fl. oz. [½ cup] water
2 lb. fresh rhubarb, trimmed,
   washed and chopped
8 fl. oz. [1 cup] gin
1 tablespoon finely grated orange
   rind
¼ teaspoon grated nutmeg
½ teaspoon ground ginger
1 tablespoon preserved ginger,
   finely chopped

In a large, heavy-based saucepan, dissolve the sugar in the water over low heat, stirring frequently. When the sugar has dissolved, increase the heat to moderately high and bring the syrup to the boil, without stirring.

Add the rhubarb, gin, orange rind, nutmeg and ground ginger to the pan and reduce the heat to low. Simmer the mixture for 25 minutes or until the rhubarb is tender. Using a slotted spoon, transfer the rhubarb to a serving dish.

Increase the heat to high and bring the cooking liquid to the boil. Boil for 10 to 12 minutes or until the liquid has reduced by about one-third. Remove the pan from the heat and pour the syrup over the rhubarb. Sprinkle the chopped ginger over the top and put the dish in the refrigerator to chill for at least 30 minutes.

Remove the dish from the refrigerator and serve immediately.

Russian Gooseberry Cream

An easy-to-make dessert, Russian Gooseberry Cream has a delicate creamy texture. Serve with langues de chats.

4 SERVINGS

1 lb. gooseberries, trimmed and
   washed
1 tablespoon dried elderflowers
   (optional)
10 fl. oz. [1¼ cups] water
4 fl. oz. [½ cup] dry white wine
   very finely grated rind of 1
   lemon
4 oz. [½ cup] sugar
3 eggs, separated

In a medium-sized saucepan, bring the goosebarries, elderflowers if you are using them, water, wine and lemon rind to the boil over moderate heat. Reduce the heat to low and simmer, stirring occasionally, for 20 minutes or until the gooseberries are soft.

Remove the pan from the heat. Using the back of a wooden spoon, rub the gooseberry mixture through a strainer into a bowl. Discard the pulp left in the strainer. Rinse and thoroughly wipe dry the saucepan.

Return the purée to the saucepan. Add the sugar and place the pan over low heat. Using the wooden spoon, stir the purée mixture until the sugar has dissolved. Remove the pan from the heat.

Beat the egg yolks into the gooseberry mixture and set it aside to cool to lukewarm.

In a medium-sized mixing bowl, beat the egg whites with a wire whisk or rotary beater until they form stiff peaks. Set aside.

With a metal spoon, fold the egg whites into the gooseberry mixture. Pour the gooseberry mixture into a large glass serving bowl or individual serving dishes. Set aside in a cool place for 1 hour or until the cream has set. Either serve immediately or chill the cream in the refrigerator until required.

This unusual dessert combines gooseberries, elderflowers, wine, lemon, sugar and eggs, in a rich purée. Serve Russian Gooseberry Cream, after a light main course, with delicate langues de chats.

Sachertorte

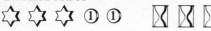

A rich moist chocolate cake, Sachertorte, the speciality of the elegant Sacher Hotel in Vienna, is almost the national cake of Austria. Sachertorte is traditionally served with lots of freshly whipped cream.

6-8 SERVINGS

4 oz. [½ cup] plus 1 teaspoon butter
6 oz. dark [semi-sweet] cooking
   chocolate, broken into pieces
6 oz. [¾ cup] sugar
1 teaspoon vanilla essence
6 egg yolks
3 oz. [¾ cup] flour
8 egg whites, stiffly whipped
6 tablespoons apricot jam

CHOCOLATE ICING

8 oz. dark [semi-sweet] cooking
   chocolate, broken into pieces
4 fl. oz. double cream [½ cup heavy
   cream]
12 oz. icing sugar [3 cups
   confectioners' sugar]

Preheat the oven to moderate 350°F (Gas Mark 4, 180°C). With the teaspoon of butter, grease a 9-inch cake tin with a removable base. Set aside.

In a heatproof bowl set over a pan of simmering water, melt the chocolate over low heat. Remove the pan from the heat and lift the bowl out of the pan. Set aside.

In a mixing bowl, beat the remaining butter and the sugar together until they are light and fluffy. Beat in the melted chocolate and the vanilla essence.

Gradually beat in the egg yolks, one at a time, adding a tablespoon of flour with each yolk. With a metal spoon, fold in the remaining flour, and then the egg whites. Spoon the batter into the prepared cake tin and smooth over the top with the back of the spoon. Place the tin in the centre of the oven. Bake for 50 minutes to 1 hour or until a skewer inserted into the centre of the cake comes out clean.

Remove the cake from the oven and set it aside to cool in the tin for 30 minutes.

The dessert to end all desserts—rich, elegant Sachertorte.

Turn the cake out of the tin on to a wire rack and slice it in half, crosswise. Set aside to cool completely.

Meanwhile, in a small saucepan, melt the apricot jam over low heat, stirring constantly. Remove from the heat and set the jam aside to cool to lukewarm.

Meanwhile, make the icing. In a heat-proof bowl set over a pan of simmering water, melt the chocolate over low heat. Remove the pan from the heat and lift the bowl out of the pan. Set aside to cool for 10 minutes. Beat in the cream and icing [confectioners'] sugar, beating until the mixture is smooth.

Using a flat-bladed knife, spread half the apricot glaze over the top of the bottom cake half and sandwich the two halves together. Spread the rest of the glaze over the top and sides of the cake.

Rinse the knife and spread the chocolate icing over the top and sides of the cake, ensuring that the icing is smooth.

Place the cake on a decorative serving plate and set aside in a cool place for 2 hours, or until the icing has set.

Sherry Jelly [Gelatin]

This simple-to-make dish may be made well in advance and, for the best flavour, removed from the refrigerator and un-moulded 30 minutes before serving.

4-6 SERVINGS

1½ oz. gelatine
4 fl. oz. [½ cup] cold water
8 fl. oz. [1 cup] boiling water
4 oz. [½ cup] sugar
¼ teaspoon salt
4 fl. oz. [½ cup] orange juice
2 tablespoons lemon juice
12 fl. oz. [1½ cups] medium sherry

Place the gelatine and cold water in a mixing bowl. Pour over the boiling water and stir until the gelatine has dissolved. Add the sugar and stir until it has dissolved. Stir in the salt. Set the gelatine mixture aside to cool for 10 minutes.

In a large jug, combine the orange juice, lemon juice and sherry. Pour the gelatine mixture into the jug, stirring constantly.

Rinse a 1½-pint [1-quart] mould in water. Pour the sherry mixture into the mould and chill in the refrigerator for 4 hours or until the jelly [gelatin] has set.

Remove the mould from the refrigerator. Pull the mixture away from the sides of the mould and quickly dip the bottom of the mould in hot water. Invert a chilled serving dish over the mould and reverse. The jelly [gelatin] should slide out easily. Serve immediately.

Sorbet with Apricots

Sorbet with Apricots is a light, refreshing dessert to serve after a rich main course.

4 SERVINGS

1 lb. canned apricot halves, drained and juice reserved
2 oz. [¼ cup] castor sugar
2 tablespoons fresh orange juice
2 tablespoons fresh lemon juice
2 egg whites, stiffly beaten
2 drops vanilla essence

Set the thermostat of the refrigerator to its coldest setting.

Put half the apricots in a blender and purée them at high speed. Pour the purée into a large measuring jug and repeat the process with the remaining apricots. Measure the purée and mix in enough of the reserved can juice to make 16 fluid ounces [2 cups].

Transfer the purée to a mixing bowl and stir in the sugar, orange and lemon juice. Using a wire whisk or rotary beater, whisk the egg whites into the

Smooth Sorbet with Apricots.

mixture until it is smooth. Stir in the vanilla essence. Pour the mixture into a freezer tray and place the tray in the frozen food storage compartment of the refrigerator. Freeze for 30 minutes or until the mixture has begun to set around the edges.

Remove the tray from the refrigerator and scrape the apricot mixture into a medium-sized mixing bowl. Using a wire whisk or rotary beater, beat the mixture until it is smooth. Return the mixture to the freezer tray and the tray to the frozen food storage compartment. Freeze for a further 4 hours or until the sorbet is firm.

Meanwhile, chill 4 individual serving glasses in the refrigerator for 30 minutes before you serve the sorbet.

Remove the glasses from the refrigerator and the freezer tray from the frozen food storage compartment. Using a table-spoon which has been dipped in hot water, spoon the sorbet into the chilled glasses. Serve immediately.

Strawberries Romanoff

 ① ① ① ✕ ✕

This glorious dish makes a perfect dessert for a summer dinner party. Serve after a fairly filling main course.

4-6 SERVINGS

2 lb. fresh strawberries, hulled and washed
4 fl. oz. [½ cup] orange-flavoured liqueur
2 fl. oz. [¼ cup] fresh orange juice, strained
CREME CHANTILLY
10 fl. oz. double cream [1¼ cups heavy cream], chilled
1 teaspoon vanilla essence
1 teaspoon castor sugar

Place the strawberries in a deep bowl and pour the orange-flavoured liqueur and orange juice over them. Cover the bowl and place it in the refrigerator.

Leave the strawberries to chill for 2 hours, basting them occasionally with the liquid in the bowl. Transfer the strawberries and liquid to a serving dish.

To make the crème, in a chilled, medium-sized mixing bowl, beat the cream with a wire whisk or rotary beater until it forms soft peaks. Add the vanilla essence and sugar and beat until the mixture forms stiff peaks.

Fill a forcing bag with the crème chantilly and pipe it around the strawberries, or in decorative swirls over the top of them. Serve at once.

Strawberry Shortcake

 ① ① ✕

A lovely dessert for a summer lunch or dinner, Strawberry Shortcake is an attractive way to serve strawberries.

4-8 SERVINGS

6 oz. [¾ cup] plus 1 teaspoon butter, softened
8 oz. [2 cups] flour
2 oz. icing sugar [½ cup confectioners' sugar]
1 egg yolk
10 fl. oz. double cream [1¼ cups heavy cream]
1 lb. strawberries, hulled and washed
2 tablespoons castor sugar

Using the teaspoon of butter, lightly grease two baking sheets.

Sift the flour and icing [confectioners'] sugar into a mixing bowl. With a table knife, cut the remaining butter into small pieces and add it to the mixture.

Using your hands, mix the flour and butter together to make a smooth dough.

With the knife, stir in the egg yolk and 2 tablespoons of the cream. Mix very well and form the dough into a ball. Cover the dough with greaseproof or waxed paper and place it in the refrigerator to chill for 30 minutes.

Preheat the oven to fairly hot 375°F (Gas Mark 5, 190°C).

Divide the dough into two equal pieces. On a floured surface, roll out each piece into a 9-inch circle.

Place the circles on the prepared baking sheets and place them in the oven. Bake for 12 to 15 minutes or until the edges of the shortcakes are golden brown.

Remove the sheets from the oven and carefully transfer the shortcakes to a wire rack to cool.

Meanwhile, thinly slice the strawberries. In a medium-sized mixing bowl, beat the remaining cream and the sugar with a wire whisk or rotary beater until the mixture forms stiff peaks.

Lightly fold the strawberries into the cream. Spoon the mixture into a heap in the centre of one of the shortcakes.

With a sharp knife, cut the other circle into eight equal triangles. Pile the triangles up against the strawberry mixture and serve at once.

Strawberry Ziggurat

  ① ① ① ✕ ✕ ✕

Named after the Ziggurat temple built in ancient Babylonia, Strawberry Ziggurat makes a very impressive and decorative dessert, ideal for summer buffet parties.

8-10 SERVINGS

7 egg whites
14 oz. [1¾ cups] castor sugar
FILLING
1 pint double cream [2½ cups heavy cream]
4 tablespoons orange-flavoured liqueur
2 lb. strawberries, hulled and washed

Preheat the oven to very cool 275°F (Gas Mark 1, 140°C).

Cut out a circle of non-stick silicone paper 9-inches in diameter and place it on a baking sheet.

Cut out another circle of non-stick silicone paper 5⅜-inches in diameter and place it on a second baking sheet.

In a medium-sized mixing bowl, beat 4 egg whites together with a wire whisk or rotary beater until they form stiff peaks. Add 4 teaspoons of the sugar and continue beating for 1 minute.

Using the side of a metal spoon as a cutting edge, fold in 8 ounces [1 cup] of the remaining sugar.

Spoon the mixture into a forcing bag fitted with a large plain nozzle.

Pipe the mixture on to the paper circles on the baking sheets, covering them completely.

Place the baking sheets in the centre of the oven and bake for 1 hour or until the meringues are firm and very lightly browned.

Meanwhile, rinse and dry the forcing bag and set it aside.

Remove the baking sheets from the oven. Carefully transfer the meringues from the baking sheets to a wire rack. Set aside to cool.

Cut out three more circles of non-stick silicone paper: 7⅜-inches, 4⅜-inches and 2½-inches in diameter. Place the largest circle on one baking sheet and the other two circles, well spaced, on the second baking sheet. Set aside.

In a medium-sized mixing bowl, beat the remaining egg whites with a wire whisk or rotary beater until they form stiff peaks. Add 1 tablespoon of the remaining sugar and beat for 1 minute.

Using the side of a metal spoon as a cutting edge, fold in the remaining sugar.

Spoon the mixture into the forcing bag and pipe it on to the paper circles on the baking sheets, covering them completely.

Place the baking sheets in the centre of the oven and bake for 1 hour or until the meringues are firm and light brown.

Remove the baking sheets from the oven and carefully transfer the meringues to a wire rack. Leave them to cool.

Meanwhile, make the filling. In a large mixing bowl, beat the cream and liqueur together with a wire whisk or rotary beater until they form stiff peaks.

Carefully peel off the silicone paper from the meringue circles. Discard the paper.

Place the largest meringue circle on a large, flat serving plate. Spread a thick layer of the cream mixture over the circle to cover it completely. Cover the cream with some of the strawberries, standing them broad base down.

Place the second largest circle over the strawberries. Spread a layer of cream over it and cover with strawberries.

Continue making layers until you come to the smallest circle.

Spread the remaining cream on the bottom of the smallest circle and place it on top of the pyramid.

Place the ziggurat in the refrigerator and chill for 30 minutes before serving.

Simple to make, stunning to look at, Strawberries Romanoff makes the perfect dessert for a special lunch or dinner party.

Tipsy Pudding

☆☆　　①①①✕✕

Rich with whisky and sherry, Tipsy Pudding makes a splendidly impressive dessert for a dinner party.

6 SERVINGS

1 teaspoon vegetable oil
3 eggs
3 oz. [⅜ cup] castor sugar
3 oz. [¾ cup] flour, sifted
½ teaspoon vanilla essence
2 tablespoons cornflour [cornstarch], sifted
8 oz. cherry jam
3 fl. oz. [⅜ cup] whisky
3 fl. oz. [⅜ cup] sherry
TOPPING
2 egg yolks
1 teaspoon cornflour [cornstarch]
1 tablespoon sugar
¼ teaspoon vanilla essence
10 fl. oz. [1¼ cups] milk, scalded
10 fl. oz. double cream [1¼ cups heavy cream], stiffly whipped
2 oz. [½ cup] almonds, blanched, split and lightly toasted

Preheat the oven to hot 425°F (Gas Mark 7, 220°C).

This impressive Tipsy Pudding contains whisky and sherry and makes a special treat for dinner!

Line a 10- x 16-inch Swiss [jelly] roll tin with non-stick silicone paper or foil. If you use foil, grease it with the teaspoon of vegetable oil.

Put the eggs and sugar in a medium-sized heatproof mixing bowl. Place the bowl over a pan half-filled with hot water. Set the pan over low heat.

Using a wire whisk or rotary beater, beat the eggs and sugar together until the mixture is thick and makes a ribbon trail on itself when the whisk is lifted.

Remove the bowl from the saucepan. Using a metal spoon or spatula, fold in the flour and the vanilla essence.

Pour the batter into the prepared tin and smooth it down with a knife.

Place the tin in the oven and bake for 8 minutes, or until a skewer inserted into the centre of the cake comes out clean. Remove the tin from the oven. Dust a working surface with the cornflour [cornstarch]. Reverse the cake out on to the working surface. Remove the silicone paper or foil from the bottom of the cake.

Using a knife, spread the jam evenly over the surface of the cake. Roll it up Swiss [jelly] roll style and place it in a long, deep serving dish. Set it aside.

When the roll has cooled to room temperature, pour the whisky and sherry over the surface.

To make the topping, in a heatproof bowl, beat the egg yolks, cornflour [cornstarch], sugar and vanilla essence together with a wire whisk or rotary beater.

Beat in the hot milk. Place the bowl over a pan of simmering water and cook, stirring constantly with a wooden spoon, until the custard thickens and coats the back of the spoon.

Remove the bowl from the heat and pour the custard over the cake. Chill the dish in the refrigerator for 1 hour.

Remove the cake from the refrigerator. Using a palette knife, spread the cream over the top and sides of the cake and stick in the split almonds all over the surface. Serve immediately.

Trifle

☆☆　　①①①✕✕✕

This luscious dessert should be served in

small quantities after a light meal.

4-6 SERVINGS

6 trifle sponge squares [6 small stale sponge cakes], each sliced into two layers
2 fl. oz. [¼ cup] orange-flavoured liqueur
2 tablespoons fresh orange juice
10 oz. [1¼ cups] sugar
10 fl. oz. [1¼ cups] custard
4 large oranges, peeled, white pith removed and thinly sliced
5 fl. oz. double cream [⅝ cup heavy cream], stiffly whipped

Place the sponge slices in one layer in a large dish. Sprinkle over the liqueur and orange juice and set aside for 30 minutes or until all the liquid has been absorbed.

In a heavy saucepan, dissolve the sugar over low heat, shaking the pan occasionally. Increase the heat to moderate and boil the syrup, shaking the pan occasionally, until it turns a rich golden brown.

Remove the pan from the heat. Place it in a bowl of hot water to keep the caramel hot.

Arrange one-third of the soaked sponge slices in a medium-sized glass serving dish. Spoon over one-third of the custard, smoothing it over evenly with the back of a spoon. Lay one-third of the orange slices over the custard to cover it completely. Trickle over one-third of the caramel in a thin stream.

Continue making layers in the same way, ending with a layer of caramel-coated orange slices.

Place the trifle in the refrigerator and chill it for 2 hours.

Fill a small forcing bag, fitted with a star-shaped nozzle, with the cream.

Remove the trifle from the refrigerator and pipe the cream over the top in decorative swirls. Serve immediately.

This unusual version of the classic British Trifle contains oranges, orange liqueur and caramel.

377

Vacherin aux Noisettes

Vacherin aux Noisettes is a scrumptious combination of hazelnut-flavoured meringue enclosing a chocolate-cream filling and topped with fresh, juicy apricots.

4-6 SERVINGS

2 teaspoons butter
4 egg whites
8 oz. [1 cup] castor sugar
½ teaspoon vanilla essence
4 oz. [⅔ cup] ground hazelnuts
4 oz. dark [semi-sweet] cooking chocolate, cut into pieces
2 tablespoons water
8 oz. double cream [1 cup heavy cream], stiffly whipped
3 tablespoons chopped hazelnuts, toasted
4 fresh apricots, blanched, peeled, halved and stoned

Preheat the oven to moderate 350°F (Gas Mark 4, 180°C). With the butter, lightly grease two 7-inch loose-bottomed sandwich tins and set them aside.

In a large mixing bowl, beat the egg whites with a wire whisk or rotary beater until they form stiff peaks. Beat in 2 tablespoons of the sugar and continue beating until the peaks are very stiff and glossy. (You should be able to turn the bowl upside down without the mixture falling out.) Using a metal spoon, fold in the remaining sugar. Stir in the vanilla essence and fold in the ground hazelnuts.

Pour half the meringue mixture into each of the prepared tins and smooth with a flat-bladed knife. Place the tins in the oven and bake for 30 to 40 minutes or until the meringues are light gold and firm. Remove the tins from the oven and allow the meringue cakes to cool in the tins for 5 minutes. Remove the meringues from the tins, carefully transfer them to a wire rack and leave them to cool completely.

Meanwhile, place the chocolate and water in a heatproof bowl placed over a pan of hot water. Set the pan over low heat and cook, stirring occasionally, until the chocolate has melted. Remove the pan from the heat and the bowl from the pan. Set aside to cool.

When the chocolate is cool but not set, using a metal spoon, fold in half of the cream and the toasted hazelnuts.

With a knife, spread the filling over one of the meringue cakes. Place the other cake over the top.

Wash the knife and use it to spread the remaining cream over the top of the vacherin. Arrange the apricot halves decoratively over the cream and serve immediately.

Yogurt Crumb Cake

Yogurt Crumb Cake, a combination of yogurt, cream and apricots on a crunchy biscuit [cracker] base, makes a delicious and decorative dessert.

8 SERVINGS

4 oz. [½ cup] plus 1 teaspoon butter, melted
8 oz. crushed digestive biscuits [2 cups crushed graham crackers]
1 teaspoon ground cinnamon
10 fl. oz. [1¼ cups] yogurt
16 fl. oz. double cream [2 cups heavy cream]
1 tablespoon lemon juice
2 oz. [¼ cup] castor sugar,
1 lb. fresh apricots blanched, peeled, halved, stoned and finely chopped
½ oz. gelatine, dissolved in 4 tablespoons hot water
2 oz. chocolate caraque
2 oz. [½ cup] slivered almonds, toasted

Lightly grease a 9-inch loose-bottomed cake tin with the teaspoon of butter. Set aside.

In a medium-sized mixing bowl, combine the crushed biscuits [crackers], the remaining melted butter and the cinnamon with a wooden spoon. Line the base of the cake tin with the biscuit [cracker] mixture, pressing it firmly against the bottom of the tin with your fingers or with the back of the wooden spoon. Set aside.

In a medium-sized bowl, beat the yogurt, half of the cream, the lemon juice and the sugar together with a wooden spoon until the mixture is smooth and creamy. Stir in the apricots. Beat in the dissolved gelatine mixture. Set the yogurt mixture aside in a cool place for 20 minutes or until it is on the point of setting.

Using a large metal spoon, spoon the mixture on to the biscuit [cracker] base. Place the tin in the refrigerator and chill for 30 minutes or until the mixture has set.

Meanwhile, in a medium-sized mixing bowl, beat the remaining double [heavy] cream with a wire whisk or rotary beater until it forms stiff peaks.

Remove the cake tin from the refrigerator and carefully spoon the whipped cream over the top of the cake, making decorative, swirling patterns with the back of the spoon.

Sprinkle the chocolate caraque and toasted almonds over the cream. Serve immediately or chill in the refrigerator until required.

Zuccotto

ITALIAN PUMPKIN-SHAPED CREAM AND SPONGE DESSERT

Zuccotto is a well-known Italian dessert which resembles a pumpkin in shape. Serve this rich, spectacular-looking dessert at a special dinner party.

8-10 SERVINGS

1 pint double cream [2½ cups heavy cream], beaten until stiff
1 oz. [¼ cup] plus 2 tablespoons icing [confectioners'] sugar
2 oz. [½ cup] hazelnuts, toasted
8 oz. fresh cherries, halved and stoned
4 oz. dark [semi-sweet] dessert chocolate, finely chopped or grated
2 fl. oz. [¼ cup] brandy
2 fl. oz. [¼ cup] orange-flavoured liqueur
2 x 8-inch chocolate sponge cakes, sliced in 2 horizontally
2 tablespoons cocoa powder

In a small mixing bowl, combine the cream and 1 ounce icing sugar [¼ cup confectioners' sugar]. Using a metal spoon, fold in the hazelnuts, cherries and chocolate. Chill the bowl in the refrigerator.

In a small mixing bowl, mix together the brandy and orange-flavoured liqueur and set aside.

Line a 2-pint [1½-quart] pudding basin with three-quarters of the sponge, cutting it into pieces with a sharp knife so that it fits the shape of the basin. Sprinkle the brandy mixture over the sponge lining.

Remove the cream mixture from the refrigerator and spoon it into the sponge case. Use the remaining sponge to cover it. Chill the basin in the refrigerator for 2 hours.

Remove the basin from the refrigerator. Run a knife around the edge of the pudding to loosen it. Invert a serving plate over the basin and, holding the two firmly together, reverse them. The zuccotto should slide out easily.

Sprinkle half of the remaining icing [confectioners'] sugar neatly over one-quarter of the pudding. Sprinkle half the cocoa powder over a second quarter, then repeat this over the other half of the pudding so that the zuccotto has 4 alternating segments of colour.

Serve immediately.

Zuccotto is an unusual-shaped Italian dessert containing cream, cherries, chocolate and liqueurs. Serve as a rich finale to a special dinner.

Apple Pudding

A delicious, sustaining dish of Scandinavian origin, this pudding is the perfect dessert for either a dinner party or a family meal. If zwieback is not available use a dark, dry brown bread.

4 SERVINGS

- 4 oz. [1 cup] zwieback, crushed
- ½ teaspoon ground allspice
- 1½ oz. [3 tablespoons] butter, melted
- 1½ lb. thick apple purée
- ½ teaspoon ground cinnamon
- 12 fl. oz. double cream [1½ cups heavy cream]
- 8 oz. white grapes, coated with egg white and sugar

In a mixing bowl, combine the zwieback, allspice and butter. Using one-half of the mixture, line the bottom of a medium-sized round cake tin with a removable base. Top with half the apple purée and sprinkle over half the cinnamon.

In a second medium-sized mixing bowl, beat the cream with a wire whisk or rotary beater until it forms stiff peaks. Spoon about one-half of the cream over the apple purée and cinnamon. Top with the remaining crushed zwieback, apple

purée and cinnamon and then with the remaining cream. Bring it up into decorative swirls with a flat-bladed knife. Arrange the white grapes decoratively over the top of the mixture and chill in the refrigerator for 1 hour.

To serve, remove the tin from the refrigerator, remove the pudding from the tin and place it on a serving dish. Serve at once.

Banana Cream Pie

This delicious and inexpensive American banana pie is made with shortcrust pastry and topped with meringue.

6 SERVINGS

PASTRY
- 6 oz. [1½ cups] flour
- ¼ teaspoon salt
- 3¼ oz. [½ cup] vegetable fat or lard
- 2 tablespoons iced water

FILLING
- 3 egg yolks

Apple Pudding, a mixture of apple purée, zwieback and cream, makes a delightfully inexpensive dessert.

- 3 oz. [⅜ cup] castor sugar
- ¼ teaspoon salt
- 2 tablespoons cornflour [cornstarch]
- 1 tablespoon butter
- 16 fl. oz. [2 cups] milk
- 1 teaspoon vanilla essence
- 2 ripe bananas, peeled and sliced

TOPPING
- 3 egg whites
- 6 oz. [¾ cup] castor sugar
- 2 tablespoons shredded almonds

Sift the flour and salt into a mixing bowl. Add the vegetable fat and with your fingertips rub it into the flour until it resembles coarse breadcrumbs. Add a tablespoon of iced water and mix and knead the dough until it is smooth. Add more water if the dough is too dry. Roll the dough into a ball, cover it and chill it in the refrigerator for 30 minutes.

Preheat the oven to fairly hot 400°F (Gas Mark 6, 200°C).

On a floured board, roll the dough out and line a 9-inch pie tin. Put the lined pie tin in the refrigerator for 10 minutes.

When you remove the pie tin from the refrigerator, prick the dough with a fork, line it with greaseproof paper and weigh it down with dried beans or peas. Bake the shell for 10 minutes.

Remove the greaseproof paper and bake for 5 minutes more, or until the shell is golden.

Reset the oven to cool 300°F (Gas Mark 2, 150°C).

To prepare the filling, beat the egg yolks in a heatproof bowl with a whisk. Gradually beat in the sugar, salt, cornflour [cornstarch] and butter.

Put the milk in a small saucepan and, over moderate heat, bring it almost to boiling point. Pour slowly on to the egg mixture, stirring continuously. Place the bowl in a pan of boiling water and cook the custard until it thickens. Cool the custard and then add the vanilla essence. Arrange the banana slices in the pie shell. Pour the custard over them.

Beat the egg whites in a small bowl with a rotary beater until they are stiff. Beat in one tablespoon of sugar and then fold in the remaining sugar. Pile the meringue on top of the custard and spread to cover completely. Sprinkle with the almonds and bake for 15 to 20 minutes or until the meringue is lightly browned. Serve cold.

Fig Flutter

This light, steamed pudding must be served as soon as it is ready because it falls as it cools. Serve with custard.

6 SERVINGS

3 oz. [⅜ cup] plus 1 teaspoon butter
5 slices of white bread, crusts
   removed, cut into pieces
10 fl. oz. [1¼ cups] milk
6 egg yolks
4 oz. [½ cup] sugar
3 oz. [½ cup] ground almonds
½ teaspoon grated nutmeg
5 oz. [1 cup] dried figs, stalks
   removed and chopped
½ teaspoon almond essence
6 egg whites

Grease a 2-pint [1½-quart] soufflé dish with the teaspoon of butter. Tie a double band of greaseproof or waxed paper 5 inches wide around the soufflé dish.

In a small saucepan, combine the bread and milk over low heat. Simmer, stirring occasionally, until the bread has blended into the milk. Remove the pan from the heat and stir in the remaining butter until it has melted. Set aside.

In a large mixing bowl, beat the egg yolks and sugar together with a wire whisk or rotary beater until the mixture is pale and fluffy. Stir in the almonds, nutmeg, figs, almond essence and the milk and bread mixture.

In another large mixing bowl, beat the egg whites with a wire whisk or rotary beater until they are stiff. With a metal spoon, carefully fold the egg whites into the egg yolk mixture.

Pour the mixture into the soufflé dish. Place the dish in the top part of a steamer, the lower half of which is three-quarters filled with hot water. Cover and place over high heat. Bring the water to the boil. Reduce the heat to moderate and steam the pudding for 50 minutes.

Remove the pudding from the steamer and serve immediately.

Honeydew Melon with Blackcurrant Iced Mousse

A cool dessert to finish a summer dinner party, Honeydew Melon with Blackcurrant Iced Mousse is superb.

6 SERVINGS

10 fl. oz. [1¼ cups] blackcurrant juice
5 fl. oz. [⅝ cup] water
2 oz. [¼ cup] sugar
   grated rind and juice of 1 lemon
½ oz. gelatine, dissolved in 2
   tablespoons hot water
1 egg white
1 large honeydew melon

Set the thermostat of the refrigerator to its coldest setting.

In a saucepan, combine the black-

Honeydew Melon with Blackcurrant Iced Mousse.

currant juice, water, sugar and lemon rind. Bring to the boil over moderately high heat and boil for 4 minutes. Remove the pan from the heat and stir in the lemon juice and dissolved gelatine. Pour the mixture through a strainer into a freezer tray. Place the freezer tray in the frozen food storage compartment of the refrigerator and chill for 30 minutes.

In a small bowl, beat the egg white with a wire whisk or rotary beater until it forms stiff peaks. Whisk the blackcurrant mixture into the egg white. Spoon the mixture back into the freezer tray and return to the storage compartment. Freeze the mixture for a further 1 hour.

Remove the freezer tray from the refrigerator and turn the blackcurrant mixture into the mixing bowl. Whisk for 1 minute. Return the mixture to the freezer tray and replace it in the storage compartment. Continue whisking every hour for 4 hours, then leave the iced mousse to freeze overnight.

With a sharp knife, slice the melon crossways into six slices. Scoop out the seeds and place the slices on individual plates. Spoon the mousse into the centre of each piece. Serve at once.

Cold Lemon Soufflé

A light, refreshing dessert, Cold Lemon Soufflé is particularly good after a heavy meal. The soufflé looks most attractive if it is set in a 6-inch soufflé dish, tied with a raised collar of greaseproof or waxed paper. The paper is removed after the soufflé is set and the top of the soufflé may then be decorated with chopped or slivered nuts, biscuits [cookies] or glacé cherries and cream. The soufflé may also be set in a decorative glass or china serving bowl or it may be used as a flan filling.

6 SERVINGS

5 egg yolks
4 oz. [½ cup] castor sugar
  finely grated rind and juice of
  3 lemons
½ oz. gelatine, dissolved in 4
  tablespoons hot water
10 fl. oz. double cream [1¼ cups
  heavy cream]
5 egg whites

In a medium-sized heatproof mixing bowl, combine the egg yolks and sugar. Put the bowl over a saucepan half full of hot water. Place the pan over moderate heat and, using a wire whisk or rotary beater, beat the mixture for 15 to 20 minutes or until it is thick.

Add the lemon rind and juice and continue beating until well mixed and the mixture makes a ribbon trail on itself when the whisk is lifted.

Alternatively, beat the egg yolks, sugar and lemon rind for 5 minutes or until thick in an electric mixer. Add the lemon juice to the egg mixture and continue beating for 15 to 20 minutes or until the mixture makes a ribbon trail on itself when the beater is lifted.

Remove the bowl from the pan and set it in a large bowl or baking dish containing cold water. Continue whisking until the mixture and the bowl are both quite cold.

Pour in the gelatine and stir well.

In a medium-sized mixing bowl, beat the cream with a wire whisk or rotary beater until it is thick but not stiff, then carefully fold it into the egg and lemon mixture. Place the bowl in the refrigerator and chill the mixture for 45 minutes to 1 hour, or until it is cold but not quite set.

In a large bowl, beat the egg whites with a wire whisk until they form stiff peaks. Using a large metal spoon, carefully fold the egg whites into the soufflé mixture. Turn the mixture into a soufflé dish or serving bowl and place in the refrigerator to set for 4 hours or overnight before serving.

382

Mixed Fruit Cream

A refreshing dessert, Mixed Fruit Cream takes only a few minutes to prepare and makes a delightful ending to a summer meal.

4 SERVINGS

8 oz. cream cheese
5 fl. oz. single cream [⅝ cup light
  cream]
1 tablespoon light rum
2 tablespoons sugar
1 medium-sized pear, peeled,
  cored and finely chopped
2 medium-sized peaches, peeled,
  stoned and finely chopped
¼ medium-sized melon, peeled,
  seeded and finely chopped
1 oz. chocolate, grated
4 oz. grapes, halved and seeded

In a medium-sized mixing bowl, beat the cream cheese, cream and rum together with a wooden spoon until they are blended. Stir in the sugar. Add the pear, peaches and melon and mix well to blend.

Spoon the mixture into four individual serving bowls or dessert glasses. Sprinkle the grated chocolate over the top, and arrange the grapes in a circle around the edge of each serving bowl. Serve immediately.

October Cobbler

A traditional English fruit pie, October Cobbler may be made with any fruit plentiful in the autumn — blackberries, apples, pears, damson plums, etc. Serve October Cobbler hot, with whipped cream.

4 SERVINGS

PASTRY
6 oz. [1½ cups] flour
⅛ teaspoon salt
3 oz. [⅜ cup] butter
2 tablespoons sugar
1 small egg
1 to 2 tablespoons iced water
1 egg yolk, well beaten with 2
  tablespoons milk

FILLING
1 lb. fruit, prepared and
  washed
2 medium-sized tart cooking
  apples, peeled, cored and chopped
3 tablespoons water
2 oz. [⅓ cup] soft brown sugar
  grated rind of 1 small orange
¼ teaspoon ground cinnamon

Cooling, tangy Cold Lemon Soufflé makes a beautifully elegant end to a heavy meal.

2 teaspoons arrowroot dissolved in
  1 tablespoon orange juice

First, make the pastry. Sift the flour and salt into a medium-sized mixing bowl. Add the butter and cut it into small pieces with a table knife. With your fingers, rub the butter into the flour until the mixture resembles fine breadcrumbs. Stir in 1 tablespoon of the sugar.

In a small mixing bowl, beat the egg and 1 tablespoon of the water together with a fork. Make a well in the centre of the flour mixture and pour in the egg and water mixture. With a knife, quickly mix the ingredients into a firm dough. Add a little more of the water if the dough is too dry. With your fingertips, lightly knead the dough until it is smooth.

Shape the dough into a ball and wrap it in greaseproof or waxed paper. Chill the dough in the refrigerator for 30 minutes.

Meanwhile, make the filling. Place the fruit, apples, water, sugar, orange rind and cinnamon in a medium-sized saucepan. Set the pan over moderately high heat and bring the mixture to the boil, stirring constantly. Reduce the heat to low, cover the pan and simmer, stirring occasionally, for 6 to 8 minutes or until

the fruit is tender.

Stir in the dissolved arrowroot and cook the mixture, stirring constantly, for 3 minutes, or until the liquid has thickened.

Remove the pan from the heat. Spoon the fruit mixture into a medium-sized pie dish. Set aside.

Preheat the oven to fairly hot 400°F (Gas Mark 6, 200°C).

Remove the dough from the refrigerator and place it on a lightly floured board. With a floured rolling pin, roll out the dough into a circle approximately ¼-inch thick.

Using a 2-inch round fluted pastry cutter, cut the dough into circles. Gather the remaining dough into a ball and knead it lightly until it is smooth. Roll the dough out into a strip approximately ⅛-inch thick. With a sharp knife, trim the dough strip to make it ½-inch wide.

Wet the rim of the pie dish with a little cold water. Place the dough strip on the rim of the dish to cover it completely. Trim off any excess dough with a sharp knife and press the ends of the strip together to seal them.

Place the dough circles over the dough strip, pressing them down lightly. The circles should overlap slightly forming a border around the pie and leaving a gap in the middle to expose the filling.

Lightly prick the circles with a fork and brush them with the egg yolk and milk mixture. Sprinkle over the remaining tablespoon of sugar.

Place the cobbler in the centre of the oven and bake for 20 to 30 minutes, or until the pastry is cooked and golden brown.

Remove the cobbler from the oven and serve immediately, straight from the dish.

Peach Dessert

This Peach Dessert makes a wonderfully light and refreshing ending for a summer lunch or dinner.

4 SERVINGS

4 fresh peaches, blanched, peeled, halved and stoned
3 tablespoons double [heavy] cream
1 tablespoon castor sugar
¼ teaspoon vanilla essence
1 oz. dark dessert chocolate, finely grated
4 tablespoons blanched slivered almonds

Arrange two peach halves, rounded sides

down, in each of 4 individual dessert dishes. Set aside.

In a medium-sized mixing bowl, whisk the cream, sugar and vanilla essence together with a wire whisk or rotary beater until the mixture forms soft peaks. With a spoon or spatula, gently fold half of the chocolate and half of the almonds into the cream mixture. Place a little of the mixture in each peach half.

Sprinkle each dish with equal amounts of the remaining grated chocolate and almonds. Chill in the refrigerator for at least 1 hour before serving.

Raspberry Pudding

Raspberry Pudding is a light and pleasant dessert to make when fresh raspberries are in season. Serve it with lots of whipped cream.

4 SERVINGS

2 oz. [¼ cup] plus 1 teaspoon butter
5 fl. oz. [⅝ cup] water
6 oz. [1½ cups] flour
3 eggs
1 tablespoon finely grated orange rind
1 lb. fresh raspberries, washed and hulled
3 tablespoons castor sugar
1 teaspoon icing [confectioners'] sugar

Using the teaspoon of butter, lightly grease a baking sheet. Set aside. Preheat the oven to fairly hot 400°F (Gas Mark 6, 200°C).

In a large saucepan, bring the water to the boil over moderate heat. Add the butter. When the butter has melted, remove the pan from the heat and beat in the flour. Continue beating until the mixture pulls away from the sides of the pan.

Beat the eggs into the mixture one by one, beating each one into the dough until it is well blended before adding the next. When the eggs have been completely absorbed, the mixture should be thick and glossy. Stir in the orange rind.

Spread one-quarter of the mixture on the baking sheet to make a 7-inch circle. Spoon the remaining mixture around the edge of the circle to make a case.

Put the raspberries and sugar into the pastry case. Place the baking sheet in the oven and bake for 40 minutes or until the pastry has risen and is deep golden brown in colour. Remove the baking sheet from the oven and transfer the pudding to a serving dish. Sprinkle the pudding with the icing [confectioners'] sugar and serve immediately.

Viennese Coffee Cake

This decorative and delicious dessert cake is very easy to make.

4 SERVINGS

4 oz. [½ cup] butter
4 oz. [1 cup] self-raising flour
4 oz. [½ cup] plus 2 teaspoons sugar
2 eggs
2 oz. [½ cup] crushed walnuts plus a few halves for decoration
6 fl. oz. [¾ cup] strong black coffee
2 fl. oz. [¼ cup] brandy
10 fl. oz. double cream [1¼ cups heavy cream]
½ teaspoon vanilla essence

Preheat the oven to moderate 350°F (Gas Mark 4, 180°C). Using a little of the butter, grease a 7-inch cake tin, then dust with a little flour.

In a bowl, beat the butter with a wooden spoon until it is soft. Add 4 ounces [½ cup] sugar and beat until the mixture is creamy. Add the eggs, one at a time, with 1 tablespoon of flour. Beat to mix and then fold in the remaining flour and the crushed walnuts. Turn the batter into the prepared cake tin. Bake for 50 minutes, or until a skewer inserted into the centre of the cake comes out clean.

Remove the cake from the tin and place on a rack to cool. Mix the coffee and brandy. Put the cake back in the cake tin and slowly pour the coffee and brandy over it. When all the liquid has been absorbed, turn out on to a dish.

Whip the cream with the remaining 2 teaspoons of the sugar and the vanilla essence. Using a spatula, spread the cream in whirls over the cake to cover it completely. Decorate with walnut halves.

Yeast Buckwheat Pancakes with Blackberries and Sour Cream

Yeast Buckwheat Pancakes with Blackberries and Sour Cream makes a really special dessert.

6 SERVINGS

½ oz. fresh yeast
2 oz. [¼ cup] plus 1 teaspoon sugar
10 fl. oz. [1¼ cups] milk, lukewarm
10 oz. [2½ cups] buckwheat flour
¼ teaspoon salt
2 eggs, lightly beaten
1 oz. [2 tablespoons] butter, melted
2 oz. [¼ cup] butter
2 tablespoons icing [confectioners'] sugar
1 lb. blackberries, washed and drained
10 fl. oz. [1¼ cups] sour cream

Yeast Buckwheat Pancakes with Blackberries and Sour Cream.

Crumble the yeast into a small bowl and mash in 1 teaspoon of the sugar with a fork. Add 2 tablespoons of the milk and cream the mixture to form a smooth paste. Set the bowl aside in a warm, draught-free place for 15 to 20 minutes or until the mixture is puffed up.

In a large mixing bowl, combine the flour and salt. Make a well in the centre and pour in the yeast, the remaining milk and sugar, the eggs and melted butter.

Using your fingers, gradually draw the flour mixture into the liquid. Continue mixing until all the flour is incorporated and the mixture is smooth.

Set the batter aside in a warm draught-free place for 30 minutes.

In a large frying-pan, melt half of the butter over high heat. Drop tablespoonfuls of the batter into the pan and fry, turning once, for 30 seconds on each side or until the pancakes are golden brown. Transfer the pancakes to a warmed serving plate and keep hot while you fry the remaining batter in the same way.

When all the pancakes have been fried, sprinkle over the icing [confectioners'] sugar. Place the blackberries in one bowl and the sour cream in another and serve immediately, with the pancakes.